Travelers' Medical Resource

Travelers' Medical Resource

A guide to health & safety worldwide

By William W. Forgey, M.D.

Dr. Forgey is a member, Medical Advisory Board, International Association for Medical Assistance to Travelers (IAMAT), Toronto, Canada; Assistant Clinical Professor of Family Medicine, Indiana University, Northwest Campus, Gary, Indiana; Chairman, Department of Family Practice, St. Mary Mercy Hospital Center of Gary and Hobart, Indiana; and Medical Director, Herchmer Medical Consultants, Merrillville, Indiana.

ICS BOOKS, INC.
Merrillville, Indiana

TRAVELERS' MEDICAL RESOURCE

Copyright © 1990 by William W. Forgey

10 9 8 7 6 5 4 3 2 1

DEDICATION

This book is dedicated to the many members of the worldwide voluntary organization IAMAT (The International Association for Medical Assistance to Travelers) and to the Marcolongo Family who have worked diligently to make the organization the success that it has become.

Library of Congress Cataloging-in-Publication Data

Forgey, William W., 1942-
    Travelers' medical resource / by William W. Forgey ; illustrations
by Scott Power.
        p.   cm.
    Includes index.
    ISBN 0-934802-62-9 : $19.95
    1. Travel--health aspects.   I. Title.
RA783.5.F67   1990
613.6'8--dc20

                                                                90-4977
                                                                CIP

ABOUT THE AUTHOR

Dr. Forgey is Assistant Clinical Professor of Family Medicine, Indiana University School of Medicine, Northwest Indiana Campus; a member of the Medical Advisory Board of the International Association for Medical Assistance to Travelers (IAMAT), Toronto, Canada; Department Chairman, Family Practice, St. Mary Mercy Medical Center at Gary and Hobart, Indiana; Trustee of the Wilderness Education Association, Saranac Lake, New York; Adjunct Faculty Member, Western Illinois University, College of Health, Physical Education & Recreation, Macomb, Illinois; Adjunct Faculty Member, Slippery Rock University, Department of Parks & Recreation, Slippery Rock, Pennsylvania; and currently is in private practice in Merrillville, Indiana.

Prior to going to medical school he held the rank of Captain, Infantry, and had over two years of service in the former Republic of Vietnam.

He is an Active Member of the American Medical Writers Association and the Outdoor Writers Association of America. A Fellow of the Explorer's Club, New York City, Dr. Forgey is also an Associate Member of the University Association for Emergency Medicine.

Other publications by Dr. Forgey include *Wilderness Medicine* (1979, 2d Ed 1983, 3rd Ed 1987), *Hypothermia* (1985), *Campfire Stories* (1985), *Basic Essentials of Outdoor First Aid* (1989), *Campfire Tales* (1989), and *The Travelers' Self Help Guide* (1990) all published by ICS Books. Dr. Forgey contributed to the current edition of the Field Book, published by the Boy Scouts of America. He is a consultant for many outdoor programs, camps, and expeditions.

TABLE OF CONTENTS

SECTION 1
INTRODUCTION TO THE MEDICAL RISKS OF FOREIGN TRAVEL

Chapters

1.1 Preparing For Departure **1-1**

1.2 Using This Book **1-11**

1.3 Books and Periodicals **1-17**

SECTION 2
RESOURCES AND SERVICES

Chapters

2.1 U.S. Governmental Help for the Traveler **2-1**

2.2 Department of State Travel Information **2-9**

2.3 WHO and CDC Bulletins **2-13**

2.4 State Boards of Health **2-17**

2.5 Travelers' Medical Clinics **2-23**

2.6 Travel Insurance And Assistance **2-39**

2.7 International Association of Medical Assistance for Travelers **2-53**

2.8 Herchmer Country Database Program **2-57**

SECTION 3

MAKING TRAVEL SAFE AND COMFORTABLE

Chapters

3.1   Safe Vehicle Travel **3-1**

3.2   Personal Security **3-5**

3.3   Safe Air Travel **3-15**

3.4   Fear of Flying **3-23**

3.5   Jet Lag **3-27**

3.6   Safe Cruise Ship Travel **3-35**

3.7   Motion Sickness **3-39**

SECTION 4

TRAVELING WITH MEDICAL PROBLEMS

Chapters

4.1   Mobility Restricted Travel **4--1**

4.2   Pregnancy and Travel **4-5**

4.3   Children and Travel **4-11**

4.4   Diabetes and Travel **4-21**

4.5   Cardiac/Pulmonary Disease and Travel **4-27**

4.6   AIDS, Compromised Immunity, and Travel **4-31**

4.7   The Return Home **4-41**

SECTION 5

DISEASE PREVENTION AND IMMUNIZATION

Chapters

5.1   Food and Dairy Product Safety **5-1**

5.2   Water Purification **5-7**

5.3   Travelers' Diarrhea **5-13**

5.4   Insect Protection **5-21**

5.5   Immunizations for Foreign Travel **5-31**

5.6   Immunization Complications and Contraindications **5-45**

SECTION 6

INFECTIOUS DISEASES OF INTEREST TO THE TRAVELER

Chapters

6.1   Anthrax **6-1**

6.2   Bartonellosis **6-2**

6.3   Brucellosis **6-3**

6.4	Chikungunya Fever	**6-3**
6.5	Cholera	**6-4**
6.6	Ciguatera Poisoning	**6-6**
6.7	Clonorchiasis and Opisthorchiasis	**6-7**
6.8	Colorado Tick Fever	**6-8**
6.9	Dengue Fever	**6-9**
6.10	Diphtheria	**6-10**
6.11	Dracunculiasis	**6-10**
6.12	Dysentery, Amoebic and Bacillary	**6-11**
6.13	Echinococcus	**6-12**
6.14	Japanese Encephalitis	**6-13**
6.15	Tick-borne Encephalitis	**6-15**
6.16	Venezuelan Equine Encephalitis	**6-15**
6.17	Fasciolopsiasis	**6-16**
6.18	Filariasis	**6-17**
6.19	Giardiasis	**6-17**
6.20	Hemorrhagic Fevers, Viral	**6-19**
6.21	Helminthic Diseases	**6-21**
6.22	Hepatitis A	**6-23**
6.23	Hepatitis B	**6-24**
6.24	Hepatitis C	**6-25**
6.25	Lassa Fever	**6-26**
6.26	Leishmaniasis	**6-27**
6.27	Leprosy	**6-28**
6.28	Leptospirosis	**6-29**
6.29	Loiasis	**6-30**
6.30	Lyme Disease	**6-31**
6.31	Malaria	**6-32**
6.32	Melioidosis	**6-40**
6.33	Meningococcal Meningitis	**6-40**
6.34	Measles/Mumps/Rubella	**6-41**
6.35	Onchocerciasis	**6-42**
6.36	Paragonimiasis	**6-43**
6.37	Paralytic Shellfish Poisoning	**6-44**
6.38	Plague	**6-45**
6.39	Poliomyelitis	**6-47**
6.40	Rabies	**6-48**
6.41	Relapsing Fever	**6-51**

6.42   Rift Valley Fever **6-52**
6.43   Rocky Mountain Spotted Fever **6-52**
6.44   Sandfly Fever **6-53**
6.45   Schistosomiasis **6-53**
6.46   Scromboid Poisoning **6-55**
6.47   Sexually Transmitted Diseases **6-55**
6.48   Smallpox **6-57**
6.49   Tapeworms **6-58**
6.50   Tetanus **6-59**
6.51   Trachoma **6-61**
6.52   Trichinosis **6-61**
6.53   Trypanosomiasis (African Sleeping Sickness) **6-62**
6.54   Trypanosomiasis (American or Chaga's Disease) **6-63**
6.55   Tuberculosis **6-64**
6.56   Tularemia **6-65**
6.57   Tungiasis **6-65**
6.58   Typhoid Fever **6-66**
6.59   Typhus, Endemic (Flea-Borne) **6-67**
6.60   Typhus, Epidemic (Louse-Borne) **6-68**
6.61   Typhus, Scrub (Mite-Borne) **6-69**
6.62   West Nile Fever **6-69**
6.63   Yellow Fever **6-70**

SECTION 7

TRAVELERS' SELF CARE MANUAL

Chapters

7.1   Trauma **7-1**
7.2   Eye, Ear, Nose, Mouth Symptoms **7-9**
7.3   Abdominal Problems **7-23**
7.4   Sprains, Fractures, Dislocations **7-33**
7.5   Bites and Stings **7-39**
7.6   Aquatic Injuries **7-47**
7.7   Environmental Injuries **7-51**
7.8   Travelers' Medical Kit **7-71**
7.9   Personal Information Section **7-95**

SECTION 8

HERCHMER INDIVIDUAL COUNTRY DATABASE 8-1

Countries
1 to 219

Separate Listings For All 219 Soverign Countries of the World
which includes disease risks; immunization requirements and
suggestions; food, water, dairy safety; U.S. Foreign Service and
Canadian High Commission addresses and telephone numbers.

SECTION 9

GLOSSARY 9-1

SECTION 10

INDEX 10-1

Section 1
Introduction to the Medical Risks of Foreign Travel

Most persons traveling to a foreign land are going to be concerned about a realistic evaluation of the risks from infection, insurgency or other dangers from fellow human beings, climate, the peculiar problems associated with travel itself, and receiving advice on how to handle these predicaments.

There are two aspects of most books on travel medical information that detract from their usefulness. One is the total lack of information concerning dangers from one's fellow man. Indeed, this has recently become a significant factor. Drug dealers in certain Central American countries, political unrest in the Near East, urban and rural crime, and despotic governments in various parts of the world, have added a new dimension of concern to business travel and tourism as well as trekking off the beaten path. Probably the best source of information concerning this human unrest comes from US Department of State Travel Advisories. The country database (page 8–1) in this book lists and reprints all of the advisories that were in effect at the time of publication. The database update discussed in Chapter 2.8 and a direct line to the Department of State [(202) 647-5225] provide current travel advisory information.

Remaining current is another problem of travel books. These books are out of date by the time they are off the press. This has been overcome in this publication by the establishment of an accessible database system. As indicated in Chapter 2.8, current intelligence regarding disease information, changes in requirements and recommendations concerning immunizations, and travel advisories can be obtained from this database.

Coalescing information about the dangers of travel and the environment into a book to be read by prospective travelers has the potential for dissuading the timid from making the trip. That is certainly not its intention and in fact would be a disservice. Some travel agents have been noted to ignore or minimize basic knowledge of potential dangers—perhaps fearful that likely travelers might cancel their tickets if they were to hear of diseases and hardships that exist in some foreign paradise. This also is a disservice.

Trips should not be made with ignorance and bliss, but rather with relative safety and the reasonable opportunity to enjoy the experience and remain healthy in the process. It is to that purpose that this book has been written.

The problem of infectious disease in travel has taken on a new meaning with the emergence of AIDS. Medical care in developing countries has been tainted with the concerns about contaminated local medical products as well as the competency of training and the ability to communicate. Finding safe medical care, and avoiding unnecessary care, is of potential concern to many travelers. Included in the latter case is insuring that all required immunizations have been obtained at home prior to arrival in the foreign land. Multiple use vials of vaccine and reusable needles/syringes pose a particular hazard for hepatitis B and AIDS that must be avoided.

There are many less life threatening concerns about travel that can be minimized by proper knowledge. Areas of interest for many travelers include control of fear of flying, avoidance of motion sickness, travel with chronic medical conditions, travel while pregnant or with small children, safe and sanitary cruise ship conditions, and in general being able to cope with medical conditions that might arise.

Intercontinental travelers must add concerns about jet lag, travelers' diarrhea, immunizations, malaria, obtaining medical help overseas, avoiding exotic foreign diseases (and some not so exotic), and possibly obtaining embassy help—to name a few.

A unique provision made for the overseas traveler is the inclusion within this book of the Traveler's Self Care Manual, which provides information concerning the care of medical problems (see Section 7). This section of the book has been designed with large inner margins, thus facilitating making photocopies. A special insert card will allow the

*book purchaser to receive a copy of this book, separately bound, from
the publisher.*

*The chapter page numbering system allows this book to be
updated, virtually constantly, prior to publication, and as time passes
between this and its next edition, without disrupting the entire page
numbering sequence. This book, and the various resources to which the
reader is directed, can serve as a living tool to help you plan your trip
in a safe, organized manner, and to aid you in ensuring that your
business and vacation plans are fulfilled safely and to your satisfaction.*

Chapter 1.1

Preparing for Departure

It might appear that properly preparing for a foreign trip seems almost overwhelming. Arrangements for transportation, passports, visas, immunizations, travel medications and advice, language problems, foreign country transportation permits and modes of travel—as well as housing, money conversion, insurance coverage, fears and concerns of terrorism or flying, travel timetables, concerns about home—the more one considers it, the more complicated the whole process becomes. If special medical problems exist, such as heart problems, pregnancy, diabetes, or locomotion handicaps, the problems seem to compound. And the responsibility of the travel planner for someone else, such as a boss or a loved one, does nothing to lessen these complications.

What sequencing and checklist is necessary to ensure that all of these details have been resolved properly? How do I get started towards planning a successful trip?

The information found in this book is the answer to your dilemma. Part of the solution is in forming a checklist so that no critical steps have been overlooked. The remainder of the problem is to ensure that adequate time is available for a proper sequencing of activities so that all details have been completed by the time the traveler is heading towards the airport, bags packed.

The traveler's goal is to be fully prepared financially, legally, and medically for the trip. Many factors are out of the control of the traveler, such as the length of time that a difficult foreign consulate might take to return a passport with their visa. Because of that, start obtaining the necessary legal documents, travel insurance, reservations, and medical consultations as soon as possible. This book provides many resources to enable your successful accomplishment of this goal.

MEDICAL PREPARATION

Obtain appropriate medical consultation. Chapter 2.5, Travelers' Medical Clinics, lists specialists and clinics in the U.S. and parts of Canada who specialize in travel medicine, pre-trip consultations, and immunizations. Some members listed in that chapter have a particular interest in post travel evaluation (see Chapter 4.7), while others are listed that restrict their practice to professional consultation with other physicians. Most infectious disease specialists are interested, and ideally suited, in providing advice and immunizations for travel. You can also contact your state board of health (see Chapter 2.4) for the names of persons and organizations in your area who can provide travel immunizations.

The first visit should be made a minimum of 8 weeks before the trip. If hepatitis B immunization is required, the first dose must be obtained 7 months prior to departure. An immunization sequencing schedule must be developed and initiated (see Chapter 5.5).

Obtain medical supplies which might be required for personal use, or which may be unique to the trip (such as antimalarials, medicine for travelers' diarrhea, prophylaxis for acute mountain sickness, and so forth as indicated), and personal medications for both chronically treated and any acute medical problems.

Modify the medical kit described in this book (see Chapter 7.8) or as suggested by your medical consultant and obtain the non-prescription items which are indicated. Non-prescription products should be carried in their original packaging.

Obtain a physician's letter describing the prescription medications which you will be taking on the trip. This letter should contain the name of the medication, its generic name, the dosage, and the reason that it has been prescribed. A sample of a suggested letter is illustrated below:

William W. Forgey, M.D.
109 East 89th Avenue
Merrillville, IN 46410
Telephone (219) 769–6055

15 March 1991

Patient Name: John Q. Traveler

The individual above is traveling with the need to take certain prescription medications. He is doing this with my prescriptions and according to the dosage and uses which I have outlined below.

Medication Name (Generic Name)	Dosage	Purpose of Medication
Inderol LA 80 (propranolol)	1 daily	high blood pressure
Lozol 2.5 mg (indapamide)	1 daily	high blood pressure
Lopid 600 mg (gemfibrozil	2 daily	high triglycerides

Cordially,
William W. Forgey, M.D.

FIGURE 1–1
A sample physician's letter to justify a traveler carrying prescription medications through international customs. Note that the letter contains both the brand and generic names for the medication, the dosage, and the intended use.

An example of a letter which would describe the prescription medications recommended for the travelers' medical kit described in Chapter 7.8, as part of the *Travelers' Self Care Manual,* is illustrated below:

William W. Forgey, M.D.
109 East 89th Avenue
Merrillville, IN 46410
Telephone (219) 769–6055

15 March 1991

Patient Name: John Q. Traveler

The individual above is traveling and carrying certain prescription medications with my advice. He is doing this with my prescriptions and according to the dosage and uses which I have outlined below.

Medication Name (Generic Name)	Dosage	Purpose of Medication
Doxycycline 100 mg (generic)	2 doses daily	For infections
Bactrim DS (trimethoprim/ sulfamethoxazole)	2 doses daily	For infections
Tobrex Ophthalmic Ointment (tobramycin .3%)	2–3 doses daily	For eye infections
Pontocaine Ophthalmic Oint (tetracaine .5%)	2–3 doses daily	To anesthetize the injured eye
Topicort Ointment .25% (desoximetasone)	2 doses daily	For allergic skin
Carafate 1 gram (sucralfate)	4 doses daily	For stomach ulcers or gastritis

Atarax 25 mg (hydroxyzine)	4 doses daily	For nausea and itch
Tylenol #3 (acetaminophen/codeine)	max of 8 daily	For pain
Transderm Scop (scopolamine)	1 patch each 3 days	For motion sickness

Cordially,
William W. Forgey, M.D.

FIGURE 1–2
This is a sample physician's letter to justify and authorize carrying the recommended traveler's medical kit through international customs. This kit is described in Chapter 7.8. Note that the letter contains both the brand and generic names for the medication, the dosage, and the intended use.

Physician's wishing a template of the above letter, without heading or signature block, for use in photocopying onto their stationary by using a plain paper copier, may write to Herchmer Medical Consultants, 109 East 89th Avenue, Merrillville, IN 46410; telephone 1–800–336–8334; FAX (219) 769–6035. This would facilitate writing the accompanying letter for persons carrying the prescription component of the proposed travelers' medical kit described in Chapter 7.8.

Photocopy or obtain a separate copy of the *Travelers' Self Care Manual* to help in case of minor medical problems. Customize the medical kit instructions and copy requisite information into Chapter 7.9, the personal information section. Carefully completing this section may prove to be a most helpful preparation in case an emergency occurs during your trip!

An alternate medical guide would be *The Pocket Doctor* by Steve Bezruchka M.D. (1988). This book is available from The Mountaineers, 306 2nd Avenue, Seattle, WA 98119, or in many outdoor speciality shops and bookstores.

TRAVEL DOCUMENTS

Obtain any necessary travel documents and make transportation and lodging arrangements well in advance, if possible.

PASSPORT:

One of the passport application forms (the DSP-82) has arrows pointing to words in bold type on the top left and top right of the form that state "Don't put it off. Apply Now. Avoid the last minute rush." Not bad advice, from the people who should know.

The form DSP-82 is an application for passport by mail. To be eligible to use it you must pass three criteria: 1). You must have been issued a U.S. passport in your name within the past 12 years; 2). You must submit your most recent U.S. passport with the application (it will be returned); and 3). You must have been age 16 or older when your most recent U.S. passport was issued. If you fail to meet any of those criteria, then you will need form DSP-11. These forms can be obtained at most U.S. Post Offices and by mail from a U.S. Passport Agency (see below). If you are a first time applicant, you must appear in person (children under the age of 13 usually can be represented by a parent or guardian) and carry proof of U.S. citizenship (certified birth certificate or previous passport are best), proof of identity, two 2 x 2 inch photographs taken within the last 6 months, and money ($42.00 for age 18 or older; $27.00 for age 17 or younger). You may appear before a clerk of any Federal or State court of record or a judge or clerk of any probate court accepting applications; a designated postal employee at a selected post office; an agent at a Passport Agency; or a U.S. consular official. The fastest service can probably be obtained at one of the Passport Agencies, but even then it may take a minimum of two weeks.

TABLE 1–1
Addresses of Passport Agencies

BOSTON PASSPORT AGENCY
Room E 123, John F. Kennedy Building
Government Center
Boston, MA 02203–0123

CHICAGO PASSPORT AGENCY
Suite 380, Kluczynski Federal Building
230 South Dearborn Street
Chicago, IL 60604–1564

HONOLULU PASSPORT AGENCY
Room C-106, New Federal Building
300 Ala Moana Boulevard
P. O. Box 50185
Honolulu, HI 96850

HOUSTON PASSPORT AGENCY
One Allen Center
500 Dallas Street
Houston, TX 77002–4878

LOS ANGELES PASSPORT AGENCY
Room 13100, 11000 Wilshire Boulevard
Los Angeles, CA 90024–3615

MIAMI PASSPORT AGENCY
16th Floor, Federal Office Building
51 SW First Avenue
Miami, FL 33130–1680

NEW ORLEANS PASSPORT AGENCY
Postal Services Building
Room T-12005
701 Loyola Avenue
New Orleans, LA 70113–1931

NORTHEAST PASSPORT CENTER
P. O. Box 22
New York, NY 10014–4896

PHILADELPHIA PASSPORT AGENCY
Room 4426, Federal Building
600 Arch Street
Philadelphia, PA 19106–1684

SAN FRANCISCO PASSPORT AGENCY
Room 200
525 Market Street
San Francisco, CA 94105–2773

SEATTLE PASSPORT AGENCY
Room 992, Federal Building
915 Second Avenue
Seattle, WA 98174–1091

WASHINGTON PASSPORT AGENCY
1425 K Street, N.W.
Washington, DC 20524–0002

VISA:

Obtaining a difficult visa may take longer than obtaining your passport. Some must be obtained prior to entering a particular country and necessitate your sending, or taking, your passport to a foreign embassy in this country. Most can be obtained at the time you are crossing the border, but "know before you go."

An official pamphlet "Foreign Visa Requirements," publication number 9517, is available for $0.50, from the Consumer Information Center, Department 438T, Pueblo, CO 81009. Guidebooks can also be a source of information about visa requirements. Visa requirements can change without warning and the rules differ by nationality of the applicant, the purpose of the visit, the length of stay anticipated, and sometimes the current political situation. Travel agents can frequently be a good source of advice on visa requirements. See also the excellent discussion on visas in *Travel Tips for the 90's* by Don Weiss and Phyllis Wachob Weiss[1]

TRANSPORTATION:

Allow adequate time to obtain any special transportation arrangements, such as Eurail passes, youth or senior citizen discount passes or special memberships, as well as tickets and reservations as required. Persons anticipating driving should inquire ahead of time concerning legal requirements, insurance, and availability of vehicles, gasoline, etc. A recent problem which demonstrates how well you need to research transportation was the March 1990 announcement by Mexican authorities to restrict private tourist vehicles with non-Mexican registration to aid with the control of air pollution in Mexico City:

---

[1]*Travel Tips for the 90's* is available from ICS Books, 107 East 89th Avenue, Merrillville, IN 46410; telephone (800) 541-7323; for $9.95 plus $1.50 shipping and handling fee.

"For non-Mexican registration, the restriction is based on the last digit of the license plates and the schedule is as follows:

Monday: No driving of vehicles with license plates with final digits of 5 or 6.

Tuesday: No driving of vehicles with license plates with final digits of 7 or 8.

Wednesday: No driving of vehicles with license plates with final digits of 3 or 4.

Thursday: No driving of vehicles with license plates with final digits of 1 or 2.

Friday: No driving of vehicles with license plates with final digits of 9 or 0.

Saturday and Sunday: All vehicles may drive.

Failure to comply with this new regulation will result in vehicle impoundment and a 300,000 Peso/ U.S. $115.00 fine."

This information was obtained from the Department of State travel advisory system as described in Chapter 2.2. Guidebooks are an excellent source of routine traffic rules and legal requirements. Allow time to study these and to enable yourself to comply.

INSURANCE:

Insurance programs for trip cancellation, medical, life, and arrangements for special assistance are described in Chapter 2.6 "Travel Insurance and Assistance." Generally, you can expect fairly rapid response to inquiries and purchase of travel insurance plans. Call the telephone numbers for applications and allow three weeks to receive your insurance certificate once you have returned them with your payment.

LEGAL AFFAIRS:

Prepare a will prior to departure. Arrange for a power of attorney, if this is appropriate, to handle selected affairs while you are gone. You will need time for an attorney to consult with you, to draw up the necessary papers, and to have them executed.

ITINERARY:

Take the time to prepare a full itinerary to be left behind with someone at home. See the excellent discussion of this topic in the

Weiss' book *Travel Tips for the 90's* mentioned above. You should include a time table with points of contact, to include hotels (if known) and the appropriate U.S. embassy addresses and telephone numbers. For this system to work, you *must* check in with the points of contact which you have established. Your person at home must realize that delays in transportation will upset even the best intentions and have pre-set rules on what to do if pre-arranged contacts are not accomplished within certain periods of time. When checking in with a U.S. embassy, you must wave at least portions, if not all, of the Privacy of Information Act to allow those calling to receive *any,* or some, information concerning you.

A photocopy of your personal information section, Chapter 7.9, would be the ideal documentation to leave behind. Take the time to fill out this section and to copy it!

As can be seen, for even a routine and basic trip, there is quite a bit of leg work required. All of this takes prior planning, and time. It is the purpose of this book to help you network with the key elements in helping you plan for a safe and healthy trip away from the United States.

Chapter 1.2

Using This Book

A book this large tends to be a bit overwhelming, but do not let that deter you. The sections following the introductory section have specific goals to aid you in planning the medical aspects of preparing for your trip and in keeping you safe and healthy while you are on your way.

The key to accomplishing this goal is "networking," or finding authorities that can provide you with written or personal advise. Many of the chapters in this book do just that, while others contain basic information on the prevention of illness or knowledge on how to care for many of the problems which you might encounter.

SECTION 1—INTRODUCTION TO THE MEDICAL ASPECTS OF FOREIGN TRAVEL

This section provides an overview of the use of this book and you are reading that right now!

The basic concepts of trip planning and a special bibliography on various aspects of general trip planning are also provided in this section.

SECTION 2—RESOURCES AND SERVICES

Consisting of 8 chapters, this section lists names, addresses, and telephone numbers of various governmental and private organizations who can provide a wide variety of help to the traveler. This is the networking section which acts as a resource planner and directory. This section directs the reader towards travel medicine specialists and various governmental agencies (both federal and state), that can provide pre-trip planning advice, immunizations, insurance, protection, overseas assistance and evacuation services. Most programs are evaluated and costs are provided. Many specialized details are included, such as how to obtain current inspection summaries on cruise ships, current information on danger areas from the Department of State, addresses and costs of travel information subscription services, experimental vaccine sources, travel insurance costs and plan evaluations, handicapped and special medical problem networking or special assistance organizations and directories, and telephone hotlines for current medical information on malaria and other health hazards.

SECTION 3—MAKING TRAVEL SAFE
AND COMFORTABLE

Chapters of advice concerning minimizing the effects of jet lag, dominating the fear of flying, controlling diabetes while changing time zones, flying with heart problems, traveling while pregnant, avoiding terrorists and planning strategies for surviving natural and man made disasters make up this section. A special section on travel restrictions for HIV positive individuals (and AIDS patients) is included. A death and injury avoidance chapter examines the common causes of foreign travel mishaps to instill caution and acquaint the traveler with knowledge of the conditions which should be avoided.

SECTION 4—TRAVELING WITH MEDICAL PROBLEMS

This section provides advice on traveling with diabetes, while pregnant, with infants and children, with cardiovascular conditions, with pulmonary problems, with mobility restrictions, and with decreased immunity. This section contains the current list of countries requiring proof of a negative AIDS antibody test in order to obtain a visa for entry. A chapter on the possible medical problems and considerations for continued medical care of the returned traveler is included.

SECTION 5—DISEASE PREVENTION AND IMMUNIZATION

Concerned with food, water, dairy product, and vector control, this section provides information involving the methods of disease spread and ways to minimize the traveler's contact. Required and recommended immunizations are described, along with dosage schedules for individual vaccines and for the occasional necessity of receiving several series. A special table of side effects of common immunizations is provided with information on how to predict which vaccines might cause an allergic reaction. The vector control chapter discusses various insects that are of medical importance in spreading disease and how to avoid, repel, or kill them.

SECTION 6—INFECTIOUS DISEASES OF INTEREST TO THE TRAVELER

This section on infectious diseases of interest to the traveler puts into perspective the dangers of over 70 contagious afflictions. It describes their distribution, causative organism, method of spread, pathology or damage caused to humans, availability of protective medications or immunizations, availability of treatment, symptoms, and the chance of delayed manifestations of illness. Some diseases considered rare in this country infect millions of persons overseas—other illnesses which have very bad reputations may not be of any significance to travelers. The emphasis of this section is to generate an awareness of potential dangers, to instill caution where it is justified, and to develop methods of minimizing chances of catching these maladies which range from nuisances to life threatening catastrophes.

SECTION 7—TRAVELERS' SELF CARE MANUAL

This book within a book is formatted with wide inner margins so that it can be easily photocopied and taken with the traveler. Consisting of 9 parts, the first 7 help the traveler diagnose, treat, or know when to seek help when faced with a variety of potential medical problems. Problems covered include trauma; eye, ear, nose and mouth symptoms; abdominal problems; sprains, fractures, and dislocations; bites and stings; aquatic injuries; and environmental injuries from altitude, heat, and cold. Part 8 is a recommended medical kit, with areas for modification depending upon the nature of the trip and recommendations made by the consulting or personal physician. Part 9 is a personal information section that encourages the traveler to obtain information about himself and various destinations for use during the trip. Much of this information should be extracted as appropriate from select portions of the basic book to customize and condense appropriate information for the traveler's particular trip and personal medical history.

While this section has been prepared to be easily photocopied, it is also available as a separately published book. Published simultaneously at $6.95, for your convenience a copy of this book may be obtained by returning the attached post card to the publisher, or by telephoning a credit card purchase request [Telephone (800) 541–7323 or (219) 769–0585].

SECTION 8—HERCHMER COUNTRY DATABASE

The largest section of this book is the database for the 219 sovereign countries of the world. Consisting of current information that is updated weekly by Herchmer Medical Consultants, prior to press the database was incorporated into Section 8 of this book. Information includes immunizations that are required and recommended, warnings about specific health hazards, an evaluation of the general safety of food, water, and dairy products sold in that country, malaria hazard evaluation with resistance patterns to normal prophylactic medications, and the addresses, telephone numbers, and hours of business of the U. S. Foreign Service representatives (embassies, etc) and the Canadian governmental representatives. Diseases of special risk for travelers are evaluated per country as "endemic", "risk", or "hazard", to help ascertain their relative importance and are cross referenced into Section 6 (Infectious Diseases) of this book. The original text of Department of State Travel Advisories, that are current as of the publication date, are included in the appropriate country section.

Pertinent information from this section can be extracted and placed into the Travelers' Self Care Manual (Section 7) for easy transportability.

Purchasers of this book are provided the opportunity to contact the Herchmer Database directly for an update of selected countries prior to their departure. This, coupled with the hotlines and other consultation resources, will allow the traveler the ability to easily update this information.

SECTION 9—GLOSSARY

The jargon and vernacular language of foreign travel experts will be explained in this dictionary of foreign medical travel. What is the difference between a toxin and a toxoid? This and many other mysteries are clarified in this important section. Listings in this section have been restricted to terms that have not been fully explained within the text and to terms that are referenced which might be unknown or confusing to the non-physician user of this book.

SECTION 10—INDEX

In a resource book an index is the critical link between the consumer and the reason they obtained the book. This index is extensively cross referenced with both technical names and common names for diseases, organizational references, and medical and travel problems. Major listings are distinguished from minor references with bold face. Major listings will include descriptions of technical terms where they appear in the text. Minor listings cross reference the appearance of terms used throughout the book, with the exception of the Individual Country Database (Section 8).

Section 8 has been indexed for country listings only as a full indexing of this section would unnecessarily bulk up references to diseases, medications, and immunizations beyond reason. Minor listings include only cross-references of possible significance to the reader and exclude simple word appearances.

Chapter 1.3

Books and Periodicals

The interested traveler and professional travel consultant can take advantage of many books and periodicals that deal with safety, well being, and health issues during domestic and international travel. The wide range of books and services now available are produced by these private sector sources as well as the governmental sources referenced elsewhere in this manual.

Medical Travel—General Audience

I particularly recommend these books that have been written for a general audience which are currently available from libraries or their respective publishers:

Dawood, R. (1988). *How to stay healthy abroad.* New York: Viking Penguin Inc.

Harkonen, W. S. (1984). *Traveling well: A comprehensive guide to your health abroad.* New York: Dodd, Mead & Company.

Sakmar, T. P., Gardner, P., & Peterson, G. N. (1986). *Health guide for international travelers: How to travel and stay well.* Lincolnwood, Illinois: Passport Books.

Scotti, A., & Moore, T. A. (1985). *The traveler's medical manual.* New York: Berkley Books.

Shales, M. (Ed.). (1988). *The traveler's handbook.* Chester, Connecticut: The Globe Pequot Press.

Silverman, H. (1986). *Travel healthy.* New York: Avon Books.

Turner, A. C. (1979). *The traveller's health guide* (2nd ed.). London: Roger Lascelles.

Weiss, D., & Weiss, P. W. (1990). *Travel Tips for the 90s.* Merrillville, IN: ICS Books.

Worring, R. W., Hibbard, W. S., & Schroeder, S. (1987). *Travel safety: Don't be a target.* Coeur d'Alene, Idaho: Uniquest Publications.

Travel Medical Update Service—General Audience

Traveling Healthy & Comfortably. Editor Karl Neuman. Published bi-monthly, subscription rate $24.00/year. 108–48 70th Road, Forest Hills, NY 11375.

Self Medical Care—General Audience

The purpose of the books listed below is the self care of medical problems, frequently encountered in wilderness settings and from exposure to extremes of the environment such as heat, cold, and altitude. While the general traveling public would not need to take the responsibility of medical care in such situations, it is possible that some travelers might find themselves in a position where the ability to develop an advanced medical kit and to administer the immediate first aid and continued care of trip members would possibly be necessary.

Auerbach, P. (1986). *Medicine for the outdoors.* Boston: Little, Brown and Co.

Bezrucka, S. (1988). *The pocket doctor.* Seattle: The Mountaineers.

Darvill, F. (1985). *Mountaineering medicine* (11th ed.). Berkely: Wilderness Press.

Forgey, W. W. (1989). *Basic essentials of outdoor first aid.* Merrillville, IN: ICS Books.

Forgey, W. (1985). *Hypothermia: Death by exposure.* Merrillville, IN: ICS Books.

Forgey, W. (1990). *Travelers' self care manual.* Merrillville, IN: ICS Books. *Included in this text as Section 7, and available as a separate publication.*

Forgey, W. (1987). *Wilderness medicine* (3rd ed.). Merrillville, IN: ICS Books.

Hackett, P. H. (1980). *Mountain sickness: Prevention, recognition, and treatment.* New York: The American Alpine Club.

Houston, C. S. (1987). *Going higher: The story of man and altitude* (rev. ed.). Boston: Little, Brown and Company.

Lentz, M. J., Macdonald, S. C, & Carline, J. (1985). *Mountaineering first aid* (3rd ed.). Seattle: The Mountaineers.

Wilkerson, J. A. (Ed). (1986). *Hypothermia, frostbite and other cold injuries.* Seattle: The Mountaineers.

Wilkerson, J. A. (Ed). (1985). *Medicine for mountaineering* (3rd ed.). Seattle: The Mountaineers.

Emergency Medical Care—Physician Audience

While the above books would also appeal to a physician facing the responsibility of caring for members of a group in a wilderness setting, the following books and articles are written specifically as reference works for the physician, or layman with a paramedic level of training.

Auerbach, P. S., & Geehr, E. C. (Eds.). (1989). *Management of wilderness and environmental emergencies.* (2d Ed.). St. Louis: C. V. Mosby Company.

Bowman, W. D. Jr. (1988). *Outdoor emergency care.* Denver: National Ski Patrol System.

Eisenberg, M., & Copass, M. (1978). *Manual of emergency medical therapeutics.* Philadelphia: W. B. Saunders Company.

Goodman, P. H., Kurtz, K. J., & Carmichael, J. (1985). Medical recommendations for wilderness travel: 3. Medical supplies and drug regimens. *Postgraduate Medicine.* 78(2). 107-115.

Nelson, R. N., Douglas, A. R., & Keller, M. D. (1985). *Environmental emergencies.* Philadelphia: W. B. Saunders Company.

Travel Medicine—Physician Audience

The following information has been written by nongovernmental organizations and authors to provide technical advice to physicians who are responsible for the counseling or care of travelers:

Committee on immunization. (1990). *Guide for adult immunization.* Philadelphia: American College of Physicians.

Doege, T. C., & Bell, J. A. (Ed.). (1982). *Travelers' health abroad: A guide for physicians.* Chicago: American Medical Association.

Halstead, S. B., & Warren, K. S. (1987). *Diseases of travelers and immigrants.* Kalamazoo, MI: The Upjohn Company.

Jong, E. C. (1987). *The travel and tropical medicine manual.* Philadelphia: W. B. Saunders Company.

Manson-Bahr, P. E. C., & Bell, D. R. (1987). *Manson's Tropical Diseases* (19th ed.). Philadelphia: Bailliere Tindall.

Neumann, H. H. (1987). *Foreign travel and immunization guide* (12th ed.). Oradell, NJ: Medical Economics Books.

Pust, R. E., Peate, W. F., & Cordes, D. H. (1986). Comprehensive Care of Travelers. *The Journal of Family Practice.* 23(6). 572–579.

Strickland, G. T. (Ed.) (1984). *Hunter's Tropical Medicine* (6th ed.). Philadelphia: W. B. Saunders Company.

Western, K. A. (Ed.). (1989). *Health hints for the tropics 1989.* Washington: The American Society for Tropical Medicine and Hygiene. *Order from the editor for $4.00; c/o Tropical Medicine and Hygiene News, 6436 31st St., NW, Washington, DC 20015-2342*

Wolfe, M. S. (1984). Diseases of travelers. *Ciba Symposia.* 36 (2).

Travel Medical Update Service—Physician Audience

Travel Health Information Service; price range from $495 to $795 for hard copy and/or computer disk updates. Contact Shoreland Medical Marketing, Inc, 5827 West Washington Boulevard Milwaukee, WI 53208–1652; Telephone (414) 774–4600.

Immunization Alert; price range $495 to $795 for monthly or weekly computer floppy disc updates. Contact Immunization Alert, P. O. Box 406, Storrs, CT 06268; Telephone (203) 487–0422.

Section 2
Resources and Services

Where can we obtain help, both before the trip, during it, and afterwards? There are many very helpful resources. Travel medical specialists exist all across the country to help. There are many insurance plans that can provide medical cost reimbursement or payment (there is a significant difference), and special plans that provide help in the form of telephonic advice or directly through local agents. The Department of State provides a variety of services, but it is also limited in what it can do for the traveler due to constraints of resources and because of U.S. and international law.

This section of the Travelers' Medical Resource provides networking information for the traveler, with points of contact and basic information on the services various specialists and agencies can provide the traveler.

Chapter 2.1

U.S. Governmental Help for the Traveler

The services which the US Embassy can, and cannot, provide

When confronting trouble in a foreign land, it is natural to think of turning to the embassy of the United States as a source of help, be it legal, medical, or financial. While the consular officers at the embassy can provide certain important services, these functions are limited by law and by the extent of their work load to specific activities.

For information concerning missing persons, emergencies, and deaths of Americans abroad, contact the telephone operator, Department of State, (202) 634-3600. Correspondence should be directed to the Overseas Citizens Services, Bureau of Consular Affairs, Department of State, Washington, D.C. 20520. A special hot line number for reporting concerns of a U.S. Citizen in trouble overseas can be contacted 24 hours per day by calling (202) 647–5225. If you have a touch tone telephone, this same number can be used to request travel advisory information (see Chapter 2.2) and to check on visa requirements by foreign governments for U.S. travelers.

U.S. consular officers are located at U.S. Embassies and consulates in most countries overseas. The telephone number and address of each of these offices, and for the local Canadian government representative, is listed in the country information database starting on page 8–1. Consular officers can advise you of any adverse conditions in the places you are visiting and can help you in emergencies. If you plan more than a short stay in one place or if you are in an area experiencing civil unrest or some natural disaster, it is advisable to register with the nearest U.S. Embassy or consulate. This will make it easier to locate you should someone at home need to contact you urgently or in the unlikely event that you need to be evacuated due to a local emergency. It will also facilitate the issuance of a new passport should yours be lost or stolen.

Should you find yourself in any legal difficulty, contact a consular officer immediately. Consular officers cannot serve as attorneys or give legal advice, but they can provide lists of local attorneys and help you find legal representation. Consular officers cannot get you out of jail. However, if you are arrested, ask permission to notify a consular official—it is your right under international law. American consular officials will visit you, advise you of your rights under local laws, attempt to ensure that you are not held under inhumane conditions, and contact your family and friends for you if you desire. They can transfer money and will try to get relief for you, including food and clothing, in countries where this is a problem. If you become destitute overseas, consular officers can help you get in touch with family, friends, bank, or employer and inform them how to wire funds to you.

Consular officers will do their best to assist U.S. nationals traveling or residing abroad. However, they must devote their priority time and energies to those Americans who are in serious legal, medical, or financial difficulties. Consular employees also provide non-emergency services, such as information on absentee voting, selective service registration, travel advisories, and acquisition and loss of U.S. citizenship. They can arrange for the transfer of Social Security and other benefits to beneficiaries residing abroad, provide U.S. tax forms, and notarize documents. They also provide information on procedures to obtain foreign public documents.

Because of the small number of consular officers abroad and the growing number of American travelers, consuls cannot provide routine or commercial-type activities. They cannot act as travel agents, lawyers, information bureaus, banks, or law enforcement officers. Do not expect them to find you employment, get residence or driving permits, act as interpreters, search for missing luggage, or settle disputes with hotel managers, although they can inform you on how to get assistance on these and other matters.

If you are injured or become seriously ill abroad, a U.S. consular officer will assist you in finding a physician or other appropriate medical services. With your permission, they will inform your next of kin or other family members and friends of your condition. In the spaces provided in your passport, enter the name, address, and telephone number of someone not traveling with you who should be informed of any emergency. If needed, consular officers will assist your family in transferring money to the foreign country to pay for your treatment.

When you are in a foreign country, you are subject to its laws. Use common sense. Avoid areas of unrest and disturbance. Deal only with authorized outlets when you exchange money or buy airline tickets and travelers checks. Do not deliver packages for anyone unless you are certain they do not contain drugs or other contraband.

On the average, 2,700 Americans are arrested aboard each year. Of these, approximately one-third are held on drug charges. Despite repeated warnings, drug arrests and convictions are still a common occurrence. If you are caught with any drugs overseas, you are subject to local—not U.S.—laws. A number of countries have imposed stiff penalties for drug violations and strict enforcement of existing drug laws. If you are arrested, you will find that:

* Few countries provide a jury trial.
* Most countries do not accept bail.
* Pretrial detention, often in solitary confinement, may last months.
* Prisons may lack even minimal comforts—bed, toilet, washbasin.
* Diets are often inadequate and require supplements from relatives and friends.
* Officials may not speak English.
* Physical abuse, confiscation of personal property, degrading or inhumane treatment, and extortion are possible.

If you are convicted, you face a sentence of:

* 2 to 10 years in most countries.
* A minimum of 6 years' hard labor and stiff fine in some countries.
* The death penalty in some countries.

Do not get involved with illegal drugs overseas. It can ruin your life!

A SUMMARY OF IMPORTANT SERVICES DURING FOREIGN TRAVEL PROVIDED BY THE U.S. DEPARTMENT OF STATE CONSULAR OFFICES

Legal Problems During Foreign Travel

Remember, you are subject to local laws. If you encounter difficulties with authorities overseas, there is very little assistance that U.S. consular officials can provide. What American officials can do is limited by both foreign and U.S. laws. The U.S. Government has no funds for your legal fees or other related expense.

Consult a consular officer if you find yourself in a dispute which could lead to legal or police action. Although U.S. consular officers cannot serve as attorneys or give legal advice, they can provide lists of local attorneys and help you find adequate legal representation. These lists of attorneys, although carefully prepared, are compiled from local bar association lists and responses to questionnaires. Neither the Department of State, nor U.S. embassies or consulates, can assume any responsibility for the caliber, competence, or professional integrity of the attorneys. Consular officers will do whatever they can to protect your legitimate interests and ensure that you are not discriminated against under local law. They cannot get you out of jail. If you are arrested, ask the authorities to notify the consular officer at the nearest U.S. embassy or consulate. Under international agreement and practice, you have the right to talk to the American consul. If you are denied this right, be persistent and try to have someone get in touch for you.

When alerted, U.S. officials will visit you, advise you of your rights (or lack thereof) under local laws, and contact your family and friends if you so desire. Consuls can transfer money, food, and clothing to the prison authorities from your family and friends. They will try to get relief if you are held under inhumane or unhealthy conditions or treated less favorably than others in the same situation.

Loss of Funds During Foreign Travel

Should you become destitute abroad, the U.S. consul will help you get in touch with your family, friends, bank, or employer and tell you how to arrange for them to send funds for you. In some cases, these funds can be wired to you through the Department of State.

Illness and Injury During Foreign Travel

If you are injured or become seriously ill abroad, the consul will help you find medical assistance and, at your request, inform your family or friends. In an emergency, when you are unable to communicate, the consul will check your passport for the name and address of any relative, friend, or legal representative whom you wish to have notified. Because the U.S. Government cannot pay for medical evacuations out of foreign countries, consider obtaining private medical insurance before you travel to cover the often exorbitant cost for getting you back to the United States for hospital care in the event of a medical emergency (see Chapter 2.6).

Marriages Performed During Foreign Travel

U.S. diplomatic and consular officials do not have the authority to perform marriages overseas. Marriages abroad must be performed in accordance with local laws. In many countries, there is a lengthy residence requirement before a marriage may take place. There are also certain documentary requirements. Consult the embassy or consulate of the country in which you plan to marry about these regulations.

Childbirth During Foreign Travel

A child born abroad to a U.S. citizen parent or parents generally acquires U.S. citizenship at birth. The parent should contact the nearest American embassy or consulate to have a "Report of Birth Abroad of a Citizen of the United States of America (Form FS-240)" prepared. This document serves as proof of acquisition of U.S. citizenship and is acceptable evidence for obtaining a passport and for most other purposes.

Death During Foreign Travel—Return of Remains

Of the 28 million Americans who traveled during 1984, 6,000 died while overseas. It can take over 100 contacts in two or more countries, involving over 300 steps to properly arrange for returning an ill, injured, or deceased traveler home from overseas. Cost can be a significant factor in returning the deceased to the United States. When shipping by air, it may be necessary to provide accompaniment—which means additional air fare. If the overseas trip was with family, the return for other family members, who have been forced to alter travel arrangements, may be at a much higher ticket rate than previously paid. Many U. S. citizens retire overseas, others have relatives in foreign lands—the importation of the deceased into this country may have application in these circumstances also.

These facts make the acquisition of travel insurance appealing. It is not simply the costs involved, but also the rather complicated liaisons that are required at a time of extreme emotional stress. Most insurance plans include a strong emphasis on providing an ombudsman to provide liaison with various governmental and commercial authorities, even paying for accompaniment of children or the deceased back to the US.

Quoting from the official publication of the Centers for Disease Control:

> *There are no federal restrictions on the importation of human remains if death does not result from any of the following communicable diseases: cholera or suspected cholera, diphtheria, infectious tuberculosis, plague, suspected smallpox, yellow fever, suspected viral hemorrhagic fevers (Lassa, Marburg, Ebola, Congo-Crimean, and others not yet isolated or named). If a person dies as a result of one of these diseases, the remains shall not be brought into a port under the control of the United States unless properly embalmed and placed in a hermetically sealed casket, or cremated.*
>
> *The remains must be accompanied by a death certificate translated into English to identify the remains and state the cause of death. The local mortician will comply with regulations of the local health department and the States concerning interstate or intrastate shipment.*

You will note that AIDS was not mentioned, but one could presume that it might be added to the restrictions concerning importation from contagious disease, and that the body will then have to be handled as indicated above.

The above regulation could pose problems for certain religious communities, such as kosher Jewish practice, with regard to the embalming or cremation requirements. Generally, health regulations—particularly international ones—do not accept religious convictions or requests as valid excuses for not complying with the letter of the law.

When a U.S. citizen dies abroad, the consular officer reports the death to the next of kin or legal representative and arranges to obtain from them necessary private funds for burial or return of the body to the United States. Because the U.S. Government cannot pay for local burial or shipment of remains to the United States, it is a worthwhile precaution to have some insurance which will cover this expense. Following a death, a "Report of the Death of An American Citizen (Form FS-192/Optional Form 180) is prepared by the consular officer to provide the facts concerning the death and the custody of the personal estate of the deceased. Under certain circumstances, a consular officer becomes the provisional conservator of a deceased American's estate and arranges for the disposition of those effects.

Incidentally, the United States has no restrictions for the exportation of the deceased, but the requirements of the country of destination must be met. This information will have to be obtained from the embassy or local consulate general of the country in question.

Chapter 2.2

Department of State Travel Information

Issued sporadically in response to urgent local conditions, the Department of State Travel Advisories are valuable, urgent communications from local embassy officials, through the State Department in Washington, D. C., that warn of local crises of health, political unrest, weather hazards, and other events of importance to travelers. The current country specific advisories can be obtained by calling number (202) 647–5225. Using a touch tone telephone automates this system, but a voice operator is also available.

All State Department Travel Advisories that were current when this book went to press are included in the country database on page 8–1. This is possible because the country database portion was set just prior to printing using the Herchmer computer database program interfaced directly into the typesetting program. The use of the Herchmer database update program, as described in Chapter 2.8, will allow readers to obtain recent information on each country of interest, including any *current* Department of State Travel Advisory information.

The possible political hazards which a traveler faces are amongst the most potentially dangerous health conditions that exist. This source of information should not be ignored by any traveler. Once inside a foreign country, the U.S. Embassy remains a source of current information and should be contacted in case of emergency—whether from political or natural causes. The address of the American embassy and consulates and Canadian High Commissions are located in the individual country database listings in this book. Update information may be obtained from the Herchmer database mentioned above. Also refer to Chapter 3.2 of this book for the special section on terrorism for techniques to generally reduce your level of vulnerability.

Addresses of U.S. embassies abroad can be obtained from the Superintendent of Documents, U.S. Government Printing Office, Washington, DC 20402–9325, by asking for the current edition of Department of State Publication Number 7877, "Key Offices of Foreign Service Posts." The 1990 edition cost was $5.00. This publication is updated three times a year.

For addresses of Canadian High Commissions, request a publication entitled "Canadian Representatives Abroad" from the Canadian Government Publishing Centre, Ottawa, Canada K1A 0S9 for $8.00 Canadian.

Travel Tips for Senior Citizens is a pamphlet containing information on passports, visas, health, currency, and suggestions for older Americans planning a trip abroad. Copies are available for $1.00 from the U.S. Government Printing Office.

A Safe Trip Abroad contains helpful precautions one can take to minimize the chance of becoming a victim of terrorism and also provides other safety tips. The cost is $1.00, also available from the U.S. Government Printing Office.

Background Notes are brief, factual pamphlets describing the countries of the world. There are about 170 *Notes* containing the most current information on each country's people, culture, geography, history, government, economy, and political conditions. *Background Notes* also include a reading list, travel notes and maps. Single copies are available from the U.S. Government Printing Office for $2.00.

Tips for Travelers provides advice prepared by the Bureau of Consular Affairs on travel to specific areas of the world. Depending on the particular region being discussed, the brochure might cover such topics as currency and customs regulations, entry requirements, dual nationality, import and export controls, vaccination requirements, restrictions on the use of photography, and warnings about the use of drugs. Single copies are for sale at $1.00 each from the U.S. Government Printing Office. This series currently includes the following titles:

Tips for Travelers to the Caribbean
Tips for Travelers to Cuba
Tips for Travelers to Eastern Europe and Yugoslavia
Tips for Travelers to Mexico
Tips for Travelers to the Middle East and North Africa
Tips for Travelers to the People's Republic of China
Tips for Travelers to South Asia
Tips for Travelers to Sub-Saharan Africa
Tips for Travelers to the USSR

While not relating directly to medical or personal safety while overseas, travelers should be aware of several other brochures that will aid in the process of returning through U.S. Customs. *Know Before You Go, Customs Hints for Returning U.S. Residents* contains information about key U.S. Customs regulations and procedures, including duty rates. Single copies are available free from any Customs office or by writing U.S. Customs Publications, P. O. Box 7407, Washington, DC 20044.

Travelers Tips on Bringing Food, Plant, and Animal Products Into the United States lists entry requirements for these items from most parts of the world. Fresh fruit and vegetables, meat, potted plants, pet birds, and other items are prohibited or restricted. The publication in English, Spanish, Italian, or Japanese is free from the Animal and Plant Health Inspection Service, U.S. Department of Agriculture, 732 Federal Building, 6505 Belcrest Road, Hyattsville, MD 20782.

Buyer Beware! provides guidelines governing restrictions on imports of wildlife and wildlife products into the United States. For a free copy, write the Publications Unit, U.S. Fish and Wildlife Service, Department of the Interior, Washington, DC 20240. Additional information on the import of wildlife products can be obtained through TRAFFIC (U.S.A.), World Wildlife Fund—U.S., 1250—24th Street, NW, Washington, DC 20037.

Chapter 2.3

WHO and CDC Bulletins

The World Health Organization and the Centers for Disease Control (a U.S. governmental agency) are valuable sources of information on various aspects of disease prevention, occurrence reports, immunization requirements and recommendations, and information of importance to world travelers in general.

Medical personnel may subscribe to the Summary of Health Information for International Travel, a biweekly publication of the CDC known as the "Blue Sheet," by requesting that their names be placed on a free mailing list. Contact CDC, Atlanta, GA 30333.

A weekly report of infectious diseases in the United States and important overseas medical developments is contained in the CDC weekly publication "Morbidity and Mortality Weekly Report." Subscriptions can be obtained from the CDC, Atlanta, GA 30333, or from the Massachusetts Medical Society, C.S.P.O. Box 9120, Waltham, MA 02254–9120, which reprints these reports as part of an inexpensive subscription service.

Another weekly summary for professional use is the CDC report "Weekly Summary—Countries with Areas Infected with Quarantinable Diseases." Subscriptions can be obtained from CDC Center for Prevention Services, Division of Quarantine, Atlanta, GA 30333.

An annual publication of the CDC is "Health Information for International Travel," 1989 Stock Number 017-023-00184-1 ($5.00 per copy). Order from the Superintendent of Documents, U.S. Government Printing Office, Washington, D.C. 20402-9325; telephone (202) 783-3238. This book is designed for physician use, but it is easily understood by non-physician readers. It is the singular most important book concerning foreign travel which is obtainable from any governmental agency. This 106 page book contains the latest recommendations from the Centers for Disease Control on malaria prophylaxis, disease immunization, specific medical conditions and travel, even information concerning pets and animal quarantines.

The official publications of the World Health Organization are not quite as reliable as those from the Centers for Disease Control as they tend to be somewhat political and less objective in reporting actual medical occurrences. The under reporting of disease incidence by countries not wishing to see a decrease in tourist dollars, or to avoid political embarrassment, is the source of this difference. Their most significant publication is "Vaccination Certificate Requirements and Health Advice for International Travel 1990." It is available through the WHO Publication Center USA, 49 Sheridan Avenue, Albany NY 12210.

WHO and CDC maintain official records of locations of endemic diseases, such as yellow fever, cholera, malaria, dracunculiasis, and other contagious or parasitic illness. At times the official locations vary between the two agencies, with one showing a specific geographical region within a country as infected, the other indicating this area disease free. The Herchmer database starting on page 8-1 takes into account the above and considers an area infected if so reported by either organization.

Physicians may obtain international vaccination requirements and travelers' health information from the Public Health Service

Quarantine Station located in their region. Regional offices and telephone numbers are:

Chicago	*(312) 686–2150*
Honolulu	*(808) 541–2552*
Los Angeles	*(213) 215–2365*
Miami	*(305) 526–2910*
New York	*(718) 917–1685*
San Francisco	*(415) 876–2872*
Seattle	*(206) 442–4519*

The Centers for Disease Control has special and general telephone numbers available for public information on specific diseases and for physician counseling. Their main switchboard number for weekday use is (404) 639–3311. Evenings, weekends, and holidays the duty office telephone number is (404) 639–2888.

Lay persons and physicians may call the Centers for Disease Control special hot line telephone number for current Malaria Prevention and Prophylaxis advice at (404) 639–1610.

Physicians may obtain counseling and availability information concerning drugs for parasitic disease treatment from the Centers for Disease Control at (404) 639–3670.

Physicians may obtain recommendations and counseling with regard to rabies risk and treatment protocols from the Rabies Branch of the Centers for Disease Control at (404) 639–3095.

Chapter 2.4

State Boards of Health

You may contact your state board of health, listed below, for the telephone number of the appropriate, local county board of health official or office which handles infectious disease, immunization, and foreign travel information. They can refer you to the nearest Yellow Fever Vaccination Center, if you find that this vaccination is required or suggested for your journey.

They will also be able to refer you for cholera immunization, if that is similarly required. They should maintain a list of physicians in your area who possess a "Uniform Stamp" that must be used to validate your cholera or yellow fever immunization. The World Health Organization suggests no longer "requiring" cholera immunization for international travel, but refer to the complete discussion of this topic in Chapter 6.5.

The epidemiologist at your county or state board of health can generally provide foreign travel information concerning yellow fever, cholera, and other epidemics. They will frequently be able to provide information concerning malaria resistance patterns. International vaccination requirements are also available from this source.

TABLE 2–1
State Boards of Health in the United States

ALABAMA
Alabama Department of Public
   Health
434 Monroe
Montgomery, AL 36130
205–261–5095

ALASKA
Division of Public Health
P.O. Box H-O6C
Juneau, AK 99811–0616
907–465–3141

ARIZONA
Arizona Department of Public
   Health Services
3008 N.Third St.
Phoenix, AZ 85012
602–230–5833

ARKANSAS
Arkansas Department of Health
4815 W. Markham
Little Rock, AR 72201
501–661–2352

CALIFORNIA
Department of Health Services
714 744 "P" Street
Sacramento, CA 95814
916–322–4787

COLORADO
Colorado Department of Health
4210 East 11th Ave.
Denver, CO 80220
303–320–8333

CONNECTICUT
State of Connecticut Department
   of Health Services
150 Washington St.
Hartford, CT 06106
203–566–4800

DELAWARE
Division of Public Health
P.O. Box 637
Dover, DE 19903
302–736–4724

DISTRICT OF COLUMBIA
D.C. Department of Human
   Services
1875 Connecticut Ave., N.W.,
   Rm. 810
Washington, D.C. 20009
202–673–6738

FLORIDA
Department of Health
2720 Blair Stone Plaza. Ste. C.
Tallahassee, FL 32301
904–488–2901

GEORGIA
Department of Human Resources
47 Trinity S.W.
Atlanta, GA 30334
404–656–5542

GUAM
Department of Public Health &
  Social Services
P O Box 2816
Government of Guam
Agana, Guam 96910
671–734–2951

HAWAII
State Department of Health
Health Promotion Education Office
P.O. Box 3378
Honolulu, HI 96801
808–548–5886

IDAHO
Department of Health and Welfare
4355 Emerald
Boise, ID 83706
208–334–6700

ILLINOIS
Illinois Department of Public
  Health
1330 West Jefferson
Springfield, IL 62601
217–633–0267

INDIANA
Indiana State Board of Health
1330 West Michigan Street
P.O. Box 1964
Indianapolis, IN 46206–1964
317–633–0267

IOWA
State Department of Health
Lucas State Office Building
3rd Floor
Des Moines, IA 50319
515–281–3583

KANSAS
Kansas Department of Health and
  Environment
60700 S.W. Topeka Blvd.,
  Building 740
Topeka, KS 66620
913–296–1500

KENTUCKY
Department of Human Resources
275 E. Main St.
Frankfort, KY 40621
502–564–6620

LOUISANA
Office of Health Services and
  Environmental Quality
325 Loyola Ave., Rm. 304.
New Orleans, LA 70160
504–568–5413

MAINE
Department of Human Services
Bureau of Health
State House, Station #11
Augusta, ME 04333
207–289–3201

MARIANA ISLANDS
Department of Health Services
Trust Territory of the Pacific
  Islands
Office of the High Commissioner
Saipan, Mariana Islands 96950

MARYLAND
Maryland Department of Health
  and Mental Hygiene
201 West Preston St.
Baltimore, MD 21201
301–225–6860

MASSACHUSETTS
Massachusetts Department of
  Public Health
150 Tremont St.
Boston, MA 02111
617-727-7170

MICHIGAN
Michigan Department of Public
  Health
3423 North Logan
P.O. Box 30195
Lansing, MI 48909
517-335-8000

MINNESOTA
Minnesota Department of Health
717 Delaware St.,S.E. Box 9441
Minneapolis, MN 55440
612-623-5100

MISSISSIPPI
Mississippi State Board of Health
2423 N. State
P. O. Box 1700
Jackson, MS 39215-1700
601-960-7463

MISSOURI
Missouri Division of Health
P.O. Box 570
Jefferson City, MO 65102
314-751-6400

MONTANA
Montana Department of Health
  and Environmental Sciences
Cogswell Building
Helena, MT 59620
406-494-4740

NEBRASKA
State of Nebraska Department of
  Health
301 Centennial Mall South
P.O. Box 95007
Lincoln, NE 68509
402-471-2101

NEVADA
Department of Human Resources
Room 200 Kinhead Building
505 E. King Street
Carson City, NV 89710
702-885-4740

NEW HAMPSHIRE
New Hampshire Division of Public
  Health
Health and Welfare Building
6 Hazen Drive
Concord, NH 03301-6527
603-271-4551

NEW JERSEY
New Jersey Department of Health
379 W. State St.
Trenton, NJ 08625
609-292-4076

NEW MEXICO
Health and Environmental
  Department
P.O. Box 968
Santa Fe, NM 87504
505-827-2623

NEW YORK
New York State Health Department
Tower Building, Rm. 1312
Empire State Plaza
Albany, NY 12237
518-474-5370

NORTH CAROLINA
North Carolina Department of
Human Resources
P.O. Box 2091
Raleigh, NC 27602
919-733-7081

NORTH DAKOTA
State Health Department
Capitol Building
Bismarck, ND 58505
701-224-2367

OHIO
Ohio Department of Health
246 North High Street
P.O. Box 118
Columbus, OH 43266-0118
614-466-4626

OKLAHOMA
Oklahoma Department of Health
N.E. 10th and Stonewall
Oklahoma City, OK 73152
405-271-5601

OREGON
Department of Human Resources
508 State Office Building
1400 S.E. 5th
P.O. Box 231
Portland, OR 97207
503-378-3033

PENNSYLVANIA
Pennsylvania Department of Health
P.O. Box 90
Harrisburg, PA 17108
717-787-5900

PUERTO RICO
Puerto Rico Department of Health
San Juan, PR 00908
809-765-4175

RHODE ISLAND
Rhode Island Department of
Health
103 Cannon Building
75 Davis Street
Providence, RI 02908-5097
401-277-2853

SOUTH CAROLINA
South Carolina Department of
Health
and Environmental Control
2600 Bull St.
Columbia, SC 29201
803-734-5360

SOUTH DAKOTA
State of South Dakota Health
Department
523 E. Capitol
Pierre, SD 57501
605-773-3737

TENNESSEE
State Department of Health
344 Cordell Hall
Nashville, TN 37219
615-741-7366

TEXAS
Texas Department of Health
1100 West 49th Street
Austin, TX 78756
512-458-7405

UTAH
Utah Department of Health
P.O. Box 16700
Salt Lake City, UT 84116-0700
801-538-6100

VERMONT
State Health Department
P.O. Box 70
Burlington, VT 05402
802-863-7200, Ext. 207

VIRGINIA
Virginia State Health Department
Room 515, 109 Governor Street
Richmond, VA 23219
804-786-3551

VIRGIN ISLANDS
Virgin Islands Department of
    Health
P. O. Box 520, Christiansted
St. Croix, U.S.V.I. 00820
809-773-1311

WASHINGTON
Department of Social and Health
    Services
1112 S. Quince MS. ET24
Olympia, WA 98504
206-753-5909

WEST VIRGINIA
West Virginia Department of
    Health
1800 Washington St., Rm. 535
Charleston, WV 25305
304-348-2971

WISCONSIN
State Health Department
P.O. Box 309
Madison, WI 53701
608-266-0923

WYOMING
Department of Health and Social
    Services
Hathaway Building, 4th Floor
Cheyenne, WY 82002
307-777-6011

Chapter 2.5

Travelers' Medical Clinics

The clinics and physicians listed below have expressed an interest in providing travelers with counseling on avoidance of hazards while traveling and in providing immunizations and prescriptions required for preventative medical care.[1] Under the line listed as "codes" each clinic is noted which provides travel immunizations and other special services.

The special code "YF" indicates that the yellow fever vaccine is also available at that facility. This special immunization can also be obtained at most state boards of health and at many county boards of health. Additional sources of immunization help can also be obtained by calling your local State Board of Health as listed in Chapter 2.4.

---

[1]Physicians and clinics wishing to be listed in this section in future editions of this book should write, indicating their interest, for an application form to William W. Forgey, M.D., 812 North West Street, Crown Point, Indiana 46307-3128.

ARIZONA

D. H. Cordes, M.D.
Codes: Travel immunizations, YF
Travelers' Clinic
University of Arizona Health Sciences Center
Department of Family and Community Medicine
Tucson, AZ 85724
Telephone: (602) 626-7900

Tim Kuberski, M.D.
Codes: Travel immunizations
5757 W. Thunderbird Road
Suite W212
Glendale, AZ 85306
Telephone: (602) 439-0274

Wayne F. Peate, M.D., MPH
Codes: Travel immunizations
Clinical Tropical Medicine, Inc.
Corporate Medical Centre
2545 E. Adams Street
Tucson, AZ 85716
Telephone: (601) 881-0050

CALIFORNIA

Elizabeth Barrett-Connor, M.D.
David Rosen, M.D.
Codes: Travel immunizations, YF
UCSD Medical Center
Family Medicine Clinic
225 W. Dickinson
San Diego, CA 92103
Telephone (619) 543-5787

Charles Beal, M.D.
Paul DeLay, M.D., DTM&H

Gordon J. Frierson, M.D., DTM&H
Robert Goldsmith, M.D. DTM&H
Edward Markell, Ph.D., M.D.
Codes: Travel immunizations, YF
Tropical Medicine—Infectious Disease Clinic
University of California, San Fransisco
350 Parnassus Street
San Fransisco, CA 94143
Telephone: (415) 476–5787

Victor L. Kovner, M.D.
Codes: Travel immunizations, YF
Travelers Immunization Center
12311 Ventura Blvd
Studio City, CA 91604
Telephone: (818) 762–1167

Claire B. Panosian, M.D.
Codes: Travel immunizations, YF
UCLA Travelers' and Tropical Medicine Clinic
Department of Medicine Practice Group
UCLA Medical Center
10833 LeConte Avenue
Los Angeles, CA 90024
Telephone: (213) 825–9711

Bob Young, M.D.
Codes: Travel immunizations
Travel Immunization Clinic
29 W. Anapamu Street
Santa Barbara, CA 93101
Telephone: (805) 965–0052

CONNECTICUT

Michele Barry, M.D.
Frank Bia, M.D., MPH
Codes: Travel immunizations, YF

Tropical Medicine and International Travelers Clinic
Yale University School of Medicine
20 York Street
New Haven, CT 06504
Telephone (203) 785–2476

Martin E. Gordon, M.D.
Codes: Consultant, Diseases of Travel
Yale School of Medicine
111 Sherman Avenue
New Haven, CT 06511
Telephone: (203) 624–5850

Kenneth R. Dardick, M.D., FACP
Codes: Travel immunizations, YF
Mansfield Family Practice
Mansfield Professional Park
Storrs, CT 06268
Telephone: (203)487–0002

David R. Hill, M.D.
Sam T. Donta, M.D.
Codes: Travel immunizations, YF, pre- and post-travel care
International Travelers Medical Service
University of Connecticut Health Center
Farmington, CT 06032
Telephone: (203) 674–3245

DISTRICT OF COLUMBIA

Vinod R. Mody, FRCP, DTM&H
Codes: Travel immunizations
Howard University Hospital
2041 Georgia Avenue, NW
Washington, D.C. 20060
Telephone: (202) 745–6641

David M. Parenti, M.D.
Carmelia Tuazon, M.D.
Gary L. Simond, M.D.
Codes: Travel immunizations, YF
Division of Infectious Diseases/Travler's Clinic
The George Washington University Medical Center
2150 Pennsylvania Avenue NW
Washington, D.C. 20037
Telephone: (202) 676-5558

Martin S. Wolfe, M.D.
Codes: Travel immunizations, YF
Travelers Medical Service
2141 K Street NW—Room 408
Washington, D.C. 20037
Telephone: (202) 466-8109

FLORIDA

Caroline L. MacLeod, M.D., MPH & TM,
Mark E. Whiteside, M.D.
Codes: Travel immunizations, YF
Institute of Tropical Medicine
1780 N.E. 168th Street
North Miami Beach, FL 33162
Telephone: (305) 947-1722

David N. Reifsnyder, M.D.
Codes: Travel immunizations, YF at nearby health department
901 N. Hercules Avenue, Suite C.
Clearwater, FL 34625
Telephone: (813) 446-3515

GEORGIA

Daniel S. Blumenthal, M.D.
Codes: Travel immunizations
Morehouse Family Practice Center

501 Fairburn Road, SW
Atlanta, GA 30331
Telephone: (404) 752-1624

Phyllis E. Kozarsky, M.D.
Codes: Travel immunizations, YF
The Emory Clinic
Crawford Long Hospital Outpatient Center
20 Linden Avenue
Atlanta, GA 30365
Telephone: (404) 892-4411 Ext 8114 or 5885

HAWAII

Vernon Ansdell, M.D., M.R.C.P., DTM&H
Codes: Travel immunizations, YF
Travel Medicine Clinic
Kaiser Permanente Honolulu Clinic
1010 Pensacola Street
Honolulu, HI 96814
Telephone (808) 529-2394

Francis D. Pien, M.D., MPH
Codes: Travel immunizations
Straub Clinic & Hospital, Inc.
888 South King Street
Honolulu, HA 96813
Telephone: (808) 523-2311

KANSAS

Larry W. Rumans, M.D.
C. Michael West, M.D.
Codes: Travel immunizations
Internal Medicine/Infectious Disease Consultants
631 Horne, Suite 420
Topeka, KS 66606
Telephone: (913) 234-8405

LOUISIANA

Rodney C. Jung, M.D., Ph.D., FACP
Codes: Travel immunizations
3600 Chestnut Street
New Orleans, LA 70115
Telephone: (504) 895–2007

William A. Sodeman, Jr., M.D.
Codes: Consultation
Louisiana State University School of Medicine
P O Box 33932
Shreveport, LA 71130
Telephone: (318) 674–5190

MAINE

Robert P. Smith, M.D.
Codes: Travel immunizations
Spurwink Internal Medicine Associates
155 Spurwink Avenue
Cape Elizabeth, ME 04107
Telephone: (207) 767–2174

MARYLAND

Stephen O. Cunnion, M.D., Ph.D., MPH
Codes: Limited to government employees
Uniformed Services University of Health Services
Bethesda, MD 20814

Deirdre A. Herrington, M.D.
G. Thomas Strickland, M.D.
J. Glenn Morris, M.D.
Carol O. Tacket, M.D.
Codes: Travel immunizations, pre- and post-travel care
Traveler's Health Service

University of Maryland Medical Group
Baltimore, MD 21201
Telephone: (301) 328-5196

Bradley R. Sack, M.D., Sc.D.
Codes: Travel immunizations, YF
Johns Hopkins International Medical Services
550 N. Broadway, Room 107
Baltimore, MD 21205
Telephone: (301) 955-6931

MASSACHUSETTS

Donna Felsenstein, M.D.
John S. Wolfson, M.D.
Codes: Travel immunizations, YF
Traveler's Advice and Immunization Center
Massachusetts General Hospital
Wang ACC 428
Boston, MA 02114
Telephone (617) 726-2748

Leonard C. Marcus, VMD, M.D.
Codes: Travel immunizations, YF
Travelers Health and Immunization Service
148 Highland Avenue
Newton, MA 02160
Telephone: (617) 527-4003

Peter F. Weller, M.D.
Codes: Travel immunizations
Division of Infectious Diseases
Beth Israel Hospital
330 Brookline Avenue
Boston, MA 02215
Telephone: (617) 735-3307

Mary E. Wilson, M.D.
Codes: Travel immunizations, YF
Mount Auburn Hospital Travel Clinic
330 Mt Auburn Street
Cambridge, MA 02238
Telephone: (617) 499-5026

David J. Wyler, M.D.
Codes: Travel immunizations
Division of Geographic Medicine and Infectious Diseases
New England Medical Center Hospitals
750 Washington Street Box 041
Boston, MA 02111
Telephone: (617) 956-7002

MICHIGAN

Jeffrey D. Band, M.D.
Codes: Travel immunizations, YF
William Beaumont Hospital, Suite 707
3535 West Thirteen Mile Road
Royal Oak, MI 48072
Telephone (313) 288-2736

MISSOURI

Donald J. Krogstad, M.D.
Codes: Consultation in parasitic and tropical diseases
Washington University School of Medicine
660 S. Euclid Avenue
St Louis, MO 63110
Telephone: (314) 362-2998

MONTANA

M. J. Winship, M.D.
Codes: Travel immunizations
2825 Ft. Missoula Road

Missoula, MT 59501
Telephone: (406) 549-4782

NEW YORK

Burke A. Cunha, M.D.
Codes: Travel immunizations
International Travelers' Center
Winthrop-University Hospital
259 First Street
Mineola, NY 11501
Telephone: (516) 663-2505

Eileen Hilton, M.D.
Carol Singer, M.D.
Miriam Smith, M.D.
Codes: Travel immunizations, YF
Division of Infectious Diseases
Department of Medicine
Long Island Jewish Medical Center (Room B202)
Lakeville Road
New Hyde Park, N.Y. 11042
Telephone (718) 470-7290

Harold Horowitz, M.D.
Codes: Travel immunizations, YF
International Travelers' Health Service
New York Medical College
Division of Infectious Disease
Room 209 Macy Pavilion S.E.
Valhalla, NY 10595
Telephone (914) 285-8867/993-4655

Richard V. Lee, M.D.
Codes: Travel immunizations
Childrens Hospital of Buffalo
219 Bryant Street

Buffalo, NY 14222
Telephone: (716) 878–7751

Harry Most, M.D.
Codes: Travel immunizations, YF
New York University Medical Center
341 E 25th Street—Room 105
New York, NY 10010
Telephone: (212) 340–6764

Thomas J. Rush, M.D.
Codes: Travel immunizations, YF
Infectious Disease & Travel Health
One South Lawn Avenue
Elmsford, NY 10523
Telephone: (914) 592–2460

Herbert Tanowitz, M.D.
Murray Wittner, M.D.
Louis M.Weiss, M.D.
Codes: Travel immunizations, YF
Albert Einstein College of Medicine
1300 Morris Park Avenue
Bronx, NY 10461
Telephone: (212) 430–2059

NORTH CAROLINA

Thomas E. Frothingham, M.D.
David T. Durack, M.D.
Duke University Medical Center
P O Box #3937
Durham, NC 27710
Telephone: (919) 684–6832

PENNSYLVANIA

Mark Hofstetter, M.D.
Robert M. Lumish, M.D.
Stephen M. Colodny, M.D.
Codes: Travel immunizations
PittsburghInfectious Disease, Ltd.
1400 Locust Street
Pittsburgh, PA 15219
Telephone (412) 232-7398

William S. Kammerer, M.D.
Codes: Travel immunizations, YF, pre- and post travel care
The Milton S. Hershey Medical Center
  of the Pennsylvania State University
Hershey, PA 17033
Telephone: (717) 531-8161

Carl W. Norden, M.D.
Frederick Ruben, M.D.
Edward Wing, M.D.
Codes: Travel immunizations, YF (Health Dept one block away)
International Travel and Infectious Disease Consulation Service
Montefiore Hospital
3459 Fifth Avenue
Pittsburgh, PA 15213
Telephone: (412) 648-6410

SOUTH CAROLINA

Ludwig A. Lettau, M.D., MPH
Codes: Travel immunizations
Department of Internal Medicine/Infectious Disease
Greenville Memorial Medical Center
701 Grove Road
Greenville, SC 29605
Telephone: (803) 242-7889

TENNESSEE

William Schaffner, M.D.
Codes: Travel immunizations (and consultation)
Vanderbilt University Hospital
21st Avenue South
Nashville, TN 37232
Telephone: (615) 322–2017

VIRGINIA

Richard L. Guerrant, M.D., Head
R. D. Pearson, M.D.
E. L. Hewlett, M.D.
W. A. Petri, Jr., M.D., Ph.D.
J. I. Ravdin, M.D.
Codes: Travel immunizations, care of returning travelers
University of Virginia Travelers Clinic
University of Virginia Hospital
Division of Geographic Medicine
Charlottesville, VA 22908
Telephone: (804) 924–9677

WASHINGTON

Elaine Jong, M.D.
Craig Karpilow, M.D.
Codes: Travel immunizations, YF , pre- and post-travel care
UW Travel and Tropical Medicine Clinic
University of Washington School of Medicine
University Hospital RC-02
1959 NE Pacific
Seattle, WA 98195
Telephone (206) 548–4000/4226/4039

Richard A. Miller, M.D.
Codes: Travel immunizations, YF
Travelers Clinic, Infectious Disease Clinic

Regional Hansen's Disease Clinic
Pacific Medical Center
1200 12th Avenue S.
Seattle, WA 98144
Telephone: (206) 326-4013

WEST VIRGINIA

John Beaumont Walden, M.D.
Codes: Travel immunizations, YF
Marshall University School of Medicine
1801 Sixth Avenue
Huntington, WV 25701
Telephone: (304) 696-7046

CANADIAN LOCATIONS

J. S. Keystone, M.D., FRCP (C), M.Sc. (CTM)
Codes: Travel immunizations, YF
Tropical Disease Unit/Travel & Inoculation Unit
Toronto General Hospital
200 Elizabeth Street, en g-214
Toronto, Ontario, Canada M5G 2C4
Telephone: (416) 595-3670/3671/3675

Dick J. MacLean, M.D., FRCP (C)
David Dawson, M.D., FRCP (C)
Robert Wittes, M.D., CCFP
Laurence Green, M.D., FRCP (C)
Zafir Ali Khan, Ph.D.,
Roger Prichard, Ph.D.
Gaetan Faubert, Ph.D.
Dorothy Moore, M.D., FRCP (C)
Joyce Pickering, M.D., FRCP (C)
Codes: Travel immunizations, YF
McGill University Centre for Tropical Disease
Montreal General Hospital
1650 Cedar Avenue—Room 787

Montreal, Quebec, Canada H3G 1A4
Telephone: (514) 937–6011 ext. 3870

William Douglas MacPherson, B.Sc., M.SC. (CTM), M.D.,
   FRCP
Codes: Travel immunizations, YF
Infectious Diseases and Tropical Medicine Clinic
2F1 Chedoke-MacMaster Hospitals (MacMaster Division)
1200 Main Street West
Hamilton, Ontario, Canada L8N 3Z5
Telephone (416) 521–2100 ext. 5014

Chapter 2.6

Travel Insurance and Assistance

Over 28 million Americans traveled overseas in 1984. Of this number, more than 17,000 required assistance from the U.S. Department of State because of illness, injury, crime, and other travel related emergencies. Unfortunately, our embassy personnel are very limited in the services which they can provide (see Chapter 2.1).

Travelers have every reason to be concerned about how vulnerable they are while traveling away from home. Unaccustomed surroundings can turn even a minor problem into an emergency.

The possible problems go far beyond medical emergencies. Lost luggage with prescription medication, lost or damaged eye glasses or hearing aids, passport problems, visa extensions, and many more problems can beset the urban traveler. Those heading into remote areas have even additional predicaments which they may face.

Finding a source of help may be the first step in solving the emergency. Locating a doctor in a strange town is always of concern, whether in the US or overseas. A voluntary membership organization providing this service is IAMAT.

International Association for Medical Assistance to Travelers

Membership is free, but a donation of any amount is appreciated. This organization maintains a directory of physicians in various countries who adhere to a fixed fee for treating IAMAT members (Office call $20.00 US; House Call—Hotels, etc $30.00; Night, Sunday and local Holidays $40.00). These physicians speak English and have passed a credentials screen by IAMAT. Many useful publications are sent to the membership concerning malaria and tropical diseases. Membership in this organization is a worthwhile must for any foreign traveler.

Further information on services provided by this organization will be found by referring to Chapter 2.7. The future traveler is well advised to send a donation to IAMAT to aid in their attempts to provide this valuable networking services.

Address: IAMAT, 417 Center Street, Lewiston, NY 14092. Telephone (716) 754-4883.

Some of the travel insurance plans listed below will also provide lists of English speaking doctors.

The names, addresses, training background, and fee schedule of English speaking doctors are available from any of the U.S. embassies, consulates, and consular agencies (see discussion in Chapter 2.1). It is important to note that the while some embassies are staffed with medical personnel, they cannot, and will not, provide direct medical services.

While abroad, you may find that a hotel can provide a physician and emergency care referral. Of course, local friends, business contacts, travel agencies, airline offices and missionaries can be sources of referral. In a dire emergency, check the telephone book for an emergency number to call. If requiring emergency room services, try to locate one affiliated with a medical school, a major university, or located in a provincial or national capital or important city.

Travelers must be certain that their travel insurance will pay for the help when they need it. Many normal policies exclude foreign travel (Medicare does) and some will only make reimbursement after application is made with substantiating documents later. Translation of itemized medical bills and diagnosis must be obtained before some companies will make payment. It is important to make certain that medical evacuation costs back to the U.S. will be provided, or to obtain a supplemental policy that will accomplish this service.

The following lists of insurance programs offer an unusual variety of services. These range from finding English speaking doctors, to full financial assistance for medical bills, emergency travel money, and even communication and ombudsman assistance.

Credit Card Programs

Many credit cards, particularly the "gold cards," provide travel insurance, lost luggage insurance, and even medical help and emergency number services—if travel tickets are purchased by charging the expenses to their card. Refer to the membership benefit packages for any gold card (VISA, Mastercharge, American Express, etc.), which you may possess or contemplate joining.

The Travelers Insurance Company

Accident protection policy by this company will pay up to $5,000 in hospital expenses. Illness coverage is optional. Policy cost is $20 to $50 for 8 days of coverage. Separate trip cancellation policy costs $5.50 per $100.00. Special emergency medical evacuation coverage is available up to ten times the policy value, maximum $25,000.00.

Address: The Travelers Insurance Company, Ticket and Travel Plans, 1 Tower Square, Hartford, CT 06118. Telephone (800) 243-3174.

American Association of Retired Persons (AARP)

Special foreign medical care coverage is offered as part of this organization's Medicare Supplement package.

Blue Cross and Blue Shield

You must check with your insurance agent about BC/BS plan coverage. It is generally available, but as a reimbursement plan. You would have to make cash payments while overseas. Keep and submit your receipts, translated into English, to BC/BS, if you have this protection. An English translation of the diagnosis must also be submitted.

Nationwide-Worldwide Emergency Ambulance Return (NEAR)

Comprehensive medical services include fully paid hospitalization and medical evacuation anywhere in the world. These services are directly paid by NEAR. It can transmit personal medical information in English and in the appropriate foreign language to attending overseas doctors. They also provide a communication service between the patient and family at home. Offering semi-annual and yearly memberships with individual ($100/$150) and family ($140/$220) rates, this organization provides a variety of services for both domestic and foreign travelers. This includes reduced rates to the "Health Care Abroad" plan described above. A brochure with their 39 point protection plan is available by mail.

Address: NEAR, 1900 North MacArthur Blvd., Oklahoma City, OK 73127-2697. Telephone (405) 949-2500; toll free in continental U.S., Hawaii and Puerto Rico (800) 654-6700; toll free in Oklahoma (800) 522-6327.

Travel Assistance International division of Europe Assistance

A comprehensive program of medical, personal, financial and legal assistance for foreign and domestic travel, this organization has been used by major American corporations to support their overseas medical programs. Short term and yearly coverage is available. The plan includes up to $5,000 in medical expense and unlimited transportation expenses. Short term coverage cost is $40 for 1-8 days; full year coverage is $450.00. Additional programs for accidental death and dismemberment, trip cancellation or delay, and baggage loss are available.

Address: Travel Assistance International, 1133 15th Street, N.W., Suite 400, Washington, D.C., 20005. Telephone (202)

347–2025; toll free (800) 821–2828.

Access America, Inc.

Two programs are available, one for travel in the US, Mexico, Caribbean, and Canada, and the other for travel in Europe, Asia, Africa, South America, and Australia. Each program has several offerings, which include trip cancellation/delay insurance, 24 hour world wide hot line phone help, separate medical insurance programs, and comprehensive policies. Medical expense insurance covers up to $10,000 (with a one time $50 deductible for out patient care). Policy prices vary from $16 to $89 for 15 days for individuals, depending upon location of travel and benefits.

Address: 600 Third Avenue, Box 807, New York, NY 10163. Telephone (212) 808–5610, or (800) 851–2800 for information. Their policies are available through many travel agents.

International SOS Assistance

This organization is also used by many corporations in support of their overseas medical programs. They have special programs that help find English speaking doctors, monitor your care, arrange hospitalization if necessary, or arrange evacuation back to the US if you fail to improve within 7 days. Membership costs $25 for 1 to 14 days, $50 per month, or $195 per year for individuals. Special rates for couples and families are available. Trip cancellation/interruption insurance costs $21 per person additional as an optional plan. Another optional program is a $10,000.00 medical expense and accidental death and dismemberment plan that costs $19.00 for two weeks; $24.00 for 20 days; or $27.00 for 30 days. This coverage can be provided for trips over 30 days for $3.00 per person per day up to a maximum of 180 days.

Address: International SOS Assistance, P O Box 11568, Philadelphia, PA 19116. Telephone (215) 244–1500; (800) 523–8930; FAX (215) 244–9617.

ARM Coverage of New York
dba Carefree Travel Insurance

This plan underwritten by the Hartford (Div of ITT), is administered by InterClaim, the International Claim Service Corporation. Plan coverage includes up to $3,000 for medical expenses for inpatient or outpatient visits due to illness or injury while overseas. Coverage includes accidental death and dismemberment, a $1,000 lost baggage provision, and provides up to $30,000 for emergency evacuation. The plan costs $74 for up to a eight day period, with additional amounts for longer travel periods. A basic plan provides 1/3 the above benefits, but at 1/3 the cost. A separate Trip Contingency Protection policy costs $5.50 for each $100.00 of coverage.

Address: Carefree Travel Insurance, P. O. Box 310, 120 Mineola Blvd., Mineola, New York 11501. Telephone (516) 294–0220 or (800) 645–2424.

HealthCare Abroad

A product of Travel Insurance Programs Corporation, a member company of the International Underwriters Group, Washington, D.C., provides a $100,000.00 medical expense and $25,000 personal accident benefit for $3.00 per day (10 day minimum/90 day maximum protection). Optional personal accident insurance can raise that amount to $100,000.00 from the $25,000.00 basic plan for $9.00 for 30 days, $18.00 for 60 days, or $27.00 for 90 days coverage. Trip cancellation/curtailment costs $0.05 per dollar of coverage, available in $500.00 to $3,500.00 amounts. Baggage coverage costs $1.00 per person per day of coverage. There is a $50.00 cash deductible, but otherwise the plan makes direct payments to foreign medical doctors and hospitals. It provides a 24 hour/day, seven days/week referral hot line for a directory of overseas hospitals and doctors. They have English speaking doctors in over 1,100 cities in 128 countries. There is an exclusion for pre-existing medical conditions. Eligibility extends to any U.S. Resident to age 76 traveling outside of the United States. Ages 76 to 85 are cover by the same company under a plan called "HealthCare Global," which has a different rate/benefit structure. Last minute purchase of coverage is available prior to departure by telephone and chargeable to major credit cards.

Address: HealthCare Abroad, 243 Church Street West, Vienna, VA 22180. Telephone (800) 237–6615; (703) 281–9500.

TravelMed

Underwritten by Monumental General Insurance Company of Baltimore, Maryland, a $3.00 per day fee provides $100,000.00 of medical and accident protection. The company also provides other services such as a coordination center to help with emergency arrangements; air fare for a family member to visit, if you are hospitalized for serious illness or injury; air fare home for persons younger than 18 years of age, if they were accompanying an ill adult; return of remains; contact with family members at home; and monitoring of your progress. A less expensive plan with reduced options is available.

Address: TravelMed, International Travelers Assistance Association, P. O. Box 10623, Baltimore MD 21204. Telephones (800) 732–5309; (301) 296–5225.

Other Programs

Various insurance companies have special foreign travel/medical coverage available. Your travel agent can be a source of valuable information concerning availability and rates. Most agencies carry travel insurance forms and can assist you in applying for adequate protection.

Some policies carry program packages that have components which you may not need. For example, many insurance carriers include trip cancellation insurance as an integral part of the basic rate. While this could be of importance to anyone taking a tour, persons paying a regular full fare would not require such a "benefit" and might wish to obtain a policy that did not include the higher rate which such policies must charge for this service.

Check your policies carefully. Travelers should expect that they will probably have to pay in full when they receive treatment. A source of cash, credit card or wire transfer (the U.S. Embassy can help) may be necessary. When paying in cash, always obtain a receipt with detailed and complete documentation of every charge, legibly written in English. Also obtain a diagnosis translated into English.

Most insurance plans will not reimburse patients for treatments that are not considered appropriate in the United States, such as Laetrile therapy, or for pre-existing conditions.

Calling Home

The ability to call home from almost anywhere in the world is an aspect of travel assistance which can and should play a role in your travel plans. AT&T has several programs that make contacting your family, your physician at home, and your business contacts, or even the Department of State Citizens Hotline[2], a much easier task.

The most ideal program is their USADIRECT program. The Dial Access Countries in this program allow you to make a call from nearly any telephone in that country and reach a U.S. based operator who can then place your call. Those who have struggled with foreign telephone exchanges will realize what a blessing this service is. The table below lists the Dial Access Countries that are part of the USADIRECT program. Dial the number shown from any telephone in that country for direct access to a U.S. operator.

TABLE 2-2
USADIRECT Dial Access Countries

Country	Telephone Number
Australia	0014–881–011
Austria(#)	022–903–011
Bahamas(2)	1–800–872–2881
Belgium(#)	11–0010
Brazil	000–8010
British Virgin Islands	1–800–872–2881
Cayman Islands	1872
Denmark(#)	0430–0010
Dominica	1–800–872–2881
Dominican Republic	1–800–872–2881
Finland(#)	9800–100–10
France(#)	19*–0011
Gambia(#)	001–199–220–0010
Germany, FRG(#)1	0130–0010
Hong Kong	008–1111
Hungary(#)(2)	171–499

[2]The Department of State Citizens Hotline can be called 24 hours per day for reporting concerns of a U. S. Citizen in trouble overseas. The number is (202) 647-5225. This number can also be called requesting current travel advisory information (see Chapter 2.2).

Italy(#)(2)	172–1011
Jamaica(2)	0–800–872–2881
Japan(#)(2)	0039–111
Korea(3)	550–4663(HOME)
Netherlands(#)	06*–022–9111
New Zealand	000–911
Norway(#)	050–12–011
Philippines(#)(2)	105–11
Singapore(#)	800–0011
St. Kitts	1–800–872–2881
St. Maartin/Saba	800–1011
(St. Martin)	
Sweden(#)	020–795–611
Switzerland(#)	046–05–0011
United Kingdom	0–800–89–0011

* Await second dial tone.
(#) Public phones require deposit of coin or phone card for dial tone.
(1) Trial basis only; Frankfurt now available.
(2) Limited availability.
(3) From U.S. military basis only.

Certain countries have a USADIRECT service from designated and specially marked telephones in certain locations. A call placed from these telephones will connect you directly to a U.S. based operator, who can then place your call within the United States.

TABLE 2–3
USADIRECT Designated Telephone Countries

Country	Telephone Location Code
Antigua	A, H, S, M
Argentina	A, T
Aruba	A
Australia	T
Bahamas	A, S
Bahrain	A, H, M, T
Barbados	A, S
Belize	A, T
Bermuda	A, S, M, D

Br. Virgin Is.	A, H, S, T
Cayman Islands	A, S, T
China, PRC	A, H, T
Colombia	A
Costa Rica	A, H, T
Dominica	A, T
Dominican Rep.	A, H
Ecuador	A, T
El Salvador	A, H
Grenada	T
Guam	A, H, M, T
Guatemala	A, H, E
Haiti	A, H, S, E
Honduras	A, H, M, T
Hong Kong	A, S, M
Israel	M
Italy	M, T
Jamaica	A, S
Japan	A, H, S, M, T
Korea	A, H, S, M, T, D
Neth/Antilles	A, H, S, T
Panama	T
Philippines	A, H, M, T
Singapore	A, T
Spain	M, T
St. Kitts	A, H, S, T
St. Lucia	A, H, S, T
Trinidad/Tobago	A, S, T
Turks/Caicos	A, H, S
United Kingdom	M
Venezuela	A, S

A Airport concourse/lounge
H Hotel lobby
S Seaport/cruise dock
M U.S. military base
T Telephone center
D Direct dial from public phone
E U.S. embassy location

With this USADIRECT service you would use your regular AT&T card number (the large number in the center of the card), not the international number. Prior to leaving on your trip, check with the USADIRECT service people to see if a country which is not listed above, and to which you are heading, may have been added to the service. You can call them at 1–800–874–4000 ext 333 for more information.

To make an AT&T Card call outside of the United States:

1. To call the U.S. using AT&T USADIRECT service in foreign countries:

* When calling from a designated telephone, just lift the receiver and an AT&T operator will come on the line

or

If dial access is available, call the country's special dial access number to reach an AT&T operator (Table 2–2 above).

*Give the operator your regular AT&T Card number(A).

2. To call the U.S. from most telephones in other countries around the world:

*Lift handset. Reach the international operator who will place your call to the U.S.

*Give the operator your international AT&T Card number(B).

(A) The regular number is the large number in the center of the card.

(B) The international number begins with 1M and is located at the bottom of the card.

To direct dial the U.S. from a foreign country, simply dial the local International Access Code (check the local telephone book), the U. S. Country Code "1," the Area Code for the location you are calling, and the local telephone number. The U. S. Country Code is always "1." The local International Access Code differs by country. The countries with direct dial service are listed below.

TABLE 2–4
International Access Codes

Country	Code
Australia	0011
Austria-Linz	00
-Vienna	900
Bahrain	0
Belgium	00
Brazil	00
Colombia	90
Costa Rica	00
Cyprus	00
Czechoslovakia	00
Denmark	009
El Salvador	0
Finland	990
France	19*
French Antilles	19
Germany, Fed Rep	00
Greece	00
Guam	001
Guatemala	00
Honduras	00
Hong Kong	001
Hungary	00
Iran	00
Iraq	00
Ireland, Rep of	16
Israel	00
Italy	00
Ivory Coast	00
Japan	001
Korea, Rep of	001
Kuwait	00
Lebanon	00
Libya	00
Liechtenstein	00
Luxembourg	00
Malaysia (Kuala Lumpur & Penang only)	00
Monaco	19*

Morocco	00
Netherlands	09*
Netherlands Antilles	00
New Zealand	00
Nicaragua	00
Norway	095
Panama	00
Philippines	00
Portugal (Lisbon only)	097
Qatar	0
Saudi Arabia	00
Senegal Republic	12
Singapore	005
South Africa/Namibia	09
Spain	07*
Sweden	009
Switzerland	00
Taiwan, Rep of China	002
Thailand	001
Tunisia	00
Turkey	99
United Arab Emirates	00
United Kingdom	010
Vatican City	00
Venezuela	00

* Await dial tone.

For example, to call the Department of State Citizens Hotline from Norway you would dial: 095 + 1 + 202 + 647–5225 (International Access Code in Norway) + (U. S. Country Code) + (Area Code) + (Local Number).

Before leaving from home, make sure to obtain an *AT&T Card*. While not an insurance card, it can provide you with access to home, business, and government agencies—all of which might be of comfort and help to you at unforseen moments during your journey.

Chapter 2.7

International Association of Medical Assistance for Travelers

IAMAT was founded more than twenty years ago by the late Dr Vincenzo Marcolongo for the purpose of providing medical assistance to travelers. IAMAT's aim is to make competent care available to the traveler around the world (even in very remote places) by doctors who usually speak either English or French and who have had medical training in Europe or North America. Professional qualifications have been reviewed by IAMAT. All registered doctors are on call to IAMAT members 24 hours a day.

Anyone can belong to IAMAT and there is no charge for membership, although a donation is requested to help support its work. Membership brings a number of excellent traveler's medical aids:

1. *Membership card.* The card identifies the bearer as an IAMAT member and entitles him/her to services and the fixed IAMAT rates ((Office call $20.00 US; House Call—Hotels, etc $30.00; Night, Sunday and local Holidays $40.00). Referrals, consultations, laboratory procedures, hospitalization, and other medical services are, of course, not subject to this fee schedule.

2. *World Directory.* The directory of IAMAT physicians guides members to centers and participating physicians in 125 countries and territories. Telephone numbers are included.

3. *Traveler clinical record.* This passport-size record is completed by one's doctor before departure. It covers patient identification, emergency medical data, glasses prescription, diagnosis summary, and immunization record, and has special sections for those with diabetes, a cardio-vascular condition, or an allergic condition. The record provides the foreign doctor with a readily accessible and complete medical history.

4. *World immunization chart.* The chart advises on immunizations for 200 countries and territories for cholera, dengue fever, viral hepatitis, plague, rabies, typhus, typhoid fever, yellow fever, diphtheria, polio, and tetanus. It also provides information on preventative measures.

5. *World malaria risk chart.* Levels of risk in various countries are described with resistance patterns to chloroquine and other antimalarials. The antimalarial drug chart includes brand names, manufacturers, generic names, dosages, and frequencies.

6. *World protection guide.* With this aid the traveler is alerted to where disease risk occurs, how great it is, and what steps to take before, during, and after the trip. Both mechanical and pharmaceutical protection is detailed.

7. *World schistosomiasis risk chart.* A map and set of tables outlining the presence of this disease (see Chapter 6.45) throughout the world.

8. *Schistosomiasis information brochure.* This publication makes the traveler aware of the preventative measures required to avoid this snail-borne, debilitating disease, prevalent in many of the fresh water areas of the tropics and subtropics.

And to those who make a "substantial" donation to support IAMAT's work:

9. *World climate charts.* These 24 charts report on climate in every part of the world and on seasonal clothing required and sanitary conditions of water, milk, and food.

As mentioned, there is no set fee for receiving a membership card and all of the above publications, nor is there a suggested membership fee. This non-profit organization provides many valuable benefits and deserves full support from the traveling public.

Memberships can be obtained by sending a donation to any of the following IAMAT membership offices:

U.S.A.: 417 Center Street, Lewiston, NY 14092
Canada: 188 Nicklin Road, Guelph, Ontario, N1H 7L5
          1287 St. Clair Avenue West, Toronto, M6E 1B8
Australia: 575 Bourke Street, 12th Floor, Melbourne 3000
Switzerland: 57 Voirets, 1212 Grand-Lancy, Geneva
New Zealand: P. O. Box 5049, Christchurch 5

The late founder of IAMAT, Dr. Marcolongo, was instrumental in developing an improved mosquito netting device. This was typical of his endeavors to find solutions to make travel a safe and rewarding experience. Insect spread disease (see Chapter 5.4) is a significant risk in most tropical and subtropical regions of the world. This specially constructed, easily transportable, fine mesh netting with frame is designed to fit over almost any style of bed or cot. It is sold by IAMAT (International Association for Medical Assistance to Travelers), 417 Center Street, Lewiston, NY 14092 for $75.00 plus mailing costs. The rectangular frame and generous size allows plenty of room to sit up in bed. It also helps preclude accidentally brushing up against the side of the netting while asleep, thus preventing insects biting through from the outside. The weight of this device is 5 pounds. It is sold by the name of "LaMosquette." I have one for my use as it is easily transportable and provides a significant improvement over traditional mosquito netting. See Chapter 5.4 for an illustration of this device.

Chapter 2.8

Herchmer Country
Database Program

A combination of sources (including CDC, WHO, IAMAT, State Department, several consulting sources, the Morbidity and Mortality Weekly Report of the US Public Health Service, and many medical journals) is used to update an extensive computer database of medical information of interest to travelers. This information is updated constantly, at least weekly. Much of the information concerning infectious disease relies upon the willingness of a given country to provide accurate data in compliance with international health regulations. Users of this information must take this into account and at no time assume that the extent of infection is limited to the areas reported or that a specific disease does not exist in countries in which it is not listed.

The medical information in the individual country databases in this book (see Section 8) was current when this publication went to press. This is possible because the country database portion was set just prior to printing using the Herchmer computer database program interfaced directly into the typesetting program. The use of the Herchmer database will allow readers to obtain recent information on each country of interest, including current Department of State travel advisory information as well as changes in disease status and immunization recommendations.

The Herchmer Individual Country Database is divided into sections discussing: vaccinations (required and/or recommended for all travelers and recommended for specific types of activities in the country which might place the traveler at special risk); malaria risk (to include geographical distribution within the country, seasons of danger, and appropriate medications to take for the strains and resistance patterns which have been reported within that country); a special section on diseases of special risk (with a table of frequency and a discussion of geographical distribution of specific diseases such as schistosomiasis); food, water and dairy safety assessment; the location of U.S. Embassy and Canadian Government Representatives, to include telephone numbers; and the complete text of any Department of State Travel Advisories. The entire database, current as of the publication date of this book, starts on page 8-1.

Regardless of the last minute accuracy at press time, the urgent and critical nature of this information dates this book before it is out of the shipping carton. By sending $15.00 for the first country and $10.00 for each additional selection, persons may acquire a copy of the current Herchmer database for any country listed in this book. The address is Herchmer Medical Consultants, 109 East 89th Avenue, Merrillville, IN 46410. Telephone 1-800-336-8334. FAX (219) 769-6035. VISA and MC are accepted for telephone, FAX, or written requests.

Section 3
Making Travel Safe and Comfortable

The most significant risk to Americans traveling abroad is trauma from motor vehicle accidents. Knowing a few basic concepts will help alleviate some of the dangers of vehicular travel.

It is a strange phenomena, but persons traveling in foreign lands will frequently walk through neighborhoods of a city, or countryside location, which they would never dream of visiting at home. Potential dangers from robbery, muggers, and even politically motivated terrorists and kidnappers, do exist. There are common sense means of minimizing exposure to these dangers and actions to be taken when confronted by threats or hazards from fellow human beings.

Many of the problems facing the traveler are not life threatening, but are a matter of comfort such as combating the effects of motion sickness, jet lag, or even the fear of flying.

There is a considerable body of resource information helping travelers prepare for the above potential problems. This section deals with the medical and potentially traumatic aspects of travel—to include minimizing the chances of robbery and the dangers of terrorism or hijacking.

Chapter 3.1

Safe Vehicle Travel

The majority of injuries and deaths that occur to Americans during foreign travel come as a result of vehicle injuries. Even with relatively safe roads, licensed drivers, enforced traffic laws, and generally mechanically safe vehicles, the death toll within our country is significant. Remove one or more of these elements and the morbidity and mortality per mile driven climbs astronomically.

In developing areas, roads are generally not as well engineered as in the United States and road hazards are common. Breathing and swallowing dust when traveling on unpaved roads, or in arid areas, may be followed by nausea and malaise and may cause increased susceptibility to infections of the upper respiratory tract.

Most vehicle accidents are preventable. Defensive driving is the most important preventative measure. Make sure the car is in good repair. Try the steering and test out the brakes by driving a few feet in front of the rental agency. Look at the tire treads to see if they are fairly deep. Check the lights and windshield wiper. If the weather is cold, check to make sure that the vehicle has been winterized. If you are paying for air conditioning, make sure that it works. Check the ashtrays in the rear seat. If they are full of rubbish, it suggests the car has not been checked over thoroughly after the previous customer returned it.

Wear seat belts. Be familiar with local traffic laws and customs. Observe how well these are followed. Find out about insurance requirements or special license prerequisites before you attempt to drive in a foreign country.

Drive the more common kinds of locally available cars. If there are not many American cars in use, do not insist on an American model. Repair parts would probably be in short supply and local mechanics would be unfamiliar with routine maintenance. In case of mechanical problems while traveling away from the point where you obtained the car, repair parts and mechanical ability for making a repair may be nonexistent.

Driving a car model which is common to the country you are visiting also helps decrease your attracting attention. Keep the car doors locked at all times. Never pick up hitchhikers. Do not get out of the car if there are suspicious individuals nearby. Drive away. Do not stop at the scene of an accident, unless a fairly large crowd has already gathered—and, in that case, your services are probably not required. Ideally an accident should be bypassed and authorities contacted further down the road. Do not return to an accident site without local authorities accompanying you.

Do not park your car on the street overnight if the hotel has a garage or secure area. If you must park it on the street, select a well-lit area. Do not leave valuables in the car.

If you are hiring a cab, you may be treated to a kamikaze ride. Sometimes this is being done to impress you and the driver will respond to your demand that he slow down and take his time. At other times he will ignore you and drive like a mad man anyway. I would threaten to withhold his tip, or take the opposite approach and offer a larger tip, for a slower ride. Tell him you wish to see out better. Actually *you* are just trying to survive the ride and frequently *he* is just trying to bolster his income which can only be accomplished by discharging you as soon as possible and acquiring another fare.

Bus drivers in many developing nations drive too fast on unimproved roads with obviously over crowded and faulty equipment. While a bus trip may be a cheap way to really get the feel of a country, sometimes discretion is the better part of valor.

Chapter 3.2

Personal Security

The U.S. Department of State, Bureau of Consular Affairs, has guidelines that aid in minimizing the chance of loss of property, injury, or death due to theft, thugs, or terrorists. The following has been written in consultation with their guidelines and Department of State Publication 9493.

Normal common sense should prevail when traveling abroad, just as it would at home. Be especially cautious in, or avoid situations where you are more likely to be victimized such as crowded subways, train stations, elevators, market places, and festivals. Do not, for instance, get on an elevator alone if there is a suspicious-looking individual inside. You may wish to consider staying in larger hotels that have more elaborate security.

Find out about local rules and obey them. American citizenship cannot protect you if you break the laws of the foreign country you are visiting.

PRECAUTIONS WHILE TRAVELING

Keep track of the news to be aware of any potential problems in areas where you may travel. Your own state of alertness and the precautions you take should increase as you travel in areas where the potential for violence or terrorism is greater. Before continuing on to such areas, inquire at the nearest U.S. Embassy or consulate whether there are any adverse conditions of which you should be aware. Ask for the American Citizens Service Unit in the consular section. Embassy/consulate addresses and telephone numbers are located in the country database in this book found in Section 8. For general information on travel advisories, also see the Section 8 individual country database section of this publication. A special hot line number for travel advisory information can be called in Washington, D.C. by calling (202) 647–5225. This number can be accessed from anywhere in the world, as long as telephone communications are still functioning. When periods of isolation are anticipated, carry a small short wave radio and tune to one of the English language broadcasts that is beamed to your geographical area by the U.S. or British governments. In short, assess your situation and surroundings, and try to remain in that healthy gray area between complacency and paranoia.

GUARDING YOUR VALUABLES

Carry travelers checks instead of cash. Change some checks for local currency before you leave or upon arrival. Don't flash large amounts of money when paying a bill. Only countersign travelers checks in front of the person who will cash them, and be sure your credit card is returned to you after each transaction.

Make sure you receive a claim check for each piece of luggage you check.

Instead of keeping all your money, airline tickets, passport, and other valuables in your wallet, conceal them in several places to prevent easy theft. Keep them in your accompanying hand-luggage, on your person, or in a hotel safety-deposit box. Do not leave them in your room while you are out.

Don't leave your bags unattended in public areas. Traveling light will help.

Women should carry handbags in a secure manner to prevent

snatch-and-run type thievery, and men should place their wallets in their inside jacket pockets. To guard against thieves on motorcycles, walk on the inside of sidewalks and carry your purse on the side away from the street. Wrapping rubber bands around your wallet or keeping it in a zipped portion of a handbag makes it more difficult for a pickpocket to remove. Keep hotel and car keys on your person.

Be alert to the possibility of street gangs operating in large cities abroad. If confronted by superior force, don't fight attackers: give up valuables.

If any of your possessions are lost or stolen, report the loss immediately to the police and other appropriate authorities. Keep a copy of the police report for insurance claims and as an explanation of your plight. Also report the loss of travelers checks to the nearest office of the issuing company or its agent, airline tickets to the airline company or travel agent, and passport to the nearest U.S. Embassy or consulate.

PERSONAL SECURITY

Keep a low profile. Dress and behave conservatively, avoiding flashy dress, jewelry, luggage, rental cars, or conspicuous behavior which would draw attention to you as a potentially wealthy or important foreigner.

Be polite and low-key. Avoid loud conversations and arguments.

Avoid dangerous areas; don't use short cuts, narrow alleys or poorly lit streets. Try not to travel alone at night.

Let someone know when you expect to return, especially if out late at night.

Don't give your room number to persons you don't know well. Meet visitors in the lobby. Keep your hotel door locked at all times.

Remember when you are in a foreign country, you are subject to its laws and are not protected by the U.S. Constitution. Penalties for drug violations, including possession of small amounts of marijuana or cocaine, are severe in many foreign countries and rigorously enforced.

Deal only with authorized agents when you exchange money,

buy airline tickets, or purchase souvenirs; don't make exchanges for local currency at black market rates. In many countries travelers should refrain from photographing police and military personnel and installations, border areas, and transportation facilities. Be wary about selling personal effects such as clothing and jewelry. The penalties you risk may be severe.

If possible, book a room between the second and fifth floors above ground level to prevent easy entrance from the outside and low enough for fire equipment to reach or to make step climbing more feasible during power outages and other emergencies.

Read the fire safety instructions in your hotel room, know how to report a fire, and make sure you know where the nearest fire exit and an alternate are. Count the doors between your room and the nearest exit—this could be a life-saver if you have to crawl through a smoke filled corridor.

Make a note of emergency telephone numbers you may need: police, fire, your hotel, the nearest U.S. Embassy or consulate. Know how to use a pay telephone and have the proper change or token on hand.

Learn a few phrases in the local language so you can signal your need for help, the police, or a doctor. These can be obtained from an appropriate foreign language phrase book available at bookstores and libraries.

PROTECTING YOURSELF AGAINST THE POSSIBILITY OF TERRORISM

Terrorist acts occur in a random and unpredictable fashion which makes it impossible to protect oneself absolutely. The first and best way is to avoid travel to unsafe areas—areas where there has been a persistent record of terrorist attacks or kidnappings. The vast majority of foreign states have a good record of maintaining public order and protecting residents and visitors within their borders from terrorism. Most terrorists attacks are the result of long and careful planning. Just as a car-thief will first be attracted to an unlocked car with the key in the ignition, terrorists are looking for defenseless, easily accessible targets who follow predictable patterns. The chances that a tourist, traveling with an unpublicized program or itinerary, would be the victim of terrorism are slight: generally a tourist will face just the random possibility of being in the wrong place at the wrong time. In addition, many terrorist groups, seeking publicity for political causes within their own country or region, are not looking for American targets.

Nevertheless, the pointers below may help you avoid becoming an American "target of opportunity." They should be considered as adjuncts to the tips listed in the previous section for ways to protect yourself against the far greater likelihood of falling prey to ordinary criminal activity. The following are additional reasonable precautions which may provide some degree of protection, and can serve as practical and psychological deterrents to would-be terrorists.

Schedule direct flights if possible. Try to minimize the time spent in the public area of an airport, which is a less secure area. Move quickly from the check-in counter to the secured areas. On arrival, leave the airport as soon as possible.

Be aware of what you discuss with strangers, or what may be overheard by others.

Avoid luggage tags, dress, and behavior which may identify you as an American. While sweat shirts and T-shirts with American university logos are commonly worn throughout Europe, leave other obvious U.S. logos or apparel at home.

Keep an eye out for suspicious abandoned packages or briefcases. Report them to airport security or other authorities and leave the area promptly.

Avoid obvious terrorist targets and places where Americans and Westerners are known to congregate.

HIGH-RISK AREAS

If you must travel in an area where there has been a history of terrorist attacks or kidnappings, also make it a habit to discuss with your family what they would do in case of an emergency, in addition to making sure your affairs are in order before leaving home.

Be sure that you register with the U.S. Embassy upon arrival. Keep in touch with Embassy officials.

Remain friendly, but be cautious about discussing personal matters, your itinerary, or program.

Leave no personal or business papers in your hotel room.

Watch for people following you or "loiterers" observing your comings and goings.

Keep a mental note of safe havens, such as police stations, hotels, and hospitals.

Let someone else know what your travel plans are. Keep them informed if you make any changes.

Avoid predictable times and routes of travel, and report any suspicious activity to local police, and the nearest U.S. Embassy or consulate.

Select your own taxicabs at random—don't take a cab which is not clearly identified as a taxi. Compare the face of the driver with one posted on his license.

If possible, travel with others.

Be sure of the identity of visitors before opening the door of your hotel room. Don't meet strangers at unknown or remote locations.

Refuse unexpected packages.

Formulate a plan of action for what you will do if a bomb explodes or there is gunfire nearby.

Check for loose wires or other suspicious activities pertaining to your car. Be sure your vehicle is in good operating condition in case you need to resort to high speed or evasive driving. Drive with the windows closed in crowded streets; bombs can be thrown through open windows.

If you are ever in a situation where somebody starts shooting, drop to the floor or get down as low as possible and don't move until you are sure the danger has passed. Do not attempt to help rescuers and do not pick up a weapon. If possible shield yourself behind or under a solid object. If you must move, crawl on your stomach.

HIJACKING/HOSTAGE SITUATION

While every hostage situation is different and the chance of becoming a hostage is remote, some considerations are important. The U.S. Government's policy not to negotiate with terrorists is firm—doing so only increases the risk of further hostage-taking by terrorists. When Americans are abducted overseas, the U. S. government looks to the host government to exercise its responsibility under international law to protect all persons within its territories and to bring about the safe release of the hostages. The Department of State works closely with these governments from the outset of a hostage-taking incident to attempt to ensure that U.S. citizens and other innocent victims are released as quickly and safely as possible.

The most dangerous phases of most hijacking or hostage situations are the beginning and, if there is a rescue attempt, the end. At the outset, the terrorists typically are tense, high-strung, and may behave irrationally. It is extremely important that you remain calm and alert and manage your own behavior.

Avoid resistance and make no sudden or threatening movements. Do not struggle or try to escape unless you are certain of being successful.

Make a concerted effort to relax. Breathe deeply and prepare yourself mentally, physically, and emotionally for the possibility of a long ordeal.

Try to remain inconspicuous, avoid direct eye contact and the appearance of observing your captor's actions.

Avoid alcoholic beverages.

Consciously put yourself in a mode of passive cooperation. Talk normally. Do not complain, avoid belligerency, and comply with all orders and instructions.

If questioned, keep your answers short. Don't volunteer information or make unnecessary overtures.

Don't try to be a hero, endangering yourself and others.

Maintain your sense of personal dignity, and gradually increase your requests for personal comforts. Make these requests in a reasonable low-key manner.

If you are involved in a lengthier, drawn-out situation, try to establish a rapport with your captors, avoiding political discussions or other confrontational subjects.

Establish a daily program of mental and physical activity. Don't be afraid to ask for anything you need or want—medicines, books, pencils, papers.

Eat what they give you, even if it does not look or taste appetizing. A loss of appetite and weight is normal.

Think positively; avoid a sense of despair. Rely on your inner resources. Remember that you are a valuable commodity to your captors. It is important to them to keep you alive and well.

SURVIVING CATASTROPHES

In case of a local civil emergency or natural catastrophe, there are several actions that you should take. As soon as possible, notify the U. S. Embassy of your location and follow their instructions.

Conserve water consumption; avoid non-essential use; fill the bath tub in your hotel room as soon as possible. This may have to be your entire source of water for an extended period of time. You should continue filling it, if water supplies do not fail. It can also be used to prevent your toilet from becoming down right nasty when the water source fails.

Conserve food supplies. Try to obtain non-perishable foods, such as crackers, candies, or canned goods early during the course of such an emergency—as long as you are not exposing yourself to local danger. Do not loot, or be in an area where looting is taking place.

Always include a small overnight bag with your luggage which can be used to carry your essential items, realizing that you may have to abandon most of your property in case things get really unpleasant. A small bag with a shoulder strap can be very handy.

Consider bringing into the country your full allotment of duty free items such as liquor, perfume, and cigarettes, to be used for barter and in exchange for favors if the money exchange and banks suddenly close.

Try to locate yourself in a hotel room near a fire escape. Place glass objects on the floor against a wall, remove mirrors from the wall, drape mirrors and pictures that cannot be removed with blankets or sheets to prevent flying glass in case of firearms use.

Carry a small backpacking stove and cook set (they nestle and weigh mere ounces) and can be used to heat water to make it potable, to cook soup, or prepare hot drinks or food. The best stove to take would be a multi-fuel device which could burn perfume, drinking alcohol, white gas, kerosene, and other fuels which you could obtain locally. Do not try to fly with liquid fuel in your possession. Carry tea or instant coffee packs to be used as a stimulating hot drink, or for barter. Carry pilot biscuits and a small amount of food rations. Numerous delicious varieties are available through backpacking specialty stores. There are several mail order services specializing in this type of equipment and light weight food items.

TABLE 3-1
Mail Order Sources of Emergency Supplies

Brigade Quartermaster

    While primarily a military style clothing and specialty item outfitter, this organization has many unique survival items. Avoid purchasing camouflaged or military style clothing when planning trips to third world countries. Address: 1025 Cobb International Boulevard, Kennesaw, GA 30144-4300.

Cabela

    Primarily a hunting and fishing supply house, their catalog has a unique selection of cooking and camping specialty items. Address: 812—13th Avenue, Sidney, Nebraska 69160.

Campmore

    A wide range of camping tents, cook gear, and a selection of outdoors clothing at reasonable prices. Address: 810 Route 17 North, Paramus, NJ 07653.

Eddie Bauer

    Originally known for their goose down clothing, upscale travel suitable clothing seems to be their specialty. Quality is superb, but prices are higher than the other catalogs listed. Address: 5th and Union Streets, Seattle, WA 98124-3700.

Indiana Camp Supply

    Their catalog has the largest selection of trail foods that can be found. They also have the most extensive listing of medical supplies and first aid kits in the business, all at very reasonable prices. Address: 111 Center Street, Hobart, Indiana 46342.

REI

Recreational Equipment Incorporated has a wide selection of travel and expedition clothing, camping tents, and camping equipment and very reasonable prices. They also have an Adventure Travel program. Address: P O Box 88125, Seattle, Washington 98138–2125.

Chapter 3.3

Safe Air Travel

A variety of concerns surface for most persons traveling by air. The safety of the whole process, the hassles of airport and baggage handling, the traffic around an airport, and special medical problems which might be exacerbated by flight, all provide the basis for these concerns. Many of these subjects have been addressed in separate chapters in this book due to their relative importance to the traveler and since some of them are cross concerns shared when taking other modes of transportation.

SAFETY:
This issue involves not only the process of flying, but the well-being and protection the traveler might expect while airborne. Lloyds of London has estimated that it is 25 times safer to travel by air than by car. The safety of air transport over other modes of transport does not mean all flyers will still not have a certain amount of apprehension of flying, at least in their subconscious thoughts. For some, this apprehension is more than a subconscious phenomenon. Fear of flying is discussed in Chapter 3.4.

Certain airlines, particularly in developing countries, have better, or worse, individual safety records than others. In fact, even the Department of State Travel Advisory system occasionally carries a warning when a local or national airline has defective maintenance procedures. This information may be gleaned from the appropriate individual country database which starts on page 8-1.

Recent events have also caused official sources within the U.S. government to release bulletins when an aircraft has been threatened by terrorists. While this may be allowing terrorists a cheap and easy way to disrupt the air travel system, not to warn passengers of even questionable threats is a liability issue with which even the U.S. Government does not wish to tangle. The individual traveler will have to decide for himself just how seriously the threat should be taken and how extensive the protection authorities can provide against bomb and sabotage to a threatened aircraft.

IN-FLIGHT HEALTH:

There is currently no available data concerning the risk of precipitating illness during, or because of, flight in previously healthy individuals. Several recent scientific papers have studied the incidence of in-flight medical emergencies, which included chronically ill, as well as previously healthy persons. The statistics revealed in these studies indicate the low frequency of illness amongst air travelers. A study of passengers arriving at Los Angeles International Airport from October 1985 through March 1986 indicated a 0.003% rate of passengers requiring assistance while in flight.[1] A study evaluating the use of the enhanced medical kit (see below) on United Airlines flights showed an incidence of use of 0.0006% or one use for every 150,000 air travelers.[2] The access to

---

[1]Speizer, C. (1989). Prevalence of in-flight medical emergencies on commercial airlines. *Annals of Emergency Medicine. 18*:1. 26–29.

[2]Cottrell, J. J., Callaghan, J. T., Kohn, G. M., Hensler, E. C., & Rogers, R. M. (1989). In-flight medical emergencies: One year of experience with the enhanced medical kit. *Journal of the American Medical Association. 262*(12). 1653–1656.

the kit was restricted to physicians and select other health care providers, which would result in a lower incidence than the previous study.

A study of passengers using the Seattle-Tacoma airport reported the incidence rate of emergency calls for air passengers to be 1 call per 39,600 (0.0025%).[3] The above percentage rates apply to the airborne traveler. The majority of emergencies among air travelers (75%) occur on the ground within the air terminal.

Although there is no doubt that the risk of an in-flight medical emergency amongst the general flying public (to include both healthy and ill individuals) is quite low, on 1 August 1986, the Federal Aviation Administration instituted new regulations requiring all U.S. aircraft to carry an enhanced medical kit aboard all craft capable of carrying 30 or more passengers (see Table 3-2).

TABLE 3-2
THE FAA REQUIRED AIRCRAFT MEDICAL KIT

1 ea	Sphygmomanometer (blood pressure cuff)
3 ea	Oropharyngeal airways (air passage aid)
6 ea	Needles
2 ea	Epinephrine 1:1000 (asthma, shock, cardiac)
1 ea	Stethoscope
4 ea	Syringes
50 ml	Dextrose 50% solution (diabetes)
2 ea	Diphenhydramine injections (allergy)
1 ea	Instruction book

Evaluations reported on the use of this kit have been quite favorable, with a primary recommendation that is could be improved with the addition of an inhaled product for asthma. Additional modifications have been suggested in a number of studies, but all indications are that the risk of having a medical emergency while in flight is quite low and that the outcome of these events is favorable.

[3]Cummins, R. O., & Schubach, J. A. (1989). Frequency and types of medical emergencies among commercial air travelers. *Journal of the American Medical Association. 216*(9). 1295-1299.

STAYING HEALTHY IN-FLIGHT:

Sitting too long in cramped conditions is not only uncomfortable, but can increase the risk of venous stasis (decreased blood return from the legs), blood clots, and pulmonary emboli. Persons who must fly frequently all run the risk of decreased physical conditioning from too much sitting, too much snacking, too much drinking, and too little exercise.

Brisk walking in the airport before flights, or during layovers, is much healthier than sitting in a lounge. If your carry-on luggage can be secured, you will find airports make remarkably interesting exercise tracks for walkers.

Do not be in a hurry to board your plane. You will be sitting long enough, soon enough, so there is no need to slide into those cramped quarters any sooner than necessary.

During long flights be sure to request an aisle seat. As a minimum, take a walk up and down the aisle every 30 minutes. Stretch your legs occasionally (another reason for requesting that aisle seat). Loosen and tighten abdominal and gluteal muscles periodically. Take occasional slow, deep breaths. Various isometric exercises help prevent cramping and travel fatigue as well as enhance blood flow.

Wear loose clothing and shoes. Use layers of clothing so that you can adjust to changes in cabin temperature. Have something warm with you, even in the summer and in tropical areas. The air conditioning system can be quite uncomfortable when it is working too well.

Wearing elastic support stockings further decreases the chance of venous stasis and blood clots. Taking one aspirin daily has also been shown to reduce the chance of blood clot formation.

Be sure to remain well hydrated. Some persons find it advisable to avoid carbonated beverages, due to the gas expansion in their bowels as the cabin pressure lowers during climbs in altitude. Try to avoid beverages with diuretic actions, such as beer, tea, and high caffeine containing drinks. Avoid alcoholic beverages in general.

SPECIAL MEDICAL CONDITIONS:

Carry any personally required medical supplies with you in

your carry on luggage. Not only may the medications prove useful in an emergency, but they can also provide an abbreviated medical history to knowledgeable medical personnel. Also, your checked baggage may not arrive at the airport with you. Bring an extra pair of glasses (these can be checked). Carry you physician's telephone number with you on all trips. If you have a medical problem, carry a Medic Alert bracelet or neck chain and wallet card.[4]

Persons with chronic medical problems such as diabetes, cardiac and pulmonary problems, those traveling with infants or children, persons with restricted mobility, and ladies traveling while pregnant should refer to the appropriate chapters in Section 4 of this book.

EAR PROTECTION:

Rapid ascents or descents in vehicles and airplanes can cause significant pain from pressure or vacuum in the middle ear. This is particularly true if the passenger is suffering from head congestion. Congestion can lead to blockage of the Eustachian tube. Failure to equilibrate pressure through this tube between the middle ear and the throat—and, thus, the outside world—can result in damage to the ear drum.

When flying, it will be noted that blocked Eustachian tubes will cause more pain upon descent than ascent. While ascending, the pressure in the inner ear will increase and blow out through the Eustachian tube. While descending, increased outer atmospheric pressure is much less apt to clear the plugged tube and a squeeze of air against the ear drum will result. Normally when there is only a 20 mm Hg difference between the middle ear and the outside air pressure, the Eustachian tube will open. If this does not occur, a feeling of fullness develops when the pressure difference reaches 100 to 150 mm Hg. Upon further descent, increased difference in pressure causes inward bulging of the ear drum and significant pain. Try to equalize this pressure by pinching the nose shut and gently increasing the pressure in your mouth and throat against closed lips. This will generally clear the Eustachian tube

---

[4]Medic Alert enrollment forms can be obtained by calling 1–800–ID–ALERT. Lifetime membership is $25.00 which includes the wallet card and a stainless steel bracelet or neck chain.

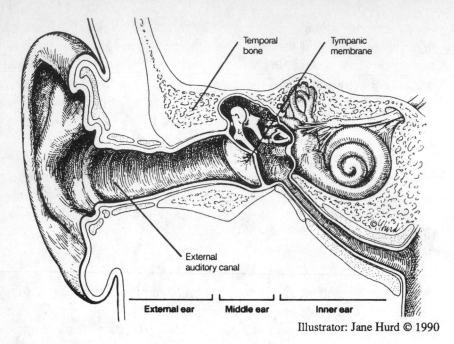

Illustrator: Jane Hurd © 1990

FIGURE 3-1
Anatomical drawing of an ear, with the portions labeled which have been referenced in the text.

and relieve the air squeeze on the ear drum. Do not over-do this;
that can also be painful. This process may need to be continuously,
and gently, repeated during the entire descent from cruising altitude to runway touch-down.

Head congestion should be vigorously treated to prevent Eustachian tube blockage. Take a decongestant, such as Actifed.
Drink larger amounts of fluid than normal to over hydrate. This
tends to thin mucous secretions and can result in less clogging of
both sinus cavities and the Eustachian tubes. Before a flight use a
long acting nasal spray, such as Afrin (2 sprays 1 hour before flight
time). Persons using such products longer than 3 days are apt to
suffer from a rebound congestion when ceasing their use. However, this medication will help to shrink the membranes around the
Eustachian tube openings in the pharynx and decrease mucous
secretion quite effectively. The chance of Eustachian tube blockage
and experiencing barotrauma (pressure change damage) is, thus,
greatly reduced.

If barotrauma results in ear drum rupture, the pain should instantly cease. There may be bloody drainage from the ear canal. Do not place drops in the ear canal, but drainage can be gently wiped away or frequently changed cotton plugs can be superficially inserted to catch the bloody fluid. Seek medical attention as soon as possible. Surgical repair may not be necessary, so one can generally seek a specialist's care upon returning home. Avoid swimming, diving, or any activities that might allow water to enter the ear. The hearing loss will be pronounced until the ear drum either heals itself or a surgical repair is obtained.

Fluid accumulation in the middle ear from sinus congestion or barotrauma will also cause a significant, yet fortunately a temporary, hearing loss. Treat as indicated for sinus congestion and seek medical attention when possible.

ENJOYMENT:

Flying can be an enjoyable and educational experience, as well as serve an utilitarian purpose. It is a safe mode of transportation with a demonstrated low frequency of illness and injury. Many pilots point out interesting geographic features and the unusual beauty of weather patterns, moon rings, sun glow, and the aurora when visible. And where do the airlines find those flying angels who somehow serve meals, drinks, as well as provide safety and comfort during flights?

Persons interested in learning more about the wonderful technology of flying are encouraged to obtain *The Air Traveler's Handbook: The complete guide to air travel, airplanes, and airports* (1989) by Bill Gunston, Ed., available at many airport bookstores, or St. Martin's Press, 175 Fifth Avenue, New York, NY 10010, for $12.95.

Chapter 3.4

Fear of Flying

A survey by the Boeing aircraft company discloses that 1 out of 7 persons has a fear of flying. This ranges from a heart in the throat feeling to pure unadulterated fear. Exaggerated or irrational fear is termed a "phobia".

Fear can be an unreasonable commodity. As mentioned, Lloyds of London has estimated that it is 25 times safer to travel by air than by car. Yet, many people will be terrified at the thought of crowding into an airliner, having the doors sealed shut, and finding themselves lifted 5 miles above the dangerous auto traffic below.

There are certainly medical indications for not flying in some select instances, but usually flying to one's destination is the safest means of transportation available.

Behavioral therapists have proven the effectiveness of systematic desensitization to alleviate phobias. These techniques can combine educational programs on the function and noises of various aspects of the airport operation, air craft boarding and take off, flight operations, and landing procedures. Programs which include a therapist tend to be the most successful. The analysis of a conditioned fear of flying (such as a previous bad experience) may require specific alterations in the desensitization program. Generally a customized approach will require an evaluation in which the client and therapist recognized precipitating factors and possibly other factors which might bear on this phobia developing. The underlying phobia of flying might be secondary to a fear of inclosed spaces for example. Once the fears have been clearly defined, the therapist can help design a desensitization program.

Desensitization generally goes through several phases. Progressive relaxation might include self guided projects at home, after the client has been taught relaxation techniques, and then considers, on a progressive basis, thinking about, or reviewing, photographs of various aspects of the pre-flight, flight, and post-flight situations. These activities are generally placed in a suggested hierarchy and can include such events as thinking about an airplane, viewing a photograph of an airliner, looking at a passing plane, getting ready to take a trip, buying airline tickets, and driving to the airport. Over a period of several sessions, the therapist exposes the client to progressively stressful stimuli and then helps implement the various relaxation and coping techniques that have been taught.

The therapist usually sets as a goal the teaching of the client's control or toleration of the natural anxieties associated with plane flights, in contrast to the goal of total anxiety ablation.

While it may be possible to rely on books and other modes of personal or automated desensitization, it has been demonstrated by several studies that therapist involvement, especially in the early stages of therapy, is particularly important. Many of the books that I have reviewed contain sound desensitization advice, but some also combine—or rely too heavily—upon various unproven modes of behavior manipulation such as dietary or vitamin protocols. Most psychologists and psychiatrists should be able to refer you to a person in your vicinity that specializes in phobia reductions. Consulting such a person is advised. Many times a referral to a special class on desensitization of flying fear can be made through an airline, a local airport, or through a travel agent.

Mild cases might be controlled with the use of a minor tranquilizer. You should consult your physician about this possibility. A tranquilizer will enhance the effects of alcohol, so alcoholic beverages should be avoided when taking this class of drugs.

Articles and books which you may find of interest include the following:

Angel-Levy, Penny, and Levy, George. (1981). *The Complete Book of Fearless Flying.* Weatherall Publishing.

Forgione, Albert, and Bauer, Frederick. (1980). *Fearless Flying.* Houghton Mifflin Co.

Gunston, William. (1989) *The Air Traveler's Handbook.* New York: St Martin's Press.

Karoly, Paul. (1974). Multi-component Behavioral Treatment of Fear of Flying: A Case Report. *Behavior Therapy.* 5: 265–270.

Lafferty, Perry. (1980). *How to Lose Your Fear of Flying.* Price, Stern, Sloan.

Chapter 3.5

Jet Lag

The use of jet airplanes allows us to rapidly cross many time zones, thus upsetting our natural biological clock. Called "jet lag," several methods have been developed that seem to minimize this disruption and which will allow the body rhythm to adjust to a new time zone.

Jet lag is distinct from the fatigue which occurs with any long distance travel. The jet lag symptoms most frequently noted are diminished coordination, disturbances in sleeping and waking patterns, abdominal upsets, mild anxiety, and fatigue . . . all significant problems when faced with an important activity upon arrival at your destination. Generally jet lag is more noticeable on eastern flights and when crossing 6 times zones or more.

The importance for athletic, or hunting endeavors, was demonstrated by a study of US residents traveling to Germany and returning 18 days later. Coordination was unfavorably affected for 10 to 12 days and changes in visual reaction time required 6 to 9 days for recovery. Certainly this problem could be more important on a big game hunt, skiing, and other sports requiring hand-eye coordination, than fatigue and sleep disturbance, the more obvious symptoms of jet lag.

These rather profound disturbances in reflex and mental function are an example of disruptions in the body's normal 24 hour clock, called the circadian rhythm. The normal wake-sleep cycle follows an obvious 24 hour pattern, but for it to work, many physiological functions must be coordinated. Aspects of body function such as daily temperature variations are actually the end result of very complex patterns of heat generation, conservation, and loss that the body causes due to hormone regulation, breathing patterns, and enzyme fluctuations of many kinds. The biological clock of the body resides in a portion of the brain. Many different signals reach this area and it in turn controls the function of liver, adrenals and other body organs in preparation for either activity or rest that the body expects and requires.

There are five basic ways of adjusting to jet lag.

First Technique: **The Argonne Jet Lag Diet.**

This process has been scientifically studied by Dr Charles Ehret at the Argonne National Laboratory in Illinois. Dr. Ehret has devised a diet plan that helps overcome jet lag.[5]

Diet can take advantage of the daily oscillations in energy reserves. In the normal circadian cycle, the high energy substance called liver glycogen builds to a high level of 15% of liver weight during the day, but will be down to 2% of liver weight just before morning. A low liver glycogen level is involved in telling the body that it is time to awaken and start the glycogen storage phase over again. However, the act of eating breakfast is an even stronger signal of phase change in the circadian rhythm.

The type of food eaten is also important in causing phase shift in the circadian rhythm. High protein foods stimulate the catecholamine pathway, which the body normally would like to turn on in the morning. High carbohydrate meals stimulate the indoleamine pathway, which is characteristic of the evening phase of the circadian cycle. In fact, when you have a high carbohydrate breakfast, you are in effect telling your body to go back to sleep. It is only

[5]Ehret and Scanlon, *Overcoming Jet Lag*, Berkley Press, New York City, 1983.

one signal, of which many others such as daylight, social interaction, and exercise, which all hopefully work in concert to get you started in the morning. A high protein diet would augment this waking phase rather than dampen it.

In preparing for long distance jet travel, the Argonne Jet Lag diet takes advantage of several days of relative feasting and fasting to focus on building up and depleting glycogen stores. The traveler starts the phase shift in circadian rhythm by manipulating the diet through the combination of fasting and depletion of glycogen stores, and feasting on either protein or carbohydrate meals, thus stimulating either the catecholamine or indoleamine metabolic pathways. The fast depletes liver glycogen and stimulates hormones, such as tyrosine aminotransferase, which speeds up catecholamine metabolism. Breaking the fast with a high protein feast—also stimulating to catecholamine metabolism—is a very strong signal to the body to wake up and become physically and mentally active. Thus a phase shift—either advance or delay—can be stimulated by this dietary manipulation.

Activity and rest, social interaction, being in light or dark, are all signals to the body to either rest or to become active. These activities also induce phase shift and can be used to manipulate a delay or advance of the biological clock. It is easiest to use these stimuli in conjunction with the dietary manipulations. *Alcohol consumption must be avoided* during the feast-fast days and during the day of travel.

While diet is important, the use of certain drugs can also induce metabolic activity. The most important class of drugs, normally consumed by Americans, are the methylxanthines, which include the caffeine and other compounds contained in coffee, tea, and chocolate.

The magnitude and direction of phase shift caused by coffee, etc., depends upon when it is consumed in the circadian cycle. *Phase delay* will be caused the later they are taken in the morning, reaching a peak effect at about 11 AM. After 11, they decrease in their effectiveness until between 3 and 5 PM when they are relatively ineffective. The later they are taken after 5:30 PM, the more powerful their effect on causing *phase advance*. They are most effective in stimulating phase advance when taken between 7 and

11 PM. They again become less effective until the very early morning, when they have minimal effect.

PHASE CHANGE USING COFFEE, TEA, OR CHOCOLATE:

In the days before the flight, the above items should only be ingested between 3 and 5 PM home time in order to not effect any time phase shift.

East bound travelers require a phase advance, so the above should be taken only between 6 and 11 PM home time.

West bound travelers require a phase delay. so the above should be taken only between 8 and 11 AM home time.

PHASE CHANGE USING MEAL ADJUSTMENTS:

In the days before the flight, start the feast-fast-feast-fast regimen. The last fast day will be the travel day; the first feast day will occur three days before leaving.

Feast on high protein breakfasts and lunches to stimulate the body's active cycle. Suitable meals include steak, eggs, hamburgers, high-protein cereals, green beans. Feast on high-carbohydrate suppers to stimulate sleep. They include spaghetti and other pastas (no meatballs), crepes (no meat filling), potatoes, other starchy vegetables, and sweet desserts.

Fast days help deplete the liver's store of carbohydrates and prepare the body's clock for resetting. Suitable foods include fruit, light soups, broths, skimpy salads, un-buttered toast, half pieces of bread. Keep calories and carbohydrates to a minimum.

Final day of fast is the travel day. Activity and eating should be timed to the activity and meal times of the destination. If you drink coffee and are going east bound, take it only between 6 and 11 PM. Going west bound, take it early the morning of departure— ideally between 8 and 11 AM. Activity on the flight should match the level of activity at that time of day at the destination.

WEST BOUND—say Chicago to Hong Kong—prepare as above. The day of the flight have a light breakfast with lots of coffee before you leave home, to effect a phase delay, and have none the rest of the day. Have a light "fast" lunch. In the hours before breakfast destination time, be placid, meditate, sleep if possible, even if it is an unusual hour like 4 or 5 in the afternoon home time. At 7 AM Hong Kong time have a high protein breakfast—frequently supper is being served at that time on the flight and would do just fine. Afterward stay awake, taking in all of the social clues that you can. When you arrive at about 4 in the afternoon, get to the hotel, have a high carbohydrate supper, and get to bed early. Get up at the proper time the next morning in Hong Kong. You should be on the Hong Kong biological clock, rested and ready for work.

EAST BOUND—say Chicago to Nairobi—prepare as above. The day of the flight you would fast. Avoid caffeinated beverages all day long, but ingest them between 6 and 11 PM home time. Then avoid any disturbances in the hours before what would be breakfast time in Nairobi. Do not watch the movie and avoid social interactions. Then at what would be 7 AM at the arrival point, get up, do some isometric exercises, wash up, watch the sunrise or turn the lights around you on, and break the fast with a high-protein breakfast. Have a high-protein lunch around noon and a high-carbohydrate supper at around 5:30 to 6:30 PM destination time and go to bed early. The next day when you awaken you will have set your biological cycle to local time.

Second Technique: The ICAO Rest Period Method

An alternate plan is simply resting at the destination for a least two days prior to significant activity. The International Civil Aviation Organization (ICAO) of Montreal, Quebec, Canada developed a formulation to compute the time needed to rest to allow the circadian rhythm a chance to return to normal. This formula is based on length of travel time, time zones crossed, and a set of local departure and arrival time coefficients.

The rest period is rounded to the nearest higher half day; travel time is rounded to the nearest hour; departure and arrival time coefficients depend on local times and are given in the table below:

TABLE 3–3
ICAO Travel Time Coefficients

Period	Departure Time Coefficient	Arrival Time Coefficient
8 AM to Noon	0	4
Noon to 6 PM	1	2
6 PM to 10 PM	3	0
10 PM to 1 AM	4	1
1 AM to 8 AM	3	3

Rest period needed (in tenths of days) = travel time in hrs/2 + (time zones crossed − 4) + departure time coefficient (local time) + arrival time coefficient (local time).

Third Technique: Melatonin Level Alteration

The hormone melatonin, produced in the pineal gland deep in the brain, plays a crucial role in setting the biological clock. Melatonin production virtually halts with sunrise as the sun detecting retina of the eye sends wake up signals to the brain. At night melatonin production resumes. The various cyclic functions such as the core temperature fluctuations and the formation of various other hormones are influenced in part by the rise and fall of melatonin levels.

A melatonin-related drug, Luzindole, has been tested in humans and has been shown to reset the biological clock by blocking melatonin receptors. Treatment with natural melatonin has also been shown experimentally to alleviate the symptoms of jet lag. Alteration of melatonin levels or blocking its activity may prove to be the most successful way yet to alleviate the long term effects of jet lag. It may be several years until products of this nature are available in the United States for prescription use.

Fourth Technique: Short Acting Sleeping Pill Method

Dr Thomas Roth, director of the sleep center at Henry Ford Hospital in Detroit feels than a good 8 hour sleep will override the body's natural sleep-wake cycle and restore alertness the next day. He states that left to its own devices the body will be restless for several nights and sleepy for several days. A controlled study he performed demonstrated that the use of a short acting sleeping pill, Halcion, taken at bed time at the destination worked better than a long acting sleeping pill (Dalmane) or placebo in restoring a sense of well being and high level of function. Incidentally, either of these sleeping pills would require a prescription to obtain them.

The experimental dose of Halcion studied was 0.5 mg taken at bedtime. The drug has a short serum half life (2 hours), so that it decays and leaves the system by morning of the following day. Alcohol ingestion should be avoided when taking this drug.

My personal experience with Halcion is that, regardless of the short half life, use of the 0.5 mg dosage leaves the person lethargic the next day. I would suggest taking the 0.25 mg, or even the 0.125 mg tablet, although the studies proving its effectiveness in combating jet lag were done with the higher, 0.5 mg dose. The manufacturer has removed a formerly available 0.5 mg tablet strength from the market.

Fifth Technique: Mental Attitude

A method that many find useful is to change their watch the moment they board the plane to the destination time zone. Think in terms of this new time zone, rather than the one which you are leaving behind. Stay awake until the new bed time, if possible. Mentally changing your time to match the new zone can help considerably in minimizing the effects of jet lag, and may remove them altogether.

I have placed the techniques of approaching the jet lag problem in decreasing order of complexity and also, most likely, in a decreasing order of effectiveness. There are avid proponents for each method. With time and experience you will find how significant the jet lag phenomena is for you and which of the above techniques, if any, you need to employ in order to maximally enjoy the time spent at your destination. It should be obvious that travel fatigue plays a role developing symptoms that could be attributed to jet lag. Many travelers leave on a trip fatigued by last minute preparations. Simply starting out rested and relaxed may be of considerable benefit in avoiding these symptoms.

Chapter 3.6

Safe Cruise Ship Travel

All passenger ships arriving at ports under the control of the United States are subject to unannounced inspection by the Public Health Service. Ships are rated to determine if they meet sanitation standards on: 1. Water; 2. Food preparation and holding; 3. Potential contamination of food; and 4. General cleanliness, storage, and repair.

The results of these inspections are published biweekly and are available free to the public by writing the Department of Health & Human Services, Public Health Services, Centers for Disease Control, Atlanta, GA 30333 and asking for the current "Summary of Sanitation Inspections of International Cruise Ships."

These inspections are stringent with approximately one half of the vessels being inspected failing to pass one or more portions of this examination! If you desire more specific information after reviewing this report, you can request a copy of the most recent inspection report on an individual vessel by writing to: Chief, Vessel Sanitation Activity, Center for Environmental Health and In-

U.S. DEPARTMENT OF HEALTH AND HUMAN SERVICES/PUBLIC HEALTH SERVICE
CENTERS FOR DISEASE CONTROL/Center for Environmental Health and Injury Control

BIWEEKLY SUMMARY OF
SANITATION INSPECTIONS OF INTERNATIONAL CRUISE SHIPS*

NAME OF VESSEL	Most Recent Inspection by CDC	Sanitation Satisfactory? YES	NO	Rev.	Most Recent Inspection by Contractor	Sanitation Satisfactory? YES	NO
REGULARLY SAIL FROM U.S. PORTS (More than 6 months during the year)							
Amerikanis	06/26/88		X				
Atlantic	02/09/88	X					
Azure Seas	07/11/88		X				
Bermuda Star	09/12/87		X				
Britanis	07/03/88	X					
Caribe I	12/12/87	X					
Carla C	06/17/88	X					
Carnivale	05/23/88	X					
Celebration	04/23/88	X					
Costa Riviera	06/04/88		X				
Cunard Countess	06/18/88		X				
Cunard Princess	11/07/87		X				
Daphne	02/20/88		X				
Discovery I	05/28/88		X				
Dolphin IV	06/13/88	X					
Emerald Seas	01/04/88	X					
Explorer Starship	08/29/87		X				
Fairsea	03/10/87	X					
Fairsky	05/05/88	X					
Fairwind	03/16/88		X				
Festivale	06/19/88	X					
Galileo	04/10/88	X					
Holiday	02/06/88	X					
Homeric	02/13/88	X					
Island Princess	07/26/88	●					
Jubilee	03/13/88	X					
Mardi Gras	04/07/88	X					
Nieuw Amsterdam	12/19/87	X					
Noordam	10/17/87	X					
Nordic Prince	12/02/87	X					
North Star	07/28/88		●				
Norway	06/11/88		X				
Pacific Princess	12/05/87		X				
Queen Elizabeth 2	08/01/87		X				
Queen of Bermuda	06/25/88		X				
Regent Sea	12/20/87		X				
Rotterdam	11/12/87	X					
Royale	03/25/88	X					
Royal Princess	05/14/88		X				
Royal Viking Sea	05/18/88		X				
Royal Viking Sky	11/04/87	X					
Royal Viking Star	07/22/88		●				
Sagafjord	10/16/87		X				
Scandinavian Saga	07/17/88		X				
Scandinavian Sky	06/06/88		X				
Scandinavian Star	09/25/87		X				
Scandinavian Sun	04/27/88		X				
Sea Goddess I	08/28/87		X				
Skyward	01/10/88	X					
Song of America	06/05/88	X					
Song of Norway	01/09/88	X					
Southward	07/08/88	X					
Sovereign of the Seas	05/17/88	X					
Stardancer	07/24/88		●				
Starship Oceanic	09/04/87	X					
Starward	07/26/87	X					
Sun Princess	10/31/87		X				
Sun Viking	11/21/87	X					

NAME OF VESSEL	Most Recent Inspection by CDC	Sanitation Satisfactory? YES	NO	Rev.	Most Recent Inspection by Contractor	Sanitation Satisfactory? YES	NO
REGULARLY SAIL FROM U.S. PORTS (More than 6 months during the year)							
Sunward II	07/04/88		X				
Tropicale	07/10/88	X					
Universe	12/23/87		X				
Veracruz I	07/16/88		X				
Victoria	05/16/88		X				
Viking Princess	06/02/88	X					
SEASONALLY SAIL FROM U.S. PORTS (From 3-6 months during the year)							
Azur	02/22/88		X				
Danae	01/02/88		X				
Golden Odyssey	07/23/88	●					
Mermoz	12/22/87		X				
Oceanos	02/21/88		X				
Regent Star	05/08/88		X				
Royal Odyssey	04/11/87	X					
Sea Princess	04/26/87		X				
Stella Solaris	07/18/87	X					
Vistafjord	04/08/88	X					
OCCASIONALLY SAIL FROM U.S. PORTS (Less than 3 months during the year)							
Canberra	01/16/88		X				
Eugenio C	01/25/88		X				
Europa	06/24/88		X				
Stella Oceanis							

Legend:
- A score of 86-100 is satisfactory.
- A score of 0-85 is not satisfactory.
- Rev. - Inspection results under review at request of owner/operator.
- Contractor — Some cruise lines may contract with private consultants to perform inspections as an adjunct to CDC inspections. CDC will on request of the cruise line company publish the results of those inspections in the Biweekly Summary provided the private consultant agrees to follow CDC guidelines in performing the inspections.

All passenger cruise ships arriving at ports under the control of the United States are subject to unannounced inspection. The purpose of these inspections is to achieve levels of sanitation that will minimize the potential for gastrointestinal disease outbreaks on these ships. Such outbreaks are infrequent, but serious, occurrences on board cruise ships. Ships are rated on the following items to determine if they meet CDC sanitation standards:

1. Water
2. Food preparation and holding
3. Potential contamination of food
4. General cleanliness, storage, and repair.

Failure to obtain a satisfactory score indicates failure to achieve and maintain generally accepted standards of sanitation and denotes the occurrence of deficiencies which require corrections; it does not necessarily imply an imminent risk of an outbreak. CDC reserves the right to recommend that a ship not sail, regardless of its inspection score, when circumstances so dictate (such as, but not restricted to, contamination of the potable water supply).

A copy of the most recent inspection report on an individual vessel may be obtained by writing to:

Chief, Vessel Sanitation Activity
Center for Environmental Health and Injury Control
1015 North America Way, Room 107
Miami, FL 33132

● = Vessels inspected during the previous two weeks.
* As of 08/05/88 Vessels for which there is no entry have not yet been inspected.

FIGURE 3-2
A sample copy (reduced size) of the biweekly cruise ship inspection summary.

jury Control, 1015 North America Way, Room 107, Miami, Florida 33132.

International vessels carrying 13 or more passengers are required by regulation to report the occurrence of diarrheal illness on board 24 hours prior to arrival at a U.S. port. The CDC investigates gastrointestinal disease outbreaks on board cruise ships if, and when, they occur.

Cruise ships are a safe way to visit many exotic ports in a restful manner. Cruise lines have a reputation to preserve and as such take precautions to maintain cleanliness aboard ship, thus providing descent accommodations and meal service. Visits can be made to shore, while eating and beverage consumption can be restricted to shipboard, thus minimizing the chance of travelers' diarrhea.

Ships are equipped with stabilizers that prevent much of the wave motion one would otherwise expect. Motion illness problems can be further reduced by one of two basic techniques while on board. Obtaining a room near the water line will minimized some of the remaining pitch and yawl which the ship experiences. Another technique is to go on deck and fix one's gaze on the horizon. This minimizes the effect of movement on the brain. Avoid reading, this seems to accent the difficulty. Alcohol use increases problems dealing with balance control and the effects of movement. Avoid even slight amounts of alcohol if you are prone to "mal de mer" or motion sickness. Additional information on prevention and treatment of motion sickness will be found in Chapter 3.7 which follows.

Sun exposure can be particularly treacherous aboard a ship. The movement of air from sea breezes has a cooling effect that, while very soothing, may mask the effects of the sun. Both eyes and skin should be protected from the ultraviolet B rays, which are the predominate tanning (and burning) rays. Water can reflect from 10% to 100% of these rays, so the intensity of the effect can be much greater than imagined. Thin cloud layer can absorb much of the infrared heat rays, but allow ultraviolet radiation through. Thin cotton clothing can similarly block the heat rays and allow passage of considerable ultraviolet. Cruise ships are equipped with swimming pools, another source of sun burn. Cooling dips manage to remove sun screens and tanning oils, eliminate the heat of the day, and lull one into become medium-well done on the first day out. See also the section on sun injury for more on the topic of sun blindness and burn care (Chapter 7.1 and 7.7).

Chapter 3.7

Motion Sickness

Motion induced nausea and vomiting can be minimized by various techniques. When traveling by a vehicle it helps to ride in the portion less subjected to movement. For a bus this would be between the front and rear wheels. That location, incidentally, is not exactly in the middle of the bus, but somewhat forward of the apparent middle of the coach. In a car, the front seat is far preferable to the rear seat. On a plane, position yourself at a location near the center. The safest location in a plane is in the back row of seats towards the trail of the aircraft, but motion problems would be greatly magnified. On a ship, locate yourself as near the center of the ship as possible. However, these are not the choicest rooms for view or amenities.

Activity can also minimize motion problems. Avoid reading. Choose a focal point for your gaze that is as near the horizon as possible. When in a car, look at houses or scenery in the distance. Aboard a plane, look at distant cloud formations. At night, or when a white out blocks outside viewing, focus your attention as far up the aisle as possible. On a ship, stare at the horizon, or as far along the ship deck as you can.

Repeated exposure to motion will allow a person to adapt and eventually experience less motion sickness. If you are motion sickness prone, this will not occur with only one or two trips, but will gradually improve after many. This improvement depends upon your sensitivity and the amount of motion encountered during the various trips.

Avoid the use of alcohol and tranquilizers which tend to upset the equilibrium. While you might imagine that these items would settle nerves, their effect is quite the opposite on the balance control mechanism in the cerebellum of the brain.

Ear pressure from sinus congestion, due to allergy or illness, might also bother the balance input area of the inner ear. A decongestant, such as Actifed, might be useful in minimizing inner ear induced vertigo and nausea.

Diet modifications which might be helpful, besides elimination of alcohol, is the reduction of fatty foods, deep fried foods, chocolate, and over-eating in general. Well cooked items, soups, toast, tea, and various carbonated beverages can be soothing—or at least palatable.

Several medications are available over the counter for control of nausea. Dramamine, Bonine, and Marezine are the most commonly available. Dramamine also has a liquid formulation. A curious fact is the Bonine (meclizine 25 mg), one tablet daily is an non-prescription product to prevent motion sickness, while Antivert (meclizine 25 mg), up to one tablet three times daily, is a prescription required dose to prevent or treat vertigo or motion sickness. There tends to be minimal drowsiness, or other side effects, when using the above medications.

Transderm Scop, a patch containing scopolamine, has been developed for prevention of motion sickness, but this requires a prescription. Each patch may be worn behind the ear for 3 days. It is fairly expensive, but also very effective and well worth the cost, if you are prone to this malady. There tends to be a higher frequency of side effects with this medication in elderly people, such as visual problems, confusion, even psychotic behavior and loss of temperature regulation. Avoid touching your eye after handling this patch and before washing your fingers, as this may result in dilation of the pupil and blurring of vision. This is not serious and will pass within 48 hours. Persons should avoid scopolamine if they have glaucoma, are pregnant or are nursing, have liver or kidney disease, have a metabolic disorder, have trouble urinating, have obstructions of the stomach or intestine, or have very sensitive skin.

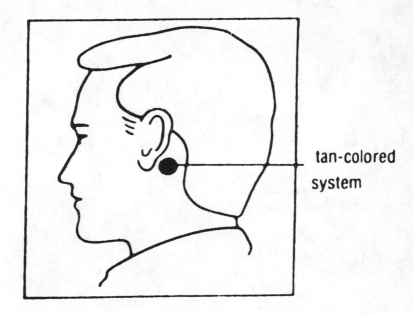

tan-colored system

FIGURE 3–3
The proper placement of Transderm Scop, a precription product used to prevent motion sickness.

Section 4

Traveling with Medical Problems

Some travelers have underlying medical concerns that should be acknowledged due to increased risk, such as pregnancy, extremes of age, diabetes, cardiac, pulmonary problems, or handicaps in locomotion, to include blindness.

Some persons may have lowered resistance to disease. These people are called "immune compromised." Travel for them becomes more complex due to increased chances of contracting infectious disease and potential side effects from immunizations. The disease "AIDS" is only one of the conditions that causes loss of immunity. Taking certain medications, such as cortisone derivatives, and various inherited disorders, also cause a total or partial loss of immunity. A discussion of the special precautions and problems of travel for the immune compromised traveler is a significant aspect of foreign travel.

One must hope that upon their return home, the traveler will no longer be "traveling with a medical problem." The potential concerns of the returned traveler need to be addressed, from suggestions for routine post-trip examinations to more urgent medical considerations.

Chapter 4.1

Mobility Restricted Travel

Those handicapped by mobility, to include loss or diminished eyesight, have a special travel problem that does not directly affect their health, but for which special pre-trip planning is required.

Easy access concepts for travel to airports, public transportation and buildings are now being considered in most countries.

A pamphlet has been prepared for travelers planning automobile trips in the United States. Titled "Highway Rest Area Facilities Designed for Handicapped Travelers," it is available free of charge. It may be obtained by writing to the President's Committee on Employment of the Handicapped, Washington, D.C. 20210.

While train travel has decreased in the United States, Amtrak provides a special publication for the handicapped traveler called "Access Amtrak." It is available at no charge from the Public Affairs Office, Amtrak, 400 North Capital Street, N.W., Washington, D.C. For information on rail travel for the handicapped in the United Kingdom, contact The Royal Association for Disability and Rehabilitation to obtain a copy of their publication "A Guide to

British Rail for the Physically Handicapped" by writing to them at 25 Mortimer Street, London W1N 8AB.

Air travel will be the most important mode of transportation for all travelers, to include the handicapped. Airport access information can be obtained by writing to the Consumer Information Center, Pueblo, CO 81009, and asking for the free publication item 832K titled "Access Travel: Airports." The Department of Transportation also has a free publication available by writing them ATTN: Distributing Unit, TAD-443.2, Washington, D.C. 20590, and requesting the item titled "Air Transportation of Handicapped Persons." For a charge of $2.00, the Rehabilitation Research and Training Center, the George Washington University, will provide a pamphlet called "Coping with Inaccessibility: Assisting the Wheelchair User. Write to them at Room 714, 2300 I Street N.W., Washington, D.C. 20037. Another publication describing facilities available at various airports for the disabled traveler can be obtained by requesting "Access Travel: A Guide to Accessibility of Airport Terminals," from the Airport Operators Council International, Inc., 1700 K Street N. W., Washington, D.C. 20006.

Getting there is only half the fun. Ease of access to various private and public buildings, ground transportation systems, and other areas are available in booklets from several organizations that can provide you with a list of guides for the disabled traveler. The "International Directory of Access Guides" can be obtained from Rehabilitation International, USA Access Guide Directory, Suite 704, 1123 Broadway, New York, NY 10010. Another organization that can provide information is the Society for the Advancement of Travel for the Handicapped, 26 Court Street, Brooklyn, NY 11242.

The hearing impaired can contact several major transportation agencies via a TTY/TDD system. These teletypewriters will allow schedule information and reservations to be made directly.

A special brochure titled "Consumer Information about Air Travel for the Handicapped" is available from the TWA Sales Department, 2 Penn Plaza, New York, NY 10010. United Airlines also has a brochure for the handicapped traveler which can be obtained by writing them at P. O. Box 66100, Chicago, IL 60666.

TABLE 4–1
TELEPHONE/TELETYPE ACCESS FOR THE
HEARING IMPAIRED

Bus Lines

Greyhound Bus Lines	TTY	(800) 345–3109

Air Lines

American Air Lines	TTY	(800) 534–1586
		Ohio: (800) 582–1573
National Air Lines	TTY	(800) 432–1537
Pan American	TTY	(800) 659–5454
TWA	TTY	(800) 421–8489 (except AL/IL)
		California: (800) 252–0622
United Airlines	TTY	(800) 323–0170
		Illinois: (800) 942–8819

The "Incapacitated Passengers Air Travel Guide" can be acquired by writing to the Traffic Services Administrator, International Air Transport Association, 2000 Peel Street, Montreal, Quebec, CANADA H3A 2R4.

Additional information on the general aspects of travel for the handicapped can be obtained from the following books on the subject:

READING LIST

Barish, F. (1984). Frommer's: *A Guide for the Disabled Traveler—The United States, Canada, and Europe.* New York: Frommer Books, Simon & Schuster.

Weiss, L. (1983). *Access to the World.* New York: Facts of File.

Annand, Douglas. (1979). *The Wheelchair Traveler.* Purchase from the author at Ball Hill Road, Milford, NH 03055 for $7.95.

Reamy, L. (1978). *Travel Ability.* Riverside, NJ: Macmillian Publishing Company.

Chapter 4.2

Pregnancy and Travel

The safest time for a pregnant woman to travel would be during the second three months of her pregnancy. Most complications occur during the first three months or the last three months. Being aware of the signs and symptoms of complications are important. Travel should be avoided if the patient has been experiencing high blood pressure or vaginal bleeding. A blood pressure kit should be carried to enable close personal monitoring during the last three months of pregnancy. Urine dip sticks should be carried to detect the spillage of protein or sugar in the urine. These can be obtained without a prescription. An ideal product is the Ames Uristix.

Indications of complications are vaginal bleeding, severe abdominal pain, contractions, elevated blood pressure above the woman's normal level (and certainly anything above 140/90), protein in the urine, severe headache or visual complaints, ankle/leg swelling or rapid weight gain, and suspected rupture of membranes.

As pregnancy in general carries a higher medical risk than a woman would normally have, it is even more important for her to obtain adequate travel and medical insurance. Some insurance policies have clauses which terminate benefits if the patient is outside of a normal delivery area. Knowledge of where to obtain help in an emergency is especially important. This topic has been covered in Chapters 2.6 and 2.7.

Dr. Alan Dedoyan, Chief Medical Director of International SOS Assistance (see Chapter 2.6) has a word of caution for ladies expecting to deliver overseas. When asked about his experiences he stated, "With regard to pregnancy, women are advised to return to their country of origin since there are very few centers in developing countries equipped to take over." This is due to the wide variations in cultural attitude about child birth, level of training, and medical biases. He warns that these potential dangers are of even greater concern for women with a high risk pregnancy. The SOS group further warns that the lack of adequate facilities in developing countries to care for premature and full term babies with complications cannot be emphasized enough.

TABLE 4-2
SELECT PREDICTORS OF HIGH RISK PREGNANCY#
 *Age 35 or older
  *Maternal heart disease
   *Maternal kidney disease
    *Maternal diabetes
     *Difficulties in becoming pregnant
      *Prior miscarriage
       *Prior ectopic pregnancy
        *Previous delivery difficulties
#There are many other conditions that can place a lady in a high risk category. Any pregnant traveler should consult her physician on the advisability of foreign travel.

Airport security x-ray machines that check baggage are well shielded and pose no threat of radiation to the mother or fetus. The large devices that passengers must walk through are magnetic field generators (magnetometers) and pose no threat.

Pregnant women who are within one month of delivery should be advised to avoid air travel if possible. Those who are within one week of their estimated date of confinement must not fly. The anticipated hypoxia (low oxygen) effects on the fetus are minimal in a healthy woman, however there is a small association between flight and pre-term labor. Attempting a delivery while on a crowded plane would be a very difficult proposition for all concerned. Most foreign airlines will not allow a woman at 35 weeks gestation to fly. A letter from the patient's physician indicating the expected delivery date is sometimes required, showing that the gestation period is less than 35 weeks. Domestic airlines generally prohibit flight when the fetus has reached 36 weeks of gestational age, with no exceptions.

The pregnant traveler should try to avoid certain destinations which might pose a serious risk to the mother or the fetus. Altitudes above 6,000 feet should be avoided during the last three months of pregnancy due to the decreased oxygen supply at high altitudes (see also the discussion of this topic in Chapter 4.5). Areas which lack proper medical services should be shunned. Areas which require a vaccine that would be of risk in pregnancy, or those which would cause unusual exposure to parasitic or insect born diseases, should also be avoided (see Table 4–3 and risk factors as listed for specific areas in the country information database starting on page 8–1).

Malaria is a particularly dangerous disease during pregnancy. The weekly doses of chloroquine (see Chapter 6.31) appear to be quite safe for fetus and mother, but the other drugs used when chloroquine resistance develops are of concern. Of the new drugs available, Lariam (mefloquine) may be safe for use in pregnancy, but adequate experience with drug has not yet been obtained. It is not approved by the CDC or FDA for use while pregnant. Proguanil (Paludrine) has been used safely in pregnant patients for many years, but this medication is not available in the United States. Travel to areas with known chloroquine resistance should be avoided. Treatment of a pregnant patient who has contracted malaria is necessary as the potential harm to both the mother and the fetus from the disease outweighs the risk of the medications, but a risk from medication does exist.

Terminal prophylaxis (the killing of the parasite after the trip is completed and the person has returned home) of the forms of

	Vaccine	Indications for vaccination during pregnancy
Live virus vaccines		
Measles	Live-attenuated	Contraindicated.
Mumps		
Rubella		
Yellow fever	Live-attenuated	Contraindicated except if exposure is unavoidable.
Poliomyelitis	Trivalent live-attenuated (OPV)	Persons at substantial risk of exposure may receive live-attenuated virus vaccine.
Inactivated virus vaccines		
Hepatitis B	Plasma derived, purified hepatitis B surface antigen	Pregnancy is not a contraindication.
Influenza	Inactivated type A and type B virus vaccines	Usually recommended only for patients with serious underlying disease. It is prudent to avoid vaccination during the first trimester. Consult health authorities for current recommendations.
Poliomyelitis	Killed virus (IPV)	OPV not IPV, is indicated when immediate protection of pregnant females is needed.
Rabies	Killed virus Rabies IG	Substantial risk of exposure.
Inactivated bacterial vaccines		
Cholera	Killed bacterial	Should reflect actual risks
Typhoid		of disease and probable benefits of vaccine.
Plague	Killed bacterial	Selective vaccination of exposed persons.
Meningococcal	Polysaccharide	Only in unusual outbreak situations.
Pneumococcal	Polysaccharide	Only for high-risk persons.
Toxoids		
Tetanus-diphtheria (Td)	Combined tetanus-diphtheria toxoids, adult formulation	Lack of primary series, or no booster within past 10 years. It is prudent to avoid vaccination during first trimester.
Immune globulins, pooled or hyperimmune	Immune globulin or specific globulin preparations	Exposure or anticipated unavoidable exposure to measles, hepatitis A, hepatitis B, rabies, or tetanus.

TABLE 4–3
VACCINATIONS DURING PREGNANCY

malaria which remain dormant in the liver cells (*P. vivax* and *P. ovale*), requires the use of primaquine. This drug should not be taken while pregnant. There is a possibility that the drug may be passed transplacentally to a G6PD-deficient fetus and cause a life-threatening hemolytic anemia *in-utero* (see Chapter 6.31). If there is concern about these forms of relapsing malaria being present and requiring terminal prophylaxis, the pregnant patient should remain on weekly chloroquine therapy until delivery, at which time the decision to give primaquine may be made.

There are no safe drugs for use during pregnancy to treat or suppress the other parasitic diseases. The pregnant woman should avoid areas of high risk. Careful water treatment (Chapter 5.2) and food/dairy precautions (Chapter 5.1) should be observed. Shoes should be worn in rural areas and insect prevention should be strictly observed (Chapter 5.4).

Venous circulation is hampered late in pregnancy due to increased clotting factors, venous dilation due to progesterone effect, and pelvic compression from the growing fetus. Elastic support hose should be worn. Long periods of sitting should be avoided. On long air flights an aisle seat should be chosen that will allow frequent strolls. Relaxation and tightening of leg muscles during periods of enforced inactivity should be practiced.

Travelers' diarrhea during pregnancy poses special problems. It is not worth the risk to take antibiotic or other medication to prevent this problem. Pepto-bismol has never been associated with fetal defects, but the high salicylate level of this medication may cause bleeding during pregnancy. There is a theoretical possibility of fetal damage from salicylates. Other drugs used in the prevention or treatment of travelers diarrhea also pose concerns for the pregnant traveler. Doxycycline can harm the bones and teeth of the fetus and therefore cannot be used during the last three months of pregnancy. Bactrim or Septra may be used in the second three months of pregnancy, but should be avoided in the first three months due to possible harmful effects of the trimethoprim component on early fetal development, and after the 32nd week due to the sulfa component causing possible problems of neonatal jaundice. Lomotil and Imodium are safe to use in treatment of symptoms, and erythromycin has been shown to be somewhat effective in treating infectious causes of diarrhea and is safe in pregnancy. The ideal dosages would be Imodium 2 mg, taken 2 capsules initial dose, followed by 1 capsule after each loose stool up to a maximum of 8 capsules per day. I find the best tolerated erythromycin to be PCE 333, taken 1 tablet three times daily after meals.

A new adsorbent, Diasorb, has ten times the adsorption capability of kaolin and shows great promise in safely treating diarrhea. It is non-prescription and is available in liquid and tablet formulation at most drug stores in the United States. It should be perfectly safe for consumption by women at any stage of pregnancy.

Chapter 4.3

Children and Travel

The particular difficulties a child may encounter while traveling will vary by age, mode of transportation, and geographical areas to be visited. Many of the concerns about children traveling are expressed in various special sections of this book, to include the individual country database section.

The preparation for a foreign trip with a child is much more complex than that for adults. While concerns of exotic diseases, extremes of temperature, and unusual or dangerous wildlife may seem the significant problem, in reality the provision of entertainment, normal functions of eating, drinking water, and comfort, and the usual injuries of childhood make up the bulk of your problems.

The dwellings you will be inhabiting on your trip will have a major impact on the ease, or problems, of managing the comfort and safety of your children. The availability of air-conditioning, home services such as laundry, cooking, and cleaning help—or the availability of modern appliances—make a considerable difference in what you will need to bring. Depending upon disposable items is frequently not best, as their availability in developing countries is usually limited.

FOOD AND NUTRITION

Generally infants can travel very well. Breast feeding is the best method of ensuring an ideal and safe source of nutrition. Once a woman has weaned her infant, her milk supply will generally cease within a week. Planning to wean after the trip makes the best travel arrangement. If you are moving to a third world country, maintain breast feeding for as long as possible. Not only is this the safest and most nutritious way of feeding the baby, but authorities are attempting to convince third world mothers to do the same and setting an example assists in this endeavor. A breast fed infant does not require additional water or fluid, unless the baby is feverish or having diarrhea.

Bring high energy food snacks and a suitable water container (with a method of purification) on any trips with children as these items may not always be available. The use of these items is mentioned in the section on modifying the travelers' medical kit in Chapter 7.8. A list of sources for these items is found at the end of Chapter 3.3.

A calculation of the minimal fluid requirement and the maximal fluid tolerance of a child can be made by knowing the child's body surface area. The minimal requirement is 870 ml (30.7 oz) per square meter and the maximum tolerated is 4,700 ml (10.3 pints) per square meter of body surface area. The normal maintenance fluid requirement for a child is 1,500 ml per square meter of body surface area.

The surface area of a child can be calculated from the nomogram on the next page. This nomogram allows you to estimate the surface area of a child of normal height and weight directly from the weight (center boxed area) or by connecting the left "height" column to the right "weight" column and reading the surface area from the scale on the right center.

Taking the example of a 6 year old who weighed 45 pounds, let us assume that the child is of average height which would be 46 inches. Entering the center table we find that his body surface area is 0.81 meters square (you need only the weight to enter this table). His minimal fluid requirement would calculate out at 0.81 x 870 ml = 704 ml.

Using the left and right nomogram scales, we fond that a 45 pound, 46 inch high child would have a surface area of 0.81, which matches the calculation above for surface area from the simple center table, since we are using an average height and weight. Using the expanded nomogram to enter height and weight will provide the most accurate body surface area measurement for the child, and will result in a more accurate determination of minimal (and maximal) daily fluid requirements.

Taking the above calculations we would find that this child would have a minimal daily fluid requirement of 700 ml (1 1/2 pints) with a maximal daily fluid tolerance of 4,700 ml x .81 = 3,800 ml or 136 ounces (7 pints).

You will need to pay particular attention to the source of these fluids to insure safety. Water purification is discussed in Chapter 5.2. Dairy product safety is considered in Chapter 5.1.

Parents should ask their pediatrician or family physician for guidance on normal fluid intake. Heat stress and play activity will increase the need of fluid. An infant should not be exposed to heat to the point that sweat loss is a significant factor in fluid replacement. The most extreme requirement necessitating an increase in fluid for a child will be in the eventuality of diarrhea. Not only is it important to replace the normal maintenance fluid requirement for the child, but *the diarrhea losses must be replaced volume for volume*. Diarrhea also causes electrolyte (or mineral) losses as well as fluid loss. The replacement of these losses is best done with the oral replacement cocktail recommended by the Centers for Disease Control (see Chapter 5.3). Throughout the world UNICEF and WHO (World Health Organization) distribute an electrolyte replacement product called Oralyte. It must be reconstituted with adequately purified water.

Antibiotic prophylaxis, or prevention, is not feasible in a child. Most of the medications that can be used for this are best not used, or are contra-indicated for use, in the pediatric age group.

Diarrhea in infants is best treated with a clear liquid diet. This must be maintained the two or more days that the diarrhea

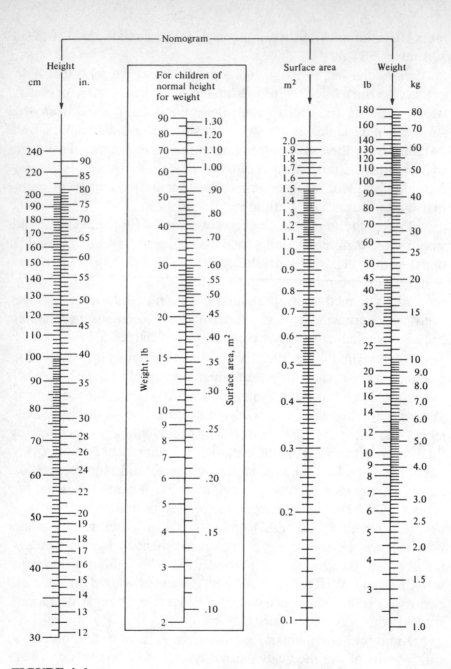

FIGURE 4–1

A nomogram for the determination of the body surface area of an infant or a child.

continues, until one-half strength formula can be restarted—and, if tolerated—progressed to full strength formula over 12 to 24 hours. Infants develop diarrhea for a variety of reasons to include simple readjustment of the normal bowel bacteria or other, sometimes serious, infections. Ear infections will frequently result in diarrhea in an infant. An infant with diarrhea needs professional medical evaluation. The breast fed infant who develops diarrhea should be maintained on breast milk, but receive augmentation of oral electrolyte fluid replacement equal in volume to the diarrhea losses.

Older children generally develop diarrhea from a viral, or bacterial, infection of the gastrointestinal tract. Fluid and electrolyte replacement is essential and the most important aspect of therapy. Anti-diarrhea agents will stop diarrhea, or at least slow it down. Their use is not without potential problems. Diarrhea is a body defense mechanism to rid itself of an unwanted infection. The most effective diarrhea agent currently available, with or without a prescription, is Imodium A-D. Children 6 years and older can use this preparation according to the instructions on the package. Younger children should be given this only on the advice of your physician. Have him instruct you on specific dosage and frequency of use for the younger child.

Antibiotics can aid in combating many of the bacterial causes of diarrhea in the older child. The safest medication available is Bactrim Suspension (trimethoprim and sulfamethoxazole), available only with a prescription. Again, your physician can instruct you on the quantity required for the twice daily dosing schedule. The combination of Bactrim Suspension and Imodium A-D can be quite effective in eliminating travelers' diarrhea. Be sure to include your physician's instructions on the child's family member information page in Chapter 7.9 to photocopy and take with you.[1]

HEALTH INSURANCE AND PROFESSIONAL HELP

These topics are even more important for the traveling child than they are for an adult. Adequate preparations for your trip include arranging for insurance (Chapter 2.6) and professional

[1]Section 7 has been printed with wide inner margins to facilitate photocopying so that it can be taken with you on your journey. This Section has been published separately as the *Traveler's Self Care Manual* and is available from the publisher, ICS Books, 107 East 89th Avenue, Merrillville, IN 46410, Telephone (219) 769-0585 or (800) 541-7323, for $6.95 plus $1.50 postage and handling.

help (Chapter 2.7). Be sure to carry your physician's or pediatrician's telephone number with you. They can be contacted from nearly every country in the world. Place this information in the child's family member information page in Chapter 7.9 to photocopy and take with you as indicated above. Be sure to take advantage of the international telephone direct dialing information as described at the end of Chapter 2.6.

IMMUNE STATUS OF CHILD

The status of the child with regard to having received his normal childhood immunizations is an important aspect of preparing the youngster for any travel. The normal immunization schedule is listed below. Primary importance must be given to assuring that this schedule has been kept current. If not, the child must be brought up to date on these basic immunizations.

TABLE 4–4
Current Recommendations for Routine Immunization
of Infants and Children in the United States

Recommended Age	Immunizations	Remarks
2 months	DTP, OPV	Given as early as 2 weeks in areas of high risk or during epidemics.
4 months	DTP, OPV	OPV should be given in a 2 month interval to avoid interference from the previous dose.
6 months	DTP	A 3rd dose of OPV is not indicated in the U.S., but is recommended in areas where polio is endemic.
15 months	MMR	Tuberculin testing may be done at this visit or at a 1 year routine examination.
15–18 months	DTP	DTP should be given 6–12 months after the 3rd dose; it may be given simultaneously with MMR at 15 months of age.

15–18 months	OPV	OPV booster may be given as early as 12 months or may be given simultaneously with MMR at 15 months of age.
18 months	HIB-conj.	Several HIB-conjugate vaccines have been licensed for use as early as this age.
4–6 years	DTP, OPV	At or before school entry. At age of 7 or older the child should receive dT, not DTP.
14–16 years	dT	Repeat every 10 years throughout life—see discussion in Chapter 5.5.

DTP = diphtheria-tetanus-pertussis vaccine
OPV = oral polio vaccine
MMR = measles-mumps-rubella vaccine
HIB-conj. = *Haemophilus influenza* b-conjugate vaccine
dT = diphtheria-tetanus vaccine

REFERENCES:
American Academy of Pediatrics. 1988. Active immunization. *Report of Committee on Infectious Diseases.* (21st ed.). 204–210.
CDC Immunization Practices Advisory Committee. 1989. General recommendations on immunization. *MMWR. 38.* 205–214, 219–227.

FOREIGN TRAVEL IMMUNIZATIONS

Part of the basic research which you need to do for your trip is to ascertain the probable infectious disease risk to which your children may be subjected. A good guide to this can be found in the individual country database in Section 8. Read about the diseases listed in the countries which you are about to visit in Section 6 and consult a physician or travel medical specialist (Chapter 2.4 and 2.5).

For your convenience, pediatric dosages of the common travel related immunizations are listed in Chapter 5.5. Concerns about allergies and reactions to these immunizations are covered in Chapter 5.6.

MALARIA

An infant is vulnerable to malaria from birth and protection must be provided from the start. If the mother is taking anti-malaria medication, it will not be protective for the baby, even if she is breast feeding. The chapter on malaria (Chapter 6.31) should be read carefully. This is a most serious problem and adequate protection for children must be obtained.

The use of insect repellants and netting is also useful in tropical countries, for not only malaria is transmitted by insect vectors. Chapter 5.4 has a full discussion of prevention of insect bites in children, as well as adults. The use of the IAMAT insect screen is discussed in that chapter as well.

AIR TRAVEL CONSIDERATIONS

Infants less than two weeks of age should not fly as their lungs may not have fully expanded by this time. They can be very sensitive to atmospheric pressure changes at this age.

Infants cannot be safely held in an adult's lap or buckled into a seat with the adult. Air turbulence can place significant force upon the child causing crush injury from the seat belt or can exert such force upon the holder that infants cannot be safely held. It does not seem too difficult to hold a 15 pound infant, but when that child instantly weights 70 pounds due to an air pocket, the adult's grasp may not be protective.

Infant seats manufactured after 1 January 1981 comply with Federal safety standards to adequately protect infants on airplanes. A special sticker will identify the seat as having met all of the Federal requirements. This sticker must be present for the airline to allow it on the plane. Some airlines have special infant seat policies about which you may inquire at the time your reservations are being obtained.

The descent on an airplane is generally the time most likely to cause ear pain for an adult or, especially, a child. Bottle or breast feeding an infant or young child may help alleviate the pressure differential between the middle ear and the ambient, or outside, pressure. This topic is discussed further in Chapter 3.3.

PROTECTIVE CLOTHING

Insist that children wear protective footwear in tropical countries. The penetration of their feet by hookworms is only one problem. The tumbu fly from East and Central Africa, and the tropical warble fly found throughout South America, can also penetrate the skin of bare feet and cause discomfort, and worse, from their infestations. Going bare foot increases the chance of snake bite injury, trauma to feet, and exposure to biting insects, many of which are found along the ground.

Head protection from heat loss, or heat gain, and from the effects of the sun, is also very important. Chapter 7.7 discusses environmental injuries and makes the point in several discussions on the importance of head cover. Clothing must be tightly woven and dry to protect youngsters from sunburn. Children can be particularly sensitive to the development of prickly heat, which is fully discussed in Chapter 7.2. Protection from sun injury to the eye will also require the availability of adequate sunglasses for the children (also refer to Chapter 7.2).

INJURY

Most of the problems which you will encounter with children will be minor, similar to those you routinely have to handle at home. Review Section 7 which describes reasonable treatments for a wide variety of injuries and illness. Discuss the medical kit recommendations with your physician and receive modified dosage instructions for the suggested medical kit. As previously mentioned, have networking prearranged with insurance and overseas help organizations to handle the more serious problems (Chapters 2.6 and 2.7) and be capable of calling for help—either to home or an overseas contact—if the situations so warrants.

SOCIALIZATION

It has been said that there are two types of travel—traveling first class and traveling with children. But for all the concern, extra effort, and frank inconvenience, taking children along can be the most rewarding aspect of travel. The increase in cultural awareness and exposure to the natural wonders of the world that children can gain from this experience, makes your efforts to include them the greatest gift which you can bestow upon them. However, this gift does not come without forethought and extra effort. You must research the wonders of the areas which you are about to visit so that you can act as an interpretive naturalist and historian, as well as their protector, mentor, and—if more than one is going with you—sometimes the referee.

If you are moving for long term residence in a foreign land, take advantage of the local culture, within the constraints of safety, and your family will have gained much more than the employment or your work assignment could possibly provide.

Chapter 4.4

Diabetes and Travel

Persons with uncontrolled diabetes should not fly. Irregular meals, and confusion in insulin dosing due to crossing of time zones, may lead to wide fluctuations in their sugar with the complications of low or high sugar (hypoglycemia or ketoacidosis). Long distance travel should be attempted only by reliable persons with the ability to maintain tight control of their blood sugar.

There is no vacation from diabetes. The basis of diabetes control is diet. Oral intake may be increased if the level of physical activity is increased, and must be reduced on those days when inactivity is anticipated.

Persons using oral medication to aid in control of their diabetes should take their medication at the prescribed time, but they should use local time.

As mentioned, only diabetics with good blood sugar control should attempt to travel. Ensure that good control continues. Routine blood sugar testing should be performed before breakfast and supper on a daily basis. On days when the normal routine is altered, possibly even closer monitoring every six hours is required.

TABLE 4–5
Supplies to be Carried by Insulin-Dependent Diabetics

Insulin	Types normally used in quantities sufficient to last the entire trip
Regular insulin	One bottle for emergency use
U-100 syringes	Quantity sufficient to last the entire trip
Lancets	Quantity equal to allow twice daily blood sugar testing
Reagent strips	Quantity equal to allow twice daily blood sugar testing
Alcohol swabs	Quantity equal to the total number of syringes and lancets.
Sugar packets	At least 5 packets or hard candies
Snacks	High energy snacks should be carried on person at all times
ID Tag*	Tag or bracelet should be worn at all times. Also carry a billfold card with your normal insulin schedule and you doctor's name and telephone number

*An ID Tag or bracelet and wallet identification card can be obtained from Medic Alert Foundation International, Turlock, CA 95381–1009, Telephone (800) 432–5378.

Some authorities suggest carrying a vial of glucagon and diluent for emergency administration in case hypoglycemia (very low blood sugar) causes unconsciousness and the victim is unable to swallow a sweet drink or suck on a hard candy or snack. It is also recommended that ketone-detecting urine test strips be carried to detect the onset of the complication of ketosis that can occur when blood sugar is allowed to remain too high as this can also lead to coma and death. However, persons with blood glucose testing strips should not require ketone testing as ketone production from prolonged high sugar concentrations should never be allowed to develop. The traveling diabetic must also assure that they never allow a low blood sugar situation to deteriorate to the point of hypoglycemic coma, requiring glucagon or even intravenous glucose.

North-South travel will require no specific changes in insulin dosage, but East-West travel greater than 6 time zones will. One rough rule of thumb that has been advocated for years has been that an insulin dependent person traveling east by air should increase his insulin dose by 25 percent for each six time zone changes; going west he should decrease it by 25 percent. A nomogram published by Benson and Metz[2] describes a method of tighter insulin control when making these significant time zone changes.

INSULIN ADJUSTMENT—EASTERN TRAVEL

As mentioned, travel through less than 6 times zones should require no change in insulin dosage. Persons normally taking one dose daily should take their usual dose before breakfast at the usual time on the day of departure. At their destination, the next morning will have come sooncr than usual and the morning dose should be reduced by one third. They, therefore, should take an insulin dosage equal to two thirds of their usual dose at the local time corresponding to their usual schedule. They should check their blood sugar levels before supper (10 hours later). Only if their blood sugar level is greater than 240 mg/dl, should they take the remaining one third dose at that time. The next morning they should resume their normal dosing schedule.

Persons who usually take two insulin doses daily will follow a similar pattern. On the travel day they should take their customary doses of insulin according to the normal routine and on the same time schedule as at home. They should take two thirds of the morning dose, as mentioned above, at their destination on the morning of their arrival. Ten hours later the blood sugar should be checked. If the blood sugar level is 240 mg/dl or less, they should take their normal evening dose. If the blood sugar is higher than 240 mg/dl, they should add the remaining one third of the morning dose to their evening dose. The following day they should plan on taking insulin according to their routine schedule, adjusted, of course, to local time and following the usual coverage adjustments as per their routine guidelines.

[2]Benson, E. A., and Metz, R. Management of diabetes during intercontinental travel. *Bulletin Mason Clinic 1984–1985*

Persons on mixed insulin regimes would also follow the same plan, but both the long acting and short acting dosages would be similarly cut or expanded according to the same guidelines.

When persons who have traveled east through greater than six times zones return home, they will have to follow the west bound schedule to readjust to their home routine.

INSULIN ADJUSTMENT—WESTERN TRAVEL

Once again, travel through less than 6 time zones should not require any change in the usual insulin dosage. The traveler should take their normal dose(s) on the day of departure at the usual times and the following day, at their destination, simply follow local times to take their usual insulin amounts.

Persons traveling further than six time zones will have lengthened their day sufficiently that they will require larger insulin amounts. Those routinely taking one dose daily should take their normal dose on the day of departure at their usual time. In flight, meals should be taken at the times they are offered by the airline. Eighteen hours after the morning dose of insulin, the blood sugar should be tested. If the glucose level is 240 mg/dl or less, the patient can wait until the first morning at the destination, where the normal dose schedule will be resumed on local time. A longer interval than normal will have occurred between the person's daily morning doses, but this should be well tolerated. If the blood sugar level is found to be greater than 240 mg/dl, however, a supplemental dose equal to one third of the usual morning dose should be taken.

Westward traveling persons who normally take two doses of insulin should leave their watches unchanged during the flight. They should take the normal morning insulin dose and twelve hours later by their watch take their second normal dose, followed by a snack or meal. Six hours later (eighteen hours from their first dose), they should check their blood sugar. An extra dose of insulin equal to one third of the normal morning dose should be taken only if the blood sugar is greater than 240 mg/dl.

Considerable changes in levels of physical activity, food intake, and even health status can be expected during long distance travel, especially in foreign lands. It will be mandatory to check blood sugar levels at least twice daily to aid in the daily insulin dose adjustments. Symptoms of hypoglycemia will have to be carefully watched for and extra snacks and sugar or hard candies should be carried by the diabetic traveler on their person at all times. Insulin and diabetic supplies should be divided amongst separate pieces of luggage to prevent loss of everything at one time. Names of English speaking doctors and organizations or services providing medical care to travelers can be found in Chapters 2.6 and 2.7. Particular attention to proper care of the feet must be taken by a diabetic traveler. Blisters should be carefully avoided and, if contracted, managed as indicated in Chapter 7.1.

Chapter 4.5

Cardiac/Pulmonary Disease and Travel

Most persons contemplating air travel will do so in commercial jet aircraft. Although these planes are pressurized, cabin pressure is not comparative to the air pressure at sea level. While the percentage of oxygen in the air at high elevations remains the same, since there is less atmosphere there are correspondingly fewer oxygen molecules. This decrease in the available oxygen can exacerbate certain underlying heart or lung conditions.

The pressurization attempted by commercial airlines is usually 8.6 pounds per square inch above the outside pressure. This means that at an altitude of 35,000 feet, the aircraft interior would be equivalent to a flight at 5,000 feet. In reality the pressure difference is usually kept at less than 8.6 pounds, with an equivalent cabin interior elevation of between 6,000 and 9,000 feet. The decreased availability of oxygen could cause harmful effects on a person's heart that was unstable, or in a heart that was having to labor unusually hard, due to a recent myocardial infarction, uncontrolled hypertension, severe congestive heart failure, symptomatic valvular disease, uncontrolled arrhythmia, or unstable angina. Pulmonary contra-indications to air travel include persons who obtain inadequate oxygen on room air, have severe restrictive lung disease, have pulmonary cysts, pneumothorax, or have had cardiothoracic surgery within the previous 3 weeks. It is currently felt that persons with heart attacks should not fly for at least 4 weeks, and then only if they have returned to normal activity in everyday life.

A wag once said "If a man can walk a city block and climb a flight of stairs without difficulty, and if he looks, acts and smells normal, he is fit to fly." But there is no substitute for clinical judgement and common sense when determining whether or not a person is capable of withstanding the rigors of flight. I have often felt that the flight, even with its relative hypoxia, was far less demanding than the stress of airport traffic, the hustle and bustle of the airport terminal with its check in lines, baggage hassle, security lines, far flung departure gates, and struggle to squeeze what's left into an overhead storage shelf and personally slither into a mid-row seat, only to soon face the whole process of beating the others out of the plane, anticipate a round of baggage problems, transportation arrangements, and eventual escape into a strange new world. But then, I generally have to fly in and out of O'Hare—perhaps your destinations will be kinder and allow you to bypass some of this hassle.

Generally a gain in altitude is well tolerated by most individuals. The development of altitude related illness (Acute Mountain Sickness, High Altitude Pulmonary Edema, and High Altitude Cerebral Edema) is discussed in Chapter 7.7. The table below lists altitude restrictions for patients with various cardiopulmonary problems without supplemental oxygen.

Arrangements for supplemental oxygen can be effected by prior contact with several major airlines. This would allow persons with stable, yet marginal, cardiac conditions, and those suffering from inadequate or marginal room air oxygen blood saturation to fly. Persons with unstable cardiac conditions, pulmonary cysts,

TABLE 4-6*
Altitude Restrictions for Patients with
Cardiopulmonary Disease Without Supplemental Oxygen

Altitude Limit	Patient difficulty
10,000 feet	Suspected or symptomatic heart/lung disease
8,000 feet	More than mildly symptomatic heart/lung disease Marked ventilatory restriction
6,000 feet	Recent myocardial infarction (8 to 24 weeks) Angina pectoris Sickle cell anemia Cyanosis, regardless of cause Cor pulmonale Respiratory acidosis

4,000 feet	Severe cardiac disease with cyanosis or recent
	decompensation
	Patients with two of the following:
	    Cyanosis
	    Cor Pulmonale
	    Respiratory acidosis

2,000 feet	Congestive heart failure Recent myocardial infarction (less than 8 weeks) Concurrent cyanosis, cor pulmonale, and respiratory acidosis

*Adapted from Rodenberg, H. Prevention of Medical Emergencies During Air Travel. AFP 1988;37(2):263–271.

pneumothorax, or recent cardiothoracic surgery, would still be at risk.

Low flying aircraft, or even specially pressurized aircraft, can allow even unstable patients to fly. Generally these activities are restricted to medical evacuations and are extremely expensive.

Persons with American Heart Association Functional Classification I and II may fly on commercial airlines quite safely. Impairment classification III individuals should have their physician's clearance before flying. Persons with a functional Class IV rating must have supplemental oxygen to fly and should avoid commercial air flight if possible.

TABLE 4–7
American Heart Association
Functional Capacity Limitations

Functional Capacity	Limitation
Class 1	No limitation
Class 2	Slight limitation
Class 3	Marked limitation
Class 4	Complete limitation

Additional information can be obtained by writing for the booklet "Travel for the Patient with Chronic Obstructive Pulmonary Disease" available from the Rehabilitation Research and Training Center, The George Washington University, Ross Hall, Room 714, 2300 I Street, N.W., Washington, D.C. 20037. The cost for this booklet is $1.25.

Chapter 4.6

AIDS, Compromised Immunity, and Travel

Partial loss of immunity, or as a physician might put it "compromised immunity," is a common problem. It greatly affects our ability to ward off infection, both the normal diseases of our daily environment, as well as the effects of micro-organisms which would normally not be able to infect a human. It is a common problem, not simply because of the emergence of AIDS, but because many medical disorders result in a compromised immunity. Aging, severe infections, diabetes, kidney problems, sickle cell disease, malnutrition (ever go on a crash diet), and the use of certain medications (especially cortisone derivatives and chemotherapy) can all decrease the immune response. The list is much longer than this, but suffice to say, if you are suffering from a chronic medical problem, you should check with your physician to see if you might have a decreased immune response to infectious diseases, or if you might have an unusual reaction or response to immunizations.

The problem of AIDS should be of particular concern to the international traveler for several reasons. A primary problem is the increasing, and already high rate, of the AIDS virus infection in some developing countries—not to mention our own.

The possibility of being forced to undergo emergency surgery in a country with a high risk of contaminated blood, surgical instruments, or medications from multi-use vials (which have a higher risk of cross-contamination) should be considered. Having adequate access to evacuation for definitive surgery after stabilization is a service that some insurance and special organizations can provide (see Chapter 2.6).

The failure to receive a required immunization for entry into a country might also result in potential exposure to re-used needles, syringes, and multi-dose vaccine vials at the port of entry. What in the past might have been inconvenient, now could become a disaster.

The United States has the second highest per capita incidence of AIDS infection in the world. This fact does not escape countries concerned about preventing the emergence of this disease in their country. More and more countries, attempting to protect themselves from the AIDS epidemic, are implementing requirements that certain travelers have laboratory proof that they are AIDS negative. Although some countries allow this test to be performed in the U.S. prior to departure, others insist that it be obtained while in their country.

Reporting statistics on AIDS will often be misleading and confusing. An "AIDS test" refers to testing for antibodies to the AIDS virus, which demonstrates exposure to the virus and possibly infection. This is generally reported as "HIV positive." False positive and false negative test results can occur. An HIV positive antibody test requires confirmation with special tests. When an accurate test for the AIDS virus particle is developed (as opposed to testing for an antibody response as the current tests do) and becomes commercially available, the chance of false negative results will be greatly reduced.

As time passes we are learning that most people who test

positive to the AIDS antibody are developing the AIDS disease. There is a latent period of 5 to 10 years between becoming infected with the virus and actually developing the complex of infections that provides the clinical definition that the patient is officially suffering from the AIDS disease (or its precursor, the Aids Related Complex, or ARC). This means that a large pool of HIV positive persons will represent a significant number of persons with active disease at a much later date. The full extent of this disease in the world is still unknown. There is considerable disagreement amongst various specialists as to how many have been exposed to the virus and how many people can be expected to loose their lives because of it. The predictions for what will occur with regard to disease spread over the next 5 years is also a matter of scientific conjecture. The World Health Organization reported that as of 31 March 1990 there were 237,110 cases of clinical AIDS being reported in the world from 153 countries. This is undoubtedly a low figure.

The method of spread of AIDS is quite different in various places of the world. In the United States the spread is predominately from contaminated needles by drug addicts, contaminated blood supplies used in transfusions, and homosexual activity. In Africa the spread is predominately by heterosexual activity. In countries with heterosexual spread, women seem much more likely to contact the disease, usually running ratios of three to four times greater in finding HIV positive tests than in men. Female prostitutes are extremely vulnerable to this disease. This is of particular concern in the United States due to a large number of prostitutes who could catch the disease by not only sexual transmission, but also by intravenous drug use. The percentage of HIV positive prostitutes in most large American cities is greater than 80%! The transmission of AIDS in various countries is generally characterized by its mode of spread. Where this information is known it has been indicated below.

The World Health Organization provides a four page pamphlet on how to avoid AIDS while traveling. For this free publication titled "AIDS Information for Travelers," write the Global Program on AIDS, World Health Organization, Avenue Appia, 1211 Geneva 27, Switzerland.

Many countries are unable to afford to test persons and the incidence may be vastly under-identified. Other countries, who rely on tourist dollars, may wish to under-report the incidence of positive carriers.

All persons with compromised immunity, regardless of its cause, must exercise particular caution during their travels to avoid unnecessary exposure to micro-organisms (see Chapters 5.1, 5.2 and 5.4). Such persons will need to take full advantage of immunizations (see Chapters 5.5 and 5.6) which are available *with special counseling* as impaired immunity can decrease a vaccine's effectiveness and other vaccines become more risky to accept. Patients planning to travel, who are HIV positive, must be particularly concerned as some vaccines seem to activate the progression of AIDS.

The traveler who is HIV positive, or who has developed Aids Related Complex, or clinical AIDS, will have special problems with regard to entry into some countries. On a sporadic basis notification of changing visa requirements is being received by WHO, CDC, and State Department sources. This information is constantly updated into the Herchmer country database. Refer to Section 8 to obtain a current country update. The following are entry requirements and AIDS information made available current as of 21 April 1990.

Australia: All persons applying for residence visas will be tested for antibodies to the AIDS virus.

Austria: Foreign workers applying for a residence permit in the City of Klagenfurt require a proof of a negative HIV test. Results of tests performed in the U.S. and other foreign countries are accepted by officials.

Belgium: Persons arriving to attend school on a state scholarship are required to show proof of a negative HIV test. Results of tests performed in the U.S. and other foreign countries are accepted by officials.

Belize: Foreign or migrant workers must be able to show proof of a negative HIV test which has been taken within the prior three months.

Bulgaria: The Bulgarian state news agency has reported that AIDS testing at border check points began on 12/26/87. Mandatory testing is in effect for resident foreigners, newlyweds, pregnant women, and Bulgarians who have lived abroad. Foreigners planning to stay longer than one month must comply with HIV antibody testing within 1 to 3 days of their arrival in Bulgaria. The government has imposed a ban on blood donations from prostitutes, foreigners and intravenous drug users.

Bulgaria has officially reported 104 positive HIV results in the native population and has deported 51 foreigners who have tested HIV positive.

China: Proof of a negative HIV test is required from anyone 17 years of older who plans to live in China longer than one year.

China has officially reported 2 cases of AIDS.

Christmas Island: Persons applying for residence visas will be tested for antibodies to the HIV virus.

Costa Rica: This country has suspended a requirement that merchant seamen provide proof of a negative HIV test before being allowed ashore.

Costa Rica has officially reported 39 AIDS cases through September 1987.

Cuba: All foreigners, other than tourists, must show proof of a negative HIV test when arriving in Cuba. Over one-fourth of the entire population has been screened for the HIV virus, with 248 persons having HIV positive tests and 28 persons ill with the disease. All donated blood in Cuba is screened for the HIV antibody.

Cyprus: HIV testing is performed upon arrival on all students from Africa and foreign nationals working in nightclubs or cabarets.

Czechoslovakia: All persons entering the country from areas of high risk are being tested for HIV antibody, including citizens returning from those areas. Areas considered high risk include all countries in Western Europe, North and South America, and Africa. All blood donors are being screened with HIV testing. This country reports 11 AIDS cases and 66 known carriers.

Ecuador: All foreign visitors intending to stay longer than 60 days will be tested for HIV virus antibody, but the starting date of this testing period has not been announced.

Egypt: All foreigners living in Egypt longer than one month will be tested for HIV antibodies. All tests must be done by Egyptian authorities. In the case of families, only the head of the household will be tested—although it is possible that spouses may also be tested. An HIV antibody test will be required for all foreign contractors entering Egyptian military facilities.

American organizations with qualified health personnel can collect their own blood samples which are then to be turned over to Egyptian authorities for testing.

France: 3,073 cases of AIDS have been reported, the highest level in Europe, with 40% of these cases being located in Paris. No testing of foreign travelers is required. Blood donors are being checked. Premarital HIV antibody testing is performed. Prenatal exams include HIV antibody testing.

East Germany: Travelers wishing to stay for extended periods will be required to show that they are free of the HIV virus antibody, per reports in East Germany's official newspaper.

West Germany: 1,760 cases of AIDS were reported through Jan 1988. No official requirement exists for testing travelers, but travelers suspected of carrying the HIV virus may be refused entry. The state of Bavaria requires an HIV antibody test for persons planning on staying there longer than 90 days. Results of US tests are not accepted.

Haiti: Researchers report 1,000 to 2,000 cases of AIDS have been diagnosed, with between 100,000 to 200,000 persons estimated to be infected with the virus. Projections are that 1 million of the country's 6 million inhabitants will become infected with the virus within the next 5 years.

50% of Haitian prostitutes carry the AIDS virus. Four out of every 10 AIDS patients are female.

Hong Kong: Government sources report 110 people have tested positive for HIV antibody and that 10 persons have died of this disease as of March 1988.

Hungary: Mandatory testing for HIV virus antibody has begun for persons infected, or suspected to be infected with, venereal disease, sexual partners of AIDS victims, prostitutes, prison inmates, blood donors, IV drug users, and travelers planning on staying longer than 30 days.

India: Proof of a negative HIV antibody test is required by all students and other persons planning to stay for more than 1 year. U.S. test results are accepted. These test results should be validated with the uniform stamp used to certify yellow fever and cholera vaccinations (see Chapter 5.5).

Health officials in Bombay have indicated that they number of AIDS carriers doubles in that city every six months. A survey of the country's blood supply in 1989 indicated that more than 1% of the country's blood supply is contaminated with the AIDS virus. There is a very poor blood donor screening program. Approximately 10,000 prostitutes in Bombay are believed to carry the AIDS virus.

Iraq: Travelers planning on staying longer than 14 days must be tested for HIV antibody. Results of US tests are not accepted. This requirement does not apply to persons older than 60 years of age.

Israel: The government is debating the testing for HIV antibody in all foreign volunteers coming to work at kibbutzim, or communal farms. Some kibbutzim are currently conducting tests. Blood donors have been screened since 1986. The number of persons infected with the virus is known to be 237; persons with active AIDS disease 45; and deaths from AIDS, 33 through July 1987.

Kenya: Government researchers randomly tested 200 Nairobi prostitutes and indicated that 85% were HIV antibody positive.

Korea, South: Long term work or resident visa applicants must show negative HIV antibody test results. U.S. tests are accepted. Employees in places which cater to tourists have undergone HIV antibody testing since July 1987. Thirty active cases of AIDS have been reported as of February 1988.

Kuwait: Contractors applying for residence visas must show proof of a negative HIV antibody test. U.S. test results are accepted.

Libya: Proof of a negative HIV antibody test is required from persons seeking residence visas for work or study. Other visitors and official delegation members are reportedly exempt.

Mexico: As of 31 January 1989 a total of 2,777 AIDS cases have been reported, with 32,000 projected cases expected by the year 1991. AIDS is spreading fastest amongst heterosexual women. One-third of the blood supply in Mexico comes from 25,000 professional donors who are running 10% HIV virus positive. The general population is running 0.8% positive. There is no requirement for HIV antibody test by travelers or those applying for work visas, but it is possible that those applying to immigrate must present proof of a negative HIV antibody test.

Mongolia: All foreign students must show proof of negative HIV antibody tests. Results from the U.S. are acceptable.

Nigeria: From 8% to 85% of the blood supply is screened at the nation's nine blood banks as of February 1988. Nigeria has officially reported 20 cases of AIDS to WHO. The Minister of Health has announced that Nigeria will reciprocate against any country that introduces mandatory testing for Nigerian travelers.

Pakistan: This country plans to start HIV antibody testing on all foreigners living in Pakistan longer than 6 months and for Pakistani citizens who are returning after living abroad. The effective date of this testing requirement has not been announced.

Papau New Guinea: Foreign workers will be required to show proof of a negative HIV antibody test. Results from the U.S. will be accepted. Spread of AIDS in this country is following the African pattern, primarily via heterosexual contact.

Phillipine Islands: All applicants for permanent resident visas are required to show proof of a negative HIV antibody test. Results from a U.S. laboratory are accepted.

Twenty two cases of AIDS have been reported as of April 1989. The Ministry of Health reports positive HIV antibody testing in prostitutes working near Clark Air Base and the Subic Bay Naval Base. One half of the known carriers in the Phillipines work as prostitutes near these bases. U.S. governmental employees and servicemen and their families are exempted from this test.

Poland: Blood donor screening has been started, but lack of funds has prevented full implementation of this program. Thirty seven cases have been reported. There are plans to broaden the extent of HIV antibody testing to persons arriving from countries "known for their bad epidemiological situation." Currently, proof of a negative HIV antibody test is required by all foreign students.

Qatar: All persons applying for foreign work permits must show proof of a negative HIV antibody test within the previous 6 months. Diplomates are exempted.

As of October 1988 this country reported 32 AIDS cases. The

extent of the HIV positive population is unknown.

Romania: Lack of medical supplies raises the concern of the accidental spread of AIDS in this country. Needles are reused hundreds of times. The extent of HIV positive cases in this country is unknown.

Rwanda: Approximately 30% of the adults between the ages of 18 and 45 in the capital city of Kigali are infected with the HIV virus. The countryside rate is between 2% and 3%, but increasing.

Saudi Arabia: Of the 4 different classifications of visas (work, business, visitor, and resident), the application for a work visa requires accompanying proof of a negative HIV antibody test. Foreign workers will be re-tested for HIV antibody three months after their arrival. Blood transfusions are routinely tested for AIDS.

Senegal: Donated blood is currently screened for HIV antibodies at Dakar's principal hospital and the National Transfusion Center. Plans to test the entire country's blood supply have been announced, but the date of starting this screening was not set.

Singapore: Foreigners without "permanent residence" status found to be carrying the HIV virus antibodies will be expelled. No compulsory testing guidelines were announced, however, except that all new foreign housemaids entering the city must present proof of a negative HIV antibody test. Blood donations have been tested since 1985.

South Africa: All foreigners infected with the HIV virus, cholera, or yellow fever will be deported. The measure is primarily targeted against migrant mine workers. No testing guidelines were announced.

Spain: Authorities report 624 persons with AIDS through September 1987. Deaths from the disease total 322, with Madrid reporting 195 cases and 102 deaths and Catalonia reporting 127 cases and 61 deaths. No updated information has been received as of April 1990.

Syria: All persons applying for foreign work permits and all foreign students must undergo HIV antibody testing at official government approved laboratories upon their arrival in Syria.

Thailand: There are 10,000 cases of HIV antibody positive carriers and known cases amongst drug users in Thailand. The virus is spreading rapidly amongst female prostitutes. Heterosexual women now make up the second largest group of persons infected with the virus.

Turkey: Seventy-five testing centers are being established at border areas and in tourism areas, but formal testing requirements have not been announced.

Uganda: Official government sources report that 1 in 10 residents of the capital city of Kampala is infected with the HIV virus. The eastern towns of Malaba and Busia have enormous infection rates with 80% of women and 30% of men. The country has reported 2,300 cases of AIDS, the third highest per capita rate behind the United States and Haiti.

United Arab Emirates: HIV antibody test results are required for all persons applying for work visas and any person staying longer than 30 days. Results of US tests are not acceptable. Screening of workers wishing to renew their permits is performed.

United States: Persons with active AIDS will be denied tourist visas, but can be granted 30 day visas to enter the country to attend conferences, obtain medical help, for business purposes, and to visit relatives. Since 1987 AIDS was added to the list of contagious diseases which serve as grounds for refusing tourist or permanent visa applications.

USSR: Beginning Feb 1989, all persons staying longer than 3 months in the Soviet Union will be required to undergo HIV antibody testing. This includes diplomats, journalists, students, and businessmen. Reports from countries that have a "mutually accepted agreement" will be honored, but there is no list of which countries were included in this arrangement. Previously U.S. tests were not accepted. Any person who knowingly infects another with AIDS can be jailed up to 8 years. The number of HIV antibody positive persons in the country is reported as slightly more than 100.

Zaire: The health minister reports an AIDS exposure rate of 12% in Kinshasa and a 5% exposure rate in the rural towns in Shaba Province, including Lumbumbashi and Kolwezi.

Chapter 4.7

Medical Considerations After the Return Home

A review of the disease descriptions in this book demonstrates quite clearly the delayed effects of travel and even lists some diseases whose impact on the traveler may not surface for decades. Such long delays in symptoms are the exception, but they demonstrate that the prudent traveler should have a passing knowledge of the potentials for infectious disease and environmental injuries which may affect his well-being after the return home. Even years later it will be wise to mention your travel history to your physician or consultants.

When should the return physical be arranged? Clearly an appointment should be made immediately if the traveler develops symptoms. Otherwise, authorities differ in the optimum time for scheduling this examination from one week[3] to eight weeks[4]. The

---

[3]Hall, A. (1987). Post-tropical check-up. in Dawood, R. (Ed.). *How to stay healthy abroad*. New York: Penguin Books.

[4]Pust, R. E., Peate, W. F., & Cordes, D. H. (1986). Comprehensive Care of Travelers. *The Journal of Family Practice*. 23(6). 572–579.

value of the one week examination is to attempt to identify a problem and treat it at the earliest stage possible. The rationale for delaying until the eight week interval is that latent infections are more apt to have manifested signs and symptoms and become more feasible to diagnose.

Authorities differ upon the importance of arranging a physical examination upon returning from an overseas trip. Clearly, a person without symptoms, who has stayed in first class hotels, had no direct contact with the native population, whose trip lasted less than a week, and who remained in an urban area, can generally feel safe in not arranging a post-trip physical. More important than where the traveler went, is what he was doing when he got there. Those who have been in close contact with native peoples, or who have worked with livestock, or who have been in close contact with the land and water, are much more apt to have encountered locally endemic diseases than a person traveling in first class hotels in a country with a greater disease burden.

As mentioned, persons with symptoms must absolutely obtain medical consultation as soon after their return as possible. This is particularly true for those returning with diarrhea, with a skin rash, with a fever, with a cough, with urinary tract symptoms, or if you had been ill while on the trip but are now feeling well.

Those who have been ill should bring any foreign medications which they may have used to their physician. Retain the original container and a sample of one of the pills. The identification of what was used may have a great bearing on future tests or treatment. Your treatment may have subdued the infection without eradicating it. Many foreign pharmaceuticals can be very dangerous to use and specific side effects might need to be evaluated with regard to liver function, kidney function, and blood formation disorders. Their use may have altered the normal laboratory tests used to identify suspicious diseases, and this may also have to be taken into account by your physician. Your physician will also need to know the symptoms you experienced, as well as any fever fluctuations, how long the illness lasted, in what countries and regions you were traveling before the illness started, and what responses occurred to any therapy that was used.

The advisability of obtaining a post-trip examination is based upon:

*Where you were.
*Contacts with the native population.
*Contact with water.
*Contact with the earth.
*What you were doing there.
*Insect exposure
*What you experienced while there.

The extent of the post-trip physical and laboratory evaluation will depend upon your activities while there, even more than it does on where you had actually been. However, it should be obvious from perusing the individual country database in this book (Section 8), that location *does* matter. In general the world can be divided into three zones of general risk for the traveler.

ZONE I

Your general health risk in these countries is the same as you would expect here at home. In fact Zone I includes the United States and Canada, the nations of northern Europe (to include France), and New Zealand and Australia.

ZONE II

You would have experienced an increased health risk in these countries which include European countries bordering the Mediterranean (except France), all islands of the Caribbean (except Haiti and the Dominican Republic), Israel, South Africa, Japan, Eastern Europe, and the Soviet Union. Besides the routine illnesses of Zone I, you will have had increased exposure to the food- and water-borne diseases (see Chapters 5.1 and 5.2 as well as the specific country as listed in Section 8).

ZONE III

Countries in this highest risk area include all nations in Central and South America, Mexico, the Dominican Republic, Haiti, and all nations in Asia and Africa, except Japan, Israel, and South Africa. Besides the exposure risks of Zones I and II, you will have had significant exposure to insect-borne illness (see Chapter 5.4), as well as increased risk to the food- and water-borne diseases (see Chapters 5.3, 6.12, 6.21, 6.22, 6.45 as well as the diseases as indicated under the specific country listing in Section 8).

For the travel medicine specialist, the *history* of travel, activities, and an assessment of your level of awareness and avoidance of the potential infectious diseases, will be the most important part of your evaluation. The *physical examination* will add some clues as to specific tests that may be required. Last in importance are *routine laboratory tests.* Our vast medical technology misleads many laymen into thinking that we can identify nearly any disorder by sophisticated laboratory tests and radiology procedures. This is just not the case. Sophisticated tests *can* identify very exotic diseases, but only if the medical practitioner knows what specifically to look for. This information comes primarily from the history which the patient volunteers.

LABORATORY ASSESSMENT:

The routine laboratory tests which may be ordered will likely include:

BLOOD: A complete blood count with a manually performed differential count of the white blood cells can indicate anemia and various infections. The presence of eosinophilia (an increase in a specific white cell count) might indicate a parasitic infection and indicate the need for more specific tests.

A thick blood smear can sometimes identify blood-borne parasites such as malaria, trypanosomiasis, and filariasis.

Liver function tests performed on a blood sample can indicate possible hepatitis, parasitic liver infections, exposure to toxic substances, or significant alcoholic beverage abuse.

Antibody tests on blood samples can indicate exposure to syphilis and AIDS. Specific antibody tests can be ordered for a number of tropical diseases depending upon probable exposure history.

STOOL: An examination of one stool for ova and parasites is generally considered adequate in the person with no symptoms. However, multiple samples, even colonoscopy and other specialized tests, may be required in the patient with symptoms.

URINE: A variety of problems can be surmised with a microscopic and chemical analysis of urine, to include eggs in schistosomiasis infection (Chapter 6.45).

SKIN TEST: A post-trip TB test is indicated in persons with exposure to native people in areas of risk.

EMOTIONAL ASSESSMENT:

Mental status survey is another reason for a post-trip evaluation. Trips can be stressful to the point that the traveler may need special counseling or assistance in resolving concerns. Perhaps the traveler watched someone else in the party come down with a terrible illness. Special assessment may be needed to assure the worried bystander that the contagion was not shared.

Did you suffer physical and/or emotional abuse from foreign officials? This does not happen too often, but when it does it is a severe emotional stress, particularly for persons used to a responsible government as is generally found in the United States.

The above are two examples of potential causes of Post-Traumatic Stress Disorder (PTSD). Witnessing, or experiencing, any distressing event that is outside the range of usual human experience can cause this syndrome to occur. Usually, the distressing event is re-experienced in a variety of ways, such as recurrent dreams. The victim can develop feelings of detachment, irritability, outbursts of anger, difficulties with attention span, extreme vigilance, or abrupt reactions to real or perceived future threats. Diagnosed early, rapid intervention can resolve PTSD. Delayed treatment can result in a chronic condition with very severe morbidity.

MEDICATION RECOMMENDATIONS:

The identification of possible continued risk may require that prescription medications be taken post-travel. Certainly malaria prophylaxis must continue for four weeks after leaving the area of malaria risk. Eradication of *Plasmodium vivax* and *P. ovale* will require a daily dosage of Primaquine for fourteen days as described in Chapter 6.31. The necessity of this can be determined by the mosquito exposure history of the traveler and the percentage of malaria which has been identified as *P. vivax* and *P. ovale* as per the individual country database (Section 8). Prior to the use of Primaquine, the physician may wish to order a blood test for G6PD deficiency as per the discussion in Chapter 6.31.

Other signs and symptoms of illness may also require the use of medication upon the return home. While this book has gone into great detail on the chemical prophylaxis and avoidance techniques of various diseases, it is beyond the scope and intention of this work to detail the diagnosis and treatment of the many diseases which have been discussed. This is best left in the hands of the infectious disease and tropical medicine specialists.

LONG TERM FOLLOW-UP:

Conditions which should alert the traveler in future years that the travel history should be offered include any of the following:

—Onset of weight loss
—Fevers of unknown origin
—Unusual blood chemistry changes
—Evidence of a "spot on the lung" in x-ray studies
—Evidence of a liver problem
—Abdominal pain of unknown cause
—Onset of anemia of unknown cause
—Onset of congestive heart failure
—Onset of blood in the urine of unknown cause
—Onset of edema, or swelling, of the legs
—Unusual skin eruptions

—Onset of neurological problems

—Any condition which cannot be rapidly diagnosed, or which does not respond to usual treatment protocols.

If the traveler does not develop signs or symptoms of a problem within one month of his/her return, the chances of carrying an occult infection become very slight. This possibility diminishes even further if the traveler remains symptom free after one year. Yet, the chronic nature of some parasitic diseases, particularly, demand that we remember our travel histories whenever a difficult medical condition surfaces, even if it occurs decades after the trip. Taking that into consideration, perhaps in some small way, all of our future trips to the doctor potentially become post-trip examinations.

Section 5

Disease Prevention and Immunization

The organisms that penetrate into our body have bypassed our first line of defense—our skin. The ingestion of food and water borne germs is a prime example of this penetration. Another is the inclusion of germs in the wounds of insect bites and stings. Traumatic wounds are the least likely method of penetration, but the most obvious when they occur.

To keep healthy we need to aid our first line of defense by following basic food, water, and sanitation precautions. Keeping ourselves healthy with adequate nutrition, rest, and hydration is part of this process. While all germs cannot be avoided, the numbers which we ingest and to which we are exposed can be minimized, perhaps to the point that our natural immune response, our second line of defense, can provide complete protection. Prophylactic medications can also decrease the numbers of pathogens, or germs, with which our immune system must contend. Learning techniques to aid our first line of defense in protecting us from disease is one of the most important aspects of safe travel.

The second line of defense, our immune response, can be aided by immunizations and prophylactic medications. This is not accomplished without potential side effects, cost, and certain concerns for safety as well as efficacy. Sections on immunizations, which are commonly available for foreign travel, discuss dosage and indications for various age groups. Side effects and means of predicting potential reactions to various vaccines are also discussed.

Chapter 5.1

Food and Dairy Product Safety

Just how does one go about minimizing the chances of ingesting food contaminated with virus, bacteria, parasites, or toxins from natural or man-made causes?

The first step is to be aware of the magnitude of the problem in various countries that are to be visited. The country information database starting on page 8–1 will indicate the current general hygienic situation with regard to water, food, and dairy products for each country of the world. Each country listing also indicates various diseases that occur, with relative risk indications. Look up these diseases via the index to learn about their mode of transmission. Some of these diseases are parasitic contaminates of various specific foods. Methods of decontamination, such as cooking guidelines, are listed for each of the potentially harmful diseases. Some toxins cannot be destroyed and certain foods must be avoided. At times this is seasonal. Some examples of specific commodities and contaminates are listed below.

TABLE 5-1
Common Contaminants of Foodstuff*

Disease	Meat	Dairy	Water	Unique Foodstuff
Anthrax	x			
Brucellosis	x	x		
Cholera			x	
Ciguatera				Ocean fish, 400 species
Clonorchiasis				Fresh water fish
Dracunculiasis			x	
Dysentery			x	
Echinococcus	x			
Encephalitis, tick		x		Milk of infected victim
Fasciolopsiasis				Water chestnuts, bamboo
Giardiasis			x	
Hepatitis A			x	
Leptospirosis			x	
Opisthorchiasis				Fresh water fish
Paragonimiasis				Fresh water crabs, crayfish
Paralytic shellfish poisoning				Mussels, clams, oysters, scallops
Poliomyelitis			x	
Schistosomiasis			x	
Scromboid poisoning				Dark meat ocean fish
Tapeworms	x			
Trichinosis	x			
Tuberculosis		x		
Tularemia	x			
Typhoid fever	x		x	

*Many of the above contaminants are seasonal and geographically limited in distribution. All water borne diseases can contaminate virtually any foodstuff due to improper handling techniques. Refer to the individual disease descriptions for further information on distribution, prevention, signs and symptoms of disease, and availability of treatment.

Avoidance of these items, or following suggested decontamination procedures, will help minimize the chance of turning your trip into a medical nightmare. Frequently the warnings must be general and apply to all food consumed within a country.

Dairy products, to include milk, ice cream, and creamed pastries, have caused outbreaks of *Salmonella* in the United States several times within the past two years. *Yersinia* contamination of chocolate milk, and *Listeria* infection of "Latin" cheeses, are also bacterial diseases encountered in the United States and Canada. Brucellosis infection occurs in travelers to Malta and Spain who have eaten contaminated soft cheeses and milk. Kuwait has one of the highest exposure rates to brucellosis in the world. Australian goat milk is often not pasteurized. I once treated a elderly lady who had tuberculosis of the intestinal lymph nodes from drinking non-pastcurizcd goat milk from right hcrc in good old Indiana. Dairy products might carry a variety of diseases, even if stored by refrigeration from the time of gathering until your consumption. In many countries cattle are inspected for tuberculosis, anthrax, and other potentially harmful pathogens. If the country you are visiting does not do so, then consumption of butter, meat, or milk could allow you to catch tuberculosis and other contagious conditions such as brucellosis, hookworm (*A. duodenale* species), and anthrax. Regardless of where one travels, insist upon consuming only properly pasteurized dairy products, taken from tuberculin free, otherwise healthy animals, and then only when satisfied that the products have been properly refrigerated from the moment of collection, through processing, transportation, and storage until your consumption. Products failing any one of the above requirements should not be consumed.

Salmonella infections occur world-wide with various species infecting such diverse commodities as Kenyan cashew nuts, Thai smoked salmon, Indonesian raw prawns, Taiwanese frozen "cooked" shrimp, Malaysian black pepper, even US and foreign sources of marijuana. An outbreak of salmonellosis affected 631 passengers and 135 crew members on international flights from contaminated aspic powder sprinkled on catered hors d'oeuvres.

But decontamination procedures are not always easy to accomplish. The Peace Corp instruction to cook it, peel it, or forget it, is an excellent guideline to follow. Care must be taken in the peeling process, however. I will point out that it is hard to peel anything with contaminated hands and miss ingesting the germs you are trying to avoid. Your hands will become contaminated the instant that you touch the soiled exterior of the food item. During the peeling, it will be next to impossible to keep from touching the skinned fruit. If you were to do so with fingers that had already touched the fruit surface, then you have transferred literally millions of germs to the peeled surface.

The chance of contracting travelers' diarrhea can be minimized by several approaches. Being aware of poor hygienic practices in developing countries goes a long way toward developing personal habits that can reduce the number of pathogens that one might otherwise ignorantly consume. A microbiologist once told of an experience while studying the causes of diarrhea in Guadalajara, Mexico. Taking samples of food items from a first class restaurant back to his lab, he noticed chicken feathers in a dish not noted to have chicken meat as a normal content (to say nothing of feathers). This mystery caused his return to the establishment to investigate. The manager assured him of their cleanliness, all employees having been instructed to wash their hands, etc. It was noted, however, that the restaurant received its chickens from the market in crates. After the dishes were carefully washed in nice, hot water, they were stacked in these convenient crates. The crates were, however, still covered in chicken dung and feathers! Such can be the incomprehension of basic hygiene in even a first class restaurant in a developing country.

The above illustrates that restricting your diet to well cooked foods may not be enough to prevent bacterial, viral, or parasitic ingestion. However, it sure helps. Raw foods of any sort are a frequent source of trouble to the unwary. Often, in countries lacking refrigeration, fruits and vegetables are "freshened" on the way to market by sprinkling these items frequently with water from road side drainage ditches. The use of human fertilizer makes this water very contaminated. This contamination is not eliminated by drying or wiping with a cloth.

Pickling and freezing food prevents bacterial decomposition, but neither is a guaranteed means of destroying disease causing bacteria or parasites. If food products have been gathered under unsanitary conditions, from animal sources that are diseased, or from water sources that are polluted, they will be unsafe to eat.

The country database in this book indicates the probable safety of water supply, dairy products, and food items. If water precautions are listed, remember that anything that this water touches has also been made unsafe. Ice would also be unsafe. Its use in alcoholic beverages has been shown experimentally not to be protective. High concentrations of alcohol in a drink made with contaminated ice will still place you at risk—not only from the effects of the alcohol, but also from any bacterial, viral, or parasitic contamination. This water is also unsafe, without further treatment, for use in brushing your teeth.

Chapter 5.2

Water Purification

Water can be purified adequately for drinking by mechanical, physical, and chemical means. The clearest water possible should be chosen or attempts made to clarify the water prior to starting any disinfectant process. Water with high particulate count, with clay or organic debris, allows higher bacterial counts and tends to be more heavily contaminated. In preparing potable, or drinkable, water we are attempting to lower pathogenic micro-organism counts to the point that the body can defend itself against the remaining numbers. We are not trying to produce sterile water—that would generally be impractical.

The use of chlorine based systems has been effectively used by municipal water supply systems for years. There are two forms of chlorine readily available to the traveler. One is liquid chlorine laundry bleach and the other is Halazone tablets. Laundry bleach that is 4 to 6 percent can make clear water safe to drink if 2 drops are added to 1 quart of water. This water must be mixed thoroughly and let stand for 30 minutes before drinking. This water should have a slight chlorine odor. If not, the original laundry bleach may have lost some of its strength and you should repeat the dose and let the mixture stand an additional 15 minutes prior to drinking.

Halazone tablets from Abbott Laboratories are also effective. They are actually quite stable with a shelf life of 5 years, even when exposed to temperatures over 100°F occasionally. Recent articles have stated that Halazone has a short shelf life and that it loses 75% of its activity when exposed to air for two days. Abbott Labs has proven the efficacy of use for Halazone sufficiently to receive FDA approval. A clue to their stability is that they turn yellow and have an objectionable odor when they decompose. Check for this before use. Five tablets should be added to a quart of clear water for adequate chlorination.

Chlorine based systems are very effective against virus and bacteria. They work best in neutral or slightly acid waters. As the active form of the chlorine, namely hypochlorous acid (HClO), readily reacts with nitrogen containing compounds such as ammonia, high levels of organic debris decrease its effectiveness. The amount of chlorine bleach or Halazone added must be increased if the water is alkaline or contaminated with organic debris.

Iodine is a very effective agent against protozoan contamination, such as *Giardia lamblia* and *Entamoeba hystolytica,* which tend to be resistant to chlorine. Further, iodine is not as reactive to ammonia or other organic debris by-products, thus working better in cloudy water. Tincture of iodine, as found in the home medicine chest, may be used as the source of the iodine. Using the commonly available 2% solution, 5 drops should be added to clear water or 10 drops to cloudy water, and the resultant mix should be allowed to stand 30 minutes prior to drinking.

The Armed Forces were responsible for developing a solid tablet that provided a source of iodine. Tetraglycine hydroperiodide is available as Globuline or Potable Aqua, or as Army surplus water purification tablets. An elemental iodine concentration of 3 to 5 ppm (parts per million) is necessary to kill amoeba and their cysts, algae, bacteria and their spores, and enterovirus. One tablet of Potable Aqua will provide 8 ppm iodine concentration per quart. If the water is clear a ten minute wait is required;

TABLE 5–2
Chemical Water Purification Methods

Substance	Amount Used	contact Time
Laundry Bleach 4–6%	2 drops/quart	Let stand 30 minutes
(water should have a slight chlorine odor; if not, repeat dose and let stand an additional 15 minutes)		
Halazone Tablets	5 tablets/quart	Let stand 30 minutes
(defective Halazone tablets have an objectionable odor)		
Tincture of Iodine 2%	5 drops/quart clear water	30 minutes
	10 drops/quart cloudy water	
Potable Aqua	1 tablet/quart clear water	10 minutes
(Globuline—	1 tablet/quart cloudy water	20 minutes
Tetraglycine	if very cold	30 minutes
hydroperiodide)		

for cloudy water wait 20 minutes before consuming. At near freezing temperatures, wait a full 30 minutes before drinking.

Crystals of iodine can also be used to prepare a saturated iodine-water solution for use in disinfecting drinking water. Four to eight grams of USP grade iodine crystals can be placed in a 1 ounce glass bottle. Water added to this bottle will dissolve an amount of iodine based upon its temperature. It is this saturated iodine-water solution which is then added to the quart of water. The amount added to produce a final concentration of 4 ppm will vary according to temperature as indicated in the chart:

TABLE 5–3
Saturated Iodine Treatment Volumes

TEMPERATURE	VOLUME	CAP FULLS*
37°F (3°C)	20.0 cc	8
68°F(20°C)	13.0 cc	5+
77°F(25°C)	12.5 cc	5
104°F(40°C)	10.0 cc	4

*Assuming 2 $\frac{1}{2}$ cc capacity for a standard 1 ounce glass bottle cap.

This water should be stored for 15 minutes before drinking. If the water is turbid, or otherwise contaminated, the amounts of saturated iodine solution indicated above should be doubled and the resultant water stored 20 minutes before using. This product is now commercially available as Polar Pure through many outdoor stores and catalog houses (see listing of suppliers at the end of Chapter 3.2).

Mechanical filtration methods are also useful in preparing drinking water. They normally consist of a screen with sizes down to 6 microns in size which are useful in removing tapeworm eggs (25 microns) or Giardia lamblia (7 to 15 microns). These screens enclose an activated charcoal filter element which removes many disagreeable tastes. As most bacteria have a diameter smaller than 1 micron, bacteria and the even smaller viral species are not removed by filtration using these units. Bacteria and virus can be held by adsorption to the surface of the carbon particles, thus effectively removing them from the water—at least until the particles are saturated and the bacteria and virus are allowed to pass on through. For water to be guaranteed safe with the use of one of these devices, it must be pre-treated with chlorine or iodine exactly as indicated above prior to passage through the filter. While these filters remove clay and organic debris, they will plug easily if the water is very turbid. A concern with the charcoal filter usage is the possibility for them to become contaminated with bacteria while being used and possibly allowing considerable passage of bacteria when they are used the next time. Pre-treating the water helps prevent this. I have frequently used a charcoal filter system to insure safe, good tasting water after chemical treatment.

Another filtration method is perhaps one of the oldest, namely filtering through unglazed ceramic material. This was done in large crocks—a slow filtration method popular in tropical countries many years ago. A modern version of this old system is the development of a pressurized pump method. Made in Switzerland, the Katadyn Pocket Filter has a ceramic core inclosed in a tough plastic housing, fitted with an aluminum pump. The built in pump forces water through the ceramic filter at a rate of approximately three fourths of a quart per minute. Turbid water will plug the filter, but a brush is provided to easily restore full flow rates. This filter has a .2 micron size, which eliminates all bacteria and larger pathogens. Pre-treating of the water is not required. There is evidence that viral particles are also killed by this unit as the ceramic material is silver impregnated which appears to denaturate virus as they pass through the filter. This possibility is being evaluated by the FDA at this time. These units are not cheap, costing about $200.00 retail. They weigh 23 ounces.

Bringing water to a boil will effectively kill pathogens and make water safe to drink. One reads variously to boil water 5, 10, even 20 minutes. But simply bringing the water temperature to 150 °F (65.5 °C) is adequate to kill the pathogens discussed above, and all others besides. At high altitude the boiling point of water is reduced. For example, at 24,000 feet the boiling point of water would be about 166 °F (74.5 °C). Thus, bringing water to a boil, even at high altitude, is adequate to destroy all harmful organisms.

The subject of the minimal length of time and temperature required to make water safe to drink is important. Bringing water to a boil is the minimal safe time for preparation. At times fuel or water supply may be in short supply and this minimal time must be used. It will never be necessary to boil water longer than 5 minutes and the shortest time mentioned (ie just bringing the water to a boil) will suffice for safe drinking water. This water will not be sterile, but it will be safe to drink.

Chapter 5.3

Travelers' Diarrhea

More than 8 million US travelers will visit developing countries in a year and approximately one third of this number will develop diarrhea.

Travelers' diarrhea is caused by a variety of infectious causes. The percentage of travelers contracting this difficulty will differ by destination of their travel, with attack rates ranging from 20% to 50% amongst visitors to high risk areas. Destinations regarded as high risk include most of the developing countries of Latin America, Africa, the Middle East, and Asia. Intermediate risk destinations include most of the Southern European countries and a few Caribbean islands. Low risk destinations include Canada, Northern Europe, Australia, New Zealand, the United States, and a number of the Caribbean islands.

Typical travelers' diarrhea usually results in 4 to 5 loose or watery stools per day. It is generally a self limiting disease, lasting 3 to 4 days. Duration of symptoms longer than one week will occur in only 10% of victims, however 2% will experience diarrhea longer than one month and 1% longer than three months.

As many as 75% of those afflicted will have abdominal pain and cramps, 50% will have nausea, and 15% will have vomiting, and 2% to 10% may have diarrhea accompanied by fever or bloody stools or both. In a study of several hundred thousand Swiss travelers, no deaths could be attributed to travelers' diarrhea.

PREVENTION OF TRAVELERS' DIARRHEA

Prevention of this problem can be attempted in several ways. One is through the use of specially prepared drinking water and foodstuff, as discussed in the sections on food and dairy products and water purification. The use of standard hygienic practices, such as hand washing by the traveler prior to eating, goes without saying.

Certain medications have been shown useful in providing protection from developing travelers' diarrhea. Pepto Bismol, 2 tablets taken four times daily with meals and at bedtime decreased the incidence of travelers' diarrhea from 61% to 23% in American students in Guadalajara in a recent well controlled study performed by the University of Texas-Houston Medical School. Side effects included dark stools, occasionally ringing in the ears, and rarely a black coating on the tongue. It is safe to take this dosage of Pepto Bismol for periods of up to three weeks. Products containing aspirin should not be taken concurrently. About 8 aspirin tablets worth of salicylate would be consumed in that quantity of Pepto Bismol on a daily basis. Persons taking coumadin are advised against this method of preventing travelers' diarrhea.

Several antibiotics have also been shown to be an effective preventative in well controlled studies. Antibiotics have several drawbacks, primarily the chance of developing an allergic reaction with prolonged use, the possibility of side effects (such as sun sensitivity), the emergence of resistant bacterial strains in the environment if over-use of antibiotic is encouraged, and the chance that the traveler will nurture the growth of a resistant strain to the antibiotic being employed. Of the antibiotics studied, doxycycline 100 mg, taken once daily on an empty stomach, seems to be the best choice. It has a greater degree of protection than the other antibiotics studied (60 to 90%). It may not be taken by ladies in the third trimester of pregnancy, children 8 years or younger, or those allergic to tetracycline.

Bactrim DS (or Septra DS), 1 tablet daily has also been shown to be effective in preventing travelers' diarrhea. It is a sulfa drug, a class of drugs generally associated with higher probabilities of sun sensitivity and allergic reactions.

Iodochlorhydroxyquin (Clioquinol) is widely used as a preventative agent in many countries, but its effectiveness has not been proven and it is not recommended. In fact, travelers should be wary of buying local remedies while overseas as many of these products have been associated with serious side effects and their efficacy is chancy.

A consensus of government and private professional experts on travelers' diarrhea was published in 1985 which came to several conclusions. One was that travelers' diarrhea was caused by infectious agents (virus or bacterial generally). The other was that taking prophylactic antibiotic was unjustified for several reasons in all but certain notable exceptions. The reasons to avoid antibiotic use were centered around the fact that travelers' diarrhea is generally very benign, with a short course and no after effects, and that prophylactic antibiotics might cause serious side effects and could allow the emergence of resistant strains due to antibiotic overuse. Persons who fall into the category which some experts feel should receive prophylactic antibiotic would be persons engaged in international athletic contests, important government or business leaders involved with negotiations, or those in whom an underlying medical condition would warrant aggressive prevention. I would add several other categories. If from previous experience the traveler knew they were at high risk from contracting diarrhea, or if the trip was very important and the traveler did not want to chance spending 1 to 10 days with diarrhea, then that person should also be considered for aggressive prophylaxis.

TREATMENT OF TRAVELERS' DIARRHEA

Treatment of travelers' diarrhea is the other side of the coin when dealing with this topic. Indeed, one approach to the problem is to simply treat it, if, and when, it occurs, thus avoiding prolonged—and unnecessary—exposure to prophylactic medications.

Pepto Bismol liquid, taken 1 oz every 30 minutes for eight doses, has been shown to decreased the rate of stooling by half. Adsorbents such as kaolin and pectin give stools more consistency, but do not decrease the frequency, abdominal cramping, or length of affliction. Pepto-bismol has never been associated with fetal defects, but the high salicylate level of this medication may cause bleeding during pregnancy. There is a theoretical possibility of fetal damage from salicylates. A new adsorbent, Diasorb, has ten times the adsorption capability of kaolin and shows great promise in safely treating diarrhea. It is non-prescription and is available in liquid and tablet formulation at most drug stores in the United States. It should be perfectly safe for consumption by women at any stage of pregnancy.

Replacement of fluid loss is the most important aspect of diarrhea treatment. Carbonated water found in most developing countries is generally considered safe. Water consumed must be either heated to boiling or be bottled water from a reputable source. More than water is lost with the diarrhea. Various minerals are also excreted in large amounts, notably sodium and potassium. The patient must receive adequate fluid replacement, equaling fluid loss plus about 2 quarts per day.

The Centers for Disease Control has recommended an oral replacement cocktail to replace the water and mineral (electrolyte) losses of profound diarrhea as described in Table 5–4.

Throughout the world UNICEF and WHO (World Health Organization) distribute an electrolyte replacement product called Oralyte. It must be reconstituted with adequately purified water.

Anti-motility agents rapidly stop the symptoms of diarrhea. Products such as paregoric, Lomotil, and Imodium are widely used in the treatment of diarrhea. Imodium, in liquid form, was made an non-prescription drug in the United States in mid-1988 and the 2 mg capsules became non-prescription in 1989. There is a significant danger in the use of these drugs. Diarrhea is your body's way of attempting to eliminate disease. If the bowel is paralyzed, the germs causing the problem are allowed to sit just where they want to be, in the nice, warm human intestine. The human response of antibody production may soon eliminate these germs and no harm will have been done. However, certain germs are

TABLE 5–4
The CDC Oral Fluid/Electrolyte
Replacement Cocktail

Prepare two separate glasses of the following:

Glass 1) Orange, apple or other fruit juice
(rich in potassium)............................8 ounces

Honey or corn syrup (glucose necessary
for absorption of essential salts) ....^{1}/$_2$ teaspoon

Salt, table (source of sodium and chloride) ....1 pinch
Glass 2) Water (carbonated or boiled).....................8 ounces

Soda, baking (sodium bicarbonate) ....^{1}/$_4$ teaspoon

* Drink alternately from each glass. Supplement with carbonated beverages or water and tea made with boiled or carbonated water as desired. Avoid solid foods and milk until recovery.

It should be noted that the use of Gatorade, available in a powdered form, may be used to replace Glass 1, except that the water used to reconstitute it must be boiled or carbonated, as mentioned under Glass 2. It should also be diluted with twice the volume of fluid recommended by the manufacturer.

considered "invasive." They will, given the chance, work their way through the bowel lining and gain access to the lymphatic system, the liver circulation system, the abdominal cavity, etc., and great harm can then result. The use of anti-motility agents should be restricted to urgent situations, such as long bus rides or trips without toilet facilities, impending dehydration, attendance at meetings that cannot be cancelled, and the like. The risk versus benefit of using such drugs must rest in part with both the prescribing physician and the traveler.

Among various antibiotic treatments that have been proven effective is the use of doxycycline 100 mg, one tablet twice daily— but only if this medication was not being taken as a preventative. Another proven treatment is with Bactrim DS (Septra DS or trimethoprim/sulfamethoxazole), one tablet twice daily—or in the event of sulfa allergy, trimethoprim alone, 200 mg taken twice daily. Three days of treatment is recommended, although 2 days may be sufficient. Nausea and vomiting without diarrhea should not be treated with antibiotics. Erythromycin has been advocated for treatment of travelers' diarrhea. An antibiotic that has been proven quite effective in treatment is Cipro (ciprofloxacin), taken 500 mg twice daily for three to four days. While more effective in a controlled study than Bactrim, its cost is much higher (Cipro costs almost $2.50 per tablet). Noroxin (norfloxacin) at a dose of 400 mg twice daily for three to four days is also effective. This medication is also quite expensive.

The most effective combination treatment that has been demonstrated to date has been the use of Imodium (loperamide) and Bactrim DS (trimethoprim/sulfamethoxazole) which resulted in nearly 100% cure of cramping and diarrhea stools. Dosages taken were as described in the package inserts for both medications. The Bactrim DS was taken one tablet twice daily. The Imodium 2 mg capsule was taken 2 capsules immediately, followed by 1 capsule after each loose stool, with a maximum dose of 8 per day.

Frequently the traveler will not develop diarrhea until returning home. It is best to take medications under the supervision of a physician, rather than ingesting medications brought home from a trip. This is especially true if blood has been noted in the diarrhea stools, an indication of an invasive organism that may require specific therapy.

There are certain risk factors for travelers' diarrhea. This problem is slightly more common in young adults than in older people. The most significant risk factors are the destination and activity of the traveler, as mentioned above. Persons having reduced stomach acid levels (such as those taking antacids or medications for ulcers) are at increased risk. Tagamet, Pepcid, Zantac, and Axid are examples of medications that reduce stomach acid formation. The safest ulcer medication for foreign travel is probably Carafate, as its coating action is not only effective in promoting ulcer healing, but it does not reduce stomach acid levels. Those contemplating using marijuana should be advised that it also causes a decrease in stomach acid secretion, thus increasing the risk of diarrhea.

After all of the above has been said, perhaps the most important advise which can be given is to refer to the sections on food, dairy (Chapter 5.1), and water treatment (Chapter 5.2) for methods to avoid the many infectious causes of travelers' diarrhea.

Chapter 5.4

Insect Protection

Protection from bites of insects is a mainstay of avoiding the contraction of many devastating diseases. The table below is only a sample of the illness that is spread by insect vectors.

Mosquito Protection

There are several techniques to employ for maximum protection from mosquito bites and their possible subsequent effects. These are classified into protective clothing, repellent and insecticide use, avoidance of attraction, and minimizing habitat contact.

A. Clothing—Clothing should be thick enough to prevent the insect's penetration. This can be accomplished in warm weather more comfortably by wearing a string underwear beneath a light, and loose, outer garment. Sleeve cuffs may need to be cinched tight. This can generally be accomplished with velcro strips sewn in such a way as to allow easy cinching of the opening. Fashionable vents should be velcro lined for easy closure. Slacks or trousers should be chosen that can tuck into boots or shoes, or a boot

TABLE 5-5
The Vector Spread of Significant Diseases*

DISEASE	SANDFLIES	FLIES	MOSQUITOS	TICKS	OTHER
Bartonelliosis	x				
Chikungunya Fever			x		
Colorado Tick Fever				x	
Dengue			x		
Encephalitis,					
Japanese Equine			x		
Venezuelan Equine			x		
Filariasis				x	
Leishmaniasis	x				
Loiasis			x		
Lyme Disease				x	
Malaria		x			
Onchoceriasis	x				
Bubonic Plague					Flea
Rabies					Mammals
Relapsing Fever					Lice
Rift Valley Fever			x		
Rocky Mtn Spotted Fever			x		
Sandfly Fever	x				
Trachoma		x			
Trypanosomiasis					
African		x			
American					Reduviidae bug
Tularemia		x	x	x	
Tungiasis					Flea "chigoe"
Typhus, Endemic					Flea
Typhus, Epidemic					Lice
Typhus, Scrub					Rodent Mite
West Nile Fever			x		
Yellow Fever			x		

*Many of the above diseases are seasonal and geographically limited in distribution. Refer to the individual disease descriptions for further information on distribution, prevention, signs and symptoms of disease, and availability of treatment. Some diseases can be spread by more than one vector, by contaminated foodstuff, or directly from infected humans. The above table is representative of the importance of vector control only.

garter obtained to effectively seal the pants leg opening. Spraying clothing with a permethrin compound (see below) can cut mosquito bites by 93% as shown by clinical trials in Alaska by the U.S. Air Force.

B. Repellent—An ideal insect repellent is a formulation of "deet" (n,n diethyl-m-toluamide) which is 12% or greater. I have found the most effective mixture to be 75% deet and 25% isopropyl (rubbing) alcohol—which is the formulation of "GI Jungle Juice" used in Vietnam and which is still in supply for Armed Forces use. Several brands of pure deet are available, such as Muskol, and Repel 100. I always cut them with the rubbing alcohol 4:1. Strong deet formulations should be avoided on children as toxic side effects have been reported in this age group. A better product for children would be Skin-So-Soft, mentioned below. Other effective formulations contain ethyl hexanediol (sold as 6/12 insect repellent), dimethyl phthalate, Indalone, and compounds containing citronella. I have not found Vitamin B-1 (thiamine) to be an effective preventative oral agent, but the recommended dose by those who do is 100 mg daily for 1 week prior to departure and daily thereafter.

C. Insecticide—To treat an inclosed area spray with a pyrethrin containing insecticide, ideally $1/2$ hour before a stay in the room is anticipated. Make sure that sleeping and living quarters are free of mosquitos, or re-spray.

D. Netting—Use netting over cots or beds when sleeping. Have adequate netting, or screens, to prevent mosquito entry. A specially constructed, fine mesh netting with frame designed to fit over a bed is sold by IAMAT (International Association for Medical Assistance to Travelers), 417 Center Street, Lewiston, NY 14092 for $75.00 plus mailing costs. The rectangular frame and generous size allows plenty of room to sit up in bed. It also helps preclude accidentally brushing up against the side of the netting, thus preventing insects biting through from the outside. The weight of this device is 5 pounds. It is sold by the name of "La-Mosquette."

E. Electronic sound devices—These devices designed to repel these critters have never dented mosquito buzzing or their biting enthusiasm in the far north in my experience, but I have friends

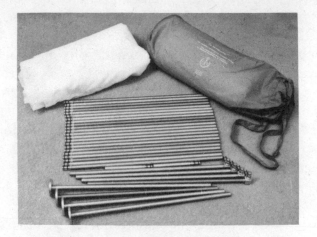

FIGURE 5–1
The LaMosquitte netting system, providing unique advantages over traditional
net systems. Developed and distributed by the International Association for
Medical Assistance to Travelers.

who use them enthusiastically under circumstances that are less obnoxious.

F. Things to avoid—Avoid the use of perfumes, colognes, deodorants, or after shave lotions as these tend to attract mosquitos.

G. Location—As mosquitos are generally dusk and nocturnal feeders, avoid outside exposures during these times. There are species variations in feeding patterns, so pay attention to local swarming times. Avoid areas that have heavy mosquito populations, if possible. Mosquitos love stagnant water, which can include water sitting in pots, old tires, and puddles as well as swamps. Choose windy locations to camp.

Blackfly, Sand fly, Gnat Protection

Blackflies, sand flies, biting gnats, and no-see-ums seem to share much of the outdoors with us. Their bites cause sores to develop which allow more secondary infections than mosquitos can generally cause.

A. Clothing—These creatures are very adept at crawling under netting. Head netting must be fastened around the neck. Similarly all openings, must be securly closed.

B. Repellent—The ideal repellent for blackflies, and related flying insects, is 2-ethyl-1,3-hexanediol (Rutgers 6/12) and dimethyl phthalate. Deet in high concentration will also work, but more frequent applications are required. An ideal preparation is Skin So Soft, sold by Avon. This later product is much easier on children than the stronger repellents. Skin So Soft is more effective in repelling blackflies than mosquitos. Some authorities have indicated that they felt this product worked by trapping the insects in the oily coating on the skin. But it actually seems to have a repellent quality.

Skin So Soft is not sold, or advertised, as an insect repellent by Avon, or approved for this use by the Food and Drug Administration. The product's significant protective characteristics have been recognized since the 1940's. While more effective in providing protection from various blackflies, it also works as a mosquito repellent. Skin So Soft is safer to use on children and on people with sensitive skin than harsher repellents. See a further discussion of this product at the end of this chapter.

C. Insecticide—The techniques described under mosquito also apply here.

D. Netting—As mentioned above, it is important to have secure fastenings of netting to prevent these insects from wriggling their way through on their way to dinner.

E. Avoid—Avoiding perfumes, colognes, deodorants, or after shave lotions is also important in minimizing attacks from flies.

F. Location—Blackflies tend to bite during the day. They prefer running water for breeding. Local species variation exists in feeding patterns. These insects tend to swarm close to the ground so that adequate foot, ankle, and lower leg protection is a must.

Ticks

Ticks are somewhat resistant to the effects of insect repellent, but their use should be as described under blackfly above. Use similar clothing protection. Ensure that closures on clothing are secure, particularly around the waist and at pants leg openings. When in tick country it is essential to visually check over each other for ticks and then remove them.

There are multiple folk remedies on ways to remove a tick, but controlled experiments and personal experience has shown me that they simply do not work. Manual removal is without a doubt the best, if not the only, way to rid yourself of these wee beasties. Do not handle ticks with your bare hands as infectious agents may infect you through breaks in your skin. Use good quality tweezers. You may wish to shield your hands from infection by grasping the tweezers with your hand covered by a rubber glove, tissue, or paper towel. Do not twist or jerk the tick out, but rather pull upward with a steady, even pressure. Most importantly, grasp the tick as close to the skin as possible, taking care not to squeeze, crush, or puncture the body of the tick.

The tick's fluids and body parts, such as saliva, hemolymph, and gut contents, may contain infective agents. When the tick has been removed, disinfect the bite site with rubbing (isopropyl) alcohol, surgical scrub, or soap, and wash your hands with soap and water. Dispose of the tick by placing it in alcohol or by flushing it down a toilet.

A. Clothing—A one-minute application of pressurized spray of 0.5% permethrin provided 100% protection against ticks, while a one-minute application of 30% deet provided 92% protection in tests performed in Massachusetts and California.

B. Repellent—as above.

C. Insecticide—permethrin mentioned above is actually an insecticide and not a repellent. It is effective enough at killing ticks that it can be used for both purposes. It is sold in the U.S. as "Permanone Tick Repellent" for use on clothing and shoes.

D. Netting—Netting provides no protection against ticks.

E. Avoid—Ticks are so universal in the outdoor habitat that avoidance is virtually impossible when in weeds, brush, and grass. Examination of the entire body to find and remove ticks is essential after outdoors exposure in tick infested areas.

Fleas, Lice

Travelers are generally not prone to problems with these critters as they have hygienic codes which eliminate cohabitation with rats, animals, filthy humans and they maintain bodily cleanliness that decreases the infestation rate. Permethrin is an effective insecticide for treatment of lice and is available in the U.S. under the brand name "Nix" for that purpose. Applied to cloths, as mentioned above, it also provides protection against fleas and ticks.

The combination of a one-minute application of 0.5% spray concentration of permethrin on clothing and a long acting 35% deet preparation on the skin provided 100% protection against mosquitos for an eight hour period in studies performed in Alaska. The long-acting cream formulation of 35% deet will be available to the U.S. Army in 1989 and for the general public in 1991. When used in tests against Alaskan mosquitos, it provided 89% protection for 8 hours. Two long acting deet preparations were previously studied in Australia which were not quite as effective. They were "3-M Insect Repellent Lotion" (33% deet which was 56% effective over 14 hours) and Biotek "Long-Acting Insect Repellent" (42% deet which was 61% effective over 14 hours). In the Australian studies the standard military jungle juice formula of 75% deet and 25% alcohol was found to be 54% protective over 14 hours in protecting from mosquito bites.

TABLE 5-6
Chemical Components of Some Insect Repellents and Insecticides

diethyl toluamide n,n diethyl meta-toluamide (deet)	mosquitos, ticks, insects avoid contact with eyes and mouth melts plastics
Dibutyl phthalate	mite, tick, and insect repellent rubbed into clothes may last 2 weeks
dimethyl phthalate (DMP)	Insect, mite, tick repellent
Gamma benzene hexachloride	Eradicates lice and scabies mite
Crotamitron (Eurax)	Eradicates scabies mite
Ethyl hexanediol	Blackfly repellent
.5% lindane or 2% malathion	To eradicate bedbugs from furniture, walls
butyl 3,4-dihydro-2,2-dimethyl-4-oxo-2H-pyran-6-carboxylate (Indalone)	Mosquito repellent
Di-isopentyl malate	Tsetse fly repellent, especially for use on net jackets.

Deet is absorbed through the skin with about 10 to 15% of the dose being excreted in the urine. Toxic and allergic reactions have been reported, particularly in children. These reports are rare and the repellent is generally quite safe. However, the 35% concentration should probably be the maximum dose used on the skin of children.

Avon "Skin-So-Soft" has been shown to be effective against the yellow fever carrying *Ae. aegypti* mosquito. "Skin-So-Soft" is a formulation of di-isopropyl adipate, mineral oil, isopropyl palmitate, dioctyl sodium sulfosucinate, fragrance, and the sun screen benzophenone-11. It is most effective against blackflies and biting gnats, but it also works well enough on mosquitos that I recommend its use in children. There have been no long term studies of side effects from frequent applications of this product, but the contents are such that harm would not be expected.

Check the Individual Country Database (Section 8) for potential risk of disease. Examine the disease listing for its method of spread. Vector control is an important aspect of preventing many of these terrible illnesses. If special aspects of vector control exist, these will be discussed in the individual disease discussions in this book.

Several pieces of specialized equipment have been developed to aid in insect control. The "LaMosquette" mosquito netting distributed by IAMAT is a notable example. Certainly one of the most useful items is the "bug jacket." Bug jackets made from a wide mesh netting are impregnated with a variety of repellents to provide long term relief from biting insects, to include hordes of flies and mosquitos.

FIGURE 5–2
The "bug jacket" has proven to be an effective way to protect the wearer from mosquito and blackfly pests when impregnated with repellant as described in the text.[1]

[1]The bug jacket can be purchased from Indiana Camp Supply, Box 211, Hobart, IN 46342; Telephone (219) 947-2525

A cream containing pyrethrum is effective against bites of the tsetse fly for up to 6 hours. The net jacket impregnated with dimethyl phthalate and ethylhexanediol can provide up to 83% protection for wearers for periods up to 8 days. These jackets have long sleeves and hoods for maximum protection. The same jackets impregnated with deet or permethrin are extremely useful against mosquitos and black flies.

Chapter 5.5

Immunizations for Foreign Travel

Vaccination is an artificial method of exposing a person to a hostile organism in such a manner that the immune system can be activated to recognize and defend itself later, if and when contact is made with natural strains of the same disease. While many diseases can be prevented by avoiding habitats or vectors carrying them, immunization frequently represents the single most effective approach for prevention.

Immunization schedules for domestic and foreign travel are listed below. Some of these schedules do not provide total protection, but they will at least frequently ameliorate the disease. Prevention is a lot safer and less traumatic than attempting to cure a patient. Further information can be obtained from a booklet published annually by the U. S. Public Health Service titled, "Health Information for International Travel," 1989 Stock Number 017–023–00184–1. Order from the Superintendent of Documents, U.S.

Government Printing Office, Washington, D.C. 20402–9325; telephone (202) 783–3238 ($5.00 per copy).

Receipt of immunizations should be recorded in an International Certificate of Vaccination, Form PHS-731, Jan 82. These forms must be completed in every detail. If they are incomplete or inaccurate, they are not valid. Revisions of this certificate dated 9–66, 9–69, 9–71, 1–74, 9–77, or 1–82 are acceptable. These International Certificates of Vaccination, PHS-731 may be purchased by physicians from the Superintendent of Documents, U.S. Government Printing Office, Washington, D.C., address and telephone as indicated above. The stock number is 017–001–004405 and the price is $2.00 each or $14.00 for 100.

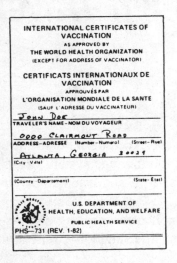

FIGURE 5–3

The International Certificates of Vaccination has areas for recording required and other immunizations, health history, blood type, and emergency notification information for the traveler.

Yellow fever vaccination must be validated by the physician providing the injection with the use of a "Uniform Stamp." Cholera vaccination, while no longer required by World Health Organization regulations, may still be demanded by some border officials. This vaccination must also be validated by a uniform stamp. An imprint of my Uniform Stamp is reproduced below as an example of its appearance.

OFFICIAL VACCINATION
INDIANA
26236
U.S.A.

FIGURE 5–4
Uniform Stamp required to validate cholera and yellow fever immunizations. This particular stamp is that of the author.

Yellow fever immunization can only be given at designated centers and these centers will, of course, provide the Form 731 and properly validate it for you. Other immunizations may be entered without validation of a Uniform Stamp, the signature of the physician, dosage provided, and sometimes the vaccine lot number, sufficing.

REQUIRED IMMUNIZATIONS FOR FOREIGN TRAVEL

Only one immunization, yellow fever, is generally required for foreign travel, and then only to selected countries. At times local epidemics of meningitis, encephalitis, or other disease may cause a country to require specific immunization of travelers. This information is generally disseminated by State Department Travel Advisories.

Until recently cholera immunization was officially required by many countries for entry through their borders. A recent ruling by the World Health Organization (WHO) has rescinded this requirement. Most countries are subscribers to WHO regulations, promising to abide by their promulgations, but some border officials might still require proof of receipt of this immunization before they will approve your entry. A warning of this discrepancy is posted in the Individual Country Database, page 8-1, if this intelligence is known.

No excuses, other than medical reasons, for not obtaining these vaccines will be accepted by authorities of requiring countries. A letter from your physician, written on his stationary, as well as a comment from your physician written into an international certificate of immunization, stating that the vaccination in question is contra-indicated due to medical reasons, would be required. Even with this evidence it is possible that you will be denied entry by the host country. It is best to check with the embassy of the country that you will be visiting to determine if that country will accept a medical exemption. Religious belief, and other grounds for refusing vaccination, are not acceptable reasons for failing to obtain required immunizations.

Required immunizations must be documented by proper completion of an International Certificate of Vaccination and signed by a licensed physician, or a properly designated individual (signature stamps will not do).

IMMUNIZATION DOSAGE SCHEDULES

CHOLERA—Primary immunization consists of two doses given subcutaneous or intramuscular 1 week to 1 month or more apart. Booster injections are required every 6 months. Dosages are: children 6 months to 5 years, 0.2ml; 5 to 10 years, 0.3 ml; over 10 years, 0.5 ml. This immunization only provides approximately 30% to 50% protection. Immunization is effective 6 days after receiving an injection, immediately, if it was a booster. The International Certificate of Immunization must be validated with the use of a Uniform Stamp (see above) and will not be considered valid for 6 days from the time of immunization. This vaccine is generally not recommended for use in travelers due to its low level of effectiveness. If it is to be taken, a new dosage regimen of 0.1 ml given intradermally causes less side effects and still fulfills potential requirements for this vaccination that some governments might demand. See a further discussion of the use of cholera vaccine in the section on cholera disease, Chapter 6.5.

HEPATITIS A (Infectious Hepatitis)—A single does of pooled immune globulin (10% solution) protects against or modifies this form of hepatitis which is commonly caught from tainted food or water supplies. It must not be given at the same time as the Measles, Mumps, Rubella (MMR) vaccine. It may be given at least 14 days after MMR or 6 weeks to 3 months (preferably 6 months) before MMR. There are no apparent problems in the administration of Oral Polio Vaccine or Yellow Fever vaccine with or near immune globulin administration. Dosage depends upon body weight and length of time of required protection. At maximal doses it still must be repeated every 6 months for continued protection. If the traveler finds himself still overseas after six months, it is best to avoid receiving booster doses from questionable sources, but rather to take one's chances with possibly contracting Hepatitis A. It is better to contend with a miserable, yet very seldom serious disease such as Hepatitis A, than to risk acquiring more serious diseases such as Hepatitis B or AIDS from contaminated local supplies. Travelers making frequent foreign journeys to areas at risk for Hepatitis A should consider having their Hepatitis A IgG levels measured, as the presence of natural antibodies would indicate lifelong immunity without need for booster shots of immune globulin. See page 5-36, Tables 5-7 and 5-8.

HEPATITIS B (Serum Hepatitis)—This disease is most commonly spread by hypodermic usage, sexual contact, and blood transfusions. It has a very high prevalence in many areas of the world. Immunization is from 1.0 ml IM injections of Hepatitis B Vaccine (Recombinant), called "Recombivax HB" by the manufacturer, Merck, Sharp & Dome, given on day 0, 1 month, and 6 months. Wholesale cost as of May 1990 is about $190.00 for 1 full course of immunization. Duration of protection and need for revaccination has not been defined. A blood test to determine resis-

TABLE 5–7
Immune Globulin Dosage*

WEIGHT	SHORT TERM (< 3 MONTHS)	LONG TERM (>3 MONTHS)	
< 50 pounds	0.5 ml	1.0 ml	(repeat
50–100 pounds	1.0 ml	2.5 ml	every
> 100 pounds	2.0 ml	5.0 ml	6 mos.)

*Also called immune serum globulin and gamma globulin.

The above chart shows the recommended total dosage of immune globulin for various weights and lengths of trip suggested by the Centers for Disease Control. The formula for calculating a more precise dose, as suggested by the FDA, is given by the following chart:

TABLE 5–8
Calculation of Precise
Immune Globulin Dosage

LENGTH OF STAY	DOSE VOLUME
Less than 3 months	0.02 ml/Kg
3 months or longer	0.06 ml/Kg (repeat this dose every 4–6 months)

tance can be performed. If the antibody level falls below 10 SRUs, revaccination should be considered. The injection must be given in the deltoid muscle.

JAPANESE ENCEPHALITIS—Immunization requires 3 doses to be given at weekly intervals, with a booster dose at 12 to 18 months and at 4 year intervals thereafter, if risk continues. This vaccine is not made in the US. The Japanese manufacturer has withdrawn the vaccine from the U.S. due to liability concerns. The Department of Defense can provide it only to its own members. Persons traveling to areas of risk may check at the U.S. Embassy within that particular country for possible availability.

INFLUENZA—Vaccines are prepared that give 1 to 2 years of immunity for prevalent strains of influenza A or B. New strains are constantly arising that require formulation of new vaccines to compensate for this "antigenic drift." Dosage is 0.5 ml IM in the deltoid muscle, given in the fall of the year. This vaccine is not required for routine travel, unless heading into an epidemic area.

MALARIA—No vaccine is currently available. See Chapter 6.31.

MEASLES, MUMPS, RUBELLA—One 0.5 ml dose given subcutaneously should provide life long immunity. The MMR vaccine provides adequate protection against all three viral diseases, but each vaccine is available separately. May not be given if allergic to eggs or neomycin without special desensitization. This vaccine must be given at least 14 days prior to or 6 weeks to 3 months after immune serum globulin.

MENINGOCOCCAL—This vaccine need be used only under special circumstances (military personnel in the U.S. and persons traveling to areas of the world where meningococcal infection is epidemic). Epidemic areas are listed in the country database in this book. The A/C/Y/W135 vaccine by Squibb-Connaught is given 0.5 ml subcutaneously. Duration of protection is unknown, but appears to be at least 3 years in those over 4 years of age.

PLAGUE—In most countries of Africa, Asia and the Americas where plague is reported, the risk of exposure exists primarily in rural mountainous or upland areas. Adult immunization consists of 3 injections of 0.5 ml, 0.5 ml, and 0.2 ml (in that order) about 4 weeks apart and two boosters of 0.2 ml 6 months apart, then 1 dose every 1 to 2 years if needed.

PNEUMOCOCCUS—A vaccine against streptococcal (formerly called pneumococcal) pneumonia has been developed for high risk patients with chronic diseases or respiratory problems. One 0.5 ml IM injection in the deltoid muscle probably provides a life-long immunity.

POLIOMYELITIS—Trivalent oral polio vaccine (OPV) is the vaccine of choice for all infants, children, and adolescents (up to their 18th birthday). The primary series is 3 doses, with dose 2 given at least 6 weeks after 1 and dose 3 given 8–12 months after dose 2. A supplemental dose is given to children at age 4 to 6 years. Anyone having a partial series may continue with the next dose(s), regardless of how long before the last dose was given.

Unimmunized adults should be given the four full dose series of injectable inactivated polio vaccine (IPV) (3 doses given at 1 to 2 month intervals, followed by a 4th dose 6 to 12 months after the 3rd dose), if time allows, or a minimum of 2 doses of IPV given a month apart. If less than a month remains prior to departure, the administration of a single dose of OPV may be justified due to potential high risk of exposure to wild poliovirus and the more rapid protective effect of OPV.

Areas of increased risk include Mexico, Central America and South America. Prior to travel to these areas, anyone who has completed the primary OPV series in the past should be given a single additional dose of OPV.

RABIES—A pre-exposure regimen of rabies vaccine is appropriate for persons routinely exposed to potential rabid animals—including skunks, fox, raccoon and bats. It does not eliminate the need for additional therapy after rabies exposure, but simplifies post-exposure therapy by eliminating the requirement for rabies immune globulin (RIG) and by decreasing the number of doses of vaccine required. Prevention with human diploid cell vaccine (HDCV) is 3 doses given 1.0 ml IM in the deltoid muscle on days 0, 7, and 21 or 28. A new dosage of 0.1 ml intradermally given on the same dosage schedule also seems effective for prophylaxis. Caution should be taken to avoid taking chloroquine for malaria prophylaxis while receiving rabies immunization as it has been shown to reduce the antibody response.

Post-exposure immunization for those previously immunized is 2 doses (1 ml each) on days 0 and 3, with no RIG. If no prior immunization, give RIG 20 IU/kg ($^1/_2$ in bite site and $^1/_2$ IM) and 5 doses (1 ml each) of HDCV on days 0, 3, 7, 14, and 28. These injections must be given in the deltoid muscle as 2 incidents of failure of post-exposure immunization with RIG and HDCV have occurred when these injections were given in the gluteal muscle.

ROCKY MOUNTAIN SPOTTED FEVER
TICK FEVER; TICK TYPHUS—England
FIEBRE MANCHODA—Mexico

FIEBRE PETEQUIAL—Colombia
FIEBRE MACULOSA—Brazil

This disease is spread by ticks with cases being reported from 47 states in the U.S. Most of these cases are from the states of North Carolina, Virginia, Maryland, the Rocky Mountain states and the state of Washington. The vaccine for this disease has been removed from the market, but prevention by use of insect repellent and frequent tick removal checks is effective.

SMALLPOX—This disease was declared eradicated by the World Health Organization in May 1980. A vaccine is available only to military and laboratory personnel working with this virus.

TETANUS—DIPHTHERIA—Officially, all persons should have a tetanus booster every 10 years; 5 years for puncture wounds, bites, and other contaminated wounds. Because of this, any trip member should have a booster so recent as to be no older than 5 years before the calculated return date of the trip. This alters the official recommendation considerably, but precludes requiring booster shots in the field or emergency protection with tetanus immune globulin. Dosage is 0.5 ml of dT vaccine given IM. A different vaccine is prepared for use in children. Infants receive a special diphtheria-tetanus-pertussis vaccine which is also a different formulation than that used in children. Family physicians, pediatricians, and travel medicine clinics generally have all three vaccines in stock at all times.

TYPHOID—Immunization should be completed before heading into areas where typhoid fever is known to be epidemic (many countries of Africa, Asia, and Central and South America). The vaccine is from 70% to 90% effective in preventing the disease and also decreases the severity of the disease. Immunization consists of two 0.5 ml doses given 1 month apart, with a booster dose every 3 years. A intradermal dose of 0.1 ml may be substituted after the initial 0.5 ml dose has been received. A new higher potency oral vaccine should become available in 1991 which will require only one dose that will provide at least 80% effective protection, and which will have considerably less side effects than the current vaccine.

TYPHUS—A disease spread worldwide, it is prevented by eliminating lice. Production of the vaccine in the US has been discontinued and there are no plans for commercial production of new vaccine. No typhus cases are known to have occurred in an American traveler since 1950. This disease is frequent after major disasters; approximately 3 million people died of it during World War II.

YELLOW FEVER—Immunization is required for travel to many countries in South America, Africa and Asia. The immunization consists of one 0.5 ml injection, which confers immunity for 10 years. It is available only at designated Yellow Fever Vaccination Centers (check your County or State Board of Health for the nearest facility—see Chapter 2.4).

SCHEDULE PRIOR TO DEPARTURE

Taking into account the incompatibility of some vaccines, the number of doses required to effectively complete some series, and the delay until some immunizations are considered valid, an immunization schedule has to be established starting approximately 8 weeks prior to departure.

A sample immunization schedule for someone requiring various series of live and killed vaccines is diagrammed below. This schematic also indicates the start of malaria prophylaxis with chloroquine or mefloquine.

PROLONGED TRIP IMMUNIZATION
BOOSTER REQUIREMENTS

Once the trip has commenced, if the traveler plans to stay in areas of risk beyond the protection time afforded by the primary vaccine administration, booster immunization doses will be needed to continue providing maximal protection. The following table indicates the booster requirements for the most commonly suggested travel related immunizations.

TABLE 5–9
General Immunization Schedule
Weeks Prior to Departure

8	7	6	5	4	3	2	1	Depart
	Killed vaccines, primary series			All live virus vaccines		Killed vaccine SIG* boosters		

Start chloroquine
or
*SIG (immune serum globulin   mefloquine
for hepatitis A prevention)

Pre-exposure rabies vaccine must be completed before starting chloroquine

Hepatitis B vaccine must be taken starting 7 months before departure date, boosted 1 month before departure

Pre-trip TB test (mantoux) should be considered when heading into developing countries for extended times or for trips to endemic areas

Providing adequate time for proper pre-trip medical travel consultation and immunization cannot be stressed too strongly. Not only must vaccine administration be sequenced properly, but a recovery time from reactions and the acquisition of personal and prophylactic medications must be accomplished.

TABLE 5–10
Booster Immunization Requirements

Cholera: Dosage of booster is by age:
                children 6 months to 5 years 0.2 ml
                5 to 10 years 0.3 ml
                over 10 years 0.5 ml
                Booster required every 6 months

Hepatitis A: Dosage of booster is by weight:
                      weight   Immune Globulin Dosage
                < 50 pounds   1.0 ml (repeat
                50–100 pounds   2.5 ml every
                > 100 pounds   5.0 ml 6 mos.)
                Booster is maximal dose every 6 months

Hepatitis B: Booster schedule has not been determined. If antibody
                      test level is below 10 SRUs, a booster of 1.0 ml is
                      required.

Japanese Encephalitis: 12 to 18 months after primary series, provide a
                         booster, then repeat every 4 years thereafter.

Influenza: Booster of 0.5 ml yearly

Meningococcal: Booster of 0.5 ml every 3 years

Plague: Booster of 0.2 ml every 6 months x 2 doses; then every
                      1 to 2 years thereafter.

Pneumococcus: No boosters required

Poliomyelitis: Booster indicated prior to departure to endemic areas,
                      but none during travel

Rabies: Antibody testing every two years, with booster if
                      inadequate level; 5% adverse reaction rate with booster.

Tetanus: Booster for adults every 10 years; unless a crush injury,
                      bite, or dirty wound, then every 5 years.

                      Special vaccine required for children.

                      Both adult and children's vaccine should be given with
                      diphtheria toxoid in combination.

                      Infants should follow the routine pediatric immunization
                      schedule with tetanus-diphtheria-pertussis combination
                      vaccine

Typhoid: Dosage 0.5 ml subcutaneously (or 0.1 ml intradermal)
                      every 3 years.

Yellow Fever: Dosage of 0.5 ml every 10 years.

Tetanus and rabies post exposure treatment requires the use of special immune globulin with a high titer against these diseases. This substance is not required when an adequate pre-exposure immunization and booster schedule has been followed. Post-rabies exposure does require additional injections of rabies vaccine as indicated in Chapter 6.40.

When travel is expected to last beyond the initial immunization protection time and boosters are required, as per the above schedule, a plan must be formulated to obtain safe vaccine and to have it administered.

Chapter 5.6

Immunization Complications and Contra-indications

No vaccine will provide complete immunity from disease. Some (such as the cholera vaccine) result in notoriously low levels of protection. The value of receiving them must be balanced with cost, proven level of effectiveness, danger of the disease, and potential for side effects from the immunization itself. These side effects are generally restricted to the person receiving them. A noted exception is the oral polio virus, which might induce disease in persons living with the recipient. In the United States the requirements and suggestions for immunization against domestic illness (such as mumps, measles, rubella, polio, diphtheria, tetanus, whooping cough, and at times others) have been well studied by epidemiologists taking these considerations into account. With regard to foreign travel, other important factors are introduced such as political requirements of a particular country and the possible lack of adequate medical care at the destination.

Political decisions do not always follow medical indications and therefore a traveler may be required to obtain a vaccination when the chance of encountering a particular disease is so low that the risk of side effects from the vaccine simply would otherwise not warrant its use. Complying with REQUIRED immunizations is mandatory for admission within the host country's borders. The traveler must obtain the immunizations under the safest conditions possible. This would be at the home of the visitor, not at some border crossing point.

Reactions to vaccines, while infrequent, are best treated at home. Completing a series of immunizations while at home also allows the use of sterile medication, single use syringes and needles—all something that might not be available in the host country. With the emergence of AIDS as an international epidemic, this consideration has become even more significant.

Most reactions, or ill effects, of an immunization will be restricted to the person receiving it. As mentioned, a notable exception is the oral polio vaccine. The oral virus is a live virus and provides its immunity by causing a low grade infection in the bowel of the recipient. This virus can be shed by the recipient, thus placing others living in close proximity at danger of acquiring the disease if they are not immune. Regardless, the use of oral polio vaccine is the method of choice for infants and pre-school children in the United States. Inactivated injectable polio vaccine is the safest to use, and is the vaccine of choice for use in persons 18 years and older. Adequate time for immunization must be provided, or a single dose of the oral vaccine may have to be taken— as per the dosage schedule indicated in Chapter 5.5. Many physicians do not stock the injectable polio vaccine. Time must be allowed for it to be ordered when planning your immunization schedule, if it is to be used.

Many other vaccines can cause local reactions with redness and soreness. Sometimes a particular vaccine, such as the injectable typhoid vaccine, is quite painful. Local reactions can be minimized with the use of newly introduced 0.1 ml intradermal dosages for some vaccines which can be given as indicated in the section on vaccine dosages.

The location of the injection is sometimes mandated by medical considerations. Some must be given in the deltoid muscle of the arm, for studies show they are more effective there than in the gluteal region. Others must be given in the gluteal region (such as immune globulin) due to the volume of the injection.

Many must be given in a certain sequence—for example one cannot have the live virus for MMR immunization too soon after receiving gamma globulin or adequate protection may not be obtained. Rabies immunization does not take well if the person is taking chloroquine for malaria protection.

Some vaccines must not be used due to other medical considerations. Physicians like to avoid giving rubella vaccine to a pregnant woman, even though no serious effects have been shown when it has been done inadvertently. Males past puberty are at increased risk of complications from mumps vaccine. Concurrent illness is frequently a contra-indication to receiving many immunizations, while others may be quite safe to give. Patients planning to travel who are HIV positive must receive special counseling as some vaccines seem to activate the progression of AIDS.

Purity of vaccines produced in the United States is not an issue. Hepatitis B vaccine, formerly produced from pooled sera and now produced by genetic engineering, has been demonstrated conclusively to be free of danger of the AIDS virus. Similarly, immune globulin (gamma globulin) production techniques have been shown suitable to prevent possible contamination with the AIDS virus. Production purity might be a factor if vaccines from a developing country are to be used.

Allergies to a vaccine, or to by-products of the media in which it is grown, or to preservatives used in its production, are also a possible problem. Persons allergic to eggs are at risk for an allergic reaction to several vaccines. Yellow fever and influenza vaccine are produced in embryonated chicken eggs, while measles and mumps vaccine are prepared in duck embryo tissue culture.

The following table lists the most frequently reported reactions to various commonly used immunizations:

TABLE 5–11
Adverse Reactions to Immunizations

VACCINE	FREQUENTLY REPORTED SIDE EFFECTS
Cholera	Pain at injection site for 24–48 hrs; possible local redness and swelling; fever, headache, malaise develop in most recipients and persist for 1–2 days.
Immune Globulin (gamma globulin)	Pain at the injection site for 24–hours. Must be given in the gluteal muscles.
Measles	Low grade fever (99 to 102 F) may occur 5–12 days after injection, rarely a generalized rash develops; fever higher than 103 F occurs less than 15% of the time.
	Allergy to chicken eggs and neomycin may cause an allergic reaction.
Meningococcal	Local redness at injection site for 1–2 days. Reactions are uncommon and usually mild.
Mumps	Burning and stinging of short duration at injection site; occasional mild fever; fever above 103 F is uncommon; allergic reactions at the injection site are extremely rare; swelling of parotid salivary gland—low incidence; testicle inflammation is very rare. Seizures, deafness, encephalitis are very rare.
	Allergy to chicken eggs or feathers or to neomycin may cause an allergic reaction.
	Any active infection is reason to delay receiving this vaccine. Also any blood disorders, immune deficiency or use of corticosteroids is a contra-indication for vaccination.
Poliomyelitis (oral)	Vaccine associate disease in 1 per 8.7 million doses; disease in contacts incidence is 1 per 5.1 million doses

Any active infection is reason to delay receiving this vaccine. Also any blood disorders, immune deficiency or use of corticosteroids is a contra-indication for vaccination.

Poliomyelitis (injectable)

No vaccine associated disease reported with this vaccine.

Slight chance of allergy in people sensitive to cow serum, neomycin, and streptomycin.

Rabies

Very low incidence of side effect with the new diploid cell vaccine; some local irritation possible. Occasional muscle ache and headache. In persons receiving booster shot up to 6% may have hives, lymph node enlargement, and fever.

Rubella

Occasional moderate fever (101–102 F) less commonly high fever (over 103 F) burning at injection site; reactions are usually mild and transit, but include fever, rash, sore throat, nausea, vomiting, joint ache.

Avoid giving to pregnant females, persons with blood disorders, or to those receiving corticosteroids.

Allergy to neomycin may cause an allergic reaction. Avoid giving if active illness is present.

Tetanus/Diphtheria

Local reaction at injection site is possible; fever may occur; severe allergic reactions are rare.

Typhoid Fever

Local pain at the injection site occurs in most recipients; fever, lethargy, headache may last for 1–2 days.

Save for use when pregnant.

Allergy to phenol may cause an allergic reaction.

Yellow Fever

5 to 10% of recipients have headache, lethargy, muscle ache and fever which occurs 5–10 days after vaccination.

Overall, a low incidence of side effects and unfavorable reactions occurs with pre-trip immunizations. These risk levels are far lower than the potential risks that could be incurred by the diseases they are given to prevent, when given to appropriate travelers. Not all travelers require, nor should they receive, many of these inoculations. The advice of a travel medicine consultant, or a physician who has access to appropriate emporiatric (travel medicine) reference material, is necessary to aid your decision of which immunization you should receive.

The Federal immunization liability act does not provide adverse reaction insurance settlements to foreign travel related immunizations—only to selected common childhood immunizations. While your travel immunizations are generally benign, it should be understood that serious reactions can occur. By referring to the above chart, it may be possible to identify allergy risk factors that would warn you and your physician of an increased risk.

Section 6

Infectious Diseases of Interest to the Traveler

Many of the infections discussed in this section are world-wide in distribution, while others are located in only one small area. To determine which may be of importance to you, refer to the country information database starting on page 8–1.

Some of these illnesses may not develop until decades later, and then with quite diverse symptoms—perhaps swelling of the face, congestive heart failure, anemia, or central nervous system destruction. If you are aware of the possible contagions which you may have encountered in your past travels, you may be able to alert your attending physician at some future time of a rare diagnosis that would not be otherwise considered.

Treatment of rare disease is beyond the scope of this book, but prevention is not. In fact, after examining the country information database, refer back to this section, learn how the various diseases you will be at risk of acquiring are spread, and note what techniques of prevention you should be aware of and probably use.

Some of these illnesses have immunizations that are commonly available and which may be recommended—or even required—before your trip. Others may have special vaccines that are available only at certain locations or with special restrictions. Some diseases can be prevented or modified by taking medication prophylactically. And finally, others require prevention of certain insect bites, avoidance of specific food stuffs, or life style modifications with regard to contact with water, trekking or travel technique, and especially sexual activity.

Self medication to treat disease, or injury, while on an extended, or remote area, trip will be important for some travelers. Refer to the "book within a book" portion of the Travelers' Medical Reference titled The Travelers' Self Care Manual, starting on page 7-1, for advice on the development of an appropriate medical kit and methods of treatment of most travel related problems.

A specific over-view of the prevalence of each disease is indicated in the country information database for each country (Section 8). World distribution patterns are mentioned in this section. While some of these diseases may seem rare to us, they may be quite common in countries that you are about to visit, perhaps infecting millions of inhabitants. The morbidity and mortality of some of these diseases are quite high, while others are generally only a nuisance. This information is also indicated in this section.

Travelers' diarrhea prevention and treatment has been discussed in Chapter 5.3 as part of the section of disease prevention and immunization due to its importance to many travelers to the developing nations. Various specific causes of diarrhea are further discussed in this section of the book.

Chapter 6.1

Anthrax

Caused by a bacterium, *Bacillus anthracis,* it is a disease of sheep, cattle, goats, horses, and pigs. Distribution of this disease is world-wide. Transmission to man is usually from spores of the bacterium that have contaminated hide or wool, or by ingestion of infected meat. This disease will occur in countries that have poor public health laws which fail to protect consumers from contaminated animal products.

This disease can cause skin infection, pneumonia, or gastrointestinal disease in humans, with death occurring from the pulmonary disease due to inadequate treatment or complications of meningitis. The skin infection, or malignant pustule, has an incubation period of 12 hours to 5 days, then evolves into a red-brown boil that enlarges with considerable redness and ulceration with drainage. Fever, muscle ache, headache, nausea and vomiting ensue. The pulmonary form is often fatal and results from inhalation of the spores (wool sorter's disease). Severe coughing leads to respiratory distress within a few days, then to shock, coma, and death.

The disease can be treated with antibiotic. There is a special vaccine which has been prepared for high risk occupations (veterinarians, laboratory technicians, persons handling wool or hides from possibly contaminated sources). Travelers are at low risk, but caution should be exercised with regard to food products and purchase of hides and goat hair or wool items in areas with suspected contamination.

Chapter 6.2

Bartonellosis

This infection, caused by the bacterium *Bartonella bacilliformis,* is found only in valleys of the Andes in Bolivia, Peru, Chilie, Equador and Colombia. It is spread from human to human by the bite of a sandfly. After the bite the bacterium invades the blood stream and attaches to the red blood cells destroying them and causing an anemia. Blood vessels are blocked and other bacteria can cause super-infections. Over 90% of the red blood cells can be attacked, although not all of them are destroyed. Two phases of the disease occur, the first called *Oroya fever* and the second a chronic skin eruption called *veruga peruana.* This disease is sometimes called Carrion's Disease.

Oroya fever occurs 2 to 3 weeks after the bite, but can take as long as 16 weeks to develop. The illness presents with fever, headache, and pain in the bones and joints. Mortality rates can exceed 50% in untreated victims. As immunity develops, the number of bacteria on the blood cells decreases. After a dormant period, bacteria reappear in the skin where they cause the formation of nodules, frequently on the face and limbs (veruga peruana). The nodules are very vascular and therefore bleed easily. They persist for 1 to 12 months before healing. They generally heal without scar formation. The skin lesions can form without the initial Oroya fever developing.

As the sandfly bites after sundown, prevention includes the use of insect repellent and netting in the evenings when in endemic areas.

Chapter 6.3

Brucellosis

This disease, caused by several species of the bacterial genus *Brucella,* is world-wide in distribution. It is acquired from unpasteurized milk, milk products, or cheese, or contact with infected meat or placenta of contaminated animals. Other names for this disease are Bang's disease, Undulant fever, Malta fever, Mediterranean fever, or Gibraltar fever.

The incubation period lasts from 5 days to several months (average is 2 weeks). A variety of symptoms are present early in the disease course, with headache, occasionally diarrhea, muscle ache, pain in the back of the neck, and malaise being the most common. As the disease develops, fevers increase to 105° F (40.5° C), then subside in the mornings with profuse sweating. This persists for 1 to 5 weeks, followed by a 2 to 14 day remission, then a return to the typical febrile phase. Only one course of fever may occur, or this pattern may continue for months or years.

Antibiotic treatment is available. The uncomplicated disease results in recovery within 2 to 3 weeks. The disease is rarely fatal.

Chapter 6.4

Chikungunya Fever

This disease is caused by a virus that is spread from human to human by the bite of the *A. aegypti* mosquito. It is found in eastern, southern, western and central Africa and in southeastern Asia where it infects thousands of individuals.

The symptoms are very similar to dengue fever and to yellow fever, and it may be easily confused with these diseases, particularly when both are endemic to an area. This illness usually lasts 3 to 7 days and consists of the sudden onset of chills, fever, headache, nausea, vomiting, joint pain and rash.

Fatalities are rare, but the joint pain may be very persistent. There is no specific medical treatment.

Chapter 6.5

Cholera

This intestinal infection is caused by a bacterium, *Vibrio cholerae,* which can produce profuse, painful diarrhea. This disease can result in dehydration and death. Indeed, the death toll can reach tens of thousands during an epidemic. The organism is ingested with growth occurring in the small bowel. The disease is passed by contaminated stool from the infected person. Ingestion of water tainted by human fecal material is the most common means of catching this disease. Poor hygiene by food servers can contaminate any food product. Travelers in cholera infected areas are advised to avoid eating uncooked foods and to peel fruits themselves. Bottled carbonated water and soft drinks are usually safe. Refer to the section on prevention of traveler's diarrhea (Chapter 5.3).

The significant symptom of cholera is the explosive onset of frequent, watery stools. Vomiting may occur early in the disease and accelerate a rapid onset of dehydration. This can lead to decreased blood pressure, muscle cramps, decreased urine output, shallow breathing, and eventually shock and death. The essential medical treatment is the rapid replacement of lost fluids. Refer to Table 5–4 on Oral Fluid Replacement Therapy (also in Chapter 5.3). Antibiotic therapy is helpful in terminating diarrhea caused by cholera.

Cholera can be very active at times in India and Southeast Asia, Africa, the Middle East, and Southern Europe. The last major epidemic in the Western Hemisphere occurred in 1866–67. The risk of cholera to tourists is extremely small. There have only been 7 cases reported of an American tourist catching this disease since 1961.

A vaccine is available to prevent cholera. Its effectiveness is probably less than 50% and, for that reason, it is not recommended by the Centers for Disease Control or the World Health Organization for routine use by travelers. There are two exceptions to this. One is for persons in areas of high risk or active disease who will be far from immediate medical attention. The other is for persons with impaired gastric defense mechanisms. Persons taking acid suppressors (such as Tagamet, Zantac, Axid, Losec and Pepcid) and antacids fall into this category. Persons who use marijuana are also at risk, as it also suppresses stomach acid secretion. Normal stomach acid levels help destroy the cholera bacterium.

There is another important use of the cholera vaccine. Some countries require that travelers receive at least one dose before entry into their country is permitted. The dose must have been received 6 days prior to attempted entry, and not more than 6 months before entry. Prior visitation to a country with active disease, or to a country in which the disease is endemic, is a conditional requirement for vaccination by some countries.

In 1988 the World Health Organization (WHO) officially recommended eliminating cholera as a required immunization for entry into any country. It may be many years before affected countries adapt this resolution and do not require cholera vaccination. At this time it is important to obtain a cholera vaccine if a country has recently required vaccination. Border officials in many developing countries are very slow to adjust their protocols to match those of officials in the capital city, or WHO. Avoid harassment at the border by continuing to obtain cholera immunization in the countries noted as requiring this vaccine in the country information database starting on page 8-1.

Many countries require a cholera vaccination if travelers have visited cholera-infected areas. Of significant importance would be the probable insistence of local health authorities that travelers arriving without proof of vaccination receive one upon arrival in their country. The possible use of contaminated needles, syringes, or multi-use vaccine bottles could increase the travelers' risks of contracting hepatitis B, AIDS, or other infections.

Table 6–1
Countries with Currently Active Cholera Reported
as of 4/2/90

Angola	Malaysia
Burundi	Mali
Cameroon	Mauritania
Ghana	Nepal
Guinea	Niger
India	Nigeria
Indonesia	Sao Tome & Principe
Ivory Coast	Tanzania
Kenya	Vietnam
Liberia	Zaire
Malawi	Zambia

Chapter 6.6

Ciguatera Poisoning

This problem is caused by a toxin released by a small ocean organism called a dinoflagellate. As various species of fish eat this small plant they acquire the toxin. Larger fish that in turn prey upon these smaller fish acquire larger and larger amounts of the toxin and thus result in more severe cases of ciguatera toxin poisoning in humans. Over 400 species of fish from the tropical reefs of Florida, the West Indies, and the Pacific have been implicated. There is no change in flavor, texture, or color of the fish flesh and there is no way of detecting contamination. Worse yet, no method of preserving, cooking, or treating fish can destroy this toxin. One must rely on local knowledge to avoid potentially polluted species. As a rule of thumb, avoid the larger, more predatory, and older fish which are most likely to be contaminated.

Symptoms usually start with numbness and tingling of the lips and tongue, and then progress to dry mouth, abdominal cramping, vomiting and diarrhea that lasts 6 to 17 hours. Muscle and joint pain, muscle weakness, facial pain, and unusual sensory phenomena such as reversal of hot and cold sensations develop. Death may result from respiratory failure in severe cases. Treatment is supportive only as no specific antidote is available.

See also the chapters on scromboid poisoning (Chapter 6.46) and paralytic shellfish poisoning (Chapter 6.37).

Chapter 6.7

Clonorchiasis and Opisthorchiasis

These liver flukes are found only in fresh water fish. Cooking destroys these parasites, but pickling, smoking, or drying fish may not. The Clonorchiasis species is found in China, Hong Kong, Vietnam, Korea, Japan, and Taiwan. Opisthorchiasis is found in Asia, Eastern Europe and the USSR.

These flukes can live for 20 to 50 years in the bile tract, passing eggs into the intestines. The eggs hatch in fresh water were they are ingested by snails. An active form is released from the snail which can then penetrate freshwater fish. Eating the infected fish allows a larvae to be released which then matures into the adult fluke that migrates into the bile duct system, thus completing the cycle.

Light infections may cause no symptoms, but a large number of flukes can result in lethargy, fever, and abdominal pain. Chronic infection can result in jaundice, low grade fever, lethargy, diarrhea, and prolonged abdominal pain. Specific medication is available for treatment.

Chapter 6.8

Colorado Tick Fever

Colorado tick fever is a viral disease of the Orbivirus group (only 1 serotype known) spread by Ixodid (hard-shelled) ticks. This disease is 20 times more common than Rocky Mountain Spotted Fever in Colorado. It is also found in the other states of the Western Rocky Mountains and provinces of Western Canada. It is most frequent in April-May at low altitudes and June-July at high altitudes.

Onset is abrupt, with chills, fever of 100.4° to 104° F (38° to 40° C), muscle ache, headache, eye pain, and eye sensitivity to light (photophobia). The patient feels weak and nauseated, but vomiting is unusual. During the first 2 days up to 12% of victims develop a rash. In half the cases the fever disappears after 2 to 3 days and the patient feels well for 2 days. Then a second bout of illness starts which lasts intensely for 2 to 4 days. This second phase subsides with the patient feeling weak for 1 to 2 additional weeks.

This disease requires no treatment other than bed rest, fluids to prevent dehydration, and medications to treat fever and aches. However, as the same ticks can also spread potentially dangerous Rocky Mountain Spotted Fever, the differential diagnosis can be confusing. Treatment with antibiotic should be accomplished without waiting for the characteristic rash of Rocky Mountain Spotted Fever or the fever pattern of Colorado Tick Fever to develop or for a firm diagnoses of either to be established.

Chapter 6.9

Dengue Fever

Also called breakbone fever or dandy fever, this viral infection is caused by a virus (Group B arbovirus or flavivirus) and is spread by bites from the *Aedes aegypti* mosquito. Dengue is endemic throughout the tropics and subtropics.

After an incubation period of 3 to 15 (usually 5 to 8) days, there is a sudden onset of fever (104° F, 40° C), chills, headache, low back ache, pain behind the eyes with movement of the eyes, and extreme aching in the legs and joints. The eyes are red and a transient flushing or pale pink rash occurs, mostly on the face. There is a relatively slow pulse rate for the temperature. The fever lasts 48 to 96 hours, followed by 24 hours of no fever and a sense of well being. A second rapid temperature increase occurs, but generally not as high as the first. A bright rash spreads from the arms/legs to the trunk, but generally not the face. Palms and soles may be bright red and swollen. There is a severe headache and other body aches as well. The fever, rash, and headache constitute the "dengue triad."

The illness lasts for weeks, but mortality is nil. Treatment is rest and the use of pain and fever medication.

A condition called Dengue Hemorrhagic Fever Shock Syndrome is lethal and occurs in patients younger than 10 exclusively; generally only in infants under 1 year of age.

Dengue may be confused with Colorado tick fever, typhus, yellow fever, or other hemorrhagic fevers.

Chapter 6.10

Diphtheria

This disease, caused by the bacterium *Corynebacterium diphtheriae,* is located world-wide with epidemic outbreaks common in temperate as well as tropical zones. Spread is direct from one person to another.

A short incubation period of 1 to 4 days leads to a sore throat, with frequent nausea, vomiting, chills, fever, and headache. A severe sore throat, coated with a dirty white membrane, is frequently noted. If the disease strain produces a toxin (some do not), then the patient can become prostrate with a infection of cardiac tissue appearing on the 10th to 14th day. Heart failure or sudden death may follow.

Treatment with antitoxin and extensive supportive therapy must be given to aid survival. Prevention is with adequate immunization (see tetanus).

Chapter 6.11

Dracunculiasis

Also called Guinea worm, dracontiasis, or fiery serpent. It is endemic in India, Pakistan, the Near East, northern and central Africa, certain West Indies islands, and the Guianas. The current annual toll world-wide is 10 million persons infected, but few deaths. Contraction is by drinking water infected with larvae, or eating produce that has been washed with this water.

The larvae penetrate the intestinal wall and mature deep in the abdominal cavity. They then migrate to the skin surface from whence they discharge their larvae. This process takes about 11 to

13 months, and diagnosis is only possible at that time. An intensely itchy and burning ulcer forms with the adult worm head seen at the ulcer base.

Treatment consists of the slow extraction of the worm from the ulcers by gradual traction on its head over a period of 10 days, generally by winding it around a toothpick, etc. Specific medical treatment is also possible at this time that helps with symptomatic improvement. This nightmare can be prevented by normal purification of drinking water and avoiding uncooked food that may have been in contact with contaminated water.

Chapter 6.12

Dysentery

Organisms which invade and inflame the bowel lining cause severe diarrhea which becomes bloody. The amoebic dysentery is found primarily, but not exclusively, in the tropics while bacterial (or bacillary) dysentery occurs world-wide.

Amoebic dysentery is ingested in food or drink containing inactive cysts of *Entamoeba histolytica,* which become active motile organisms capable of invading the bowel lining, gaining access to the circulation system to the liver. More cysts are formed which are then excreted. Cysts survive in the soil about 8 days. They are resistant to low doses of chlorine, but are instantly killed by boiling.

The infected victim develops symptoms of abdominal pain, cramping, diarrhea or constipation, usually two to four weeks after exposure. Cases may not present until years later, however. Severe infections cause fever, chills, and bloody specked liquid stools. Liver abscess formation can occur.

In some areas of the world, 50% of the population are carriers of this disease. *Entamoeba histolytica* infects the lower intestine of nearly 500 million people and kills at least 40,000 people yearly. Specific treatment is available.

Bacillary dysentery is caused by *Shigella* bacteria which are also ingested due to fecal contamination of food. Man is the only host, but flies may serve as vectors contaminating food after crawling in sewage.

The incubation period is 1 to 4 days. After onset there is severe intermittent cramping with formed stools and temporary relief of symptoms. Eventually liquid stools containing mucus, pus, and often blood are formed at the rate of up to 20 per day. Mild cases last 4 to 8 days; severe cases 3 to 6 weeks. The disease can be fatal to children and debilitated adults.

A significant concern in treating diarrhea with medications such as Lomotil and Imodium is that they result in sudden stoppage of the flushing action of diarrhea, which in the case of one of the dysenteries can allow the causative organism a chance to invade the bowel lining and cause serious complications. The proper treatment is adequate fluid replacement with the oral rehydration formula as shown in Table 5–4. Specific antibiotics are available for treatment.

Chapter 6.13

Echinococcus

Also called hydatid disease, this infection is caused by the larval stage of a tapeworm found in dogs (with sheep as an intermediate host), or in wilderness areas found in wolves (with moose as the intermediate host). This disease is world-wide, but most commonly a problem in Europe, Russia, Japan, Alaska, Canada, and the continental United States.

When ingested by sheep, moose, or humans, the eggs form embryos which pass through the intestinal circulation into the liver and sometimes beyond into the lungs, brain, kidney and other tissue. There a fluid filled cyst forms which contains scolices, brood capsules, and second generation (daughter) cysts containing infectious scolices. The hydatid cysts maintain their presence, sometimes bursting and spreading in a malignant fashion causing destruction of liver, lung and other critical tissues. After remaining without symptoms for decades, abdominal pain, jaundice, or chest pain and coughing may commence. If the intermediate host is eaten by a carnivore (dog, wolf, or man), the infectious scolices are released into the GI tract where they develop into adult worms and the life cycle continues.

Most hydatid disease is from a particular tapeworm known as *Echinococcus granulosis*, but a rapidly progressive form develops when infection is caused by the *Echinococcus multilocularis* tapeworm. This tape worm is carried primarily by domestic dogs, cats, and by foxes. Multiple small cysts form that multiply rapidly. The result is often fatal.

There is no adequate medical treatment, with attempts at surgical removal of multiple cysts being the only hope of cure.

Chapter 6.14

Encephalitis, Japanese

This infection of the brain is caused by a virus known as a flavivirus of the family *Togaviridae*. Infected mosquitos spread the disease to humans, horses, swine, birds, and various domestic animals. The virus has caused annual epidemics in Japan with up to 8,000 cases at a time, in China with 10,000 cases annually, and large outbreaks in Korea, Okinawa, Taiwan, Bangladesh, Burma, Democratic Kampuchea, Indonesia, Loas, Malaysia, the Philippines, Singapore, Sri Lanka, Vietnam , and eastern portions of the Union of Soviet Socialist Republics. The risk to most American travelers is considered low, especially on short trips to urban areas. High risk areas are rural rice and pig farming regions and for persons staying for longer than three weeks during times of high disease activity. In temperate zones, this is only the summer months; in the tropics, disease activity is all year.

The symptoms appear after an incubation period of 4–14 days, with either abrupt or gradual onset of headache, lethargy, sore throat, loss of appetite, nausea, vomiting, and aching or weakness in the arms and legs. Fever is intermittent or continuous, generally ranging from 101° to 102° F (38.5° C). In severe infections symptoms progress to eventual coma, convulsions, paralysis, and possible death. Between 20 to 50% of people with disease symptoms die; those surviving frequently have serious neurological side effects to include mental retardation, movement and speech disorders, and personality changes.

Deaths from Japanese encephalitis have occurred in American travelers to the People's Republic of China in recent years. Threats of possible exposure for various occupational or travel itineraries are listed in the appropriate country's database, starting on page 8–1.

A vaccine (produce by a Japanese firm) is available which is probably about 80% effective in preventing the disease. A three dose schedule was being evaluated in clinical trials here in the United States. The manufacturer of the vaccine, The Research Foundation for Microbial Diseases of Japan [Biken], became concerned about the liability problem in the United States and has withdrawn their vaccine from clinical trials. It is available in the United States only through the Defense Department, which assumes all liability for its use in service personnel. Travelers who are unable to receive the vaccine prior to overseas travel may inquire at the U.S. Embassy abroad, if visiting infected countries. JE vaccine is currently available in Japan, Taiwan, Hong Kong, Korea, Thailand, India, Nepal, Singapore, Sri Lanka, and other Asian countries.

There is no specific treatment available, other than supportive care.

Chapter 6.15

Encephalitis, Tick-Borne

Also known as Russian spring-summer encephalitis, this viral infection of the brain is spread by a tick bite, or the ingestion of contaminated, unpasteurized dairy products. It is prevalent in forested areas of eastern Europe and USSR from April through August when the tick vectors are thriving. The individual country database indicates areas at high risk.

Symptoms develop 1 to 2 weeks from the tick bite or ingestion of contaminated dairy products. These symptoms are similar to the mosquito-borne encephalitis (see Japanese encephalitis). Vaccines have been developed and are available in endemic areas, but are not available in the US. Avoid tick bites with the use of insect repellent and avoid consumption of unpasteurized dairy products.

No specific treatment is available.

Chapter 6.16

Encephalitis, Venezuelan Equine

This mosquito-borne encephalitis is similar to Japanese encephalitis, but it occurs in South America, Panama, and Mexico. Outbreaks are possible in the Gulf states. There is no vaccine available for general use. Prevention is with the use of mosquito repellents and avoidance of bites (see Chapter 5.4).

It should also be noted that there are over 250 different viral encephalitis diseases spread by insects to man, such as the ones mentioned above. Also of note are Western Equine, Eastern Equine, St Louis, California—all native to the US, and many others with exotic names. Significant ones are listed elsewhere in this book (Colorado tick fever, yellow fever, dengue, sandfly fever, Rift Valley fever, West Nile fever, and Lassa fever). See also Chapter 6.20.

Chapter 6.17

Fasciolopsiasis

This parasite of man and pigs is also known as the "giant intestinal fluke." It is common in central and south China, Taiwan, Southeast Asia, Indonesia, India, and Bangladesh. This fluke infects man through the ingestion of contaminated water chestnuts or bamboo shoots. As with other fluke infections, the eggs are shed into water in the feces of an infected host, which is usually humans or pigs. The eggs hatch to produce larvae which infect snails. The organisms are shed and then form cysts on water plants, which are then ingested by humans or pigs, and the cycle is complete. In the human these cysts form immature flukes in the small intestine, which in about 3 months form the adult worms.

Several months after ingestion, severely infected people develop abdominal pain, lack of appetite, nausea, and diarrhea and/or constipation. Swelling of the face or body may occur. Death is rare, but can occur.

To prevent this disease, avoid partially or uncooked water plants in areas of known contamination. There is a specific medical treatment available.

Chapter 6.18

Filariasis

A disease caused by several species of round worms, *Wuchereria bancrofti,* found only in humans, is spread by many species of mosquito, and is widely distributed throughout Africa, southern and southeastern Asia, the Pacific, and the tropical and subtropical regions of South America. *Brugia malayi* is spread to man from animal hosts by mosquitos, but is found only in southern and southeastern Asia.

Infected larvae from the mosquito bite pass into the human lymphatic system where they develop into mature round worms in 6 to 12 months. The fertilized female worms then release motile larvae into the blood stream at night, to coincide with the biting times of the vector mosquitos. Chills, fever and headache may be presenting symptoms, but other presenting symptoms are infections of the testicles, skin surfaces, or any portion of the lymphatic system. Severe infections cause the development of elephantitis, an extreme swelling of the scrotum and legs.

Medical and surgical treatment is available.

Chapter 6.19

Giardiasis

Intestinal infection by *Giardia lamblia,* a single cell parasite, is becoming a significant problem in wilderness travel in the United States and is a very common cause of traveler's diarrhea in the Middle East, India, and the western USSR, particularly the city of Leningrad. The stools of infected individuals contain the infective cyst form of the parasite. These cysts can live in water for longer than 3 months. Other mammalian vectors, such as the beaver, are responsible for much of the wilderness spread of this disease.

In the active disease, the trophozoite form attaches to the small bowel by means of a central sucker. Multiplication is by binary fission, or division. Approximately 2 weeks after ingestion of the cysts there is either a gradual or abrupt onset of persistent watery diarrhea which usually resolves in 1 to 2 weeks, but which may persist less severely for several months. Abdominal pain, bloating, nausea, and weight loss from malabsorption may occur. Giardiasis is often without symptoms at all and a chronic carrier state exists. In the US about 4% of stools submitted for parasitology examination contain *G. lamblia* cysts.

Diagnosis is by finding cysts in stools or trophozoites from gastric suction or the "string test" from the duodenum. This later test is performed by having the patient swallow a string, allowing the far end to pass into the first part of the bowel, or duodenum. When the string is pulled out, a microscopic examination may demonstrate the presence of trophozoites. In active disease the cysts are routinely secreted, but in the chronic carrier state repeated stool examinations (at least three) are required to provide a 95% accuracy of test results.

Treatment is with one of several drugs available in the US. Prevention is by proper filtration of water, adequate chemical treatment, or heating water to 150° F (66° C). See page CCC for a full discussion of water treatment.

Chapter 6.20

Hemorrhagic Fevers, Viral

The term "hemorrhagic fever," as listed in the individual country database, refers to the viral hemorrhagic fevers, a group of diseases caused by various viruses. Some of the names associated with these diseases fairly smack of tropical, exotic locations. While these conditions can be mild, all of them can also result in fatalities and sometimes in ravaging epidemics. Several of the more common ones have sections describing them (yellow fever, dengue, Lassa fever).

Various vectors spread these diseases and avoidance is essential as there are no specific treatments for any of them. Only yellow fever has an effective immunization to help with prevention. Treatment for each of these illnesses is supportive, which means that intravenous fluids and blood are frequently required. Victims of these diseases must be kept in strict isolation as their blood, and sometimes other body fluids, can be highly infective.

The mosquito born fevers have the tendency to the the most aggressive in their potential spread. Those noted as being carried by rodents are generally spread by infected urine. It is known that person-to-person spread of Lassa Fever and Machupo virus disease occurs. Lassa fever, Bolivian hemorrhagic fever, Argentinian hemorrhagic fever, as well as the African hemorrhagic fevers caused by the Marburg and Ebola viruses have surfaced as human illnesses only in the last twenty years, possibly due to the encroachment of mankind on wilderness locations which have been isolated reservoirs of infection. As closer contact with wild animals continues through the destruction of their natural rain forest and other habitat, there is every reason to believe that new viral diseases will be encountered.

Protection from insect vectors will be the mainstay of protection from these, and other yet to be discovered, diseases of tropical and sub-tropical environments.

TABLE 6-2
Viral Hemorrhagic Fevers

DISEASE	VECTOR	GEOGRAPHICAL AREA
Dengue	mosquito	Tropics and subtropics world-wide
Chikungunya Hemorrhagic Fever	mosquito	Africa, Southeast Asia, India
Rift Valley Fever	mosquito	East Africa, Egypt
Yellow Fever	mosquito	Central & South America, Africa
Omsk Hemorrhagic Fever	tick	USSR
Kyasanur Forest Disease	tick	India
Crimea-Congo Hemorrhagic Fever	tick	USSR, Central Africa, West Pakistan
Hantaan Virus Hemorrhagic Fever with Renal Syndrome	small rodents	Northern Asia, Europe possibly USA
Junin Virus Argentinian Hemorrhagic Fever	rodents	South America
Machupo virus Bolivian Hemorrhagic Fever	rodents	South America
Lassa Fever	rodents	Africa
Marburg Virus Disease	unknown	Africa
Ebola Virus Disease	unknown	Africa

Chapter 6.21

Helminthic Diseases

The country information database starting on page 8-1 indicates disease risk by name. At times the term "helminthic diseases" is used, especially in countries with mixed infections of these parasites. The helminths are round worms. Included in this classification are the following diseases discussed in this book with a general description of their geographical distribution.

List of Helminthic Infections & Locations

Diphyllobothrium lata
        fish tapeworm—world-wide.

Dracunculiasis round worm—India; Pakistan; the Near East; Northern and central Africa; certain West Indies Islands; the Guianas.

Echinococcus a tape worm—South America; South Africa; USSR; Middle East.

Fasciolopsiasis giant intestinal fluke—China; Taiwan; Southeast Asia; Indonesia; India; Bangladesh

Filariasis   round worm—*Bancroftian:* Africa; South & Southeast Asia; Pacific; South America. *Malayan*—only South and Southeast Asia.

Loiasis   round worm—Tropical West and Central Africa.

Opisthorchiasis liver fluke—Asia; Eastern Europe; USSR.

&

Clonorchiasis liver fluke—China; Hong Kong; Vietnam; Korea; Japan; Taiwan.

Onchocerciasis round worm—Tropical Africa; tropical Americas, esp Mexico, Guatamala, Venezuela, northern Brazil, Colombia.

Paragonimiasis liver fluke—Far East; West Africa; South Asia; Indonesia; New Guinea; Central America; northern South America.

Schistosomiasis blood flukes—*S. mansoni* in tropical Africa; Venezuela; the Caribbean; the Guianas; Brazil; and the Middle East and *S. japonicum* in China; Japan; the Philippines; and Southeast Asia and *S. haematobium* in Africa; the Middle East, portions of Indian and islands in the Indian Ocean.

Tapeworm   tape worm as per chapter on this subject *as follows:*

Taenia saginata beef tapeworm—Mexico; South America; Eastern Europe; the Middle East; and Africa.

Taenia solium pork tapeworm—South America; Eastern Europe; Russia; and Asia.

Trichinosis   roundworm—world-wide.

Other helminthic diseases have not been described. Some are common, such as the intestinal parasite ascaris, but there are many rarer forms as well. Those chosen have been selected due to their potential for infection of the traveler or a person engaged in a select

Chapter 6.22

Hepatitis A (Infectious Hepatitis)

A viral infection of the liver, this disease is world-wide in distribution. It is transmitted by ingestion of infected feces, either through water supplies contaminated by human sewage, food handled by persons with poor hygiene, or contaminated food such as raw shellfish grown in impure water. Contaminated milk, even infusion of infected blood products (see Hepatitis B), can spread this disease.

The period from the time of exposure to the appearance of symptoms takes 15 to 50 days. The disease can range from minor flu-like symptoms to fatal liver disease. Most cases resolve favorably within 6 to 12 weeks. Symptoms start abruptly with fever, lethargy, and nausea. Occasionally a rash develops. A characteristic loss of taste for cigarettes is frequent. In 3 to 10 days the urine turns dark, followed by jaundice—or yellowing of the whites of the eyes and the skin. The stool may turn light colored. There is frequently itching and joint pain. The jaundice peaks within one to two weeks and fades during the two to four week recovery phase. There is no specific treatment, other than rest during the first few days of illness. The hepatitis A patient stops shedding virus in the stool prior to the jaundice developing, and is therefore not contagious by the time the diagnosis is normally made. Full activity can be resumed once the jaundice clears. Chronic forms of hepatitis are unusual after hepatitis A, but the patient should be monitored by a physician.

A single dose of pooled immune globulin (10% solution) protects against or modifies this form of hepatitis. It must not be given at the same times as the Measles, Mumps, Rubella (MMR) vaccine. The MMR vaccine should be given at least 14 days before immune globulin and should not be given for at least 6 weeks, but preferably 3 months, after the administration of immune globulin. There are no apparent problems with the administration of Oral Polio Vaccine or Yellow Fever vaccine with or near immune globulin administration. Dosage depends upon body weight and length of time of required protection. At maximal doses it still must be repeated every 6 months for continued protection.

TABLE 6–3
Immune Globulin Dosage*

WEIGHT	SHORT TERM (< 3 MONTHS)	LONG TERM (>3 MONTHS)	
< 50 pounds	0.5 ml	1.0 ml	(repeat
50–100 pounds	1.0 ml	2.5 ml	every
> 100 pounds	2.0 ml	5.0 ml	6 mos.)

*Also called immune serum globulin and gamma globulin.

Increased risk factors and recommendations for hepatitis A protection are indicated in the appropriate country database listing beginning on page 8-1.

Chapter 6.23

Hepatitis B (Serum Hepatitis)

A different viral infection of the liver, this disease is also world-wide in distribution. Transmission is primarily through infusion of infected blood products, sexual contact, use of contaminated needles, syringes, or even sharing contaminated razor blades. Dental procedures, acupuncture, and ear piercing with contaminated equipment will also spread this disease.

Incubation period from time of exposure to the development of symptoms is longer than with hepatitis A, namely 30 to 180 days. The symptoms are similar, but the onset is less abrupt and the incidence of fever is lower. There is a greater chance of developing chronic hepatitis (5 to 10% of cases). Mortality is higher, especially in elderly patients were it ranges from 10 to 15%.

Immunization is available and is very effective. Dosage consists of 1.0 ml IM injections of Hepatitis B Vaccine (Recombinant) given on day 0, 1 month, and 6 months. Wholesale cost as of July 1990 is about $190.00 for 1 full course of immunization. Duration of protection and need for revaccination has not been defined. A blood test to determine resistance can be performed. If the antibody level falls below 10 SRUs, revaccination should be considered. The injection must be given in the upper arm.

Increased risks and recommendations for immunization are indicated in the appropriate country database listing beginning on page 8–1.

Chapter 6.24

Hepatitis C (Non-A, Non-B)

A form of hepatitis, with similar manifestations to Hepatitis B, has been designated as Hepatitis C (formerly Non-A, Non-B since blood tests for evidence of exposure to those virus particles was not previously found). There may be more than one, as yet undiscovered virus, resulting in this symptom complex. The transmission is probably the same as for Hepatitis B, although spread via contaminated water sources may also occur. There is no preventative vaccine.

Incubation period is from less than 2 weeks, to more than 25 weeks, with an average of 7 weeks for the development of clinical disease.

There is no specific treatment.

Chapter 6.25

Lassa Fever

This serious "arenavirus" infection has been found in the western African countries of Nigeria, Liberia, and Sierra Leone. It probably spreads by exposure to urine or feces of a small rat which appears to be the vector. Patient to patient spread is possible and strict isolation of victims must be maintained. This disease is highly contagious and causes a severe illness that is fatal 16% to 50% of the time.

After exposure the incubation period lasts 1 to 24 days (10 days average). The initial symptoms are sore throat, fever, headache, muscle ache—followed by loss of appetite, vomiting, pains in the chest and stomach. The sore throat becomes severe and forms a white or yellow exudate much like strep throat, mononucleosis, or diphtheria. During the second week patients who will recover break their fever, while fatally ill patients deteriorate and lapse into coma.

Persons returning from West Africa, who develop a high fever within 21 days of return, should mention to their physician their possible exposure to lassa fever so that proper tests and therapy can be initiated. IV injections of an anti-viral drug (ribavirin) have proven beneficial, but without this therapy the mortality is over 50%. Patients must be strictly isolated.

Chapter 6.26

Leishmaniasis

The single cell protozoan Leishmania has three species that cause various, frequently terrible diseases in man. The manifestations of these illnesses are changed by the victim's immune response and probably various strains of the attacking organism. All forms of leishmaniasis are spread by bites from sandflies. One form, visceral leishmaniasis, can also be spread by sexual contact and through blood transfusions.

CUTANEOUS LEISHMANIASIS—ORIENTAL SORE; TROPICAL SORE; DELHI BOIL; ALEPPO BOIL

Found in central Asia, China, India, the Near East, the Mediterranean coastal plain, and West Africa, either single or multiple sharply demarcated lesions, which ulcerate, are formed 2 to 8 weeks after sandfly bites. Ulcers usually heal within 2 to 18 months, leaving a depressed scar. Special treatment is available.

MUCOCUTANEOUS LEISHMANIASIS—FOREST YAWS, ESPUNDIA, UTA, AMERICAN LEISHMANIASIS

A disease of Central and South America, the ulcers of this form of the disease spread into the membranes of the nose, mouth, and nasal septum causing severe and extensive facial deformity.

VISCERAL LEISHMANIASIS—KALA-AZAR, DUMDUM FEVER

Wide spread around the world, it occurs in India, China, Russia, the Mediterranean coastal plain, East Africa, and several countries in Central and South America. The spread through the blood stream allows the parasite to lodge in the spleen, bone marrow, liver, lymph nodes, and skin. After an incubation period of 2 to 6 months, symptoms including fever, weakness, and weight loss begin. The destruction of the immune system leads to complications with other infections. Untreated the fatality rate in 90%, but generally it is less than 10% with therapy.

Chapter 6.27

Leprosy

Also known as Hansen's Disease, leprosy is caused by the *Mycobacterium leprae* bacteria. It possibly spreads via infected nasal discharge. Contaminated cloth and other material, and even insects have been implicated in the spread of this contagion. Only approximately 5% of contacts catch the disease. While this is an important illness in the world (there are an estimated 12 to 20 million cases), it is rare for a traveler to contract leprosy. This problem is tropical in distribution and includes countries in Southeast Asia, Africa, and South America. Approximately 2,000 cases are located in the United States.

A variety of classifications are applied to the victim's response and to the changing clinical picture of leprosy. In all stages, skin and peripheral nerve lesions are the earliest clinical findings. It has a prolonged incubation period of 1 to 30 years. Diagnosis is usually made with the aid of a skin biopsy. Loss of nerve sensations cause tissue destruction, particularly of the hands and feet, from lack of attention to skin injury. Various reactions can cause eye damage. Nasal congestion can be an early sign with eventual bleeding. If the disease is not treated this may result in ulceration and destruction of nasal cartilage.

Persons exposed to leprosy should be watched carefully. An examination for clinical signs and symptoms should be made every 6 months. There are several very effective medications available for treatment.

Chapter 6.28

Leptospirosis

Also called Weil's disease, swamp fever, Canicola fever, or swineherd's disease, this bacterial infection of the genus *Leptospira* occurs world-wide. It is shed in the urine by infected host animals, which include many domestic and wild animals, and man. If the organism reaches water it can survive for more than a month, but it dies almost instantly upon drying. It is caught by ingesting contaminated flesh, or exposure to urine contaminated water, or foods washed with this water. Swimming or wading in stagnate ponds or slow moving streams which may have been contaminated should be avoided. It is an occupational hazard of those working with contaminated animals, soil, or water. Medical prophylaxis is possible by taking one tablet daily of doxycycline 100 mg.

After an incubation period of 1 to 2 weeks, chills, fever, headache, and muscle ache begins. Recurrent fevers up to 102° F (38.9° C) transpire over the next 4 to 9 days. The fever breaks, then on the 6th to 12th day of the illness a similar fever pattern returns. Weil's syndrome is a serious form of the disease with severe jaundice and other signs of liver and kidney damage. Without jaundice mortality is zero, with jaundice the death rate is 15% to 30%.

Treatment is with large doses of antibiotics, with the best results being obtained when they are given within 4 days of the onset of symptoms.

Chapter 6.29

Loiasis

Also known as African eyeworm, *Loa loa* infection, Calabar swellings, and fugitive swellings, this disease is caused by filariasis, or small worms, spread by bites from infected *Chrysops* deerflies. It is widely distributed in tropical west and central Africa. In the Congo River basin, up to 90% of some villagers are infected.

Symptoms consist of local, transient swellings of the skin caused by migrating adult worms. These worms might also migrate beneath the conjunctiva across the eye. Fever, large welts, lip and tongue swellings are common, with up to 20% of cases showing evidence of cardiac and kidney problems. Symptoms are very delayed, in fact they do not customarily appear until several years after the infected fly bite. The small microfilariae can be found in the blood within 5 to 6 months of infection and have been shown to remain for as long as 17 years.

Prevention is possible with adequate fly protection by using insect repellents, wearing protective clothing, sleeping in protected areas, and with the use of diethylcarbamazine 300 mg, one tablet weekly. This same drug, in much larger doses, is used for treatment of the disease, but should only be used under the close supervision of a physician.

Chapter 6.30

Lyme Disease

Lyme Disease is caused by a bacterial spirochete, *Borrelia burgdorferi*. The disease lives in various mammals, but is transmitted to humans by the bite of several species of ticks. The disease is most common in the northeastern United States, extending through Connecticut and Massachusetts down to Maryland; in Wisconsin and Minnesota; throughout the states of California and Oregon; and in parts of California and Utah. It has also been found in various south Atlantic and south central states, the southern portions of most Canadian provinces, and in several European countries.

The disease goes through several phases. In Stage 1, after an incubation of 3 days to a month, from 30% to 80% of victims develop a circular lesion in the area of the bite. Called an erythema chronicum migrans (ECM) rash, it has a clear center, raised border, is painless, and ranges from 1 to 23 inches in diameter. There are usually several such patches. The patient feels lethargy, has headache, muscle and joint pain, and enlarged lymph nodes. In stage 2, 10% to 15% of patients can develop a meningitis, fewer than 10% heart problems. Symptoms may last for months, but are generally self-limited. Approximately 60% enter stage 3—the development of actual arthritis. Frequently a knee is involved. The swelling can be impressive. Stage 3 can start abruptly several weeks to 2 years after the onset of the initial rash.

Lyme disease is treatable in all stages with antibiotic, but it responds to therapy most readily when treated while still in stage 1.

Chapter 6.31

Malaria

Malaria is the most important infectious disease in the world (over 100 million cases, with just under 1 million deaths yearly world-wide) and the most important health risk to Americans traveling to malaria infected areas. While the disease is present in most tropical countries, risk differs according to rainy season, altitude, and urban or rural settings. During the period 1980–1988,

1,534 cases of malaria in US civilian travelers were reported, with 37 fatal cases resulting. 80% of the cases and 27 of the fatalities resulted from malaria contact in sub-Saharan Africa.

Quoting from the Centers for Disease Control publication "Recommendations for the prevention of malaria among travelers," MMWR 1990 supplement 39 (No. RR-3):

> "... *most imported malaria among U.S. travelers was acquired in sub-Saharan Africa, even though only an estimated 90,000 Americans travel to sub-Saharan Africa each year. In contrast, an estimated 900,000 Americans travel to malarious areas of Asia and South America each year. This disparity in the risk of acquiring malaria reflects the fact that travelers to Africa are at risk in most rural and many urban areas, and, moreover, tend to spend considerable time, including evening and nighttime hours, in rural areas where malaria risk is highest. Most travelers to Asia and South America, however, spend most of their time in urban or resort areas where there is limited, if any, risk of exposure, and they travel to rural areas mainly during daytime hours when there is limited risk of infection.*
>
> *Estimating the risk of infection for different categories of travelers is difficult, even if persons travel or temporarily reside in the same general areas within a country. For example, tourists staying in air-conditioned hotels may be at lower risk than backpackers or adventure travelers. Similarly, longer-term residents living in screened and air-conditioned housing are less likely to be exposed than are missionaries or Peace Corps volunteers."*

There are four species of malaria, each spread by the bite of the infected female anopheles mosquito. The parasite primarily lives in red blood cells and it, thus, circulates throughout the body. The illness is characterized by an incubation period of 10 to 35 days, followed by 2 to 3 days of low grade fever, headache, muscle ache, and general ill feeling.

In *Plasmodium falciparum* the illness starts as a chilly sensation with a fever lasting 20 to 36 hours with considerable prostration and severe headache. During interludes between paroxysms of high fever, the patient feels miserable and generally maintains a low grade fever. Fevers of 104° F (40° C), severe headache, coma, or convulsions, may indicate impending cerebral infection, a frequently fatal complication. Falciparum malaria is the most dangerous variety and it is the one that kills.

With *Plasmodium malariae* the illness presents abruptly with high fever which then recurs at 72 hour intervals. In *Plasmodium vivax* and *ovale* infections the abrupt onset of fever may be preceded by a short period of malaise or chill, but generally the fever begins abruptly and lasts 1 to 8 hours. Afterwards the patient feels well until the next febrile episode, which usually occurs every 48 hours.

Prevention is complicated by several factors. First, guidelines for avoiding mosquito bites as indicated in Chapter 5.4 should be observed. Avoiding all mosquito bites is a very difficult proposition. A person can be at risk during an airport lay-over while in a malarious zone. Swarms of mosquitos frequently encountered in rural tropical areas make accidental exposure almost unavoidable. Second, *P. falciparum*—the most dangerous of the species—is becoming resistant to the medication most commonly used to protect travelers, namely chloroquine. Effective in 1990, mefloquine is now recommended by the CDC for use in the many chloroquine resistant areas of the world (see discussion below). The alternate medication, Fansidar, can have serious side effects, so that its use is limited and care must be taken to avoid complications. Other alternate drugs exist, a few are only available overseas. Some medications sold outside of the United States are dangerous and must not be used; some are valuable and may be used. Resistance to these alternate medications is developing rapidly.

An understanding of medications used to prevent *P. falciparum* malaria is so important to the traveler at risk that a full discussion of these medications and dosages is found below. *P. vivax* and *ovale* are capable of living in liver cells for an extended period of time where they are safe from the medications otherwise used to prevent or kill the malaria parasite. In areas with an increased incidence of these species of malaria, terminal eradication with primaquine is advised, as indicated below.

MEDICAL PREVENTION OF MALARIA

All travelers, including infants, children, and pregnant women, to an area with malaria are advised to use the appropriate drug for protection against malaria, as well as avoiding mosquito bites as discussed in Chapter 5.4.

In March 1990, the Centers for Disease Control released new guidlines for the chemical prophylaxis of malaria. Chloroquine remains the drug of choice for those areas which have not developed resistance. One chloroquine tablet weekly (equal to 300 mg of base, or 500 mg of the salt compound), starting two weeks prior to departure and continuing for four weeks after leaving the malarious area, is the recommended dose. Starting two weeks prior to the trip allows the proper blood level to be obtained for adequate protection prior to arrival. This would also allow the traveler's physician at home a chance to monitor and advise on any complications or side effects of chloroquine therapy that may develop. Side effects of this medication are minimal, usually consisting of headache, gastrointestinal disturbance, dizziness, blurred vision, and itching—but this does not require discontinuing the medication. Most persons experience no side effects. It is not harmful to a fetus and this drug is recommended for pregnant women who must travel to a malarious zone. The drug can exacerbate psoriasis and may interfere with the antibody response to rabies vaccine. Risk of damage to the eye can occur after 6 *years* of continuous use. Chloroquine has a bitter taste. The tablets may be crushed and placed in gelatin capsules in calculated pediatric doses. In many countries in malarious zones, a pediatric suspension is available. Be sure to note the concentration when providing it to a child, paying particular attention whether or not the concentration is expressed as the salt or the base. The dosage tables below will help you convert to the proper dosage quantity. Antimalarial drugs are *very* toxic and must be stored in child-proof containers.

Mefloquine (Lariam) is another new drug that appears highly effective against both chloroquine and Fansidar resistant malaria. In July 1989 mefloquine was approved by the FDA for sale in the United States. In March of 1990, the Centers for Disease Control made mefloquine the official drug to use for malaria prevention in most areas of chloroquine resistance.

Side effects appear minimal and consist of dizziness and gastrointestinal problems which soon resolve, even with continued dosing. This drug may cause electrocardiogram changes and should be used with caution in persons taking calcium channel blockers, quinidine, and beta blockers for high blood pressure or heart problems. Concurrent use with quinine may also cause irregular heart beats. If anticonvulsion drugs are being used, the blood levels should be monitored as breakthrough seizures and unexpectedly low anti-epileptic drug blood levels have been reported with simultaneous use of mefloquine. It is not approved for use during pregnancy.

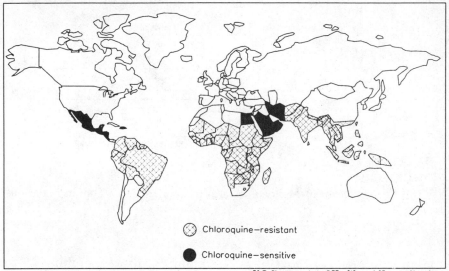

U.S. Department of Health and Human Services

FIGURE 6–1
Malarious Areas with *Plasmodium falciparium*
Resistant and Sensitive to Chloroquine, 1990

For prophylaxis the dose schedule is one 250 mg tablet weekly, starting 1 week prior to entering a malarious zone, for four weeks, followed by one tablet every other week for the duration of stay and for two doses after leaving the endemic area, thus providing an additional 4 weeks of coverage after departure (see Figure 6–2).

The FDA has not yet approved mefloquine for use in children. The U.S. Public Health Service, however, does recommend a prophylactic dose for children by weight: 1/4 tablet for those weighing

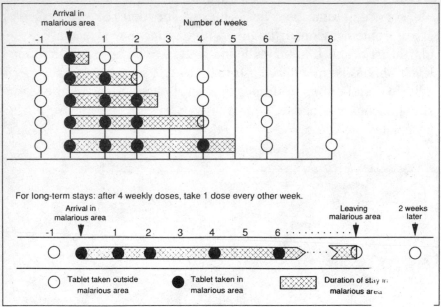

U.S. Department of Health and Human Services

FIGURE 6–2

Recommended Doses of Mefloquine for Various Lengths of Stay in Malarious Areas

33 to 42 pounds (15 to 19 kg), $^1/_2$ tablet for those weighing 43 to 66 pounds (20 to 30 kg), and $^3/_4$ tablet for those weighing 67 to 99 pounds (31 to 45 kg). The U.S. Public Health Service does not recommend the use of mefloquine in children who weigh less than 33 pounds (15 kg) and by pregnant women.

In some foreign countries a fixed combination of mefloquine and Fansidar is marketed under the trade name "Fansimef." Fansimef should not be confused with mefloquine, and it is not recommended for prevention of malaria by the Centers for Disease Control.

Previously, when travel was planned for less than three weeks into an area of chloroquine resistance travelers were advised to continue their weekly use of chloroquine as indicated above. They were also instructed to carry a 3 tablet dose of Fansidar to be taken at one time if a febrile illness occurs and professional medical help is not available. They were to continue taking their chloroquine even if they took the Fansidar dose. Medical help should be promptly sought in any case of possible malaria infection due to the seriousness of this disease. Fansidar is a sulfa drug and may not be taken by persons allergic to this class of medications. It may not be taken by infants younger than 2 months of age. Under periods of prolonged exposure to chloroquine resistant malaria (ie trips lasting longer than 3 weeks), Fansidar had been previously prescribed to be taken one tablet weekly prophylactically, along with the weekly chloroquine dose. The CDC has dropped this recommendation and no longer recommends using Fansidar for preventative use, only for presumptive treatment use. A fatal reaction can occur in persons taking weekly Fansidar which first manifests itself as a skin rash, itch, sore throat, or the development of mouth or genital lesions. This fatal reaction has never been reported in persons taking the three tablet presumptive treatment dose of Fansidar.

An alternate drug to be used in areas of high resistance is doxycycline 100 mg, taken 1 tablet daily. When this drug is used, the chloroquine is not taken. It may be started a day prior to arrival in the malarious area, but it must be continued for 4 weeks after departure. As this medication is a tetracycline, it may not be taken by children under the age of 8, ladies during the third trimester of pregnancy, or in persons allergic to this class of drugs. This is a drug that has been shown to be useful in preventing travelers' diarrhea in the same dosage (refer to Chapter 5.3 for a full discussion).

Amadiaquine is available in the United Kingdom, Switzerland, and in many tropical countries for malaria prevention. The Centers for Disease Control recommends that this drug not be used due to the high incidence of a fatal blood disorder. In 1988 an expedition that I was the medical advisor to was told by local medical authorities in Venezuela that this was the drug to take. This medication should *not* be taken (and it certainly was not by that expedition).

Proguanil (Paludrine) is not commercially available in the United States. It is felt to be effective in East Africa in Fansidar resistant areas, but probably not in Thailand, Papua New Guinea, and West Africa. Dosage is a daily 200 mg dose, along with weekly chloroquine. Proguanil has been widely used for several decades, and no adverse effects on pregnancy or fetus have been established.

Primaquine is used only to eradicate *P. vivax* and *ovale*. These forms can persist in the liver and cause relapses months and years later, hence the term relapsing malaria. Destruction of the liver phase of these species of malaria is accomplished by taking primaquine, 1 tablet daily for 14 days during the last two weeks of chloroquine therapy after returning home. This medication causes an adverse reaction in persons who have an inherited disorder known as G6PD deficiency. A blood test can safely determine the existence of this deficiency and should be performed on all persons contemplating taking primaquine. The presence of species of *P. vivax* and *ovale* can be determined by referring to the country information data base in this book (Section 8). Primaquine should not be used while pregnant, as per the discussion in Chapter 4.2.

TABLE 6–4
CDC Recommended Dosages of Drugs Used for Malaria Prevention

DRUG	ADULT DOSE	PEDIATRIC DOSE
Chloroquine phosphate (Aralen)	300 mg base (500 mg salt) orally, once per week	5 mg/kg base (8.3 mg/kg salt) orally, once per week, up to adult dose
Hydroxy-chloroquine sulfate (Plaquenil)	310 mg base (400 mg salt) orally, once per week	5mg/kg base (6.5 mg/kg salt) orally once per week, up to adult dose
Doxycycline (Vibramycin)	100 mg orally, once per day	>8 years of age: 2 mg/kg of body weight orally, once per day up to adult dose
Mefloquine (Lariam)	250 mg orally, once per week for 4 doses, then once every other week	>33 lbs: 1/4 tablet 34–44 lbs: 1/2 tablet 45–99 lbs: 3/4 tablet interval as for adult

Proguanil (Paludrine)	200 mg orally, once/day, in combination with weekly chloroquine	>2 yrs: 50/mg/day* 2–6 yrs: 100 mg/day* 7–10 yrs: 150 mg/day* >10 yrs: 200 mg/day*
Pyrimethamine sulfadoxine (Fansidar)#	1 tablet (25 mg pyrimethamine and 500 mg sulfadoxine) orally, once per week*	2–11 mos: 1/8 tab/wk* 1–3 yrs: 1/4 tab/wk* 4–8 yrs: 1/2 tab/wk* 9–14 yrs: 3/4 tab/wk* >14 yrs: 1 tab/wk*
Primaquine	15 mg base (26.3 mg salt) orally, once/day for 14 days *after* return	0.3 mg/kg base (0.5 mg/kg salt) orally, once/day for 14 days after return

*Use in addition to the weekly dose of chloroquine.

#Indicated dosage is for prolonged (>3 weeks) of exposure only. See text for precautions and alternate dose for presumptive therapy during shorter trips.

Detailed recommendations for the prevention of malaria may be obtained 24 hours a day by calling the CDC Malaria Hotline at (404) 332–4555. Persons experiencing an adverse reaction to preventative malarial medication, especially to mefloquine, should consult their physician, who should report these reactions to the Malaria Branch of the Centers for Disease Control (404) 488–4046. Physicians should also report adverse drug reactions to the Food and Drug Administration, Division of Epidemiology and Surveillance (HFD-730), 5600 Fishers Lane, Rockville, MD 20852, requesting Form FDA 1639(7 86). The telephone number for assistance in reporting adverse reactions to the FDA is (301) 443–4580.

Chapter 6.32

Melioidosis

This bacterial infection caused by *Pseudomonas pseudomallei* can be caught from infected soil or water through skin abrasions or burns, but is not caught from infected animals or persons directly. It is found in Southeast Asia, North Queensland Australia, and recently identified in Central, West, and East Africa.

The incubation period is unknown, but apparently it is variable. The infection may lay dormant for years, then erupt into an acute pulmonary infection or spleen infection. Secondary infections may develop in skin, lymph nodes, lungs, or any organ, leading to blood poisoning and death. Diagnosis is made by several lab tests, including the growth of the bacteria from sputum, blood cultures, or biopsies.

Antibiotic treatment is available.

Chapter 6.33

Meningococcal Meningitis

This acute bacterial infection causes inflammation in linings of the brain and central nervous system. While the disease is found world-wide, large epidemics are more common in tropical countries, especially sub-Saharan Africa in the dry season, New Delhi (India), and in Nepal.

Many cases are without symptoms or consist of a mild upper respiratory illness. Severe cases begin with sudden fever, chills, headache, stiff neck, nausea, and vomiting. Within 24 to 48 hours the victim becomes drowsy, mentally confused, followed by convulsions, coma, and death. The disease is spread by contact with the nasal secretions of infected persons (sneezing and coughing). Incubation period is short, from 1 to 3 days, never longer than one week. Victims of the disease shed virus as long as symptoms persist. Carriers without symptoms can shed virus for up to six months.

A vaccine is available. The A/C/Y/W135 vaccine by Squibb-Connaught is given 0.5 ml subcutaneously. Duration of protection is unknown, but appears to be at least 3 years in those over 4 years of age. Physicians can obtain the vaccine by calling the manufacturer at 1–800–VACCINE. Increased risk and recommendation for immunization are indicated in the appropriate country information database listing beginning on page 8–1.

Immediate, and appropriately large, doses of the proper antibiotic are critical to save the patient's life.

Chapter 6.34

Measles/Mumps/Rubella

These common diseases are world-wide in distribution. Measles is also known as rubeola, hard measles, or 10 day measles. Rubella is also called German measles and 3 day measles. Proof of immunization is not required for entry into any country. The MMR vaccine, providing life-long immunity to each of these diseases, is currently given all infants in the United States, generally at 15 months of age. Immunization is available individually, or in combination, against each of these diseases.

In some states women are required to obtain rubella titers prior to obtaining a marriage license, as having this disease during pregnancy frequently results in birth defects. Rubella immunization should be sought by nonpregnant women in child bearing age who may become pregnant and who have not had the vaccine, or who have not had a titer to prove immunity to this disease.

In 1988 and 1989 a measles (rubeola) epidemic in young adults caused the State Boards of Health in Illinois, Indiana, and select other states to recommend booster inoculations for persons younger than 32 years of age who had received their MMR, or their rubeola immunization, before 1980. The annual world-wide toll of rubeola in the world, reported in 1989, is 2 million deaths, mostly of children.

Mumps can cause significant infections in the salivary glands and in a mature male's testicles. Mumps and measles are potentially serious diseases. Measles and mumps immunization should be sought by unvaccinated persons without documented disease, born in 1957 or latter.

The recommended pediatric immunization schedule for the United States is discussed in Chapter 4.3.

Chapter 6.35

Onchocerciasis

This disease is spread by infected female *Simulium* black fly bites. The infectious agent is a nematode (round worm) called *Onchocerca volvulus*. Other names for this disease are river blindness, Robles' disease, mal morado, and volvulosis. Distribution is tropical Africa and parts of the New World, especially Mexico, Guatemala, Venezuela, northern Brazil, and Colombia. There are 18 million cases of this disease in the world, with 340,000 people made blind as a consequence.

The biting black fly injects the larvae just beneath the skin. These larvae penetrate deeper into the skin layers and in about 1 year develop into an adult worm. The female worm then produces large numbers of active larvae called microfilariae that migrate throughout the body. Biting black flies are thus infected when biting a host with the microfilariae in their circulation. The life span of the female worms is 15 years, and the microfilariae about 2 $^1/_2$ years.

Obviously with the delay in symptomatic development and the generalized symptoms that this disease can cause, diagnosis long after the traveler has returned home can be difficult. A key to the diagnosis is the formation of chronic skin nodules at the bite site. In Africa the bites are primarily on the trunk and around the pelvis, while in the Americas the bites are predominantly on the head and scalp. Microfilariae penetration into the eye can be detected by eye examination. Symptoms of widespread disease include fever, headache, and lethargy. Blindness can occur depending upon severity of disease.

Cure is with specific medical therapy and surgical removal of skin nodules.

Chapter 6.36

Paragonimiasis

This parasitic flat worm, or liver fluke, is found throughout the Far East, West Africa, South Asia, Indonesia, New Guinea, Central America and northern South America. As with most flukes its life span is complex, involving several hosts before reaching man. Eggs are shed through sputum or feces into water, where the organisms hatch, next infecting freshwater snails. They then enter crayfish and freshwater crabs where tissue cysts develop. These are ingested by humans eating raw or pickled crayfish or crabs containing these cysts. Immature flukes are released by the cysts in the bowel system of the human host. They penetrate the bowel lining and gain free access to the abdominal cavity where they migrate to other tissues, especially the lung.

Symptoms begin when adult flukes develop in various body tissues and start releasing eggs, about 6 weeks after cyst ingestion.

Mild infections do not have any symptoms, but heavily infected people become quite ill. Pulmonary manifestations are common with a low grade fever and a dry cough—progressing to a productive, blood specked sputum. Shortness of breath, weight loss, and loss of energy develop. Infestations of the abdominal cavity or central nervous system produce symptoms in these areas.

Medical treatment is available. Sometimes surgery is required to remove cysts. The average traveler is unlikely to have prolonged, or significant, exposure to this disease, if ingestion of raw, partially cooked, or pickled crabs, crayfish, or other freshwater crustaceans are avoided.

Chapter 6.37

Paralytic Shellfish Poisoning

Mussels, clams, oysters, and scallops may ingest poisonous dinoflagellates known as the "red tide" during June to October along the New England and Pacific coasts.

Numbness around the mouth may occur within 5 to 30 minutes after eating. Other symptoms are similar to ciguatera poisoning. These include gastrointestinal illness, loss of coordination, and paralysis progressing to complete respiratory paralysis with 12 hours in 8% of cases.

No specific treatments or antidotes are available, but purging of stomach contents should be encouraged. Supportive medical care is available to alleviate symptoms.

Chapter 6.38

Plague

Plague is caused by a bacterium, *Yersinia pestis,* that infects wild rodents in many parts of the world, including the western United States and parts of South America, Africa, the Near East, India, and China. The disease is most prevalent during warm, humid weather and is found primarily in rural mountainous or upland areas. Epidemics occur when domestic rats become infected and spread the disease to man. Bubonic plague is transmitted by infected fleas, while pneumonic plague is spread directly to other people by coughing. Plague is accompanied by fever, enlarged lymph nodes (bubonic plague) and less commonly pneumonia (pneumonic plague).

The most common form of the disease is the bubonic plague, which begins abruptly 1 to 5 days after exposure to the infected flea bite with high fever, severe headache, rapid heart rate, weakness and muscle aches. A pus filled lesion may form at the site of the bite, with local lymph nodes (buboes) becoming enlarged, tender, and draining pus. The skin hemorrhages, with black, purple spots forming under the skin surface (thus the term, black plague or black death). The death rate in untreated bubonic plague is 60%, with most deaths occurring from overwhelming infection in 3 to 5 days.

If the plague victim develops pneumonia, the disease can be easily spread to others by coughing. The pneumonic plague victim develops sudden fever 2 to 3 days from exposure. The cough appears over the next 20 to 24 hours. At first the cough is not especially notable, but it soon becomes productive with bloody flecks, then bright red (raspberry syrup appearance) and foamy. In untreated patients death occurs within 48 hours of onset. Prompt treatment in both types reduces mortality below 5%.

A vaccine exists that might be helpful in reducing the risk of persons who must work in rural areas where avoidance of fleas or rodents is impossible, or for health care workers who will be exposed to plague victims. Adult immunization consists of 3 injections of 0.5 ml, 0.5 ml, and 0.2 ml (in that order) about 4 weeks apart and two boosters of 0.2 ml 6 months apart, then 1 dose every 1 to 2 years if needed. Increased risk and recommendation for immunization are indicated in the appropriate country database listing beginning on page 8–1.

Antibiotic treatment is available and it is essential that the patient receive appropriate therapy immediately.

Chapter 6.39

Poliomyelitis

Also known as infantile paralysis, or polio, this world-wide disease is caused by a virus. It infects only man and is transmitted through contaminated water (fecal-oral route) or through cough droplet (respiratory route) from an infected individual. Most polio infections are mild and go undetected. A small proportion of victims develop severe muscle paralysis. World-wide there are 250,000 cases of polio reported annually, resulting in a yearly toll of 25,000 deaths.

From time of exposure to onset of symptoms is 3 to 5 days for the mild disease and 7 to 14 days for the paralytic form. Paralysis appears to be more common and severe in adults. Prevention is adequate water purification and immunization with polio vaccine.

In 1984 the distribution of polio cases world-wide was 63% from Southeast Asia, 19% in the Western Pacific, 8% in the Eastern Mediterranean, 8% Africa, 2% in the Americas, and 1% in Europe. The only countries considered disease free of wild polio virus strains are the United States, Canada, Japan, Australia, New Zealand, and most of Eastern and Western Europe. Before visiting other countries it is best for every traveler to receive at least a complete primary series.

Trivalent oral polio vaccine (OPV) is the vaccine of choice for all infants, children, and adolescents (up to their 18th birthday). The primary series is 3 doses, with dose 2 given at least 6 weeks after 1 and dose 3 given 8–12 months after dose 2. The supplemental dose is given to children at age 4 to 6 years. Anyone having a partial series may continue with the next dose(s), regardless of how long before the last dose was given.

Anyone who has completed the primary OPV series in the past should be given a single additional dose of OPV. Unimmunized adults should be given the four full dose series of injectable inactivated polio vaccine (IPV) (3 doses given at 1 to 2 month intervals, followed by a 4th dose 6 to 12 months after the 3rd dose), if time allows or a minimum of 2 doses of IPV given a month apart. If less than a month remains prior to departure, the administration of a single dose of OPV may be justified due to potential high risk of exposure to wild poliovirus and the more rapid protective effect of OPV. The OPV should not be given to immune compromised people, nor to people whose households have such a person or a non-immune person at home.

The routine polio immunization schedule for children, recommended in the United States, is described in Chapter 4.3.

Chapter 6.40

Rabies

Rabies is a virus that causes encephalitis. It is usually transmitted via the saliva from an infected animal bite to another animal or to a human. Saliva in contact with an open wound or mucous membrane may allow transmission of this disease. Two cases have been reported of rabies developing due to inhalation of infected bat cave guano.

The incubation period in a human is 1 to 2 months. Rabies is a vicious disease that is usually fatal once it clinically develops. There is frequently pain at the bite site. The local skin becomes sensitive to temperature and ever air currents. The victim becomes restless, behaves with uncontrollable excitement, develops excessive salivation and has severe pain and spasm of the muscles used in swallowing. Convulsions occur and death results in 3 to 5 days, without intensive supportive care. Even so, the disease is usually fatal. Because of this, there is generous use of rabies vaccine and immune globulin.

Approximately 20,000 people are vaccinated in the US yearly to prevent this disease. In the United States there have been 9 cases of rabies reported between 1980 and 1987. In India 40,000 people die yearly from rabies, with a high incidence also reported in the other developing counties of Asia, Africa, and Latin America.

Rabies can be transmitted on the North American continent by several species of mammals, namely skunk, bat, fox, coyote, racoon, bobcat, and wolf. Any unprovoked attack by one of these mammals should be considered an attack by a rapid animal. Dogs and cats in the United States have a low incidence of rabies. Information from local departments of health will indicate if rabies is currently of concern in these animals. In many foreign countries the bite of a cat or dog should be considered rabid. Animals whose bites have never caused rabies in humans in the US are livestock (cattle, sheep, horse), rabbit, gerbil, chipmunk, squirrel, rat, and mouse. Hawaii is the only rabies free state. Countries free of rabies are England, Australia, Japan, and parts of the Caribbean. In Europe the red fox is the animal most often rapid with documented cases spreading to dogs, cats, cattle, and deer. Canada's rabies occurs mostly in foxes and skunks in the province of Ontario. Mongoose rabies is found in South Africa and the Caribbean islands of Cuba, Puerto Rico, Hispaniola, and Grenada.

TABLE 6–5
Countries Reporting No Cases of Rabies

The following countries and politcal units have reported to the WHO and the Pan American Zoonoses Center that rabies is not present. Bat rabies should be considered separately.

AFRICA: Mauritius*

AMERICAS: NORTH: Bermuda; St. Pierre and Miquelon.

CARIBBEAN: Anguilla; Antigua and Barbuda; Bahamas; Barbados; Cayman Islands; Dominica; Guadeloupe; Jamaica; Martinique; Montserrat; Netherlands Antilles (Aruba, Bonaire, Curacao, Saba, St. Maarten, and St. Eustatius); Redonda; St Christopher (St. Kitts) and Nevis; St. Lucia; St. Martin; St. Vincent; Turks and Caicos Islands; Virgin Islands (U.K. and U.S.).

SOUTH: Uruguay.*

ASIA: Bahrain; Brunei Darussalam; Japan; Kuwait; Malaysia (Malaysia-Sabah*); Maldives*; Oman*; Singapore; Taiwan.

EUROPE: Bulgaria*; Cyprus; Faroe Islands; Gibraltar; Iceland; Ireland; Malta; Norway (mainland); Portugal*; Sweden; United Kingdom.

OCEANIA: America Samoa; Australia; Belau (Palau); Cook Islands;
            Federated States of Micronesia (Kosrae, Ponape, Truk, and
            Yap); Fiji; French Polynesia; Guam; Kiribati; New Caledonia;
            New Zealand; Niue; Northern Mariana Islands; Papua New
            Guinea; Samoa; Solomon Islands; Tonga; Vanuatu.

*Countries that have only recently reported no cases of rabies; these
classifications should be considered provisional.

#Source: Centers for Disease Control, Center for Prevention Services,
Division of Quarantine (E-03); Health Information for Travelers (1989)

Most of Pacific Oceania is "rabies-free." For information on
specific islands not listed above, contact the Centers for Disease
Control, Division of Quarantine. The CDC main switchboard
number for weekday use is (404) 639–3311.

Persons having to work with potentially rabid animal populations can be immunized with the human diploid cell vaccine
(HDCV) or with rabies vaccine adsorbed (RVA) with 1 ml given
intramuscular (IM) in the deltoid area of the shoulder on days 0, 7,
and 21 or 28, and with 1 ml of HDCV given every two years as a
booster shot.

Only the HDCV may be given with an alternate intradermal
dose of 0.1 ml on days 0, 7, and 21 or 28. This three dose series
must be completed 30 or more days prior to departure. If this is
not possible, the IM dose/route should be used. RVA may not be
given via the intradermal route.

Chloroquine (the anti-malaria drug) blocks effective immune
response to rabies immunization with HDCV, so its concurrent use
during the immunization period should be avoided. If it must be
taken, then the *intramuscular dosage of HDCV* must be used in the
deltoid area of the shoulder.

The treatment for rabies exposure in the person not previously immunized is with Rabies Immune Globulin (RIG) 20 IU/kg
with half infiltrated around the wound and the remaining half in
the gluteal area (upper outer quadrant of the bottom) and human
diploid cell vaccine (HDCV) or rabies vaccine adsorbed (RVA) 1
ml given IM in the shoulder on days 0, 3, 7, 14, and 28.

If the person has been previously immunized as indicated above, then a post-exposure treatment conists of two doses of HDCV or RVA given 1.0 ml in the deltoid muscle of the shoulder on days 0 and 3. RIG should not be administered.

Chapter 6.41

Relapsing Fever

This bacterial infection is caused by several species of *Borrelia* spirochete and is spread by body lice in Asia, Africa and Europe, or by soft body ticks in the Americas (including the western United States), Asia, Africa and Europe.

Symptoms occur 3 to 11 days from contact with the tick or louse vector and start with an abrupt onset of chills, headache, muscular pains and sometimes vomiting. A rash may appear and small hemorrhages present under the skin surface. The fever remains high from 3 to 5 days, then clears suddenly. After 1 to 2 weeks a somewhat milder relapse begins. Jaundice is more common during relapse. The illness again clears, but 2 to 10 similar episodes reoccur at intervals of 1 to 2 weeks until immunity fully develops.

Antibiotic is available for effective treatment. Mortality is low. Personal hygiene is effective in preventing louse borne disease, while control of ticks with insect repellent and frequent body checks and tick removal minimize the chance of tick borne disease.

Chapter 6.42

Rift Valley Fever

This disease is a viral illness, found in East Africa and Egypt, transmitted to humans by bites from infected mosquitos or by contaminated wounds or breathing aerosols of contaiminated blood or fluid of infected animals.

Symptoms are similar to other arbovirus illness, such as dengue fever. The illness is usually brief and victims recover without after effects.

Chapter 6.43

Rocky Mountain Spotted Fever

This is an acute and serious infection caused by a microorganism called *Rickettsia rickettsii* and transmitted by *Ixodid* (hard-shelled) ticks. It is most common in the states of North Carolina, Virginia, Maryland, the Rocky Mountain States, and the state of Washington. It is also located in other countries of Central and South America. The peak incidence of cases is during late spring and summer.

Onset of infection is abrupt, after a 3 to 12-day incubation period (average 7 days from the tick bite). Fever reaches 103 to 104 F (40 C) within two days. There is considerable headache, chills, and muscle pain at the onset. In four days a rash appears on wrists, ankles, soles, palms, and then spreads to the trunk. Initially pink, this rash turns to dark blotches and even ulcers in severe cases.

Any suspected case of Rocky Mountain Spotted Fever should be considered a MEDICAL EMERGENCY. Antibiotic therapy is urgent and reduces mortality from 20% to nearly zero.

Prevention is by the careful removal of ticks, the use of insect repellent and protective clothing.

Chapter 6.44

Sandfly Fever

This viral disease, also known as Phlebotomus fever, is spread by bites of infected sandflies, which generally bite at night. The disease is found in hot, dry regions of Europe, Africa, Asia, Central and South America.

Symptoms appear 3 to 6 days after exposure and consist of headache, fever, weakness, and nausea. Pains in the back, arms and legs are characteristic. The symptoms are significant, but this disease is self limited and does not result in death.

There is no specific therapy. Protection from sandfly bites is preventative.

Chapter 6.45

Schistosomiasis

Also called Bilharziasis and Safari Fever, blood trematodes or flukes are responsible for this disease. The eggs are deposited in fresh water and hatch into motile miracidia which infect snails.

After development in the snails, active cercariae emerge which penetrate exposed human skin. Swimming, wading, or drinking fresh water must be avoided in infected areas.

Schistosoma mansoni is found in tropical Africa, part of Venezuela, several Caribbean islands, the Guianas, Brazil and the Middle East. *S. japonicum* is encountered in China, Japan, the Philippines, and Southeast Asia. *S. haematobium* is in Africa, the Middle East, and small portions of India and islands in the Indian Ocean. The former two species are excreted in the stools and the latter in urine. Shedding may occur for years. No isolation is required of patients.

Initial penetration of the skin causes an itchy rash. After entry, the organism enters the blood stream, migrates through the lungs, and eventually lodges in the blood vessels draining either the intestines or the bladder, depending upon the species. While the worms are maturing the victim will have fever, lethargy, cough, rash, abdominal pain, and frequently nausea. In acute infections caused by *S. mansoni* and *S. japonicum,* victims develop a mucoid, bloody diarrhea and tender liver enlargement. Chronic infection leads to fibrosis of the liver with distention of the abdomen. In *S. haematobium* infections, the bladder becomes inflamed and eventually fibrotic. Symptoms include painful urination, urgency, blood in urine, and pelvic pain.

Specific treatments for the various species are available. Each country information database listing in this book indicates areas of known infection at the time of publication. Check for current information on dangerous areas by contacting Herchmer Medical Group for specific country database updates (see Section 8).

Chapter 6.46

Scromboid Poisoning

The flesh of dark meat fish, such as tuna, mackerel, albacore, bonito, amberjack and mahi-mahi (dolphin) contain large amounts of histadine. Improper storage after catching these fish allows bacterial enzymatic changes of this meat releasing large amounts of histamine and other toxic by-products which are not destroyed by cooking.

Symptoms of scromboid poisoning include flushing, dizziness, headache, burning of the mouth and throat, nausea, vomiting, and diarrhea. Severe poisoning can cause significant respiratory distress.

Benadryl has been reported to cause an increase in symptoms at times which is surprising since it is an excellent anti-histamine. Tagamet has been shown to block the effects of scromboid poisoning. While normally a prescription product used to control stomach acid formation, its mode of action is known as an H-2 histamine blocker. Other similar compounds in this class will have to be tested (Zantac, Pepcid, Axid), but if they are available they might be tried in an emergency.

Chapter 6.47

Sexually Transmitted Diseases

The sexual spread of disease has become a front page event due to the emergence of the AIDS virus. Other serious diseases are also commonly spread by sexual intercourse. Hepatitis B can be found in high incidence amongst many populations of the world. This disease, like AIDS, can be spread via blood and blood product transfusions, by sexual intercourse, and less commonly by ingestion of tainted food products or water. Also similar to AIDS, this disease can be carried by people who have no symptoms, it is not treatable by any antibiotic, and it places the victim at risk for future medical complications including severe illness and death.

Persons traveling tend to be on holiday and this may lead to relaxed morals and contact with persons whose occupation it is to prey on the unwary. A doubly dangerous combination with high risk. The various venereal diseases are totally preventable by abstention, any other technique falls short of being foolproof. Most venereal infections cause symptoms in the male, but frequently do not in the female. Either gender may note increased discomfort with urination, the development of sores or unusual growths around the genitalia, and discharge from the portions of the anatomy used in sex (pharynx, penis, vagina, anus). Some venereal diseases can be very difficult to detect, such as syphilis, hepatitis B, hepatitis C, and AIDS. There is no vaccine protection available against any of the venereal diseases, except hepatitis B.

Gonorrhea is common and easy to detect in the male. The appearance of symptoms is 2 to 8 days from time of contact and basically consists of a copious greenish-yellow discharge. The female will frequently not have symptoms. It is treatable with several antibiotics, but highly resistant strains are emerging. Untreated this disease can cause pelvic infections in the woman and urethral obstructions and deeper infections of the prostate, spermatic cord, and testes in the male.

Syphilis has an incubation period of 2 to 6 weeks before the characteristic sore appears. The development of a painless ulcer (1.4 to $^1/_2$ inch in size), generally with enlarged, non-tender lymph nodes in the region, is a hallmark of this disease. A painful ulcer formation is more characteristic of herpes simplex. The lesion may not appear in a syphilis victim, making the early detection of this disease very difficult. A second stage consisting of a generalized skin rash (generally which does not itch, does not produce blisters, and which frequently appears on the soles of the feet and palms of the hands) appears about 6 weeks after the lesions mentioned above. The third phase of the disease may develop in several years, during which nearly any organ system in the body may be affected. The overall study of syphilis is so complicated that Sir William Osler, a great medical instructor, once said, "To know syphilis is to know medicine." Treatment of syphilis is with antibiotics.

The development of a clear, scanty discharge in the male may be due to chlamydia or other nonspecific urethral infections. Symptoms appear 7 to 28 days after contact. Antibiotic treatment should be started immediately. Women may have no symptoms. Blood tests for syphilis should be performed before treatment and again in 3 months. 20% of victims with nonspecific urethritis will have a relapse, therefore adequate medical follow-up after the trip is essential.

Upon return home, trip members who may have experienced a sexual disease should be seen by their physician for serology tests for syphilis, hepatitis B tests, chlamydial smears, gonorrheal cultures, herpes simplex titers, and possibly HIV studies for AIDS. Lesions or growths should be examined, as molluscum contagiosum and venereal warts should be treated.

Chapter 6.48

Smallpox

The last case of smallpox in the world occurred in Somalia in 1977, although a laboratory accident caused a case in the United Kingdom in 1978. The World Health Organization proclaimed the disease eradicated from the world in 1980. No country in the world requires smallpox vaccination for international travel at this time. There is no vaccine available for civilian use in the United States.

Chapter 6.49

Tapeworms

Three species of tapeworms infect humans, *Taenia saginata* larvae found in beef, *Taenia solium* in pork, and *Diphyllobothrium latum* in fish. In all three the human ingests under-cooked flesh of the host animal, acquiring the infective cysts.

The beef tapeworm can be huge, forming lengths of 10 to 30 feet inside the human host. It is common in Mexico, South America, Eastern Europe, the Middle East, and Africa. Symptoms can include stomach pain, weight loss, and diarrhea, but frequently the human host has no clue of the infestation.

The pork tapeworm infests South America, Eastern Europe, Russia and Asia. Generally without symptoms, at times vague abdominal complaints are noted. A complication of this disease is cystocercosis. In this condition the tapeworm larvae penetrate the human intestinal wall and invade body tissues, frequently skeletal muscle and the brain. There they mature into cystic masses. After several years the cysts degenerate and produce local inflammatory reactions that can then cause convulsions, visual problems, or mental disturbances.

Fish tapeworm occurs world-wide, but is particularly a hazard in Scandinavia and the Far East. A single tapeworm, usually without symptoms, results. The worm's absorption of Vitamin B-12 may cause the development of pernicious anemia in the host.

Persons who may have been exposed to tapeworm infection should indicate this to their physician during their post-trip medical evaluation. Specific tests for diagnosis and treatments are available.

Chapter 6.50

Tetanus

Caused by a bacterium, *Clostridium tetani,* that is located world-wide, most cases occur from very minor wounds, such as blisters or even paper cuts, rather than rusty barbed wire as so many people seem to think.

Onset is gradual, with an incubation period of 2 to 50 (usually 5 to 10) days. The earliest symptom is stiffness of the jaw, with subsequent symptoms developing that include sore throat, stiff muscles, headache, low grade fever, and muscle spasm. As the disease progresses, the patient is unable to open his jaw and the facial muscles may be fixed in a smile with elevated eyebrows. Painful generalized spasms of muscles occur with minor disturbances such as drafts, noise, or someone jarring their bed. Death from loss of respiratory muscle function, or even unknown causes, may ensue. The disease is frequently fatal.

Prevention is obtained by adequate immunization. The primary series is obtained during infancy, with boosters every 10 years. Unimmunized adults would require 3 doses of vaccine given at 0, 1 month, and 6 months. Tetanus toxin should be combined with diphtheria toxin to simultaneously provide adequate immunity against that disease.

The recommended immunization schedule for infants is indicated in Chapter 4.3.

While routine immunization boosters of tetanus are required only every ten years, wounds which are considered as "dirty," such as puncture wounds, crush injuries, and bites, should receive a tetanus toxoid booster within five years, as per Table 6–6.

To avoid the necessity of receiving a booster immunization of the tetanus and diphtheria toxoid while overseas, the traveler may wish to have a tetanus booster prior to the trip, so that it will not be older than 5 years by the return date. This modifies the CDC recommended immunization schedule, but precludes a situation where the last immunization being 6 to 10 years old, a dirty wound being acquired, and the victim suddenly finding himself in the situation where it is recommended that he obtain an immediate booster of tetanus and diphtheria toxoid.

TABLE 6–6
Tetanus Prophylaxis in Routine Wound Management

History of Adsorbed Tetanus Toxoid Doses	Clean, Minor Wounds		All Other Wounds	
	Td	TIG	Td	TIG
Unkown or <3	Yes	No	Yes	Yes
Three or more(a)	No(b)	No	No(c)	No

Td   = combined tetanus and diphtheria toxoids adsorbed.
TIG = tetanus immune globulin.
(a)   = If only 3 doses of fluid toxoid have been received, a fourth dose of toxoid, preferably an absorbed toxoid, should be given.
(b)   = Yes, if more than 10 years since the last dose.
(c)   = Yes, if more than 5 years since the last dose. More frequent boosters are not needed and can accentuate side effects.

All other wounds include those contaminated with dirt, feces, soil, saliva; puncture wounds; avulsions; and wounds resulting from missles, crushing, burns, and frostbite.

For persons 7 years of age and older, combined tetanus and diphtheria toxoid adsorbed is preferred to tetanus toxoid alone.

REF: Centers for Disease Control. Diphtheria, tetanus and pertussis: guidelines for vaccine prophylaxis and other preventive measures. MMWR. 1985; 34:405–14, 419–26.

American College of Physicians. Guide for adult immunization, 2nd ed. 1990; 37–38.

Chapter 6.51

Trachoma

This infectious disease due to the intracellular parasite *Chlamydia trachomatis* is a leading cause of blindness in underdeveloped countries. It is prevalent in Mediterranean countries and in the Far East. It is spread by direct contact, by the use of dirty towels or wash cloths, and by flies.

The early symptoms are eye irritation, redness, and discharge. The traveler should be spared from this eye infection by good hygienic practices.

The disease is treatable with topical antibiotic ointments and oral antibiotics.

Chapter 6.52

Trichinosis

Human infection is caught by eating improperly cooked meat infected with the cysts of the parasitic roundworm *Trichinella spiralis*. Risk is world-wide. It is most common in pigs, bears (particularly polar bears) and some marine mammals.

Nausea and diarrhea or intestinal cramping may appear within 1 to 2 days, but it generally takes 7 days after indigestion. Swelling of the eyelids is very characteristic on the 11th day. Afterwards, muscle soreness, fever, pain in the eyes and hemorrhages in the whites of the eye frequently develop. If enough contaminated food is ingested, this disease can be fatal. Most symptoms disappear in 3 months.

Specific medical treatment is available. The best prevention is cooking suspected flesh at 150° F (66° C) for 30 minutes for each pound of meat.

Chapter 6.53

Trypanosomiasis, African

African Trypanosomiasis is also called African sleeping sickness. Two species of trypanosomes (protozoan hemoflagellates) cause this disease which is transmitted by the bite of the tsetse fly. The severity of the disease depends upon the species encountered.

The infection is confined to the area of Africa between 15 degrees north and 20 degrees south of the equator—the exact distribution of the tsetse fly. Man is the only reservoir of *Trypanosoma gambiense* found in West and Central Africa, while wild game is the principle reservoir of *T. rhodesiense* of East Africa.

T. gambiense infection starts with a nodule or a chancre that appears briefly at the site of a tsetse fly bite. Generalized illness appears months to years later and is characterized by lymph node enlargement at the back of the neck and intermittent fever. Months to years after this development invasion of the central nervous system may occur, noted by behavioral changes, headache, loss of appetite, back ache, hallucinations, delusions, and sleeping. In *T. rhodesiense* infection the generalized illness begins 5 to 14 days after the nodule or chancre develops. It is much more intense than the gambian variety and may include acute central nervous system and cardiac symptoms, fever, and rapid weight loss. It has a high rate of mortality. If untreated, death usually occurs within one year.

Chapter 6.54

Trypanosomiasis, American

Also known as Chaga's disease, this affliction is caused by *Trypanosoma cruzi*, a protozoan hemoflagellate, which is transmitted through the feces of a brown insect called the "kissing bug" or "assassin bug" in North American. This bug is a member of the *Reduviidae* family. A name popular in South America is "vinchuca" derived from a word which means "one who lets himself fall down." These bugs live in palm trees, thatching in native huts, and like to drop on their victims while sleeping, frequently biting them on the face or exposed arms. Bitten patients rub the feces into the bite site, thus causing the inoculation of the infectious agent. This disease is located in parts of South and Central America where it is a leading cause of death, generally due to heart failure. As many as 15 million people in South America may be infected. The individual country database in this book indicates specific areas of risk.

At first this disease may have no symptoms. A "chagoma" or red nodule develops at the site of the original infection. This area may then lose its pigmentation. After 1 to 2 weeks, a firm swelling of one eyelid occurs, known as Ramoana's sign. The swelling becomes purplish in color, lymph node swelling in front of the ear on the same side may occur. In a few days a fever develops, with generalized lymph node swelling. Rapid heart rate, spleen and liver enlargement, swelling of the legs, and meningitis or encephalitis may occur. Serious conditions also can include acute heart failure. In most cases, however, the illness subsides in about 3 months and the patient appears to be living a normal life. The disease continues, however, slowly destroying the heart until 10 to 20 years later when chronic congestive heart failure becomes apparent. The underlying cause may never be known, especially in a traveler who has left the endemic area. In some areas of Brazil, the disease attacks the colon, causing flaccid enlargement with profound constipation.

A diagnostic blood test is available through State Boards of Health and Centers for Disease Control. Supportive treatment is given during acute disease and specific treatments are being developed.

Chapter 6.55

Tuberculosis

This infection is caused by one of two bacteria, *Mycobacterium tuberculosis* or *M. bovis*. It results in a very chronic illness that can reactivate many years after it has been apparently killed. In the United States there are 20,000 new cases, with 1,800 deaths, yearly. World-wide there are 8 to 10 million new cases, with 2 to 3 million deaths yearly. This disease is spread primarily by inhalation of infected droplets. The disease also spreads by drinking infected milk or dairy products such as butter.

Active disease usually develops within a year of contact. The early symptoms of fever, night sweats, lethargy, and weight loss can be so gradual that they are initially ignored. Tuberculosis usually infects the lungs, but can spread throughout the body causing neurological damage and overwhelming infection. Diagnosis is usually made with a chest x-ray which has characteristic findings.

A traveler heading to an area with epidemic tuberculosis should have a pre- and post-trip TB skin test. A negative TB skin test does not exclude a diagnosis of TB, but the Mantoux intradermal test can be a very useful aid in evaluating the chance that a traveler has contracted tuberculosis.

Specific antibiotic therapy is available.

Chapter 6.56

Tularemia

Also known as rabbit fever or deer fly fever, this bacterial disease, caused by *Francisella tularensis,* is located in Europe, Russia, Japan, and the United States. It can be contracted through exposure to ticks, deer flies, or mosquitos. It is also possible to have cuts infected when working with the pelts, or eating improperly cooked, infected rabbits. Similarly, muskrats, foxes, squirrels, mice and rats can spread the disease via direct contact with the carcasses. Stream water may become contaminated by these animals.

After an incubation period of 1 to 10 days (average 2 to 4), an ulcer appears when a wound is involved and lymph nodes become enlarged first in nearby areas and then throughout the body. Symptoms start abruptly with fever, chills, headache, and nausea. Pneumonia normally develops. The disease lasts 4 weeks in untreated cases.

Antibiotic treatment is available. Mortality in treated cases is almost zero, while in untreated cases it ranges from 6% to 30%.

Chapter 6.57

Tungiasis

This skin condition can be contracted in Africa, the West Indies, and South America. It is caused by a burrowing flea, *Tunga penetrans,* usually called a chigoe or jigger. This is not the same creature as the chigger so familiar to outdoorsmen in the United States.

The flea burrows under the skin where she is able to suck blood and eventually expel eggs. A localized, nodular rash containing live fleas develops. Skin ulcers, gangrene and blood poisoning may result, even proving fatal in some cases.

These fleas may be removed from lesions with tweezers after applying alcohol. Antibiotic creams can soothe and protect these wounds, but avoid excessive warmth which can aggravate the condition. Avoidance is through flea control by disinfecting clothing, furniture, bed clothes, and the use of insect repellents when needed.

Chapter 6.58

Typhoid Fever

Caused by a bacterium, *Salmonella typhi,* this disease is spread by the fecal-oral route since the germs are shed in the urine and feces of infected persons. In developed countries the disease is usually spread by food contaminated by poor hygiene of food servers, who are carriers of this disease. There are approximately 400 cases of typhoid fever in this country yearly, with half in returning international travelers.

This disease is characterized by headache, chills, loss of appetite, back ache, constipation, nosebleed, and tenderness of the abdomen to touch. The temperature rises daily for 7 to 10 days. The fever is maintained at a high level for 7 to 19 more days, then drops over the next 10 days. The pulse rate is low for the amount of fever (generally, the pulse rate will increase 10 beats per minute for every one degree of temperature elevation over normal for that individual.) With typhoid fever, a pulse rate of only 84 may occur with a temperature of 104° F (40° C). Between the 7th and 10th day of illness, rose-colored splotches—which blanche when pressure is applied—appear in 10% of patients. Treatment is with antibiotic and replacement of fluids.

Prevention is via proper food handling and water purification. Immunization against typhoid fever is an important aid and is recommended if traveling to many developing countries (see individual country immunization recommendations starting on page 8–1). The vaccine is from 70% to 90% effective in preventing the disease and also decreases the severity of the disease. Immunization consists of two 0.5 ml doses given 1 month apart, with a booster dose every 3 years. In 1990 a new oral vaccine will become available for use in the United States.

Chapter 6.59

Endemic Typhus, Flea-Borne

This disease is also known as murine typhus, rat-flea typhus, New World typhus, Malaya typhus, and urban typhus. This is one of several diseases caused by rickettsia, which resemble both virus and bacteria. Other diseases caused by this order are Rocky Mountain spotted fever, Q-fever, trench fever, and the various typhus diseases listed in the next two sections. Endemic typhus is due to *Rickettsia typhi*. It is located world-wide, including the southern Atlantic and Gulf coast states of the US. It is spread to humans through infected rat flea feces.

After an incubation period of 6 to 18 days (mean 10), shaking chills, fever, and headache develops. A rash forms primarily on the trunk, but fades fairly rapidly. The fever lasts about 12 days. This is a mild disease and fatalities are rare.

Antibiotic treatment is very effective. Prevention is directed toward vector (rat and flea) control.

Chapter 6.60

Epidemic Typhus, Louse-Borne

This malady is also called classic typhus, European typhus, and jail fever. This disease killed 3 million people during World War II. On the positive side, no American traveler has contracted this disease since 1950. It is most likely to be encountered in mountainous regions of Mexico, Central and South America, the Balkans, eastern Europe, Africa, and many countries of Asia. The causative agent is *Rickettsia prowazekii,* which is transmitted by infected lice.

Following a 7 to 14 day incubation period, there is a sudden onset of high fever (104° F, 40° C) which remains at a high level, with a usual morning decrease, for about 2 weeks. There is an intense headache. A light pink rash appears on the 4th to 6th day, soon becoming dark red. There is low blood pressure, pneumonia, mental confusion, and bruising in severe cases.

Mortality is rare in children less than 10 years of age, but may reach greater than 60% in those over 50. Antibiotics are available and are very effective if given early in the disease. Prevention is proper hygiene and delousing when needed. A vaccine was formerly made in the United States, but is no longer available and is not needed due to the low incidence observed in American travelers.

Chapter 6.61

Scrub Typhus

Also called mite-borne typhus, tropical typhus, and tsutsuga-mushi disease, scrub typhus is located in Southeast Asia, the western Pacific (including India and Japan) and Australia. The causative agent in *Rickettsia tsutsugamushi*. This disease is spread by mites which feed upon forest and rural rodents. The mite larva (chigger) is deposited upon vegetation where is comes into contact with humans, biting and thus infecting them.

After an incubation period of 6 to 21 days (average 10 to 12), a sudden onset of fever, headache, cough, and lymph node enlargement occurs. When the fever starts a local lesion develops at the original bite site. It eventually forms a black scab. Fever continues to rise over the next week to 104° or 105° F (40° C). A rash develops on the trunk during the 5th to 8th day of fever, often extending to the legs and arms. Pneumonia develops during the second week. In severe cases the blood pressure drops, muscle twitching can start, and the victim becomes delirious.

Death can occur, but prompt antibiotic therapy can promote rapid recovery.

Chapter 6.62

West Nile Fever

This viral disease of birds is transmitted to humans by mosquito bites. Distribution is wide spread and includes the Middle East, India, southern France, parts of the USSR, Africa, and the northern Mediterranean area.

The symptoms include fever, malaise, muscle ache, and joint ache. A rash usually develops. The illness is short term with complete recovery as a rule.

No specific therapy is available.

Chapter 6.63

Yellow Fever

An arbovirus, this disease is found in tropical areas of South and Central America and Africa. This viral disease is contracted by the bite of the *Aedes aegypti* mosquito (among others).

There is a 2 week incubation period. Onset is sudden with a fever of 102° to 104° F (38.8° to 40° C). The pulse is usually rapid the first day, but becomes slow by the second day. In mild cases the fever falls by crises 2 to 5 days after onset. This remission lasts for hours to several days. Next the fever returns, but the pulse remains slow. Jaundice, vomiting of black blood, and severe loss of protein in the urine (causing it to become foamy) occurs during this stage. Hemorrhages may be noted in the mouth and skin (petechiae). The patient is confused and senses are dulled. Delirium, convulsions and coma occur at death in approximately 10% of cases. If the patient is to survive, this last febrile episode lasts from 3 to 9 days. With remission the patient is well, with no after effects from the disease.

Immunization consists of one 1 ml injection of yellow fever vaccine. This injection is valid for ten years. It should be noted that the yellow fever immunization does not become valid until 10 days after administration. Your International Certificate of Vaccination must be validated and stamped with an official "Uniform Stamp." The administration of other live virus vaccines (such as oral polio vaccine, measles, mumps, or rubella) should either be given simultaneously or three weeks apart to prevent a decrease in antibody response. The simultaneous administration of gamma globulin (for hepatitis A prevention) does not interfere with yellow fever antibody response.

The use of yellow fever vaccine is generally contra-indicated in infants younger than 6 months due to a high incidence of encephalitis in reaction to the vaccine. It is strongly recommended by the Centers for Disease Control that children younger than 9 months not be immunized for the same reason, although some countries require immunization in this young age group. The CDC recommends the following guidelines when considering yellow fever immunization in a child under 9 months of age:

Infants 6 to 9 months: These children should only be vaccinated if the child will be traveling in an area of currently active yellow fever when the travel cannot be postponed and a high level of protection against possible mosquito bites is not possible.

Infants 4 to 6 months: Vaccination in this age group should only be contemplated in unusual circumstances and in consultation with the CDC.

Infants younger than 4 months: These children should not be vaccinated under any circumstances.

To avoid a yellow fever vaccination in the above age groups, obtain a letter from your physician, written on his stationary, as well as a comment from your physician written into the infant's international certificate of immunization, stating that the yellow fever vaccination is contra-indicated due to medical reasons. You should check with the embassy of the country you will be visiting to ensure that they will accept this medical exemption.

It is also best to avoid this vaccination if you are pregnant, unless travel to high risk areas is unavoidable. If the travel itinerary of the pregnant woman does not indicate a substantial risk, efforts should be made to obtain a waiver letter from the consulting physician. However, those who must travel to areas of high risk should be vaccinated. The small theoretical risk for mother and fetus, under this circumstance, is far outweighed by the risk of yellow fever infection.

Persons with decreased immunity (to include those being treated with certain steroids, chemotherapy, radiation) and those with leukemia, lymphoma, generalized cancer, or AIDS must consider the risk versus benefit of receiving the yellow fever vaccine.

Persons with asymptomatic HIV infections, who cannot avoid potential exposure to the yellow fever virus, should be immunized. The patient should be monitored for possible adverse effects of the vaccine. In the HIV patient, it may be desirable to measure the neutralizing antibody response following vaccination prior to travel. The physician will wish to contact his State Board of Health (Chapter 2.4) or the Centers for Disease Control, Fort Collins, Colorado at (303) 221–6400, for information on performing this test.

Persons with egg allergy might have a reaction. A skin test with the vaccine may be performed prior to receiving the normal vaccine dose to indicate if this problem may be severe enough to warrant avoiding this immunization.

Immunization with yellow fever vaccine is *required* for travel to many countries. FAILURE TO RECEIVE THE VACCINE MAY RESULT IN VACCINATION, DENIAL OF ENTRY, MEDICAL FOLLOW-UP AND/OR QUARANTINE. As some countries with this requirement are developing countries, many with significant AIDS activity, you will probably wish to avoid receiving a vaccination in their country. Should this be demanded, insist on purchasing your own packaged needle and syringe and the use of a previously unopened bottle of vaccine. You may require the help of embassy officials in this matter.

The countries listed in Table 6–7 all require that the traveler receive a yellow fever vaccination when traveling directly from the United States to their country.

Recent visitation to a country with active disease, or to a country in the endemic zone for the disease, can result in a mandatory requirement for yellow fever immunization prior to entry into the new host country. The countries with currently active disease are listed in Table 6–8.

The World Health Organization formerly established a list of countries universally recognized as being in a yellow fever endemic zone—countries that have had the disease and where conditions are such that the disease might appear in the future. Although there may not be active yellow fever in a country on this list, you may find that having visited such a country, you will be required by another country on your itinerary to have a valid yellow fever certificate. Follow these requirements carefully. Failure to do so could lead to denial of your entry into a country, or require that you be immunized or detained prior to entry.

TABLE 6–7
Yellow Fever Vaccination Certificate Required
for Direct Travel from the United States

Benin	Liberia
Burkina Faso	Mali
Cameroon	Mauritania (for stay of > 2 weeks)
Central African	Niger
Republic	Rwanda
Congo	Sao Tome and Principe (for stay of
Cote d'Ivoire	> 2 weeks)
French Guiana	Senegal
Gabon	Togo
Ghana	

TABLE 6–8
Countries with Currently Active Yellow Fever Reported
as of 4/2/90

Angola	Guinea
Bolivia	Mali
Brazil	Nigeria
Colombia	Peru
Gambia	Sudan
Ghana	Zaire

TABLE 6–9
Yellow Fever Endemic Zones

AFRICA: Angola, Benin, Botswana, Burkina Faso, Burundi, Cameroon,
Central African Republic, Cape Verde, Chad, Congo, Djibouti,
Equatorial Guinea, Ethiopia, Gabon, Gambia, Guinea, Guinea-Bissau,
Ivory Coast, Kenya, Liberia, Malawi, Mali, Mauritania, Niger, Nigeria,
Rwanda, Sao Tome and Principe, Senegal, Sierra Leone, Somalia,
Sudan (south of 15 deg. N.), Tanzania, Togo, Uganda, Zaire, Zambia
AMERICAS: Belize, Bolivia, Brazil, Canal Zone, Colombia, Costa Rica,
Ecuador, French Guiana, Guatemala, Guyana, Honduras, Nicaragua,
Panama, Peru, Surinam, Venezuela
CARIBBEAN: Trinidad and Tobago

Check for information on active disease areas, and countries
requiring yellow fever immunization, by referring to the appropriate entry in the country information database in this book starting
on page 8–1. CAUTION: Requirements can change at a moment's
notice. Contact Herchmer Medical Group for a current specific
country update (Chapter 2.8).

Section 7
The Travelers' Self Care Manual

How to personally take care of the medical problems which you might encounter.

Regardless of our attempts to find qualified local medical help, there will be times when it will not be available. Whether by necessity or design, many travelers will feel much more secure if they are capable of resolving medical problems on their own without depending upon local assistance.

As the parent book, The Travelers' Medical Resource, *is simply too large to carry while actually traveling, this book within a book has been printed to allow its removal or to facilitate photocopying it for use as a ready reference. This section of the book,* The Travelers' Self Care Manual, *has been bound separately and is available from the publisher, ICS Books[1]*

More extensive information on self care can be found in my book Wilderness Medicine, 3rd Edition, *also published by ICS Books,[2] and in the additional books listed in Chapter 1.3.*

[1]*The Travelers' Self Care Manual* is available from ICS Books, Inc., 107 East 89th Avenue, Merrillville, IN 46410, Telephone (800) 541-7323 for $6.95 plus $1.50 handling.

[2]*Wilderness Medicine, 3rd Edition* is available from ICS Books, Inc., 107 East 89th Avenue, Merrillville, IN 46410, telephone (800) 541-7323 for $7.95 plus $1.50 handling.

Chapter 7.1

Trauma

WOUND CARE

The most common minor injuries while traveling will be sun burn, friction blisters, and twisted ankles and knees. Although the first two are certainly preventable, they will never-the-less still occur to even the most experienced traveler.

Friction Blisters

A relatively new and easily obtainable substance has revolutionized the prevention and care of friction blisters. The substance is Spenco 2nd Skin, available at most athletic supply and drug stores. Made from an inert, breathable gel consisting of 4% polyethylene oxide and 96% water, it has the feel and consistency of cold jello. It comes in various sized sterile sheets, sealed in water-tight packages. It is very cool to the touch, in fact large sheets are sold to cover infants to reduce a fever. It has three valuable properties that make it so useful. One, it will remove all friction between two moving surfaces (hence its use in prevention) and two, it cleans and deodorizes wounds by absorbing blood, serum, or pus. Three, its cooling effect is very soothing, which aids in pain relief.

After opening the sealed package, you will find the Spenco 2nd Skin sandwiched between two sheets of cellophane. Remove the cellophane from the side which will be applied to the wound or hot spot. It must be secured to the wound and for that purpose the same company produces an adhesive knit bandage.

For treatment of a hot spot, remove the cellophane from one side and apply this gooey side against the wound, securing it with the knit bandaging. If a friction blister has developed, it will have to be lanced. Cleanse with soap or surgical scrub and open along an edge with a clean, thin blade. After expressing the fluid, apply a fully stripped piece of 2nd Skin. This is easiest done by removing the cellophane from one side, then apply it to the wound. Once on the skin surface, remove the cellophane from the top surface. Over this you will need to place the adhesive knit. The bandage must be kept moist with clean water. Applied through the adhesive knit, routine moistening will allow the same bandage to be used for days or until the wound is healed.

Thermal Burns

Sun burns have ruined more vacations than any other single injury. These burns are generally first degree (with red, painful skin) or second degree (with red, blistered, painful skin), and can even result in shock from fluid loss and pain. The victim will feel relief with cool compresses (or even soaked sheets), but care must be taken to avoid too much cooling or they may become hypothermic. Various ointments have been developed to help with first and second degree burns, such as topical anesthetics (which are usually formulations of dibucaine) and various antispetic combinations. Dibucaine can be sensitizing and might result in an allergic reaction or increased skin rash, but generally works quite well.

The Spenco 2nd Skin mentioned above also works quite well for burn treatment, but will seldom be available in sheets large enough to treat sun burn.

Pain medication should be provided. Early inflammation will respond to topical steroids, but the major effort should be to provide pain relief and moisturizing creams. Aloe vera ointment also works quite well in treating minor, first degree burns.

Thermal burns can also be first and second degree, but may also result in charred tissue, or third degree burns. As soon as possible remove the source of the burn—quick immersion into cool water will help eliminate additional heat from scalding water or burning fuels and clothing. Or otherwise suffocate the flames with clothing, sand, etc.

The field treatment of burns has also been revolutionized by the development of Spenco 2nd Skin. It is the perfect substance to use on 1st, 2nd, or 3rd degree burns. Its cooling effect relieves pain, while its sterile covering absorbs fluid easily from the wound. If applied to a charred 3rd degree burn, it provides a sterile cover that does not have to be changed. When the patient arrives at a hospital, it can easily be removed in a whirlpool bath.

Burn patients can generally be self managed

quite well if the wounds are not worse than 2nd degree and as long as they do not cover more than 15% of the body surface area of an adult (10% of a child). Burns more extensive than this, and burns which involve the face or include more than one joint of the hand, are best treated professionally. The first aid treatment will be as above, but additionally, treat for shock and try to find professional help.

Lacerations

Direct pressure is the best method of stopping bleeding—in fact pressure alone can stop bleeding from amputated limbs! When the accident first occurs, you may even need to use your bare hand to stem the flow of blood. This direct pressure may have to be applied 5, 10, even 30 minutes or longer. Apply it as long as it takes! With the blood stopped, even if only with your hand, and the victim on the ground in the shock treatment position, the actual emergency is over. The victim's life has been saved. And you have bought the time to gather together various items you need to perform the definitive job of caring for this wound. You have also treated for psychogenic shock—the shock of "fear". For obviously someone knows what to do: they have taken charge, they have stopped the bleeding, they are giving orders to gather materials together. This shock caused by fear is more of a problem than that caused by the loss of blood.

In the first aid management of this wound, the next step is simply bandaging and then transporting the victim to professional medical care. Further care of a wound takes the practitioner beyond the first aid phase. It is generally best to seek professional help for aggressive wound cleansing and closure technique. However, after thorough cleansing, most wounds can be closed with strips of tape, such as butterfly closures, or more sophisticated tape closures (Steri-Strips, Cover-Strips). A complete description of wound closure techniques can be found in *Wilderness Medicine.*

Abrasions

An abrasion is the loss of surface skin due to a scraping injury. The best treatment is cleansing with Hibiclens surgical scrub, application of triple antibiotic ointment, and the use of Spenco 2nd Skin with Adhesive Knit Bandage—all components of the Travel Medical Kit. This type of wound oozes profusely, but the above bandaging allows rapid healing, excellent protection, and considerable pain relief. Avoid the use of alcohol on these wounds as it tends to damage the tissue, to say nothing of causing excessive pain. Lacking first aid supplies, cleanse gently with mild detergent and protect from dirt, bugs, etc., the best that you can. Tetanus immunization should have been received within 10 years.

Puncture Wounds

Allow puncture wounds to bleed, thus hoping to effect an automatic irrigation of bacteria from the wound. If available apply suction with the Extractor (venom suction device) immediately and continue the vacuum for 20 to 30 minutes. The Extractor is recommended for inclusion in a Travel Medical Kit under certain circumstances as mentioned in that section. Cleanse the wound area with surgical scrub—or soapy water—and apply triple antibiotic ointment to the surrounding skin surface. Do not tape shut, but rather start warm compress applications for 20 minutes, every 2 hours for the next 2 days.

These soaks should be as warm as the patient can tolerate without danger of burning the skin. Larger pieces of cloth work best—such as undershirts—as they hold the heat longer. If sterile items are in short supply, they need not be used on this type of wound. Use clean clothes, or boil such items and allow to cool and dry before use. Tetanus immunization should be within 5 years for dirty injuries such as puncture wounds. Red coloration of the skin, extending more than 1/4th inch from the wound edge could indicate a wound infection. If this develops, start the patient on oral antibiotics such as the doxycycline 100 mg twice daily.

Shock Treatment

Injury care can be broken into chronological phases. The first phase consists of SAVING THE VICTIM'S LIFE—by stopping the bleeding and treating for shock. Even if the victim is not bleeding, you will want to treat for shock. Shock has many fancy medical definitions, but on the bottom line it amounts to an inadequate oxygenated blood supply getting to the head. Lay the patient down, elevate feet above the head, and provide protection from the environment—from both the ground and the atmosphere. Grab anything which you can find for this at first—use jackets, newspapers, pieces of cardboard, or whatever.

Patients with head injuries are best allowed to have slight head elevation, unless concern for a neck injury exists. It is essential to immobilize the patient with an injured neck to prevent spinal cord damage.

Wound Infection

The formation of slight red discoloration

around a wound edge is generally part of the healing process. However, an excessive spread of this red discoloration—say 1/4th of an inch beyond the wound margin—usually indicates that an infection is forming.

The best treatment is to allow this wound to gape open (remove tape closures, etc., if they have been applied). Apply warm, wet soaks for fifteen to twenty minutes every two hours to promote drainage and increase circulation in the area to aid the body in defending itself against the infection.

If antibiotics are available, this is the time to use them. From the recommended prescription medical kit use the doxycycline 100 mg, giving one tablet twice daily. Your physician may recommend an alternate antibiotic which should then be included in your medical kit, with the instructions he has given you also recorded in the instruction section provided at the end of this section.

Splinter Removal

Prepare the wound with Hibiclens surgical scrub, soapy water, or other cleansing solution that does not discolor the skin. Minute splinters are hard enough to see without discoloring the skin and disguising them even more. If the splinter is shallow, or the point buried, use a needle or thin knife blade to tease the tissue over the splinter to remove this top layer. The splinter can then be pried up or more easily grasped with the tweezers or splinter forceps.

It is best to be aggressive in removing this top layer of skin and obtaining a substantial bite on the splinter with the tweezers, rather than nibbling off the end while making futile attempts to remove it due to inadequate exposure. When using the splinter forceps, grasp the instrument between the

FIGURE 7- 1
Hold splinter forceps or
tweezer parallel to the skin
surface and grasp the splinter only after obtaing an adequate exposure by un-
roofing it adequately.

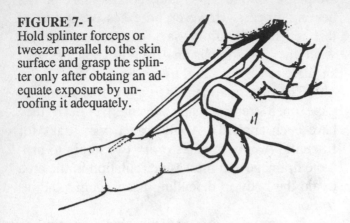

thumb and forefinger, resting the instrument on the
middle finger and further resting the entire hand
against the victim's skin, if necessary, to prevent
tremor. Approach the splinter from the side, if
exposed, grasping it as low as possible. Remove
it along the same direction as its entry path. Apply triple antibiotic afterwards.

Tetanus immunization should be current
within 10 years, or if a dirty wound, within 5
years. If the wound was dirty, scrub afterwards
with Hibiclens or soapy water. If deep, treat as
indicated above under PUNCTURE WOUND
with hot soaks and antibiotic as indicated.

Chapter 7.2

Eye, Ear, Nose, Mouth

No portion of our general well being affects us as much as our five senses, and four of them relate to proper function of the above organs.

Eye

Foreign bodies, abrasions, and infections (conjunctivitis) are the most frequently encountered eye problems. Therapy for these problems is virtually the same, except that it is very important to remove any foreign body that may be present.

Foreign Body

A calm, careful examination is necessary to adequately examine the eye for a foreign body.

Very carefully shine a small light at the cornea (the surface of the eye lying over the pupil and iris) from one side to see if a minute speck becomes visible. By moving the light back and forth, one might see movement of a shadow on the iris of the eye and thus confirm the presence of a foreign body. A shadow that consistently stays put with blinking is probably a foreign body.

In making the foreign body examination, also be sure to check under the eyelids. Evert the upper lid over a Q-tip stick, thus examining not only the eyeball, but also the under-surface of the eyelid. See figure 2. This surface may be gently brushed with the cotton applicator to eliminate minute particles. Always use a fresh Q-tip when touching the eye or eyelid each additional time.

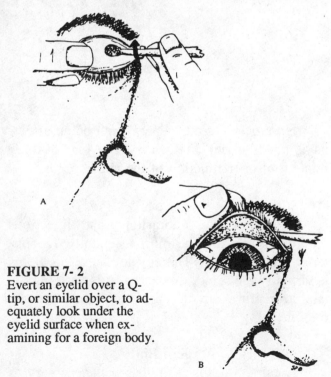

FIGURE 7- 2
Evert an eyelid over a Q-tip, or similar object, to adequately look under the eyelid surface when examining for a foreign body.

When a foreign body has been found, it can frequently be rinsed off with running water. One method is for the victim to hold their face under water and blink their eyes. Sometimes it can be easily prodded off with the edge of a clean cloth.

Leave stubborn foreign bodies for removal by a physician in all but the most desperate circumstances. The patient should be evacuated to a physician at once, if at all possible. If you are stuck without professional help and have a difficult time removing an obvious foreign body from the surface of the cornea, a wait of two to three days may allow the cornea to ulcerate slightly so that removal by gentle prodding with a Q-tip handle may be *much* easier. Deeply lodged foreign bodies will have to be left for surgical removal.

Patching the eye will help alleviate pain. Patch techniques for the eye must allow for gentle closure of the eyelid and retard blinking activity. Generally both eyes must be patched for this to succeed. Simple strips of tape holding the eyelids shut may suffice. In case of trauma, a ring of cloth may be constructed to pad the eye without pressure over the eyeball. A simple eye patch with over-size gauze or cloth may work fine, as the bone of the orbital rim around the eye acts to protect the eyeball which is recessed. Try to avoid patching both eyes, except at times when the patient is resting. If eye drops are available, they can provide some relief, but antibiotic drops are prescription medications. Seek professional help for any eye condition as soon as possible.

Eye Abrasion

Carefully examine the eye surface to insure that no foreign body is present. Check under the eyelids as indicated above. An abrasion on the eye will feel like a foreign body is present. Treat with soothing eye drops if available. Patch for comfort as indicated above.

Eye infection
An infection of the eye will be heralded by a scratchy feeling, almost indistinguishable from a foreign body in the eye. The sclera, or white of the eye, will be pink or red. Generally the eye will be matted shut in the morning with pus or granular matter.

Rinse with clean water frequently during the day. Eye infections such as bacterial conjunctivitis, the most common infection, are self limiting and will generally clear themselves within two weeks. They can become much worse, however, so medical attention should be sought. Do not patch, but protect the eyes from sunlight. When one eye is infected, treat both eyes as the infection spreads easily to the non-infected eye.

Eye infections should be treated with a prescription antibiotic such as Tobrex ophthalmic ointment. If nasal congestion is also present, treatment with a decongestant, such as Actifed, is quite appropriate.

Styes
Many persons form styes upon exposure to sun. This can be prevented by wearing sunglasses, wide brimmed hats, or other eye protection that prevents direct and reflected sun exposure to the eye lids.

Treatment is with warm compresses, antibiotic eye ointment. Frequently, oral antibiotics are prescribed for this condition.

Sun and Snow Blindness
This severely painful condition is primarily caused by ultraviolet B rays of the sun which are

considerably reflected by snow (85%), water (10–100%), and sand (17%). Thin cloud layers allow the transmission of this wavelength, while filtering out infra-red (heat) rays of the sun. Thus, it is possible on a rather cool, overcast day under bright snow conditions to become sunburned or snow blind.

Properly approved (ANSI) sunglasses will block 99.8% of the ultraviolet B wavelength. Suitable glasses should be tagged as meeting these standards[1]

In 1989 the Food and Drug Administration announced a new system of labeling sunglasses based on their effectiveness in removing both the short-wave UVB and the longer wave and more penetrating UVA. Sunglasses will be in three categories:

1. Cosmetic. They will block at least 70 percent of the UVB and 20 percent of the UVA radiation. Cosmetic sunglasses will be recommended for shopping or other "around town" activities away from harsh sunlight.
2. General Purpose. These will block from 60 percent to 92 percent of visible light and range in shade from medium to dark. They keep out at least 95 percent of UVB and at least 60 percent of UVA rays. These are recommended for a sunny environment and activities such as boating, driving, flying, or hiking.
3. Special Purpose. This model will block at least 97 percent of the visible light and at least 99 percent of UVB and 60 percent UVA radiation. They are recom-

[1]The American National Standards Institute, or ANSI, establishes specifications for many manufactured products.

mended for very bright environments such as tropical beaches or snowy ski slopes.

The fit of sunglasses is extremely important. Side protection must be sought in conditions of reflective light. Slippage of sunglasses by as little as one fourth of an inch can increase UV exposure by 20%.

A suitable retention strap must be worn, as I recently once again learned while rafting on the Green River in Colorado. And for those of us who must learn these things more than once, a second pair of glasses—particularly if prescription lenses are worn—is essential. Lacking sunglasses, any field expedient method of eliminating glare, such a slit glasses made from wood or any material at hand, to include the ubiquitous bandana, will help. An important aspect of sun blindness is the delayed onset of symptoms. The pain and loss of vision may not be evident until after damaging exposure has been sustained.

Sun blindness is a self limiting affliction. However, not only is the actual loss of vision a problem, but so is the terrible pain, usually described as feeling like red hot pokers were massaging the eye sockets. Lacking any first aid supplies, the treatment would be gentle eye patch and the application of cold packs as needed for pain relief. Generally both eyes are equally affected with a virtual total loss of vision. If there is partial sight, then patching the most affected eye may be practical. Otherwise, rest both eyes.

The prescription Pontocaine ophthalmic ointment will help ease the pain, but long term use can delay eye surface healing. Oral pain medication will be of help and should be used. The severe pain can last from hours to several days. In case a drainage of pus, or crusting of the eyelids occurs, start antibiotic ophthalmic ointment applications as indicated in the section on conjunctivitis. Further information on sun injury may be found on page 2.

Ear

The development of ear pain is a sure way to ruin a trip. Pain in the ear can be due to a number of causes. Air squeeze, or barotrauma, or a history of injury will be an obvious source of pain. Most ear pain is due to an *otitis media* or infection behind the ear drum (tympanic membrane), *otitis externa* or infection in the outer ear canal (auditory canal), or due to infection elsewhere (generally a dental infection, infected tonsil, or lymph node in the neck near the ear). Allergy can result in pressure behind the ear drum and is also a common source of ear pain.

Air Squeeze

Air squeeze, or barotrauma, can result in a painful ear. Rapid ascents or descents in vehicles and airplanes can cause significant pain from pressure or vacuum in the middle ear. This is particularly true if the passenger is suffering from head congestion. Congestion can lead to blockage of the eustachian tube. Failure to equilibrate pressure through this tube between the middle ear and the throat—and, thus, the outside world—can result in damage to the ear drum.

The descent on an airplane is generally the time most likely to cause ear pain for an adult or, especially, a child. Bottle or breast feeding an infant or young child may help alleviate the pressure differential between the middle ear and the ambient pressure.

Try to equalize this pressure by pinching the nose shut and gently increasing the pressure in your mouth and throat against closed lips. This will generally clear the eustachian tube and relieve the air squeeze on the ear drum. Do not over-do this; that can also be painful.

Head congestion should be vigorously treated to prevent eustachian tube blockage. Take a decongestant, such as Actifed. Drink larger amounts of fluid than normal to over hydrate. This tends to thin mucous secretions and can result in less clogging of both sinus cavities and the eustachian tube. While I do not recommend nasal sprays for long-term application, before a flight use a long acting nasal spray, such as Afrin (2 sprays 1 hour before flight time). Persons using such products longer than 3 days are apt to suffer from a rebound congestion when ceasing their use. However, these drops will help to shrink the membranes around the eustachian tube opening in the pharynx and decrease mucous secretion quite effectively. The chance of eustachian tube blockage and experiencing barotrauma, or ear pressure squeeze, is thus greatly reduced.

If barotrauma results in ear drum rupture, the pain should instantly cease. There may be bloody drainage from the ear canal. Do not place drops in the ear canal, but drainage can be gently wiped away or frequently changed cotton plugs used to catch the bloody fluid. Seek medical attention as soon as possible.

Ear Infections

A simple physical examination and a little additional medical history will readily (and generally accurately) distinguish the difference between an *otitis media* or *otitis externa*, and sources of pain beyond the ear. Pushing on the knob at the front of the ear (the tragus) or pulling on the ear lobe will elicit pain with an *otitis externa*. This will not hurt if the patient has *otitis media*. The history of head congestion also favors *otitis media*.

Otitis Externa—Outer Ear Infection

This infection of the auditory canal is commonly called "swimmer's ear". The external auditory canal generally becomes inflamed from conditions of high humidity, accumulation of ear wax, or contact with contaminated water. Scratching the ear after itching the nose or scratching elsewhere may also be a source of this common infection.

Prevent cold air from blowing against the ear. Warm packs against the ear or instilling comfortably warm sweet oil, or even clean cooking oil, can help. Provide pain medication. Obtain professional help if the patient develops a fever, the pain becomes severe, or lymph nodes or adjacent neck tissues start swelling. Significant tissue swelling will require antibiotic treatment such as doxycycline 100 mg twice daily. Non-prescription ear drops will not clear infections, but can help with pain and local irritation.

Otitis media—Middle Ear Infection

This condition will present in a person who has sinus congestion and possibly drainage from allergy or infection. The ear pain can be excruciating. Fever will frequently be intermittent, normal at one moment and over 103° F at other times. Fever indicates bacterial infection of the fluid trapped behind the ear drum. If the ear drum ruptures, the pain will cease immediately and the fever will drop. This drainage allows the body to cure the infection, but will result in at least temporary damage to the ear drum and decreased hearing until it heals.

Treatment will consist of providing decongestant, pain medication and oral antibiotic such as the doxycycline. An ideal decongestant is Actifed, 1 tablet 4 times daily. Give oral pain medication.

Foreign body in the Ear

These are generally of three types. Accumulation of wax plugs (cerumen), foreign objects, and living insects. Wax plugs can usually be softened with a warmed oil. This may have to be placed in the ear canal repeatedly over many days. Irrigating with room temperature water may be attempted with a bulb syringe. If a wax plugged ear becomes painful, treat as indicated in the section on *otitis externa*.

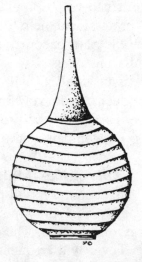

FIGURE 7-3
Bulb syringe for irrigating wounds, ear, or eye as described in the text.

The danger in trying to remove inanimate objects is the tendency to shove them further into the ear canal or to damage the delicate ear canal lining, thus adding bleeding to your troubles. Of course, rupturing the ear drum by shoving against it would be a real unnecessary disaster.

Attempt to grasp a foreign body with a pair of tweezers if you can visualize it. Do not poke blindly with anything. Irrigation may be attempted as indicated above.

A method of aiding in the management of insects in the ear canal is to drown the bug with cooking or other oil, then attempt removal. Oil seems to kill bugs quicker than water. The less struggle, the less chance for stinging, biting, or other trauma to the delicate ear canal and ear drum. Tilt the ear downward, thus hoping to slide the dead bug towards the entrance where it can be grappled. Shining a light at the ear to coax a bug out is probably futile.

Nose Bleed (Epistaxis)

If nose bleeding is caused from a contusion to the nose, the bleeding is usually self limited. Bleeding that starts without trauma is generally more difficult to stop. Most bleeding is from small arteries located near the front of the nose partition, or nasal septum.

The best treatment is direct pressure. Have the victim squeeze the nose between his fingers for ten minutes by the clock (a very long time when there is no clock to watch), in the location as illustrated in figure 4. If this fails, squeeze another ten minutes. Do not blow the nose for this will dislodge clots and start the bleeding all over again.

If the bleeding is severe, have the victim sit up to prevent choking on blood and to aid in the reduction of the blood pressure in the nose. Cold compresses do little good. The field treatment of nose fractures and dislocations and advanced techniques of dealing with severe bloody noses are described in my book *Wilderness Medicine*.

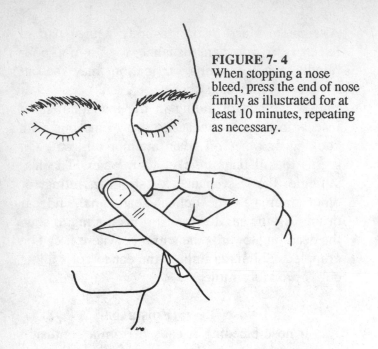

FIGURE 7- 4
When stopping a nose bleed, press the end of nose firmly as illustrated for at least 10 minutes, repeating as necessary.

Dental Pain, Lost Filling, and Trauma

Cavities may be identified by visual examination of the mouth in most cases. Dry the tooth and try to clean out any cavity found. For years oil of cloves, or eugenol, has been used to deaden dental pain. A daub of topical anesthetic such as 1% dibucaine ointment will also help deaden dental pain. Avoid trying to apply an aspirin directly to a painful tooth, it will only make a worse mess of things.

When you examine a traumatized mouth and find a tooth that is rotated, or dislocated in any direction, do not push the tooth back into place. Further movement may disrupt the tooth's blood and nerve supply. If the tooth is at all secure, leave it alone. The musculature of the lips and tongue will generally gently push the tooth back into place and keep it there.

A broken tooth with that is bleeding or that displays an exposed pink substance, will also have exposed the nerve. This tooth will need protection with eugenol as indicated above. This is a dental emergency that should be treated by a dentist immediately.

If a tooth is knocked out, replace it into the socket immediately. If this cannot be done, have the victim hold the tooth under their tongue or in their lower lip until it can be implanted. In any case hours is a matter of great importance. A tooth left out too long will be rejected by the body as a foreign substance. All of the above problems will mean that a soft diet and avoidance of chewing with the affected tooth for many days will be necessary. Persons suffering dental trauma should be taken to a dentist as soon as possible.

Chapter 7.3

Abdominal Pain

Even with years of clinical experience and unlimited laboratory and x-ray facilities, abdominal pain can be a diagnostic dilemma. For the traveler confronted with abdominal pain, the major decision is concerning the seriousness of the problem—should professional help be obtained or can the condition be safely self-medicated.

Diagnosis is frequently discerned by the type of pain, location, cause, fever—all from the history—as well as certain aspects of the physical exam and the clinical course that develops.

Burning—upper part of the stomach in the middle (mid-epigastrium) is probably **GASTRITIS**. If allowed to persist this can develop into an

TABLE 7.1
Symptoms and Signs of Abdominal Pathology

	Burning	Nausea	Food Related	Diarrhea	Fever
Gastritis/ulcer	xx	x	xx		
Pancreatitis	xx	x	x		x
Hiatal Hernia	xx		x		
Gall Bladder		xx	xx		(x)
Appendicitis		x			x
Gastro-enteriti		xx		xx	x
Diverticulitis				xx	x
Hepatitis		xx	x		x
Food Poisoning		xx	xx	xx	x

ULCER—which is a crater eaten into the stomach wall. Severe persistent mid-epigastric pain, that is frequently burning in nature, can be **PANCREATITIS**. This is a serious problem, but rare. Alcohol consumption can cause pancreatitis, as well as gastritis and ulcer formation. Alcohol must be avoided if pain in this area develops. Reflux of stomach acid up the esophagus, sometimes caused by a **HIATAL HERNIA**, will cause the same symptoms. Treatment for all of the above is aggressive antacid therapy. These conditions can be made worse with spicy food, tomato products, and other foods high in acid content and these should be avoided. Avoid any medication that contains aspirin or ibuprofen, but Tylenol (acetaminophen) containing products are all right. Acid suppression medication such as Tagamet, Zantac, Axid, or Pepcid can help greatly, but these medications can make the user more vulnerable to traveler's diarrhea and other infectious disease from which normal or high stomach acid would otherwise help provide protection. A safer medication for persons afflicted with frequent heart burn, not responsive to antacids, would be Carafate taken 1 gram 4 times daily. This prescription drug should be added to the traveler's medical kit, if necessary.

Nausea with pain in the patient's right upper quadrant may be from a **GALL BLADDER** problem. This discomfort is made worse with eating—sometimes even smelling—fatty foods. While cream would initially help the pain of gastritis or ulcer, it would cause an immediate increase in symptoms if the gall bladder is involved. Part of the treatment is avoidance of fatty foods. Nausea can be treated with the meclizine 25 mg tablets from the non-prescription kit, but would respond much better to the Atarax 25 mg given every 4 to 6 hours from the prescription kit. There is no burning sensation with gall bladder pain. A safe medication would be the use of Tylenol #3. The development of a fever is an important sign which could indicate an infection in an obstructed gall bladder. An infection of the gall bladder is a surgical emergency. Treat the nausea and pain as indicated. Offer as much fluid as tolerated. Gall bladder disease is most common in overweight people in their 40's. It is more common in women.

The possibility of **APPENDICITIS** is a major concern as it can occur in any age group, and that includes even healthy travelers. It is fortunately rare. While surgery is the treatment of choice, probably as many as 70% of people not treated with surgery can survive this disaster, even more with appropriate IV therapy. The classic presentation of this illness is a vague feeling of discomfort around the umbilicus (navel). Temperature may be a low grade fever, 99.6 to 100.6

at first. Within a matter of hours the discomfort turns to pain and localizes in the right lower quadrant, most frequently on a point $1/3$ of the way between the navel and the very top of the right pelvic bone (anterior-superior iliac spine), the so-called Mc Burney's point (see figure 5). This pain syndrome can be evaluated by asking two questions: Where did you first start hurting? (belly button); Now where do you hurt? (right lower quadrant as described). Those answers give an 80% probability of appendicitis. Obtain professional help when abdominal pain persists longer than 12 hours, regardless of suspected cause.

FIGURE 7- 5
The location of McBurney's Point, the location of maximum pain in classic appendicitis.

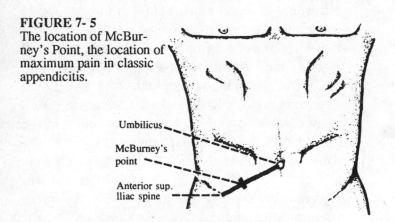

Umbilicus

McBurney's
point

Anterior sup.
lliac spine

Bladder Infection

The symptoms of a bladder infection are the urge to urinate frequently, burning upon urination, small amounts of urine being voided with each attempt, and discomfort in the suprapublic region, the lowest area of the abdomen. Frequently the victim has fever with its attendant chills and muscle ache. Cloudiness and discoloration of the urine is generally not of help in the diagnosis of bladder infections. The ideal treatment is with prescription antibiotics such as the Bactrim DS or doxycycline 100 mg, one tablet twice daily.

Vomiting

Nausea and vomiting are frequently caused by infections known as gastroenteritis. Many times these are viral so that antibiotics are of no value. These infections will usually resolve without treatment in 24 to 48 hours. Fever seldom is high, but may briefly be high in some cases. Fever should not persist above 100 degrees longer than 12 hours. Treatment may be with meclizine, or Atarax—as indicated in the discussions of those drugs—for symptomatic relief. Vomiting without diarrhea will not require the use of an antibiotic. If the vomiting is caused from severe illness, such as an ear infection, then use of antibiotic to treat the underlying cause is justified.

Diarrhea

Pepto Bismol liquid, taken 1 oz every 30 minutes for eight doses, has been shown to decreased the rate of stooling by half. Adsorbents such as kaolin and pectin give stools more consistency, but do not decrease the frequency, abdominal cramping, or length of affliction. A new adsorbent, Diasorb, has ten times the adsorption capability of kaolin and shows great promise in safely treating diarrhea. It is non-prescription and is available in liquid and tablet formulation at most drug stores in the United States. It should be perfectly safe for consumption by women at any stage of pregnancy. Replacement of fluid loss is the important aspect of diarrhea treatment. Carbonated water found in most developing countries is generally considered safe. Water consumed must be either heated to boiling or be bottled water from a reputable source. More than water is lost with the diarrhea. Various minerals are also excreted in large amounts, notably sodium and potassium. The patient must receive adequate fluid replacement, equaling fluid loss plus about 2 quarts per day.

The Centers for Disease Control has developed an oral replacement cocktail to replace the water and mineral (electrolyte) losses of profound diarrhea.

TABLE 7–2
The CDC Oral Fluid Replacement Cocktail

Prepare two separate glasses of the following:

Glass 1) Orange, apple or other fruit juice rich in potassium)
8 ounces

Honey or corn syrup (glucose necessary for absorption of essential salts)
1/2 teaspoon

Salt, table (source of sodium and chloride)
1 pinch

Glass 2) Water (carbonated or boiled)
8 ounces

Soda, baking (sodium bicarbonate)
1/4 teaspoon

Drink alternately from each glass. Supplement with carbonated beverages or water and tea made with boiled or carbonated water as desired. Avoid solid foods and milk until recovery.

Throughout the world UNICEF and WHO (World Health Organization) distribute an electrolyte replacement product called Oralyte. It must be reconstituted with adequately purified water.

Anti-motility agents rapidly stop the symptoms of diarrhea. Products such as paregoric, Lomotil, and Imodium are widely used in the treatment of diarrhea. Imodium, in liquid form, was made a non-prescription drug in the United States in mid-1988, while the capsules were made non-prescription in 1989. The adult dose of Imodium is two 2 mg capsules at the onset of treatment, followed by 1 capsule with each loose stool up to a maximum of 8 capsules a day. The use of anti-motility agents should be restricted to urgent situations, such as long bus rides or trips without toilet facilities, impending dehydration, attendance at meetings that cannot be cancelled, and the like.

Antibiotic treatment that has been proven effective in the use of doxycycline 100 mg, one tablet twice daily — if this medication was not being taken as a preventative. Bactrim DS (Septra DS), one tablet twice daily — or in the event of sulfa allergy, trimethoprim alone, 200 mg taken twice daily. Three days of treatment is recommended, although 2 days may be sufficient. Nausea and vomiting without diarrhea should not be treated with antibiotics. Erythromycin has been advocated for treatment of travelers' diarrhea. An antibiotic that has been proven quite effective in treatment is Cipro (ciprofloxacin), taken 500 mg twice daily for three to four days. While more effective in a controlled study that Bactrim, its cost is much higher (Cipro costs almost $2.50 per tablet).

Motion Sickness

Motion induced nausea and vomiting can be minimized by various techniques.

When traveling by a vehicle, it helps to ride in the portion less subjected to movement. For a bus this would be between the front and rear wheels. That location, incidentally, is not exactly in the middle of the bus, but somewhat forward of the apparent middle of the coach. In a car, the front seat is far preferable to the rear seat. On a plane, position yourself at the location of the center wings. Generally this obstructs your view. The ideal seat would also be the one next to the wing emergency exit. The safest location in the plane is in the back row of seats towards the trail of the aircraft, but motion problems would be greatly magnified. On a ship, locate yourself as near the center of the ship as possible. However, these are not the choicest rooms for view or amenities.

Activity can also minimize motion problems. Avoid reading. Choose a focal point for your gaze that is as near the horizon as possible. When in a car, look at houses or scenery in the distance. Aboard a plane, look at distant cloud formations. At night, or when a white out blocks outside viewing, focus your attention as far up the aisle as possible. On a ship, stare at the horizon, or as far along the ship deck as you can.

Several medications are available over the counter for control of nausea. Dramamine, Bonine, and Marezine are the most commonly available. Dramamine also has a liquid formulation. A curious fact is the Bonine (meclizine 25 mg), one tablet daily is an non-prescription product to prevent motion sickness, while Antivert (meclizine 25 mg), up to one tablet three times daily, is a prescription required dose to prevent or treat vertigo or motion sickness. There tends to be minimal drowsiness or other side effects when using the above medications.

Transderm Scop, a patch containing scopolamine, has been developed for prevention of motion sickness, but this requires a prescription. Each patch may be worn behind the ear for 3 days. It is fairly expensive, but also very effective and well worth the cost if you are prone to this malady. There tends to be a higher frequency of side effects with this medication in elderly people, such as visual problems, confusion, even psychotic behavior and loss of temperature regulation. Avoid touching your eye after handling this patch and before washing your fingers, as this may result in dilation of the pupil and blurring of vision. This is generally not serious and will pass within 48 hours. Persons should avoid this product if they have glaucoma, are pregnant or are nursing, have liver or kidney disease, have a metabolic disorder, have trouble urinating, have obstructions of the stomach or intestine, or have very sensitive skin.

An excellent prescription drug that effectively treats nausea and vomiting from all causes, and which works very well in treating motion sickness, is Atarax. This medication is listed in the recommended prescription medical kit. Dosage for motion sickness treatment is one 25 mg tablet every four hours as needed.

Chapter 7.4

Sprains, Fractures, and Dislocations

ACUTE JOINT INJURY

Proper care of joint injuries must be started immediately. *R*est, *I*ce, *C*ompression, and *E*levation (RICE) form the basis of good first aid management. Cold should be applied for the first 2 days, as continuously as possible. Afterward, applying heat for 20 minutes, 4 times daily is helpful. Cold decreases the circulation, which lessens bleeding and swelling. Heat increases the circulation, which then aids the healing process. This method applies to all injuries including muscle contusions and bruises.

Elevate the involved joint, if possible. Wrap with an elastic bandage to immobilize the joint and provide moderate support once walking or use of the joint begins. Take care that the wrappings are not so tightly applied that they cut off the circulation.

Use crutches or other support to take enough weight off an injured ankle and knee to the point that increased pain is not experienced. The patient should not use an injured joint if use causes pain, as this indicates further strain on the already stressed ligaments or the existence of a fracture. Conversely, if use of the injured part does not cause pain, additional damage is not being done even if there is considerable swelling.

If the victim must walk on an injured ankle or knee, and doing so causes pain, then support it the best way possible (wrapping, crutches, decreased carrying load, tight boot for ankle injury) and realize that further damage is being done, but that in your opinion the situation warrants such a sacrifice.

Wrapping an ankle with an ace bandage is easy. The so-called figure eight technique is illustrated in figure 6A. Simply wrap around the ankle, under and around the foot and layer as shown.

Wrapping a knee is similarly performed using a figure eight technique, as shown in figure 6B. These wraps provide compression and slight support. They should never be applied so tight that they cause discomfort or cut off circulation.

Pain medications may be given as needed, but elevation and decreased use will provide considerable pain relief.

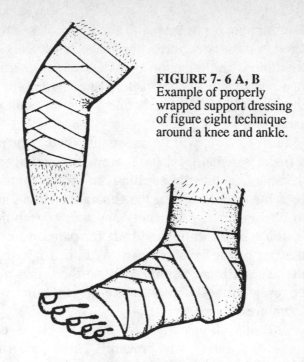

FIGURE 7- 6 A, B
Example of properly wrapped support dressing of figure eight technique around a knee and ankle.

Dislocations

If the joint in question is deformed and/or the patient cannot move it, then the joint has suffered either a severe sprain or dislocation. Support the joint with sling or splinting in such a manner that further stress is not applied to the joint.

For the advanced treatment of specific dislocations, please refer to my book *Wilderness Medicine*. These techniques are beyond the scope of first aid, but if you are unable to obtain medical help, reductions of shoulder, elbow, finger, and nose dislocations can reduce pain and facilitate long evacuations.

Fractures

Fracture is the medical term for a broken bone. Fractures have several critical aspects to consider during management: 1) loss of circulation or nerve damage if bone spicules press against these structures due to deformity of the fracture; 2) introduction of infection if the skin is broken at or near the fracture site; 3) failure of the bone to mend properly due to improper alignment of bone fragments.

At times it will be uncertain whether or not a fracture actually exists. There will be point tenderness, frequently swelling and discoloration over the fracture site or the generalized area, and in obvious cases, deformity and loss of stability. If doubt exists, splint and treat for pain, avoiding the use of the involved part. Within a few days the pain will have diminished and the crises may be over. If not, the suspicion of fracture will loom even larger.

People frequently will say: "Well, I can move it, it must not be broken!" This is not true. The pain associated with activity may discourage movement, but it certainly does not prevent it. With proper splinting the pain involved with a fracture will decrease dramatically. Pain medication should be provided as soon as possible. A proper splint is well padded to protect underlying skin from developing pressure sores. It should also immobilize the joint above and below the fracture site. Fracture splinting requires common sense—and sometime imagination when fabricating some first aid device from available items such as ski poles, rolled newspapers, tree branches—even boots, eye glass frames, and articles of clothing.

Reduction, or correction, of fractures should be left to the hands of skilled persons. The adage "splint them as they lie" is the golden rule in handling fractures. However, if obvious circulation damage is occurring, namely the pulses beyond the fracture site have ceased, the extremity is turning blue and cold to the touch, or numbness is apparent in the portion of the limb beyond the fracture, angulations of the fracture should be straightened to attempt to eliminate the pressure damage. Broken bone edges can be very sharp—in fact a laceration of the blood vessels and nerves may have already occurred, thus causing the above symptoms.

Chapter 7.5

Bites and Stings

ANIMAL BITES

Animal bite wounds must be vigorously cleaned. While surgical scrubs (such as the Hibiclens recommended for your travel medical kit) are ideal, any *very* dilute solution of clean water and soap or detergent will work quite well. The wound should generally be covered with triple antibiotic ointment and a pressure dressing. The patient should be seen by a physician as soon as possible. Tetanus immunization must be current within 5 years.

Rabies

This disease can be transmitted on the North American continent by several species of mammals, namely skunk, bat, fox, coyote, racoon, bobcat, and wolf. Any unprovoked attack by one of these mammals should be considered an attack by a rabid animal. Dogs and cats in the United States have a low incidence of rabies. Information from local departments of health will indicate if rabies is currently of concern in these animals. *In many foreign countries the bite of a cat or dog should be considered rabid.* Animals whose bites have never caused rabies in humans in the US are livestock (cattle, sheep, horse), rabbit, gerbil, chipmunk, squirrel, rat, and mouse. Hawaii is the only rabies free state. Countries free of rabies are England, Australia, Japan, and parts of the Caribbean. In Europe the red fox is the animal most often rabid with documented cases spreading to dogs, cats, cattle, and deer. Canada's rabies occurs mostly in foxes and skunks in the province of Ontario. Mongoose rabies is found in South Africa and the Caribbean islands of Cuba, Puerto Rico, Hispaniola, and Grenada. In the United States there have been 11 cases of rabies reported between 1980 and 1989. In India 40,000 to 50,000 people die yearly from rabies, with an equal incidence in the other developing counties of Asia, Africa, and Latin America.

The treatment for rabies is initiated with Rabies Immune Globulin 20 IU/kg. Half is infiltrated around the wound and the remaining half is given IM in the gluteal area (upper outer quadrant of the bottom). Also, human diploid cell vaccine (HDCV) 1 ml must be given IM in the shoulder on days 0, 3, 7, 14, and 28.

Treatment of Insect Bites and Stings

Prevention of insect bites and stings is important for comfort and to minimize the chance of catching insect borne diseases. The use of insect repellent, sprays, netting, proper clothing, and avoiding the times and locations of significant insect swarming are all necessary techniques. This topic is discussed in Chapter 5.4 of the *Travelers' Medical Resource*.

Honey bee—also wasp, yellow jackets, and hornets are members of the order *Hymenoptera*. Stings from these insects hurt instantly and the pain lingers. The danger comes from the fact that some persons are "hypersensitive" to the venom and can have an immediate *anaphylactic shock* which is life-threatening. Fire ants and other insects may also cause an anaphylactic reaction.

The pain of stings and local skin reactions to bites can be alleviated by almost anything applied topically. Best choices are cold packs, dibucaine ointment from the medical kit, or a piece of Spenco 2nd Skin and the use of oral pain medication. Swelling can be prevented and/or treated with oral antihistamine such as Benadryl 25 mg taken 4 times daily.

The puss caterpillar (*Megalopyge opercularis*) of the southern US and the gypsy moth caterpillar (*Lymantria dispar*) of the northeastern US have bristles that cause an almost immediate skin rash and welt formation. Treatment includes patting the victim with a piece of adhesive tape to remove these bristles. Thoroughly cleanse the area with soap and water. A patch of Spenco 2nd Skin is very cooling. Give Benadryl 25 mg, one capsule 4 times daily.

Tick bites are of increased concern due to the diseases that can be transmitted by these little fellows. Lyme disease, Rocky Mountain spotted fever, Colorado tick fever, relapsing fever, tularemia, babesiosis, ehrlichiosis and tick paralysis are amongst the tick borne diseases found just in the United States. Remove the tick by grasping the victim's skin with the splinter forceps (tweezers) just where the tick has bitten the victim as illustrated in figure 1. Remove by pulling straight up, probably also taking a small piece of skin as the tick pincers hang on tightly. I have seldom found heating the tick with a hot paper clip, using alcohol, finger nail polish remover, or other chemical means very successful.

Anaphylactic Shock

While most commonly due to insect stings, this severe form of life-threatening shock may be encountered as a serious allergic reaction to medications, shell fish and other foods, or anything to which one has become profoundly allergic. Those developing anaphylaxis generally have warnings of their severe sensitivity in the form of welts (urticaria) forming all over their body immediately after exposure, the development of an asthmatic attack with respiratory wheezing, or the onset of symptoms of shock. After an exposure with such severe warning symptoms, the concern is that the next exposure might produce increased symptoms or even the shock state known as anaphylaxis.

This deadly form of shock can begin within seconds of exposure. It cannot be treated as shock would normally be handled, with elevation of the feet above heart level. The only life-saving remedy is to administer the drug called epinephrine (Adrenalin). It is available for emergency use as a component of a prepackaged prescription kit called the "Anakit" or in a special automatic injectable syringe called the EpiPen. Note illustrations of each type of kit in figure 7.

The Anakit is recommended as it contains two injections of epinephrine, rather than one and the cost is about half that of the EpiPen. Nor-

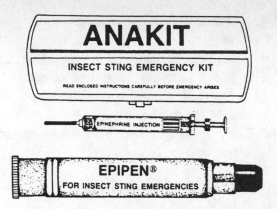

FIGURE 7-7
The "Anakit" and "EpiPen" used to treat severe insect reactions.

mal dosage is .3 cc for an adult of the 1:1000 epinephrine solution given "subQ" (in the fatty layer beneath the skin). This may have to be repeated in 15 to 20 minutes if the symptoms of wheezing or shock start to return. The Anakit contains a chewable antihistamine which should also be taken immediately, but antihistamines are of no value in treating the shock or asthmatic component of anaphylaxis.

Anyone experiencing anaphylactic reactions should be evacuated to medical care, even though they have responded to the epinephrine. They are at risk of the condition returning and they should be monitored carefully over the next 24 hours.

First Aid Management of Snake Bite

Snake bite prevention is easier than treatment. Wear boots that cover the ankle and avoid placing your hands or reaching into areas where your view is obstructed in habitats of poisonous snakes. Avoid poisonous snakes when seen, rather than trying to kill them. These steps will prevent most snake bite incidents from occurring

Nonpoisonous Snake Bite

Get away from the snake. Cleanse the bitten area with surgical scrub—apply suction with the Extractor to promote evacuation of puncture debris. No constriction band should be used. Treat for shock. Manage the wound as a puncture wound. The victim should have had a tetanus shot within 5 years.

Poisonous Snake Bite

Not everyone bitten by a poisonous snake will have envenomation injury—fully 20% of rattlesnake and 30% of cotton mouth water moccasin and copperhead bites will not envenomate during their bite. DO NOT APPLY COLD—this is associated with increased tissue damage. 1) Immobilize the injured part at heart level or slightly above in a position of function. 2) Apply

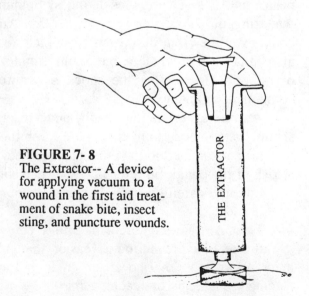

FIGURE 7- 8
The Extractor-- A device for applying vacuum to a wound in the first aid treatment of snake bite, insect sting, and puncture wounds.

an elastic bandage with a firm wrap from the bite site towards the body, leaving the bite exposed if you have an Extractor for further treatment, covered if you do not. 3) Apply suction with the Extractor (see figure 8). Making incisions actually decreases the amount of venom that can be removed with this device. If applied within 3 minutes as much as 35% of the venom may be removed with the Extractor. After $^1/_2$ hour, less than 3% more will be removed so further suction can be terminated. 4) Treat for shock and evacuate to professional medical help.

Antivenin and pharmacologic management of poisonous snake bites, to include cobra and other species, as well as specific therapies for poisonous spiders and scorpions, is discussed in *Wilderness Medicine*.

Chapter 7.6

Aquatic Injuries

CATFISH STINGS

Apply hot water as indicated under STING RAY. The wound must be properly cleaned and irrigated using surgical scrub, if available, or soap. Place the patient on an oral antibiotic for several days to decrease the chance of wound infection which is common with this injury. Treat an infected wound as described on page 6.

Coral Cuts, Barnacle Cuts

Clean the wound thoroughly—trivial wounds can later flare into real disasters that may go on for years. Scour thoroughly with a coarse cloth or soft brush and surgical scrub or soapy water. Then apply hydrogen peroxide to help bubble out fine particles and bacteria. Apply triple antibiotic ointment. Manage this wound as discussed in the section on laceration care.

Coral Stings
These injuries are treated as indicated under JELLYFISH.

Jellyfish
Tentacles can cause mild pricking to burning, shooting, terrible pain. The worse danger is shock and drowning. Avoid the use of hot water in treating this injury. First, pour ocean water over the injury. Try to remove the tentacles with gloved hands. Pour alcohol (or ideally formalin) over the wound, which will prevent the nematocysts from firing more poison. Both ammonia or vinegar would work, but not as well as formalin or alcohol. Urine may be used, but do not use fresh water. Powder the area with a dry powder such as flour or baking powder. Gently scrape off the mess with a knife, clam shell or other sharp instrument, but avoid cutting the nematocysts with a sharp blade. Apply hydrocortisone cream .5% four times daily from the Traveler's Medical Kit, or the prescription product Topicort .25% twice daily for inflammation.

Scorpion Fish
Same treatment as STING RAY.

Sea Urchin
Punctures from sea urchin spines cause severe pain and burning. Besides trauma from the sharp spines, some species inject a venom. The wound can appear red and swollen or even blue to black from a harmless dye which may be con-

tained in the spines. Generalized symptoms are rare, but may include weakness, numbness, muscle cramps, nausea, and occasionally shortness of breath. The spines should be removed thoroughly—a very tedious process. Very thin spines may be absorbed by the body without harm, but some may form a reactive tissue around them (granulomas) several months later. Spines may migrate into joints and cause pain and inhibit movement or lodge against a nerve and cause extreme pain. The discoloration of the dye causes no problems, but may be mistaken for a thin spine. Relief may be obtained by soaking in hot water (110° to 113° F) for 20 to 30 minutes. Vinegar or acetic acid soaks several times a day may help dissolve spines that are not found. Evacuation and treatment by a physician is advisable.

Sponge Rash

Sponges handled directly from the ocean can cause an allergic reaction that appears immediately. Fine spicules may also break off in the outer layer of skin also causing inflammation. It will be difficult to tell whether your victim is suffering from the allergic reaction or the spicules, or both. Soak the affected skin by applying vinegar to a cloth and covering for 15 minutes. Dry the skin and pat with the adhesive side of tape to remove sponge spicules. Again soak in vinegar for 5 minutes. An application of rubbing alcohol for 1 minute has been suggested. Then apply hydrocortisone cream .5% four times a day or Topicort .25% twice daily for several days until the inflammation subsides.

Sting Ray

The damage is done by the barbed tail,

which lacerates the skin, imbedding pieces of tail material and venom into the wound. The wound bleeds heavily. Pain increases over 90 minutes and takes 6 to 48 hours to abate.

Immediately rinse the wound with sea water and remove any particles of the tail sheath which are visible as these particles continue to release venom. Hot water is the treatment of choice— applied as soon as possible and as hot as the patient can stand it (110°–113° F). The heat will destroy the toxin rapidly and remove the pain that the patient is experiencing. After hot water has been applied and all tail particles removed, the wound may be loosely closed with taping techniques. Elevation of the wound is important. If particularly dirty, leave the wound open and continue to use intermittent hot soaks 20 minutes at a time, every 2 hours. Questionably dirty wounds should be treated with Bactrim DS 1 tablet twice daily or doxycycline 100 mg twice daily. As these are nasty, painful wounds, treat for shock from the onset.

Chapter 7.7

Environmental Injuries

COLD WEATHER INJURIES

The term "hypothermia" refers to the lowering of the body's core temperature to 95° F (35° C); "profound hypothermia" is a core temperature lower than 90° F (32° C). Another important point is that the term "hypothermia" applies to two distinctly different diseases. One is "chronic hypothermia," the slow onset hypothermia of the outdoors traveler exposed to conditions too cold for their equipment to adequately protect them; the other is "acute," or "immersion hypothermia," the rapid onset hypothermia of a person immersed in cold water.

Hypothermia is the most likely of the environmental injuries that will be encountered in the outdoors. Prevention is the hall mark of survival, in fact hypothermia has been called the killer of the unprepared. It is most important to attempt to prevent hypothermia. The factors that protect trip members include being in good physical condition, maintaining adequate nutrition, prevention of physical exhaustion, prevention of dehydration, wearing adequate clothing, and having replacement clothing available in case of emergencies. More extensive information on various aspects of hypothermia prevention, diagnosis, and treatment can be found in my book *Hypothermia: Death by Exposure*, published by ICS Books.[2]

Chronic Hypothermia

The essential aspects of surviving this situation are: being prepared to prevent it, recognizing it when it occurs, and knowing how to treat it. Dampness and wind are the most devastating factors to be considered. Dampness as it can reduce the insulation of clothing and cause evaporative heat loss. Wind as the increased convection heat loss can readily strip away body energy, the so called "wind chill" effect. Remember, it is possible to die of hypothermia in temperatures far above freezing—in fact most hypothermia deaths occur in the 30° to 50° F (-1° to 10° C) range.

Detection of hypothermia is generally made by two observations. The first is to watch for exhaustion. Exhausted victims are not necessarily hypothermic, yet. But they will be unless they can obtain adequate rest and have adequate cloth-

[2]*Hypothermia: Death by Exposure* is available from ICS Books, Inc., 107 East 89th Avenue, Merrillville, IN 46410, telephone (219) 769-0585 for $9.95 plus $1.50 handling.

FAHRENHEIT WIND CHILL EQUIVALENT TEMPERATURE

Wind Speed MPH	TEMPERATURE FAHRENHEIT																						
	50	45	40	35	30	25	20	15	10	5	0	-5	-10	-15	-20	-25	-30	-35	-40	-45	-50	-55	-60
Calm	50	45	40	35	30	25	20	15	10	5	0	-5	-10	-15	-20	-25	-30	-35	-40	-45	-50	-55	-60
5	48	42	37	33	28	21	16	12	6	1	-5	-11	-15	-20	-26	-31	-36	-41	-47	-52	-57	-65	-70
10	40	34	28	21	16	9	4	-2	-9	-15	-24	-27	-33	-38	-46	-52	-58	-64	-70	-75	-83	-90	-95
15	36	29	22	16	9	1	-5	-11	-18	-25	-32	-40	-45	-51	-58	-65	-72	-77	-85	-90	-99	-105	-110
20	32	25	18	12	4	-4	-10	-17	-25	-32	-39	-46	-53	-60	-67	-75	-82	-89	-96	-102	-110	-115	-120
25	30	23	16	7	0	-7	-15	-22	-29	-37	-44	-52	-59	-67	-74	-83	-88	-96	-104	-111	-118	-125	-135
30	28	20	13	5	-2	-11	-18	-26	-33	-41	-48	-56	-63	-70	-79	-87	-94	-101	-109	-115	-125	-130	-140
35	27	19	11	3	-4	-13	-20	-27	-35	-43	-51	-60	-67	-72	-82	-90	-98	-105	-113	-120	-129	-135	-146
40	26	18	10	1	-6	-15	-21	-29	-37	-45	-53	-62	-69	-76	-85	-94	-100	-107	-115	-125	-132	-140	-150

Exposed Flesh Can Freeze in 60 Seconds

Exposed Flesh Can Freeze in 30 Seconds

"WIND CHILL CHART--FAHRENHEIT"

NOTE 1: The above chart has been based upon the Siple Equation and reflects Wind Chill Equivalent temperatures in Fahrenheit.

NOTE 2: At low wind speeds, relative humidity and radiant heat are more important than wind speed in determining equivalent temperate comfort.

NOTE 3: Most charts indicate that at wind speeds over 40 mph there is little additional wind chill effect. This is a reflection of an error in the basic equation at these higher wind speeds and is not correct. Heat loss IS magnified by these higher wind speeds, but the chart is an accurate indicator of equivalent temperature at speeds lower than 40 mph.

TABLE 7.3
Knowing the fahrenheit temperature and the wind speed one can calculate wind chill temperature by using this chart. Freezing points for exposed flesh are given in the lower margins.

ing to protect them from heat loss during rest, or after they actually reach exhaustion.

The second is loss of coordination. People who cannot walk a straight 30 foot (9 meter) line are hypothermic. This same test was formerly used by the police to detect inebriation, which also causes loss of coordination. Both impair mental process. For that reason, when hypothermia is detected in travelers, their judgement must

SIGNS AND SYMPTOMS OF HYPOTHERMIA

CORE TEMP.	SIGNS AND SYMPTOMS
99° to 97°F (37° to 36°C)	Normal temperature range Shivering may begin
97° to 95°F (36° to 35°C)	Cold sensation, goose bumps, unable to perform complex tasks with hands, shivering can be mild to severe, skin numb
95° to 93°F (35° to 34°C)	Shivering intense, muscle incoordination becomes apparent, movements slow and labored, stumbling pace, mild confusion, may appear alert, unable to walk 30 ft. line properly — BEST FIELD TEST FOR EARLY HYPOTHERMIA
93° to 90°F (34° to 32°C)	Violent shivering persists, difficulty speaking, sluggish thinking, amnesia starts to appear and may be retrograde, gross muscle movements sluggish, unable to use hands, stumbles frequently, difficulty speaking, signs of depression
90° to 86°F 32° to 30°C)	Shivering stops in chronic hypothermia, exposed skin blue or puffy, muscle coordination very poor with inability to walk, confusion, incoherent, irrational behavior, BUT MAY BE ABLE TO MAINTAIN POSTURE AND THE APPEARANCE OF PSYCHOLOGICAL CONTACT
86° to 82°F (30° to 27.7°C)	Muscles severely rigid, semiconscious, stupor, loss of psychological contact, pulse and respirations slow, pupils can dilate
82° to 78°F (27 to 25.5°C)	Unconsciousness, heart beat and respiration erratic, pulse and heart beat may be inapparent, muscle tendon reflexes cease
78° to 75°F (25° to 24°C)	Pulmonary edema, failure of cardiac and respiratory centers, probable death, DEATH MAY OCCUR BEFORE THIS LEVEL
64°F (17.7°C)	Lowest recorded temperature of chronic hypothermia survivor, Chicago 1951
48.2°F (9°C)	Lowest recorded temperature of induced hypothermia in surgical patient with survival, 1958

TABLE 7.4
Know what signs to look for in an potential hypothermia victim by the comparing the symptoms to the
relative core temperature.

be suspect. More than not trusting their decisions, these people actually need help. They
must be treated for hypothermia.

The treatment for hypothermia is basically:

1. Prevent further heat loss. Wet clothing
   must be removed and replaced with dry
   clothing. At the very least, it must be
   covered with a rain jacket and pants—
   and this in turn covered with more insulation.

2. Treat dehydration. Hypothermia causes vasoconstriction which in effect shrinks the fluid volume of the victim. This is only one reason for dehydration, but all hypothermic people are, indeed, very dehydrated. This volume needs replacement.

3. Treat the victim gently. Very cold people can suffer cardiac rhythm problems if they are jarred around. If they are being carried during an evacuation, avoid bumping them along the ground or dropping them from a stretcher.

4. Add heat. If victims can stand, and you can build a fire, do it! And have them stand comfortably near it. A roaring fire can replace a massive number of calories and practically speaking, if patients can stand on their own by the fire, they are not so profoundly hypothermic that you would have to worry about rewarming shock.

5. Avoid rewarming shock. Persons who are unable to stand are so ill that if they were reheated too rapidly, they could be adversely affected. The dehydration of hypothermia causes a substantial decrease in their fluid volume. So much so that a sudden rewarming can result in shock, even death. Note: this is a concern of the chronic hypothermic, not the acute (immersion) hypothermic victim.

6. Be aware of after-drop. As victims were being reheated it was noted that their core temperature continued to drop before starting to rise. This is called "after-drop." It was originally thought to be a cause of death, but the significant reason

for death in the chronic hypothermic is actually rewarming shock. All persons will have after-drop, which is related to the rate of cooling that was taking place before the rewarming process started. It amounts to an equilibration phenomenon. After-drop *is* a serious problem in the treatment of acute (immersion) hypothermia, but is probably not of much concern in the chronic hypothermic.

7. Avoid adding cold. Never rub the person with snow or allow further exposure to the cold. It is probably best to avoid undressing the victim while exposed to the environment—do this in a sleeping bag or other sheltered area if at all possible. Try to warm water before giving the patient, if possible.

8. Allow rest. These patients are at or near exhaustion. Rest is mandatory to replace the high energy compounds that are required to shiver, work, and otherwise generate heat. If resting victims are being adequately insulated from further heat loss, there is no reason why they cannot be allowed to sleep. It is therapeutic. Do not shake or slap a hypothermic individual (see item 3 above).

Deepening hypothermia will lead to a semicomatose state and worse. This victim needs to be evacuated to help. Wrap to prevent further heat loss and transport. Chemical heat packs, warmed rocks or water bottles, etc., can be added to the wrap to help offset further heat loss, but care must be taken not to burn the victim. If evacuation is not feasible, heat will have to be added slowly to avoid re-warming shock. Huddling with two rescuers naked with the victim in an adequate sleeping bag may be the only alternative.

Acute Hypothermia

Acute hypothermia is the term applied to hypothermia which occurs in less than 2 hours. This generally means cold water immersion. If the air temperature and the water temperature add to less than 100° F (38° C), there is a risk of acute hypothermia if a person falls into the water. As a rule of thumb, a person who has been in water of 50°F (10° C) or less for a period of 20 minutes or longer, is suffering from a severe amount of heat loss. That individual's thermal mass has been so reduced that they are in potentially serious condition. They should not be allowed to move around as this will increase the blood flow to their very cold skin and facilitate a profound circulatory induced after-drop; one that is so great as to be potentially lethal. If this same person is simply wrapped as a litter case and not provided outside heat, there is a real danger of them cooling below a lethal level due to this profound amount of heat loss.

The ideal treatment is rapid re-warming of the acute hypothermic by placing them in hot water (110° F, or 43° C), forcing rapid replacement of heat. These people may have an almost normal core temperature initially, but one that is destined to drop dramatically as their body equilibrates the heat store from their core to their very cold mantle. A roaring fire can be a life saver. If not available, huddling two naked rescuers with the victim in a large sleeping bag may be the only answer—the same therapy that might have to be employed in the field treatment of chronic hypothermia under some conditions.

Frostbite

Frostbite is the freezing of tissue. Surface skin goes through several phases before this occurs. The freezing process requires predisposing risk factors to be present before the events leading to frostbite are initiated. Outside temperatures must be below freezing for frostbite to occur, in fact skin temperature must be cooled to between 22° to 24° F (-5.5° C to-4.4° C) before tissue will freeze. The underlying physical condition of the victim, length of cold contact, and type of cold contact (such as cold metal or fuel) are other important factors leading to frostbite.

Traditionally, several degrees of frostbite are recognized. Generally, deeply frostbitten flesh will not indent when pressed upon, while superficial injury will also be waxy colored and cold, but will indent. When superficial frost bite is suspected, thaw immediately so that it does not become a more serious, deep frostbite. Warm the hands by withdrawing them into the parka through the sleeves—avoid opening the front of the parka to minimize heat loss. Feet should be thawed against a companion or cupped in your own hands in a roomy sleeping bag, or otherwise in an insulated environment. NEVER, NEVER rub snow on a frostbitten area.

For victims with deep frostbite, rapid rewarming in 110° F (43° C) water is the most effective treatment. This thawing may take 20 to 30 minutes, but it should be continued until all paleness of the tips of the fingers or toes has turned pink or burgundy red, but no longer. This will be very painful and will require pain medication. Refreezing would result in substantial tissue loss. The frozen part should not be thawed if there is any possibility of refreezing the part. Also, once the victim has been thawed, very careful management of the thawed part is required. The patient will become a stretcher case if the foot is involved. For that reason, it may be necessary to leave the foot or leg(s) frozen and allow the victim to walk back to the evacuation point. Tissue damage increases with the length of time that it is allowed to remain frozen, but this damage is less than the refreezing destruction.

Immersion Foot

It is essential that anyone going into the outdoors know how to prevent this injury. It results from wet, cool conditions with temperature exposures from 68° F (20° C) down to freezing. To prevent this problem avoid non-breathing (rubber) footwear when possible, dry the feet and change wool or polypro socks when feet become wet or sweaty (every 3 to 4 hours, at minimum), and periodically elevate, air, dry, and massage the feet to promote circulation. Avoid tight, constrictive clothing. *At night footwear must absolutely be removed and socks changed to dry ones, or simply removed and feet dried before retiring to the sleeping bag.*

There are two clinical stages of immersion foot. In the initial stage the foot is cold, swollen, waxy, mottled with dark burgundy to blue splotches. This foot is spongy to touch, whereas the frozen foot is very hard. Skin is sodden and friable. Loss of feeling makes walking difficult. The second stage lasts from days to weeks. The feet are swollen, red and hot. Blisters form and infection and gangrene are common problems. The pain from immersion foot can be life-long and massive tissue injury can easily develop.

Treatment would include providing the victim 10 grains of aspirin every 6 hours to help decrease platelet adhesion and promote blood circulation. This injury is one of the few medical situations in which alcohol plays a proper role. Providing 1 ounce of hard liquor every hour while awake and 2 ounces every 2 hours during sleeping hours, helps vasodilate and increase the flow of blood to the feet. Immediate stretcher evacuation is necessary.

Other cold injuries such as chilblains, frozen lung, etc., are less threatening and will not seriously injure trip participants. A full treatment of the prevention, diagnosis, and treatment of cold injuries is covered in my book *Hypothermia: Death by Exposure.*

SUN AND HEAT INJURIES

Ultraviolet radiation causing sun burns, eye injuries, and other skin damage, and infrared rays potentially leading to the various forms of illness caused by over-heating, result in many uncomfortable and even lethal situations for the unwary traveler.

Sun and snow blindness is discussed in the section on eye injuries found on page 12 in this manual.

Prickly Heat

Prickly heat is a common problem many people have on exposure to hot, even sub-tropical sun. It is caused by the closure of sweat glands which leads to the formation of small, red blisters on mildly pink skin. This problem is encountered in areas of the body which tend to stay damp or which tend to have contact with damp clothing— such as under the arm pits, hollow of the knee, front of the elbows and forearm, over the collarbone and the front of the chest.

Two factors cause this sogginess. One is high humidity which prevents sweat evaporation as the atmosphere is already saturated. The second is wearing clothes that either prevent sweat from evaporating or from being absorbed. Clothes that help sweat evaporate are loose-fitting. This provides an essential layer of air between the garment and the skin. Fabrics should be chosen that have a high moisture absorption capability, such as cotton, as these wick moisture away from the skin.

It has also been shown that providing adequate air conditioning for 8 hours a day tends to decrease the incidence of prickly heat. British army studies demonstrate a peak incidence of prickly heat after 4 to 5 months of exposure to high humidity-heat conditions, so the average tourist should be spared this malady.

Treatment is accomplished with thorough drying of the skin, bathing with a bland soap, application of drying powders, and seeking increased time in air-conditioned settings.

Sun Burn

Infrared rays from the sun provide heat, but do not burn or tan skin. Long-wave ultraviolet rays, called UVA, between 320 and 400 nanometers cause most drug-induced sun reactions, which can be a problem when the traveler is taking doxycycline or a sulfa drug (such as Bactrim), frequently used to prevent diarrhea or treat infection. Midrange ultraviolet light (UVB), between 290 and 320 nanometers, is the major cause of sunburn. In temperate latitudes only a small portion of UVB reaches the earth's surface before 10:00 AM, or after 3:00 PM. UVA reaches the ground fairly constantly throughout the daylight hours.

Most sun screens are designed to block UVB, but do not block UVA. For persons using the above drugs, special care must be taken during any daylight hours to minimize the chance of a drug reaction. Proper attire, consisting of large brimmed hats and tight knit, dry clothing that covers the front of the neck and the extremities, is a must. Many solar dermatitis reactions are seen in the "V" of the neck, arms, nape of the neck, and legs. Wet clothing, or loosely knit cloth, can allow UV radiation penetration and thus do not provide adequate protection.

People with a pale complexion are at the greatest risk from sun burn. While they need to be primarily concerned about UVB radiation, even a 60 minute exposure to UVA will result in a burn. As mentioned above, the morning and evening hours provide safe initial exposure times, except from UVA. It is best to limit sun exposure on non-tan body surfaces to a 15 minute exposure the first day, 30 minutes the next, 1 hour the day after and increasing exposure times by 1 hour daily from then on. Within 2 weeks, naked skin is tanned adequately to prevent sun burn with even an all day exposure. Problems of sun related skin aging and increased cancer risk remain a concern. Sunblocks are opaque preparations containing titanium dioxide, talc, or zinc oxide that scatter light, preventing any solar ultraviolet radiation from reaching the skin surface. Originally white, there are fashionable brands now available in various bright colors. These products are useful on limited areas, such as the nose, lips and tips of ears.

Sun Protection Factor is a term applied to sun screens that describes the *additional* time that a person may be exposed to the same intensity of sunlight and have the same amount of skin erythema, or reaction. If a person who would normally burn in 1 hour of exposure were to wear a sunscreen with a SPF rating of 5, that person could tolerate 5 hours of sun exposure to reach the same level of burn. Sunscreens are commonly sold with SPF ratings of 2 to 15. Some newly developed products are now available with SPF ratings of 50, allowing a theoretical exposure time beyond the hours of sunlight availability.

The SPF ratings given by the manufacturer can be misleading for several reasons. In 1982 a study of 30 sunscreen products labeled SPF 15 found that none had an actual SPF of greater than 12! Proper application is also very important. Applying too thin of a coat decreases the SPF automatically. The official amount that should be applied is 2 mg/cm::, but your guess is as good as mine as to how thick that turns out to be. Sunscreens are most effective when applied 30 minutes to 1 hour before sun exposure. This allows adequate penetration of the skin. They must be reapplied after sweating or swimming. Waterproof and water-resistant products will still be removed by sweating or toweling off and must be reapplied.

Multiple applications, however, do not increase the SPF rating of the product. For example, if a SPF 5 product is used, the amount of skin redness that develops in 5 hours will not be decreased by multiple applications of this product.

The SPF factor protection increases dramatically the higher the protection rating as indicated in the table on the next page.

Thus, sun protective factor ratings of 15 or greater should be chosen for adequate UV protection. Eighty percent of sun exposure is acquired during the first 20 years of life. The deadly skin cancer called melanoma is directly related to the amount of blistering sunburn re-

Table 7.5
Sun Protective Factor versus
Percentage of UV Protection

SPF	Percent Protection
2	50
4	75
8	87
15	93
29	97

ceived as a child. The incidence of this deadly condition has increased alarmingly. In 1933 the incidence was one case per 10,000 members of the U.S. population. In 1988 the frequency became one case per 150, and in 1990 the estimated frequency is one case per 100 members of our population!

Most sun screen formulae do not protect the traveler from ultraviolet A damage. The only products that provide some protection from UVA are those containing benzophenones and anthranilates, other than the sun blocks mentioned above.

An increase in elevation places a person at more risk from ultraviolet exposure. Each 1,000 foot gain in elevation increases the intensity of the UV effect by 4%. These means that the intensity of sunlight at 5000 feet is greater than that experienced at sea level by 20%.

As mentioned under snow blindness, reflection from snow, sand, and water can increase the effect of this radiation by up to 100%! Not only is this reflective light additive, but the UV radiation can also strike areas of skin that are not normally exposed and are therefore more vulnerable to burn.

Wet skin may make the bather feel cooler, but it does nothing to protect from UV damage or sun burn. UV light can significantly penetrate one fourth an inch of water. Bright cloudy days will block the infrared heat rays from the sun, but will allow 60 to 80% of the ultraviolet rays through.

Many a vacation has been ruined in the attempt to soak up too much sun by beach and pool. One indiscreet hour too many and the traveler will not only be in excruciating pain, but will be readily avoiding all contact with the sun for the next two weeks!

In case of a sun burn, one of the best products to apply would be sheets of Spenco 2nd Skin. This is sold at most athletic supply stores and at many pharmacies across the US. It provides immediate pain relief and helps the skin heal rapidly. Various "caine" ointments and creams are sold for anesthetizing burnt skin. Creams and foams sold to treat hemorrhoids actually make good sun burn creams. Traditional burn ointments provide less relief, but aid in treating this problem. Cold compresses are useful for significant, immediate relief, but most burn victims easily become quite cold and care must be taken not to cool them too much. Oral pain medications are frequently required.

Heat Cramps

Salt depletion can result in nausea, twitching of muscle groups and at times severe cramping of abdominal muscles, legs, or elsewhere. Treatment consists of stretching the muscles involved (avoid overly aggressive massage), resting in a cool environment, and replacing salt losses. Generally 10 to 15 grams (¹/₃ to ¹/₂ oz) of salt and generous water replacement should be adequate treatment.

Heat Exhaustion

This is a classic example of SHOCK, but in this case encountered while working in a hot environment and due to a heat stress injury. The body has dilated the blood vessels in the skin, attempting to divert heat from the core to the surface for cooling. However, this dilation is so pronounced, coupled with the profuse sweating and loss of fluid—also a part of the cooling process—that the blood pressure to the entire system falls too low to adequately supply the brain and the other organs. The patient will have a rapid heart rate, and will have the other findings associated with shock: Pale color, nausea, dizziness, headache, and a light-headed feeling. Generally the patient is sweating profusely, but this may not be the case. Skin temperature may be low, normal, or mildly elevated.

Treat for shock. Have the patient lie down immediately, and elevate the feet to increase the blood supply to the head. Also, provide copious water; 10 to 15 grams of salt would also be helpful, but water is the most important. Give a minimum of 1 to 2 quarts. Obviously, fluids can only be administered if the patient is conscious. If unconscious, elevate the feet 3 feet above head level and try to protect from the potential of accidentally inhaling vomit. Try to revive with stimulation, such as contact with the person or, if available, an ammonia inhalant. Give water when the patient awakens.

Heat Stroke

Heat stroke, or sun stroke as it is also called, represents the complete breakdown of the heat control process (thermal regulation). There is a total loss of the ability to sweat, core temperatures rise over 105° F (40.5° C) *rapidly* and will soon exceed 115° F (46° C) and result in death if this condition is not treated aggressively. THIS IS A TRUE MEDICAL EMERGENCY. The patient will be confused and rapidly become unconscious.

Immediately move the victim into shade or erect a hasty barrier for shade. If possible employ immediate immersion in ice water to lower the temperature. Once the core temperature lowers to 102° F the victim is removed and the temperature carefully monitored. It may continue to fall or suddenly rise again.

Further cooling with wet cloths may suffice. IV solutions of normal saline are started in the clinic setting—otherwise, douse the victim with the coolest water possible. Massage limbs to allow the cooler blood of the extremities to return to the core circulation more readily. Sacrifice your water or other beverage supply if necessary, fan and massage to provide the best coolant effect possible. Heat stroke victims should be evacuated as soon as possible, for their thermal regulation mechanism is quite unstable and will be labile for an unknown length of time. They should be placed under a physician's care as soon as possible.

HIGH ALTITUDE ILLNESS

The high altitude related illnesses can generally be avoided by gradual exposure to higher elevation, with the ascent rate not exceeding 1,000 feet per day when above 6,000 feet. The three major clinical manifestations of this disease complex are outlined on the next page.

Acute Mountain Sickness (AMS)

Rarely encountered below 6,500 feet (2,000 meters), it is common in persons going above 10,000 feet (3,000 meters) without taking the time to acclimatize for altitude. Symptoms beginning soon after ascent consist of headache (often severe), nausea, vomiting, shortness of breath, weakness, sleep disturbance and occasionally a periodic breathing known to physicians as Cheyne-Stokes breathing.

Prevention, as with all of the high altitude illness problems, is gradual ascent to any altitude above 9,000 feet and light physical activity for the first several days. For persons especially prone to AMS, it may be helpful to take acetazolamide (Diamox) 250 mg every 12 hours starting the day before ascent and continuing the next 3 to 5 days. This prescription drug should be added to your medical kit if you expect rapid ascents of elevations above 9,000 feet.

Treatment is descent and relief can often be felt even if the descent is only 2,000 to 3,000 feet (600 to 900 meters). Full relief can be obtained by descending to below 6,500 feet (2,000 meters). Stricken individuals should avoid heavy exercise, but sleep does not help as the breathing is slower during sleep and oxygen deprivation is worse. Oxygen will only help if taken continuously for 12 to 48 hours. Aspirin may be used for headache. Mobigesic from the non-prescription kit may be used. In addition to descent, Decadron (dexamethasone) 4 mg tablets every 6 hours until below the altitude at which symptoms appeared has been shown to help treat AMS. Decadron tablets should be added to your medical kit if you expect to encounter elevations above 9,000 feet.

High Altitude Pulmonary Edema (HAPE)

This problem is rare below 8,000 feet (2,50 meters), but occurs at higher altitude in those poorly acclimatized. It is more prone to occur in persons between the ages of 5 and 18 (the incidence is apparently less than .4% in persons over 21 and as high as 6% in those younger); in persons who have had this problem before; and in persons who have been altitude acclimatized and who are returning to high altitude after spending 2 or more weeks at sea level.

Symptoms develop slowly within 24 to 60 hours of arrival at high altitude with shortness of breath, irritating cough, weakness, rapid heart rate and headache which rapidly progress to intractable cough with bloody sputum, low-grade fever and increasing chest congestion. Symptoms may progress at night. Climbers should be evaluated by listening to their chests for a fine crackling sound (called rales) and have their resting pulse rate checked nightly. A pulse rate of greater than 110 per minute or respirations greater than 16 per minute after a 20 minute rest is an early sign of HAPE. Respirations over 20 per minute and pulse over 120 per minute indicates a medical emergency and the patient must be evacuated immediately. Without treatment, death usually occurs within 6 to 12 hours after onset of coma.

Descent to lower altitude is essential and should not be delayed. Oxygen may be of value if given continuously over the next 12 to 48 hours, starting at 6 liters/minute for the first 15 minutes, then reduced to 2 liters/minute. A snug face mask is better than nasal prongs. Oxygen may provide rapid relief in mild cases, however it should be continued for a minimum of 6 to 12 hours, if possible. Oxygen is not a substitute for descent in severe cases. A descent of as little as

2,000 to 3,000 feet (600 to 900 meters) may result in prompt improvement. Further methods of treatment are described in *Wilderness Medicine*.

Cerebral Edema (CE)

This is a less common event than AMS or HAPE just mentioned, but it is more dangerous. Death has occurred from CE at altitude as low as 8,000 feet (2,500 meters), but CE is rare below 11,500 feet (3,500 meters). The symptoms are increasingly severe headache, mental confusion, emotional behavior, hallucinations, unstable gait, loss of vision, loss of dexterity, and facial muscle paralysis. The victim may fall into a restless sleep, followed by a deep coma and death.

Descent is essential. Oxygen should be administered. Decadron (dexamethasone) should be given in large doses, namely 10 mg intravenous, followed by 4 mg every 6 hours intramuscular until the symptoms subside. Response is usually noted within 12 to 24 hours and the dosage may be reduced after 2 to 4 days and gradually discontinued over a period of 5 to 7 days. Immediate descent and oxygen are recommended to prevent permanent neurological damage or death.

As can be noted from the above discussions of AMS, HAPE, and CE, the symptoms progress rather insidiously. They are not clear-cut, separate diseases—they often occur together. The essential therapy for each of them is recognition and descent. This is life saving and more valuable than the administration of oxygen or the drugs mentioned. To prevent them it is helpful to "climb high, but camp low"—ie, spend nights at the lowest camp elevation feasible.

Chapter 7.8

Travelers' Medical Kit

This select list of medications and equipment relies primarily on non-prescription products to reduce the cost and the problems of acquiring safe and effective components. A list of suggested prescription items is included and described that is keyed to the *Travelers' Self Care Manual* and to the main text of the *Travelers' Medical Resource*. An additional section is included for adding special use drugs for certain travel conditions (such as malaria prophylaxis, acute mountain sickness prophylaxis, etc), as well as personal prescription medications. Finally, a location for telephone numbers, addresses, and other information that might be required in a medical emergency is included.

NON-PRESCRIPTION KIT COMPONENTS

Item: *Spenco 2nd Skin Blister Kit*

Qty: 1 kit

Purpose: Blister and burn treatment

This kit is truly a major advance in first aid. This inert hydrogel consists of 96% water and 4% polyethylene oxide. It is used on wet, weeping wounds to absorb these fluids and to protect the injury. This is a perfect prevention and even cure for friction blisters. It revolutionized the field treatment of 1st, 2nd, and 3rd degree burns, as it can be applied to all three as a perfect sterile covering and for pain relief. This item should be in every medical kit. The ideal covering pad is the Spenco Adhesive Knit Bandage, which comes with the Blister Kit. If used in treating hot spots, remove only the outer covering of cellophane from the Second Skin, cover with the Knit Bandaging, and occasionally dampen with clean water to maintain the hydrogel's hydration. For treatment of developed blisters, apply as above, but remove the top layer of cellophane also before applying the knit bandaging. Moisten as above. This product should not be confused with "Nu Skin" which is useless for treatment of the above problems

Item: *Potable Aqua and 1 liter poly bottle*

Qty: 1 bottle of 50 tablets/1 poly bottle

Purpose: Water purification and storage

Add one tablet per quart of water and allow to stand for 10 minutes prior to consumption. If the water is cloudy, let stand 20 minutes; if very cold increase the waiting period to 30 minutes.

Item: *Hibiclens Surgical Scrub*

Qty: 4 ounces

Purpose: Cleanse and disinfect wounds

This Stuart Pharmaceutical Company product [chlorhexidine gluconate 4%] far surpasses hexachlorophene (pHiso-Hex) and povidone-iodine (Betadine) scrub in its antiseptic action. Its onset and duration of action is also much more impressive than either of those two products. It is safe to use on skin and in open wounds. It should be irrigated from the eye, but will not cause damage with a short period of contact.

Item: *Cover-Strip*

Qty: 1 pkg of 6 each $1/2''$ × $4''$ strips

Purpose: Wound closure tapes

Several brands are available such as Cover-Strip by Beiersdorf, Steri-Strip by 3-M Corp, or even Butterfly Closures by Johnson & Johnson. Cover-Strips are perhaps the best tape wound closure system that can be obtained. These strips can be removed and re-applied while trying to adjust the wound edges and yet they will still retain their adhesive property, a quality that other products do not do as well. These strips breathe and can be left on as long as necessary for the wound to heal, often without an outer covering. Far better than "butterfly" bandages, the latter can be substituted if cost and availability is a factor.

Item: *Triple Antibiotic Ointment*

Qty: 1 one ounce tube

Purpose: Surface wound antibiotic protection

Each gram of this ointment contains bacitracin 400 units, neomycin sulfate 5 mg and polymyxin B sulfate 5000 units. For use as a topical antibiotic in the prevention and treatment of minor infections of abrasions and burns. A light coat should be applied twice daily. If a rash develops after use, it may mean a sensitivity to this product and its use should be discontinued.

Item: *Splinter Forceps*

Qty: 1 pair

Purpose: Splinter removal

Splinter forceps are fine pointed tweezers used to remove foreign bodies from the skin. Regular tweezers may be substituted.

Item: *#11 Scalpel Blade*

Qty: 1

Purpose: Sharp knife blade

This sharp instrument is used to uncover splinters, open boils or blisters, and for other minor procedures. A sharp knife blade can substitute, but it would not be as thin or as sharp.

Item: *Q-Tips*

Qty: 10 pkgs of 2 each, sterile

Purpose: Sterile applicator

Q-Tips can be used to remove foreign bodies from the eye, cleanse wounds, apply medications, or even used as a tooth pick.

Item: *Tape, ¹/₂ Inch*

Qty : 1 Roll

Purpose: Splinting, taping bandages

Old fashion water-proof tape is more versatile than newer knit tapes.

Item: *Actifed*

Qty: 24 Tablets

Purpose: Decongestant

Each tablet contains 60 mg of pseudoephedrine (a vasoconstrictor that dries up mucous formation) and 2.5 mg of triprolidine (an antihistamine to block allergic reactions). Normal dose is 1 tablet every 6 hours to relieve congestion in nasal and sinus passages, and to treat pressure in the middle ear due to eustachian tube blockage.

Item: *Bulb Syringe*

Qty: 1

Purpose: Wound irrigation

A bulb syringe easily and safely jets water into a wound with considerable force to remove residue that would allow infection. It can also be used to remove foreign bodies due to rinsing action as described in the text.

Item: *Antacid Tablets*

Qty: 24 tablets

Purpose: Treat stomach acid

Be sure to choose high potency antacid tablets. Various brands may be substituted, but do not forget an antacid!

Item: *Meclizine 25 mg*

Qty: 10 tablets

Purpose: Treat nausea, motion sickness

This item is very effective for nausea and vomiting, particularly when due to motion sickness. Dosage is 1 tablet daily. While sold non-Rx only for motion sickness, with prescription this may be taken 3 times daily for dizziness due to inner ear dysfunction. It will work against nausea from virtually any cause.

Item: *Benadryl 25 mg*

Generic Name: Diphenhydramine

Qty: 24 capsules

Purpose: Antihistamine

These capsules can be taken 1 or 2 every 6 hours to suppress allergy conditions of the skin and allergy or viral induced congestion. Benadryl is also a powerful cough suppressor, the dose being 1 capsule every 6 hours.

Item: *Mobigesic* (or equal)

Qty: 24 tablets

Purpose: Pain relief

A powerful, yet non-prescription, medication, Mobigesic relieves pain, fever, inflammation, and muscle spasm. Each tablet contains 325 mg of magnesium salicylate and 30 mg of phenyltoloxamine citrate. Ideal for arthritis and injuries of joints and muscles, as well as aches from infections. One of the most useful non-Rx drugs obtainable.

Item: *Hydrocortisone Cream .5%*

Qty: 1 ounce

Purpose: Skin allergy

This non-Rx steroid cream treats allergic skin rashes, such as those from poison ivy. A cream is ideal for treating weeping lesions, as opposed to dry scaly ones, but will work on either. To potentiate this medication apply an occlusive dressing (plastic cover) overnight.

Item: *Miconazole Cream 2%*

Qty: 1 ounce

Purpose: Antifungal

This is one of the most effective antifungal preparations available for foot, groin, or body fungal infections. Brand names are Monistat Derm and Micatin. The former is sold by Rx only, but Micatin and the generic product have been available without Rx since 1983.

Item: *Diasorb*

Qty: 24 Tablets

Purpose: Anti-diarrhea

The safest non-Rx anti-diarrhea agent made, it works as well as Imodium, which is a strong antimotility product. Available in liquid or tablets, the latter are easier to carry. Take 4 tablets at the first sign of diarrhea and repeat after each subsequent bowel movement or every 2 hours, whichever comes first. Maximum dose for an adult is 12 tablets per day. Use 2 tablets for children 6–12 and 1 tablet for children 3–6. Tablets should not be chewed, but rather swallowed whole with water. Carry the liquid for children who cannot swallow pills. This product controls diarrhea, but it also does not trap dangerous bacteria or parasites in the bowel as the indiscriminate use of Imodium or Lomotil is apt to due.

Item: *Imodium 2 mg*

Generic Name: Loperamide

Qty: 12 capsules

Purpose: Diarrhea

Imodium brand of loperamide lessens the secretion of fluid into the colon and decreases excess cramping of the colon, thus stopping diarrhea. It must be used with caution, especially if bloody diarrhea is present. A bloody diarrhea can indicate invasive organisms which will cause more harm if trapped in the colon. It is very effective, however, and provides rapid, symptomatic relief of diarrhea. The dose is two capsules immediately, followed by one capsule after each loose stool, up to a maximum of eight capsules per day. A pediatric form of liquid Imodium is also available without a prescription. Note the further description concerning the treatment of diarrhea on page 26.

PRESCRIPTION MEDICATIONS

The following prescription items may be necessary for use in prevention or treatment of medical problems during your travels. The quantities suggested are meant to support one person for treatment, not prophylaxis, purposes. Two antibiotics have been suggested for this kit. One or the other should suffice. These have been chosen based on their wide spectrum of activity against common travel infections, their general low level of side effects, and their reasonable cost. Your physician may suggest an alternate antibiotic. This information can then be entered into the notebook section of this handbook.

Suggested Prescription Kit Components

Item: *Doxycycline 100 mg*

Qty: 10

Purpose: Antibiotic

This antibiotic can be used to treat diarrhea and most infections at a dose of one tablet taken twice daily. When used for prevention of traveler's diarrhea or malaria prophylaxis the dosage is one tablet taken once daily. This product is not to be used in children 8 years or younger or during pregnancy. It may cause skin sensitivity on exposure to sunlight, thus causing an exaggerated sunburn. This does not usually happen, but be cautious during your first sun exposure when on this product. Many people traveling in the tropics have used this antibiotic safely. Common brand names are Vibramycin, Vibra-tabs, Vivox, and Doryx. Recommended quantity of 10 tablets would have to be increased if this medication is being used for disease prophylaxis rather than treatment.

Item: *Bactrim DS*

Generic Name: Sulfamethoxazole/
trimethoprim

Qty: 10 tablets

Purpose: Antibiotic

This is a brand name of a combination of
two antibiotics, namely 800 mg of sulfamethoxazole and 160 mg of trimethoprim. Another common brand name is Septra DS. It is useful in
treating traveler's diarrhea and many other infections utilizing a dose of one tablet twice daily. It
should not be used at term of pregnancy or when
nursing. Stop using in case of a skin rash as this
may precede a more serious reaction. When used
to prevent traveler's diarrhea, the dose is one tablet taken once daily. This product can also cause
photosensitization, as indicated under doxycycline listed above.

Item: *Tobrex Ophthalmic Ointment .3%*

Generic Name: Tobramycin

Qty: 1/8 ounce tube

Purpose: Antibiotic ointment for eye and
ear

Tobrex is a brand name for tobramycin ophthalmic ointment. While designed as an antibiotic
for the eye, it is safe to apply to infected ear
canals. This is useable on any surface infection,
but too expensive to be carried for general skin
use.

Item: *Pontocaine Ophthalmic Ointment* *.5%*

Generic Name: Tetracaine

Qty: $1/8$ ounce tube

Purpose: Eye pain

This sterile medication is packed especially for use in the eye, but it can be used to numb pain on the eye surface or to treat ear pain. Do not reapply to eye if pain returns without examining for the presence of a foreign body on the eye surface very carefully. Apply once daily as needed for eye pain. Do not use in an ear if there is considerable drainage as an ear drum may have ruptured—avoid use if ear drum is ruptured. Allow to melt into the ear canal and do not poke it in with a Q-Tip.

Item: *Topicort ointment .25%*

Generic Name: Desoximetasone

Qty: $1/2$ ounce tube

Purpose: Allergic skin reactions

This prescription steroid ointment treats severe allergic skin rashes. Ointments work best on dry, scaly lesions. Weeping, blistered areas are best treated with creams, or even wet soaks of dilute salt solution. Dosage is a thin coat twice daily. It should be used with caution over large body surface areas or in children. Use should be limited to 10 days or less.

Item: *Carafate 1 gram*

Generic Name: Sucralfate

Qty: 20 or more

Purpose: Heartburn or ulcer

Carafate is the brand name of sucralfate, an aluminum starch complex that heals and prevents ulcers and other damage to the gastric system from acid, medications, or other irritants. It does not affect acidity in the stomach, which is a plus for travelers. Reduced stomach acidity makes a person more vulnerable to bacteria and virus infections potentially causing traveler's diarrhea. Its healing action is due to a coating process. Very little is absorbed into the blood stream. This is a safe medication with few side effects.

Item *Atarax 25 mg tablet*

Generic Name: Hydroxyzine

Qty: 20 tablets

Purpose: nausea, anti-histamine, pain medication augmentation

Atarax is the brand name of hydroxyzine hydrochloride. These tablets have multiple uses. They are a very powerful anti-nausea agent, muscle relaxer, antihistamine, anti-anxiety agent, sleeping pill, and narcotic potentiator. For sleep 50 mg at bed time; for nausea 25 mg every 4 to 6 hours; to potentiate a narcotic, take two 25 mg tablets with each dose of the pain medication.

This medication helps with rashes of all types and has a drying effect on congestion.

Item *Tylenol #3*

Generic Name: Acetaminophen/codeine

Qty: 24 tablets

Purpose: pain, diarrhea, cough

Tylenol #3 is the brand name of a combination of 300 mg of acetaminophen and 30 mg of codeine phosphate. The principle use of this drug is in the relief of pain. Codeine is one of the most powerful cough suppression and anti-diarrhea agents known. Also useful in treating abdominal cramping. The dosage of 1 tablet every 4 hours will normally control a toothache. Maximum dosage is 2 tablets every 3 to 4 hours, augmented with Atarax—see above. Codeine tablets can be obtained without the acetaminophen, but they are considered a Class II narcotic which increases the difficulty of obtaining a prescription and which could complicate border crossing inquiries. Tylenol #3 is considered a Class III narcotic, even though the codeine content per tablet is the same strength as in the more restricted plain codeine tablet.

Item: *Transderm Scōp*

Generic Name: Scopolamine

Qty: 1 box of 4 patches

Purpose: To prevent motion sickness

Transderm Scop, a patch containing scopolamine, has been developed for prevention of motion sickness using the transdermal method of
providing medication. Each patch may be worn
behind the ear for 3 days. It is fairly expensive,
but very worth while if you are prone to this malady. There tends to be a higher frequency of side
effects with this medication in elderly people,
such as visual problems, confusion, and loss of
temperature regulation.

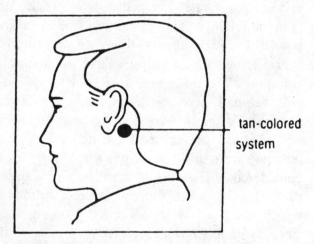

tan-colored
system

FIGURE 7-9
The proper placement of Transderm Scop, a prescription product used to prevent sickness.

Customizing Your Medical Kit

Additional quantities, substitutions for the above recommended products, and additional components may be indicated depending upon the traveler's activities, destination, remoteness from identified sources of acceptable medical help, and personal medical history. The best source for advice on these changes would be your physician or a travel medicine clinic in conjunction with your physician. The chapter on "Obtaining Help" in the *Travelers' Medical Resource* lists addresses and telephone numbers of many travel medical clinics and specialists who may be able to help you if you do not have a personal physician who is interested in travel medicine.

There are a variety of items that you will want to consider carrying on your trip. While some of these are not medical supplies, their existence can make your medical "survival" and comfort much more likely.

You cannot bring too many zip-lock baggies. They seem to have dozens of uses, and more keep presenting themselves all of the time.

Carry a strong 1 quart poly bottle in which to purify or carry water. It may be a long time between safe sources of water. Carry some water purification tablets, even if you do not think you may need to use them. While the nonprescription kit mentioned above includes Potable Aqua and a poly bottle for a water purification system, a coffee cup heating coil may suffice for many travelers. Be certain to also include a electrical current conversion system when traveling overseas, or the heating coil may not be operable.

Carry some high calorie trail munchies—edible food may be scarce at times for a number of reasons.

Keep medication in carry-on luggage to help with compliance in following prescribed dosage times, prevent loss, and to serve as a rough medical history in an emergency.

Persons with chronic illnesses should wear a "Medic Alert" bracelet or other attention getting device listing their disabilities. The address for Medic Alert is : Medical Alert Foundation International, Turlock, CA 95381–1009. Telephone is 1–800-ID-ALERT (1–800–736–3342).

Consideration should be given to a dental kit. As a minimum, a small bottle of oil of cloves (eugenol) can serve as a topical toothache treatment or a tube of toothache gel can be obtained.

A fever thermometer should be included on trips.

People wearing contact lenses should carry the special suction cup or rubber pincer device to aid in their removal.

Do not forget mosquito netting and insect repellent if you are visiting the tropics or bug infested areas, particularly if insect borne disease is a possibility. The Extractor, as described on page 42, is recommended when travel is contemplated into areas where first aid care of snake bite or severe insect sting may be encountered.

Access to hydrogen peroxide, vinegar, alcohol and formalin may be useful when potential harm from jelly fish, coral, or ocean sponges is possible. Fishermen should carry a pair of side-cutting wire cutters, if fishing with barbed hooks, to facilitate their removal from human puncture wounds by the push-through-snip-off method.

To help you gather and organize your travel medical kit, the following outlines and quantities are provided in table format to match the text description of the non-prescription and recommended prescription components:

TABLE 7-6
THE TRAVEL MEDICAL KIT
NON-PRESCRIPTION COMPONENTS

QTY*	ITEM DESCRIPTION
1 ea	Spenco 2nd Skin Blister Kit
1 bottle	Potable Aqua—50 tablets
1 ea	Poly bottle—1 liter
1 ea	Hibiclens Surgical Scrub—4 oz
1 ea	Coverstrip—6/pack—$1/2''$ × 4'' strips
1 ea	Triple Antibiotic—1 oz tube
1 ea	Splinter Forceps
1 ea	#11 Scalpel Blade
10 pks	Q Tips—2/pack, sterile
1 roll	Tape, Waterproof—$1/2$'' wide
1 bottle	Actifed—24 tablets
1 ea	Bulb Syringe
1 bottle	Antacid Tablets—24 tablets
1 bottle	Meclizine 25 mg—10 tablets
1 bottle	Benadryl 25 mg—24 capsules
1 bottle	Mobigesic—24 tablets
1 tube	Hydrocortisone Cream .5%—1 oz
1 tube	Miconazole Cream 2%—1 oz
1 bottle	Diasorb—24 tablets
12 capsules	Imodium 2 mg

* Quantity recommended per individual traveler.

TABLE 7-7
THE TRAVEL MEDICAL KIT
RECOMMENDED PRESCRIPTION COMPONENTS

QTY*	ITEM DESCRIPTION
10 tablets	Doxycycline 100 mg
10 tablets	Bactrim DS
1 tube	Tobrex Ophthalmic Ointment .3%—1/8 oz
1 tube	Pontocaine Ophthalmic Ointment .5%—1/8 oz
1 tube	Topicort Ointment—1/2 oz
20+ tablets	Carafate 1 gram
20 tablets	Atarax 25 mg
24 tablets	Tylenol #3
1 box	Transderm Scop—4 patches ea

* Quantity recommended per individual traveler.

Assembling Your Medical Kit

The above kit, excluding prescription items, can be purchased pre-packed, and/or the individual items may be purchased separately from Indiana Camp Supply, Inc., PO Box 211, Hobart, Indiana 46342—telephone (219) 947–2525. Since 1972 Indiana Camp Supply has specialized in supporting wilderness expeditions and many governmental agencies with medical components. Besides the Travelers' Medical Kit recommended above, they carry an extensive listing of all manner of non-prescription medical articles available by mail order. *Wilderness Medicine, 3rd Edition* describes medical kit construction in detail for the problems of travel that extend beyond the requirements of the average foreign travel adventure.[3]

Customizing Your Medical Kit
While this book offers basic suggestions for antibiotic and other medication, your physician advisors may wish to substitute other products. If alternate medications are to be used, fill in their names (brand name and generic), purpose, and dosage instructions in the following section. Special purpose items should also be obtained and included in the spaces provided.

[3]*Wilderness Medicine, 3rd Edition*, is available from ICS Books, 107 East 89th Avenue, Merrillville, IN 46410, telephone (219) 769-0585, for $7.95 plus $1.50 shipping and handling.

Medications Recommended By My Doctor

The Customized Medical Kit
Purpose: Antibiotic
Qty:
Item: *Name, strength, and dosage instructions—*

Purpose: Alternate Antibiotic
Qty:
Item: *Name, strength, and dosage instructions—*

Purpose: Anti-diarrhea
Qty:
Item: *Name, strength, and dosage instructions—*

Purpose: Acute Mountain Sickness
Qty:
Item: *Name, strength, and dosage instructions—*

Purpose: Malaria Prophylaxis
Qty:
Item: *Name, strength, and dosage instructions—*

Purpose: Motion Sickness
Qty:
Item: *Name, strength, and dosage instructions—*

Purpose: Jet Lag
Qty:
Item: *Name, strength, and dosage instructions—*

Purpose: Water purification
Qty:
Item: *Name, strength, and dosage instructions—*

Purpose: Allergies
Qty:
Item: *Name, strength, and dosage instructions—*

Purpose: Pain Medication
Qty:
Item: *Name, strength, and dosage instructions—*

Purpose: Heart Burn/Gastritis
Qty:
Item: *Name, strength, and dosage instructions—*

Purpose: Cough/Cold Relief
Qty:
Item: *Name, strength, and dosage instructions—*

Chapter 7.9

Personal Information Section

Full Name _____

Street Address _____

City _____ State ____ ZIP _____

Telephone _____

Social Security Number _____

Passport Number _____

Birth Date _____ Place _____

My Special Health Problems:
Include allergies, surgeries, current medical problems for which you routinely or occasionally take medication

Personal Prescription Medications:
Brand name, generic name, purpose, dosage instructions for each

Emergency Contacts at Home:
Names, addresses, telephones, relationship

Travel Medical Insurance:
Company, U.S. telephone, local country contact information, policy identification number

Names of Significant Other Traveling Companions
Names, home addresses, home telephones, relationship

Additional Family Member Information Page

Full Name _____

Social Security Number _____

Passport Number _____

Birth Date _____ **Place** _____

Special Health Problems:
Include allergies, surgeries, current medical problems for which you routinely or occasionally take medication

Personal Prescription Medications:
Brand name, generic name, purpose, dosage instructions for each

Travel Medical Insurance:
Policy identification number

Country Information Page

Country:

Dates visit planned:

VISA requirements:

Immunizations required:

U.S. Embassy *addresses and telephone numbers:*
Refer to Travelers' Medical Resource, Country
Information Database, beginning on page ____

IAMAT Physician *names, addresses, telephone*
numbers:
Refer to Travelers' Medical Resource, page ____

Canadian High Commission *addresses and*
telephone numbers:
Refer to Travelers' Medical Resource, Country
Information Database, beginning on page ____

Business and other local contacts:

Country Information Page

Country:

Dates visit planned:

VISA requirements:

Immunizations required:

U.S. Embassy *addresses and telephone numbers:*
Refer to Travelers' Medical Resource, Country
Information Database, beginning on page ____

IAMAT Physician *names, addresses, telephone*
numbers:
Refer to Travelers' Medical Resource, page ____

Canadian High Commission *addresses and*
telephone numbers:
Refer to Travelers' Medical Resource, Country
Information Database, beginning on page ____

Business and other local contacts:

Section 8
Herchmer Individual Country Database

A combination of sources (including CDC, WHO, IAMAT, State
Department, several consulting sources, the Morbidity and Mortality
Weekly Report of the US Public Health Service, and many medical
journals) are used to update an extensive computer database of medical
information of interest to travelers. Called the Herchmer Individual
Country Database, this information is updated constantly, at least weekly.
Much of the information concerning infectious disease relies upon the
willingness of a given country to provide accurate data in compliance
with International Health Regulations. Users of this information must
take this into account and at no time assume that the extent of infection
is limited to the areas reported or that a specific disease does not exist
in countries in which it is not listed.

The Herchmer Individual Country Database is divided into sections
discussing: vaccinations (required and/or recommended for all travelers
and recommended for specific types of activities in the country which
might place the traveler at special risk); malaria risk (to include
geographical distribution within the country, seasons of danger, and
appropriate medications to take for the strains and resistance patterns
which have been reported within that country); a special section on
diseases of special risk (with a table of frequency and a discussion of
geographical distribution of specific diseases such as schistosomiasis);
food, water and dairy safety assessment; the location of U.S. Embassy
and Canadian Government Representatives, to include telephone
numbers; and the complete text of any Department of State Travel
Advisories.

The disease risk tables indicate a frequency, or risk, pattern. "Endemic" indicates that a disease is potentially present in a country at all times, or conditions are such that this disease could be reintroduced at any time. "Risk" reflects an increased chance of catching a particular condition and that special caution is advised. "Hazard" signifies a very high degree of risk and that caution is necessary to avoid the conditions and vectors by which this disease can be spread. Diseases in this list are frequently prevalent amongst native populations.

When various agencies and experts differ in their recommendations, a consensus opinion has been included in the Herchmer Individual Country Database, current as of the time of this book's publication.

In spite of this last minute accuracy, the urgent and critical nature of the information dates this book before it is out of the shipping carton. Special hot lines will help update much of this critical information. The Department of State consumer hot line (202-647-5225) can be consulted for updates on travel advisory bulletins (see also Chapter 2.2). The Centers for Disease Control hot line (404-639-1610) can be consulted for their current recommendations on malaria prophylaxis (see also Chapter 2.3).

Continuous access to the Herchmer Individual Country Database is available. By sending $15.00 for the first country and $10.00 for each additional selection, persons may acquire a copy of the current Herchmer database for any country listed in this book. The address is Herchmer Medical Consultants, 109 East 89th Avenue, Merrillville, IN 46410. Telephone (219) 769-0866. FAX (219) 769-6035. VISA and MC are accepted for telephone, FAX, or written requests.

Afghanistan

INFECTIOUS DISEASE RISK

Malaria Risk

Malaria risk is from May through November. Malaria may be encountered throughout the country below 2000 meters, to include urban areas. The malaria in this country is resistant to chloroquine. The CDC recommends the use of mefloquine (Lariam) as described in Chapter 6.31 for chemical prophylaxis.

Falciparum malaria represents < 1% of malaria, therefore there is a risk of p. vivax malaria exposure. Consider the use of primaquine upon return home (see Chapter 6.31).

Diseases of Special Risk

In addition to the worldwide hazard of tetanus, the routine and special immunizations required or recommended below, and malaria as indicated above, the traveler should be aware that risk of exposure to the following diseases exists in this country.

DISEASE RISK PROFILE

Disease	endemic	risk	hazard
Brucellosis		x	
Cholera		x	
Echinococcosis		x	
Giardiasis		x	
Diarrheal Diseases		x	
Helminthic Infections		x	
Hepatitis, Viral		x	
Leishmaniasis			x
Sandfly Fever			x
Tapeworms		x	
Trachoma		x	
Trichinosis		x	
Typhoid Fever		x	

Food/Water Safety

Water, milk products, and cold food unsafe.

VACCINATIONS

Yellow fever—A vaccination certificate is required for travelers coming from infected areas. A vaccination is required for children of all ages. Children under one year of age should not be vaccinated due to health considerations. Please refer to the discussion in Chapter 6.63 on avoiding yellow fever vaccination in this age group.

Routine immunizations should be current. For infants and children through 16 years of age, refer to Chapter 4.3. A rubeola (measles) booster should be considered. Persons age 16 to 65 should receive a booster of tetanus and diphtheria every ten years. Healthy adults under age 65 do not require pneumococcal vaccine, but this should be considered for those with chronic medical conditions. Influenza vaccine may be considered for those providing essential community services, health care workers, and those wishing to reduce the likelihood of becoming ill with influenza. Adults over 65 years of age are urged to obtain yearly influenza immunization, and to insure that their tetanus and diphtheria immunizations are current. Pneumococcal vaccination is also suggested for this age group.

Poliomyelitis—A poliomyelitis booster is indicated for this country.

Viral Hepatitis A—Vaccination is recommended for all travelers for their protection.

Typhoid Fever—Vaccination is recommended for all travelers for their protection.

Viral Hepatitis B—Because of the high rate of healthy carriers of hepatitis B in this country, vaccination is recommended for persons on working assignments in the health care field (dentists, physicians, nurses, laboratory technicians), or working in close contact with the local population (teachers, missionaries, Peace Corps), or persons foreseeing sexual relations with local inhabitants.

Plague—Vaccination is recommended only for persons who may be occupationally exposed to wild rodents (anthropologists, geologists, medical personnel, missionaries, etc). The standard vaccination course must be completed before entering the plague infested area. Georgraphical distribution of the area of risk for this country is a small region in the extreme northeastern part of the country.

Typhus—Louse-borne typhus is cosmopolitan in distribution and is present wherever groups of persons are crowded together under conditions of poor sanitation and malnutrition. Risk exists for persons living or working in remote areas of the country (anthropologists, archeologists, geologists, medical personnel, missionaries, etc.). Freedom from louse infestation is the most effective protection against typhus.

U.S. Foreign Service
   Wazir Akbar Khan Mina
   Kabul, Telephone 24230-9
   Available Sunday—Thursday

DEPARTMENT OF STATE TRAVEL ADVISORY
9FB DN37 1-1 1LA71 1 02/15/89 02:39
SECSTATE WSH SUBJECT:
TRAVEL ADVISORY— AFGHANISTAN— WARNING

1. THE DEPARTMENT OF STATE CONTINUES STRONGLY TO URGE U.S. CITIZENS TO AVOID TRAVEL TO AFGHANISTAN. A HIGH LEVEL OF RISK AND INSTABILITY PREVAILS DUE TO CONTINUED COMBAT BETWEEN AFGHAN GOVERNMENT AND AFGHAN RESISTANCE FORCES.
2. ALL PERSONNEL AT THE U.S. EMBASSY IN KABUL WERE EVACUATED ON JANUARY 31, 1989, AND THERE ARE NO PROVISIONS FOR ANY OTHER DIPLOMATIC MISSION TO PROVIDE SERVICES TO AMERICAN CITIZENS.
3. DUE TO THE VERY DOUBTFUL RECORD OF MAINTENANCE OF AIRCRAFT, THE DEPARTMENT OF STATE STRONGLY RECOMMENDS AGAINST TRAVEL ON ALL FLIGHTS BY BAHAR (ARIANA) AFGHAN AIRLINES.
4. THIS TRAVEL ADVISORY CANCELS THE ADVISORY CONTAINED IN 88 STATE 235788, DATED JULY 31, 1988.
5. EXPIRATION DATE: INDEFINITE. DEPARTMENT OF STATE OC/T ROOM 5440 WASHINGTON D.C. 20520

Country Number 8.2
Albania

INFECTIOUS DISEASE RISK

Diseases of Special Risk

In addition to the worldwide hazard of tetanus, the traveler should be aware that risk of exposure to the following diseases exists in this country.

DISEASE RISK PROFILE

Disease	endemic	risk	hazard
Brucellosis	x		
Echinococcosis	x		
Encephalitis, Tick-Borne	x		
Leishmaniasis	x		
Rabies	x		
Sandfly Fever	x		
Typhus, Endemic Flea-Borne	x		
West Nile Fever	x		

Food/Water Safety

Water probably safe, although not recommended. Milk and food safe. Dysentery, other diarrheas and typhoid fever are more common in the summer and autumn in southeastern and southwestern areas.

VACCINATIONS

Yellow fever—A vaccination certificate is required for travelers coming from infected areas. A vaccination certificate is required for children over one year of age.

Routine immunizations should be current. For infants and children through 16 years of age, refer to Chapter 4.3. A rubeola (measles) booster should be considered. Persons age 16 to 65 should receive a booster of tetanus and diphtheria every ten years. Healthy adults under age 65 do not require pneumococcal vaccine, but this should be considered for those with chronic medical conditions. Influenza vaccine may be considered for those providing essential community services, health care workers, and those wishing to reduce the likelihood of becoming ill with influenza. Adults over 65 years of age are urged to obtain yearly influenza immunization, and to insure that their tetanus and diphtheria immunizations are current. Pneumococcal vaccination is also suggested for this age group.

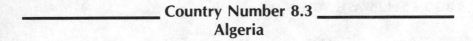

Country Number 8.3
Algeria

INFECTIOUS DISEASE RISK

Malaria Risk

Malaria risk is from May through November. There is no malaria risk in urban areas. There is very limited risk in the Sahara region. See Chapter 6.31 for use of Chloroquine. Centers for Disease Control does not currently recommend preventative medication.

Falciparum malaria represents < 1% of malaria, therefore there is a slight risk of p. vivax malaria exposure. Consider the use of primaquine upon return home.

Diseases of Special Risk

Schistosomiasis may be found in this country. Avoid contact with contaminated fresh water lakes, ponds, or streams. Infection is present in the area of Biskra; along the river (Oued) Djidioua and in Khemis el Khechna in Northern Algeria; in the Oasis of Djanet (Fort Charlet) near the border with Libya, and in the area of Be'ni-Abbe's in the western part of the country near the border of Morocco.

Diarrheal diseases, to include helminthic infections and dysentery are common in this country. Hepatitis A and typhoid fever are common.

In addition to the worldwide hazard of tetanus, the routine and special immunizations required or recommended below, and specific diseases indicated above, the traveler should be aware that risk of exposure to the following diseases exists in this country.

DISEASE RISK PROFILE

Disease	endemic	risk	hazard
Brucellosis		x	
Dengue Fever	x		
Echinococcosis	x		
Giardiasis		x	
Lassa Fever	x		
Leishmaniasis	x		
Rabies	x		
Relapsing Fever	x		
Sandfly Fever	x		
Trachoma	x		
Tungiasis		x	
Typhoid Fever		x	
Typhus, Endemic Flea-Borne			
Typhus, Epidemic Louse-Borne	x		

Food/Water Safety

Water, milk products and cold food are not safe in this county.

VACCINATIONS

Yellow fever—A vaccination certificate is required for travelers coming from infected areas. A vaccination certificate is required for children over one year of age.

Routine immunizations should be current. For infants and children through 16 years of age, refer to Chapter 4.3. A rubeola (measles) booster should be considered. Persons age 16 to 65 should receive a booster of tetanus and diphtheria every ten years. Healthy adults under age 65 do not require pneumococcal vaccine, but this should be considered for those with chronic medical conditions. Influenza vaccine may be considered for those providing essential community services, health care workers, and those wishing to reduce the likelihood of becoming ill with influenza. Adults over 65 years of age are urged to obtain yearly influenza immunization, and to insure that their tetanus and diphtheria immunizations are current. Pneumococcal vaccination is also suggested for this age group.

The following vaccinations listed for this country are listed for the traveler's protection, but they are not required for entry.

Poliomyelitis—A poliomyelitis booster is indicated for this country.

Viral Hepatitis A—Vaccination is recommended when traveling outside the areas usually visited by tourists, traveling extensively in the interior of the country (trekkers, hikers) and for persons on working assignments in remote areas.

Typhoid fever—Vaccination is recommended when traveling outside the areas usually visited by tourists, traveling extensively in the interior of the country (trekkers, hikers) and for persons on working assignments in remote areas.

Selective vaccinations—These apply only to specific groups of travelers or persons on specific working assignments.

Rabies—In this country, where rabies is a constant threat, a pre-exposure rabies vaccination is advised for persons planning an extended stay or on working assignments (naturalists, agricultural advisors, archeologists, geologists, etc.). Although this provides adequate initial protection, a person bitten by a potentially rabid animal would still require post exposure immunization. Children should be cautioned not to pet dogs, cats, or other mammals.

U.S. Foreign Service
   4 Chemin Cheich Bachir Brahimi
   Algiers, Telephone 60-14-25/255/186

   14 Square de Bamako
   Oran, Telephone 39-09-72, 39-99-41
   (Workweek:Saturday—Wednesday)

Canadian Embassy Address:
   27 Bis Rued' Anjou
   Hydra, Telephone 60-66-11

Country Number 8.4
American Samoa

INFECTIOUS DISEASE RISK

Malaria Risk
   None.

Diseases of Special Risk
   This country must be considered receptive to dengue fever. Intermittent epidemics in the past make renewed activity or reintroduction of the virus possible.
   In addition to the worldwide hazard of tetanus and the routine and special immunizations required and recommended below, the traveler should be aware that risk of exposure to the following diseases exists in this country.

DISEASE RISK PROFILE

Disease	endemic	risk	hazard
Dengue Fever	x		
Encephalitis, Japanese	x		
Filariasis			x

Food/Water Safety
Water is safe, but is not recommended without treatment. Milk products and food safe.

VACCINATIONS

*Yellow fever—A vaccination certificate is required for travelers coming from infected areas. A vaccination certificate is required for children over one year of age.

Routine immunizations should be current. For infants and children through 16 years of age, refer to Chapter 4.3. A rubeola (measles) booster should be considered. Persons age 16 to 65 should receive a booster of tetanus and diphtheria every ten years. Healthy adults under age 65 do not require pneumococcal vaccine, but it is appropriate for those with chronic medical conditions. Influenza vaccine may be considered for those providing essential community services, health care workers, and those wishing to reduce the likelihood of becoming ill with influenza. Adults over 65 years of age are urged to obtain yearly influenza immunization, and to insure that their tetanus and diphtheria immunizations are current. Pneumococcal vaccination is also suggested for this age group.

Viral Hepatitis A—Vaccination is recommended for all travelers for their protection.

Typhoid fever— Vaccination is recommended for all travelers for their protection.

Selective vaccinations—These apply only to specific groups of travelers or persons on specific working assignments:
Viral Hepatitis B—Because of the high rate of healthy carriers of hepatitis B in this country, vaccination is recommended for persons on working assignments in the health care field (dentists, physicians, nurses, laboratory technicians), or working in close contact with the local population (teachers, missionaries, Peace Corps), or persons foreseeing sexual relations with local inhabitants.

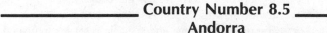

Country Number 8.5
Andorra

INFECTIOUS DISEASE RISK

Food/Water Safety
Water is probably safe, but due to local variations in bacterial counts, using bottled water for the first few weeks will help the traveler adjust and decrease the chance of traveler's diarrhea. Local meat, poultry, seafood, vegetables, and fruits are safe to eat.

VACCINATIONS

Routine immunizations should be current. For infants and children through 16 years of age, refer to Chapter 4.3. A rubeola (measles) booster should be considered. Persons age 16 to 65 should receive a booster of tetanus and diphtheria every ten years. Healthy adults under age 65 do not require pneumococcal vaccine, but it is appropriate for those with chronic medical conditions. Influenza vaccine may be considered for those providing essential community services, health care workers, and those wishing to reduce the likelihood of becoming ill with influenza. Adults over 65 years of age are urged to obtain yearly influenza immunization, and to insure that their tetanus and diphtheria immunizations are current. Pneumococcal vaccination is also suggested for this age group.

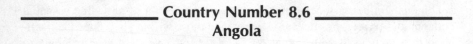

Country Number 8.6
Angola

INFECTIOUS DISEASE RISK

Malaria Risk

Malaria is present in all parts of this country, including urban areas. The risk exists all year. Resistance has developed in this country to chloroquine. The CDC recommends the use of mefloquine for prophylaxis as described in Chapter 6.31.

Falciparum malaria represents 90% of malaria, therefore there is a slight risk of p. vivax malaria exposure. Consider use of primaquine upon return home (see Chapter 4.7).

Diseases of Special Risk

This country must be considered receptive to dengue fever. Intermittent epidemics in the past make renewed activity or reintroduction of the virus possible.

Schistosomiasis may be found in this country. Avoid contact with contaminated fresh water lakes, ponds, or streams. It is present except in the Districts of Cabinda, Zaire, and Uige in the north-western part of the country.

In addition to the worldwide hazard of tetanus, the routine and special immunizations required or recommended below, and specific diseases indicated above, the traveler should be aware that risk of exposure to the following diseases exists in this country.

DISEASE RISK PROFILE

Disease	endemic	risk	hazard
Cholera			x
Dysentery			x
Dracunculiasis/Guinea Worm	x		
Filariasis			x
Giardiasis			x
Hepatitis A		x	
Helminthic Infections			x
Leishmaniasis	x		
Onchocerciasis			x
Relapsing Fever	x		
Tapeworms	x		
Trachoma			x
Trypanosomiasis, African Sleeping Sickness	x		
Typhoid Fever		x	
Typhus, Endemic Flea-Borne	x		
Typhus, Epidemic Louse-Borne	x		
Typhus, Scrub	x		

Food/Water Safety

All tap water used for drinking, brushing teeth, and making ice cubes should be boiled prior to use. Insure that bottled water is uncapped in your presence. Milk should be boiled to insure safety. Powdered and evaporated milk are available and safe. Avoid butter and other dairy products. All meat, poultry and seafood must be well cooked and served while hot. Pork is best avoided. Vegetables should be well cooked and served hot. Salads and mayonnaise are best avoided. Fruits with intact skins should be peeled by you just prior to consumption. Avoid cold buffets, custards, and any frozen dessert.

VACCINATIONS

Cholera—A cholera vaccination certificate is not required for entry to this country. The disease is active in this country and a cholera vaccination may be required for travel to other countries.

Yellow fever—A vaccination certificate is required for travelers coming from infected areas. A vaccination certificate is required for children over one year of age. CDC recommends a yellow fever vaccination for all travelers over 9 months of age who will travel outside of urban areas.

Routine immunizations should be current. For infants and children through 16 years of age, refer to Chapter 4.3. A rubeola (measles) booster should be considered. Persons age 16 to 65 should receive a booster of tetanus and diphtheria every ten years. Healthy adults under age 65 do not require pneumococcal vaccine, but it is appropriate for those with chronic medical

conditions. Influenza vaccine may be considered for those providing essential community services, health care workers, and those wishing to reduce the likelihood of becoming ill with influenza. Adults over 65 years of age are urged to obtain yearly influenza immunization, and to insure that their tetanus and diphtheria immunizations are current. Pneumococcal vaccination is also suggested for this age group.

Poliomyelitis—A poliomyelitis booster is indicated for this country.

Viral Hepatitis A—Vaccination is recommended for all travelers for their protection.

Typhoid fever—Vaccination is recommended for all travelers for their protection.

Selective vaccinations—These apply only to specific groups of travelers or persons on specific working assignments:

Viral Hepatitis B—Because of the high rate of healthy carriers of hepatitis B in this country, vaccination is recommended for persons on working assignments in the health care field (dentists, physicians, nurses, laboratory technicians), or working in close contact with the local population (teachers, missionaries, Peace Corps), or persons foreseeing sexual relations with local inhabitants.

Plague—Vaccination is recommended only for persons who may be occupationally exposed to wild rodents (anthropologists, geologists, medical personnel, missionaries, etc). The standard vaccination course must be completed before entering the plague infested area. Geographical distribution of the area of risk for this country is in the southern part of the country along the border with Nambia (middle third).

Country Number 8.7
Anguilla
(Formerly, Leeward Islands)

INFECTIOUS DISEASE RISK

Malaria

No malaria risk is present in this country.

Food/Water Safety

No reliable information exists with regard to safety of water, food, or dairy products. Discretion is advised.

VACCINATIONS

Routine immunizations should be current. For infants and children through 16 years of age, refer to Chapter 4.3. A rubeola (measles) booster

should be considered. Persons age 16 to 65 should receive a booster of tetanus and diphtheria every ten years. Healthy adults under age 65 do not require pneumococcal vaccine, but it is appropriate for those with chronic medical conditions. Influenza vaccine may be considered for those providing essential community services, health care workers, and those wishing to reduce the likelihood of becoming ill with influenza. Adults over 65 years of age are urged to obtain yearly influenza immunization, and to insure that their tetanus and diphtheria immunizations are current. Pneumococcal vaccination is also suggested for this age group.

Country Number 8.8
Antigua and Barbuda

INFECTIOUS DISEASE RISK

Malaria Risk
No malaria risk is present in this country.

Diseases of Special Risk
In addition to the worldwide hazard of tetanus and the routine and any special immunizations recommended below, the traveler should be aware that risk of exposure to the following diseases exists in this country. This list is not all inclusive, but it is a caution concerning the more likely endemic disease risks.

DISEASE RISK PROFILE

Disease	endemic	risk	hazard
Dengue Fever	x		
Hepatitis, Viral	x		
Rabies	x		

Food/Water Safety
Local water is considered safe without further treatment. Milk is pasteurized and safe to drink. Butter, cheese, yogurt and ice-cream are safe. Local meat, poultry, seafood, vegetables, and fruits are generally safe to eat, however, bacillary and amoebic dysentary are encountered .

VACCINATIONS
Yellow fever—A vaccination certificate is required for travelers coming from infected areas. A vaccination certificate is required for children over one year of age.
Routine immunizations should be current. For infants and children through 16 years of age, refer to Chapter 4.3. A rubeola (measles) booster

should be considered. Persons age 16 to 65 should receive a booster of tetanus and diphtheria every ten years. Healthy adults under age 65 do not require pneumococcal vaccine, but it is appropriate for those with chronic medical conditions. Influenza vaccine may be considered for those providing essential community services, health care workers, and those wishing to reduce the likelihood of becoming ill with influenza. Adults over 65 years of age are urged to obtain yearly influenza immunization, and to insure that their tetanus and diphtheria immunizations are current. Pneumococcal vaccination is also suggested for this age group.

U.S. Foreign Service
St. Johns, Telephone (809) 462-3505/06

Country Number 8.9
Argentina

INFECTIOUS DISEASE RISK

Malaria Risk
Malaria risk is from October through May, only below 1200 meters, in the rural Departments of Iruya, Oran, San Martin, Santa Victoria (northern Salta Provence) and eastern Ledesma (Jujuy Province). There is no risk of malaria in urban areas. The CDC recommends taking chloroquine for malria prophylaxis in this country. See Chapter 6.31.

Falciparum malaria represents 1% of malaria, therefore there is a risk of p. vivax malaria exposure. Consider the use of primaquine upon return home.

Diseases of Special Risk
In addition to the worldwide hazard of tetanus and the routine and any special immunizations recommended below, the traveler should be aware that risk of exposure to the following diseases exists in this country. This list is not all inclusive, but it is a caution concerning the more likely endemic disease risks.

DISEASE RISK PROFILE

Disease	endemic	risk	hazard
Anthrax		x	
Giardiasis		x	
Hepatitis, Viral	x		
Rabies			x
Tapeworms		x	
Trachoma	x		
Typhoid Fever	x		

Food/Water Safety

Water is probably safe, but due to local variations in bacterial counts, using bottled water for the first few weeks will help the traveler adjust and decrease the chance of traveler's diarrhea. Milk is pasteurized and safe to drink. Butter, cheese, yogurt and ice-cream are safe. Local meat, poultry, seafood, vegetables, and fruits are safe to eat.

Salmonellosis is relatively common in suburban areas and is a particular risk in children below 5 years of age.

VACCINATIONS

Routine immunizations should be current. For infants and children through 16 years of age, refer to Chapter 4.3. A rubeola (measles) booster should be considered. Persons age 16 to 65 should receive a booster of tetanus and diphtheria every ten years. Healthy adults under age 65 do not require pneumococcal vaccine, but it is appropriate for those with chronic medical conditions. Influenza vaccine may be considered for those providing essential community services, health care workers, and those wishing to reduce the likelihood of becoming ill with influenza. Adults over 65 years of age are urged to obtain yearly influenza immunization, and to insure that their tetanus and diphtheria immunizations are current. Pneumococcal vaccination is also suggested for this age group.

No vaccinations are required to enter this country. The vaccinations listed are recommended for the traveler's protection.

Viral Hepatitis A—Vaccination is recommended when traveling outside the areas usually visited by tourists, traveling extensively in the interior of the country (trekkers, hikers) and for persons on working assignments in remote areas.

Typhoid fever—Vaccination is recommended when traveling outside the areas usually visited by tourists, traveling extensively in the interior of the country (trekkers, hikers) and for persons on working assignments in remote areas.

Yellow fever—Vaccination is recommended when traveling outside the areas usually visited by tourists, traveling extensively in the interior of the country (trekkers, hikers) and for persons on working assignments in remote areas. CDC recommends vaccination for all persons over 9 months of age planning to visit the northeastern forest areas.

U.S. Foreign Service
4300 Colombia, 1425
Buenos Aires, Telephone 774-7611/8811/9911

Canadian High Commission/Embassy Office:
Brunetta Building, 25th Floor
Sulpacha 1111
Buenos Aires, Telelephone 312-9081/8

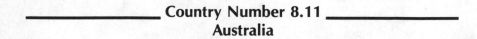

Country Number 8.10
Aruba

INFECTIOUS DISEASE RISK

Malaria Risk
There is no malaria risk in this country.

Diseases of Special Risk
In addition to the worldwide hazard of tetanus and the routine and any special immunizations recommended below, the traveler should be aware that risk of exposure to the following diseases exists in this country. This list is not all inclusive, but it is a caution concerning the more likely endemic disease risks.
Dengue has been reported in this country. The virus is present in this country at all times and may give rise to major outbreaks.

Food/Water Safety
Food and water precautions should be taken as bacillary and amoebic dysentary are common.

VACCINATIONS
Routine immunizations should be current. For infants and children through 16 years of age, refer to Chapter 4.3. A rubeola (measles) booster should be considered. Persons age 16 to 65 should receive a booster of tetanus and diphtheria every ten years. Healthy adults under age 65 do not require pneumococcal vaccine, but it is appropriate for those with chronic medical conditions. Influenza vaccine may be considered for those providing essential community services, health care workers, and those wishing to reduce the likelihood of becoming ill with influenza. Adults over 65 years of age are urged to obtain yearly influenza immunization, and to insure that their tetanus and diphtheria immunizations are current. Pneumococcal vaccination is also suggested for this age group.

Country Number 8.11
Australia

INFECTIOUS DISEASE RISK

Malaria Risk
There is no malaria risk in this country.

Diseases of Special Risk

In addition to the worldwide hazard of tetanus and the routine and any special immunizations recommended below, the traveler should be aware that risk of exposure to the following diseases exists in this country. This list is not all inclusive, but it is a caution concerning the more likely endemic disease risks.

Potential risk of dengue fever exists. The virus is present in this country at all times and may give rise to major outbreaks. Areas of greatest risk are along the coast from Cornavon to Port Darwin to Townsville and occasionally northern New South Wales.

Lyme arthritis is present. Avoid ticks.

Viral encephalitis may occur in some rural areas. Avoid mosquitos.

Food/Water Safety

Local water is considered safe without further treatment. Milk is pasteurized and safe to drink. Butter, cheese, yogurt and ice-cream are safe. Local meat, poultry, seafood, vegetables, and fruits are safe to eat.

VACCINATIONS

Yellow fever—A vaccination certificate is required for travelers coming from infected areas and from or in transit through countries any part of which is considered infected. A vaccination certificate is required for children over one year of age. Vaccination certificate is required for travelers who have been in or passed through an infected yellow fever area within six days prior to arrival. Australia is not bound by International Health Regulations. Australian officials currently have added Cameroon, Ecuador, Ivory Coast, Senegal, Togo, Trinidad and Tobago, and Venezuela to the infected country list. Any country is considered infected when it has been so listed in the Weekly Epidemiological Record.

Routine immunizations should be current. For infants and children through 16 years of age, refer to Chapter 4.3. A rubeola (measles) booster should be considered. Persons age 16 to 65 should receive a booster of tetanus and diphtheria every ten years. Healthy adults under age 65 do not require pneumococcal vaccine, but it is appropriate for those with chronic medical conditions. Influenza vaccine may be considered for those providing essential community services, health care workers, and those wishing to reduce the likelihood of becoming ill with influenza. Adults over 65 years of age are urged to obtain yearly influenza immunization, and to insure that their tetanus and diphtheria immunizations are current. Pneumococcal vaccination is also suggested for this age group.

Selective vaccinations—These apply only to specific groups of travelers or persons on specific working assignments:

Viral Hepatitis B—Because of the high rate of healthy carriers of hepatitis B among the local Aboriginal population in the interior (mainly in the Warburton Creek area of Central Australia), vaccination is recommended for persons working in health care, education, or in close contact with them.

U.S. Foreign Service
Moonah Pl.
Canberra, Telephone (62) 73-3711

24 Albert Road
Melbourne, Telephone (3) 699-2244

T & G Tower 36th Floor
Hyde Park Square, Park and Elizabeth Streets
Sydney, Telephone (2) 264-7044

383 Wickhamler Ter.
Brisbane, Telephone (7) 839-8955

246 St. George's Ter.
Perth, Telephone (9) 322-4466

Canadian High Commission/Embassy Office:
Commonwealth Avenue
Canberra, Telephone (62) 73-3844

6th Floor
1 Collins Street
Melbourne, Telephone (3) 654-1433

A.M.P. Center
8th Floor
50 Bridge Street
Sydney, Telephone (2) 231-6522

160 St George's Ter.
Perth, Telephone (9) 322-6288

_____ **Country Number 8.12** _____
Austria

INFECTIOUS DISEASE RISK

Malaria Risk
There is no malaria risk in this country.

Food/Water Safety

Water is probably safe, but due to local variations in bacterial counts, using bottled water for the first few weeks will help the traveler adjust and decrease the chance of traveler's diarrhea. Milk is pasteurized and safe to drink. Butter, cheese, yogurt and ice-cream are safe. Local meat, poultry, seafood, vegetables, and fruits are safe to eat.

VACCINATIONS

Routine immunizations should be current. For infants and children through 16 years of age, refer to Chapter 4.3. A rubeola (measles) booster should be considered. Persons age 16 to 65 should receive a booster of tetanus and diphtheria every ten years. Healthy adults under age 65 do not require pneumococcal vaccine, but it is appropriate for those with chronic medical conditions. Influenza vaccine may be considered for those providing essential community services, health care workers, and those wishing to reduce the likelihood of becoming ill with influenza. Adults over 65 years of age are urged to obtain yearly influenza immunization, and to insure that their tetanus and diphtheria immunizations are current. Pneumococcal vaccination is also suggested for this age group.

Selective vaccinations—These apply only to specific groups of travelers or persons on specific working assignments:

Tick-borne encephalitis—(Central European encephalitis) Vaccination is recommended for persons involved in recreational activities in forested areas (camping, hiking) or working in forestry occupations. Risk season: March to November. Risk is present in all forested areas of southern, eastern, and northern Austria (areas around Klagenfurt, Graz, Wiener Neustadt, Vienna, and Linz, extending to the border with Germany along the Danube).

U.S. Foreign Service

    IX Boltzmanngasse 16A-1091
    Vienna, Telephone (222) 31-55-11

    A-5020 Salzburg Giselakai 51
    Salzburg, Telephone (662) 28-6-01

Canadian High Commission/Embassy Office:

    Dr. Karl Lueger Ring 10
    Vienna, Telephone (222) 63-36-91/95

Country Number 8.13
Azores

INFECTIOUS DISEASE RISK

Malaria Risk

There is no malaria risk in this country.

Diseases of Special Risk

Food/Water Safety

Water is probably safe, but due to local variations in bacterial counts, using bottled water for the first few weeks will help the traveler adjust and decrease the chance of traveler's diarrhea. Some milk is pasteurized and safe to drink, but caution is advised. Pasteurized butter, cheese, yogurt and ice-cream are safe. Local meat, poultry, seafood, vegetables, and fruits are generally safe to eat.

VACCINATIONS

Routine immunizations should be current. For infants and children through 16 years of age, refer to Chapter 4.3. A rubeola (measles) booster should be considered. Persons age 16 to 65 should receive a booster of tetanus and diphtheria every ten years. Healthy adults under age 65 do not require pneumococcal vaccine, but it is appropriate for those with chronic medical conditions. Influenza vaccine may be considered for those providing essential community services, health care workers, and those wishing to reduce the likelihood of becoming ill with influenza. Adults over 65 years of age are urged to obtain yearly influenza immunization, and to insure that their tetanus and diphtheria immunizations are current. Pneumococcal vaccination is also suggested for this age group.

Viral Hepatitis A—Vaccination with gamma globulin is recommended when traveling outside the areas usually visited by tourists, traveling extensively in the interior of the country and for persons on working assignments in remote areas.

U.S. Foreign Service
Avenida D. Henrique
Ponta Delgada
Sao Miguel, Telephone 22216/7

Country Number 8.14
Bahamas

INFECTIOUS DISEASE RISK

Malaria Risk

There is no malaria risk in this country.

Diseases of Special Risk

In addition to the worldwide hazard of tetanus and the routine and any special immunizations recommended below, the traveler should be aware that risk of exposure to the following diseases exists in this country. This list is not all inclusive, but it is a caution concerning the more likely endemic disease risks.

DISEASE RISK PROFILE

Disease	endemic	risk	hazard
Dengue Fever	x		
Dysentery		x	
Hepatitis, Viral	x		
Rabies	x		

Food/Water Safety

All tap water used for drinking, brushing teeth, and making ice cubes should be boiled prior to use. Insure that bottled water is uncapped in your presence. Milk should be boiled to insure safety. Powdered and evaporated milk are available and safe. Avoid butter and other dairy products. All meat, poultry and seafood must be well cooked and served while hot. Pork is best avoided. Vegetables should be well cooked and served hot. Salads and mayonnaise are best avoided. Fruits with intact skins should be peeled by you just prior to consumption. Avoid cold buffets, custards, and any frozen dessert. First class hotels and restaurants serve purified drinking water and reliable food. However, the hazard is left to your judgement.

Ciguatera fish poisoning may prove to be a hazard.

VACCINATIONS

Yellow fever—A vaccination certificate is required for travelers coming from infected areas and from or in transit through countries in which this disease is active. A vaccination certificate is required for children over one year of age.

Routine immunizations should be current. For infants and children through 16 years of age, refer to Chapter 4.3. A rubeola (measles) booster should be considered. Persons age 16 to 65 should receive a booster of tetanus and diphtheria every ten years. Healthy adults under age 65 do not require

pneumococcal vaccine, but it is appropriate for those with chronic medical conditions. Influenza vaccine may be considered for those providing essential community services, health care workers, and those wishing to reduce the likelihood of becoming ill with influenza. Adults over 65 years of age are urged to obtain yearly influenza immunization, and to insure that their tetanus and diphtheria immunizations are current. Pneumococcal vaccination is also suggested for this age group.

U.S. Foreign Service
Mosmar Building, Queen Street
Nassau, Telephone (809) 322-1181/1700

Canadian Consulate:
Out Island Traders Building
Office Z1
P.O. Box SS6371
Nassau, Telephone (809) 323-2123/2124

Country Number 8.15
Bahrain

INFECTIOUS DISEASE RISK

Malaria Risk
There is no malaria risk in this country.

Diseases of Special Risk
In addition to the worldwide hazard of tetanus and the routine and any special immunizations recommended below, the traveler should be aware that risk of exposure to the following diseases exists in this country. This list is not all inclusive, but it is a caution concerning the more likely endemic disease risks.

DISEASE RISK PROFILE

Disease	endemic	risk	hazard
Brucellosis			x
Cholera	x		
Dracunculiasis/Guinea Worm	x		
Echinococcosis	x		
Hepatitis, Viral		x	
Leishmaniasis (cutaneous)	x		
Leishmaniasis (visceral)	x		
Rabies	x		
Relapsing Fever	x		

Disease	endemic	risk	hazard
Tapeworms	x		
Trachoma	x		
Typhoid Fever		x	
Typhus, Endemic Flea-Borne	x		
Typhus, Scrub	x		

Food/Water Safety

All tap water used for drinking, brushing teeth, and making ice cubes should be boiled prior to use. Insure that bottled water is uncapped in your presence. Milk should be boiled to insure safety. Powdered and evaporated milk are available and safe. Avoid butter and other dairy products. All meat, poultry and seafood must be well cooked and served while hot. Pork is best avoided. Vegetables should be well cooked and served hot. Salads and mayonnaise are best avoided. Fruits with intact skins should be peeled by you just prior to consumption. Avoid cold buffets, custards, and any frozen dessert. First class hotels and restaurants serve purified drinking water and reliable food. However, the hazard is left to your judgement.

VACCINATIONS

Yellow fever—A vaccination certificate is required for travelers coming from infected areas. A vaccination certificate is required for children over one year of age.

Routine immunizations should be current. For infants and children through 16 years of age, refer to Chapter 4.3. A rubeola (measles) booster should be considered. Persons age 16 to 65 should receive a booster of tetanus and diphtheria every ten years. Healthy adults under age 65 do not require pneumococcal vaccine, but it is appropriate for those with chronic medical conditions. Influenza vaccine may be considered for those providing essential community services, health care workers, and those wishing to reduce the likelihood of becoming ill with influenza. Adults over 65 years of age are urged to obtain yearly influenza immunization, and to insure that their tetanus and diphtheria immunizations are current. Pneumococcal vaccination is also suggested for this age group.

The following vaccinations listed for this country are listed for the traveler's protection, but they are not required for entry:

Viral Hepatitis A—Vaccination is recommended for all travelers for their protection.

Typhoid fever—Vaccination is recommended for all travelers for their protection.

U.S. Foreign Service
Shalkh Isa Road
Manama, Telephone 714151
(Workweek: Saturday-Wednesday)

Country Number 8.16
Bangladesh

INFECTIOUS DISEASE RISK

Malaria Risk
The malaria in this country is resistant to chloroquine. The CDC recommends the use of mefloquine (Lariam) as described in Chapter 6.31 for chemical prophylaxis. Malaria is present in all parts of this country, including urban areas, with the exception of Dhaka City, where there is no risk. The risk in the remainder of this country exists all year.

Diseases of Special Risk
In addition to the worldwide hazard of tetanus and the routine and any special immunizations recommended below, the traveler should be aware that risk of exposure to the following diseases exists in this country. This list is not all inclusive, but it is a caution concerning the more likely endemic disease risks.

Potential risk of dengue fever exists. The virus is present in this country at all times and may give rise to major outbreaks.

It should be noted that 58% of the country's 103 million people are infected with tuberculosis, causing 500,000 positive cases annually.

DISEASE RISK PROFILE

Disease	endemic	risk	hazard
Brucellosis		x	
Cholera		x	
Dysenteries		x	
Echinococcosis		x	
Encephalitis, Japanese	x		
Filariasis		x	
Helminthic Diseases		x	
Hepatitis A		x	
Leishmaniasis (Visceral)			x
Rabies			x
Sandfly Fever			x

Food/Water Safety
All tap water used for drinking, brushing teeth, and making ice cubes

should be boiled prior to use. Insure that bottled water is uncapped in your presence. Milk should be boiled to insure safety. Powdered and evaporated milk are available and safe. Avoid butter and other dairy products. All meat, poultry and seafood must be well cooked and served while hot. Pork is best avoided. Vegetables should be well cooked and served hot. Salads and mayonnaise are best avoided. Fruits with intact skins should be peeled by you just prior to consumption. Avoid cold buffets, custards, and any frozen dessert.

VACCINATIONS

Yellow fever—A vaccination certificate is required for travelers coming from infected areas and from or in transit through countries any part of which is infected. A yellow fever vaccination is also required from all countries the yellow fever endemic zones in South and Central America and Central Africa (see Chapter 6.63). It is also required from all persons arriving from Botswana, Malawi, Mauritania, Belize, Costa Rica, Guatemala, Honduras, and Nicaragua. When required, this vaccination must be obtained by persons of all ages (including infants) or they will face isolation up to 6 days. This vaccine should not be given to infants younger than 6 months, as explained in Chapter 6.63.

Cholera—Cholera is present in this country. Risk to western travelers is low. Immunization is not required or recommended for travel to this country due to its low effectiveness. Avoid uncooked foods and untreated water. Vaccination is advised only for persons living or working under inadequate sanitary conditions and for those with impaired defense mechanisms. Cholera immunization is only REQUIRED of Bangladesh nationals on leaving the country.

Routine immunizations should be current. For infants and children through 16 years of age, refer to Chapter 4.3. A rubeola (measles) booster should be considered. Persons age 16 to 65 should receive a booster of tetanus and diphtheria every ten years. Healthy adults under age 65 do not require pneumococcal vaccine, but it is appropriate for those with chronic medical conditions. Influenza vaccine may be considered for those providing essential community services, health care workers, and those wishing to reduce the likelihood of becoming ill with influenza. Adults over 65 years of age are urged to obtain yearly influenza immunization, and to insure that their tetanus and diphtheria immunizations are current. Pneumococcal vaccination is also suggested for this age group.

The following vaccinations listed for this country are listed for the traveler's protection, but they are not required for entry:

Poliomyelitis—A poliomyelitis booster is indicated for this country.

Viral Hepatitis A—Vaccination is recommended for all travelers for their protection.

Typhoid fever—Vaccination is recommended for all travelers for their protection.

Selective vaccinations—These apply only to specific groups of travelers or persons on specific working assignments:

Viral Hepatitis B—Because of the high rate of healthy carriers of hepatitis B in this country, vaccination is recommended for persons on working assignments in the health care field (dentists, physicians, nurses, laboratory technicians), or working in close contact with the local population (teachers, missionaries, Peace Corps), or persons foreseeing sexual relations with local inhabitants.

Japanese encephalitis—Vaccination is indicated for persons traveling extensively in rual areas or living and working near rice growing rural and suburban areas and other irrigated land, when exposure to the disease carrying mosquitoes is high. Children are especially susceptible to the infection. Sporadic cases are reported throughout the country. Period of transmission is all year, but greatest risk is June through October. You may obtain information about a vaccine for this disease from the CDC at (303) 221-6429. See also Chapter 6.14.

Rabies—In this country, where rabies is a constant threat, a pre-exposure rabies vaccination is advised for persons planning an extended stay or on working assignments (naturalists, agricultural advisors, archeologists, geologists, etc.). Although this provides adequate initial protection, a person bitten by a potentially rabid animal would still require post exposure immunization (see Chapter 6.40). Children should be cautioned not to pet dogs, cats, or other mammals.

U.S. Foreign Service
Adamjee Court Building (5th Floor)
Motijheel Commercial Area, Ramma
Dhaka, Telephone 237161/63, 235093/99

Canadian High Commission/Embassy Office:
House CWN 16/A
Road 48
Gulshan, Telephone 413553, 600181/2/3/4

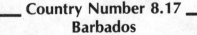

Country Number 8.17
Barbados

INFECTIOUS DISEASE RISK

Malaria Risk
There is no malaria risk in this country.

Diseases of Special Risk

In addition to the worldwide hazard of tetanus and the routine and any special immunizations recommended below, the traveler should be aware that risk of exposure to the following diseases exists in this country. This list is not all inclusive, but it is a caution concerning the more likely endemic disease risks.

Potential risk of dengue fever exists. The virus is present in this country at all times and may give rise to major outbreaks.

Viral hepatitis occurs on this island.

Animal rabies is present, particularly in the mongoose.

Food/Water Safety

First class hotels and restaurants serve purified drinking water and reliable food. However, the hazard is left to your judgement. Amoebic and bacillary dysenteries are common.

VACCINATIONS

Yellow fever—A vaccination certificate is required for travelers coming from infected areas and from or in transit through countries any part of which is infected. A vaccination certificate is required for children over one year of age.

Routine immunizations should be current. For infants and children through 16 years of age, refer to Chapter 4.3. A rubeola (measles) booster should be considered. Persons age 16 to 65 should receive a booster of tetanus and diphtheria every ten years. Healthy adults under age 65 do not require pneumococcal vaccine, but it is appropriate for those with chronic medical conditions. Influenza vaccine may be considered for those providing essential community services, health care workers, and those wishing to reduce the likelihood of becoming ill with influenza. Adults over 65 years of age are urged to obtain yearly influenza immunization, and to insure that their tetanus and diphtheria immunizations are current. Pneumococcal vaccination is also suggested for this age group.

U.S. Foreign Service

P.O. Box 302
Bridgetown, Telephone 426-3574/7

Commonwealth Development
Corporation Building
Culloden Road
St Michael, Telephone 429-3550

_____ **Country Number 8.18** _____
Barbuda
See entry under ANTIGUA and BARBUDA.

_____ **Country Number 8.19** _____
Belgium

INFECTIOUS DISEASE RISK

Malaria Risk
There is no malaria risk in this country.

Diseases of Special Risk
In addition to the worldwide hazard of tetanus and the routine and any special immunizations recommended below, the traveler should be aware that risk of exposure to the following diseases exists in this country. This list is not all inclusive, but it is a caution concerning the more likely endemic disease risks.
Heavy concentrations of bacterial contamination (salmonella) have caused authorities to warn against swimming in the Ourthe and Semois Rivers in the Ardennes. Officials report that 75% of the waterways in northern Belgium are heavily polluted.

Food/Water Safety
Local water is considered safe without further treatment. Milk is pasteurized and safe to drink. Butter, cheese, yogurt and ice-cream are safe. Local meat, poultry, seafood, vegetables, and fruits are safe to eat.

VACCINATIONS
Routine immunizations should be current. For infants and children through 16 years of age, refer to Chapter 4.3. A rubeola (measles) booster should be considered. Persons age 16 to 65 should receive a booster of tetanus and diphtheria every ten years. Healthy adults under age 65 do not require pneumococcal vaccine, but it is appropriate for those with chronic medical conditions. Influenza vaccine may be considered for those providing essential community services, health care workers, and those wishing to reduce the likelihood of becoming ill with influenza. Adults over 65 years of age are urged to obtain yearly influenza immunization, and to insure that their tetanus and diphtheria immunizations are current. Pneumococcal vaccination is also suggested for this age group.

U.S. Foreign Service
27 Boulevard du Regent, B-1000
Brussels, Telephone (02) 513-38-30

Rubens Center, Nationalestraat 5, B-2000
Antwerp, Telephone (03) 321-8000

Canadian High Commission:
Rue de Loxum 6
Brussels, Telephone (02) 513-79-40

Country Number 8.20
Belize
Formerly British Honduras

INFECTIOUS DISEASE RISK

Malaria Risk
Malaria risk is year round. Malaria may be encountered throughout the country below 400 meters, except urban areas. There is no risk of malaria in Belize District. See Chapter 6.31 use of Chloroquine.

Falciparum malaria represents 1% of malaria, therefore there is a risk of p. vivax malaria exposure. Consider the use of primaquine upon return home.

Diseases of Special Risk
In addition to the worldwide hazard of tetanus and the routine and any special immunizations recommended below, the traveler should be aware that risk of exposure to the following diseases exists in this country. This list is not all inclusive, but it is a caution concerning the more likely endemic disease risks.

This country must be considered receptive to dengue fever. Intermittent epidemics in the past make renewed activity or reintroduction of the virus possible.

Schistosomiasis has been reported in this country. Avoid swimming or wading in fresh water lakes or rivers unless an authoritative local source can assure you that the water is safe (see Chapter 6.45).

DISEASE RISK PROFILE

Disease	endemic	risk	hazard
Brucellosis	x		
Dysentery (amoebic and bacillary)		x	
Encephalitis, Venezuelan Equine	x		

Disease	endemic	risk	hazard
Helminthic Diseases		x	
Hepatitis, Viral	x		
Leishmaniasis	x		
Rabies			x
Trypanosomiasis, American Chaga's Disease	x		
Typhoid Fever		x	

Food/Water Safety

All tap water used for drinking, brushing teeth, and making ice cubes should be boiled prior to use. Insure that bottled water is uncapped in your presence. Milk should be boiled to insure safety. Powdered and evaporated milk are available and safe. Avoid butter and other dairy products. All meat, poultry and seafood must be well cooked and served while hot. Pork is best avoided. Vegetables should be well cooked and served hot. Salads and mayonnaise are best avoided. Fruits with intact skins should be peeled by you just prior to consumption. Avoid cold buffets, custards, and any frozen dessert. First class hotels and restaurants serve purified drinking water and reliable food. However, the hazard is left to your judgement.

VACCINATIONS

Yellow fever—A vaccination certificate is required for travelers coming from infected areas and from or in transit through countries with active yellow fever. A vaccination is required for children of all ages. Children under nine months of age should not be vaccinated due to health considerations. Please refer to the discussion in Chapter 6.63 on avoiding yellow fever vaccination in this age group. Although yellow fever is not active at this time, this country is in the endemic zone. Other countries may require a yellow fever certificate after visiting this country.

Routine immunizations should be current. For infants and children through 16 years of age, refer to Chapter 4.3. A rubeola (measles) booster should be considered. Persons age 16 to 65 should receive a booster of tetanus and diphtheria every ten years. Healthy adults under age 65 do not require pneumococcal vaccine, but it is appropriate for those with chronic medical conditions. Influenza vaccine may be considered for those providing essential community services, health care workers, and those wishing to reduce the likelihood of becoming ill with influenza. Adults over 65 years of age are urged to obtain yearly influenza immunization, and to insure that their tetanus and diphtheria immunizations are current. Pneumococcal vaccination is also suggested for this age group.

The following vaccinations listed for this country are listed for the traveler's protection, but they are not required for entry:

Viral Hepatitis A—Vaccination is recommended when traveling outside the areas usually visited by tourists, traveling extensively in the interior of the country (trekkers, hikers) and for persons on working assignments in remote areas.
Typhoid fever—as above.

U.S. Foreign Service
Gabourel Lane and Hutson Street
Belize City, Telephone 02-7161/2/3

Canadian High Commission/Embassy Office:
P.O. Box 1229
Belize City, Telephone 02-7463, 02-3639

Country Number 8.21
Benin
(formerly Dahomey)

INFECTIOUS DISEASE RISK

Malaria Risk
Malaria is present in all parts of this country, including urban areas. The risk exists all year. The malaria in this country is resistant to chloroquine. The CDC recommends the use of mefloquine (Lariam) as described in Chapter 6.31 for chemical prophylaxis.

Falciparum malaria represents 87% of malaria, therefore there is a slight risk of p. vivax malaria exposure. Consider the use of primaquine upon return home.

Diseases of Special Risk
In addition to the worldwide hazard of tetanus and the routine and any special immunizations recommended below, the traveler should be aware that risk of exposure to the following diseases exists in this country. This list is not all inclusive, but it is a caution concerning the more likely endemic disease risks.

This country must be considered receptive to dengue fever. Intermittent epidemics in the past make renewed activity or reintroduction of the virus possible.

Schistosomiasis may be found in this country. Avoid contact with contaminated fresh water lakes, ponds, or streams. Risk is present in the entire country, to include urban areas.

Parasitic worm infections are common. Dysentery and diarrheal diseases, including giardiasis, typhoid fevers, and viral hepatitis, are widespread.

DISEASE RISK PROFILE

Disease	endemic	risk	hazard
Dracunculiasis/Guinea Worm	x		
Echinococcosis		x	
Filariasis			x
Lassa Fever	x		
Leishmaniasis (Cutaneous)	x		
Leishmaniasis (Visceral)	x		
Onchocerciasis			x
Rabies	x		
Relapsing Fever	x		
Tapeworms			x
Trachoma			x
Trypanosomiasis, African Sleeping Sickness	x		
Tungiasis			x
Typhoid Fever		x	
Typhus, Endemic Flea-Borne	x		
Typhus, Epidemic Louse-Borne	x		
Typhus, Scrub	x		

Food/Water Safety

All tap water used for drinking, brushing teeth, and making ice cubes should be boiled prior to use. Insure that bottled water is uncapped in your presence. Milk may be unsafe due to poor refrigeration, but other dairy products may be safe. All meat, poultry and seafood must be well cooked and served while hot. Pork is best avoided. Vegetables should be well cooked and served hot. Salads and mayonnaise are best avoided. Fruits with intact skins should be peeled by you just prior to consumption. Avoid cold buffets, custards, and any frozen dessert.

VACCINATIONS

Yellow fever—A vaccination certificate is required on arrival from all countries. A vaccination certificate is required for children over one year of age, but the CDC recommends vaccinations for everyone over 9 months of age who will be traveling outside of urban areas.

Routine immunizations should be current. For infants and children through 16 years of age, refer to Chapter 4.3. A rubeola (measles) booster should be considered. Persons age 16 to 65 should receive a booster of tetanus and diphtheria every ten years. Healthy adults under age 65 do not require pneumococcal vaccine, but it is appropriate for those with chronic medical conditions. Influenza vaccine may be considered for those providing essential community services, health care workers, and those wishing to reduce the likelihood of becoming ill with influenza. Adults over 65 years of age are urged to obtain yearly influenza immunization, and to insure that their tetanus and diphtheria immunizations are current. Pneumococcal vaccination is also suggested for this age group.

The following vaccinations listed for this country are listed for the traveler's protection, but they are not required for entry:

Poliomyelitis—A poliomyelitis booster is indicated for this country.

Viral Hepatitis A—Vaccination is recommended for all travelers for their
protection.

Typhoid fever—Vaccination is recommended for all travelers for their protection.

Selective vaccinations—These apply only to specific groups of travelers or
persons on specific working assignments:

Viral Hepatitis B—Because of the high rate of healthy carriers of hepatitis
B in this country, vaccination is recommended for persons on working assignments in the health care field (dentists, physicians, nurses, laboratory technicians), or working in close contact with the local population (teachers,
missionaries, Peace Corps), or persons foreseeing sexual relations with local
inhabitants.

Meningococcal meningitis—Vaccination is advised for persons traveling
extensively or on working assignements in the meningitis belt of Africa's northern savannah, which stretches from the Red Sea to the Atlantic Ocean. Peak
season is March and April. The entire country is in this zone.

U.S. Foreign Service
Rue Caporal Anani Bernard
Cotonou, Telephone 30-06-50, 30-17-92

Country Number 8.22
Bermuda

INFECTIOUS DISEASE RISK

Malaria Risk
There is no malaria risk in this country.

Diseases of Special Risk
In addition to the worldwide hazard of tetanus and the routine and any
special immunizations recommended below, the traveler should be aware that
risk of exposure to the following diseases exists in this country. This list is not
all inclusive, but it is a caution concerning the more likely endemic disease
risks.

The is a very low incidence of communicable disease on this island.
Rocky Mountain spotted fever, encephalitis, and tularemia all occur in low frequency. Snake bites and Portuguese man-of-war injuries occur.

Food/Water Safety
    Local water is considered safe without further treatment. Milk is pasteur-
ized and safe to drink. Butter, cheese, yogurt and ice-cream are safe. Local
meat, poultry, seafood, vegetables, and fruits are safe to eat.

VACCINATIONS
    Routine immunizations should be current. For infants and children
through 16 years of age, refer to Chapter 4.3. A rubeola (measles) booster
should be considered. Persons age 16 to 65 should receive a booster of tetanus
and diphtheria every ten years. Healthy adults under age 65 do not require
pneumococcal vaccine, but it is appropriate for those with chronic medical
conditions. Influenza vaccine may be considered for those providing essential
community services, health care workers, and those wishing to reduce the likelihood of becoming ill with influenza. Adults over 65 years of age are urged to
obtain yearly influenza immunization, and to insure that their tetanus and diphtheria immunizations are current. Pneumococcal vaccination is also suggested
for this age group.

U.S. Foreign Service
    Vallis Building, Front Street
    Hamilton, Telephone (809) 295-1342

Country Number 8.23
Bhutan

INFECTIOUS DISEASE RISK

Malaria Risk
    Malaria risk is year around. Malaria may be encountered in the southern
districts bordering India and only below 1600 meters. The malaria in this country is resistant to chloroquine. The CDC recommends the use of mefloquine
(Lariam) as described in Chapter 6.31 for chemical prophylaxis.
    Falciparum malaria represents 10% of malaria, therefore there is a risk of
p. vivax malaria exposure. Consider the use of primaquine upon return home.

Diseases of Special Risk
    In addition to the worldwide hazard of tetanus and the routine and any
special immunizations recommended below, the traveler should be aware that
risk of exposure to the following diseases exists in this country. This list is not
all inclusive, but it is a caution concerning the more likely endemic disease
risks.
    Louse-borne typhus is cosmopolitan in distribution and is present wher-
ever groups of persons are crowded together under conditions of poor sanitation

and malnutrition. Risk exists for persons living or working in remote areas of the country (anthropologists, archeologists, geologists, medical personnel, missionaries, etc.). Freedom from louse infestation is the most effective protection against typhus.

DISEASE RISK PROFILE

Disease	endemic	risk	hazard
Brucellosis		x	
Cholera	x		
Echinococcosis		x	
Encephalitis, Japanese	x		
Giardiasis	x		
Helminthic Infections			
Hepatitis, Viral	x		
Leishmaniasis			x
Sandfly Fever			x
Tapeworms	x		
Typhoid Fever	x		

Food/Water Safety

All tap water used for drinking, brushing teeth, and making ice cubes should be boiled prior to use. Insure that bottled water is uncapped in your presence. Milk should be boiled to insure safety. Powdered and evaporated milk are available and safe. Avoid butter and other dairy products. All meat, poultry and seafood must be well cooked and served while hot. Pork is best avoided. Vegetables should be well cooked and served hot. Salads and mayonnaise are best avoided. Fruits with intact skins should be peeled by you just prior to consumption. Avoid cold buffets, custards, and any frozen dessert.

VACCINATIONS

Yellow fever—A vaccination certificate is required for travelers coming from infected areas. A vaccination is required for children of all ages. Children under nine months of age should not be vaccinated due to health considerations. Please refer to the discussion in Chapter 6.63 on avoiding yellow fever vaccination in this age group.

Routine immunizations should be current. For infants and children through 16 years of age, refer to Chapter 4.3. A rubeola (measles) booster should be considered. Persons age 16 to 65 should receive a booster of tetanus and diphtheria every ten years. Healthy adults under age 65 do not require pneumococcal vaccine, but it is appropriate for those with chronic medical conditions. Influenza vaccine may be considered for those providing essential community services, health care workers, and those wishing to reduce the likelihood of becoming ill with influenza. Adults over 65 years of age are urged to obtain yearly influenza immunization, and to insure that their tetanus and diphtheria immunizations are current. Pneumococcal vaccination is also suggested for this age group.

The following vaccinations listed for this country are listed for the traveler's protection, but they are not required for entry:

Poliomyelitis—A poliomyelitis booster is indicated for this country.

Viral Hepatitis A—Vaccination is recommended for all travelers for their protection.

Typhoid fever—Vaccination is recommended for all travelers for their protection.

Selective vaccinations—*These apply only to specific groups of travelers or persons on specific working assignments:*

Viral Hepatitis B—Because of the high rate of healthy carriers of hepatitis B in this country, vaccination is recommended for persons on working assignments in the health care field (dentists, physicians, nurses, laboratory technicians), or working in close contact with the local population (teachers, missionaries, Peace Corps), or persons foreseeing sexual relations with local inhabitants.

Country Number 8.24
Bolivia

INFECTIOUS DISEASE RISK

Malaria Risk

Malaria is present below 2500 meters. Malaria is not a risk in the provinces of Ingavi, La Paz, Los Andes, Omasuyos, Pacajes, and the departments of Oruro, Southern and Central Potosi. Where found, the risk exists all year. The malaria in this country is resistant to chloroquine. The CDC recommends the use of mefloquine (Lariam) as described in Chapter 6.31 for chemical prophylaxis.

Falciparum malaria represents 13% of malaria, therefore there is a risk of p. vivax malaria exposure. Consider the use of primaquine upon return home.

Diseases of Special Risk

In addition to the worldwide hazard of tetanus and the routine and any special immunizations recommended below, the traveler should be aware that risk of exposure to the following diseases exists in this country. This list is not all inclusive, but it is a caution concerning the more likely endemic disease risks.

Chaga's Disease risk is present in rural and suburban areas below 3600 meters in the following departments: Beni, Chiquisaca, Cochabamba (including the city of Cochabamba), La Paz, Potosi, Santa Cruz, and Tarija. The main vectors are triatoma species known locally as "vinchuca."

Louse-borne typhus is cosmopolitan in distribution and is present wherever groups of persons are crowded together under conditions of poor sanitation and malnutrition. Risk exists for persons living or working in remote areas of the country (anthropologists, archeologists, geologists, medical personnel, missionaries, etc.). Freedom from louse infestation is the most effective protection against typhus.

DISEASE RISK PROFILE

Disease	endemic	risk	hazard
Brucellosis		x	
Dysentery		x	
Echinococcosis	x		
Hepatitis, Viral		x	
Helminthic Infections		x	
Leishmaniasis (Cutaneous)	x		
Leishmaniasis (Mucocutaneous)	x		
Leishmaniasis (Visceral)	x		
Plague	x		
Rabies	x		
Irypanosomiasis, American Chaga's Disease	x		

Food/Water Safety

All tap water used for drinking, brushing teeth, and making ice cubes should be boiled prior to use. Insure that bottled water is uncapped in your presence. Milk should be boiled to insure safety. Powdered and evaporated milk are available and safe. Avoid butter and other dairy products. All meat, poultry and seafood must be well cooked and served while hot. Pork is best avoided. Vegetables should be well cooked and served hot. Salads and mayonnaise are best avoided. Fruits with intact skins should be peeled by you just prior to consumption. Avoid cold buffets, custards, and any frozen dessert. First class hotels and restaurants serve purified drinking water and reliable food. However, the hazard is left to your judgement.

Travelers' diarrhea is common. Also common are parasitic worm infections and viral hepatitis.

VACCINATIONS

Yellow fever—A vaccination certificate is required for travelers coming from infected areas. CDC recommends vaccination of all persons over 9 months of age who go outside of urban areas. Yellow fever is currently active in this country and is present in the departments of Beni, Cochabamba, La Paz, Pando, Tarija, and Santa Cruz. Bolivia recommends obtaining yellow fever vaccination when visiting these areas.

Routine immunizations should be current. For infants and children through 16 years of age, refer to Chapter 4.3. A rubeola (measles) booster should be considered. Persons age 16 to 65 should receive a booster of tetanus and diphtheria every ten years. Healthy adults under age 65 do not require

pneumococcal vaccine, but it is appropriate for those with chronic medical conditions. Influenza vaccine may be considered for those providing essential community services, health care workers, and those wishing to reduce the likelihood of becoming ill with influenza. Adults over 65 years of age are urged to obtain yearly influenza immunization, and to insure that their tetanus and diphtheria immunizations are current. Pneumococcal vaccination is also suggested for this age group.

The following vaccinations listed for this country are listed for the traveler's protection, but they are not required for entry:
Poliomyelitis—A poliomyelitis booster is indicated for this country.
Viral Hepatitis A—Vaccination is recommended for all travelers for their protection.
Typhoid fever—Vaccination is recommended for all travelers for their protection.

Selective vaccinations—These apply only to specific groups of travelers or persons on specific working assignments:
Plague—Vaccination is recommended only for persons who may be occupationally exposed to wild rodents (anthropologists, geologists, medical personnel, missionaries, etc). The standard vaccination course must be completed before entering the plague infested area. Geographical distribution of the area of risk for this country is: along the border with Peru (middle third) north of Lake Titicac (province of La Paz) and the Cordillera Oriental between the provinces of Cochabama and Santa Cruz.
Rabies—In this country, where rabies is a constant threat, a pre-exposure rabies vaccination is advised for persons planning an extended stay or on working assignments (naturalists, agricultural advisors, archeologists, geologists, etc.). Although this provides adequate initial protection, a person bitten by a potentially rabid animal would still require post exposure immunization (see Chapter 6.40). Children should be cautioned not to pet dogs, cats, or other mammals.

U.S. Foreign Service
   Banco Popular del Peru Building
   Corner of Calles Mercado and Colon
   La Paz, Telephone 35-0251, 35-0120

Canadian High Commission/Embassy Office:
   Edificio Alborada
   Office 505
   1420 J. De la Riva Street
   La Paz, Telephone 37-5224

Country Number 8.25
Bonaire

INFECTIOUS DISEASE RISK

Malaria Risk
There is no malaria risk in this country.

Diseases of Special Risk
No information on the current level of disease activity.

Food/Water Safety
No reliable information exists with regard to safety of water, food, or dairy products. Discretion is advised.

VACCINATIONS
Routine immunizations should be current. For infants and children through 16 years of age, refer to Chapter 4.3. A rubeola (measles) booster should be considered. Persons age 16 to 65 should receive a booster of tetanus and diphtheria every ten years. Healthy adults under age 65 do not require pneumococcal vaccine, but it is appropriate for those with chronic medical conditions. Influenza vaccine may be considered for those providing essential community services, health care workers, and those wishing to reduce the likelihood of becoming ill with influenza. Adults over 65 years of age are urged to obtain yearly influenza immunization, and to insure that their tetanus and diphtheria immunizations are current. Pneumococcal vaccination is also suggested for this age group.

Country Number 8.26
Botswana

INFECTIOUS DISEASE RISK

Malaria Risk
Malaria risk is from November through May in the northern part of the country above 21 degrees south, including urban areas. The malaria in this country is resistant to chloroquine. The CDC recommends the use of mefloquine (Lariam) as described in Chapter 6.31 for chemical prophylaxis.

Falciparum malaria represents 95% of malaria, therefore there is a slight risk of p. vivax malaria exposure. Consider use of primaquine upon return home.

Diseases of Special Risk

In addition to the worldwide hazard of tetanus and the routine and any special immunizations recommended below, the traveler should be aware that risk of exposure to the following diseases exists in this country. This list is not all inclusive, but it is a caution concerning the more likely endemic disease risks.

Schistosomiasis may be found in this country. Avoid contact with contaminated fresh water lakes, ponds, or streams. Known endemic areas of infection are present in the area of Maun, along the Okavango River, in the north of the country.

DISEASE RISK PROFILE

Disease	endemic	risk	hazard
Plague	x		
Rabies	x		
Relapsing Fever	x		
Rift Valley Fever	x		
Trypanosomiasis, African Sleeping Sickness	x		
Typhus, Scrub	x		

Food/Water Safety

All tap water used for drinking, brushing teeth, and making ice cubes should be boiled prior to use. Insure that bottled water is uncapped in your presence. Milk should be boiled to insure safety. Powdered and evaporated milk are available and safe. Avoid butter and other dairy products. All meat, poultry and seafood must be well cooked and served while hot. Pork is best avoided. Vegetables should be well cooked and served hot. Salads and mayonnaise are best avoided. Fruits with intact skins should be peeled by you just prior to consumption. Avoid cold buffets, custards, and any frozen dessert. Water, dairy products and food products are considered safe in Gaborone.

Amoeba and typhoid fever are common problems associated with food ingestion in this country.

VACCINATIONS

Routine immunizations should be current. For infants and children through 16 years of age, refer to Chapter 4.3. A rubeola (measles) booster should be considered. Persons age 16 to 65 should receive a booster of tetanus and diphtheria every ten years. Healthy adults under age 65 do not require pneumococcal vaccine, but it is appropriate for those with chronic medical conditions. Influenza vaccine may be considered for those providing essential community services, health care workers, and those wishing to reduce the likelihood of becoming ill with influenza. Adults over 65 years of age are urged to obtain yearly influenza immunization, and to insure that their tetanus and diph-

theria immunizations are current. Pneumococcal vaccination is also suggested for this age group.

No vaccinations are required to enter this country. The vaccinations listed are recommended for the traveler's protection.

Viral Hepatitis A—Vaccination is recommended for all travelers for their protection.

Typhoid fever—Vaccination is recommended for all travelers for their protection.

Selective vaccinations—These apply only to specific groups of travelers or persons on specific working assignments:

Viral Hepatitis B—Because of the high rate of healthy carriers of hepatitis B in this country, vaccination is recommended for persons on working assignments in the health care field (dentists, physicians, nurses, laboratory technicians), or working in close contact with the local population (teachers, missionaries, Peace Corps), or persons foreseeing sexual relations with local inhabitants.

Viral Hepatitis B—Because of the high rate of healthy carriers of hepatitis B in this country, vaccination is recommended for persons on working assignments in the health care field (dentists, physicians, nurses, laboratory technicians), or working in close contact with the local population (teachers, missionaries, Peace Corps), or persons foreseeing sexual relations with local inhabitants.

Plague—Vaccination is recommended only for persons who may be occupationally exposed to wild rodents (anthropologists, geologists, medical personnel, missionaries, etc). The standard vaccination course must be completed before entering the plague infested area. Geographical distribution of the area of risk is scattered throughout this country.

U.S. Foreign Service
P.O. Box 90
Gaborone, Telephone 53982/3/4

Country Number 8.27
Brazil

INFECTIOUS DISEASE RISK

Malaria Risk

Malaria is found below 900 meters in Acre, Amazonas, Goias, Maranhao, Mato Grosso, and Para States; Territories of Amapa, Rondonia, and Roraima. There is generally no risk in urban areas, except in the urban areas of the Amazon region. The risk exists all year. The malaria in this country is resistant to chloroquine. The CDC recommends the use of mefloquine (Lariam) as described in Chapter 6.31 for chemical prophylaxis.

Falciparum malaria represents 40% of malaria, therefore there is a risk of p. vivax malaria exposure. Consider the use of primaquine upon return home.

Diseases of Special Risk

In addition to the worldwide hazard of tetanus and the routine and any special immunizations recommended below, the traveler should be aware that risk of exposure to the following diseases exists in this country. This list is not all inclusive, but it is a caution concerning the more likely endemic disease risks.

This country must be considered receptive to dengue fever. Intermittent epidemics in the past make renewed activity or reintroduction of the virus possible. Risk is limited to the coastal areas of the following states: Amapa, Para, Maranhao, Piaui.

Schistosomiasis may be found in this country. Avoid contact with contaminated fresh water lakes, ponds, or streams. Infection occurs in the following areas: The Federal District, including the city of Brasilia; scattered areas in the southern part of Golas; in the north in the state of Para, and in areas in the coastal region of Braganca; in the east numerous areas in the coastal regions of Maranhao from the border with the state of Para to the Bay of Sao Marcos, including the Island of Sao Luis; further to the east numerous areas scattered over the state of Ceara; the eastern states of Rio Grande do Norte, Paraiba, Pernambuco, Alagoas, and Sergipe are highly infected; the state of Bahla is heavily infected in the eastern part including the basin of the Sao Francisco River; the whole state of Espirito Santo; the state of Minas Gerais is highly infected, except the extreme western part; scattered areas throughout the state of Rio de Janeiro; the state of Sao Paulo infection is widely spread in the northern parts, including the city of Santos; and scattered areas throughout the state of Parana.

Chaga's Disease risk is present in the rural areas of Rio Grande do Sul, Santa Caterina, Parana, Sao Paulo, Rio de Janeiro, Mato Grosso do Sul, Minas Gerais, Goias, Bahia, Pernambuco. In addition infection has reached urban araes of Salvador (Bahia) and Recife (Pernambuco). Several insects are vectors, but all are known locally as "barbeiros."

DISEASE RISK PROFILE

Disease	endemic	risk	hazard
Brazilian Purpuric Fever	x		
Brucellosis		x	
Dengue Fever	x	(in North)	
Echinococcosis	x		
Encephalitis, Venezuelan Equine	x	(in North)	
Hepatitis, Viral		x	
Leishmaniasis (Cutaneous)	x		

Disease	endemic	risk	hazard
Leishmaniasis (Mucocutaneous)	x	(in North)	
Meningitis	x		
Onchocerciasis	x	(in North)	
Plague	x		
Rabies	x		
Tapeworms		x	

Food/Water Safety

All tap water used for drinking, brushing teeth, and making ice cubes should be boiled prior to use. Insure that bottled water is uncapped in your presence. Milk should be boiled to insure safety. Powdered and evaporated milk are available and safe. Avoid butter and other dairy products. All meat, poultry and seafood must be well cooked and served while hot. Pork is best avoided. Vegetables should be well cooked and served hot. Salads and mayonnaise are best avoided. Fruits with intact skins should be peeled by you just prior to consumption. Avoid cold buffets, custards, and any frozen dessert. First class hotels and restaurants serve purified drinking water and reliable food. However, the hazard is left to your judgement.

Amoebic dysentery, diarrheal diseases, parasitic worms, and viral hepatitis associated with water and food supplies are common in this country.

VACCINATIONS

Yellow fever—A vaccination certificate is required for travelers coming from infected areas and from or in transit through countries in the endemic yellow fever zone, see page HHH. A vaccination certificate is required for children over six months of age, however vaccination is not advised for children under nine months of age due to medical complications frequently encountered in the younger age group. CDC recommends vaccination of all persons over 9 months of age. See also discussion in Chapter 6.63. Vaccination is recommended for travelers to the following states: Acre, Amazonas, Goias, Maranhao, Mato Grosso, Mato Grosso do Sul, Para, Rondonia, and the Territories of Amap and Roraima.

Routine immunizations should be current. For infants and children through 16 years of age, refer to Chapter 4.3. A rubeola (measles) booster should be considered. Persons age 16 to 65 should receive a booster of tetanus and diphtheria every ten years. Healthy adults under age 65 do not require pneumococcal vaccine, but it is appropriate for those with chronic medical conditions. Influenza vaccine may be considered for those providing essential community services, health care workers, and those wishing to reduce the likelihood of becoming ill with influenza. Adults over 65 years of age are urged to obtain yearly influenza immunization, and to insure that their tetanus and diphtheria immunizations are current. Pneumococcal vaccination is also suggested for this age group.

The following vaccinations listed for this country are listed for the traveler's protection, but they are not required for entry:

Viral Hepatitis A—Vaccination is recommended when traveling outside the areas usually visited by tourists, traveling extensively in the interior of the country (trekkers, hikers) and for persons on working assignments in remote areas.

Typhoid fever—Vaccination is recommended when traveling outside the areas usually visited by tourists, traveling extensively in the interior of the country (trekkers, hikers) and for persons on working assignments in remote areas.

Selective vaccinations—These apply only to specific groups of travelers or persons on specific working assignments:

Plague—Vaccination is recommended only for persons who may be occupationally exposed to wild rodents (anthropologists, geologists, medical personnel, missionaries, etc). The standard vaccination course must be completed before entering the plague infested area. Geographical distribution of the area of risk for this country is the northwestern part of the country in the provinces of Bahia and Ceara. A small focus is present in the area of Redonda (southern part of Minas Gerais).

Rabies—In this country, where rabies is a constant threat, a pre-exposure rabies vaccination is advised for persons planning an extended stay or on working assignments (naturalists, agricultural advisors, archeologists, geologists, etc.). Although this provides adequate initial protection, a person bitten by a potentially rabid animal would still require post exposure immunization (see Chapter 6.40). Children should be cautioned not to pet dogs, cats, or other mammals.

U.S. Foreign Service
Avenida das Nocoes, Lote 3
Brasilia, Telephone (61) 223-0120

Avenida Presidente Wilson, 147
Rio De Janeiro, Telephone (21) 292-7117

Rua Padre Joao Manoel, 933
Sao Paulo, Telephone (11) 881-6511

Rua Goncalves Mala, 163
Recife, Telephone (81) 221-1412, 222-6612/6577

Avenida Presidente Vargas, 1892 (Ondina)
Salvador Da Bahia, Telephone (71) 245-6691/92

Canadian High Commission/Embassy Office:
Avenida das Nocoes, 16
Brasilia, Telephone (61) 223-7515

Edificio Top Center
Avenida Paulista 854, 5th Fl.
Sao Paulo, Telephone (11) 287-2122, 285-3217

Country Number 8.28
Brunei Darussalam

INFECTIOUS DISEASE RISK

Malaria Risk
There is no malaria risk in this country.

Diseases of Special Risk
In addition to the worldwide hazard of tetanus and the routine and any special immunizations recommended below, the traveler should be aware that risk of exposure to the following diseases exists in this country. This list is not all inclusive, but it is a caution concerning the more likely endemic disease risks.

Potential risk of dengue fever exists. The virus is present in this country at all times and may give rise to major outbreaks.

DISEASE RISK PROFILE

Disease	endemic	risk	hazard
Cholera	x		
Dengue Fever	x		
Encephalitis, Japanese	x		
Fasciolopsiasis	x		
Filariasis			x
Hepatitis, Viral	x		
Melioidosis	x		
Rabies	x		
Typhoid Fever	x		
Typhus, Scrub	x		

Food/Water Safety
All tap water used for drinking, brushing teeth, and making ice cubes should be boiled prior to use. Insure that bottled water is uncapped in your presence. Milk should be boiled to insure safety. Powdered and evaporated milk are available and safe. Avoid butter and other dairy products. All meat, poultry and seafood must be well cooked and served while hot. Pork is best avoided. Vegetables should be well cooked and served hot. Salads and mayonnaise are best avoided. Fruits with intact skins should be peeled by you just prior to consumption. Avoid cold buffets, custards, and any frozen dessert. Amoebic and bacillary dysentery occurs in this country.

VACCINATIONS

Yellow fever—A vaccination certificate is required for travelers coming from infected areas and from or in transit through countries in the endemic yellow fever zone, see Chapter 6.63 A vaccination certificate is required for children over one year of age. Vaccination certificate is required for travelers who have been in or passed through an infected yellow fever area within six days prior to arrival.

Routine immunizations should be current. For infants and children through 16 years of age, refer to Chapter 4.3. A rubeola (measles) booster should be considered. Persons age 16 to 65 should receive a booster of tetanus and diphtheria every ten years. Healthy adults under age 65 do not require pneumococcal vaccine, but it is appropriate for those with chronic medical conditions. Influenza vaccine may be considered for those providing essential community services, health care workers, and those wishing to reduce the likelihood of becoming ill with influenza. Adults over 65 years of age are urged to obtain yearly influenza immunization, and to insure that their tetanus and diphtheria immunizations are current. Pneumococcal vaccination is also suggested for this age group.

The following immunizations are not required but are recommended for persons visitng this country.

Viral Hepatitis A—Vaccination is recommended for all travelers for their protection.

Typhoid fever—Vaccination is recommended for all travelers for their protection.

The following immunization is recommended for persons traveling on special assignments or engaged in certain activities:

Viral Hepatitis B—Because of the high rate of healthy carriers of hepatitis B in this country, vaccination is recommended for persons on working assignments in the health care field (dentists, physicians, nurses, laboratory technicians), or working in close contact with the local population (teachers, missionaries, Peace Corps), or persons foreseeing sexual relations with local inhabitants.

U.S. Foreign Service:
   P.O. Box 2991
   Bandar Seri Begawan, Telephone 29670

Country Number 8.29
Bulgaria

INFECTIOUS DISEASE RISK

Malaria Risk

There is no malaria risk in this country.

Diseases of Special Risk

In addition to the worldwide hazard of tetanus and the routine and any special immunizations recommended below, the traveler should be aware that risk of exposure to tick-borne encephalitis, rabies, and a viral hemorrhagic fever exists in this country.

Food/Water Safety

Water is probably safe, but due to local variations in bacterial counts, using bottled water for the first few weeks will help the traveler adjust and decrease the chance of traveler's diarrhea. Milk is pasteurized and safe to drink. Butter, cheese, yogurt and ice-cream are safe. Local meat, poultry, seafood, vegetables, and fruits are safe to eat.

VACCINATIONS

Routine immunizations should be current. For infants and children through 16 years of age, refer to Chapter 4.3. A rubeola (measles) booster should be considered. Persons age 16 to 65 should receive a booster of tetanus and diphtheria every ten years. Healthy adults under age 65 do not require pneumococcal vaccine, but it is appropriate for those with chronic medical conditions. Influenza vaccine may be considered for those providing essential community services, health care workers, and those wishing to reduce the likelihood of becoming ill with influenza. Adults over 65 years of age are urged to obtain yearly influenza immunization, and to insure that their tetanus and diphtheria immunizations are current. Pneumococcal vaccination is also suggested for this age group.

No vaccinations are required to enter this country.

U.S. Foreign Service

1 Stamboliiski Blvd.
Sofia, Telephone 88-48-01/02/03/04/05

Country Number 8.30
Burkina Faso

INFECTIOUS DISEASE RISK

Malaria Risk

Malaria risk is all year in all sections of this country, to include urban areas. The malaria in this country is resistant to chloroquine. The CDC recommends the use of mefloquine (Lariam) as described in Chapter 6.31 for chemical prophylaxis.

Falciparum malaria represents 85% of malaria, therefore there is a 15% risk of p. vivax malaria exposure. Consider the use of primaquine upon return home.

Diseases of Special Risk

In addition to the worldwide hazard of tetanus and the routine and any special immunizations recommended below, the traveler should be aware that risk of exposure to the following diseases exists in this country. This list is not all inclusive, but it is a caution concerning the more likely endemic disease risks.

Schistosomiasis may be found in this country. Avoid contact with contaminated fresh water lakes, ponds, or streams.

DISEASE RISK PROFILE

Disease	endemic	risk	hazard
Dracunculiasis/Guinea Worm	x		
Dysentery, Amoebic		x	
Echinococcosis		x	
Filariasis			x
Giardiasis		x	
Helminthic Diseases (see Chapter 6.21)		x	
Hepatitis, Viral		x	
Meningitis		x	
Onchocerciasis			x
Rabies	x		
Relapsing Fever	x		
Sandfly Fever			
Tapeworms			x
Trachoma			x
Trypanosomiasis, African Sleeping Sickness	x		
Typhoid Fever		x	
Typhus, Endemic Flea-Borne	x		
Typhus, Epidemic Louse-Borne	x		
Typhus, Scrub	x		

Food/Water Safety

All tap water used for drinking, brushing teeth, and making ice cubes should be boiled prior to use. Insure that bottled water is uncapped in your presence. Milk should be boiled to insure safety. Powdered and evaporated milk are available and safe. Avoid butter and other dairy products. All meat, poultry and seafood must be well cooked and served while hot. Pork is best avoided. Vegetables should be well cooked and served hot. Salads and mayonnaise are best avoided. Fruits with intact skins should be peeled by you just prior to consumption. Avoid cold buffets, custards, and any frozen dessert.

Amoebic dysentery, diarrheal diseases, parasitic worms, and viral hepatitis associated with water and food supplies are common in this country.

VACCINATIONS

Yellow fever—A vaccination certificate is required on arrival from all countries. A vaccination certificate is required for children over one year of age. CDC recommends vaccination for all travelers over 9 months of age who will be traveling outside of urban areas.

Routine immunizations should be current. For infants and children through 16 years of age, refer to Chapter 4.3. A rubeola (measles) booster should be considered. Persons age 16 to 65 should receive a booster of tetanus and diphtheria every ten years. Healthy adults under age 65 do not require pneumococcal vaccine, but it is appropriate for those with chronic medical conditions. Influenza vaccine may be considered for those providing essential community services, health care workers, and those wishing to reduce the likelihood of becoming ill with influenza. Adults over 65 years of age are urged to obtain yearly influenza immunization, and to insure that their tetanus and diphtheria immunizations are current. Pneumococcal vaccination is also suggested for this age group.

The following vaccinations listed for this country are listed for the traveler's protection, but they are not required for entry:

Cholera—Cholera is present in this country. Risk to western travelers is low. Immunization is not required. Avoid uncooked foods and untreated water. Vaccination is advised only for persons living or working under inadequate sanitary conditions and for those with impaired defense mechanisms.

Poliomyelitis—A poliomyelitis booster is indicated for this country.

Viral Hepatitis A—Vaccination is recommended for all travelers for their protection.

Typhoid fever—Vaccination is recommended for all travelers for their protection.

Selective vaccinations—These apply only to specific groups of travelers or persons on specific working assignments:

Viral Hepatitis B—Because of the high rate of healthy carriers of hepatitis B in this country, vaccination is recommended for persons on working assignments in the health care field (dentists, physicians, nurses, laboratory technicians), or working in close contact with the local population (teachers, missionaries, Peace Corps), or persons foreseeing sexual relations with local inhabitants.

Meningococcal meningitis—Vaccination is advised for persons traveling extensively or on working assignements in the meningitis belt of Africa's northern savannah, which stretches from the Red Sea to the Atlantic Ocean. Peak season is March and April. The disease is currently active in this country.

Rabies—In this country, where rabies is a constant threat, a pre-exposure rabies vaccination is advised for persons planning an extended stay or on working assignments (naturalists, agricultural advisors, archeologists, geologists, etc.). Although this provides adequate initial protection, a person bitten by a potentially rabid animal would still require post exposure immunization (see Chapter 6.40). Children should be cautioned not to pet dogs, cats, or other mammals.

U.S. Foreign Service
P.O. Box 35
Ouagadougou, Telephone 33-25-05

Country Number 8.31
Burma
(Myanmar)

INFECTIOUS DISEASE RISK

Malaria Risk

Malaria is present only below 1000 meters in rural areas as noted: April—December in Tenasserim; May—December in Irrawaddy and Mandalay Division; June—December in Pegu and Rangoon Divisions, Arakan, Chin, Hachin, Karen, Mon and Shan States; June—October in Magwe and Sagaing Division. The malaria in this country is resistant to chloroquine. The CDC recommends the use of mefloquine (Lariam) as described in Chapter 6.31 for chemical prophylaxis.

Falciparum malaria represents 88% of the malaria strains, therefore there is a risk of exposure to vivax malaria. Travelers may wish to consider the use of primaquine upon their return home.

Diseases of Special Risk

In addition to the worldwide hazard of tetanus and the routine and any special immunizations recommended below, the traveler should be aware that risk of exposure to the following diseases exists in this country. This list is not all inclusive, but it is a caution concerning the more likely endemic disease risks.

Potential risk of dengue fever exists. The virus is present in this country at all times and may give rise to major outbreaks. See Chapter 6.9.

DISEASE RISK PROFILE

Disease	endemic	risk	hazard
Chikungunya Fever	x		
Cholera	x		
Dengue Fever	x		
Diarrheal Disease Risk	x		
Dysentery, Amoebic	x		
Encephalitis, Japanesex			
Fasciolopsiasis	x		
Filariasis			x
Hepatitis, Viral	x		
Leishmaniasis			
Visceral		x	
Melioidosis	x		
Plague		x	
Rabies	x		
Trachoma	x		
Typhoid Fever	x		
Typhus, Scrub	x		

Food/Water Safety

All tap water used for drinking, brushing teeth, and making ice cubes should be boiled prior to use. Insure that bottled water is uncapped in your presence. Milk should be boiled to insure safety. Powdered and evaporated milk are available and safe. Avoid butter and other dairy products. All meat, poultry and seafood must be well cooked and served while hot. Pork is best avoided. Vegetables should be well cooked and served hot. Salads and mayonnaise are best avoided. Fruits with intact skins should be peeled by you just prior to consumption. Avoid cold buffets, custards, and any frozen dessert. First class hotels and restaurants serve purified drinking water and reliable food. However, the hazard is left to your judgement.

VACCINATIONS

Yellow fever—A vaccination certificate is required for travelers coming from infected areas and from or in transit through countries in the endemic yellow fever zone. A vaccination is required for children of all ages. Children under nine months of age should not be vaccinated due to health considerations. Please refer to the discussion in Chapter 6.63 on avoiding yellow fever vaccination in this age group. Travelers leaving this country are required to possess a vaccination certificate on their departure to an infected area or to countries which still demand such a certificate. Burmese nationals are required to possess certificates of vaccination on their departure from an infected area.

Routine immunizations should be current. For infants and children through 16 years of age, refer to Chapter 4.3. A rubeola (measles) booster should be considered. Persons age 16 to 65 should receive a booster of tetanus and diphtheria every ten years. Healthy adults under age 65 do not require pneumococcal vaccine, but it is appropriate for those with chronic medical conditions. Influenza vaccine may be considered for those providing essential community services, health care workers, and those wishing to reduce the likelihood of becoming ill with influenza. Adults over 65 years of age are urged to obtain yearly influenza immunization, and to insure that their tetanus and diphtheria immunizations are current. Pneumococcal vaccination is also suggested for this age group.

The following vaccinations listed for this country are listed for the traveler's protection, but they are not required for entry:
Poliomyelitis—A poliomyelitis booster is indicated for this country.
Viral Hepatitis A—Vaccination is recommended for all travelers for their protection.
Typhoid fever—Vaccination is recommended for all travelers for their protection.

Selective vaccinations—These apply only to specific groups of travelers or persons on specific working assignments:
Viral Hepatitis B—Because of the high rate of healthy carriers of hepatitis B in this country, vaccination is recommended for persons on working assignments in the health care field (dentists, physicians, nurses, laboratory technicians), or working in close contact with the local population (teachers, missionaries, Peace Corps), or persons foreseeing sexual relations with local inhabitants.
Japanese encephalitis—Vaccination is indicated for persons traveling extensively in rual areas or living and working near rice growing rural and suburban areas and other irrigated land, when exposure to the disease carrying mosquitoes is high. Children are especially susceptible to the infection. Sporadic cases occur throughout the year, with all ages being considered equally at high risk.
Plague—Vaccination is recommended only for persons who may be occupationally exposed to wild rodents (anthropologists, geologists, medical personnel, missionaries, etc). The standard vaccination course must be completed before entering the plague infested area. Geographical distribution of the area of risk for this country is west of Mandalay.
Rabies—In this country, where rabies is a constant threat, a pre-exposure rabies vaccination is advised for persons planning an extended stay or on working assignments (naturalists, agricultural advisors, archeologists, geologists, etc.). Although this provides adequate initial protection, a person bitten by a potentially rabid animal would still require post exposure immunization (see

Chapter 6.40). Children should be cautioned not to pet dogs, cats, or other mammals.

U.S. Foreign Service
581 Merchant St.
Rangoon, Telephone 82055, 8218 1

TRAVEL ADVISORY

A U.S. Department of State Travel Advisory was in effect on 4 May 1990 when this book went to press. The entire text is included below. Travel advisories are subject to reissue, change, and cancellation at any time. Current travel advisory information is available by calling the U.S. Department of State Travel Advisory Hotline at (202) 647-5225. The current travel advisory status is also available from the Herchmer Database update system (see Chapter 2.8).

MARCH 21, 1990 SECSTATE WSH SUBJECT: TRAVEL ADVISORY— BURMA—CAUTION
1. THE DEPARTMENT OF STATE ADVISES THAT SECURITY CONDITIONS IN BURMA REMAIN UNCERTAIN AND A CURFEW IS IN EFFECT. ARMED SOLDIERS MAINTAIN A VISIBLE PRESENCE IN BURMA'S CAPITAL, RANGOON.
2. BURMA WILL HOLD ITS FIRST MULTI-PARTY ELECTION IN OVER TWENTY-FIVE YEARS IN MAY 1990. THE ELECTION PROCESS COULD RESULT IN HEIGHTENED POLITICAL TENSION, WHICH MAY LEAD TO CIVIL UNREST.
3. THE BURMESE GOVERNMENT IS NOT ISSUING INDIVIDUAL TOURIST VISAS AT PRESENT, AND ALL TOURIST TRAVEL MUST BE IN ORGANIZED GROUPS AND BE APPROVED BY THE BURMESE GOVERNMENT THREE WEEKS IN ADVANCE. AMERICANS ARE ALSO ADVISED THAT MYANMAR AIRWAYS, (FORMERLY BURMA AIRWAYS CORPORATION) HAS EXPERIENCED FOUR FATAL CRASHES IN THE PAST THREE YEARS. THE DEPARTMENT OF STATE THEREFORE RECOMMENDS AGAINST FLYING ON BURMESE AIRCRAFT. TRAVEL BY SURFACE TO MAJOR TOURIST ATTRACTIONS IS TIME CONSUMING, BUT GROUP VISAS VALID FOR 14 DAYS ARE NOW BEING ISSUED.
4. AMERICANS PLANNING TRIPS TO BURMA ARE ENCOURAGED TO CHECK FOR POSSIBLE LATE BREAKING DEVELOPMENTS IN BURMA BY CALLING THE CITIZENS EMERGENCY CENTER OF THE DEPARTMENT OF STATE (TEL: 202/647-5225) THE U.S. EMBASSY IN BANGKOK, THAILAND (TEL: 252-5040 x2212) OR THE U.S. EMBASSY IN RANGOON (TEL: 82055 x320).
5. EXPIRATION DATE: DECEMBER 31, 1990

_____ Country Number 8.32 _____
Burunda

INFECTIOUS DISEASE RISK

Malaria Risk

Malaria is present in all parts of this country, including urban areas. The risk exists all year. The malaria in this country is resistant to chloroquine. The CDC recommends the use of mefloquine (Lariam) as described in Chapter 6.31 for chemical prophylaxis.

Falciparum malaria represents 80% of malaria, therefore there is a 20% risk of p. vivax malaria exposure. Consider the use of primaquine upon return home.

Diseases of Special Risk

In addition to the worldwide hazard of tetanus and the routine and any special immunizations recommended below, the traveler should be aware that risk of exposure to the following diseases exists in this country. This list is not all inclusive, but it is a caution concerning the more likely endemic disease risks.

Louse-borne typhus is cosmopolitan in distribution and is present wherever groups of persons are crowded together under conditions of poor sanitation and malnutrition. Risk exists for persons living or working in remote areas of the country (anthropologists, archeologists, geologists, medical personnel, missionaries, etc.). Freedom from louse infestation is the most effective protection against typhus.

DISEASE RISK PROFILE

Disease	endemic	risk	hazard
Dracunculiasis/Guinea Worm	x		
Dysentery, Amoebic			x
Echinococcosis		x	
Filariasis			x
Giardiasis			x
Helminthic Diseases (see Chapter 6.21)			x
Hepatitis, Viral			x
Leishmaniasis			
Cutaneous	x		
Visceral	x		
Onchocerciasis			x
Rabies	x		
Relapsing Fever	x		
Trachoma			x
Trypanosomiasis, African			
Sleeping Sickness	x		
Typhoid Fever			x

Disease	endemic	risk	hazard
Typhus, Endemic Flea-Borne	x		
Typhus, Epidemic Louse-Borne	x		
Typhus, Scrub	x		

Food/Water Safety

All tap water used for drinking, brushing teeth, and making ice cubes should be boiled prior to use. Insure that bottled water is uncapped in your presence. Milk should be boiled to insure safety. Powdered and evaporated milk are available and safe. Avoid butter and other dairy products. All meat, poultry and seafood must be well cooked and served while hot. Pork is best avoided. Vegetables should be well cooked and served hot. Salads and mayonnaise are best avoided. Fruits with intact skins should be peeled by you just prior to consumption. Avoid cold buffets, custards, and any frozen dessert.

VACCINATIONS

Yellow fever—A vaccination certificate is required for travelers coming from infected areas. A vaccination certificate is required for children over one year of age. Vaccination is recommended for travelers over 9 months of age for their protection. Also refer to Chapter 6.63.

Routine immunizations should be current. For infants and children through 16 years of age, refer to Chapter 4.3. A rubeola (measles) booster should be considered. Persons age 16 to 65 should receive a booster of tetanus and diphtheria every ten years. Healthy adults under age 65 do not require pneumococcal vaccine, but it is appropriate for those with chronic medical conditions. Influenza vaccine may be considered for those providing essential community services, health care workers, and those wishing to reduce the likelihood of becoming ill with influenza. Adults over 65 years of age are urged to obtain yearly influenza immunization, and to insure that their tetanus and diphtheria immunizations are current. Pneumococcal vaccination is also suggested for this age group.

The following vaccinations listed for this country are listed for the traveler's protection, but they are not required for entry:

Poliomyelitis—A poliomyelitis booster is indicated for this country.

Cholera—Cholera is present in this country. Risk to western travelers is low. Immunization is not required or recommended for travel to this country due to its low effectiveness. Avoid uncooked foods and untreated water. Vaccination is advised only for persons living or working under inadequate sanitary conditions and for those with impaired defense mechanisms.

Viral Hepatitis A—Vaccination is recommended for all travelers for their protection.

Typhoid fever—Vaccination is recommended for all travelers for their protection.

Selective vaccinations—These apply only to specific groups of travelers or persons on specific working assignments:

Viral Hepatitis B—Because of the high rate of healthy carriers of hepatitis B in this country, vaccination is recommended for persons on working assignments in the health care field (dentists, physicians, nurses, laboratory technicians), or working in close contact with the local population (teachers, missionaries, Peace Corps), or persons foreseeing sexual relations with local inhabitants.

U.S. Foreign Service
Chaussee Prince Louis Rwagasore
Bujumbura, Telephone 34-54

Country Number 8.33
United Republic of Cameroon

INFECTIOUS DISEASE RISK

Malaria Risk
Malaria is present in all parts of this country, including urban areas. The risk exists all year. The malaria in this country is resistant to chloroquine. The CDC recommends the use of mefloquine (Lariam) as described in Chapter 6.31 for chemical prophylaxis.

Falciparum malaria represents 85% of malaria, therefore there is a 15% risk of p. vivax malaria exposure. Consider the use of primaquine upon return home.

Diseases of Special Risk
In addition to the worldwide hazard of tetanus and the routine and any special immunizations recommended below, the traveler should be aware that risk of exposure to the following diseases exists in this country. This list is not all inclusive, but it is a caution concerning the more likely endemic disease risks.

This country must be considered receptive to dengue fever. Intermittent epidemics in the past make renewed activity or reintroduction of the virus possible.

Schistosomiasis may be found throughout this country, including urban areas. Avoid contact with contaminated fresh water lakes, ponds, or streams.

Typhus—Louse-borne typhus is cosmopolitan in distribution and is present wherever groups of persons are crowded together under conditions of poor sanitation and malnutrition. Risk exists for persons living or working in remote areas of the country (anthropologists, archeologists, geologists, medical personnel, missionaries, etc.). Freedom from louse infestation is the most effective protection against typhus.

Lake Nyos contains large amounts of dissolved carbon dioxide gas which represents a potential threat for the release of another cloud of asphyxiating gas. Caution is advised.

DISEASE RISK PROFILE

Disease	endemic	risk	hazard
Dracunculiasis/Guinea Worm	x		
Diarrheal Disease Risk			x
Dysentery, Amoebic			x
Echinococcosis		x	
Filariasis			x
Giardiasis			x
Helminthic Diseases (see Chapter 6.21)			x
Hepatitis, Viral			x
Leishmaniasis			
Cutaneous	x		
Visceral	x		
Loiasis			x
Onchocerciasis			x
Relapsing Fever	x		
Trachoma			x
Trypanosomiasis, African			
Sleeping Sickness	x		
Typhoid Fever			x
Typhus, Endemic Flea-Borne	x		
Typhus, Epidemic Louse-Borne	x		
Typhus, Scrub	x		

Food/Water Safety

All tap water used for drinking, brushing teeth, and making ice cubes should be boiled prior to use. Insure that bottled water is uncapped in your presence. Milk should be boiled to insure safety. Powdered and evaporated milk are available and safe. Avoid butter and other dairy products. All meat, poultry and seafood must be well cooked and served while hot. Pork is best avoided. Vegetables should be well cooked and served hot. Salads and mayonnaise are best avoided. Fruits with intact skins should be peeled by you just prior to consumption. Avoid cold buffets, custards, and any frozen dessert.

VACCINATIONS

Yellow fever—A vaccination certificate is required on arrival from all countries. A vaccination certificate is required for children over one year of age. CDC recommends vaccination for all children over 9 months of age.

Routine immunizations should be current. For infants and children through 16 years of age, refer to Chapter 4.3. A rubeola (measles) booster should be considered. Persons age 16 to 65 should receive a booster of tetanus and diphtheria every ten years. Healthy adults under age 65 do not require pneumococcal vaccine, but it is appropriate for those with chronic medical

conditions. Influenza vaccine may be considered for those providing essential community services, health care workers, and those wishing to reduce the likelihood of becoming ill with influenza. Adults over 65 years of age are urged to obtain yearly influenza immunization, and to insure that their tetanus and diphtheria immunizations are current. Pneumococcal vaccination is also suggested for this age group.

The following vaccinations listed for this country are listed for the traveler's protection, but they are not required for entry:

Poliomyelitis—A poliomyelitis booster is indicated for this country.

Cholera—Cholera is present in this country. Risk to western travelers is low. Immunization is not required or recommended for travel to this country due to its low effectiveness. Avoid uncooked foods and untreated water. Vaccination is advised only for persons living or working under inadequate sanitary conditions and for those with impaired defense mechanisms.

Viral Hepatitis A—Vaccination is recommended for all travelers for their protection.

Typhoid fever—Vaccination is recommended for all travelers for their protection.

Selective vaccinations—These apply only to specific groups of travelers or persons on specific working assignments:

Viral Hepatitis B—Because of the high rate of healthy carriers of hepatitis B in this country, vaccination is recommended for persons on working assignments in the health care field (dentists, physicians, nurses, laboratory technicians), or working in close contact with the local population (teachers, missionaries, Peace Corps), or persons foreseeing sexual relations with local inhabitants.

Meningococcal meningitis—Vaccination is advised for persons traveling extensively or on working assignements in the meningitis belt of Africa's northern savannah, which stretches from the Red Sea to the Atlantic Ocean. Peak season is March and April. Local area of greatest danger is the northern third of the country.

U.S. Foreign Service
   Rue Nachtigal, B.P. 817
   Yaounde, Telephone 23-40-14,23-05-12
   21 Avenue du General De Gaulle, B.P. 4006
   Douala, Telephone 42-53-31, 42-60-03

Canadian High Commission/Embassy Office:
   Immeuble Stamatiades
   Place de L'Hotel de Ville
   Yaounde, Telephone 23-02-03, 22-29-22

Country Number 8.34
Canada

INFECTIOUS DISEASE RISK

Malaria Risk

There is no malaria risk in this country.

Diseases of Special Risk

In addition to the worldwide hazard of tetanus and the routine and any special immunizations recommended below, the traveler should be aware that risk of exposure to the following diseases exists in this country. This list is not all inclusive, but it is a caution concerning the more likely endemic disease risks.

DISEASE RISK PROFILE

Disease	endemic	risk	hazard
Encephalitis	x		
Lyme Disease	x		
Rabies	x		
Rocky Mountain Spotted Fever	x		
Tularemia	x		

Food/Water Safety

Local water is considered safe without further treatment. Milk is pasteurized and safe to drink. Butter, cheese, yogurt and ice-cream are safe. Local meat, poultry, seafood, vegetables, and fruits are safe to eat.

VACCINATIONS

Routine immunizations should be current. For infants and children through 16 years of age, refer to Chapter 4.3. A rubeola (measles) booster should be considered. Persons age 16 to 65 should receive a booster of tetanus and diphtheria every ten years. Healthy adults under age 65 do not require pneumococcal vaccine, but it is appropriate for those with chronic medical conditions. Influenza vaccine may be considered for those providing essential community services, health care workers, and those wishing to reduce the likelihood of becoming ill with influenza. Adults over 65 years of age are urged to obtain yearly influenza immunization, and to insure that their tetanus and diphtheria immunizations are current. Pneumococcal vaccination is also suggested for this age group.

No vaccinations are required to enter this country.

Selective vaccinations—These apply only to specific groups of travelers or persons on specific working assignments:

*Viral Hepatitis B—*Because of the high rate of healthy carriers of hepatitis B among the local Inuit (Eskimo) population of northern Canada, vaccination is recommended for persons working in health care, education, or in close contact with them.

U.S. Foreign Service
100 Wellington St.
Ottawa, Telephone (613) 238-5335

Rm. 1050
615 Macleod Trail S.E.
Calgary, Telephone (403) 266-8962

Suite 910
Cogswell Tower, Scotia Sq.
Halifax, Telephone (902) 429-2480

Suite 1122, South Tower
Place Desjardins
Montreal, Telephone (514) 281-1886

1 Ave. Ste-Genevieve
Quebec, Telephone (418) 692-2095

360 University Ave.
Toronto, Telephone (416) 595-1700/1224

21st Fl.
1075 West Georgia St.
Vancouver, Telephone (604) 685-4311

6 Donald St.
Winnipeg, Telephone (204) 475-3344

Country Number 8.35
Canal Zone

INFECTIOUS DISEASE RISK

Malaria Risk
There is no malaria risk in this country, but see listing for Panama.

VACCINATIONS

Routine immunizations should be current. For infants and children through 16 years of age, refer to Chapter 4.3. A rubeola (measles) booster should be considered. Persons age 16 to 65 should receive a booster of tetanus and diphtheria every ten years. Healthy adults under age 65 do not require pneumococcal vaccine, but it is appropriate for those with chronic medical conditions. Influenza vaccine may be considered for those providing essential community services, health care workers, and those wishing to reduce the likelihood of becoming ill with influenza. Adults over 65 years of age are urged to obtain yearly influenza immunization, and to insure that their tetanus and diphtheria immunizations are current. Pneumococcal vaccination is also suggested for this age group.

No vaccinations are required to enter this area.

Country Number 8.36
Canary Islands

INFECTIOUS DISEASE RISK

Malaria Risk
There is no malaria risk in this country.

Food/Water Safety
Water is probably safe, but due to local variations in bacterial counts, using bottled water for the first few weeks will help the traveler adjust and decrease the chance of traveler's diarrhea. Milk is pasteurized and safe to drink. Butter, cheese, yogurt and ice-cream are safe. Local meat, poultry, seafood, vegetables, and fruits are safe to eat.

VACCINATIONS

Routine immunizations should be current. For infants and children through 16 years of age, refer to Chapter 4.3. A rubeola (measles) booster should be considered. Persons age 16 to 65 should receive a booster of tetanus and diphtheria every ten years. Healthy adults under age 65 do not require pneumococcal vaccine, but it is appropriate for those with chronic medical

conditions. Influenza vaccine may be considered for those providing essential community services, health care workers, and those wishing to reduce the likelihood of becoming ill with influenza. Adults over 65 years of age are urged to obtain yearly influenza immunization, and to insure that their tetanus and diphtheria immunizations are current. Pneumococcal vaccination is also suggested for this age group.

No vaccinations are required to enter this country.

Country Number 8.37
Cape Verde

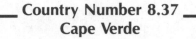

INFECTIOUS DISEASE RISK

Malaria Risk

Malaria risk is all year in the rural areas of Concelho de Santa Cruz (Sao Tiago Island). See Chapter 6.31 for use of Chloroquine.

Diseases of Special Risk

In addition to the worldwide hazard of tetanus and the routine and any special immunizations recommended below, the traveler should be aware that risk of exposure to the following diseases exists in this country. This list is not all inclusive, but it is a caution concerning the more likely endemic disease risks.

DISEASE RISK PROFILE

Disease	endemic	risk	hazard
Diarrheal Disease Risk			x
Dysentery, Amoebic			x
Echinococcosis		x	
Filariasis			x
Giardiasis			x
Helminthic Diseases (see Chapter 6.21)			x
Hepatitis, Viral			x
Lassa Fever	x		
Leishmaniasis			
Cutaneous	x		
Visceral	x		
Relapsing Fever	x		
Trachoma			x
Tungiasis	x		
Typhoid Fever			x
Typhus, Endemic Flea-Borne	x		
Typhus, Epidemic Louse-Borne	x		
Typhus, Scrub	x		

Food/Water Safety

All tap water used for drinking, brushing teeth, and making ice cubes should be boiled prior to use. Insure that bottled water is uncapped in your presence. Milk should be boiled to insure safety. Powdered and evaporated milk are available and safe. Avoid butter and other dairy products. All meat, poultry and seafood must be well cooked and served while hot. Pork is best avoided. Vegetables should be well cooked and served hot. Salads and mayonnaise are best avoided. Fruits with intact skins should be peeled by you just prior to consumption. Avoid cold buffets, custards, and any frozen dessert.

VACCINATIONS

Yellow fever—A vaccination certificate is required for travelers coming from infected areas. A vaccination certificate is required for children over one year of age. The requirement does not apply to travelers arriving in Sao Vincente, Sal, Maio, Boa Vista, and Santiago. Vaccination is recommended for all travelers for their protection. Vaccination is not advised for children under nine months of age.

Routine immunizations should be current. For infants and children through 16 years of age, refer to Chapter 4.3. A rubeola (measles) booster should be considered. Persons age 16 to 65 should receive a booster of tetanus and diphtheria every ten years. Healthy adults under age 65 do not require pneumococcal vaccine, but it is appropriate for those with chronic medical conditions. Influenza vaccine may be considered for those providing essential community services, health care workers, and those wishing to reduce the likelihood of becoming ill with influenza. Adults over 65 years of age are urged to obtain yearly influenza immunization, and to insure that their tetanus and diphtheria immunizations are current. Pneumococcal vaccination is also suggested for this age group.

The following vaccinations listed for this country are listed for the traveler's protection, but they are not required for entry:

Poliomyelitis—A poliomyelitis booster is indicated for this country.

Viral Hepatitis A—Vaccination is recommended for all travelers for their protection.

Typhoid fever—Vaccination is recommended for all travelers for their protection.

Selective vaccinations—These apply only to specific groups of travelers or persons on specific working assignments:

Viral Hepatitis B—Because of the high rate of healthy carriers of hepatitis B in this country, vaccination is recommended for persons on working assignments in the health care field (dentists, physicians, nurses, laboratory technicians), or working in close contact with the local population (teachers, missionaries, Peace Corps), or persons foreseeing sexual relations with local inhabitants.

U.S. Foreign Service
1st and 3rd Fls.
Rua Hoji Ya Yenna 81
Praia, Telephone 553, 761

Country Number 8.38
Cayman Islands

INFECTIOUS DISEASE RISK

Malaria Risk
There is no malaria risk in this country.

Diseases of Special Risk
In addition to the worldwide hazard of tetanus and the routine and any special immunizations recommended below, the traveler should be aware that risk of exposure to the following diseases exists in this country. This list is not all inclusive, but it is a caution concerning the more likely endemic disease risks.

DISEASE RISK PROFILE

Disease	endemic	risk	hazard
Dengue Fever	x		
Diarrheal Disease Risk		x	
Dysentery, Amoebic		x	
Hepatitis, Viral	x		
Rabies	x		

Food/Water Safety
Water is probably safe, but due to local variations in bacterial counts, using bottled water for the first few weeks will help the traveler adjust and decrease the chance of traveler's diarrhea. Milk is pasteurized and safe to drink. Butter, cheese, yogurt and ice-cream are safe. Local meat, poultry, seafood, vegetables, and fruits are safe to eat.

VACCINATIONS

Routine immunizations should be current. For infants and children through 16 years of age, refer to Chapter 4.3. A rubeola (measles) booster should be considered. Persons age 16 to 65 should receive a booster of tetanus and diphtheria every ten years. Healthy adults under age 65 do not require pneumococcal vaccine, but it is appropriate for those with chronic medical conditions. Influenza vaccine may be considered for those providing essential community services, health care workers, and those wishing to reduce the likelihood of becoming ill with influenza. Adults over 65 years of age are urged to

obtain yearly influenza immunization, and to insure that their tetanus and diphtheria immunizations are current. Pneumococcal vaccination is also suggested for this age group.

No vaccinations are required to enter this country.

——————— Country Number 8.39 ———————
Central African Republic

INFECTIOUS DISEASE RISK

Malaria Risk

Malaria is present in all parts of this country, including urban areas. The risk exists all year. The malaria in this country is resistant to chloroquine. The CDC recommends the use of mefloquine (Lariam) as described in Chapter 6.31 for chemical prophylaxis.

Falciparum malaria represents 85% of malaria, therefore there is a 15% risk of p. vivax malaria exposure. Consider the use of primaquine upon return home (see Chapter 6.31).

Diseases of Special Risk

In addition to the worldwide hazard of tetanus and the routine and any special immunizations recommended below, the traveler should be aware that risk of exposure to the following diseases exists in this country. This list is not all inclusive, but it is a caution concerning the more likely endemic disease risks.

Schistosomiasis may be found in this country. Avoid contact with contaminated fresh water lakes, ponds, or streams.

Tuberculosis, venereal disease, yaws, and leprosy are prevalent amongst the local population, but travelers are at very low risk in contracting these diseases.

DISEASE RISK PROFILE

Disease	endemic	risk	hazard
Dracunculiasis/Guinea Worm	x		
Diarrheal Disease Risk			x
Dysentery, Amoebic			x
Echinococcosis		x	
Filariasis			x
Giardiasis			x
Helminthic Diseases (see Chapter 6.21)			x
Hepatitis, Viral			x
Leishmaniasis			
Cutaneous	x		
Visceral	x		
Loiasis			x

Disease	endemic	risk	hazard
Onchocerciasis			x
Relapsing Fever	x		
Trachoma		x	
Trypanosomiasis, African Sleeping Sickness	x		
Typhoid Fever			x
Typhus, Endemic Flea-Borne	x		
Typhus, Epidemic Louse-Borne	x		
Typhus, Scrub	x		

Food/Water Safety

All tap water used for drinking, brushing teeth, and making ice cubes should be boiled prior to use. Insure that bottled water is uncapped in your presence. Milk should be boiled to insure safety. Powdered and evaporated milk are available and safe. Avoid butter and other dairy products. All meat, poultry and seafood must be well cooked and served while hot. Pork is best avoided. Vegetables should be well cooked and served hot. Salads and mayonnaise are best avoided. Fruits with intact skins should be peeled by you just prior to consumption. Avoid cold buffets, custards, and any frozen dessert.

VACCINATIONS

Yellow fever—A vaccination certificate is required on arrival from all countries. A vaccination certificate is required for children over one year of age. CDC recommends vaccination for all travelers over 9 months of age.

Routine immunizations should be current. For infants and children through 16 years of age, refer to Chapter 4.3. A rubeola (measles) booster should be considered. Persons age 16 to 65 should receive a booster of tetanus and diphtheria every ten years. Healthy adults under age 65 do not require pneumococcal vaccine, but it is appropriate for those with chronic medical conditions. Influenza vaccine may be considered for those providing essential community services, health care workers, and those wishing to reduce the likelihood of becoming ill with influenza. Adults over 65 years of age are urged to obtain yearly influenza immunization, and to insure that their tetanus and diphtheria immunizations are current. Pneumococcal vaccination is also suggested for this age group.

The following vaccinations listed for this country are listed for the traveler's protection, but they are not required for entry:

Poliomyelitis—A poliomyelitis booster is indicated for this country.

Viral Hepatitis A—Vaccination is recommended for all travelers for their protection.

Typhoid fever—Vaccination is recommended for all travelers for their protection.

Selective vaccinations—These apply only to specific groups of travelers or persons on specific working assignments:

Viral Hepatitis B—Because of the high rate of healthy carriers of hepatitis B in this country, vaccination is recommended for persons on working assignments in the health care field (dentists, physicians, nurses, laboratory technicians), or working in close contact with the local population (teachers, missionaries, Peace Corps), or persons foreseeing sexual relations with local inhabitants.

Meningococcal meningitis—Vaccination is advised for persons traveling extensively or on working assignements in the meningitis belt of Africa's northern savannah, which stretches from the Red Sea to the Atlantic Ocean. Peak season is March and April, but the danger extends from December through June. Local area of greatest danger is the northern third of the country.

Rabies—In this country, where rabies is a constant threat, a pre-exposure rabies vaccination is advised for persons planning an extended stay or on working assignments (naturalists, agricultural advisors, archeologists, geologists, etc.). Although this provides adequate initial protection, a person bitten by a potentially rabid animal would still require post exposure immunization (see Chapter 6.40). Children should be cautioned not to pet dogs, cats, or other mammals.

U.S. Foreign Service
Avenue President Dacko
Banjui, Telephone 61-02-00/05/10

Country Number 8.40
Chad

INFECTIOUS DISEASE RISK

Malaria Risk

Malaria risk is present in the entire country, all year long, including urban areas. The malaria in this country is resistant to chloroquine. The CDC recommends the use of mefloquine (Lariam) as described in Chapter 6.31 for chemical prophylaxis.

Falciparum malaria represents 78% of the malaria present in this country, therefore there is a risk of vivax exposure. Consider the use of primaquine upon your return home. (Refer also the Chapter 6.31).

Diseases of Special Risk

In addition to the worldwide hazard of tetanus and the routine and any special immunizations recommended below, the traveler should be aware that risk of exposure to the following diseases exists in this country. This list is not

all inclusive, but it is a caution concerning the more likely endemic disease risks.

Schistosomiasis may be found in this country. Avoid contact with contaminated fresh water lakes, ponds, or streams.

The local population suffers from leprosy, tuberculosis, influenza, tropical ulcers, eye diseases, pneumonia, measles, cholera, polio, and fungal infections. Travelers are low risk in contracting these illnesses.

DISEASE RISK PROFILE

Disease	endemic	risk	hazard
Dracunculiasis/Guinea Worm	x		
Diarrheal Disease Risk			x
Dysentery, Amoebic			x
Echinococcosis		x	
Filariasis			x
Giardiasis			x
Helminthic Diseases (see Chapter 6.21)			x
Hepatitis, Viral			x
Leishmaniasis			
Cutaneous	x		
Visceral	x		
Loiasis			x
Onchocerciasis			x
Relapsing Fever	x		
Trachoma			x
Trypanosomiasis, African			
Sleeping Sickness	x		
Typhoid Fever			x
Typhus, Endemic Flea-Borne	x		
Typhus, Epidemic Louse-Borne	x		
Typhus, Scrub	x		

Food/Water Safety

All tap water used for drinking, brushing teeth, and making ice cubes should be boiled prior to use. Insure that bottled water is uncapped in your presence. Milk should be boiled to insure safety. Powdered and evaporated milk are available and safe. Avoid butter and other dairy products. All meat, poultry and seafood must be well cooked and served while hot. Pork is best avoided. Vegetables should be well cooked and served hot. Salads and mayonnaise are best avoided. Fruits with intact skins should be peeled by you just prior to consumption. Avoid cold buffets, custards, and any frozen dessert.

VACCINATIONS

Yellow fever—Vaccination is recommended for all travelers for their protection. Vaccination is advised for all travelers over 9 months of age who will be traveling outside of urban areas.

Routine immunizations should be current. For infants and children through 16 years of age, refer to Chapter 4.3. A rubeola (measles) booster should be considered. Persons age 16 to 65 should receive a booster of tetanus and diphtheria every ten years. Healthy adults under age 65 do not require pneumococcal vaccine, but it is appropriate for those with chronic medical conditions. Influenza vaccine may be considered for those providing essential community services, health care workers, and those wishing to reduce the likelihood of becoming ill with influenza. Adults over 65 years of age are urged to obtain yearly influenza immunization, and to insure that their tetanus and diphtheria immunizations are current. Pneumococcal vaccination is also suggested for this age group.

The following vaccinations listed for this country are listed for the traveler's protection, but they are not required for entry:
Poliomyelitis—A poliomyelitis booster is indicated for this country.
Viral Hepatitis A—Vaccination is recommended for all travelers for their protection.
Typhoid fever—Vaccination is recommended for all travelers for their protection.

Selective vaccinations—*These apply only to specific groups of travelers or persons on specific working assignments:*
Viral Hepatitis B—Because of the high rate of healthy carriers of hepatitis B in this country, vaccination is recommended for persons on working assignments in the health care field (dentists, physicians, nurses, laboratory technicians), or working in close contact with the local population (teachers, missionaries, Peace Corps), or persons foreseeing sexual relations with local inhabitants.
Meningococcal meningitis—Vaccination is advised for persons traveling extensively or on working assignments in the meningitis belt of Africa's northern savannah, which stretches from the Red Sea to the Atlantic Ocean. Peak season is March and April, but danger extends from December trough June. Local area of greatest danger is the southern half of this country.
Rabies—In this country, where rabies is a constant threat, a pre-exposure rabies vaccination is advised for persons planning an extended stay or on working assignments (naturalists, agricultural advisors, archeologists, geologists, etc.). Although this provides adequate initial protection, a person bitten by a potentially rabid animal would still require post exposure immunization (see Chapter 6.40). Children should be cautioned not to pet dogs, cats, or other mammals.

U.S. Foreign Service
Avenue Felix Ebove
N'Djamena, Telephone 23-29, 28-62, 30-94, 32-69, 35-15

TRAVEL ADVISORY

A U.S. Department of State Travel Advisory was in effect on 4 May 1990 when this book went to press. The entire text is included below. Travel advisories are subject to reissue, change, and cancellation at any time. Current travel advisory information is available by calling the U.S. Department of State Travel Advisory Hotline at (202) 647-5225. The current travel advisory status is also available from the Herchmer Database update system (see Chapter 2.8).

JANUARY 26, 1990
CHAD—CAUTION
THE DEPARTMENT OF STATE ADVISES THAT CAUTION MUST BE EXERCISED WHEN TRAVELING IN PARTS OF CHAD AND THAT TRAVEL IS RESTRICTED IN SOME AREAS.
ALTHOUGH CHAD AND LIBYA HAVE AGREED TO NEGOTIATE THEIR DIFFERENCES PEACEFULLY, CHAD'S NORTHERN FRONTIER WITH LIBYA IS STILL A MILITARIZED ZONE, PORTIONS OF WHICH ARE HEAVILY MINED. ALSO, CHAD'S EASTERN BORDER WITH SUDAN HAS BEEN THE SCENE OF RECENT HOSTILITIES BETWEEN CHADIAN GOVERNMENT FORCES AND ARMED INSURGENT GROUPS. THE GOVERNMENT OF CHAD RESTRICTS TOURIST TRAVEL TO BOTH OF THESE AREAS.
FOR LATEST TRAVEL INFORMATION, VISITORS SHOULD CHECK UPON ARRIVAL WITH THE U.S. EMBASSY IN N'DJAMENA. THE EMBASSY IS LOCATED ON AVENUE FELIX EBOUE, TELEPHONE 51-40-09 OR 51-62-18.
EXPIRATION: FEBRUARY 1, 1991

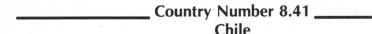

Country Number 8.41
Chile

INFECTIOUS DISEASE RISK

Malaria Risk
There is no malaria risk in this country.

Diseases of Special Risk
In addition to the worldwide hazard of tetanus and the routine and any special immunizations recommended below, the traveler should be aware that risk of exposure to the following diseases exists in this country. This list is not all inclusive, but it is a caution concerning the more likely endemic disease risks.

Chaga's Disease is present in rural and suburban areas in the following northern and central provinces: Tarapaca, Antofagasta, Coquimbo, Aconcagua, Valparaiso, Santiago, O'Higgins, and Colchagua.

DISEASE RISK PROFILE

Disease	endemic	risk	hazard
Anthrax		x	
Echinococcosis	x		
Hepatitis, Viral	x		
Tapeworms	x		
Typhoid Fever	x		

Food/Water Safety

All tap water used for drinking, brushing teeth, and making ice cubes should be boiled prior to use. Insure that bottled water is uncapped in your presence. Milk should be boiled to insure safety. Powdered and evaporated milk are available and safe. Avoid butter and other dairy products. All meat, poultry and seafood must be well cooked and served while hot. Pork is best avoided. Vegetables should be well cooked and served hot. Salads and mayonnaise are best avoided. Fruits with intact skins should be peeled by you just prior to consumption. Avoid cold buffets, custards, and any frozen dessert. First class hotels and restaurants serve purified drinking water and reliable food. However, the hazard is left to your judgement.

VACCINATIONS

Routine immunizations should be current. For infants and children through 16 years of age, refer to Chapter 4.3. A rubeola (measles) booster should be considered. Persons age 16 to 65 should receive a booster of tetanus and diphtheria every ten years. Healthy adults under age 65 do not require pneumococcal vaccine, but it is appropriate for those with chronic medical conditions. Influenza vaccine may be considered for those providing essential community services, health care workers, and those wishing to reduce the likelihood of becoming ill with influenza. Adults over 65 years of age are urged to obtain yearly influenza immunization, and to insure that their tetanus and diphtheria immunizations are current. Pneumococcal vaccination is also suggested for this age group.

No vaccinations are required to enter this country.

The vaccinations listed are recommended for the traveler's protection.

Viral Hepatitis A—Vaccination is recommended when traveling outside the areas usually visited by tourists, traveling extensively in the interior of the country (trekkers, hikers) and for persons on working assignments in remote areas.

Typhoid fever—Vaccination is recommended when traveling outside the areas usually visited by tourists, traveling extensively in the interior of the country (trekkers, hikers) and for persons on working assignments in remote areas.

U.S. Foreign Service
Codina Bldg.
1343 Agustinas
Santiago, Telephone 710133/90, 710326/75

Canadian High Commission/Embassy Office:
Ahumada 11
10th Floor
Santiago, Telephone 62256/7/8/9

_____ Country Number 8.42 _____
People's Republic of China

INFECTIOUS DISEASE RISK

Malaria Risk

Malaria risk is present from June–November north of 33 degress North latitude; from May–December at 25–33 degrees North latitude; and all year south of 25 degrees North latitude. Malaria is found in parts of Anhui, Fujian, Guandong, Guangxi, Guizhou, Hebei, Henan, Hubei, Hunan, Jiangsu, Jiangxi, Liaoning, Shanxi, Shenxi, Shandong, Sichuan, Yunnan, Xingjiang, and Zhejiang provivences/auton. regions. Resistance to chloroquine has developed in parts of Guangdong (Hainan), Guangxi and Yunnan; adjacent to Burma, Lao People's Democratic Republic, and Vietnam. The CDC recommends the use of mefloquine (Lariam) as described in Chapter 6.31 for chemical prophylaxis.

Diseases of Special Risk

This country must be considered receptive to dengue fever (see Chapter 6.9). Intermittent epidemics in the past make renewed activity or reintroduction of the virus possible. Risk is limited to the southern provinces of Yunnan, Guangxi, and Guangdong.

Schistosomiasis may be found in this country. Avoid contact with contaminated fresh water lakes, ponds, or streams. The major endemic area is located in the central and lower Chang Jiang (Yangtze River) valley, including its tributaries and adjacent lakes. The reas extends from the western city of Yichang (Ich'ang) in Hubei (Hupeh) Province to and including the suburbs of Shanghai in on the mouth of the river. In the north the area is limited by the cities of Tianmen (T'ienmen) on the Han River, Zaoshih (Tsaoshi) and the surrounding lake areas (Hubei Province); the area of Hufei (Hofei) in Anhui (Anhwei) Province, and the area of Yngzhou (Yangchou) in central Jiangsu (Kiangsu) Province. To the south of the Chang Jiang the risk extends to the lake area of Dongting (Tungt'ing) and the areas of the cities of Changde (Ch'angte) on the Yuan River. Xiangtan (Hsiangt'an) on the Xiang Jiang (Hsiang) River, and to the east of the lake (Hunan Province). In the province of Zhejian (Chekiang) the risk extends from the Tai Lake area to the delta of Fuchun River and the coastal areas of Hangzhou (Hangchou) Bay. A restricted focus of infection is present in Fujian (Fukien) Province: the area of Changle (Ch'anglo) on the Min River delta, south of Fuzhou (Fuchou). In southern China two restricted areas of infection are prsent: one on the Han River north of Shantou in Guangdong (Kwangtung) Province, the other in the area of Binyang (pinyang) north of Naning in Guangxi (Kwangsi) Province. A restricted focus is present in western China, in the province of Sichuan (Szechuan), south of Chengdu (Cheng'tu) in the villages of Renshou (Jenshowsien) and Rongxian (Junghsien).

Polio epidemics occur sporadically in China. Tuberculosis occurs at 55 times the United States rate.

In addition to the worldwide hazard of tetanus and the routine and any special immunizations recommended below, the traveler should be aware that risk of exposure to the following diseases exists in this country. This list is not all inclusive, but it is a caution concerning the more likely endemic disease risks.

DISEASE RISK PROFILE

Disease	endemic	risk	hazard
Brucellosis	x		
Clonorchiasis	x		
Dengue Fever	x		
Diarrheal Disease Risk		x	
Dysentery, Amoebic		x	
Encephalitis, Japanese	x		
Encephalitis, Tick-Borne	x		
Fasciolopsiasis	x		
Filariasis	x		
Helminthic Diseases (see Chapter 6.21)	x		
Hepatitis, Viral		x	
Leishmaniasis			
Visceral	x		
Leptospirosis	x		
Paragonimiasis	x		
Plague	x		
Trachoma	x		
Typhus, Scrub (in southern areas)	x		

Food/Water Safety

All tap water used for drinking, brushing teeth, and making ice cubes should be boiled prior to use. Insure that bottled water is uncapped in your presence. Milk should be boiled to insure safety. Powdered and evaporated milk are available and safe. Avoid butter and other dairy products. All meat, poultry and seafood must be well cooked and served while hot. Pork is best avoided. Vegetables should be well cooked and served hot. Salads and mayonnaise are

best avoided. Fruits with intact skins should be peeled by you just prior to consumption. Avoid cold buffets, custards, and any frozen dessert. First class hotels and restaurants in Beijing (Peking), Guangzhou (Canton), Nanjing (Nanking), Tianjin (Tientsin), and Xi'in (Sian) serve purified drinking water and reliable food. However, the hazard is left to your judgement.

VACCINATIONS

Yellow fever—A vaccination certificate is required for travelers coming from infected areas. A vaccination is required for children of all ages. Children under nine months of age should not be vaccinated due to health considerations. Please refer to the discussion in Chapter 6.63 on avoiding yellow fever vaccination in this age group.

Routine immunizations should be current. For infants and children through 16 years of age, refer to Chapter 4.3. A rubeola (measles) booster should be considered. Persons age 16 to 65 should receive a booster of tetanus and diphtheria every ten years. Healthy adults under age 65 do not require pneumococcal vaccine, but it is appropriate for those with chronic medical conditions. Influenza vaccine may be considered for those providing essential community services, health care workers, and those wishing to reduce the likelihood of becoming ill with influenza. Adults over 65 years of age are urged to obtain yearly influenza immunization, and to insure that their tetanus and diphtheria immunizations are current. Pneumococcal vaccination is also suggested for this age group.

The following vaccinations listed for this country are listed for the traveler's protection, but they are not required for entry:

Viral Hepatitis A—Vaccination is recommended for all travelers for their protection.

Typhoid fever—Vaccination is recommended for all travelers for their protection.

Selective vaccinations—These apply only to specific groups of travelers or persons on specific working assignments:

Viral Hepatitis B—Because of the high rate of healthy carriers of hepatitis B in this country, vaccination is recommended for persons on working assignments in the health care field (dentists, physicians, nurses, laboratory technicians), or working in close contact with the local population (teachers, missionaries, Peace Corps), or persons foreseeing sexual relations with local inhabitants.

Japanese encephalitis—Vaccination is indicated for persons traveling extensively in rual areas or living and working near rice growing rural and suburban areas and other irrigated land, when exposure to the disease carrying mosquitoes is high. Children are especially susceptible to the infection. Cases have been reported from all provinces except Xinzang (Tibet), Xinjiang

(Sinkiang) and Qinghai. Disease is most prevalent in central and eastern China. Period of transmission: June to October. High risk group: children under 15 years of age.

Plague—Vaccination is recommended only for persons who may be occupationally exposed to wild rodents (anthropologists, geologists, medical personnel, missionaries, etc). The standard vaccination course must be completed before entering the plague infested area.

Rabies—This disease kills 5,000 persons yearly in mainland China. As many as 1 million yearly are bitten by possibly rapid dogs. Rabies vaccine in China is in short supply.

U.S. Foreign Service:

Guang Hua Lu 17
Beijing, Telephone 52-2033

Dong Fang Hotel
Guangzhou, Telephone 69-900(ext. 1000)

1469 Huai Hai Middle Rd.
Shanghai, Telephone 37-9880

Liaoning Mansions
Shenyang

Canadian High Commission/Embassy Office:

10 San Li Tun Road
Chao Yang District
Beijing, Telephone 52-1475, 52-1571

TRAVEL ADVISORY

A U.S. Department of State Travel Advisory was in effect on 4 May 1990 when this book went to press. The entire text is included below. Travel advisories are subject to reissue, change, and cancellation at any time. Current travel advisory information is available by calling the U.S. Department of State Travel Advisory Hotline at (202) 647-5225. The current travel advisory status is also available from the Herchmer Database update system (see Chapter 2.8).

JANUARY 12, 1990
CHINA—CAUTION
THE DEPARTMENT OF STATE ADVISES AMERICAN CITIZENS THAT MARTIAL LAW WAS LIFTED IN BEIJING ON JANUARY 11, 1990.
THERE ARE OVER 600 CITIES AND AREAS IN CHINA OPEN TO VISITORS WITHOUT SPECIAL TRAVEL PERMITS, INCLUDING MOST MAJOR SCENIC AND HISTORICAL SITES. HOWEVER, VISITORS

SHOULD BE AWARE THAT CHINESE GOVERNMENT REGULATIONS STILL PROHIBIT TRAVEL IN CERTAIN AREAS WITHOUT SPECIAL PERMISSION. FOR MORE INFORMATION TRAVELERS SHOULD CONTACT THE NEAREST CHINESE EMBASSY OR CONSULATE, OR THE AMERICAN EMBASSY OR NEAREST AMERICAN CONSULATE IN CHINA.

AMERICANS PLANNING TO VISIT TIBET SHOULD BE AWARE THAT THERE ARE SPECIAL RESTRICTIONS ON TRAVEL TO LHASA. LHASA IS OPEN TO FOREIGN VISITORS, BUT IT HAS BEEN UNDER MARTIAL LAW SINCE MARCH 8, 1989. ALTHOUGH INDIVIDUALS ARE GENERALLY UNABLE TO PURCHASE AIRPLANE TICKETS TO LHASA, SMALL GROUPS HAVE ENTERED LHASA WITH TRAVEL COMPANIES FROM HONG KONG OR CHENGDU. AFTER ARRIVAL IN LHASA, SPECIAL PERMISSION TO VISIT ANY OF THE CLOSED AREAS IN TIBET MUST BE OBTAINED FROM THE TIBETAN AUTONOMOUS REGION PUBLIC SECURITY BUREAU.

AMERICANS VISITING CHINA SHOULD ENSURE THAT ALL PASSPORTS AND VISAS ARE CURRENT. CHINESE AUTHORITIES HAVE REQUESTED THE DEPARTURE OF CERTAIN INDIVIDUALS WHO THEY CLAIMED EXCEEDED THE TERMS OF THEIR VISITOR VISAS. AMERICANS SHOULD BE CAUTIOUS ABOUT CARRYING INTO CHINA DOCUMENTS, LITERATURE, LETTERS, ETC., THAT MIGHT BE REGARDED AS OBJECTIONABLE BY CHINESE AUTHORITIES. AUTHORITIES HAVE SEIZED WHAT THEY DEEM TO BE RELIGIOUS, PORNOGRAPHIC AND POLITICAL MATERIALS.

AMERICANS WHO WILL HAVE AN EXTENDED STAY IN CHINA ARE STRONGLY URGED TO REGISTER WITH THE AMERICAN EMBASSY IN BEIJING OR WITH THE AMERICAN CONSULATE GENERAL IN SHANGHAI, GUANGZHOU, SHENYANG OR CHENGDU UPON ARRIVAL IN CHINA. THIS APPLIES EVEN TO AMERICANS WHO HAVE PREVIOUSLY REGISTERED WITH THE EMBASSY OR CONSULATES GENERAL.

EXPIRATION: INDEFINITE

Country Number 8.43
Taiwan—Republic of China

INFECTIOUS DISEASE RISK

Malaria Risk

There is no malaria risk in this country.

Food/Water Safety

All tap water used for drinking, brushing teeth, and making ice cubes should be boiled prior to use. Insure that bottled water is uncapped in your presence. Milk should be boiled to insure safety. Powdered and evaporated milk are available and safe. Avoid butter and other dairy products. All meat, poultry and seafood must be well cooked and served while hot. Pork is best avoided. Vegetables should be well cooked and served hot. Salads and mayonnaise are best avoided. Fruits with intact skins should be peeled by you just prior to consumption. Avoid cold buffets, custards, and any frozen dessert. First class hotels and restaurants in Taipei serve purified drinking water and reliable food. However, the hazard is left to your judgement.

VACCINATIONS

Yellow fever—A vaccination certificate is required for travelers coming from infected areas. A vaccination is required for children of all ages. Children under nine months of age should not be vaccinated due to health considerations. Please refer to the discussion in Chapter 6.63 on avoiding yellow fever vaccination in this age group.

Routine immunizations should be current. For infants and children through 16 years of age, refer to Chapter 4.3. A rubeola (measles) booster should be considered. Persons age 16 to 65 should receive a booster of tetanus and diphtheria every ten years. Healthy adults under age 65 do not require pneumococcal vaccine, but it is appropriate for those with chronic medical conditions. Influenza vaccine may be considered for those providing essential community services, health care workers, and those wishing to reduce the likelihood of becoming ill with influenza. Adults over 65 years of age are urged to obtain yearly influenza immunization, and to insure that their tetanus and diphtheria immunizations are current. Pneumococcal vaccination is also suggested for this age group.

The following vaccinations listed for this country are listed for the traveler's protection, but they are not required for entry:

Poliomyelitis—Vaccination is recommended when traveling outside the areas usually visited by tourists, traveling extensively in the interior of the country (trekkers, hikers) and for persons on working assignments in remote areas.

Viral Hepatitis A—Vaccination is recommended when traveling outside the areas usually visited by tourists, traveling extensively in the interior of the country (trekkers, hikers) and for persons on working assignments in remote areas.

Typhoid fever—Vaccination is recommended when traveling outside the areas usually visited by tourists, traveling extensively in the interior of the country (trekkers, hikers) and for persons on working assignments in remote areas.

Selective vaccinations—These apply only to specific groups of travelers or persons on specific working assignments:

Viral Hepatitis B—Because of the high rate of healthy carriers of hepatitis B in this country, vaccination is recommended for persons on working assignments in the health care field (dentists, physicians, nurses, laboratory technicians), or working in close contact with the local population (teachers, missionaries, Peace Corps), or persons foreseeing sexual relations with local inhabitants.

Japanese encephalitis—Vaccination is indicated for persons traveling extensively in rual areas or living and working near rice growing rural and suburban areas and other irrigated land, when exposure to the disease carrying mosquitoes is high. Children are especially susceptible to the infection. Occasional outbreaks occur throughout the country. Period of transmission June to October.

U.S. Representative:
American Institute in Taiwan
7 Lane 134
Hsin Yi Road, Section 3
Taipei, Telephone 709-2000

88 Wu Fu 3rd Road
Kaohsiung, Telephone 221-2918

Country Number 8.44
Christmas Island—Indian Ocean

INFECTIOUS DISEASE RISK

Malaria Risk
There is no malaria risk in this country.

Food/Water Safety
Water is probably safe, but due to local variations in bacterial counts, using bottled water for the first few weeks will help the traveler adjust and decrease the chance of traveler's diarrhea. Milk and food products probably safe.

VACCINATIONS
Yellow fever—A vaccination certificate is required for travelers coming from infected areas and from or in transit through countries any part of which is infected with this disease. A vaccination certificate is required for children over one year of age. Vaccination certificate is required for travelers who have been in or passed through an infected yellow fever area within six days prior to arrival.

Routine immunizations should be current. For infants and children through 16 years of age, refer to Chapter 4.3. A rubeola (measles) booster should be considered. Persons age 16 to 65 should receive a booster of tetanus and diphtheria every ten years. Healthy adults under age 65 do not require pneumococcal vaccine, but it is appropriate for those with chronic medical conditions. Influenza vaccine may be considered for those providing essential community services, health care workers, and those wishing to reduce the likelihood of becoming ill with influenza. Adults over 65 years of age are urged to obtain yearly influenza immunization, and to insure that their tetanus and diphtheria immunizations are current. Pneumococcal vaccination is also suggested for this age group.

Country Number 8.45
Cocos (Keeling) Island

INFECTIOUS DISEASE RISK

Malaria Risk
There is no malaria risk in this country.

Food/Water Safety
Water is probably safe, but due to local variations in bacterial counts, using bottled water for the first few weeks will help the traveler adjust and decrease the chance of traveler's diarrhea. Milk and food products probably safe.

VACCINATIONS
Routine immunizations should be current. For infants and children through 16 years of age, refer to Chapter 4.3. A rubeola (measles) booster should be considered. Persons age 16 to 65 should receive a booster of tetanus and diphtheria every ten years. Healthy adults under age 65 do not require pneumococcal vaccine, but it is appropriate for those with chronic medical conditions. Influenza vaccine may be considered for those providing essential community services, health care workers, and those wishing to reduce the likelihood of becoming ill with influenza. Adults over 65 years of age are urged to obtain yearly influenza immunization, and to insure that their tetanus and diphtheria immunizations are current. Pneumococcal vaccination is also suggested for this age group.
No vaccinations are required to enter this country.

Country Number 8.46
Colombia

INFECTIOUS DISEASE RISK

Malaria Risk

Malaria is present only below 800 meters in rural areas of Uraba (Antioquia), Bajo Cauca-Nechi (Cauca and Antioquia), Magdelana Medio, Caqueta (Caqueta), Sarare (Arauca), Catatumbo (Norte de Santander, Pacifico Central and Sur, Putumayo (Putumayo), Ariari (Meta), Alto Vaupes (Vaupes), and Amazonas. The risk exists all year. There is no malaria risk in Bogota and vacinity. The malaria in this country is resistant to chloroquine. The CDC recommends the use of mefloquine (Lariam) as described in Chapter 6.31 for chemical prophylaxis.

Falciparum malaria represents 48% of malaria, therefore there is a 52% risk of p. vivax malaria exposure. Consider the use of primaquine upon return home.

Diseases of Special Risk

In addition to the worldwide hazard of tetanus and the routine and any special immunizations recommended below, the traveler should be aware that risk of exposure to the following diseases exists in this country. This list is not all inclusive, but it is a caution concerning the more likely endemic disease risks.

Chaga's Disease risk is present below 2500 meters in the following provinces: Boyaca, Caqueta, Cesar, Cuncinamarca, Guajira, Huila, Magdalena, Meta, Santander del Norte, Santander del Sur, Tolima, and Valle del Cauca.

Potential risk of dengue fever exists. The virus is present in this country at all times and may give rise to major outbreaks.

Bartonellosis exists on the western slopes of the Andes, primarily in river valleys, up to 3000 meters.

DISEASE RISK PROFILE

Disease	endemic	risk	hazard
Brucellosis		x	
Diarrheal Disease Risk		x	
Dysentery, Amoebic		x	
Echinococcosis	x		
Helminthic Diseases (see Chapter 6.21)		x	
Hepatitis, Viral		x	
Leishmaniasis			
Cutaneous	x		
Mucocutaneous	x		
Visceral	x		
Onchocerciasis	x		

Disease	endemic	risk	hazard
Trypanosomiasis, American	x		
Chaga's Disease			
Typhus, Scrub	x		

Food/Water Safety

All tap water used for drinking, brushing teeth, and making ice cubes should be boiled prior to use. Insure that bottled water is uncapped in your presence. Milk should be boiled to insure safety. Powdered and evaporated milk are available and safe. Avoid butter and other dairy products. All meat, poultry and seafood must be well cooked and served while hot. Pork is best avoided. Vegetables should be well cooked and served hot. Salads and mayonnaise are best avoided. Fruits with intact skins should be peeled by you just prior to consumption. Avoid cold buffets, custards, and any frozen dessert. First class hotels and restaurants in Bogota serve purified drinking water and reliable food. However, the hazard is left to your judgement.

VACCINATIONS

Routine immunizations should be current. For infants and children through 16 years of age, refer to Chapter 4.3. A rubeola (measles) booster should be considered. Persons age 16 to 65 should receive a booster of tetanus and diphtheria every ten years. Healthy adults under age 65 do not require pneumococcal vaccine, but it is appropriate for those with chronic medical conditions. Influenza vaccine may be considered for those providing essential community services, health care workers, and those wishing to reduce the likelihood of becoming ill with influenza. Adults over 65 years of age are urged to obtain yearly influenza immunization, and to insure that their tetanus and diphtheria immunizations are current. Pneumococcal vaccination is also suggested for this age group.

No vaccinations are required to enter this country.

The vaccinations listed are recommended for the traveler's protection.
Poliomyelitis—A poliomyelitis booster is indicated for this country.
Viral Hepatitis A—Vaccination is recommended when traveling outside the areas usually visited by tourists, traveling extensively in the interior of the country (trekkers, hikers) and for persons on working assignments in remote areas.
Typhoid fever—Vaccination is recommended when traveling outside the areas usually visited by tourists, traveling extensively in the interior of the country (trekkers, hikers) and for persons on working assignments in remote areas.
Yellow fever—Vaccination is recommended for all travelers for their protection. Vaccination is advised for all persons traveling outside of urban areas who are nine months or older. Yellow fever is frequently active in this country in Arauca, Caqueta, Casanare. Cucuta, Meta and Putumayo Intendencias; and Antioquia, Boyaca, Cundinamarca, Cesar, Guaviare, Santander and Norte de Santander Departments.

U.S. Foreign Service:
Calle 37, 8-40
Bogota, Telephone 285-1300/1688

Centro Comercial Mayorista
Calle 77, Carrera 68
Barranquilla, Telephone 45-7088/7560

Edificio Pieiroja
Carrera 3, No. 11-55
Cali, Telephone 881-7098

Canadian High Commission/Embassy Office:
Calle 76, No. 11-52
Bogota, Telephone 235-5066

TRAVEL ADVISORY

A U.S. Department of State Travel Advisory was in effect on 4 May 1990 when this book went to press. The entire text is included below. Travel advisories are subject to reissue, change, and cancellation at any time. Current travel advisory information is available by calling the U.S. Department of State Travel Advisory Hotline at (202) 647-5225. The current travel advisory status is also available from the Herchmer Database update system (see Chapter 2.8).

SECSTATE WSH MARCH 2, 1990
COLOMBIA—WARNING
THE DEPARTMENT OF STATE RECOMMENDS THAT AMERICANS EXERCISE CAUTION WHEN TRAVELING TO COLOMBIA. ALTHOUGH ALMOST ALL AMERICANS WHO VISIT COLOMBIA DO SO WITHOUT INCIDENT, SOME PARTS OF THE COUNTRY ARE DANGEROUS DUE TO GUERRILLA AND NARCOTIC ACTIVITIES. EVEN RELATIVELY SAFE AREAS LIKE BOGOTA HAVE URBAN CRIME AND RANDOM NARCO-TERRORIST ACTS. THE TERRORIST ASSASSINATIONS AND BOMBINGS THAT FLARED UP IN 1989 HAVE DECREASED, BUT COLOMBIA CONTINUES TO EXPERIENCE RANDOM CRIMINAL AND POLITICAL VIOLENCE.
GENERAL SECURITY: SEVERAL TERRORIST/GUERRILLA GROUPS ARE ACTIVE THROUGHOUT THE COUNTRY. IN EARLY 1990, ONE GROUP ANNOUNCED ITS INTENTION TO TARGET OFFICIAL AMERICAN CITIZENS AND U.S. INTERESTS IN COLOMBIA AND KIDNAPPED THREE PRIVATE AMERICAN CITIZENS FOR POLITICAL PURPOSES. IN THE PAST, AMERICANS ALSO HAVE BEEN ABDUCTED FOR RANSOM. AMERICAN RESIDENTS OF COLOMBIA SHOULD EXERCISE CAUTION AND CONSTANTLY REVIEW THEIR

SECURITY PRACTICES. ALL AMERICANS SHOULD CONSTANTLY BE ALERT TO THE POSSIBILITY OF THREATS TO THEIR WELL-BEING. ALTHOUGH TEMPORARY VISITORS AND TOURISTS HAVE RARELY BEEN THE TARGET OF VIOLENCE, CAUTION SHOULD BE EXERCISED TO AVOID BECOMING VICTIMS OF RANDOM VIOLENCE. VISITORS ARE ADVISED TO AVOID REMOTE AREAS, TAKE SPECIAL PRECAUTIONS AGAINST STREET CRIME IN BOGOTA, USE ONLY OFFICIAL TAXIS, AND CONTACT THE EMBASSY OR CONSULATE FOR UP-TO-DATE SECURITY INFORMATION.

RECOMMENDED PRECAUTIONS:

—RESIDENTS, ESPECIALLY THOSE IN DANGEROUS AREAS (SEE BELOW), SHOULD PRACTICE GOOD SECURITY BY ALTERING THEIR TRAVEL PATTERNS, CHANGING TRAVEL SCHEDULES (ESPECIALLY TO AND FROM WORK), AND BY BEING ALERT TO UNUSUAL ACTIVITY IN THEIR NEIGHBORHOODS WHICH MIGHT INDICATE THE POSSIBILITY THAT THEY ARE BEING WATCHED.

—ALL AMERICANS SHOULD AVOID REMOTE AREAS DUE TO THE OCCASIONAL LACK OF GOVERNMENT CONTROL AND THE PRESENCE OF NARCO-TRAFFICKERS AND GUERRILLAS IN MANY AREAS. OVERLAND NIGHT TRAVEL IS ESPECIALLY DISCOURAGED.

—VISITORS SHOULD BE WARY OF COMMON CRIMINALS IN MAJOR CITIES, ESPECIALLY BOGOTA AND MEDELLIN. PICKPOCKETS, MUGGERS AND CONFIDENCE MEN FREQUENT THE VICINITY OF MAJOR HOTELS. JEWELRY AND OTHER VALUABLES SHOULD BE LEFT AT HOME.

—VISITORS SHOULD TAKE CARE IN AIRPORTS, WHERE MANY PASSPORTS ARE STOLEN. THE MOST COMMON THEFT IS HAND LUGGAGE PLACED ON THE FLOOR NEAR THE VISITOR. ILLEGAL TAXIS, WHICH ARE SOMETIMES IDENTIFIED BY TWO DRIVERS AND IRREGULAR MARKINGS, ARE DANGEROUS. MOST AIRPORTS HAVE OFFICIAL TAXI QUEUES.

—TRAVELERS ARE URGED TO CONTACT THE EMBASSY IN BOGOTA OR THE CONSULATE IN BARRANQUILLA FOR THE LATEST INFORMATION ON TRAVEL OUTSIDE OF TOURIST RESORTS, MAJOR CITIES, OR THE BOGOTA SAVANNA.

RELATIVELY SAFE DEPARTMENTS/AREAS: IT MUST BE NOTED THAT EVEN SAFE AREAS MAY BE DANGEROUS AT TIMES, AND ALL OF COLOMBIA SHARES THE PROBLEMS NOTED ABOVE. PLACES THAT ARE NOT MENTIONED BELOW SHOULD BE CHECKED WITH THE EMBASSY PRIOR TO TRAVEL.

—CENTRAL CUNDINAMARCA INCLUDING BOGOTA AND THE SURROUNDING BOGOTA SAVANNA.

—THE HIGHLANDS OF BOYACA DEPARTMENT.

—SAN ANDRES AND PROVIDENCIA ISLANDS.

— THE CITY OF CARTAGENA AND THE ROSARIO ISLAND.
— THE CITIES OF CALI, BARRANQUILLA, AND LETICIA.
DANGEROUS DEPARTMENTS/AREAS: TRAVEL TO UNSAFE AREAS SHOULD BE AVOIDED OR ONLY UNDERTAKEN AFTER CONSULTATION WITH THE EMBASSY OR CONSULATE.
— COLUMBIA EAST OF THE ANDES (EXCEPT THE CITY OF LETICIA, AMAZONAS AND ADJACENT TOURIST AREAS).
— ALL OF ANTIOQUIA DEPARTMENT.
— MOST OF THE NORTH COAST (SOUTH TO SANTANDER, CALDAS, AND QUIBBO, CHOCO) EXCEPT FOR THE MAJOR TOURIST AREAS SUCH AS SANTA MARTA, BARRANQUILLA, CARTAGENA, AND CAPURGANA.
— THE MAGDELENA MEDIO REGION: THE MAGDELENA RIVER VALLEY SOUTH TO TOLIMA INCLUDING WESTERN BOYACA, EASTERN CALDAS, AND NORTHWESTERN CUNDINAMARCA.
— RURAL HUILA, CAUCA, AND VALLE DE CAUCA DEPARTMENTS.
— MOST OF THE CAUCA RIVER VALLEY.
— THE URABA REGION OF CHOCO IN NORTHWESTERN COLOMBIA.
INFORMATION: UPON ARRIVAL, U.S. CITIZENS SHOULD SEEK THE LATEST TRAVEL INFORMATION AND REGISTER WITH THE AMERICAN CITIZEN SERVICES UNIT OF THE EMBASSY IN BOGATA, CALLE 38 NO. 8-61, AT (571) 285-1300 (EXT. 206, 215) OR WITH THE CONSULATE IN BARRANQUILLA, CALLE 77 CARRERA 68, CENTRO COMERCIAL MAYORISTA, AT (575) 457-088. REGISTRATION FACILITATES THE PROVIDING OF EMERGENCY SERVICES SHOULD IT BECOME NECESSARY.
EXPIRATION: MARCH 1, 1991.

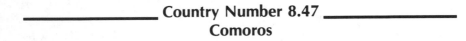

Country Number 8.47
Comoros

INFECTIOUS DISEASE RISK

Malaria Risk

Malaria is present in all parts of this country, including urban areas. The malaria in this country is resistant to chloroquine. The CDC recommends the use of mefloquine (Lariam) as described in Chapter 6.31 for chemical prophylaxis.

Falciparum malaria represents 88% of malaria, therefore there is a 12% risk of p. vivax malaria exposure. Consider the use of primaquine upon return home (see Chapter 6.31).

Diseases of Special Risk

In addition to the worldwide hazard of tetanus and the routine and any special immunizations recommended below, the traveler should be aware that risk of exposure to the following diseases exists in this country. This list is not all inclusive, but it is a caution concerning the more likely endemic disease risks.

DISEASE RISK PROFILE

Disease	endemic	risk	hazard
Dracunculiasis/Guinea Worm	x		
Diarrheal Disease Risk Dysentery, Amoebic and Bacillary			x
Echinococcosis		x	
Filariasis			x
Giardiasis			x
Helminthic Diseases (see Chapter 6.21)			x
Hepatitis, Viral			x
Leishmaniasis			
Cutaneous	x		
Visceral	x		
Onchocerciasis			x
Rabies	x		
Relapsing Fever	x		
Trachoma			x
Trypanosomiasis, African Sleeping Sickness	x		
Typhoid Fever			x
Typhus, Endemic Flea-Borne	x		
Typhus, Epidemic Louse-Borne	x		
Typhus, Scrub	x		

Food/Water Safety

All tap water used for drinking, brushing teeth, and making ice cubes should be boiled prior to use. Insure that bottled water is uncapped in your presence. Milk should be boiled to insure safety. Powdered and evaporated milk are available and safe. Avoid butter and other dairy products. All meat, poultry and seafood must be well cooked and served while hot. Pork is best avoided. Vegetables should be well cooked and served hot. Salads and mayonnaise are best avoided. Fruits with intact skins should be peeled by you just prior to consumption. Avoid cold buffets, custards, and any frozen dessert.

VACCINATIONS

Routine immunizations should be current. For infants and children through 16 years of age, refer to Chapter 4.3. A rubeola (measles) booster should be considered. Persons age 16 to 65 should receive a booster of tetanus and diphtheria every ten years. Healthy adults under age 65 do not require pneumococcal vaccine, but it is appropriate for those with chronic medical

conditions. Influenza vaccine may be considered for those providing essential community services, health care workers, and those wishing to reduce the likelihood of becoming ill with influenza. Adults over 65 years of age are urged to obtain yearly influenza immunization, and to insure that their tetanus and diphtheria immunizations are current. Pneumococcal vaccination is also suggested for this age group.

No vaccinations are required to enter this country.

The vaccinations listed are recommended for the traveler's protection.
Poliomyelitis—A poliomyelitis booster is indicated for this country.
Viral Hepatitis A—Vaccination is recommended for all travelers for their protection.
Typhoid fever—Vaccination is recommended for all travelers for their protection.

Selective vaccinations—*These apply only to specific groups of travelers or persons on specific working assignments:*
Viral Hepatitis B—Because of the high rate of healthy carriers of hepatitis B in this country, vaccination is recommended for persons on working assignments in the health care field (dentists, physicians, nurses, laboratory technicians), or working in close contact with the local population (teachers, missionaries, Peace Corps), or persons foreseeing sexual relations with local inhabitants.

Country Number 8.48
People's Republic of Congo

INFECTIOUS DISEASE RISK

Malaria Risk
Malaria is present in all parts of this country, including urban areas. The risk exists all year. The malaria in this country is resistant to chloroquine. The CDC recommends the use of mefloquine (Lariam) as described in Chapter 6.31 for chemical prophylaxis.

Falciparum malaria represents 90% of malaria, therefore there is a 10% risk of p. vivax malaria exposure. Consider the use of primaquine upon return home (see Chapter 6.31).

Diseases of Special Risk
In addition to the worldwide hazard of tetanus and the routine and any special immunizations recommended below, the traveler should be aware that risk of exposure to the following diseases exists in this country. This list is not all inclusive, but it is a caution concerning the more likely endemic disease risks.

This country must be considered receptive to dengue fever. Intermittent epidemics in the past make renewed activity or reintroduction of the virus possible.

Schistosomiasis may be found in this country. Avoid contact with contaminated fresh water lakes, ponds, or streams. Known areas of infection are in the southwestern part of the country.

Onchocerciasis is encountered in the south of the country with the major concentration along the Djoue River and the bank regions of the River Congo downstream from Brazzaville.

Typhus—Louse-borne typhus is cosmopolitan in distribution and is present wherever groups of persons are crowded together under conditions of poor sanitation and malnutrition. Risk exists for persons living or working in remote areas of the country (anthropologists, archeologists, geologists, medical personnel, missionaries, etc.). Freedom from louse infestation is the most effective protection against typhus.

DISEASE RISK PROFILE

Disease	endemic	risk	hazard
Dracunculiasis/Guinea Worm	x		
Diarrheal Disease Risk			x
Dysentery, Amoebic			x
Echinococcosis		x	
Filariasis			x
Giardiasis			x
Helminthic Diseases (see Chapter 6.21)			x
Hepatitis, Viral			x
Leishmaniasis			
Cutaneous	x		
Visceral	x		
Loiasis			x
Onchocerciasis			x
Relapsing Fever	x		
Trachoma			x
Trypanosomiasis, African	x		
Sleeping Sickness			
Typhoid Fever			x
Typhus, Endemic Flea-Borne	x		
Typhus, Epidemic Louse-Borne	x		
Typhus, Scrub	x		

Food/Water Safety

All tap water used for drinking, brushing teeth, and making ice cubes should be boiled prior to use. Insure that bottled water is uncapped in your presence. Milk should be boiled to insure safety. Powdered and evaporated milk are available and safe. Avoid butter and other dairy products. All meat, poultry and seafood must be well cooked and served while hot. Pork is best avoided. Vegetables should be well cooked and served hot. Salads and mayonnaise are

best avoided. Fruits with intact skins should be peeled by you just prior to consumption. Avoid cold buffets, custards, and any frozen dessert.

VACCINATIONS

Yellow fever—A vaccination certificate is required on arrival from all countries. A vaccination certificate is required for children over one year of age. Vaccination is recommended for all travelers for their protection. CDC recommends vaccination for all travelers over 9 months of age, but see also Chapter 6.63.

Routine immunizations should be current. For infants and children through 16 years of age, refer to Chapter 4.3. A rubeola (measles) booster should be considered. Persons age 16 to 65 should receive a booster of tetanus and diphtheria every ten years. Healthy adults under age 65 do not require pneumococcal vaccine, but it is appropriate for those with chronic medical conditions. Influenza vaccine may be considered for those providing essential community services, health care workers, and those wishing to reduce the likelihood of becoming ill with influenza. Adults over 65 years of age are urged to obtain yearly influenza immunization, and to insure that their tetanus and diphtheria immunizations are current. Pneumococcal vaccination is also suggested for this age group.

The following vaccinations listed for this country are listed for the traveler's protection, but they are not required for entry:

Poliomyelitis—A poliomyelitis booster is indicated for this country.

Viral Hepatitis A—Vaccination is recommended for all travelers for their protection.

Typhoid fever—Vaccination is recommended for all travelers for their protection.

Selective vaccinations—*These apply only to specific groups of travelers or persons on specific working assignments:*

Viral Hepatitis B—Because of the high rate of healthy carriers of hepatitis B in this country, vaccination is recommended for persons on working assignments in the health care field (dentists, physicians, nurses, laboratory technicians), or working in close contact with the local population (teachers, missionaries, Peace Corps), or persons foreseeing sexual relations with local inhabitants.

U.S. Foreign Service:
Avenue Amilcar Cabral
Brazzaville, Telephone 81-20-70, 81-26-24

_____ **Country Number 8.49** _____
Cook Islands

INFECTIOUS DISEASE RISK

Malaria Risk
There is no malaria risk in this country.

Diseases of Special Risk
In addition to the worldwide hazard of tetanus and the routine and any special immunizations recommended below, the traveler should be aware that risk of exposure to the following diseases exists in this country. This list is not all inclusive, but it is a caution concerning the more likely endemic disease risks.

This country must be considered receptive to dengue fever. Intermittent epidemics in the past make renewed activity or reintroduction of the virus possible.

DISEASE RISK PROFILE

Disease	endemic	risk	hazard
Diarrheal Disease Risk		x	
Dysentery, Amoebic		x	
Encephalitis, Japanese	x		
Filariasis			x
Helminthic Diseases (see Chapter 6.21)		x	
Typhoid Fever		x	

Food/Water Safety
Caution should be used with regard to water supplies. Food and milk products probably safe, but caution advised.

VACCINATIONS
Routine immunizations should be current. For infants and children through 16 years of age, refer to Chapter 4.3. A rubeola (measles) booster should be considered. Persons age 16 to 65 should receive a booster of tetanus and diphtheria every ten years. Healthy adults under age 65 do not require pneumococcal vaccine, but it is appropriate for those with chronic medical conditions. Influenza vaccine may be considered for those providing essential community services, health care workers, and those wishing to reduce the likelihood of becoming ill with influenza. Adults over 65 years of age are urged to obtain yearly influenza immunization, and to insure that their tetanus and diphtheria immunizations are current. Pneumococcal vaccination is also suggested for this age group.

No vaccinations are required to enter this country.

The vaccinations listed are recommended for the traveler's protection.

Viral Hepatitis A—Vaccination is recommended for all travelers for their protection.

Typhoid fever—Vaccination is recommended for all travelers for their protection.

Selective vaccinations—These apply only to specific groups of travelers or persons on specific working assignments:

Viral Hepatitis B—Because of the high rate of healthy carriers of hepatitis B in this country, vaccination is recommended for persons on working assignments in the health care field (dentists, physicians, nurses, laboratory technicians), or working in close contact with the local population (teachers, missionaries, Peace Corps), or persons foreseeing sexual relations with local inhabitants.

Country number 8.50
Costa Rica

INFECTIOUS DISEASE RISK

Malaria Risk

Malaria risk exists only below 500 meters, where it is present all year in the rural areas of Alajuela, Guanacaste, Limon, and Puntarenas. There is no risk in urban areas. See Chapter 6.31 for use of chloroquine.

Falciparum malaria represents 27% of malaria, therefore there is a 73% risk of p. vivax malaria exposure. Consider the use of primaquine upon return home.

Diseases of Special Risk

In addition to the worldwide hazard of tetanus and the routine and any special immunizations recommended below, the traveler should be aware that risk of exposure to the following diseases exists in this country. This list is not all inclusive, but it is a caution concerning the more likely endemic disease risks.

This country must be considered receptive to dengue fever (see Chapter 6.9). Intermittent epidemics in the past make renewed activity or reintroduction of the virus possible.

DISEASE RISK PROFILE

Disease	endemic	risk	hazard
Dengue Fever	x		
Diarrheal Disease Risk		x	
Dysentery, Amoebic/Bacillary		x	

Disease	endemic	risk	hazard
Encephalitis, Venezuelan Equine	x		
Helminthic Diseases (see Chapter 6.21)		x	
Hepatitis, Viral	x		
Leishmaniasis	x		
Paragonimiasis	x		
Rabies (esp dogs and bats)			x
Trypanosomiasis, American Chaga's Disease	x		
Typhoid Fever		x	

Food/Water Safety

All tap water used for drinking, brushing teeth, and making ice cubes should be boiled prior to use. Insure that bottled water is uncapped in your presence. Milk should be boiled to insure safety. Powdered and evaporated milk are available and safe. Avoid butter and other dairy products. All meat, poultry and seafood must be well cooked and served while hot. Pork is best avoided. Vegetables should be well cooked and served hot. Salads and mayonnaise are best avoided. Fruits with intact skins should be peeled by you just prior to consumption. Avoid cold buffets, custards, and any frozen dessert.

VACCINATIONS

Routine immunizations should be current. For infants and children through 16 years of age, refer to Chapter 4.3. A rubeola (measles) booster should be considered. Persons age 16 to 65 should receive a booster of tetanus and diphtheria every ten years. Healthy adults under age 65 do not require pneumococcal vaccine, but it is appropriate for those with chronic medical conditions. Influenza vaccine may be considered for those providing essential community services, health care workers, and those wishing to reduce the likelihood of becoming ill with influenza. Adults over 65 years of age are urged to obtain yearly influenza immunization, and to insure that their tetanus and diphtheria immunizations are current. Pneumococcal vaccination is also suggested for this age group.

No vaccinations are required to enter this country.

The vaccinations listed are recommended for the traveler's protection.

Viral Hepatitis A—Vaccination is recommended when traveling outside the areas usually visited by tourists, traveling extensively in the interior of the country (trekkers, hikers) and for persons on working assignments in remote areas.

Typhoid fever—Vaccination is recommended when traveling outside the areas usually visited by tourists, traveling extensively in the interior of the country (trekkers, hikers) and for persons on working assignments in remote areas.

U.S. Foreign Service:

Avenida 3 and Calle 1
San Jose, Telephone 33-11-55

Canadian High Commission/Embassy Office:
6th Floor
Cronos Building
Calle 3 y Ave. Central
San Jose, Telephone 23-04-46

_____ **Country number 8.51** _____
Cuba

INFECTIOUS DISEASE RISK

Malaria Risk
There is no malaria risk in this country.

Diseases of Special Risk
In addition to the worldwide hazard of tetanus and the routine and any special immunizations recommended below, the traveler should be aware that risk of exposure to the following diseases exists in this country. This list is not all inclusive, but it is a caution concerning the more likely endemic disease risks.

This country must be considered receptive to dengue fever (see Chapter 6.9). Intermittent epidemics in the past make renewed activity or reintroduction of the virus possible.

DISEASE RISK PROFILE

Disease	endemic	risk	hazard
Diarrheal Disease Risk	x		
Dysentery, Amoebic/Bacillary	x		
Hepatitis, Viral	x		
Rabies (esp mongoose)	x		
Typhoid Fever	x		

Food/Water Safety
All tap water used for drinking, brushing teeth, and making ice cubes should be boiled prior to use. Insure that bottled water is uncapped in your presence. Milk should be boiled to insure safety. Powdered and evaporated milk are available and safe. Avoid butter and other dairy products. All meat, poultry and seafood must be well cooked and served while hot. Pork is best avoided. Vegetables should be well cooked and served hot. Salads and mayonnaise are best avoided. Fruits with intact skins should be peeled by you just prior to consumption. Avoid cold buffets, custards, and any frozen dessert. First class hotels and restaurants serve purified drinking water and reliable food. However, the hazard is left to your judgement.

VACCINATIONS

Routine immunizations should be current. For infants and children through 16 years of age, refer to Chapter 4.3. A rubeola (measles) booster should be considered. Persons age 16 to 65 should receive a booster of tetanus and diphtheria every ten years. Healthy adults under age 65 do not require pneumococcal vaccine, but it is appropriate for those with chronic medical conditions. Influenza vaccine may be considered for those providing essential community services, health care workers, and those wishing to reduce the likelihood of becoming ill with influenza. Adults over 65 years of age are urged to obtain yearly influenza immunization, and to insure that their tetanus and diphtheria immunizations are current. Pneumococcal vaccination is also suggested for this age group.

No vaccinations are required to enter this country.

U.S. Foreign Service Representative:
Swiss Embassy
Calcado entre L & M
Vedado Section
Havana, Telephone (3) 20551, (3) 29700

TRAVEL ADVISORY

A U.S. Department of State Travel Advisory was in effect on 4 May 1990 when this book went to press. The entire text is included below. Travel advisories are subject to reissue, change, and cancellation at any time. Current travel advisory information is available by calling the U.S. Department of State Travel Advisory Hotline at (202) 647-5225. The current travel advisory status is also available from the Herchmer Database update system (see Chapter 2.8).

09 SEP 1988
UNITED STATES DEPARTMENT OF STATE TRAVEL ADVISORY
CUBA—CAUTION
DUAL NATIONALS: THE DEPARTMENT OF STATE ADVISES THAT THE GOVERNMENT OF CUBA CONSIDERS ALL CUBAN-BORN U.S. CITIZENS, AND POSSIBLY THEIR CHILDREN, TO BE SOLELY CUBAN CITIZENS. THE CUBAN GOVERNMENT DOES NOT RECOGNIZE THE RIGHT OR OBLIGATION OF THE U.S. GOVERNMENT TO PROTECT DUAL U.S./CUBAN CITIZENS AND HAS CONSISTENTLY DENIED U.S. CONSULAR OFFICERS THE RIGHT TO VISIT INCARCERATED U.S. DUAL NATIONALS IN ORDER TO ASCERTAIN THEIR WELFARE AND PROPER TREATMENT UNDER CUBAN LAW.
CHECK WITH THE U.S. TREASURY DEPARTMENT BEFORE TRAVEL; RESTRICTIONS ON BUSINESS TRAVEL AND TOURISM TRANSACTIONS; REGISTER WITH U.S. INTEREST SECTION, EMBASSY OF SWITZERLAND UPON ARRIVAL (9/9/88) TREASURY RESTRICTIONS

EXIST.
EXPIRATION DATE: INDEFINITE

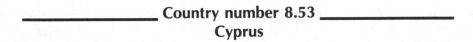

Country number 8.52
Curacao
Formerly the "Netherlands Antilles"

INFECTIOUS DISEASE RISK

Malaria Risk
There is no malaria risk in this country.

Food/Water Safety
First class hotels and restaurants serve purified drinking water and reliable food.

VACCINATIONS
Routine immunizations should be current. For infants and children through 16 years of age, refer to Chapter 4.3. A rubeola (measles) booster should be considered. Persons age 16 to 65 should receive a booster of tetanus and diphtheria every ten years. Healthy adults under age 65 do not require pneumococcal vaccine, but it is appropriate for those with chronic medical conditions. Influenza vaccine may be considered for those providing essential community services, health care workers, and those wishing to reduce the likelihood of becoming ill with influenza. Adults over 65 years of age are urged to obtain yearly influenza immunization, and to insure that their tetanus and diphtheria immunizations are current. Pneumococcal vaccination is also suggested for this age group.

No vaccinations are required to enter this country.

Country number 8.53
Cyprus

INFECTIOUS DISEASE RISK

Malaria Risk
There is no malaria risk in this country.

Diseases of Special Risk
In addition to the worldwide hazard of tetanus and the routine and any special immunizations recommended below, the traveler should be aware that risk of exposure to the following diseases exists in this country. This list is not

all inclusive, but it is a caution concerning the more likely endemic disease risks.

DISEASE RISK PROFILE

Disease	endemic	risk	hazard
Brucellosis	x		
Cholera	x		
Dracunculiasis/Guinea Worm	x		
Diarrheal Disease Risk	x		
Echinococcosis	x		
Helminthic Diseases (see Chapter 6.21)	x		
Hepatitis, Viral	x		
Leishmaniasis			
Cutaneous	x		
Visceral	x		
Rabies	x		
Tapeworms	x		
Trachoma	x		
Typhoid Fever	x		
Typhus, Endemic Flea-Borne	x		
Typhus, Scrub	x		

Food/Water Safety

Water is probably safe, but due to local variations in bacterial counts, using bottled water for the first few weeks will help the traveler adjust and decrease the chance of traveler's diarrhea. Local meat, poultry, seafood, vegetables, and fruits are safe to eat. Milk is pasteurized and safe to drink. Butter, cheese, yogurt and ice-cream are safe. At times refrigeration of dairy products during transport is unsatisfactory.

VACCINATIONS

Routine immunizations should be current. For infants and children through 16 years of age, refer to Chapter 4.3. A rubeola (measles) booster should be considered. Persons age 16 to 65 should receive a booster of tetanus and diphtheria every ten years. Healthy adults under age 65 do not require pneumococcal vaccine, but it is appropriate for those with chronic medical conditions. Influenza vaccine may be considered for those providing essential community services, health care workers, and those wishing to reduce the likelihood of becoming ill with influenza. Adults over 65 years of age are urged to obtain yearly influenza immunization, and to insure that their tetanus and diphtheria immunizations are current. Pneumococcal vaccination is also suggested for this age group.

No vaccinations are required to enter this country.

The vaccinations listed are recommended for the traveler's protection.

Viral Hepatitis A—Vaccination is recommended when traveling outside the areas usually visited by tourists, traveling extensively in the interior of the country (trekkers, hikers) and for persons on working assignments in remote areas.

Typhoid fever—Vaccination is recommended when traveling outside the areas usually visited by tourists, traveling extensively in the interior of the country (trekkers, hikers) and for persons on working assignments in remote areas.

Selective vaccinations—*These apply only to specific groups of travelers or persons on specific working assignments:*

Viral Hepatitis B—Because of the high rate of healthy carriers of hepatitis B in this country, vaccination is recommended for persons on working assignments in the health care field (dentists, physicians, nurses, laboratory technicians), or working in close contact with the local population (teachers, missionaries, Peace Corps), or persons foreseeing sexual relations with local inhabitants.

U.S. Foreign Service:
Therissos St. and Dositheos St.
Nicosia, Telephone 65151/5

TRAVEL ADVISORY
A U.S. Department of State Travel Advisory was in effect on 4 May 1990 when this book went to press. The entire text is included below. Travel advisories are subject to reissue, change, and cancellation at any time. Current travel advisory information is available by calling the U.S. Department of State Travel Advisory Hotline at (202) 647-5225. The current travel advisory status is also available from the Herchmer Database update system (see Chapter 2.8).

FEBRUARY 3, 1990 CYPRUS—CAUTION
THE DEPARTMENT OF STATE ADVISES THAT THE INTER-NATIONALLY-RECOGNIZED GOVERNMENT OF THE REPUBLIC OF CYPRUS HAS DESIGNATED LARNACA AND PAPHOS INTERNATIONAL AIRPORTS AND THE SEAPORTS OF LIMASSOL, LARNACA, AND PAPHOS AS THE ONLY LEGAL PORTS OF ENTRY INTO AND EXIT FROM CYPRUS. ALL OF THESE PORTS ARE IN THE SOUTHERN, GREEK CYPRIOT-CONTROLLED PART OF THE ISLAND. ENTRY OR EXIT THROUGH ANY OTHER AIR OR SEAPORT IS NOT AUTHORIZED BY THE GOVERNMENT OF THE REPUBLIC OF CYPRUS.
VISITORS WHO ARRIVE AT THESE GOVERNMENT-DESIGNATED PORTS OF ENTRY IN CYPRUS AND WHOSE PASSPORTS CONTAIN STAMPS REFLECTING PREVIOUS TRAVEL TO THE "TURKISH REPUBLIC OF CYPRUS OR BY THE UNITED STATES, WILL BE ASKED BY REPUBLIC OF CYPRUS IMMIGRATION OFFICIALS WHETHER

THE STAMPS CAN BE CANCELED. IF THE VISITOR AGREES, THE PRESENCE OF THE CANCELED STAMPS IN THE PASSPORT WILL NOT ACT AS A BAR TO ENTRY INTO CYPRUS.

VISITORS WHO ARRIVE AT NONDESIGNATED PORTS IN THE TURKISH CYPRIOT-CONTROLLED NORTHERN AREA SHOULD NOT EXPECT TO TRAVEL ACROSS THE UNITED NATIONS-PATROLLED "GREEN LINE" TO THE SOUTHERN AREA CONTROLLED BY THE GOVERNMENT OF THE REPUBLIC OF CYPRUS. SUCH TRAVEL IS NOT PERMITTED BY THE GOVERNMENT OF THE REPUBLIC OF CYPRUS, EVEN FOR TRANSIT PURPOSES.

VISITORS ARRIVING THROUGH THE GOVERNMENT-DESIGNATED PORTS OF ENTRY IN THE SOUTH MAY OFTEN OBTAIN PERMISSION FROM THE GOVERNMENT OF THE REPUBLIC OF CYPRUS AND FROM THE TURKISH CYPRIOT ADMINISTRATION TO CROSS THE UNITED NATIONS-PATROLLED "GREEN LINE", WHICH SEPARATES THE GREEK CYPRIOT-AND TURKISH CYPRIOT-ADMINISTERED PARTS OF CYPRUS, FOR SHORT VISITS IN THE NORTH. HOWEVER, PROSPECTIVE VISITORS SHOULD NOT ARRIVE IN CYPRUS UNDER THE ASSUMPTION THAT PERMISSION TO VISIT NORTHERN CYPURS WILL AUTOMATICALLY BE GRANTED. POLICY AND PROCEDURES REGARDING TRAVEL BETWEEN THE GREEK CYPRIOT-AND TURKISH CYPRIOT-ADMINISTERED PARTS OF CYPRUS ARE SUBJECT TO CHANGE.

U.S. CITIZENS MAY CONTACT THE U.S. EMBASSY, LOCATED AT THERISSOS ST. AND DOSITHEOS ST., NICOSIA, TELEPHONE NUMBER 465151, REGARDING CURRENT CIRCUMSTANCES.

EXPIRATION: FEBRUARY 6, 1991

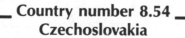

Country number 8.54
Czechoslovakia

INFECTIOUS DISEASE RISK

Malaria Risk
There is no malaria risk in this country.

Diseases of Special Risk
In addition to the worldwide hazard of tetanus and the routine and any special immunizations recommended below, the traveler should be aware that risk of exposure to the following diseases exists in this country. This list is not all inclusive, but it is a caution concerning the more likely endemic disease risks.

DISEASE RISK PROFILE

Disease	endemic	risk	hazard
Hepatitis, Viral	x		
Rabies		x	
Rocky Mountain Spotted Fever			x

Food/Water Safety

Water is probably safe, but due to local variations in bacterial counts, using bottled water for the first few weeks will help the traveler adjust and decrease the chance of traveler's diarrhea. Water should be boiled in summer months and at other times when the water table falls to low levels. Local meat, poultry, seafood, vegetables, and fruits are safe to eat. Milk is pasteurized and safe to drink. Butter, cheese, yogurt and ice-cream are safe.

VACCINATIONS

Routine immunizations should be current. For infants and children through 16 years of age, refer to Chapter 4.3. A rubeola (measles) booster should be considered. Persons age 16 to 65 should receive a booster of tetanus and diphtheria every ten years. Healthy adults under age 65 do not require pneumococcal vaccine, but it is appropriate for those with chronic medical conditions. Influenza vaccine may be considered for those providing essential community services, health care workers, and those wishing to reduce the likelihood of becoming ill with influenza. Adults over 65 years of age are urged to obtain yearly influenza immunization, and to insure that their tetanus and diphtheria immunizations are current. Pneumococcal vaccination is also suggested for this age group.

No vaccinations are required to enter this country.

The vaccinations listed are recommended for the traveler's protection.
Viral Hepatitis A—Gamma globulin is recommended for all travelers.

Selective vaccinations—These apply only to specific groups of travelers or persons on specific working assignments:
Tick-borne encephalitis—(Central European encephalitis) Vaccination is recommended for persons involved in recreational activities in forested areas (camping, hiking) or working in forestry occupations. Risk season: March to November. Risk is present in forested areas south of Prague, north of Brno, and the areas west of Plzin (Pilsen).

U.S. Foreign Service:
Trziste 15
Prague, Telephone 53-6641/8

Canadian High Commission/Embassy Office:
Mickiewiczova 6
Prague, Telephone 32-6941

_____ **Country number 8.55** _____
Democratic Kampuchea
Formerly "Cambodia"

INFECTIOUS DISEASE RISK

Malaria Risk
Malaria is present in all parts of this country, including urban areas. The risk exists all year. The malaria in this couyntry is resistant to chloroquine and mefloquine. Use doxycycline for malaria prevention as described in Chapter 6.31.
Falciparum malaria represents 71% of malaria, therefore there is a 29% risk of p. vivax malaria exposure. Consider the use of primaquine upon return home.

Diseases of Special Risk
In addition to the worldwide hazard of tetanus and the routine and any special immunizations recommended below, the traveler should be aware that risk of exposure to the following diseases exists in this country. This list is not all inclusive, but it is a caution concerning the more likely endemic disease risks.

DISEASE RISK PROFILE

Disease	endemic	risk	hazard
Chikungunya Fever	x		
Cholera	x		
Dengue Fever	x		
Diarrheal Disease Risk		x	
Dysentery, Amoebic	x		
Encephalitis, Japanese	x		
Fasciolopsiasis	x		
Filariasis			x
Hepatitis, Viral	x		
Melioidosis	x		
Rabies	x		
Typhoid Fever	x		
Typhus, Scrub	x		

Food/Water Safety
All tap water used for drinking, brushing teeth, and making ice cubes should be boiled prior to use. Insure that bottled water is uncapped in your

presence. Milk should be boiled to insure safety. Powdered and evaporated milk are available and safe. Avoid butter and other dairy products. All meat, poultry and seafood must be well cooked and served while hot. Pork is best avoided. Vegetables should be well cooked and served hot. Salads and mayonnaise are best avoided. Fruits with intact skins should be peeled by you just prior to consumption. Avoid cold buffets, custards, and any frozen dessert.

VACCINATIONS

Yellow fever—A vaccination certificate is required for travelers coming from infected areas. A vaccination is required for children of all ages. Children under nine months of age should not be vaccinated due to health considerations. Please refer to the discussion in Chapter 6.63 on avoiding yellow fever vaccination in this age group.

Routine immunizations should be current. For infants and children through 16 years of age, refer to Chapter 4.3. A rubeola (measles) booster should be considered. Persons age 16 to 65 should receive a booster of tetanus and diphtheria every ten years. Healthy adults under age 65 do not require pneumococcal vaccine, but it is appropriate for those with chronic medical conditions. Influenza vaccine may be considered for those providing essential community services, health care workers, and those wishing to reduce the likelihood of becoming ill with influenza. Adults over 65 years of age are urged to obtain yearly influenza immunization, and to insure that their tetanus and diphtheria immunizations are current. Pneumococcal vaccination is also suggested for this age group.

The vaccinations listed are recommended for the traveler's protection.
Poliomyelitis—A poliomyelitis booster is indicated for this country.
Viral Hepatitis A—Vaccination is recommended for all travelers for their protection.
Typhoid fever—Vaccination is recommended for all travelers for their protection.

Selective vaccinations—*These apply only to specific groups of travelers or persons on specific working assignments:*
Viral Hepatitis B—Because of the high rate of healthy carriers of hepatitis B in this country, vaccination is recommended for persons on working assignments in the health care field (dentists, physicians, nurses, laboratory technicians), or working in close contact with the local population (teachers, missionaries, Peace Corps), or persons foreseeing sexual relations with local inhabitants.
Japanese encephalitis—Vaccination is indicated for persons traveling extensively in rual areas or living and working near rice growing rural and suburban areas and other irrigated land, when exposure to the disease carrying mosquitoes is high. Children are especially susceptible to the infection.

Plague—Vaccination is recommended only for persons who may be occupationally exposed to wild rodents (anthropologists, geologists, medical personnel, missionaries, etc). The standard vaccination course must be completed before entering the plague infested area. Geographical distribution of the area of risk for this country is scattered throughout the country.

TRAVEL ADVISORY

A U.S. Department of State Travel Advisory was in effect on 4 May 1990 when this book went to press. The entire text is included below. Travel advisories are subject to reissue, change, and cancellation at any time. Current travel advisory information is available by calling the U.S. Department of State Travel Advisory Hotline at (202) 647-5225. The current travel advisory status is also available from the Herchmer Database update system (see Chapter 2.8).

SECSTATE WSH 29 NOVEMBER 1989
CAMBODIA—WARNING
THE UNITED STATES GOVERNMENT IS NOT IN A POSITION TO ACCORD NORMAL CONSULAR PROTECTIVE SERVICES TO UNITED STATES CITIZENS IN CAMBODIA AND DISCOURAGES TRAVEL TO THAT COUNTRY. THE UNITED STATES DOES NOT RECOGNIZE ANY GOVERNMENT IN CAMBODIA, NOR DOES IT MAINTAIN DIPLOMATIC OR CONSULAR RELATIONS WITH AUTHORITIES THERE. MOREOVER, THE UNITED STATES REGARDS THE CURRENT REGIME IN PHNOM PENH AS ILLEGALLY INSTALLED THROUGH VIETNAMESE MILITARY FORCE. NO THIRD COUNTRY REPRESENTS UNITED STATES INTERESTS. PROSPECTIVE TRAVELERS SHOULD BE AWARE THAT THEIR SECURITY CANNOT BE GUARANTEED IN LIGHT OF ONGOING MILITARY OPERATIONS IN CAMBODIA. MANY AREAS OF THE COUNTRY, INCLUDING THE AREA SURROUNDING THE MAIN POTENTIAL TOURIST ATTRACTION, THE PHRA VIHARN TEMPLE RUINS LOCATED ADJACENT TO THE BORDER WITH THAILAND, IS IN AN AREA HEAVILY MINED IN THE PAST AND POTENTIALLY THE OBJECT OF FUTURE ARMED CLASHES BETWEEN CONTENDING CAMBODIAN FACTIONS. U.S. PASSPORTS ARE VALID FOR TRAVEL TO CAMBODIA. HOWEVER, IT IS THE TRAVELER'S RESPONSIBILITY TO APPLY FOR THE REQUIRED VISA. CAMBODIA HAS DETAINED AND HELD INCOMMUNICADO FOR A LENGTHY PERIOD AN AMERICAN CITIZEN WHO HAD ENTERED CAMBODIA WITHOUT A VISA.
DUAL CITIZENSHIP
U.S. CITIZENS WHO WERE BORN IN CAMBODIA OR WHO WERE AT ONE TIME CITIZENS OF CAMBODIA, AND THE CHILDREN OF SUCH PERSONS, MAY BE CONSIDERED DUAL NATIONALS AND MAY, THEREFORE, BE SUBJECTED TO CAMBODIAN LAWS. THESE LAWS

MAY IMPOSE SPECIAL OBLIGATIONS UPON CAMBODIAN NATION-
ALS, E.G., MILITARY SERVICE, TAXES. U.S. CITIZENS CONTEMPLAT-
ING TRAVEL TO CAMBODIA SHOULD ONLY CARRY U.S. PASSPORTS
WITH THE PROPER VISA AFFIXED. UNDER NO CONDITIONS
SHOULD U.S. CITIZENS ACCEPT TRAVEL DOCUMENTS THAT IDEN-
TIFY THEM AS A CITIZEN OF CAMBODIA. SPECIFIC QUESTIONS ON
DUAL NATIONALITY MAY BE DIRECTED TO THE OFFICE OF CITI-
ZENS CONSULAR SERVICES, DEPARTMENT OF STATE, WASHING-
TON, D.C. 20520.

U.S. TREASURY REGULATIONS

INDIVIDUAL TRAVEL

UNDER THE FOREIGN ASSETS CONTROL REGULATIONS ADMINIS-
TERED BY THE TREASURY DEPARTMENT, A GENERAL LICENSE
AUTHORIZES TRANSACTIONS BY THE INDIVIDUAL TRAVELER OR-
DINARILY INCIDENT TO TO TRAVEL TO AND FROM CAMBODIA, IN-
CLUDING PAYMENT OF LIVING EXPENSES AND THE PURCHASE
OF GOODS FOR PERSONAL CONSUMPTION. IN ADDITION, ONCE
EVERY SIX MONTHS, THE GENERAL LICENSE AUTHORIZES IN
CONNECTION WITH SUCH TRAVEL THE PURCHASE OF GOODS
WITH A VALUE NOT TO EXCEED DOLS 100, AND THEIR IMPORTA-
TION INTO THE UNITED STATES AS ACCOMPANIED BAGGAGE.
THESE GOODS MUST BE FOR PERSONAL USE ONLY AND MAY NOT
BE RESOLD. JOURNALISTS, RESEARCHERS, NEWS AND DOCU-
MENTARY FILM-MAKERS, AND OTHER PERSONS TRAVELING FOR
SIMILAR PURPOSES ARE FURTHER AUTHORIZED TO ACQUIRE
FILMS, MAGAZINES, BOOKS AND OTHER PUBLICATIONS. THE AC-
QUISITIONS MUST BE DIRECTLY RELATED TO THEIR PROFES-
SIONAL ACTIVITIES AND MAY NOT BE RESOLD. THE GENERAL
LICENSE DOES NOT AUTHORIZE ANY OTHER TRAVEL RELATED
TRANSACTIONS WITH NATIONALS OF CAMBODIA. FURTHER, THE
USE OF CREDIT CARDS IN CAMBODIA IS NOT AUTHORIZED.

TRAVEL RELATED SERVICES

NO TRANSPORTATION SERVICES BY U.S. CARRIERS DIRECTLY TO
CAMBODIA ARE AVAILABLE OR AUTHORIZED. INDIVIDUALS MAY
BOOK THEIR OWN PASSAGE ABOARD A CAMBODIAN CARRIER DE-
PARTING FROM A LOCATION OUTSIDE THE UNITED STATES, BUT
NO U.S. SERVICE PROVIDER, SUCH AS A TRAVEL AGENT, MAY
PROVIDE THIS SERVICE OR RECEIVE A FEE OR COMMISSION FOR
IT. HOWEVER, A U.S. TRAVEL AGENT COULD BOOK PASSAGE FOR
AND RECEIVE FEES OR COMMISSIONS FROM INDIVIDUAL TRAV-
ELERS TO CAMBODIA, IF NONE OF THE TRAVEL IS ABOARD A
BLOCKED CARRIER (CARRIERS THAT ARE NATIONALS OF LIBYA,
CUBA, CAMBODIA, NORTH KOREA AND VIETNAM ARE CURRENTLY
BLOCKED). IN ADDITION, NO U.S. PERSON MAY ARRANGE OR

PROMOTE TOURS TO CAMBODIA, ENTER INTO BUSINESS AGREE-
MENTS OR ARRANGEMENTS WITH CAMBODIA OR ITS NATIONAL
WITH RESPECT TO TRAVEL, OR ACCEPT FEES, COMMISSIONS, OR
OTHER PAYMENTS FROM THEM. THE PROHIBITION ON THE AR-
RANGEMENTS OR PROMOTION OF TOURS TO CAMBODIA EX-
TENDS TO ARRANGEMENTS FOR SUCH TOURS MADE THROUGH
THIRD-COUNTRY INTERMEDIARIES.
THIS ADVISORY PROVIDES ONLY GENERAL GUIDANCE REGARD-
ING APPLICABLE TREASURY REGULATIONS. INDIVIDUALS CON-
TEMPLATING TRAVEL TO CAMBODIA ARE ENCOURAGED TO
CONTACT THE DEPARTMENT OF THE TREASURY FOR FURTHER
INFORMATION AT: LICENSING SECTION OFFICE OF FOREIGN AS-
SETS CONTROL DEPARTMENT OF THE TREASURY WASHINGTON,
D.C. 20220 TEL: (202) 376-0236
EXPIRATION: INDEFINITE

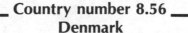

Country number 8.56
Denmark

INFECTIOUS DISEASE RISK

Malaria Risk

There is no malaria risk in this country.

Diseases of Special Risk

Rabies is prevalent in wild animals, especially foxes. Diphyllobothrias
(infection with fish tapeworm) is a risk in the Baltic Sea area.

Food/Water Safety

Local water is considered safe without further treatment. Milk is pasteurized and safe to drink. Butter, cheese, yogurt and ice-cream are safe. Local
meat, poultry, seafood, vegetables, and fruits are safe to eat.

VACCINATIONS

Routine immunizations should be current. For infants and children
through 16 years of age, refer to Chapter 4.3. A rubeola (measles) booster
should be considered. Persons age 16 to 65 should receive a booster of tetanus
and diphtheria every ten years. Healthy adults under age 65 do not require
pneumococcal vaccine, but it is appropriate for those with chronic medical
conditions. Influenza vaccine may be considered for those providing essential
community services, health care workers, and those wishing to reduce the likelihood of becoming ill with influenza. Adults over 65 years of age are urged to
obtain yearly influenza immunization, and to insure that their tetanus and diph-

theria immunizations are current. Pneumococcal vaccination is also suggested for this age group.

No vaccinations are required to enter this country.

U.S. Foreign Service:
Dag Hammarskjold Alle 24
Copenhagen, Telephone (01) 42-31-44

Canadian High Commission/Embassy Office:
Kr. Bernikowsgade 1
Copenhagen, Telephone (01) 12-22-99

Country number 8.57
Djibouti

INFECTIOUS DISEASE RISK

Malaria Risk
Malaria may be encountered throughout the country, to include urban areas. Risk is year around. See Chapter 6.31 for use of Chloroquine.

Falciparum malaria represents 80% of malaria, therefore there is a 20% risk of p. vivax malaria exposure. Consider the use of primaquine upon return home.

Diseases of Special Risk
In addition to the worldwide hazard of tetanus and the routine and any special immunizations recommended below, the traveler should be aware that risk of exposure to the following diseases exists in this country. This list is not all inclusive, but it is a caution concerning the more likely endemic disease risks.

This country must be considered receptive to dengue fever. Intermittent epidemics in the past make renewed activity or reintroduction of the virus possible.

Meningococcal meningitis may occur during the dry season (December through June) in the savannah areas.

DISEASE RISK PROFILE

Disease	endemic	risk	hazard
Dracunculiasis/Guinea Worm	x		
Diarrheal Disease Risk	x		
Dysentery, Amoebic/Bacillary		x	
Echinococcosis		x	
Filariasis			x
Giardiasis		x	
Helminthic Diseases (see Chapter 6.21)			x

Disease	endemic	risk	hazard
Hepatitis, Viral		x	
Leishmaniasis			
Cutaneous	x		
Visceral	x		
Rabies	x		
Relapsing Fever	x		
Trachoma			x
Typhoid Fever		x	
Typhus, Endemic Flea-Borne	x		
Typhus, Epidemic Louse-Borne	x		
Typhus, Scrub	x		

Food/Water Safety

Water is probably safe, but due to local variations in bacterial counts, using bottled water for the first few weeks will help the traveler adjust and decrease the chance of traveler's diarrhea. Milk should be boiled to insure safety. Powdered and evaporated milk are available and safe. Avoid butter and other dairy products. All meat, poultry and seafood must be well cooked and served while hot. Pork is best avoided. Vegetables should be well cooked and served hot. Salads and mayonnaise are best avoided. Fruits with intact skins should be peeled by you just prior to consumption. Avoid cold buffets, custards, and any frozen dessert.

VACCINATIONS

Yellow fever—A vaccination certificate is required for travelers coming from infected areas. A vaccination certificate is required for children over one year of age.

Routine immunizations should be current. For infants and children through 16 years of age, refer to Chapter 4.3. A rubeola (measles) booster should be considered. Persons age 16 to 65 should receive a booster of tetanus and diphtheria every ten years. Healthy adults under age 65 do not require pneumococcal vaccine, but it is appropriate for those with chronic medical conditions. Influenza vaccine may be considered for those providing essential community services, health care workers, and those wishing to reduce the likelihood of becoming ill with influenza. Adults over 65 years of age are urged to obtain yearly influenza immunization, and to insure that their tetanus and diphtheria immunizations are current. Pneumococcal vaccination is also suggested for this age group.

No vaccinations are required to enter this country.

The vaccinations listed are recommended for the traveler's protection.

Poliomyelitis—A poliomyelitis booster is indicated for this country.

Cholera—Cholera is present in this country. Risk to western travelers is low. Immunization is not required or recommended for travel to this country due to its low effectiveness. Avoid uncooked foods and untreated water. Vaccination is advised only for persons living or working under inadequate sanitary conditions and for those with impaired defense mechanisms.

Viral Hepatitis A—Vaccination is recommended for all travelers for their protection.

Typhoid fever—Vaccination is recommended for all travelers for their protection.

Selective vaccinations—These apply only to specific groups of travelers or persons on specific working assignments:

Viral Hepatitis B—Because of the high rate of healthy carriers of hepatitis B in this country, vaccination is recommended for persons on working assignments in the health care field (dentists, physicians, nurses, laboratory technicians), or working in close contact with the local population (teachers, missionaries, Peace Corps), or persons foreseeing sexual relations with local inhabitants.

U.S. Foreign Service:
Villa Plateau du Serpent Blvd.,
Marechal Joffre
Djibouti, Telephone 35-38-49, 35-39-95, 35-29-16/17
(Workweek: Sunday-Thursday)

_____ **Country number 8.58** _____
Dominica

INFECTIOUS DISEASE RISK

Malaria Risk
There is no malaria risk in this country.

Diseases of Special Risk
In addition to the worldwide hazard of tetanus and the routine and any special immunizations recommended below, the traveler should be aware that risk of exposure to the following diseases exists in this country. This list is not all inclusive, but it is a caution concerning the more likely endemic disease risks.

DISEASE RISK PROFILE

Disease	endemic	risk	hazard
Dengue	x		
Diarrheal Disease Risk		x	
Dysentery, Amoebic/Bacillary		x	
Hepatitis, Viral		x	
Rabies (esp. mongoose)		x	

Food/Water Safety

All tap water used for drinking, brushing teeth, and making ice cubes should be boiled prior to use. Insure that bottled water is uncapped in your presence. Milk should be boiled to insure safety. Powdered and evaporated milk are available and safe. Avoid butter and other dairy products. All meat, poultry and seafood must be well cooked and served while hot. Pork is best avoided. Vegetables should be well cooked and served hot. Salads and mayonnaise are best avoided. Fruits with intact skins should be peeled by you just prior to consumption. Avoid cold buffets, custards, and any frozen dessert.

VACCINATIONS

Yellow fever—A vaccination certificate is required for travelers coming from infected areas. A vaccination certificate is required for children over one year of age.

Routine immunizations should be current. For infants and children through 16 years of age, refer to Chapter 4.3. A rubeola (measles) booster should be considered. Persons age 16 to 65 should receive a booster of tetanus and diphtheria every ten years. Healthy adults under age 65 do not require pneumococcal vaccine, but it is appropriate for those with chronic medical conditions. Influenza vaccine may be considered for those providing essential community services, health care workers, and those wishing to reduce the likelihood of becoming ill with influenza. Adults over 65 years of age are urged to obtain yearly influenza immunization, and to insure that their tetanus and diphtheria immunizations are current. Pneumococcal vaccination is also suggested for this age group.

No vaccinations are required to enter this country.

Country number 8.59
Dominican Republic

INFECTIOUS DISEASE RISK

Malaria Risk

Malaria risk is all year long. Malaria may be encountered throughout the country below 400 meters, but not in urban areas. Malaria risk is greatest in the areas bordering Haiti. Falciparum malaria represents 100% of malaria. See Chapter 6.31 for use of chloroquine.

Diseases of Special Risk

In addition to the worldwide hazard of tetanus and the routine and any special immunizations recommended below, the traveler should be aware that risk of exposure to the following diseases exists in this country. This list is not all inclusive, but it is a caution concerning the more likely endemic disease risks.

Schistosomiasis may be found in this country. Avoid contact with contaminated fresh water lakes, ponds, or streams. Risk of infection is limited to the area of Hato Major and the surrounding villages in the interior of the eastern part of the country. Other foci of infection are present along the eastern part of the northern coast: Mitches, Nisibon, Cotui, and Nagua.

DISEASE RISK PROFILE

Disease	endemic	risk	hazard
Dengue	x		
Diarrheal Disease Risk		x	
Dysentery, Amoebic/Bacillary		x	
Hepatitis, Viral	x		

Food/Water Safety

All tap water used for drinking, brushing teeth, and making ice cubes should be boiled prior to use. Insure that bottled water is uncapped in your presence. Milk should be boiled to insure safety. Powdered and evaporated milk are available and safe. Avoid butter and other dairy products. All meat, poultry and seafood must be well cooked and served while hot. Pork is best avoided. Vegetables should be well cooked and served hot. Salads and mayonnaise are best avoided. Fruits with intact skins should be peeled by you just prior to consumption. Avoid cold buffets, custards, and any frozen dessert. First class hotels and restaurants in Santo Domingo serve purified drinking water and reliable food. However, the hazard is left to your judgement.

VACCINATIONS

Routine immunizations should be current. For infants and children through 16 years of age, refer to Chapter 4.3. A rubeola (measles) booster should be considered. Persons age 16 to 65 should receive a booster of tetanus and diphtheria every ten years. Healthy adults under age 65 do not require pneumococcal vaccine, but it is appropriate for those with chronic medical conditions. Influenza vaccine may be considered for those providing essential community services, health care workers, and those wishing to reduce the likelihood of becoming ill with influenza. Adults over 65 years of age are urged to obtain yearly influenza immunization, and to insure that their tetanus and diphtheria immunizations are current. Pneumococcal vaccination is also suggested for this age group.

No vaccinations are required to enter this country.

The vaccinations listed are recommended for the traveler's protection.
Poliomyelitis—A poliomyelitis booster is indicated for this country.
Viral Hepatitis A—Vaccination is recommended when traveling outside the areas usually visited by tourists, traveling extensively in the interior of the country (trekkers, hikers) and for persons on working assignments in remote areas.

Typhoid fever—Vaccination is recommended when traveling outside the areas usually visited by tourists, traveling extensively in the interior of the country (trekkers, hikers) and for persons on working assignments in remote areas.

Selective vaccinations—These apply only to specific groups of travelers or persons on specific working assignments:

Viral Hepatitis B—Because of the high rate of healthy carriers of hepatitis B in this country, vaccination is recommended for persons on working assignments in the health care field (dentists, physicians, nurses, laboratory technicians), or working in close contact with the local population (teachers, missionaries, Peace Corps), or persons foreseeing sexual relations with local inhabitants.

Rabies—In this country, where rabies is a constant threat, a pre-exposure rabies vaccination is advised for persons planning an extended stay or on working assignments (naturalists, agricultural advisors, archeologists, geologists, etc.). Although this provides adequate initial protection, a person bitten by a potentially rabid animal would still require post exposure immunization (see Chapter 6.40). Children should be cautioned not to pet dogs, cats, or other mammals. This disease is especially prevlent in the mongoose in this country.

U.S. Foreign Service:
> Corner of Calle Cesar Nicolas Penson and
> Calle Leopold Navarro
> Santo Domingo, Telephone (809) 682-2171

Canadian High Commission/Embassy Office:
> Mahatma Ghandhi 200
> Corner Juan Sanchez Ramirez
> Santo Domingo, Telephone (809) 689-002

_____ **Country number 8.60** _____
East Timor
Formerly "Portuguese Timor"

INFECTIOUS DISEASE RISK

Malaria Risk
> There is no malaria risk in this country.

Diseases of Special Risk
> No specific information is available.

Food/Water Safety
No specific information is available.

VACCINATIONS

Routine immunizations should be current. For infants and children through 16 years of age, refer to Chapter 4.3. A rubeola (measles) booster should be considered. Persons age 16 to 65 should receive a booster of tetanus and diphtheria every ten years. Healthy adults under age 65 do not require pneumococcal vaccine, but it is appropriate for those with chronic medical conditions. Influenza vaccine may be considered for those providing essential community services, health care workers, and those wishing to reduce the likelihood of becoming ill with influenza. Adults over 65 years of age are urged to obtain yearly influenza immunization, and to insure that their tetanus and diphtheria immunizations are current. Pneumococcal vaccination is also suggested for this age group.

No vaccinations are required to enter this country.

Country number 8.61
Ecuador

INFECTIOUS DISEASE RISK

Malaria Risk
Malaria risk is all year, only below 1500 meters, with minimal risk in urban areas. There is little or no risk in Quito vicinity and the Galapagos Islands. Malria risk is present in Esmeraldas, Guayas (including Guayaquil), Manabi, and El Oro; and rural areas of Los Rios, Morona Santiago, Napo, Pastaza, Pichincha, and Zamora Chinchipe. The malaria in this country is resistant to chloroquine. The CDC recommends the use of mefloquine (Lariam) as described in Chapter 6.31 for chemical prophylaxis.

Falciparum malaria represents 22% of malaria, therefore there is a 78% risk of p. vivax malaria exposure. Consider the use of primaquine upon return home.

Diseases of Special Risk
In addition to the worldwide hazard of tetanus and the routine and any special immunizations recommended below, the traveler should be aware that risk of exposure to the following diseases exists in this country. This list is not all inclusive, but it is a caution concerning the more likely endemic disease risks.

Chaga's Disease is present in rural and urban areas including the city of Guayaquil and the coastal provinces of Esmeraldes, Guayas, El Oro, Los Rios, and Manabi. The vector is locally known as chinchorro.

Typhus—Louse-borne typhus is cosmopolitan in distribution and is present wherever groups of persons are crowded together under conditions of poor sanitation and malnutrition. Risk exists for persons living or working in remote areas of the country (anthropologists, archeologists, geologists, medical personnel, missionaries, etc.). Freedom from louse infestation is the most effective protection against typhus.

DISEASE RISK PROFILE

Disease	endemic	risk	hazard
Bartonellosis	x		
Brucellosis		x	
Diarrheal Disease Risk			x
Dysentery, Amoebic/Bacillary			x
Echinococcosis	x		
Helminthic Diseases (see Chapter 6.21)			x
Hepatitis, Viral			x
Leishmaniasis			
Cutaneous	x		
Mucocutaneous	x		
Onchocerciasis	x		
Paragonimiasis	x		
Plague	x		x

Food/Water Safety

All tap water used for drinking, brushing teeth, and making ice cubes should be boiled prior to use. Insure that bottled water is uncapped in your presence. Milk should be boiled to insure safety. Powdered and evaporated milk are available and safe. Avoid butter and other dairy products. All meat, poultry and seafood must be well cooked and served while hot. Pork is best avoided. Vegetables should be well cooked and served hot. Salads and mayonnaise are best avoided. Fruits with intact skins should be peeled by you just prior to consumption. Avoid cold buffets, custards, and any frozen dessert. First class hotels and restaurants in Quito and Guayaquil serve purified drinking water and reliable food. However, the hazard is left to your judgement.

VACCINATIONS

Routine immunizations should be current. For infants and children through 16 years of age, refer to Chapter 4.3. A rubeola (measles) booster should be considered. Persons age 16 to 65 should receive a booster of tetanus and diphtheria every ten years. Healthy adults under age 65 do not require pneumococcal vaccine, but it is appropriate for those with chronic medical conditions. Influenza vaccine may be considered for those providing essential community services, health care workers, and those wishing to reduce the likelihood of becoming ill with influenza. Adults over 65 years of age are urged to obtain yearly influenza immunization, and to insure that their tetanus and diph-

theria immunizations are current. Pneumococcal vaccination is also suggested for this age group.

No vaccinations are required to enter this country.

The vaccinations listed are recommended for the traveler's protection.
Poliomyelitis—A poliomyelitis booster is indicated for this country.
Viral Hepatitis A—Vaccination is recommended for all travelers for their protection.
Typhoid fever—Vaccination is recommended for all travelers for their protection.
Yellow fever—Vaccination is recommended when traveling outside the areas usually visited by tourists, traveling extensively in the interior of the country (trekkers, hikers) and for persons on working assignments in remote areas. The Centers for Disease control recommend vaccination for all travelers over 9 months of age who plan travel outside of urban areas.

Selective vaccinations—*These apply only to specific groups of travelers or persons on specific working assignments:*
Plague—Vaccination is recommended only for persons who may be occupationally exposed to wild rodents (anthropologists, geologists, medical personnel, missionaries, etc). The standard vaccination course must be completed before entering the plague infested area. Geographical distribution of the area of risk for this country is the southern part of the country in Loya Province.
Rabies—In this country, where rabies is a constant threat, a pre-exposure rabies vaccination is advised for persons planning an extended stay or on working assignments (naturalists, agricultural advisors, archeologists, geologists, etc.). Although this provides adequate initial protection, a person bitten by a potentially rabid animal would still require post exposure immunization (see Chapter 6.40). Children should be cautioned not to pet dogs, cats, or other mammals.

U.S. Foreign Service:
120 Avenida Patria
Quito, Telephone 548-000

Canadian High Commission/Embassy Office:
Edificio Belmonte
6th Floor
Calle Corea
126 y Amazonas
Quito, Telephone 458-016/156/578/873

Country number 8.62
Egypt

INFECTIOUS DISEASE RISK

Malaria Risk

Malaria risk is from June through October in the Nile Delta, El Faiyum area, the Oases and part of Southern (Upper) Egypt. See Chapter 6.31 for use of chloroquine.

Falciparum malaria represents 4% of malaria, therefore there is a 96% risk of p. vivax malaria exposure. Consider the use of primaquine upon return home.

Diseases of Special Risk

In addition to the worldwide hazard of tetanus and the routine and any special immunizations recommended below, the traveler should be aware that risk of exposure to the following diseases exists in this country. This list is not all inclusive, but it is a caution concerning the more likely endemic disease risks.

Schistosomiasis may be found in this country. Avoid contact with contaminated fresh water lakes, ponds, or streams. S. haematobium is endemic throughout Egypt. S. mansoni is present in the Nile delta and does not extend further south than El Giza.

DISEASE RISK PROFILE

Disease	endemic	risk	hazard
Brucellosis		x	
Dengue Fever	x		
Diarrheal Disease Risk		x	
Dysentery, Amoebic/Bacillary		x	
Echinococcosis	x		
Filariasis	x		
Giardiasis		x	
Helminthic Diseases (see Chapter 6.21)		x	
Hepatitis, Viral		x	
Leishmaniasis	x		
Rabies	x		
Relapsing Fever	x		
Rift Valley Fever	x		
Sandfly Fever	x		
Trachoma	x		
Typhoid Fever		x	
Typhus	x		

Food/Water Safety

Water in first class hotels is probably safe, but due to local variations in bacterial counts, using bottled water for the first few weeks will help the traveler adjust and decrease the chance of traveler's diarrhea. Treat all other sources of water or use bottled water. Milk products should be considered unsafe, other than canned, evaporated or dehydrated milk. Cold food is unsafe.

VACCINATIONS

Yellow fever—A vaccination certificate is required for travelers coming from infected areas and from or in transit through countries in the endemic yellow fever zone, see Chapter 6.63. A vaccination certificate is required for children over one year of age.

Cholera—This vaccne is not required officially, but the U.S. Embassy reports that border officials may require this immunization if travelers arrive from cholera-infected areas.

Special required immunizations—Visitors arriving from the Sudan have recently been required to have immunization against cholera, meningitis, and typhoid. This requirement was no longer official as of Jan 1990. Visitors from the Sudan are required to be on malaria prophylaxis and might be given anti-malria tablets to swallow before being admitted to Egypt. Visitors from all regions of the Sudan are required to have their yellow fever vaccination.

Routine immunizations should be current. For infants and children through 16 years of age, refer to Chapter 4.3. A rubeola (measles) booster should be considered. Persons age 16 to 65 should receive a booster of tetanus and diphtheria every ten years. Healthy adults under age 65 do not require pneumococcal vaccine, but it is appropriate for those with chronic medical conditions. Influenza vaccine may be considered for those providing essential community services, health care workers, and those wishing to reduce the likelihood of becoming ill with influenza. Adults over 65 years of age are urged to obtain yearly influenza immunization, and to insure that their tetanus and diphtheria immunizations are current.

The vaccinations listed are recommended for the traveler's protection.

Meningitis—The Department of State recommends this vaccine for all persons posted to Egypt, but the CDC does not currently recommend this vaccine for travelers.

Poliomyelitis—A poliomyelitis booster is indicated for this country. There are 300 cases of polio in this country yearly amongst the native population.

Viral Hepatitis A—Vaccination is recommended for all travelers for their protection.

Typhoid fever—Vaccination is recommended for all travelers for their protection.

Selective vaccinations—These apply only to specific groups of travelers or persons on specific working assignments:

Viral Hepatitis B—Because of the high rate of healthy carriers of hepatitis B in this country, vaccination is recommended for persons on working assignments in the health care field (dentists, physicians, nurses, laboratory technicians), or working in close contact with the local population (teachers, missionaries, Peace Corps), or persons foreseeing sexual relations with local inhabitants.

Rabies—In this country, where rabies is a constant threat, a pre-exposure rabies vaccination is advised for persons planning an extended stay or on working assignments (naturalists, agricultural advisors, archeologists, geologists, etc.). Although this provides adequate initial protection, a person bitten by a potentially rabid animal would still require post exposure immunization (see Chapter 6.40). Children should be cautioned not to pet dogs, cats, or other mammals.

U.S. Foreign Service:
5 Sharia Latin American
Cairo, Telephone 28219, 774666
(Workweek: Sunday-Thursday)

110 Ave. Horreya
Alexandria, Telephone 801911, 25607, 22861, 28458
(Workweek: Monday-Friday)

Canadian High Commission/Embassy Office:
6 Sharia Mohamed Fahmiel Sayed
Garden City, Telephone 23110

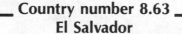

Country number 8.63
El Salvador

INFECTIOUS DISEASE RISK

Malaria Risk

Malaria exists in rural areas this country throughout the year, only below 1000 meters. There is no risk in urban areas. See Chapter 6.31 for use of chloroquine.

Falciparum malaria represents 9% of malaria, therefore there is a 91% risk of p. vivax malaria exposure. Consider the use of primaquine upon return home.

Diseases of Special Risk

In addition to the worldwide hazard of tetanus and the routine and any special immunizations recommended below, the traveler should be aware that risk of exposure to the following diseases exists in this country. This list is not all inclusive, but it is a caution concerning the more likely endemic disease risks.

This country must be considered receptive to dengue fever. Intermittent epidemics in the past make renewed activity or reintroduction of the virus possible.

Chaga's Disease is present in all rural areas below 1500 meters.

DISEASE RISK PROFILE

Disease	endemic	risk	hazard
Brucellosis	x		
Diarrheal Disease Risk		x	
Dysentery, Amoebic/Bacillary		x	
Encephalitis, Venezuelan Equine	x		
Helminthic Diseases (see Chapter 6.21)			x
Hepatitis, Viral	x		
Leishmaniasis	x		
Typhoid Fever		x	

Food/Water Safety

All tap water used for drinking, brushing teeth, and making ice cubes should be boiled prior to use. Insure that bottled water is uncapped in your presence. Milk should be boiled to insure safety. Powdered and evaporated milk are available and safe. Avoid butter and other dairy products. All meat, poultry and seafood must be well cooked and served while hot. Pork is best avoided. Vegetables should be well cooked and served hot. Salads and mayonnaise are best avoided. Fruits with intact skins should be peeled by you just prior to consumption. Avoid cold buffets, custards, and any frozen dessert.

VACCINATIONS

Yellow fever—A vaccination certificate is required for travelers coming from infected areas. A vaccination certificate is required for children over six months of age. Children under nine months of age should generally not be vaccinated due to health considerations. Please refer to the discussion in Chapter 6.63 on avoiding yellow fever vaccination in this age group.

Routine immunizations should be current. For infants and children through 16 years of age, refer to Chapter 4.3. A rubeola (measles) booster should be considered. Persons age 16 to 65 should receive a booster of tetanus and diphtheria every ten years. Healthy adults under age 65 do not require pneumococcal vaccine, but it is appropriate for those with chronic medical conditions. Influenza vaccine may be considered for those providing essential community services, health care workers, and those wishing to reduce the likelihood of becoming ill with influenza. Adults over 65 years of age are urged to

obtain yearly influenza immunization, and to insure that their tetanus and diphtheria immunizations are current. Pneumococcal vaccination is also suggested for this age group.

The vaccinations listed are recommended for the traveler's protection.
Poliomyelitis—A poliomyelitis booster is indicated for this country.
Viral Hepatitis A—Vaccination is recommended when traveling outside the areas usually visited by tourists, traveling extensively in the interior of the country (trekkers, hikers) and for persons on working assignments in remote areas.
Typhoid fever—Vaccination is recommended when traveling outside the areas usually visited by tourists, traveling extensively in the interior of the country (trekkers, hikers) and for persons on working assignments in remote areas.

Selective vaccinations—*These apply only to specific groups of travelers or persons on specific working assignments:*
Rabies—In this country, where rabies is a constant threat, a pre-exposure rabies vaccination is advised for persons planning an extended stay or on working assignments (naturalists, agricultural advisors, archeologists, geologists, etc.). Although this provides adequate initial protection, a person bitten by a potentially rabid animal would still require post exposure immunization (see Chapter 6.40). Children should be cautioned not to pet dogs, cats, or other mammals. Rabies is especially found in dogs and bats.

U.S. Foreign Service:
25 Avenida Norte No. 1230
San Salvador, Telephone 26-7100, 25-9984

TRAVEL ADVISORY
A U.S. Department of State Travel Advisory was in effect on 4 May 1990 when this book went to press. The entire text is included below. Travel advisories are subject to reissue, change, and cancellation at any time. Current travel advisory information is available by calling the U.S. Department of State Travel Advisory Hotline at (202) 647-5225. The current travel advisory status is also available from the Herchmer Database update system (see Chapter 2.8).

FEBRUARY 5, 1990
EL SALVADOR—WARNING
SUMMARY: THE DEPARTMENT OF STATE WARNS UNITED STATES CITIZENS TO EXERCISE CAUTION WHEN TRAVELING TO EL SALVADOR.
—THE GUERRILLAS OF THE FARABUNDO MARTI NATIONAL LIBERATION FRONT (FMLN) LAUNCHED AN OFFENSIVE IN NOVEMBER 1989 WHICH LASTED SEVERAL WEEKS. ALTHOUGH THE GUERRILLAS ARE GENERALLY THOUGHT TO HAVE LEFT THE CAPITAL AREA

AND ARMED CLASHES IN URBAN AREAS HAVE DIMINISHED, RANDOM GUERRILLA ATTACKS STILL OCCUR.

—TRAVEL IS DANGEROUS AND SHOULD BE AVOIDED IN THE EASTERN AND NORTHERN PARTS OF THE COUNTRY WHERE THE GUERRILLA INSURGENCY IS PARTICULARLY ACTIVE.

—TRAVELERS ARRIVING BY AIR SHOULD ARRIVE IN TIME TO BE ABLE TO CLEAR CUSTOMS AND DEPART THE AIRPORT BY 5:00 P.M. FOR THOSE ARRIVING BY ROAD, THE SAFEST ROUTE IS VIA THE SOUTHERN ENTRY POINTS ALONG THE BORDER WITH GUATEMALA. OVERLAND TRAVEL AFTER DUSK IS DANGEROUS AND SHOULD BE AVOIDED.

—ALTHOUGH THE COUNTRY WIDE CURFEW HAS BEEN LIFTED, THE DEPARTMENT OF STATE RECOMMENDS THAT AMERICANS REMAIN INDOORS AFTER 1:00 A.M.

—AMERICANS TRAVELING TO EL SALVADOR ARE STRONGLY URGED TO SEEK THE LATEST TRAVEL INFORMATION AND TO REGISTER WITH THE CONSULAR SECTION OF THE U.S. EMBASSY IN SAN SALVADOR UPON ARRIVAL.

SECURITY: THE GOVERNMENT OF EL SALVADOR IS WORKING TO CURB THE ACTIVITIES OF THE FMLN WHICH OFTEN UNDERTAKES INDISCRIMINATE ATTACKS AGAINST CIVILIAN TARGETS. COMBAT AND SABOTAGE CAN OCCUR ALMOST DAILY IN ANY REGION OF THE COUNTRY. WHILE IT DOES NOT APPEAR THAT UNITED STATES CITIZENS ARE SINGLED OUT FOR ATTACK, THERE IS RISK DUE TO THE INDISCRIMINATE NATURE OF THE VIOLENCE.

—TRAVELERS SHOULD KEEP A SAFE DISTANCE FROM MILITARY VEHICLES WHILE ON THE ROADWAYS AND FROM ARMY AND SECURITY FORCE PATROLS IN THE COUNTRYSIDE IN ORDER TO AVOID ACCIDENTAL INVOLVEMENT IN COMBAT ACTION. BEFORE VENTURING OUTSIDE OF MAJOR URBAN AREAS TRAVELERS SHOULD FAMILIARIZE THEMSELVES WITH THE LIKELY SECURITY SITUATIONS IN THE REGIONS WHERE THEY WISH TO TRAVEL. INSURGENT LAND MINES POSE A SIGNIFICANT DANGER IN BACK COUNTRY REGIONS AND HAVE CAUSED NUMEROUS UNINTENDED CASUALTIES.

CONFLICTIVE ZONES: THE GOVERNMENT OF EL SALVADOR HAS DESIGNATED SOME SECTIONS OF THE COUNTRY AS CONFLICTIVE ZONES. INDIVIDUALS SEEKING TO TRAVEL TO THOSE ZONES MUST OBTAIN A PRIOR CLEARANCE FROM BOTH THE MILITARY HIGH COMMAND AND THE DEPARTMENTAL MILITARY COMMANDER BEFORE ENTERING SUCH ZONES. MANY AMERICANS HAVE BEEN ARRESTED FOR NOT ADHERING TO THIS REGULATION. PERMISSION ONCE GRANTED TO ENTER THESE AREAS CAN LATER BE RESCINDED OR MODIFIED. THE LOCATIONS OF CONFLICTIVE

ZONES ARE SUBJECT TO CHANGE. FOR UP-TO-DATE INFORMA-
TION ABOUT THESE ZONES, TRAVELERS SHOULD CONTACT THE
U.S. EMBASSY.
INVOLVEMENT IN DOMESTIC POLITICS: THE SALVADORAN CONSTI-
TUTION PROHIBITS FOREIGNERS FROM PARTICIPATING IN DOMES-
TIC POLITICAL ACTIVITIES, INCLUDING PUBLIC DEMONSTRATIONS.
THE GOVERNMENT OF EL SALVADOR CONSIDERS SUCH INVOLVE-
MENT TO BE A VIOLATION OF THE PARTICIPANT'S TOURIST VISA
STATUS. ALTHOUGH DEMONSTRATIONS IN SAN SALVADOR SINCE
MARCH 1987 HAVE BEEN SMALL, THEY OFTEN TURN VIOLENT.
VISAS: PRIVATE U.S. CITIZENS ARE REQUIRED BY THE GOVERN-
MENT OF EL SALVADOR TO HOLD A VALID PASSPORT AND TO OB-
TAIN A VISA BEFORE TRAVELING TO EL SALVADOR. U.S. CITIZENS
SHOULD CONSULT WITH THE NEAREST EL SALVADOR CONSULATE
OR THE EMBASSY IN WASHINGTON, D.C. FOR THE MOST CUR-
RENT INFORMATION.
FOR INFORMATION: ALL AMERICAN CITIZENS VISITING EL SALVA-
DOR ARE STRONGLY ENCOURAGED TO CONTACT THE CONSULAR
SECTION OF THE U.S. EMBASSY UPON ARRIVAL IN EL SALVADOR.
THE EMBASSY IS LOCATED AT 25 AVENIDA NORTE NO. 1230, SAN
SALVADOR, TELEPHONE: (503)26-71-00
EXPIRATION: AUGUST 1, 1990

_____ **Country number 8.64** _____
Equatorial Guinea

INFECTIOUS DISEASE RISK

Malaria Risk

Malaria is present in all parts of this country, including urban areas. The
risk exists all year. The malaria in this country is resistant to chloroquine. The
CDC recommends the use of mefloquine (Lariam) as described in Chapter 6.31
for chemical prophylaxis.

Falciparum malaria represents 85% of malaria, therefore there is a 15%
risk of p. vivax malaria exposure. Consider the use of primaquine upon return
home.

Diseases of Special Risk

In addition to the worldwide hazard of tetanus and the routine and any
special immunizations recommended below, the traveler should be aware that
risk of exposure to the following diseases exists in this country. This list is not
all inclusive, but it is a caution concerning the more likely endemic disease
risks.

Schistosomiasis is endemic in this country. Avoid swimming or wading in fresh water sources such as lakes, rivers, or ponds.

DISEASE RISK PROFILE

Disease	endemic	risk	hazard
Dengue Fever	x		
Dracunculiasis/Guinea Worm	x		
Diarrheal Disease Risk			x
Dysentery, Amoebic/Bacillary			x
Echinococcosis		x	
Filariasis			x
Giardiasis		x	
Helminthic Diseases (see Chapter 6.21)			x
Hepatitis, Viral		x	
Leishmaniasis			
Cutaneous	x		
Visceral	x		
Loiasis			x
Relapsing Fever	x		
Trachoma			x
Typhoid Fever		x	
Typhus, Endemic Flea-Borne	x		
Typhus, Epidemic Louse-Borne	x		
Typhus, Scrub	x		

Food/Water Safety

All tap water used for drinking, brushing teeth, and making ice cubes should be boiled prior to use. Insure that bottled water is uncapped in your presence. Milk should be boiled to insure safety. Powdered and evaporated milk are available and safe. Avoid butter and other dairy products. All meat, poultry and seafood must be well cooked and served while hot. Pork is best avoided. Vegetables should be well cooked and served hot. Salads and mayonnaise are best avoided. Fruits with intact skins should be peeled by you just prior to consumption. Avoid cold buffets, custards, and any frozen dessert.

VACCINATIONS

Yellow fever—A vaccination certificate is required for travelers coming from infected areas and from countries with current infection. A vaccination is required for children of all ages. CDC recommends vaccination for all travelers over 9 months of age, but see the discussion in Chapter 6.63.

Routine immunizations should be current. For infants and children through 16 years of age, refer to Chapter 4.3. A rubeola (measles) booster should be considered. Persons age 16 to 65 should receive a booster of tetanus and diphtheria every ten years. Healthy adults under age 65 do not require pneumococcal vaccine, but it is appropriate for those with chronic medical conditions. Influenza vaccine may be considered for those providing essential community services, health care workers, and those wishing to reduce the likeli-

hood of becoming ill with influenza. Adults over 65 years of age are urged to obtain yearly influenza immunization, and to insure that their tetanus and diphtheria immunizations are current. Pneumococcal vaccination is also suggested for this age group.

The vaccinations listed are recommended for the traveler's protection.
Poliomyelitis—A poliomyelitis booster is indicated for this country.
Cholera—Cholera is present in this country. Risk to western travelers is low. Immunization is not required or recommended for travel to this country due to its low effectiveness. Avoid uncooked foods and untreated water. Vaccination is advised only for persons living or working under inadequate sanitary conditions and for those with impaired defense mechanisms (see Chapter 4.6).
Viral Hepatitis A—Vaccination is recommended for all travelers for their protection.
Typhoid fever—Vaccination is recommended for all travelers for their protection.

Selective vaccinations—These apply only to specific groups of travelers or persons on specific working assignments:
Viral Hepatitis B—Because of the high rate of healthy carriers of hepatitis B in this country, vaccination is recommended for persons on working assignments in the health care field (dentists, physicians, nurses, laboratory technicians), or working in close contact with the local population (teachers, missionaries, Peace Corps), or persons foreseeing sexual relations with local inhabitants.
Plague—Vaccination is recommended only for persons who may be occupationally exposed to wild rodents (anthropologists, geologists, medical personnel, missionaries, etc). The standard vaccination course must be completed before entering the plague infested area. Areas of risk are scattered throughout the country.

U.S. Foreign Service:
Calle de Los Ministros
Malabo, Telephone 2467

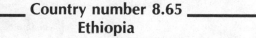

Country number 8.65
Ethiopia

INFECTIOUS DISEASE RISK

Malaria Risk
Malaria is found throughout the country, including urban areas, but excluding Addis Ababa, in all regions below 2000 meters. The malaria in this

country is resistant to chloroquine. The CDC recommends the use of mefloquine (Lariam) as described in Chapter 6.31 for chemical prophylaxis.

Falciparum malaria represents 80% of malaria, therefore there is a 20% risk of p. vivax malaria exposure. Consider the use of primaquine upon return home.

Diseases of Special Risk

In addition to the worldwide hazard of tetanus and the routine and any special immunizations recommended below, the traveler should be aware that risk of exposure to the following diseases exists in this country. This list is not all inclusive, but it is a caution concerning the more likely endemic disease risks.

This country must be considered receptive to dengue fever. Intermittent epidemics in the past make renewed activity or reintroduction of the virus possible.

Schistosomiasis may be found in this country. Avoid contact with contaminated fresh water lakes, ponds, or streams. The city of Addis Ababa is risk free. Foci of infection are scattered throughout the country. Well documented areas of infection are in the areas of Adwa and Adi Abun (along the Mai Assem and Mai Guagua streams), in the Upper and Lower Awash valley. Foci of infection are also present in Eritrea. More than 2.5 million natives are infected with this disease.

There is a risk of meningococcal meningitis in the Sahelian savannah areas from December through June.

Onchocerciasis (river blindness) affects more than 1.3 million natives. These disease is endemic in the western part of the country.

There are 10,000 cases of relapsing fever in this country annually which is the highest rate of anywhere in the world. Travelers are at low risk from this louse borne disease.

Louse-borne typhus is cosmopolitan in distribution and is present wherever groups of persons are crowded together under conditions of poor sanitation and malnutrition. Risk exists for persons living or working in remote areas of the country (anthropologists, archeologists, geologists, medical personnel, missionaries, etc.). Freedom from louse infestation is the most effective protection against typhus.

DISEASE RISK PROFILE

Disease	endemic	risk	hazard
Dracunculiasis/Guinea Worm	x		
Diarrheal Disease Risk		x	
Dysentery, Amoebic/Bacillary			x
Echinococcosis		x	
Filariasis			x
Giardiasis		x	
Helminthic Diseases (see Chapter 6.21)			x
Hepatitis, Viral		x	

Disease	endemic	risk	hazard
Leishmaniasis			
Cutaneous		x	
Visceral			x
Rabies	x		
Trachoma			x
Trypanosomiasis, African		x	
Sleeping Sickness			
Typhoid Fever		x	
Typhus, Endemic Flea-Borne	x		
Typhus, Epidemic Louse-Borne	x		
Typhus, Scrub		x	

Food/Water Safety

All tap water used for drinking, brushing teeth, and making ice cubes should be boiled prior to use. Insure that bottled water is uncapped in your presence. Milk should be boiled to insure safety. Powdered and evaporated milk are available and safe. Avoid butter and other dairy products. All meat, poultry and seafood must be well cooked and served while hot. Pork is best avoided. Vegetables should be well cooked and served hot. Salads and mayonnaise are best avoided. Fruits with intact skins should be peeled by you just prior to consumption. Avoid cold buffets, custards, and any frozen dessert. First class hotels and restaurants in Addis Ababa, Asmara, and Massawa serve purified drinking water and reliable food. However, the hazard is left to your judgement.

VACCINATIONS

Yellow fever—A vaccination certificate is required for travelers coming from infected areas and from or in transit through countries with active disease. A vaccination certificate is required for children over one year of age. CDC recommends vaccination for all travelers over 9 months of age.

Routine immunizations should be current. For infants and children through 16 years of age, refer to Chapter 4.3. A rubeola (measles) booster should be considered. Persons age 16 to 65 should receive a booster of tetanus and diphtheria every ten years. Healthy adults under age 65 do not require pneumococcal vaccine, but it is appropriate for those with chronic medical conditions. Influenza vaccine may be considered for those providing essential community services, health care workers, and those wishing to reduce the likelihood of becoming ill with influenza. Adults over 65 years of age are urged to obtain yearly influenza immunization, and to insure that their tetanus and diphtheria immunizations are current. Pneumococcal vaccination is also suggested for this age group.

The vaccinations listed are recommended for the traveler's protection.
Poliomyelitis—A poliomyelitis booster is indicated for this country.
Viral Hepatitis A—Vaccination is recommended for all travelers for their protection.

Typhoid fever—Vaccination is recommended for all travelers for their protection.

Selective vaccinations—These apply only to specific groups of travelers or persons on specific working assignments:

Viral Hepatitis B—Because of the high rate of healthy carriers of hepatitis B in this country, vaccination is recommended for persons on working assignments in the health care field (dentists, physicians, nurses, laboratory technicians), or working in close contact with the local population (teachers, missionaries, Peace Corps), or persons foreseeing sexual relations with local inhabitants.

Rabies—In this country, where rabies is a constant threat, a pre-exposure rabies vaccination is advised for persons planning an extended stay or on working assignments (naturalists, agricultural advisors, archeologists, geologists, etc.). Although this provides adequate initial protection, a person bitten by a potentially rabid animal would still require post exposure immunization (see Chapter 6.40). Children should be cautioned not to pet dogs, cats, or other mammals.

U.S. Foreign Service:
Entoto St.
Addis Ababa, Telephone 11-06-66/117/129

Canadian High Commission/Embassy Office:
African Solidarity Insurance Bldg.
Unity Square
Addis Ababa, Telephone 15 11 00, 15 12 28

TRAVEL ADVISORY

A U.S. Department of State Travel Advisory was in effect on 4 May 1990 when this book went to press. The entire text is included below. Travel advisories are subject to reissue, change, and cancellation at any time. Current travel advisory information is available by calling the U.S. Department of State Travel Advisory Hotline at (202) 647-5225. The current travel advisory status is also available from the Herchmer Database update system (see Chapter 2.8).

SUBJECT: TRAVEL ADVISORY—ETHIOPIA—WARNING SECSTATE WSH
CANCEL: NOS. 89-27, 88-30, 87-20, 84-64A
OCTOBER 20, 1989 NO. 89-66
THE DEPARTMENT OF STATE HAS HAD A TRAVEL ADVISORY IN EFFECT ON ETHIOPIA SINCE MAY 19. DUE TO AN UPSURGE IN FIGHTING BETWEEN REBELS AND GOVERNMENT FORCES IN AREAS OUTSIDE THE CAPITAL OF ADDIS ABABA, WE URGE UNITED STATES CITIZENS TO CONTINUE TO DEFER ALL NONESSENTIAL TRAVEL TO ETHIOPIA UNTIL FURTHER NOTICE. FOR THOSE WHO

MUST TRAVEL TO ETHIOPIA, NO TRAVEL OUTSIDE OF ADDIS ABABA SHOULD BE PLANNED.
WE WOULD URGE ALL TRAVELERS WHO FEEL THEY MUST TRAVEL TO ETHIOPIA TO CONSULT WITH THE EMBASSY IN ADDIS ABABA UPON ARRIVAL TO OBTAIN AN UPDATE ON LOCAL DEVELOPMENTS AND TO REPORT THEIR PRESENCE TO THE EMBASSY. THE EMBASSY IS LOCATED ON ENTOTO STREET, AND ITS TELEPHONE NUMBER IS 550-666
EXPIRATION: INDEFINITE

Country number 8.66
Falkland (Malvinas) Islands

INFECTIOUS DISEASE RISK

Malaria Risk
There is no malaria risk in this country.

Diseases of Special Risk
In addition to the worldwide hazard of tetanus and the routine and any special immunizations recommended below, the traveler should be aware that risk of exposure to the following diseases exists in this country. This list is not all inclusive, but it is a caution concerning the more likely endemic disease risks.

DISEASE RISK PROFILE

Disease	endemic	risk	hazard
Echinococcosis	x		
Hepatitis, Viral	x		
Tapeworms	x		
Typhoid Fever	x		

Food/Water Safety
Local water is considered safe without further treatment. Milk is pasteurized and safe to drink. Butter, cheese, yogurt and ice-cream are safe. Local meat, poultry, seafood, vegetables, and fruits are safe to eat.

VACCINATIONS
Routine immunizations should be current. For infants and children through 16 years of age, refer to Chapter 4.3. A rubeola (measles) booster should be considered. Persons age 16 to 65 should receive a booster of tetanus and diphtheria every ten years. Healthy adults under age 65 do not require pneumococcal vaccine, but it is appropriate for those with chronic medical conditions. Influenza vaccine may be considered for those providing essential

community services, health care workers, and those wishing to reduce the likelihood of becoming ill with influenza. Adults over 65 years of age are urged to obtain yearly influenza immunization, and to insure that their tetanus and diphtheria immunizations are current. Pneumococcal vaccination is also suggested for this age group.

No vaccinations are required to enter this country.

Country number 8.67
Faroe Islands

INFECTIOUS DISEASE RISK

Malaria Risk
There is no malaria risk in this country.

Food/Water Safety
Local water is considered safe without further treatment. Milk is pasteurized and safe to drink. Butter, cheese, yogurt and ice-cream are safe. Local meat, poultry, seafood, vegetables, and fruits are safe to eat.

VACCINATIONS
Routine immunizations should be current. For infants and children through 16 years of age, refer to Chapter 4.3. A rubeola (measles) booster should be considered. Persons age 16 to 65 should receive a booster of tetanus and diphtheria every ten years. Healthy adults under age 65 do not require pneumococcal vaccine, but it is appropriate for those with chronic medical conditions. Influenza vaccine may be considered for those providing essential community services, health care workers, and those wishing to reduce the likelihood of becoming ill with influenza. Adults over 65 years of age are urged to obtain yearly influenza immunization, and to insure that their tetanus and diphtheria immunizations are current. Pneumococcal vaccination is also suggested for this age group.

No vaccinations are required to enter this country.

Country number 8.68
Fiji

INFECTIOUS DISEASE RISK

Malaria Risk
There is no malaria risk in this country.

Diseases of Special Risk

In addition to the worldwide hazard of tetanus and the routine and any special immunizations recommended below, the traveler should be aware that risk of exposure to the following diseases exists in this country. This list is not all inclusive, but it is a caution concerning the more likely endemic disease risks.

This country must be considered receptive to dengue fever. Active cases of dengue fever and dengue hemorrhagic fever have been reported from Fiji's central and western divisions.

DISEASE RISK PROFILE

Disease	endemic	risk	hazard
Diarrheal Disease Risk	x		
Encephalitis, Japanese	x		
Filariasis			x
Helminthic Diseases (see Chp 6.21)	x		
Hepatitis, Viral	x		
Typhoid Fever	x		

Food/Water Safety

Water is probably safe, but due to local variations in bacterial counts, using bottled water for the first few weeks will help the traveler adjust and decrease the chance of traveler's diarrhea. Milk is pasteurized and safe to drink. Butter, cheese, yogurt and ice-cream are safe. Local meat, poultry, seafood, vegetables, and fruits are safe to eat.

VACCINATIONS

Yellow fever—A vaccination certificate is required for travelers coming from infected areas. A vaccination certificate is required for children over one year of age.

Routine immunizations should be current. For infants and children through 16 years of age, refer to Chapter 4.3. A rubeola (measles) booster should be considered. Persons age 16 to 65 should receive a booster of tetanus and diphtheria every ten years. Healthy adults under age 65 do not require pneumococcal vaccine, but it is appropriate for those with chronic medical conditions. Influenza vaccine may be considered for those providing essential community services, health care workers, and those wishing to reduce the likelihood of becoming ill with influenza. Adults over 65 years of age are urged to obtain yearly influenza immunization, and to insure that their tetanus and diphtheria immunizations are current. Pneumococcal vaccination is also suggested for this age group.

The vaccinations listed are recommended for the traveler's protection.
Viral Hepatitis A—Vaccination is recommended when traveling outside the

areas usually visited by tourists, traveling extensively in the interior of the country (trekkers, hikers) and for persons on working assignments in remote areas.

Typhoid fever—Vaccination is recommended when traveling outside the areas usually visited by tourists, traveling extensively in the interior of the country (trekkers, hikers) and for persons on working assignments in remote areas.

Selective vaccinations—These apply only to specific groups of travelers or persons on specific working assignments:

Viral Hepatitis B—Because of the high rate of healthy carriers of hepatitis B in this country, vaccination is recommended for persons on working assignments in the health care field (dentists, physicians, nurses, laboratory technicians), or working in close contact with the local population (teachers, missionaries, Peace Corps), or persons foreseeing sexual relations with local inhabitants.

U.S. Foreign Service:
31 Loftus St.
Suva, Telephone 314-466, 314-069

Country number 8.69
Finland

INFECTIOUS DISEASE RISK

Malaria Risk
There is no malaria risk in this country.

Diseases of Special Risk
In addition to the worldwide hazard of tetanus and the routine immunizations recommended above, the traveler should be aware that rabies is prevalent in wild animals, especially foxes.

Food/Water Safety
Local water is considered safe without further treatment. Milk is pasteurized and safe to drink. Butter, cheese, yogurt and ice-cream are safe. Local meat, poultry, seafood, vegetables, and fruits are safe to eat.

VACCINATIONS
Routine immunizations should be current. For infants and children through 16 years of age, refer to Chapter 4.3. A rubeola (measles) booster should be considered. Persons age 16 to 65 should receive a booster of tetanus and diphtheria every ten years. Healthy adults under age 65 do not require pneumococcal vaccine, but it is appropriate for those with chronic medical

conditions. Influenza vaccine may be considered for those providing essential community services, health care workers, and those wishing to reduce the likelihood of becoming ill with influenza. Adults over 65 years of age are urged to obtain yearly influenza immunization, and to insure that their tetanus and diphtheria immunizations are current. Pneumococcal vaccination is also suggested for this age group.

No vaccinations are required to enter this country.

Selective vaccinations—These apply only to specific groups of travelers or persons on specific working assignments:

Tick-borne encephalitis—(Central European encephalitis) Vaccination is recommended for persons involved in recreational activities in forested areas (camping, hiking) or working in forestry occupations. Risk season: March to November. Risk is present in forested areas along the coast of the Gulf of Finland from Kotka to the border with the USSR, and all the islands south of Turku including the Aland islands.

U.S. Foreign Service:
Itainen Puistotie 14A
Helsinki, Telephone 17-19-31

Canadian High Commission/Embassy Office:
Esplanadi 25B
Helsinki, Telephone 17-11-41

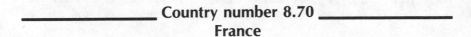

Country number 8.70
France

INFECTIOUS DISEASE RISK

Malaria Risk
There is no malaria risk in this country.

Diseases of Special Risk
In addition to the worldwide hazard of tetanus and the routine and any special immunizations recommended below, the traveler should be aware that risk of exposure to the following diseases exists in this country, primarily in the Mediterranean costal areas. This list is not all inclusive, but it is a caution concerning the more likely endemic disease risks.

DISEASE RISK PROFILE

Disease	endemic	risk	hazard
Leishmaniasis			
Cutaneous	x		
Visceral	x		
Sandfly Fever	x		
Typhus, Endemic Flea-Borne	x		
Typhus, Scrub	x		
West Nile Fever	x		

Food/Water Safety

Water is probably safe, but due to local variations in bacterial counts, using bottled water for the first few weeks will help the traveler adjust and decrease the chance of traveler's diarrhea. Milk is pasteurized and safe to drink. Butter, cheese, yogurt and ice-cream are safe. Local meat, poultry, seafood, vegetables, and fruits are safe to eat.

VACCINATIONS

Routine immunizations should be current. For infants and children through 16 years of age, refer to Chapter 4.3. A rubeola (measles) booster should be considered. Persons age 16 to 65 should receive a booster of tetanus and diphtheria every ten years. Healthy adults under age 65 do not require pneumococcal vaccine, but it is appropriate for those with chronic medical conditions. Influenza vaccine may be considered for those providing essential community services, health care workers, and those wishing to reduce the likelihood of becoming ill with influenza. Adults over 65 years of age are urged to obtain yearly influenza immunization, and to insure that their tetanus and diphtheria immunizations are current. Pneumococcal vaccination is also suggested for this age group.

No vaccinations are required to enter this country.

U.S. Foreign Service:

2 Avenue Gabriel
Paris, Telephone 4296-1202, 4261-8075

22 Cours du Marechal-Foch
Bordeaux, Telephone 5652-65-95

7 Quai General-Sarrail
Lyon, Telephone 824-68-49

No. 9 Rue Armeny, 13006
Marseille, Telephone 9154-92-00

1 Rue Du Marechal-Joffre
Nice, 9388-89-55,88-87-72

15 Avenue d'Alsace
Strasbourg, Telephone 8835-31-04/05/06

Canadian High Commission/Embassy Office:
35 Avenue Montaigne
Paris, Telephone 4723-01-01

24 Avenue du Prado
Marseille, Telephone 9137-19-37

10 Place du Temple-Neuf
Strasbourg, Telephone 8832-65-96

_____ **Country number 8.71** _____
French Guiana

INFECTIOUS DISEASE RISK

Malaria Risk

Malaria is present in all parts of this country, including urban areas. The risk exists all year. The malaria in this country is resistant to chloroquine. The CDC recommends the use of mefloquine (Lariam) as described in Chapter 6.31 for chemical prophylaxis.

Falciparum malaria represents 70% of malaria, therefore there is a 30% risk of p. vivax malaria exposure. Consider the use of primaquine upon return home.

Diseases of Special Risk

In addition to the worldwide hazard of tetanus and the routine and any special immunizations recommended below, the traveler should be aware that risk of exposure to the following diseases exists in this country. This list is not all inclusive, but it is a caution concerning the more likely endemic disease risks.

DISEASE RISK PROFILE

Disease	endemic	risk	hazard
Brucellosis		x	
Chikungunya Fever Dengue Fever	x		
Diarrheal Disease Risk	x		
Dysentery, Amoebic	x		

Disease	endemic	risk	hazard
Echinococcosis	x		
Encephalitis	x		
Filariasis			x
Helminthic Diseases (see Chapter 6.21)	x		
Hepatitis, Viral	x		
Leishmaniasis			
Cutaneous	x		
Mucocutaneous	x		
Rabies	x		
Trypanosomiasis, American	x		

Food/Water Safety

Water is probably safe, but due to local variations in bacterial counts, using bottled water for the first few weeks will help the traveler adjust and decrease the chance of traveler's diarrhea. Milk should be boiled to insure safety. Powdered and evaporated milk are available and safe. Avoid butter and other dairy products. Local meat, poultry, seafood, vegetables, and fruits are safe to eat.

VACCINATIONS

Yellow fever—A vaccination certificate is required on arrival from all countries. A vaccination certificate is required for children over one year of age. CDC recommends vaccination for all travelers over 9 months of age.

Routine immunizations should be current. For infants and children through 16 years of age, refer to Chapter 4.3. A rubeola (measles) booster should be considered. Persons age 16 to 65 should receive a booster of tetanus and diphtheria every ten years. Healthy adults under age 65 do not require pneumococcal vaccine, but it is appropriate for those with chronic medical conditions. Influenza vaccine may be considered for those providing essential community services, health care workers, and those wishing to reduce the likelihood of becoming ill with influenza. Adults over 65 years of age are urged to obtain yearly influenza immunization, and to insure that their tetanus and diphtheria immunizations are current. Pneumococcal vaccination is also suggested for this age group.

The vaccinations listed are recommended for the traveler's protection.
Poliomyelitis—A poliomyelitis booster is indicated for this country.
Viral Hepatitis A—Vaccination is recommended for all travelers for their protection.
Typhoid fever—Vaccination is recommended for all travelers for their protection.

_____ **Country number 8.72** _____
French Polynesia
Formerly "Tahiti"

INFECTIOUS DISEASE RISK

Malaria Risk
   There is no malaria risk in this country.

Diseases of Special Risk
   In addition to the worldwide hazard of tetanus and the routine and any special immunizations recommended below, the traveler should be aware that risk of exposure to the following diseases exists in this country. This list is not all inclusive, but it is a caution concerning the more likely endemic disease risks.
   Potential risk of dengue fever exists. The virus is present in this country at all times and may give rise to major outbreaks. An active epidemic of dengue and dengue hemorrhagic fever is present in this country at this time.

DISEASE RISK PROFILE

Disease	endemic	risk	hazard
Diarrheal Disease Risk		x	
Encephalitis, Japanese	x		
Filariasis			x
Helminthic Diseases (see Chapter 6.21)		x	
Typhoid Fever		x	

Food/Water Safety
   Water is probably safe, but due to local variations in bacterial counts, using bottled water for the first few weeks will help the traveler adjust and decrease the chance of traveler's diarrhea. Milk is pasteurized and safe to drink. Butter, cheese, yogurt and ice-cream are safe. Local meat, poultry, seafood, vegetables, and fruits are safe to eat.

VACCINATIONS
   Yellow fever—A vaccination certificate is required for travelers coming from infected areas. A vaccination certificate is required for children over one year of age.
   Routine immunizations should be current. For infants and children through 16 years of age, refer to Chapter 4.3. A rubeola (measles) booster should be considered. Persons age 16 to 65 should receive a booster of tetanus and diphtheria every ten years. Healthy adults under age 65 do not require pneumococcal vaccine, but it is appropriate for those with chronic medical conditions. Influenza vaccine may be considered for those providing essential

community services, health care workers, and those wishing to reduce the likelihood of becoming ill with influenza. Adults over 65 years of age are urged to obtain yearly influenza immunization, and to insure that their tetanus and diphtheria immunizations are current. Pneumococcal vaccination is also suggested for this age group.

The vaccinations listed are recommended for the traveler's protection.
Viral Hepatitis A—Vaccination is recommended for all travelers for their protection.
Typhoid fever—Vaccination is recommended for all travelers for their protection.

Selective vaccinations—These apply only to specific groups of travelers or persons on specific working assignments:
Viral Hepatitis B—Because of the high rate of healthy carriers of hepatitis B in this country, vaccination is recommended for persons on working assignments in the health care field (dentists, physicians, nurses, laboratory technicians), or working in close contact with the local population (teachers, missionaries, Peace Corps), or persons foreseeing sexual relations with local inhabitants.

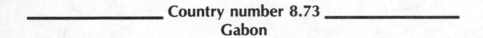

Country number 8.73
Gabon

INFECTIOUS DISEASE RISK

Malaria Risk
Malaria exists all year, in all parts of the country below 1000 meters, including urban areas. The malaria in this country is resistant to chloroquine. The CDC recommends the use of mefloquine (Lariam) as described in Chapter 6.31 for chemical prophylaxis.
Falciparum malaria represents 95% of malaria, therefore there is a 5% risk of p. vivax malaria exposure. Consider the use of primaquine upon return home.

Diseases of Special Risk
In addition to the worldwide hazard of tetanus and the routine and any special immunizations recommended below, the traveler should be aware that risk of exposure to the following diseases exists in this country. This list is not all inclusive, but it is a caution concerning the more likely endemic disease risks.
This country must be considered receptive to dengue fever. Intermittent epidemics in the past make renewed activity or reintroduction of the virus possible.

Schistosomiasis is present in this country. Avoid contact with fresh water lakes, pounds, or rivers, unless a competent local authority can assure you of the water's safety.

DISEASE RISK PROFILE

Disease	endemic	risk	hazard
Dracunculiasis/Guinea Worm		x	
Diarrheal Disease Risk			x
Dysentery, Amoebic/Bacillary			x
Echinococcosis		x	
Filariasis			x
Giardiasis		x	
Helminthic Diseases (see Chapter 6.21)			x
Hepatitis, Viral		x	
Leishmaniasis			
Cutaneous		x	
Visceral		x	
Loiasis			x
Onchocerciasis			x
Rabies	x		
Relapsing Fever	x		
Trachoma	x		
Trypanosomiasis, African Sleeping Sickness	x		
Typhoid Fever			x
Typhus, Endemic Flea-Borne	x		
Typhus, Epidemic Louse-Borne	x		
Typhus, Scrub	x		

Food/Water Safety

All tap water used for drinking, brushing teeth, and making ice cubes should be boiled prior to use. Insure that bottled water is uncapped in your presence. Milk should be boiled to insure safety. Powdered and evaporated milk are available and safe. Avoid butter and other dairy products. All meat, poultry and seafood must be well cooked and served while hot. Pork is best avoided. Vegetables should be well cooked and served hot. Salads and mayonnaise are best avoided. Fruits with intact skins should be peeled by you just prior to consumption. Avoid cold buffets, custards, and any frozen dessert.

VACCINATIONS

Yellow fever—A vaccination certificate is required for travelers coming from all countries. A vaccination certificate is required for children over one year of age. CDC recommends vaccination for all travelers over 9 months of age who go outside of urban areas.

Routine immunizations should be current. For infants and children through 16 years of age, refer to Chapter 4.3. A rubeola (measles) booster should be considered. Persons age 16 to 65 should receive a booster of tetanus

and diphtheria every ten years. Healthy adults under age 65 do not require pneumococcal vaccine, but it is appropriate for those with chronic medical conditions. Influenza vaccine may be considered for those providing essential community services, health care workers, and those wishing to reduce the likelihood of becoming ill with influenza. Adults over 65 years of age are urged to obtain yearly influenza immunization, and to insure that their tetanus and diphtheria immunizations are current. Pneumococcal vaccination is also suggested for this age group.

The vaccinations listed are recommended for the traveler's protection.
Poliomyelitis—A poliomyelitis booster is indicated for this country. Polio is prevalent in this country.
Viral Hepatitis A—Vaccination is recommended for all travelers for their protection.
Typhoid fever—Vaccination is recommended for all travelers for their protection.

Selective vaccinations—These apply only to specific groups of travelers or persons on specific working assignments:
Viral Hepatitis B—Because of the high rate of healthy carriers of hepatitis B in this country, vaccination is recommended for persons on working assignments in the health care field (dentists, physicians, nurses, laboratory technicians), or working in close contact with the local population (teachers, missionaries, Peace Corps), or persons foreseeing sexual relations with local inhabitants.

U.S. Foreign Service:
Blvd. de la Mer
P.O. Box 4000
Libreville, Telephone 76-20-03/4, 76-13-37,72-13-48

Canadian High Commission/Embassy Office:
P.O. Box 4037
Libreville, Telephone 72-41-54/56/69

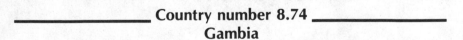

Country number 8.74
Gambia

INFECTIOUS DISEASE RISK

Malaria Risk
Malaria is present in this entire country all year around. The malaria in this country is resistant to chloroquine. The CDC recommends the use of meflo-

quine (Lariam) as described in Chapter 6.31 for chemical prophylaxis.

Falciparum malaria represents 85% of malaria, therefore there is a 15% risk of p. vivax malaria exposure. Consider the use of primaquine upon return home.

Diseases of Special Risk

In addition to the worldwide hazard of tetanus and the routine and any special immunizations recommended below, the traveler should be aware that risk of exposure to the following diseases exists in this country. This list is not all inclusive, but it is a caution concerning the more likely endemic disease risks.

This country must be considered receptive to dengue fever. Intermittent epidemics in the past make renewed activity or reintroduction of the virus possible.

Schistosomiasis may be found in this country. Avoid contact with contaminated fresh water lakes, ponds, or streams.

DISEASE RISK PROFILE

Disease	endemic	risk	hazard
Dracunculiasis/Guinea Worm	x		
Diarrheal Disease Risk			x
Dysentery, Amoebic/Bacillary		x	
Echinococcosis		x	
Filariasis			x
Giardiasis		x	
Helminthic Diseases (see Chapter 6.21)		x	
Hepatitis, Viral		x	
Leishmaniasis			
Cutaneous	x		
Visceral	x		
Rabies	x		
Relapsing Fever	x		
Rift Valley Fever	x		
Trachoma			x
Trypanosomiasis, African Sleeping Sickness	x		
Tungiasis			x
Typhoid Fever		x	
Typhus, Endemic Flea-Borne	x		
Typhus, Epidemic Louse-Borne	x		
Typhus, Scrub	x		

Food/Water Safety

All tap water used for drinking, brushing teeth, and making ice cubes should be boiled prior to use. Insure that bottled water is uncapped in your presence. Milk should be boiled to insure safety. Powdered and evaporated milk are available and safe. Avoid butter and other dairy products. All meat, poultry and seafood must be well cooked and served while hot. Pork is best avoided.

Vegetables should be well cooked and served hot. Salads and mayonnaise are best avoided. Fruits with intact skins should be peeled by you just prior to consumption. Avoid cold buffets, custards, and any frozen dessert.

VACCINATIONS

Yellow fever—A vaccination certificate is required on arrival from all countries. A vaccination certificate is required for children over one year of age. CDC recommends vaccination for all travelers over 9 months of age. This disease is active presently in the Upper River Division.

Routine immunizations should be current. For infants and children through 16 years of age, refer to Chapter 4.3. A rubeola (measles) booster should be considered. Persons age 16 to 65 should receive a booster of tetanus and diphtheria every ten years. Healthy adults under age 65 do not require pneumococcal vaccine, but it is appropriate for those with chronic medical conditions. Influenza vaccine may be considered for those providing essential community services, health care workers, and those wishing to reduce the likelihood of becoming ill with influenza. Adults over 65 years of age are urged to obtain yearly influenza immunization, and to insure that their tetanus and diphtheria immunizations are current. Pneumococcal vaccination is also suggested for this age group.

The vaccinations listed are recommended for the traveler's protection.
Poliomyelitis—A poliomyelitis booster is indicated for this country.
Viral Hepatitis A—Vaccination is recommended for all travelers for their protection.
Typhoid fever—Vaccination is recommended for all travelers for their protection.

Selective vaccinations—These apply only to specific groups of travelers or persons on specific working assignments:
Viral Hepatitis B—Because of the high rate of healthy carriers of hepatitis B in this country, vaccination is recommended for persons on working assignments in the health care field (dentists, physicians, nurses, laboratory technicians), or working in close contact with the local population (teachers, missionaries, Peace Corps), or persons foreseeing sexual relations with local inhabitants.
Meningococcal meningitis—Vaccination is advised for persons traveling extensively or on working assignements in the meningitis belt of Africa's northern savannah, which stretches from the Red Sea to the Atlantic Ocean. Peak season is March and April. Meningococcal infection is present in this country.

U.S. Foreign Service:
  Fajara (East), Pipeline Rd., Serrekanda
  Telephone 93-2856 and 93-2858

_____ **Country number 8.75** _____
German Democratic Republic
"East Germany"

INFECTIOUS DISEASE RISK

Malaria Risk
There is no malaria risk in this country.

Diseases of Special Risk
In addition to the worldwide hazard of tetanus and the routine and any special immunizations recommended below, the traveler should be aware that risk of exposure to the following disease exists in this country. Rabies is prevalent in wild animals, especially foxes.

Food/Water Safety
Local water is considered safe without further treatment. Milk is pasteurized and safe to drink. Butter, cheese, yogurt and ice-cream are safe. Local meat, poultry, seafood, vegetables, and fruits are safe to eat.

VACCINATIONS
Routine immunizations should be current. For infants and children through 16 years of age, refer to Chapter 4.3. A rubeola (measles) booster should be considered. Persons age 16 to 65 should receive a booster of tetanus and diphtheria every ten years. Healthy adults under age 65 do not require pneumococcal vaccine, but it is appropriate for those with chronic medical conditions. Influenza vaccine may be considered for those providing essential community services, health care workers, and those wishing to reduce the likelihood of becoming ill with influenza. Adults over 65 years of age are urged to obtain yearly influenza immunization, and to insure that their tetanus and diphtheria immunizations are current. Pneumococcal vaccination is also suggested for this age group.
No vaccinations are required to enter this country.

Selective vaccinations—These apply only to specific groups of travelers or persons on specific working assignments:
Tick-borne encephalitis—(Central European encephalitis) Vaccination is recommended for persons involved in recreational activities in forested areas (camping, hiking) or working in forestry occupations. Risk season: March to November. Risk is present in the forested areas south of Rostock and Schwerin, and west of Frankfort on the Oder, west of Erfurt including the areas of Gothia and Eisenach, the areas arounf Dresden and Zwickau.

U.S. Foreign Service:
108 Berlin
Neustadtische Kirchstrasse 4-5
Berlin, Telephone 2202741

Country number 8.76
Germany, Federal Republic of
"West Germany"

INFECTIOUS DISEASE RISK

Malaria Risk
There is no malaria risk in this country.

Diseases of Special Risk
In addition to the worldwide hazard of tetanus and the routine and any special immunizations recommended below, the traveler should be aware that risk of exposure to the following disease exists in this country. This list is not all inclusive, but it is a caution concerning the most likely endemic disease risk. Rabies is prevalent in wild animals, especially foxes.

Food/Water Safety
Local water is considered safe without further treatment. Milk is pasteurized and safe to drink. Butter, cheese, yogurt and ice-cream are safe. Local meat, poultry, seafood, vegetables, and fruits are safe to eat.

VACCINATIONS
Routine immunizations should be current. For infants and children through 16 years of age, refer to Chapter 4.3. A rubeola (measles) booster should be considered. Persons age 16 to 65 should receive a booster of tetanus and diphtheria every ten years. Healthy adults under age 65 do not require pneumococcal vaccine, but it is appropriate for those with chronic medical conditions. Influenza vaccine may be considered for those providing essential community services, health care workers, and those wishing to reduce the likelihood of becoming ill with influenza. Adults over 65 years of age are urged to obtain yearly influenza immunization, and to insure that their tetanus and diphtheria immunizations are current. Pneumococcal vaccination is also suggested for this age group.
No vaccinations are required to enter this country.

Selective vaccinations—These apply only to specific groups of travelers or persons on specific working assignments:
Tick-borne encephalitis—(Central European encephalitis) Vaccination is

recommended for persons involved in recreational activities in forested areas (camping, hiking) or working in forestry occupations. Risk season: March to November. Risk is present in the forested areas around Karlsruhe and Pforzheim, Stuttgart and Tubingen, and in areas around Regensburg, extending south to Landshut and to Passau on the border with Austria.

U.S. Foreign Service:
Delchmannsaue
Bonn, Telephone (0228) 339-3390

Clayalle 170
Berlin, Telephone (030) 832-40-87

Cecillenallee 5
Dusseldorf, Telephone (0211) 49-00-81

Siesmayerstrasse 21
Frankfurt, Telephone (0611) 74-00-71

Alsterufer 27/28
Hamburg, Telephone (040) 44-10-61

Koeniginstrasse 5
Munich, Telephone (089) 2-30-11

Urbanstrasse 7
Stuttgart, Telephone (0711) 21-02-21

Canadian High Commission/Embassy Office:
Friedrich Wilhelm Strasse 18
Bonn, Telephone (0228) 23-10-61

Europa-Center
Berlin, Telephone (030) 261-1161

Immermannstrasse 3
Dusseldorf, Telephone (0211) 35-34-71

Esplanade 41-47
Hamburg, Telephone (040) 35-10-85

Maximilianplatze 9
Munich, Telephone (089) 55-85-31

_____ Country number 8.77 _____
Ghana

INFECTIOUS DISEASE RISK

Malaria Risk

Malaria exists in all parts of this country, all year long. The malaria in this country is resistant to chloroquine. The CDC recommends the use of mefloquine (Lariam) as described in Chapter 6.31 for chemical prophylaxis.

Diseases of Special Risk

In addition to the worldwide hazard of tetanus and the routine and any special immunizations recommended below, the traveler should be aware that risk of exposure to the following diseases exists in this country. This list is not all inclusive, but it is a caution concerning the more likely endemic disease risks.

This country must be considered receptive to dengue fever. Intermittent epidemics in the past make renewed activity or reintroduction of the virus possible.

Schistosomiasis may be found in this country. Avoid contact with contaminated fresh water lakes, ponds, or streams.

Amoebic and bacillary dysentery, diarrheal diseases, helminthic diseases, and viral hepatitis associated with water and food supplies are particularly common in this country.

DISEASE RISK PROFILE

Disease	endemic	risk	hazard
Dracunculiasis/Guinea Worm	x		
Echinococcosis		x	
Filariasis			x
Leishmaniasis			
Cutaneous	x		
Visceral	x		
Loiasis			x
Onchocerciasis			x
Rabies	x		
Relapsing Fever	x		
Trachoma			x
Trypanosomiasis, African Sleeping Sickness	x		
Typhoid Fever		x	
Typhus, Endemic Flea-Borne	x		
Typhus, Epidemic Louse-Borne	x		
Typhus, Scrub	x		

Food/Water Safety

All tap water used for drinking, brushing teeth, and making ice cubes should be boiled prior to use. Insure that bottled water is uncapped in your presence. Milk should be boiled to insure safety. Powdered and evaporated milk are available and safe. Avoid butter and other dairy products. All meat, poultry and seafood must be well cooked and served while hot. Pork is best avoided. Vegetables should be well cooked and served hot. Salads and mayonnaise are best avoided. Fruits with intact skins should be peeled by you just prior to consumption. Avoid cold buffets, custards, and any frozen dessert.

VACCINATIONS

Yellow fever—A vaccination certificate is required for travelers coming from infected areas and from or in transit through countries in the endemic yellow fever zone, see Chapter 6.63. A vaccination certificate is required for children over one year of age. Vaccination certificate is required for travelers who have been in or passed through an infected yellow fever area within six days prior to arrival. Vaccination is recommended for all travelers for their protection. The Centers for Disease Control recommends immunization for all travelers 9 months and over.

Cholera—Cholera is present in this country. Risk to western travelers is low. Local officials may demand a cholera vaccination, therefore it is advisable to obtain one prior to arrival in this country.

Routine immunizations should be current. For infants and children through 16 years of age, refer to Chapter 4.3. A rubeola (measles) booster should be considered. Persons age 16 to 65 should receive a booster of tetanus and diphtheria every ten years. Healthy adults under age 65 do not require pneumococcal vaccine, but it is appropriate for those with chronic medical conditions. Influenza vaccine may be considered for those providing essential community services, health care workers, and those wishing to reduce the likelihood of becoming ill with influenza. Adults over 65 years of age are urged to obtain yearly influenza immunization, and to insure that their tetanus and diphtheria immunizations are current. Pneumococcal vaccination is also suggested for this age group.

The vaccinations listed are recommended for the traveler's protection.
Poliomyelitis—A poliomyelitis booster is indicated for this country.
Viral Hepatitis A—Vaccination is recommended for all travelers for their protection.
Typhoid fever—Vaccination is recommended for all travelers for their protection.

Selective vaccinations—*These apply only to specific groups of travelers or persons on specific working assignments:*
Viral Hepatitis B—Because of the high rate of healthy carriers of hepatitis

B in this country, vaccination is recommended for persons on working assignments in the health care field (dentists, physicians, nurses, laboratory technicians), or working in close contact with the local population (teachers, missionaries, Peace Corps), or persons foreseeing sexual relations with local inhabitants.

Meningococcal meningitis—Vaccination is advised for persons traveling extensively or on working assignements in the meningitis belt of Africa's northern savannah, which stretches from the Red Sea to the Atlantic Ocean. Peak season is March and April. Local area of greatest danger is in the region bordering Burkina Faso.

Rabies—In this country, where rabies is a constant threat, a pre-exposure rabies vaccination is advised for persons planning an extended stay or on working assignments (naturalists, agricultural advisors, archeologists, geologists, etc.). Although this provides adequate initial protection, a person bitten by a potentially rabid animal would still require post exposure immunization (see Chapter 6.40). Children should be cautioned not to pet dogs, cats, or other mammals.

U.S. Foreign Service:
 Ring Road, East
 Accra, Telephone 75346

Canadian High Commission/Embassy Office:
 42 Independance Ave.
 Accra, Telephone 28555/02

TRAVEL ADVISORY

A U.S. Department of State Travel Advisory was in effect on 4 May 1990 when this book went to press. The entire text is included below. Travel advisories are subject to reissue, change, and cancellation at any time. Current travel advisory information is available by calling the U.S. Department of State Travel Advisory Hotline at (202) 647-5225. The current travel advisory status is also available from the Herchmer Database update system (see Chapter 2.8).

SECSTATE WSH JANUARY 5, 1990
GHANA—CAUTION
AMERICAN CITIZENS TRAVELING TO GHANA SHOULD BE AWARE THAT GHANIAN LAWS AND PRACTICES DIFFER CONSIDERABLY FROM THOSE IN THE UNITED STATES.
AMERICAN CITIZENS WHO HAVE BEEN ARRESTED HAVE ENCOUNTERED PROBLEMS INCLUDING A LACK OF PROMPT NOTIFICATION TO THE AMERICAN EMBASSY, DENIAL OF ACCESS BY A CONSULAR OFFICER FOR EXTENDED PERIODS, HARSH AND UNHEALTHFUL JAIL CONDITIONS, AND LENGTHY LEGAL PROCESS

DURING WHICH THE DETAINEE MAY NOT BE PERMITTED TO POST BOND. AMERICANS ARE ADVISED THAT, IF DETAINED, THEY SHOULD MAKE EVERY EFFORT TO CONTACT THE U.S. EMBASSY BY ANY MEANS AVAILABLE.

SOME AMERICAN MISSIONARIES AND OTHER MEMBERS OF RELIGIOUS GROUPS VISITING OF LIVING IN GHANA HAVE BEEN DETAINED BY GHANIAN AUTHORITIES OR ORDERED TO LEAVE THE COUNTRY.

FOREIGN CURRENCY TRANSACTIONS SHOULD BE CONDUCTED ONLY THROUGH REGISTERED BANKS AND FOREIGN EXCHANGE BUREAUS. CURRENCY TRANSACTIONS WITH PRIVATE CITIZENS ARE ILLEGAL. ALL GOLD, DIAMOND AND OTHER NATURAL RESOURCE TRANSACTIONS ARE HANDLED THROUGH DESIGNATED OFFICIAL AGENCIES. TRANSACTIONS IN THESE COMMODITIES WITH PRIVATE CITIZENS ARE ILLEGAL.

THE WEARING OF ANY MILITARY APPAREL SUCH AS CAMOUFLAGE JACKETS OF PANTS OR ANY CLOTHING OR ITEMS WHICH MAY APPEAR MILITARY IN NATURE IS STRICTLY PROHIBITED.

AMERICAN CITIZENS SHOULD EXERCISE DISCRETION IN SELECTING PHOTO SUBJECTS. PHOTOGRAPHING OF CERTAIN AREAS AND FACILITIES IS PROHIBITED, AND MANY GHANIANS MAY TAKE OFFENSE AT BEING PHOTOGRAPHED WITHOUT THEIR CONSENT.

AMERICANS TRAVELING TO GHANA SHOULD REGISTER WITH THE AMERICAN EMBASSY IMMEDIATELY UPON ARRIVAL. THE U.S. EMBASSY IS LOCATED ON RING ROAD EAST, P.O. BOS 194, ACCRA; THE TELEPHONE NUMBER IS 77-53-47.

EXPIRATION : DECEMBER 31, 1990.

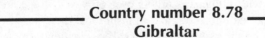

Country number 8.78
Gibraltar

INFECTIOUS DISEASE RISK

Malaria Risk

There is no malaria risk in this country.

Diseases of Special Risk

In addition to the worldwide hazard of tetanus and the routine and any special immunizations recommended below, the traveler should be aware that risk of exposure to the following diseases exists in this country. This list is not all inclusive, but it is a caution concerning the more likely endemic disease risks.

DISEASE RISK PROFILE

Disease	endemic	risk	hazard
Brucellosis	x		
Diarrheal Disease Risk	x		
Dysentery, Amoebic/Bacillary	x		
Leishmaniasis			
Cutaneous	x		
Visceral	x		
Sandfly Fever	x		
Typhoid Fever	x		
Typhus, Endemic Flea-Borne	x		
Typhus, Scrub	x		
West Nile Fever	x		

Food/Water Safety

Water is probably safe, but due to local variations in bacterial counts, using bottled water for the first few weeks will help the traveler adjust and decrease the chance of traveler's diarrhea. Milk is pasteurized and safe to drink. Butter, cheese, yogurt and ice-cream are safe. Local meat, poultry, seafood, vegetables, and fruits are safe to eat.

VACCINATIONS

Routine immunizations should be current. For infants and children through 16 years of age, refer to Chapter 4.3. A rubeola (measles) booster should be considered. Persons age 16 to 65 should receive a booster of tetanus and diphtheria every ten years. Healthy adults under age 65 do not require pneumococcal vaccine, but it is appropriate for those with chronic medical conditions. Influenza vaccine may be considered for those providing essential community services, health care workers, and those wishing to reduce the likelihood of becoming ill with influenza. Adults over 65 years of age are urged to obtain yearly influenza immunization, and to insure that their tetanus and diphtheria immunizations are current. Pneumococcal vaccination is also suggested for this age group.

No vaccinations are required to enter this country.

—————————— Country number 8.79 ——————————
Greece

INFECTIOUS DISEASE RISK

Malaria Risk

There is no malaria risk in this country.

Diseases of Special Risk

In addition to the worldwide hazard of tetanus and the routine and any special immunizations recommended below, the traveler should be aware that risk of exposure to the following diseases exists in this country. This list is not all inclusive, but it is a caution concerning the more likely endemic disease risks.

DISEASE RISK PROFILE

Disease	endemic	risk	hazard
Brucellosis	x		
Diarrheal Disease Risk	x		
Dysentery, Bacillary	x		
Echinococcosis	x		
Encephalitis, Tick-Borne	x		
Leishmaniasis			
Cutaneous	x		
Visceral	x		
Rabies	x		
Sandfly Fever	x		
Typhoid Fever	x		
Typhus, Endemic Flea-Borne	x		
Typhus, Scrub	x		
West Nile Fever	x		

Special Note: Most medications with codeine have been banned in Greece. Obtain a physician's letter explaining the need for medications containing codeine (caution—many cough preparations contain codeine). Fines of $850 to $85,000 or prison terms of up to ten years can be levied on anyone attempting to bring codeine into the country without a doctor's justification.

Food/Water Safety

Water is probably safe, but due to local variations in bacterial counts, using bottled water for the first few weeks will help the traveler adjust and decrease the chance of traveler's diarrhea. Milk is pasteurized and safe to drink. Butter, cheese, yogurt and ice-cream are safe. Local meat, poultry, seafood, vegetables, and fruits are safe to eat.

VACCINATIONS

Yellow fever—A vaccination certificate is required for travelers coming from infected areas and from or in transit through countries with active infection. A vaccination certificate is required for children over 6 months of age. See Chapter 6.63 for a discussion on avoiding immunization in children under 9 months of age with this vaccine.

Routine immunizations should be current. For infants and children through 16 years of age, refer to Chapter 4.3. A rubeola (measles) booster should be considered. Persons age 16 to 65 should receive a booster of tetanus and diphtheria every ten years. Healthy adults under age 65 do not require pneumococcal vaccine, but it is appropriate for those with chronic medical

conditions. Influenza vaccine may be considered for those providing essential community services, health care workers, and those wishing to reduce the likelihood of becoming ill with influenza. Adults over 65 years of age are urged to obtain yearly influenza immunization, and to insure that their tetanus and diphtheria immunizations are current. Pneumococcal vaccination is also suggested for this age group.

Selective vaccinations—These apply only to specific groups of travelers or persons on specific working assignments:

Viral Hepatitis B—Because of the high rate of healthy carriers of hepatitis B in this country, vaccination is recommended for persons on working assignments in the health care field (dentists, physicians, nurses, laboratory technicians), or working in close contact with the local population (teachers, missionaries, Peace Corps), or persons foreseeing sexual relations with local inhabitants.

U.S. Foreign Service:
91 Vasilissis Sophias Blvd.
Athens, Telephone 721-2951 or 721-8401

Canadian High Commission/Embassy Office:
4 Ioannou Gennadiou St.
Athens, Telephone 723-9511/12/13

Country number 8.80
Greenland

INFECTIOUS DISEASE RISK

Malaria Risk
There is no malaria risk in this country.

Diseases of Special Risk
In addition to the worldwide hazard of tetanus and the routine and any special immunizations recommended below, the traveler should be aware that risk of exposure to the following diseases exists in this country. This list is not all inclusive, but it is a caution concerning the more likely endemic disease risks.
Rabies ocurs in this country in wildlife, especially bats.
Tularemia is also endemic in Greenland.

Food/Water Safety
Local water is considered safe without further treatment. Milk is pasteur-

ized and safe to drink. Butter, cheese, yogurt and ice-cream are safe. Local meat, poultry, seafood, vegetables, and fruits are safe to eat.

VACCINATIONS

Routine immunizations should be current. For infants and children through 16 years of age, refer to Chapter 4.3. A rubeola (measles) booster should be considered. Persons age 16 to 65 should receive a booster of tetanus and diphtheria every ten years. Healthy adults under age 65 do not require pneumococcal vaccine, but it is appropriate for those with chronic medical conditions. Influenza vaccine may be considered for those providing essential community services, health care workers, and those wishing to reduce the likelihood of becoming ill with influenza. Adults over 65 years of age are urged to obtain yearly influenza immunization, and to insure that their tetanus and diphtheria immunizations are current. Pneumococcal vaccination is also suggested for this age group.

No vaccinations are required to enter this country.

Selective vaccinations—These apply only to specific groups of travelers or persons on specific working assignments:

Viral Hepatitis B—Because of the high rate of healthy carriers of hepatitis B among the local Inuit (Eskimo) population, vaccination is recommended for persons working in health care, education, or in close contact with them.

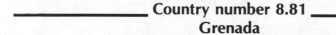

Country number 8.81
Grenada

INFECTIOUS DISEASE RISK

Malaria Risk

There is no malaria risk in this country.

Diseases of Special Risk

In addition to the worldwide hazard of tetanus and the routine and any special immunizations recommended below, the traveler should be aware that risk of exposure to the following diseases exists in this country. This list is not all inclusive, but it is a caution concerning the more likely endemic disease risks.

Potential risk of dengue fever exists. The virus is present in this country at all times and may give rise to major outbreaks.

Amoebic and bacillary dysentery, diarrheal diseases, and viral hepatitis associated with water and food supplies are particularly common in this country.

Rabies is prevalent in this country, especially in the mongoose.

Food/Water Safety
Water is probably safe, but due to local variations in bacterial counts, using bottled water for the first few weeks will help the traveler adjust and decrease the chance of traveler's diarrhea. Milk is pasteurized and safe to drink. Butter, cheese, yogurt and ice-cream are safe. Local meat, poultry, seafood, vegetables, and fruits are safe to eat.

VACCINATIONS

Yellow fever—A vaccination certificate is required for travelers coming from infected areas and from or in transit through countries with active disease. A vaccination is required for children of all ages. Children under nine months of age should not be vaccinated due to health considerations. Please refer to the discussion in Chapter 6.63 on avoiding yellow fever vaccination in this age group.

Routine immunizations should be current. For infants and children through 16 years of age, refer to Chapter 4.3. A rubeola (measles) booster should be considered. Persons age 16 to 65 should receive a booster of tetanus and diphtheria every ten years. Healthy adults under age 65 do not require pneumococcal vaccine, but it is appropriate for those with chronic medical conditions. Influenza vaccine may be considered for those providing essential community services, health care workers, and those wishing to reduce the likelihood of becoming ill with influenza. Adults over 65 years of age are urged to obtain yearly influenza immunization, and to insure that their tetanus and diphtheria immunizations are current. Pneumococcal vaccination is also suggested for this age group.

U.S. Foreign Service:
St. George's
Telephone 2255

Country number 8.82
Guadeloupe

INFECTIOUS DISEASE RISK

Malaria Risk
There is no malaria risk in this country.

Diseases of Special Risk
In addition to the worldwide hazard of tetanus and the routine and any special immunizations recommended below, the traveler should be aware that risk of exposure to the following diseases exists in this country. This list is not all inclusive, but it is a caution concerning the more likely endemic disease risks.

Potential risk of dengue fever exists. The virus is present in this country at all times and may give rise to major outbreaks.

Schistosomiasis may be found in this country. Avoid contact with contaminated fresh water lakes, ponds, or streams. The islands of Grand Terre, Basse Terre, Marie Galante and La Desirade are infected.

Rabies has been reported, especially in the mongoose, in this country.

Amoebic and bacillary dysentery, diarrheal diseases, and viral hepatitis associated with water and food supplies are particularly common in this country.

Food/Water Safety

All tap water used for drinking, brushing teeth, and making ice cubes should be boiled prior to use. Insure that bottled water is uncapped in your presence. Milk should be boiled to insure safety. Powdered and evaporated milk are available and safe. Avoid butter and other dairy products. All meat, poultry and seafood must be well cooked and served while hot. Pork is best avoided. Vegetables should be well cooked and served hot. Salads and mayonnaise are best avoided. Fruits with intact skins should be peeled by you just prior to consumption. Avoid cold buffets, custards, and any frozen dessert. First class hotels and restaurants serve purified drinking water and reliable food. However, the hazard is left to your judgement.

VACCINATIONS

Yellow fever—A vaccination certificate is required for travelers coming from infected areas and from or in transit through countries with active disease. A vaccination certificate is required for children over one year of age.

Routine immunizations should be current. For infants and children through 16 years of age, refer to Chapter 4.3. A rubeola (measles) booster should be considered. Persons age 16 to 65 should receive a booster of tetanus and diphtheria every ten years. Healthy adults under age 65 do not require pneumococcal vaccine, but it is appropriate for those with chronic medical conditions. Influenza vaccine may be considered for those providing essential community services, health care workers, and those wishing to reduce the likelihood of becoming ill with influenza. Adults over 65 years of age are urged to obtain yearly influenza immunization, and to insure that their tetanus and diphtheria immunizations are current. Pneumococcal vaccination is also suggested for this age group.

_____ **Country number 8.83** _____
Guam

INFECTIOUS DISEASE RISK

Malaria Risk

There is no malaria risk in this country.

Diseases of Special Risk

In addition to the worldwide hazard of tetanus and the routine and any special immunizations recommended below, the traveler should be aware that risk of exposure to the following diseases exists in this country. This list is not all inclusive, but it is a caution concerning the more likely endemic disease risks.

DISEASE RISK PROFILE

Disease	endemic	risk	hazard
Dengue Fever	x		
Diarrheal Disease Risk		x	
Encephalitis, Japanese	x		
Filariasis			x
Helminthic Diseases (see Chapter 6.21)		x	
Typhoid Fever	x		

Food/Water Safety

First class hotels and restaurants serve purified drinking water and reliable food. However, the hazard is left to your judgement.

VACCINATIONS

Routine immunizations should be current. For infants and children through 16 years of age, refer to Chapter 4.3. A rubeola (measles) booster should be considered. Persons age 16 to 65 should receive a booster of tetanus and diphtheria every ten years. Healthy adults under age 65 do not require pneumococcal vaccine, but it is appropriate for those with chronic medical conditions. Influenza vaccine may be considered for those providing essential community services, health care workers, and those wishing to reduce the likelihood of becoming ill with influenza. Adults over 65 years of age are urged to obtain yearly influenza immunization, and to insure that their tetanus and diphtheria immunizations are current. Pneumococcal vaccination is also suggested for this age group.

No vaccinations are required to enter this country.

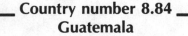

Country number 8.84
Guatemala

INFECTIOUS DISEASE RISK

Malaria Risk

Malaria risk exists all year only below 1500 meters. Risk is low in Guatemala City and Central Highlands. It is found (a) (excluding urban areas) in Baja Verapaz, Chiquimula, Escuintla, Jalapa, El Peten, El Progreso, El Quiche, Santa Rosa, Suchitpequez, Zacapa; (b) Alta Verapaz, Huehuetenago, Izabal,

Jutiapa, Retalhuleu; and in the Municipios of Coatepeque (Quetzaltenango Dep.) and Ocos (San Marcos Dept.) The CDC recommends taking cholorquine weekly (see Chapter 6.31).

Falciparum malaria represents 6% of malaria, therefore there is a risk of p. vivax malaria exposure. Consider the use of primaquine upon return home.

Diseases of Special Risk

In addition to the worldwide hazard of tetanus and the routine and any special immunizations recommended below, the traveler should be aware that risk of exposure to the following diseases exists in this country. This list is not all inclusive, but it is a caution concerning the more likely endemic disease risks.

DISEASE RISK PROFILE

Disease	endemic	risk	hazard
Brucellosis	x		
Dengue Fever	x		
Diarrheal Disease Risk		x	
Dysentery, Amoebic/Bacillary		x	
Encephalitis, Venezuelan Equine	x		
Helminthic Diseases (see Chapter 6.21)	x		
Hepatitis, Viral	x		
Leishmaniasis	x		
Onchocerciasis	x		
Trypanosomiasis, American Chaga's Disease	x		
Typhoid Fever		x	

Food/Water Safety

All tap water used for drinking, brushing teeth, and making ice cubes should be boiled prior to use. Insure that bottled water is uncapped in your presence. Milk should be boiled to insure safety. Powdered and evaporated milk are available and safe. Avoid butter and other dairy products. All meat, poultry and seafood must be well cooked and served while hot. Pork is best avoided. Vegetables should be well cooked and served hot. Salads and mayonnaise are best avoided. Fruits with intact skins should be peeled by you just prior to consumption. Avoid cold buffets, custards, and any frozen dessert. First class hotels and restaurants in Guatemala City serve purified drinking water and reliable food. However, the hazard is left to your judgement.

VACCINATIONS

Yellow fever—A vaccination certificate is required for travelers coming from infected areas and from or in transit through countries any part of which is infected with yellow fever. A vaccination certificate is required for children over one year of age.

Routine immunizations should be current. For infants and children through 16 years of age, refer to Chapter 4.3. A rubeola (measles) booster should be considered. Persons age 16 to 65 should receive a booster of tetanus and diphtheria every ten years. Healthy adults under age 65 do not require pneumococcal vaccine, but it is appropriate for those with chronic medical conditions. Influenza vaccine may be considered for those providing essential community services, health care workers, and those wishing to reduce the likelihood of becoming ill with influenza. Adults over 65 years of age are urged to obtain yearly influenza immunization, and to insure that their tetanus and diphtheria immunizations are current. Pneumococcal vaccination is also suggested for this age group.

The vaccinations listed are recommended for the traveler's protection.
Poliomyelitis—A poliomyelitis booster is indicated for this country.
Viral Hepatitis A—Vaccination is recommended for all travelers for their protection.
Typhoid fever—Vaccination is recommended for all travelers for their protection.

Selective vaccinations—*These apply only to specific groups of travelers or persons on specific working assignments:*
Rabies—In this country, where rabies is a constant threat, a pre-exposure rabies vaccination is advised for persons planning an extended stay or on working assignments (naturalists, agricultural advisors, archeologists, geologists, etc.). Although this provides adequate initial protection, a person bitten by a potentially rabid animal would still require post exposure immunization (see Chapter 6.40). Children should be cautioned not to pet dogs, cats, or other mammals. Rabies is most commonly found in this country in dogs and bats.

U.S. Foreign Service:
7-01 Avenida de la Reforma
Zone 10
Guatemala, Telephone 31-15-41

Canadian High Commission/Embassy Office:
Galerias Espana
6th Floor
7 Avendina 11-59
Zona 9
Guatemala, Telephone 32-14-11/13/17

TRAVEL ADVISORY
A U.S. Department of State Travel Advisory was in effect on 4 May 1990 when this book went to press. The entire text is included below. Travel adviso-

ries are subject to reissue, change, and cancellation at any time. Current travel advisory information is available by calling the U.S. Department of State Travel Advisory Hotline at (202) 647-5225. The current travel advisory status is also available from the Herchmer Database update system (see Chapter 2.8).

JANUARY 18, 1990 SECSTATE WSH
GUATEMALA—CAUTION
SUMMARY: THE DEPARTMENT OF STATE ADVISES U.S. CITIZENS TRAVELING TO GUATEMALA THAT GUATEMALA CITY SUFFERED A NUMBER OF RANDOM TERRORIST INCIDENTS, INCLUDING BOMB AND GRENADE EXPLOSIONS IN 1989. THE ATTACKS, THUS FAR, HAVE NOT INJURED FOREIGN NATIONALS, BUT GIVEN THEIR RANDOM NATURE THAT POSSIBILITY EXISTS. PERSONS PLANNING TO TRAVEL BY ROAD IN CERTAIN AREAS OF WESTERN GUATEMALA SHOULD EXERCISE PARTICULAR CAUTION. THE DEPARTMENT DISCOURAGES INTERCITY ROAD TRAVEL AT NIGHT ANYWHERE IN GUATEMALA. END SUMMARY.
MAJOR TOURIST AREAS: U.S. TRAVELERS TO THE TOURIST CENTERS OF GUATEMALA CITY AND ANTIGUA HAVE REPORTED NO MAJOR DIFFICULTIES. MOST VISITORS TO TIKAL FLY TO THE TOWN OF FLORES AND THEN GO BY BUS TO THE MAYAN RUINS. IN DECEMBER THERE WERE REPORTS OF ARMED ROBBERIES OF TOURISTS TRAVELING BY CAR BETWEEN TIKAL AND BELIZE. INDIVIDUAL ROAD TRAVEL IN MOST OF PETEN IS DISCOURAGED. TRAVELERS ON THE PAN AMERICAN HIGHWAY (CA-1) TO LAKE ATITLAN AND CHICHICASTENANGO ON OCCASION ENCOUNTER ROADBLOCKS AND SUFFER ARMED ROBBERIES, APPARENTLY AT THE HANDS OF LEFTIST GUERILLAS. AMERICAN CITIZENS INTENDING TO TRAVEL TO LAKE ATITLAN OR CHICHICASTENANGO BY AUTOMOBILE SHOULD CONTACT THE CITIZEN SERVICES SECTION OF THE AMERICAN EMBASSY FOR SPECIFIC AND UP-TO-DATE INFORMATION ON TRAVEL ONLY DURING DAYLIGHT, ENSURE THEIR VEHICLE IS IN GOOD CONDITION, AVOID THE SOUTH SIDE OF THE LAKE, AND NOT DRIVE OFF MAIN ROADS.
GUERRILLA ACTIVITY: ENCOUNTERS BETWEEN GUATEMALAN SECURITY FORCES AND LEFTIST GUERRILLAS OCCUR IN SEVERAL AREAS OF THE COUNTRY. SUCH ENCOUNTERS HAVE TAKEN PLACE NEAR THE BORDER WITH MEXICO WEST OF THE CITIES ON SAN MARCOS AND HUEHUETENANGO; NORTHERN EL QUICHE AND HUEHUETENANGO; SOUTHWESTERN PETEN; IN A NUMBER OF AREAS IN SOPLOLA SOUTH OF LAKE ATITLAN; AND SUCHIITEPEQUEZ, PARTICULARLY INSIDE THE AREA FRAMED BY THE TOWNS OF PATZICIA, PATZUN, POCHUTA, AND ACATENANGO. CAMPING, BACKPACKING, AND RIVER TRAVEL IS DISCOURAGED

THROUGHOUT GUATEMALA. NO U.S. TOURISTS HAVE REPORTED INJURIES. GUATEMALAN SECURITY FORCES RECENTLY HAVE IN-CREASED THEIR PRESENCE ALONG THE PAN AMERICAN HIGH-WAY AND INCIDENTS SUCH AS ROADBLOCKS AND ROBBERIES HAVE DECLINED. ROBBERIES ALSO HAVE TAKEN PLACE OCCA-SIONALLY ON THE PACIFIC HIGHWAY NEAR MAZATENANGO. THE DEPARTMENT ENCOURAGES AMERICAN VISITORS PLANNING INTERCITY HIGHWAY TRAVEL TO CONTACT THE AMERICAN CITI-ZEN SERVICES SECTION OF THE U.S. EMBASSY IN GUATEMALA CITY FOR UP-TO-DATE INFORMATION. TRAVELERS ARE ADVISED, HOWEVER, THAT INCIDENTS OCCUR ON A RANDOM BASIS, AF-FECT EVEN MAIN HIGHWAYS, AND ARE NOT PREDICTABLE. THE DEPARTMENT ADVISES MOTORISTS ENTERING FROM MEXICO TO TAKE THE TAPACHULA-TEUN UMAN CROSSING ON THE PACIFIC COAST (CA-2) OR THE COMITAN-LA MESILLA ENTRY TO THE HIGH-LANDS (CA-1).
EXPIRATION: 10 APRIL 1990

Country number 8.85
Guernsey, Alderney, and Sark (UK)

INFECTIOUS DISEASE RISK

Malaria Risk
There is no malaria risk in this country.

Diseases of Special Risk

Food/Water Safety
Local water is considered safe without further treatment. Milk is pasteurized and safe to drink. Butter, cheese, yogurt and ice-cream are safe. Local meat, poultry, seafood, vegetables, and fruits are safe to eat.

VACCINATIONS

Routine immunizations should be current. For infants and children through 16 years of age, refer to Chapter 4.3. A rubeola (measles) booster should be considered. Persons age 16 to 65 should receive a booster of tetanus and diphtheria every ten years. Healthy adults under age 65 do not require pneumococcal vaccine, but it is appropriate for those with chronic medical conditions. Influenza vaccine may be considered for those providing essential community services, health care workers, and those wishing to reduce the likelihood of becoming ill with influenza. Adults over 65 years of age are urged to

obtain yearly influenza immunization, and to insure that their tetanus and diphtheria immunizations are current. Pneumococcal vaccination is also suggested for this age group.

No vaccinations are required to enter this country.

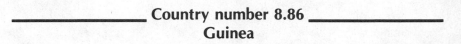

Country number 8.86
Guinea

INFECTIOUS DISEASE RISK

Malaria Risk

Malaria is present in this entire country, all year long. The malaria in this country is resistant to chloroquine. The CDC recommends the use of mefloquine (Lariam) as described in Chapter 6.31 for chemical prophylaxis.

Falciparum malaria represents 92% of malaria, therefore there is a slight risk of p. vivax malaria exposure. Consider the use of primaquine upon return home.

Diseases of Special Risk

In addition to the worldwide hazard of tetanus and the routine and any special immunizations recommended below, the traveler should be aware that risk of exposure to the following diseases exists in this country. This list is not all inclusive, but it is a caution concerning the more likely endemic disease risks.

This country must be considered receptive to dengue fever. Intermittent epidemics in the past make renewed activity or reintroduction of the virus possible.

Schistosomiasis may be found in this country. Avoid contact with contaminated fresh water lakes, ponds, or streams. In lower Guinea the following districts are free of infection: Boffa, Conacry, Fria, and Telimele.

Amoebic and bacillary dysentery, diarrheal diseases, helminthic diseases, and viral hepatitis associated with water and food supplies are particularly common in this country.

DISEASE RISK PROFILE

Disease	endemic	risk	hazard
Dracunculiasis/Guinea Worm	x		
Echinococcosis		x	
Filariasis			x
Lassa Fever	x		
Leishmaniasis			
Cutaneous	x		
Visceral	x		
Loiasis			x
Onchocerciasis			x

Disease	endemic	risk	hazard
Rabies		x	
Relapsing Fever	x		
Trachoma			x
Trypanosomiasis, African Sleeping Sickness	x		
Tungiasis			x
Typhus, Endemic Flea-Borne	x		
Typhus, Epidemic Louse-Borne	x		
Typhus, Scrubx			

Food/Water Safety

All tap water used for drinking, brushing teeth, and making ice cubes should be boiled prior to use. Insure that bottled water is uncapped in your presence. Milk should be boiled to insure safety. Powdered and evaporated milk are available and safe. Avoid butter and other dairy products. All meat, poultry and seafood must be well cooked and served while hot. Pork is best avoided. Vegetables should be well cooked and served hot. Salads and mayonnaise are best avoided. Fruits with intact skins should be peeled by you just prior to consumption. Avoid cold buffets, custards, and any frozen dessert.

VACCINATIONS

Yellow fever—A vaccination certificate is required for travelers coming from infected areas and from or in transit through countries with active disease. A vaccination certificate is required for children over one year of age. Yellow fever is active in this country at this time. CDC recommends vaccination for all travelers over 9 months of age.

Routine immunizations should be current. For infants and children through 16 years of age, refer to Chapter 4.3. A rubeola (measles) booster should be considered. Persons age 16 to 65 should receive a booster of tetanus and diphtheria every ten years. Healthy adults under age 65 do not require pneumococcal vaccine, but it is appropriate for those with chronic medical conditions. Influenza vaccine may be considered for those providing essential community services, health care workers, and those wishing to reduce the likelihood of becoming ill with influenza. Adults over 65 years of age are urged to obtain yearly influenza immunization, and to insure that their tetanus and diphtheria immunizations are current. Pneumococcal vaccination is also suggested for this age group.

The vaccinations listed are recommended for the traveler's protection.
Poliomyelitis—A poliomyelitis booster is indicated for this country.
Cholera—Cholera is present in this country. Risk to western travelers is low. Immunization is not required or recommended for travel to this country due to its low effectiveness. Avoid uncooked foods and untreated water. Vaccination is advised only for persons living or working under inadequate sanitary conditions and for those with impaired defense mechanisms.

Viral Hepatitis A—Vaccination is recommended for all travelers for their protection.

Typhoid fever—Vaccination is recommended for all travelers for their protection.

Selective vaccinations—These apply only to specific groups of travelers or persons on specific working assignments:

Viral Hepatitis B—Because of the high rate of healthy carriers of hepatitis B in this country, vaccination is recommended for persons on working assignments in the health care field (dentists, physicians, nurses, laboratory technicians), or working in close contact with the local population (teachers, missionaries, Peace Corps), or persons foreseeing sexual relations with local inhabitants.

Rabies—In this country, where rabies is a constant threat, a pre-exposure rabies vaccination is advised for persons planning an extended stay or on working assignments (naturalists, agricultural advisors, archeologists, geologists, etc.). Although this provides adequate initial protection, a person bitten by a potentially rabid animal would still require post exposure immunization. Children should be cautioned not to pet dogs, cats, or other mammals.

U.S. Foreign Service:
2d Blvd. and 9th Ave.
Conakry, Telephone 415-20/21/22/23/24

Canadian High Commission/Embassy Office:
P.O. Box 99
Conakry, Telephone 46-37-32/33

Country number 8.87
Guinea-Bissau

INFECTIOUS DISEASE RISK

Malaria Risk

Malaria is present in this entire country, all year long. The malaria in this country is resistant to chloroquine. The CDC recommends the use of mefloquine (Lariam) as described in Chapter 6.31 for chemical prophylaxis.

Falciparum malaria represents 90% of malaria, therefore there is a slight risk of p. vivax malaria exposure. Consider the use of primaquine upon return home.

Diseases of Special Risk

In addition to the worldwide hazard of tetanus and the routine and any special immunizations recommended below, the traveler should be aware that

risk of exposure to the following diseases exists in this country. This list is not all inclusive, but it is a caution concerning the more likely endemic disease risks.

This country must be considered receptive to dengue fever. Intermittent epidemics in the past make renewed activity or reintroduction of the virus possible.

Schistosomiasis may be found in this country. Avoid contact with contaminated fresh water lakes, ponds, or streams. Areas of infection are present in the northern part of the country only, in the area extending from the coastal region of Cacheu to the border with Guinea, including the valleys of the Cacheu and Geba River basins.

Amoebic and bacillary dysentery, diarrheal diseases, helminthic diseases, and viral hepatitis associated with water and food supplies are particularly common in this country.

DISEASE RISK PROFILE

Disease	endemic	risk	hazard
Dracunculiasis/Guinea Worm	x		
Echinococcosis		x	
Filariasis			x
Lassa Fever	x		
Leishmaniasis			
Cutaneous	x		
Visceral	x		
Loiasis			x
Onchocerciasis			x
Rabies	x		
Relapsing Fever	x		
Trachoma			x
Trypanosomiasis, African	x		
Sleeping Sickness			
Tungiasis			x
Typhoid Fever		x	
Typhus, Endemic Flea-Borne	x		
Typhus, Epidemic Louse-Borne	x		
Typhus, Scrub	x		

Food/Water Safety

All tap water used for drinking, brushing teeth, and making ice cubes should be boiled prior to use. Insure that bottled water is uncapped in your presence. Milk should be boiled to insure safety. Powdered and evaporated milk are available and safe. Avoid butter and other dairy products. All meat, poultry and seafood must be well cooked and served while hot. Pork is best avoided. Vegetables should be well cooked and served hot. Salads and mayonnaise are best avoided. Fruits with intact skins should be peeled by you just prior to consumption. Avoid cold buffets, custards, and any frozen dessert.

VACCINATIONS

Yellow fever—A vaccination certificate is required for travelers coming from infected areas and from or in transit through countries in the endemic yellow fever zone, see page HHH. A vaccination certificate is required for children over one year of age. CDC recommends vaccination for all travelers over 9 months of age, but see also Chapter 6.63.

Routine immunizations should be current. For infants and children through 16 years of age, refer to Chapter 4.3. A rubeola (measles) booster should be considered. Persons age 16 to 65 should receive a booster of tetanus and diphtheria every ten years. Healthy adults under age 65 do not require pneumococcal vaccine, but it is appropriate for those with chronic medical conditions. Influenza vaccine may be considered for those providing essential community services, health care workers, and those wishing to reduce the likelihood of becoming ill with influenza. Adults over 65 years of age are urged to obtain yearly influenza immunization, and to insure that their tetanus and diphtheria immunizations are current. Pneumococcal vaccination is also suggested for this age group.

The vaccinations listed are recommended for the traveler's protection.

Poliomyelitis—A poliomyelitis booster is indicated for this country.

Cholera—Cholera is present in this country. Risk to western travelers is low. Immunization is not required or recommended for travel to this country due to its low effectiveness. Avoid uncooked foods and untreated water. Vaccination is advised only for persons living or working under inadequate sanitary conditions and for those with impaired defense mechanisms.

Viral Hepatitis A—Vaccination is recommended for all travelers for their protection.

Typhoid fever—Vaccination is recommended for all travelers for their protection.

Selective vaccinations—These apply only to specific groups of travelers or persons on specific working assignments:

Viral Hepatitis B—Because of the high rate of healthy carriers of hepatitis B in this country, vaccination is recommended for persons on working assignments in the health care field (dentists, physicians, nurses, laboratory technicians), or working in close contact with the local population (teachers, missionaries, Peace Corps), or persons foreseeing sexual relations with local inhabitants.

Rabies—In this country, where rabies is a constant threat, a pre-exposure rabies vaccination is advised for persons planning an extended stay or on working assignments (naturalists, agricultural advisors, archeologists, geologists, etc.). Although this provides adequate initial protection, a person bitten by a potentially rabid animal would still require post exposure immunization (see

Chapter 6.40). Children should be cautioned not to pet dogs, cats, or other mammals.

U.S. Foreign Service:
Avenida Domingos Ramos
Bissau, Telephone 212816/7

_____ Country number 8.88 _____
Guyana

INFECTIOUS DISEASE RISK

Malaria Risk
Malaria is present in North West Region and Rupununi Region of this country below 900 meters, excluding urban areas. The risk exists all year. The malaria in this country is resistant to chloroquine. The CDC recommends the use of mefloquine (Lariam) as described in Chapter 6.31 for chemical prophylaxis.

Falciparum malaria represents 41% of malaria, therefore there is a risk of p. vivax malaria exposure. Consider the use of primaquine upon return home.

Diseases of Special Risk
In addition to the worldwide hazard of tetanus and the routine and any special immunizations recommended below, the traveler should be aware that risk of exposure to the following diseases exists in this country. This list is not all inclusive, but it is a caution concerning the more likely endemic disease risks.

Potential risk of dengue fever exists. The virus is present in this country at all times and may give rise to major outbreaks.

Amoebic and bacillary dysentery, diarrheal diseases, helminthic diseases, and viral hepatitis associated with water and food supplies are particularly common in this country.

DISEASE RISK PROFILE

Disease	endemic	risk	hazard
Brucellosis	x		
Echinococcosis	x		
Encephalitisx			
Filariasisx			
Leishmaniasis			
Cutaneous	x		
Visceral	x		
Rabies	x		
Trypanosomiasis, American	x		

Food/Water Safety

All tap water used for drinking, brushing teeth, and making ice cubes should be boiled prior to use. Insure that bottled water is uncapped in your presence. Milk should be boiled to insure safety. Powdered and evaporated milk are available and safe. Avoid butter and other dairy products. All meat, poultry and seafood must be well cooked and served while hot. Pork is best avoided. Vegetables should be well cooked and served hot. Salads and mayonnaise are best avoided. Fruits with intact skins should be peeled by you just prior to consumption. Avoid cold buffets, custards, and any frozen dessert. First class hotels and restaurants in Georgetown serve purified drinking water and reliable food. However, the hazard is left to your judgement.

VACCINATIONS

Yellow fever—A vaccination certificate is required for travelers coming from infected areas and from or in transit through countries in the endemic yellow fever zone, see Chapter 6.63. A vaccination is required for children of all ages. CDC recommends vaccination for all travelers over 9 months of age, but see also Chapter 6.63 in avoiding vaccination in infants under that age.

Routine immunizations should be current. For infants and children through 16 years of age, refer to Chapter 4.3. A rubeola (measles) booster should be considered. Persons age 16 to 65 should receive a booster of tetanus and diphtheria every ten years. Healthy adults under age 65 do not require pneumococcal vaccine, but it is appropriate for those with chronic medical conditions. Influenza vaccine may be considered for those providing essential community services, health care workers, and those wishing to reduce the likelihood of becoming ill with influenza. Adults over 65 years of age are urged to obtain yearly influenza immunization, and to insure that their tetanus and diphtheria immunizations are current. Pneumococcal vaccination is also suggested for this age group.

The vaccinations listed are recommended for the traveler's protection.
Poliomyelitis—A poliomyelitis booster is indicated for this country.
Viral Hepatitis A—Vaccination is recommended for all travelers for their protection.
Typhoid fever—Vaccination is recommended for all travelers for their protection.

U.S. Foreign Service:
31 Main St.
Georgetown, Telephone 54900

Canadian High Commission/Embassy Office:
High and Young Streets
Georgetown, Telephone 72081/5

—————— Country number 8.89 ——————
Haiti

INFECTIOUS DISEASE RISK

Malaria Risk

Malaria risk is present in this country in all areas below 300 meters, including urban areas, all year long. See Chapter 6.31 for the use of chloroquine which is the prophylaxis recommended by the CDC.

Diseases of Special Risk

In addition to the worldwide hazard of tetanus and the routine and any special immunizations recommended below, the traveler should be aware that risk of exposure to the following diseases exists in this country. This list is not all inclusive, but it is a caution concerning the more likely endemic disease risks.

Potential risk of dengue fever exists. The virus is present in this country at all times and may give rise to major outbreaks.

AIDS has been diagnosed in 2,000 cases, with up to 200,000 persons estimated as infected with the virus. It is estimated that in the next 5 years 1 million of the country's 6 million inhabitants will become infected with the AIDS virus.

DISEASE RISK PROFILE

Disease	endemic	risk	hazard
Diarrheal Disease Risk		x	
Dysentery, Amoebic/Bacillary			x
Filariasis	x		
Hepatitis, Viral	x		
Rabies (esp. mongoose)	x		
Tularemia	x		

Food/Water Safety

All tap water used for drinking, brushing teeth, and making ice cubes should be boiled prior to use. Insure that bottled water is uncapped in your presence. Milk should be boiled to insure safety. Powdered and evaporated milk are available and safe. Avoid butter and other dairy products. All meat, poultry and seafood must be well cooked and served while hot. Pork is best avoided. Vegetables should be well cooked and served hot. Salads and mayonnaise are best avoided. Fruits with intact skins should be peeled by you just prior to consumption. Avoid cold buffets, custards, and any frozen dessert.

VACCINATIONS

Yellow fever—A vaccination certificate is required for travelers coming from infected areas and from or in transit through countries with current infection. A vaccination is required for children of all ages. Children under nine months of age should not be vaccinated due to health considerations. Please refer to the discussion in Chapter 6.63 on avoiding yellow fever vaccination in this age group.

Routine immunizations should be current. For infants and children through 16 years of age, refer to Chapter 4.3. A rubeola (measles) booster should be considered. Persons age 16 to 65 should receive a booster of tetanus and diphtheria every ten years. Healthy adults under age 65 do not require pneumococcal vaccine, but it is appropriate for those with chronic medical conditions. Influenza vaccine may be considered for those providing essential community services, health care workers, and those wishing to reduce the likelihood of becoming ill with influenza. Adults over 65 years of age are urged to obtain yearly influenza immunization, and to insure that their tetanus and diphtheria immunizations are current. Pneumococcal vaccination is also suggested for this age group.

The vaccinations listed are recommended for the traveler's protection.
Poliomyelitis—A poliomyelitis booster is indicated for this country.
Viral Hepatitis A—Vaccination is recommended when traveling outside the areas usually visited by tourists, traveling extensively in the interior of the country (trekkers, hikers) and for persons on working assignments in remote areas.
Typhoid fever—Vaccination is recommended when traveling outside the areas usually visited by tourists, traveling extensively in the interior of the country (trekkers, hikers) and for persons on working assignments in remote areas.

Selective vaccinations—These apply only to specific groups of travelers or persons on specific working assignments:
Viral Hepatitis B—Because of the high rate of healthy carriers of hepatitis B in this country, vaccination is recommended for persons on working assignments in the health care field (dentists, physicians, nurses, laboratory technicians), or working in close contact with the local population (teachers, missionaries, Peace Corps), or persons foreseeing sexual relations with local inhabitants.
Rabies—In this country, where rabies is a constant threat, a pre-exposure rabies vaccination is advised for persons planning an extended stay or on working assignments (naturalists, agricultural advisors, archeologists, geologists, etc.). Although this provides adequate initial protection, a person bitten by a potentially rabid animal would still require post exposure immunization (see Chapter 6.40). Children should be cautioned not to pet dogs, cats, or other mammals.

U.S. Foreign Service:
Harry Truman Blvd.
Port-au-Prince, Telephone 2-0200

Canadian High Commission/Embassy Office:
Edifice Banque Nova Scotia
Route de Delmas
Port-au-Prince, Telephone 2-2358, 2-4231, 2-4919

TRAVEL ADVISORY
A U.S. Department of State Travel Advisory was in effect on 4 May 1990 when this book went to press. The entire text is included below. Travel advisories are subject to reissue, change, and cancellation at any time. Current travel advisory information is available by calling the U.S. Department of State Travel Advisory Hotline at (202) 647-5225. The current travel advisory status is also available from the Herchmer Database update system (see Chapter 2.8).

MARCH 31,1990
HAITI—WARNING
IN VIEW OF CONTINUED UNREST IN VARIOUS PARTS OF HAITI, IN-CLUDING THE CITY OF PORT-AU-PRINCE, THE DEPARTMENT OF STATE ADVISES AMERICAN CITIZENS TO DEFER ALL NON-ESSENTIAL TRAVEL TO HAITI. U.S. CITIZENS WHO DO TRAVEL TO HAITI SHOULD BE AWARE THAT ALTHOUGH THERE DOES NOT AP-PEAR TO BE ANY DIRECT THREAT TO AMERICAN CITIZENS IN HAITI, CAUTION SHOULD BE EXERCISED AT ALL TIMES AND CROWDS AND BARRICADES SHOULD BE AVOIDED. NIGHT TIME TRAVEL WITHIN THE CITY OF PORT-AU-PRINCE AND ELSEWHERE IN HAITI IS INADVISABLE. U.S. CITIZENS WHO DO TRAVEL TO HAITI SHOULD REGISTER UPON ARRIVAL WITH THE CONSULAR SEC-TION OF THE AMERICAN EMBASSY IN PORT-AU-PRINCE, RUE OS-WALD DURAN, TEL: 2-0200. AFTER-HOURS INQUIRIES SHOULD BE ADDRESSED TO THE AMERICAN EMBASSY, HARRY TRUMAN BLVD., TEL: 2-0200.
EXPIRATION DATE: INDEFINITE

_____ **Country number 8.90** _____
Honduras

INFECTIOUS DISEASE RISK

Malaria Risk
There is no risk of malaria in the urban areas of the Central highlands.

Malaria is found below 1000 meters from May through December in rural areas of Intibuca, La Paz, Lempira, and Olancho Departments. See Chapter 6.31 for use of chloroquine as malaria prophylaxis.

Falciparum malaria represents 3% of malaria, therefore there is risk of p. vivax malaria exposure. Consider the use of primaquine upon return home.

Diseases of Special Risk

In addition to the worldwide hazard of tetanus and the routine and any special immunizations recommended below, the traveler should be aware that risk of exposure to the following diseases exists in this country. This list is not all inclusive, but it is a caution concerning the more likely endemic disease risks.

This country must be considered receptive to dengue fever. Intermittent epidemics in the past make renewed activity or reintroduction of the virus possible.

Chaga's Disease is present in rural areas below 1500 meters in the following departments: Choluteca, Comayagua, Copan, El Paraiso, Francisco Morazan, Intibuca, La Paz, Lempira, Ocotepeque, Olancho, Santa Barbara, and Yoro.

DISEASE RISK PROFILE

Disease	endemic	risk	hazard
Brucellosis	x		
Diarrheal Disease Risk		x	
Dysentery, Amoebic/Bacillary		x	
Encephalitis, Venezuelan Equine	x		
Helminthic Diseases (see Chapter 6.21)		x	
Hepatitis, Viral	x		
Leishmaniasis	x		
Typhoid Fever		x	

Food/Water Safety

All tap water used for drinking, brushing teeth, and making ice cubes should be boiled prior to use. Insure that bottled water is uncapped in your presence. Milk should be boiled to insure safety. Powdered and evaporated milk are available and safe. Avoid butter and other dairy products. All meat, poultry and seafood must be well cooked and served while hot. Pork is best avoided. Vegetables should be well cooked and served hot. Salads and mayonnaise are best avoided. Fruits with intact skins should be peeled by you just prior to consumption. Avoid cold buffets, custards, and any frozen dessert. First class hotels and restaurants in Tegucigalpa serve purified drinking water and reliable food. However, the hazard is left to your judgement.

VACCINATIONS

Yellow fever—A vaccination certificate is required for travelers coming from infected areas. Children under nine months of age should generally not be vaccinated with yellow fever vaccine due to health considerations. Please refer to the discussion in Chapter 6.63 on avoiding yellow fever vaccination in this age group.

Routine immunizations should be current. For infants and children through 16 years of age, refer to Chapter 4.3. A rubeola (measles) booster should be considered. Persons age 16 to 65 should receive a booster of tetanus and diphtheria every ten years. Healthy adults under age 65 do not require pneumococcal vaccine, but it is appropriate for those with chronic medical conditions. Influenza vaccine may be considered for those providing essential community services, health care workers, and those wishing to reduce the likelihood of becoming ill with influenza. Adults over 65 years of age are urged to obtain yearly influenza immunization, and to insure that their tetanus and diphtheria immunizations are current. Pneumococcal vaccination is also suggested for this age group.

The vaccinations listed are recommended for the traveler's protection.

Viral Hepatitis A—Vaccination is recommended when traveling outside the areas usually visited by tourists, traveling extensively in the interior of the country (trekkers, hikers) and for persons on working assignments in remote areas.

Typhoid fever—Vaccination is recommended when traveling outside the areas usually visited by tourists, traveling extensively in the interior of the country (trekkers, hikers) and for persons on working assignments in remote areas.

Selective vaccinations—These apply only to specific groups of travelers or persons on specific working assignments:

Rabies—In this country, where rabies is a constant threat, a pre-exposure rabies vaccination is advised for persons planning an extended stay or on working assignments (naturalists, agricultural advisors, archeologists, geologists, etc.). Although this provides adequate initial protection, a person bitten by a potentially rabid animal would still require post exposure immunization (see Chapter 6.40). Children should be cautioned not to pet dogs, cats, or other mammals. Rabies frequently occurs in dogs and bats in this country.

U.S. Foreign Service:
Avenido La Paz
Tegucigalpa, Telephone 32-3120/21/22/23/24/25

TRAVEL ADVISORY
A U.S. Department of State Travel Advisory was in effect on 4 May 1990 when this book went to press. The entire text is included below. Travel advisories are subject to reissue, change, and cancellation at any time. Current travel advisory information is available by calling the U.S. Department of State Travel

Advisory Hotline at (202) 647-5225. The current travel advisory status is also available from the Herchmer Database update system (see Chapter 2.8).

06/10/89 10:31 SECSTATE WSH
SUBJECT: TRAVEL ADVISORY—HONDURAS—CAUTION
   1. SUMMARY. THE DEPARTMENT OF STATE ADVISES U.S. CITI-ZENS THAT WITH THE EXCEPTION OF AREAS BORDERING NICA-RAGUA AND EL SALVADOR WHERE ARMED ACTIVITY OCCURS, TRAVEL THROUGHOUT THE REMAINDER OF HONDURAS IS SAFE FROM A SECURITY STANDPOINT AND IS ESSENTIALLY NORMAL. TRAVELERS WHO ARRIVE BY AIR HAVE NOT ENCOUNTERED ANY DIFFICULTIES. TRAVELERS WHO ARRIVE OVERLAND BY ROAD SOMETIMES HAVE EXPERIENCED PROBLEMS.
   2. HONDURAN/SALVADORAN BORDER: OVERLAND TRAVELERS ARE CAUTIONED THAT SALVADORAN GUERRILLAS OPERATE OUT OF AREAS NEAR THE SALVADORAN/HONDURAN BORDER. THE GUERRILLAS SOMETIMES INDISCRIMINATELY ATTACK CIVILIAN TRAFFIC ON SALVADORAN ROADS. GUERRILLA-PLACED LAND MINES ON RURAL ROADS IN EL SALVADOR ARE CAUSING IN-CREASING NUMBERS OF CIVILIAN CASUALTIES.
   3. HONDURAN/GUATEMALAN Bt(ORDER: THERE ARE NO RE-PORTED PROBLEMS.
   4. HONDURAN/NICARAGUAN BORDER: TRAVELERS ARE ADVISED THAT TRAVEL BY ROAD BETWEEN NICARAGUA AND HONDURAS IS UNCERTAIN AND POTENTIALLY QUITE HAZARDOUS. ALTHOUGH EVERYDAY FIGHTING BETWEEN SANDINISTA AND NICARAGUAN DEMOCRATIC RESISTANCE FORCES HAS STOPPED, THE SITUA-TION REMAINS TENSE ALONG POORLY DELINEATED SECTIONS OF THE BORDER AND THERE ARE OCCASIONAL ARMED SKIRMISHES. THERE ARE ALSO SEVERAL REFUGEE CAMPS FOR CIVILIAN NICA-RAGUANS IN THE BORDER AREAS. THE AREAS SURROUNDING ALL OF THE CAMPS ARE CLOSELY SUPERVISED BY HONDURAN MILITARY FORCES AND TRAVELERS WITHOUT PROPER DOCU-MENTATION WILL NOT BE ALLOWED TO ENTER THESE AREAS. TRAVELERS TO THE BORDER IN THE MOSQUITIA AREA OF HON-DURAS (IN THE DEPARTMENT OF GRACIAS A DIOS) MUST CON-SULT WITH HONDURAN MILITARY AUTHORITIES IN ADVANCE.
   5. BECAUSE OF THE ABOVE CONDITIONS, THE U.S. EMBASSY RECOMMENDS THAT AMERICANS TRAVEL BETWEEN HONDURAS AND NICARAGUA ONLY BY AIR. THOSE WHO HAVE NO ALTERNA-TIVE BUT TO TRAVEL BY LAND SHOULD BE AWARE THAT:
   6. ONLY THE EL ESPINO (ALSO KNOWN AS LA FRATERNIDAD) AND LAS MANOS BORDER CROSSINGS ARE OPEN. BORDER CROSS-INGS ARE ONLY OPEN DURING DAYLIGHT HOURS.

7. A HONDURAN VISA DOES NOT GUARANTEE ADMISSION TO HONDURAS. IMMIGRATION AUTHORITIES AT THE BORDER HAVE THE RIGHT TO EXCLUDE FOREIGNERS WHO HAVE VALID VISAS BUT HAVE SPENT 30 DAYS OR MORE IN NICARAGUA, AS SECURITY RISKS. THE AUTHORITIES GENERALLY DO NOT TELL MOST APPLI-CANTS WHY THEY ARE NOT BEING ADMITTED, WHILE OTHERS ARE TOLD THEY CAN ONLY TRANSIT HONDURAS UNDER ESCORT. TRAVELERS ARE THEN CHARGED 100 LEMPIRAS (50 US DOLLARS) FOR THE ESCORT'S EXPENSES.

8. HONDURAN AUTHORITIES HAVE DETECTED A NUMBER OF FOREIGNERS CARRYING ARMS, MESSAGES, OR MONEY FROM NICARAGUA TO GUERRILLA GROUPS THROUGHOUT CENTRAL AMERICA. FOR THIS REASON, TRAVELERS CAN EXPECT A LENGTHY, METICULOUS SEARCH OF THEIR VEHICLES AND BE-LONGINGS.

9. EXPIRATION DATE: MAY 15, 1990.

10. TRAVEL ADVISORY CONTAINED IN STATE 152482 DATED MAY 12, 1988 IS HEREBY CANCELLED.

DEPARTMENT OF STATE WASHINGTON, DC 183959/0781L

Country number 8.91
Hong Kong

INFECTIOUS DISEASE RISK

Malaria Risk
There is no malaria risk in this country.

Diseases of Special Risk
In addition to the worldwide hazard of tetanus and the routine and any special immunizations recommended below, the traveler should be aware that risk of exposure to the following diseases exists in this country. This list is not all inclusive, but it is a caution concerning the more likely endemic disease risks.

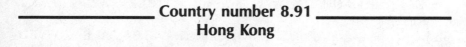

DISEASE RISK PROFILE

Disease	endemic	risk	hazard
Dengue Fever	x		
Diarrheal Diseases	x		
Encephalitis, Japanese	x		
Hepatitis, Viral	x		

Food/Water Safety

First class hotels and restaurants serve purified drinking water and reliable food.

VACCINATIONS

Routine immunizations should be current. For infants and children through 16 years of age, refer to Chapter 4.3. A rubeola (measles) booster should be considered. Persons age 16 to 65 should receive a booster of tetanus and diphtheria every ten years. Healthy adults under age 65 do not require pneumococcal vaccine, but it is appropriate for those with chronic medical conditions. Influenza vaccine may be considered for those providing essential community services, health care workers, and those wishing to reduce the likelihood of becoming ill with influenza. Adults over 65 years of age are urged to obtain yearly influenza immunization, and to insure that their tetanus and diphtheria immunizations are current. Pneumococcal vaccination is also suggested for this age group.

No vaccinations are required to enter this country.

Selective vaccinations—These apply only to specific groups of travelers or persons on specific working assignments:

Viral Hepatitis B—Because of the high rate of healthy carriers of hepatitis B in this country, vaccination is recommended for persons on working assignments in the health care field (dentists, physicians, nurses, laboratory technicians), or working in close contact with the local population (teachers, missionaries, Peace Corps), or persons foreseeing sexual relations with local inhabitants.

Japanese encephalitis—Vaccination is indicated for persons traveling extensively in rual areas or living and working near rice growing rural and suburban areas and other irrigated land, when exposure to the disease carrying mosquitoes is high. Children are especially susceptible to the infection. Sporadic cases are reported, with period of transmission all year.

U.S. Foreign Service:

26 Garden Rd.
Hong Kong, Telephone 239011

Canadian High Commission/Embassy Office:

Asian House
14th-15th Floors
1 Hennessy Road
Hong Kong, Telephone 282222/3/4/5

_____ Country number 8.92 _____
Hungary

INFECTIOUS DISEASE RISK

Malaria Risk
   There is no malaria risk in this country.

Diseases of Special Risk
   In addition to the worldwide hazard of tetanus and the routine and any special immunizations recommended below, the traveler should be aware that risk of exposure to the following diseases exists in this country. This list is not all inclusive, but it is a caution concerning the more likely endemic disease risks.

DISEASE RISK PROFILE

Disease	endemic	risk	hazard
Diarrheal Disease Risk	x		
Dysentery, Bacillary	x		
Rabies	x		
Typhoid Fever	x		

Food/Water Safety
   Water is probably safe, but due to local variations in bacterial counts, using bottled water for the first few weeks will help the traveler adjust and decrease the chance of traveler's diarrhea. Milk is pasteurized and safe to drink. Butter, cheese, yogurt and ice-cream are safe. Local meat, poultry, seafood, vegetables, and fruits are safe to eat.

VACCINATIONS

   Routine immunizations should be current. For infants and children through 16 years of age, refer to Chapter 4.3. A rubeola (measles) booster should be considered. Persons age 16 to 65 should receive a booster of tetanus and diphtheria every ten years. Healthy adults under age 65 do not require pneumococcal vaccine, but it is appropriate for those with chronic medical conditions. Influenza vaccine may be considered for those providing essential community services, health care workers, and those wishing to reduce the likelihood of becoming ill with influenza. Adults over 65 years of age are urged to obtain yearly influenza immunization, and to insure that their tetanus and diphtheria immunizations are current. Pneumococcal vaccination is also suggested for this age group.
   No vaccinations are required to enter this country.

Selective vaccinations—These apply only to specific groups of travelers or persons on specific working assignments:

Tick-borne encephalitis—(Central European encephalitis) Vaccination is recommended for persons involved in recreational activities in forested areas (camping, hiking) or working in forestry occupations. Risk season: March to November. Risk is present in forested areas extending from the Austrian border east to the outskirts of Budapest.

U.S. Foreign Service:
V. Szabadsag Ter 12
American Embassy
Budapest, Telephone 126-450

Canadian High Commission/Embassy Office:
Budakeszi ut. 32
Budapest, Telephone 387-312/512/711/712

Country number 8.93
Iceland

INFECTIOUS DISEASE RISK

Malaria Risk
There is no malaria risk in this country.

Food/Water Safety
Local water is considered safe without further treatment. Milk is pasteurized and safe to drink. Butter, cheese, yogurt and ice-cream are safe. Local meat, poultry, seafood, vegetables, and fruits are safe to eat.

VACCINATIONS
Routine immunizations should be current. For infants and children through 16 years of age, refer to Chapter 4.3. A rubeola (measles) booster should be considered. Persons age 16 to 65 should receive a booster of tetanus and diphtheria every ten years. Healthy adults under age 65 do not require pneumococcal vaccine, but it is appropriate for those with chronic medical conditions. Influenza vaccine may be considered for those providing essential community services, health care workers, and those wishing to reduce the likelihood of becoming ill with influenza. Adults over 65 years of age are urged to obtain yearly influenza immunization, and to insure that their tetanus and diphtheria immunizations are current. Pneumococcal vaccination is also suggested for this age group.

No vaccinations are required to enter this country.

_____ **Country number 8.94** _____
India

INFECTIOUS DISEASE RISK

Malaria Risk

Malaria is present in all parts of this country, including urban areas. The risk exists all year. The malaria in this country is resistant to chloroquine. The CDC recommends the use of mefloquine (Lariam) as described in Chapter 6.31 for chemical prophylaxis.

Falciparum malaria represents 19% of malaria, therefore there is a risk of p. vivax malaria exposure. Consider the use of primaquine upon return home.

Diseases of Special Risk

In addition to the worldwide hazard of tetanus and the routine and any special immunizations recommended below, the traveler should be aware that risk of exposure to the following diseases exists in this country. This list is not all inclusive, but it is a caution concerning the more likely endemic disease risks.

Potential risk of dengue fever exists. The virus is present in this country at all times and may give rise to major outbreaks.

Meningococcal meningitis—There have been outbreaks in the New Delhi area. Consider vaccination for travel to this area.

Schistosomiasis may be found in this country. Avoid contact with contaminated fresh water lakes, ponds, or streams. Risk is present in a small circumscribed area along the Vishishti River in the District of Tatnagiri, State of Maharashtra (about 250 km south of bombay).

DISEASE RISK PROFILE

Disease	endemic	risk	hazard
Brucellosis		x	
Chikungunya Fever	x		
Cholera		x	
Dengue Fever	x		
Dracunculiasis/Guinea Worm		x	
Diarrheal Disease Risk		x	
Dysentery, Amoebic/Bacillary		x	
Echinococcosis		x	
Encephalitis, Japanese	x		
Filariasis		x	
Helminthic Diseases (see Chapter 6.21)		x	
Hemorrhagic Fevers	x		
Hepatitis, Viral		x	
Leishmaniasis			
Visceral			x

Disease	endemic	risk	hazard
Rabies		x	
Relapsing Fever		x	
Sandfly Fever			x
Trachoma		x	
Typhoid Fever		x	
Typhus		x	

Food/Water Safety

All tap water used for drinking, brushing teeth, and making ice cubes should be boiled prior to use. Insure that bottled water is uncapped in your presence. Milk should be boiled to insure safety. Powdered and evaporated milk are available and safe. Avoid butter and other dairy products. All meat, poultry and seafood must be well cooked and served while hot. Pork is best avoided. Vegetables should be well cooked and served hot. Salads and mayonnaise are best avoided. Fruits with intact skins should be peeled by you just prior to consumption. Avoid cold buffets, custards, and any frozen dessert. First class hotels and restaurants in Agra, Ahmadabad, Bangalore, Bombay, Calcutta, cochin, Darjeeling, Jaipur, madras, New Delhi, Simla, Srinagar, Udaipur, and Varanasi (Benaress) serve purified drinking water and reliable food. However, the hazard is left to your judgement.

VACCINATIONS

Cholera—Cholera is present in this country. Risk to western travelers is low. Immunization is not required or recommended for travel to this country due to its low effectiveness. Avoid uncooked foods and untreated water. Vaccination is advised only for persons living or working under inadequate sanitary conditions and for those with impaired defense mechanisms. Travelers leaving this country are required to possess a vaccination certificate on their departure to countries which still demand such a certificate.

Yellow fever—A vaccination certificate is required for travelers coming from infected areas and from or in transit through countries in the endemic yellow fever zone (see Chapter 6.63) but to include all portions of the Sudan— not just that area south of 15 degrees north latitude. A vaccination is required for children up to six months of age. CDC recommends vaccination for all travelers over 9 months of age, but see also The discussion in Chapter 6.63 concerning avoiding yellow fever innoculation in children younger than 9 months of age. Vaccination certificate is required for travelers who have been in or passed through an infected yellow fever area within six days prior to arrival.

Routine immunizations should be current. For infants and children through 16 years of age, refer to Chapter 4.3. A rubeola (measles) booster should be considered. Persons age 16 to 65 should receive a booster of tetanus and diphtheria every ten years. Healthy adults under age 65 do not require pneumococcal vaccine, but it is appropriate for those with chronic medical conditions. Influenza vaccine may be considered for those providing essential

community services, health care workers, and those wishing to reduce the likelihood of becoming ill with influenza. Adults over 65 years of age are urged to obtain yearly influenza immunization, and to insure that their tetanus and diphtheria immunizations are current. Pneumococcal vaccination is also suggested for this age group.

The vaccinations listed are recommended for the traveler's protection.
Poliomyelitis—A poliomyelitis booster is indicated for this country.
Viral Hepatitis A—Vaccination is recommended for all travelers for their protection.
Typhoid fever—Vaccination is recommended for all travelers for their protection.
Selective vaccinations—These apply only to specific groups of travelers or persons on specific working assignments:
Viral Hepatitis B—Because of the high rate of healthy carriers of hepatitis B in this country, vaccination is recommended for persons on working assignments in the health care field (dentists, physicians, nurses, laboratory technicians), or working in close contact with the local population (teachers, missionaries, Peace Corps), or persons foreseeing sexual relations with local inhabitants.
Japanese encephalitis—Vaccination is indicated for persons traveling extensively in rual areas or living and working near rice growing rural and suburban areas and other irrigated land, when exposure to the disease carrying mosquitoes is high. Children are especially susceptible to the infection. The disease is most prevalent in the north, northeast, and south. Period of transmission is all year, with the high risk group being children under 15 years of age. Time of greatest risk is June through October.
Plague—Vaccination is recommended only for persons who may be occupationally exposed to wild rodents (anthropologists, geologists, medical personnel, missionaries, etc). The standard vaccination course must be completed before entering the plague infested area. Geographical distribution of the area of risk for this country is in the north: Himachal Pradesh and the northern part of Uttar Pradesh; in the south: the northwestern part of Tamil Nadu.
Rabies—In this country, where rabies is a constant threat, a pre-exposure rabies vaccination is advised for persons planning an extended stay or on working assignments (naturalists, agricultural advisors, archeologists, geologists, etc.). Although this provides adequate initial protection, a person bitten by a potentially rabid animal would still require post exposure immunization (see Chapter 6.40). Children should be cautioned not to pet dogs, cats, or other mammals.

U.S. Foreign Service:
  Shanti Path,
  Chanakyapuri New Delhi, Telephone 69-0351

Lincoln House
78 Bhulabhai Desai Rd.
Bombay, Telephone 823-611/8

5/1 Ho Chi Minh
Sarani Calcutta, Telephone 44-3611/6

Mount Rd.
Madras, Telephone 83-041/6

Canadian High Commission/Embassy Office:
7/8 Shantipath
Chanakyapuri New Delhi, Telephone 60-8161
Durga Khote Productions
Malhotra House
Bombay, Telephone 265-219

TRAVEL ADVISORY

A U.S. Department of State Travel Advisory was in effect on 4 May 1990 when this book went to press. The entire text is included below. Travel advisories are subject to reissue, change, and cancellation at any time. Current travel advisory information is available by calling the U.S. Department of State Travel Advisory Hotline at (202) 647-5225. The current travel advisory status is also available from the Herchmer Database update system (see Chapter 2.8).

UNITED STATES DEPARTMENT OF STATE TRAVEL ADVISORY 16 APR 1990
INDIA—CAUTION SUMMARY: THE DEPARTMENT OF STATE ADVISES U.S. CITIZENS TRAVELING TO INDIA OF THE FOLLOWING CONDITIONS:
—TRAVEL TO JAMMU AND KASHMIR SHOULD BE DEFERRED.
—TRAVELERS TO PUNJAB AND CERTAIN OTHER AREAS SHOULD EXERCISE CAUTION.
—SPECIAL PERMITS ARE REQUIRED FOR MANY AREAS.
EACH OF THESE SITUATIONS IS DISCUSSED LATER IN THE ADVISORY.
IN ADDITION, DEMONSTRATIONS, RALLIES AND PROCESSIONS FREQUENTLY OCCUR THROUGH-OUT INDIA ON VERY SHORT NOTICE, MAKING IT PREFERABLE FOR AMERICANS TO AVOID PARTICULAR AREAS OF INDIA, OR PARTICULAR AREAS WITHIN AN INDIAN CITY, FOR A SPECIFIC TIME PERIOD. LOCAL SITUATIONS CAN CHANGE RAPIDLY. IT IS RECOMMENDED THAT TRAVELERS IN INDIA READ THE LOCAL ENGLISH LANGUAGE NEWSPAPERS AND CHECK WITH THE CONSULAR SECTION OF THE AMERICAN EM-

BASSY IN NEW DELHI OR WITH THE CONSULAR SECTION OF THE APPROPRIATE CONSULATE GENERAL (LOCATED IN BOMBAY, CALCUTTA AND MADRAS) TO FIND OUT IF THERE IS ANY SITUATION OF RISKS. END OF SUMMARY.

JAMMU AND KASHMIR: DUE TO INCREASED POLITICAL UNREST IN JAMMU AND KASHMIR, TRAVEL TO THE STATES SHOULD BE POSTPONED UNTIL FURTHER NOTICE. THE ONLY EX-CEPTION IS TRANVEL TO THE LEH DISTRICT OF LADAKH AS LONG AS SUCH TRAVEL IS NOT BY ROAD, BUT BY AIR ON NON-STOP FLIGHTS FROM AND TO NEW DELHI. IN ADDITION, REPORTS INDICATE THAT POSTERS, POSSIBLY FROM MILITANT GROUPS, HAVE APPEARED IN THE AREA WARNING THE PUBLIC NOT TO FLY INDIAN AIRLINES TO OR FROM THE CITY OF SRINAGAR. AMERICANS ARE THEREFORE ADVISED NOT TO TAKE FLIGHTS DESTINED TO OR ORIGINATING IN SRINAGAR, BECAUSE OF THE POSSIBILITY OF TERRORIST ACTS.

PUNJAB: FOREIGNERS ARE NOT REQUIRED TO OBTAIN A SPECIAL PERMIT TO VISIT THE PUNJAB. HOWEVER, BECAUSE OF SPORADIC INCIDNETS OF POLITICAL AND CRIMINAL VIOLENCE, INCLUDING OCCASIONAL BOMBINGS OF PUBLIC TRANSPORTATION, U.S. CITIZENS SHOULD EXERCISE SPECIAL CAUTION AND AVOID TRAVELING BY BUS OR TRAIN TO OR THROUGH THE STATE. THEY SHOULD CHECK WITH THE AMERICAN EMBASSY IN NEW DELHI PRIOR TO TRAVELING TO THE PUNJAB. TRAVELERS SHOULD BE AWARE THAT THE GOVERN-MENT OF INDIA HAS DECLARED THE DISTRICTS OF AMRITSAR, FEROZEPUR, AND GURDASPUR TO BE "DISTURBED" AREAS:. THE MAJORITY OF MILITANT ACTS IN PUNJAB TAKE PLACE IN THESE DISTRICTS. SPECIAL LAWS ARE IN EFFECT CONCERNING UNLAWFUL ASSEMBLY AND DANGERS TO PUBLIC ORDER. TRAVELERS VISITING THESE AREAS SHOULD REPORT TO THE SUPERINTENDENT OF POLICE OF THE PARTICULAR DISTRICT.

RESTRICTED/PROTECTED AREAS WHICH REQUIRE SPECIAL GOVERNMENT OF INDIA PERMISSION TO VISIT ARE: THE STATES OF ARUNACHAL PRADESH, NAGALAND, MANIPUR, SIKKIM AND MIZORAN; PARTS OF KULU DISTRICT, KANNAUR DISTRICT AND LAHAUL AND SPITI DIS-TRICTS OF HIMACHAL PRADESH; PARTS OF THE DISTRICTS OF TEHRI GARHWAL, GARHWAL, ALMORA, PITHORAGARH, CHAMOLI AND UTTARKASHI OF UTTAR PRADESH; THE AREA WEST OF NATIONAL HIGHWAY NO. 15 RUNNING FROM GANGANGAR TO SANCHAR IN RAJASTHAN; THE NORTHERN AND WESTERN PARTS OF JAMMU AND KASHMIR; AS WELL AS THE STATES OF ASSAM, MEGHALAYA, TRIPURA AND THE UNION TERRITORY OF ANDAMAN AND NICOBAR ISLANDS; DISTRICTS OF COOCH BEHAR, JALPAIGURI, MALDA AND WEST DINAJPUR IN WEST BEN-

GAL; AND THE UNION TERRITORY OF THE LACCADIVE, MINICOY AND AMINDIVI ISLANDS. DARJEELING: NO PERMIT IS REQUIRED TO VISIT DARJEELING FOR TOURISM UP TO 15 DAYS PROVIDED TRAVELERS HAVE ROUND-TRIP AIR TICKETS TO BAGDOGRA.

INDIAN/PAKISTAN BORDER: THE ONLY OFFICIAL BORDER CROSSING POINT FOR FOREIGNERS IS AT ATTARA, PUNJAB/WAHAH, PAKISTAN. PERSONS TRAVELING BY LAND BETWEEN INDIA AND PAKISTAN MAY TRAVEL BETWEEN 0930 AND 1700 HOURS. A PAKISTANI VISA IS REQUIRED.

MOUNTAIN CLIMBING: BOTH INDIA AND PAKISTAN LAY CLAIM TO AN AREA OF THE KARA-KORAM MOUNTAIN RANGE WHICH INCLUDES THE SIACHEN GLACIER. THE TWO COUNTRIES HAVE ESTABLISHED MILITARY OUTPOSTS IN THE REGION AND SINCE MAY 1984 BOTH SIDES HAVE BEEN INVOLVED IN ARMED CLASHES THERE. BECAUSE OF THIS SITUATION, THE DEPT. OF STATE WARNS AMERICANS AGAINST TRAVELING TO OR CLIMBING PEAKS ANYWHERE IN THE DISPUTED AREA OF THE MOUNTAINS IN THE EAST KARAKORAM RANGE AND ESPECIALLY AGAINST VENTURING ON OR NEAR THE SIACHEN GLACIER. CLIMBERS SHOULD AVOID THE FOLLOWING PEAKS WHICH LIE WITHIN THE DISPUTED AREA CLAIMED BY BOTH INDIA AND PAKISTAN: RIMO PEAK, APSARAS AS-I, II AND III, TEHAM KANGRI-I, II AND III, SINGHI KANGRI, GHAINT I AND II, INDRA COR, AND SIA KANGRI.

VACCINATIONS: PLEASE CHECK WITH YOUR LOCAL PUBLIC HEALTH SERVICE OFFICE FOR RECOMMENDED VACCINATIONS. IN ADDITION, PLEASE NOTE THAT TRAVELERS ARRIVING FROM COUNTRIES WHERE OUTBREAKS OF YELLOW FEVER HAVE OCCURRED WILL BE REQUIRED TO FURNISH A CERTIFICATE FOR YELLOW FEVER VACCINATION. TRAVELERS SHOULD ALSO BE AWARE OF THE POSSIBILITY OF YEARLY OUTBREAKS OF CHOLERA AND GASTROENTERITIS WHICH OCCUR DURING SUMMER MONSOON MONTHS (JULY AND AUGUST), MOSTLY IN THE POORER AREAS OF DELHI. THE BEST PROTECTION INCLUDES EATING ONLY AT BETTER QUALITY RESTAURANTS OR HOTELS, DRINKING ONLY BOILED OR BOTTLED MINERAL WATER AND AVOIDING ICE. EATING UNTREATED FRUITS AND VEGETABLES AND COOKED FOODS SOLD BY STREET VENDORS CAN BE RISKY.

REGISTRATION: AMERICANS RESIDENT OR VISITING IN INDIA ARE ENCOURAGED TO REGIS-TER WITH THE AMERICAN EMBASSY IN NEW DELHI OR WITH THE AMERICAN CONSULATE GENERAL IN BOMBAY, CALCUTTA OR MADRAS.

EXPIRATION: APRIL 4, 1991

Country number 8.95
Indonesia

INFECTIOUS DISEASE RISK

Malaria Risk

Malaria exists in the rural areas only, and below 1200 meters. Risk is all year. No risk in Jakarta, Surabaya, and Bali. There may be urban exposure in Irian Jaya. The malaria in this country is resistant to chloroquine. The CDC recommends the use of mefloquine (Lariam) as described in Chapter 6.31 for chemical prophylaxis.

Falciparum malaria represents 40% of malaria, therefore there is a risk of p. vivax malaria exposure. Consider the use of primaquine upon return home.

Diseases of Special Risk

In addition to the worldwide hazard of tetanus and the routine and any special immunizations recommended below, the traveler should be aware that risk of exposure to the following diseases exists in this country. This list is not all inclusive, but it is a caution concerning the more likely endemic disease risks.

Potential risk of dengue fever exists. The virus is present in this country at all times and may give rise to major outbreaks.

Schistosomiasis may be found in this country. Avoid contact with contaminated fresh water lakes, ponds, or streams. Two areas of infection are present on the island of Sulawesi (Celebes): In the Lindu valley, in the central Sulawesi, the infection is localized around Lake Lindu in the villages of Anca, Tomado, Langko, and Puroo. A recently discovered area of infection is present in Napu valley, about 50 kn southeast of Lindu valley, affecting the villages of Wuasa, Maholo, Winowangsa, Altitupu, and Watumaeta.

Amoebic and bacillary dysentery, diarrheal diseases, helminthic diseases, and viral hepatitis associated with water and food supplies are particularly common in this country.

DISEASE RISK PROFILE

Disease	endemic	risk	hazard
Chikungunya Fever	x		
Encephalitis, Japanese	x		
Fasciolopsiasis	x		
Filariasis			x
Melioidosis		x	
Rabies		x	
Trachoma	x		
Typhus, Scrub	x		

Food/Water Safety

All tap water used for drinking, brushing teeth, and making ice cubes should be boiled prior to use. Insure that bottled water is uncapped in your presence. Milk should be boiled to insure safety. Powdered and evaporated milk are available and safe. Avoid butter and other dairy products. All meat, poultry and seafood must be well cooked and served while hot. Pork is best avoided. Vegetables should be well cooked and served hot. Salads and mayonnaise are best avoided. Fruits with intact skins should be peeled by you just prior to consumption. Avoid cold buffets, custards, and any frozen dessert. First class hotels and restaurants in Denpasar, Jakarta, Surabaya, and Yogyakarta serve purified drinking water and reliable food. However, the hazard is left to your judgement.

VACCINATIONS

Yellow fever—A vaccination certificate is required for travelers coming from infected areas and from or in transit through countries in the endemic yellow fever zone, see Chapter 6.63. A vaccination is required for children of all ages. Children under nine months of age should generally not be vaccinated due to health considerations. Please refer to the discussion on page III on avoiding yellow fever vaccination in this age group.

Routine immunizations should be current. For infants and children through 16 years of age, refer to Chapter 4.3. A rubeola (measles) booster should be considered. Persons age 16 to 65 should receive a booster of tetanus and diphtheria every ten years. Healthy adults under age 65 do not require pneumococcal vaccine, but it is appropriate for those with chronic medical conditions. Influenza vaccine may be considered for those providing essential community services, health care workers, and those wishing to reduce the likelihood of becoming ill with influenza. Adults over 65 years of age are urged to obtain yearly influenza immunization, and to insure that their tetanus and diphtheria immunizations are current. Pneumococcal vaccination is also suggested for this age group.

The vaccinations listed are recommended for the traveler's protection.

Poliomyelitis—A poliomyelitis booster is indicated for this country.

Cholera—Cholera is present in this country. Risk to western travelers is low. Immunization is not required or recommended for travel to this country due to its low effectiveness. Avoid uncooked foods and untreated water. Vaccination is advised only for persons living or working under inadequate sanitary conditions and for those with impaired defense mechanisms.

Viral Hepatitis A—Vaccination is recommended for all travelers for their protection.

Typhoid fever—Vaccination is recommended for all travelers for their protection.

Selective vaccinations—These apply only to specific groups of travelers or persons on specific working assignments:

Viral Hepatitis B—Because of the high rate of healthy carriers of hepatitis B in this country, vaccination is recommended for persons on working assignments in the health care field (dentists, physicians, nurses, laboratory technicians), or working in close contact with the local population (teachers, missionaries, Peace Corps), or persons foreseeing sexual relations with local inhabitants.

Japanese encephalitis—Vaccination is indicated for persons traveling extensively in rual areas or living and working near rice growing rural and suburban areas and other irrigated land, when exposure to the disease carrying mosquitoes is high. Children are especially susceptible to the infection. Sporadic cases are reported throughout the country all year long (highest instance in June through October), with the highest risk being in children younger than 15 years of age.

Plague—Vaccination is recommended only for persons who may be occupationally exposed to wild rodents (anthropologists, geologists, medical personnel, missionaries, etc). The standard vaccination course must be completed before entering the plague infested area. Geographical distribution of the area of risk for this country is on the island of Java south of Surakarta.

Rabies—In this country, where rabies is a constant threat, a pre-exposure rabies vaccination is advised for persons planning an extended stay or on working assignments (naturalists, agricultural advisors, archeologists, geologists, etc.). Although this provides adequate initial protection, a person bitten by a potentially rabid animal would still require post exposure immunization (see Chapter 6.40). Children should be cautioned not to pet dogs, cats, or other mammals.

U.S. Foreign Service:
Medan Merdeka Selatan 5
Jakarta, Telephone 340-001/9

Jalan Imam Bonjol 13
Medan, Telephone 322-200

Jalan Raya Dr. Sutomo 33
Surabaya, Telephone 69287/8

Canadian High Commission/Embassy Office:
5th Floor
WISMA Metropolitan
Jalan Jendral Sudirman
Jakarta, Telephone 584-031/9

_____ **Country number 8.96** _____
Islamic Republic of Iran

INFECTIOUS DISEASE RISK

Malaria Risk

Malaria is present in rural areas below 1500 meters from March through November in Sistan-Baluchestan, Hormozgan, southern part of Fars, Kohgiluyeh-Boyar, Lorestan Chahar Mahal-Bakhtiani and the north of Khuzestan. The malaria in this country is resistant to chloroquine. The CDC recommends the use of mefloquine (Lariam) as described in Chapter 6.31 for chemical prophylaxis.

Falciparum malaria represents 21% of malaria, therefore there is a risk of p. vivax malaria exposure. Consider the use of primaquine upon return home.

Diseases of Special Risk

In addition to the worldwide hazard of tetanus and the routine and any special immunizations recommended below, the traveler should be aware that risk of exposure to the following diseases exists in this country. This list is not all inclusive, but it is a caution concerning the more likely endemic disease risks.

Schistosomiasis may be found in this country. Avoid contact with contaminated fresh water lakes, ponds, or streams. . Risk exists only in the plains in the southwestern part of the country bordering Iraq. The area extends from the regions of Dezful and Sar Dasht to Khorramshar and is limited in the east by the Zagros Mountains (Khuzistan Province).

Amoebic and bacillary dysentery, diarrheal diseases, giardiasis, helminthic diseases, and viral hepatitis associated with water and food supplies are particularly common in this country.

DISEASE RISK PROFILE

Disease	endemic	risk	hazard
Brucellosis		x	
Echinococcosis		x	
Leishmaniasis		x	
Relapsing Fever		x	
Sandfly Fever			x
Trachoma		x	
Typhoid Fever		x	
Typhus		x	

Food/Water Safety

All tap water used for drinking, brushing teeth, and making ice cubes should be boiled prior to use. Insure that bottled water is uncapped in your

presence. Milk should be boiled to insure safety. Powdered and evaporated milk are available and safe. Avoid butter and other dairy products. All meat, poultry and seafood must be well cooked and served while hot. Pork is best avoided. Vegetables should be well cooked and served hot. Salads and mayonnaise are best avoided. Fruits with intact skins should be peeled by you just prior to consumption. Avoid cold buffets, custards, and any frozen dessert. First class hotels and restaurants in Abadan, Esfahan, Mashhad (Meshed), Shiraz, and Tehran serve purified drinking water and reliable food. However, the hazard is left to your judgement.

VACCINATIONS

Yellow fever—A vaccination certificate is required for travelers coming from infected areas and from or in transit through countries in the endemic yellow fever zone, see Chapter 6.63. A vaccination certificate is required for children over one year of age.

Routine immunizations should be current. For infants and children through 16 years of age, refer to Chapter 4.3. A rubeola (measles) booster should be considered. Persons age 16 to 65 should receive a booster of tetanus and diphtheria every ten years. Healthy adults under age 65 do not require pneumococcal vaccine, but it is appropriate for those with chronic medical conditions. Influenza vaccine may be considered for those providing essential community services, health care workers, and those wishing to reduce the likelihood of becoming ill with influenza. Adults over 65 years of age are urged to obtain yearly influenza immunization and to insure that their tetanus and diphtheria immunizations are current. Pneumococcal vaccination is also suggested for this age group.

The vaccinations listed are recommended for the traveler's protection.
Poliomyelitis—A poliomyelitis booster is indicated for this country.
Cholera—Cholera is present in this country. Risk to western travelers is low. Immunization is not required or recommended for travel to this country due to its low effectiveness. Avoid uncooked foods and untreated water. Vaccination is advised only for persons living or working under inadequate sanitary conditions and for those with impaired defense mechanisms.
Viral Hepatitis A—Vaccination is recommended for all travelers for their protection.
Typhoid fever—Vaccination is recommended for all travelers for their protection.

Selective vaccinations—These apply only to specific groups of travelers or persons on specific working assignments:
Viral Hepatitis B—Because of the high rate of healthy carriers of hepatitis B in this country, vaccination is recommended for persons on working assignments in the health care field (dentists, physicians, nurses, laboratory techni-

cians), or working in close contact with the local population (teachers, missionaries, Peace Corps), or persons foreseeing sexual relations with local inhabitants.

Plague—Vaccination is recommended only for persons who may be occupationally exposed to wild rodents (anthropologists, geologists, medical personnel, missionaries, etc). The standard vaccination course must be completed before entering the plague infested area. Geographical distribution of risk for this country are present in the northwest portion of the country in the areas around Manjil where the Talish Mountains meet the Elburz Mountains.

Rabies—In this country, where rabies is a constant threat, a pre-exposure rabies vaccination is advised for persons planning an extended stay or on working assignments (naturalists, agricultural advisors, archeologists, geologists, etc.). Although this provides adequate initial protection, a person bitten by a potentially rabid animal would still require post exposure immunization (see Chapter 6.40). Children should be cautioned not to pet dogs, cats, or other mammals.

Canadian High Commission/Embassy Office:
57 Darya-e-Noor Ave.
Takht-e-Tavoos, Telephone 623548/49

TRAVEL ADVISORY
A U.S. Department of State Travel Advisory was in effect on 4 May 1990 when this book went to press. The entire text is included below. Travel advisories are subject to reissue, change, and cancellation at any time. Current travel advisory information is available by calling the U.S. Department of State Travel Advisory Hotline at (202) 647-5225. The current travel advisory status is also available from the Herchmer Database update system (see Chapter 2.8).

9FB DN37 1-1 1LA71 1 01/18/89 20:10 SECSTATE WSH TRAVEL ADVISORY RECIPIENTS .
SUBJECT: TRAVEL ADVISORY—IRAN—WARNING
1. THE DEPARTMENT OF STATE CONTINUES STRONGLY TO ADVISE U.S. CITIZENS TO AVOID TRAVEL TO IRAN. WITH THE ADVENT OF A CEASEFIRE BETWEEN IRAN AND IRAQ, WARTIME CONDITIONS NO LONGER PREVAIL IN IRAN. HOWEVER, THERE IS CONTINUING TENSION BETWEEN IRAN AND IRAQ. TRAVEL TO IRAN CONTINUES TO BE DANGEROUS BECAUSE OF THE VIRULENT ANTI-AMERICA POLICIES OF THE IRANIAN GOVERNMENT. IN THE PAST, AMERICAN CITIZENS AND OTHER FOREIGN NATIONALS HAVE BEEN ARBITRARILY ARRESTED, DETAINED OR HARASSED BY IRANIAN AUTHORITIES. MOREOVER, IRAN CONTINUES TO SUPPORT INTERNATIONAL TERRORISM DIRECTED AGAINST U.S. CITIZENS.
2. THE U.S. GOVERNMENT DOES NOT MAINTAIN DIPLOMATIC OR

CONSULAR RELATIONS WITH IRAN. AMERICAN INTERESTS IN
IRAN ARE REPRESENTED BY THE SWISS GOVERNEMENT ACTING
THROUGH ITS EMBASSY IN TEHRAN. SWISS OFFICIALS, HOW-
EVER, HAVE OFTEN BEEN PREVENTED BY IRANIAN OFFICIALS
FROM PROVIDING EVEN MINIMAL PROTECTIVE SERVICES TO U.S.
CITIZENS.
3. THIS REPLACES TRAVEL ADVISORY DATED OCT. 19, 1987 CON-
TAINED IN STATE 325558.
4. EXPIRATION DATE: INDEFINITE. SHULTZ DEPT OF STATE
WASHDC 016148 / L1259

_____ Country number 8.97 _____
Iraq

INFECTIOUS DISEASE RISK

Malaria Risk
    Malaria is found below 1500 meters in the northern part of the country,
including urban areas, in the Provinces of Duhok, Erbil, Kirkuk, Ninawa, and
Sulaimaniya. The CDC recommends a weekly chloroquine dose for malaria
prophylaxis (see Chapter 6.31).
    Falciparum malaria represents < 1% of malaria, therefore there is a sig-
nificant risk of p. vivax malaria exposure. Consider the use of primaquine upon
return home.

Diseases of Special Risk
    In addition to the worldwide hazard of tetanus and the routine and any
special immunizations recommended below, the traveler should be aware that
risk of exposure to the following diseases exists in this country. This list is not
all inclusive, but it is a caution concerning the more likely endemic disease
risks.
    Schistosomiasis may be found in this country. Avoid contact with contami-
nated fresh water lakes, ponds, or streams. The mountainous regions of the
northeastern part of the country bordering Iran are not infected. Endemic areas
are the river systems of the Tigris and Euphrates, their tributaries and irrigation
canals including all urban areas (Baghdad and Al Basrah).

DISEASE RISK PROFILE

Disease	endemic	risk	hazard
Brucellosis			x
Cholera	x		
Dracunculiasis/Guinea Worm	x		
Diarrheal Disease Risk		x	

Disease	endemic	risk	hazard
Echinococcosis	x		
Hepatitis, Viral		x	
Hemorrhagic Fever (Crimean-Congo)	x		
Leishmaniasis			
Cutaneous	x		
Visceral	x		
Rabies	x		
Relapsing Fever	x		
Tapeworms	x		
Trachoma	x		
Typhoid Fever	x		
Typhus, Endemic Flea-Borne	x		
Typhus, Scrub	x		

Food/Water Safety

All tap water used for drinking, brushing teeth, and making ice cubes should be boiled prior to use. Insure that bottled water is uncapped in your presence. Milk should be boiled to insure safety. Powdered and evaporated milk are available and safe. Avoid butter and other dairy products. All meat, poultry and seafood must be well cooked and served while hot. Pork is best avoided. Vegetables should be well cooked and served hot. Salads and mayonnaise are best avoided. Fruits with intact skins should be peeled by you just prior to consumption. Avoid cold buffets, custards, and any frozen dessert. First class hotels and restaurants in Baghdad serve purified drinking water and reliable food. However, the hazard is left to your judgement.

VACCINATIONS

Yellow fever—A vaccination certificate is required for all travelers coming from infected areas and from or in transit through countries with active infection.

Routine immunizations should be current. For infants and children through 16 years of age, refer to Chapter 4.3. A rubeola (measles) booster should be considered. Persons age 16 to 65 should receive a booster of tetanus and diphtheria every ten years. Healthy adults under age 65 do not require pneumococcal vaccine, but it is appropriate for those with chronic medical conditions. Influenza vaccine may be considered for those providing essential community services, health care workers, and those wishing to reduce the likelihood of becoming ill with influenza. Adults over 65 years of age are urged to obtain yearly influenza immunization and to insure that their tetanus and diphtheria immunizations are current. Pneumococcal vaccination is also suggested for this age group.

The vaccinations listed are recommended for the traveler's protection.
Poliomyelitis—A poliomyelitis booster is indicated for this country.
Viral Hepatitis A—Vaccination is recommended for all travelers for their protection.

Typhoid fever—Vaccination is recommended for all travelers for their protection.

Selective vaccinations—These apply only to specific groups of travelers or persons on specific working assignments:
Viral Hepatitis B—Because of the high rate of healthy carriers of hepatitis B in this country, vaccination is recommended for persons on working assignments in the health care field (dentists, physicians, nurses, laboratory technicians), or working in close contact with the local population (teachers, missionaries, Peace Corps), or persons foreseeing sexual relations with local inhabitants.
Plague—Vaccination is recommended only for persons who may be occupationally exposed to wild rodents (anthropologists, geologists, medical personnel, missionaries, etc). The standard vaccination course must be completed before entering the plague infested area. Known areas of risk are present in the eastern part of the country, with a major focus of activity around Khanaqin.
Rabies—In this country, where rabies is a constant threat, a pre-exposure rabies vaccination is advised for persons planning an extended stay or on working assignments (naturalists, agricultural advisors, archeologists, geologists, etc.). Although this provides adequate initial protection, a person bitten by a potentially rabid animal would still require post exposure immunization (see Chapter 6.40). Children should be cautioned not to pet dogs, cats, or other mammals.

U.S. Foreign Service Representative:
Belgian Embassy
Opposite Foreign Ministry Club
Masbah Quarter
Baghdad, Telephone 719-6138/9
(workweek: Sunday-Thursday)

Canadian Embassy Addresses:
47/1/7 Al Mansour
Baghdad, Telephone 542-1459/1932/1933

TRAVEL ADVISORY
A U.S. Department of State Travel Advisory was in effect on 4 May 1990 when this book went to press. The entire text is included below. Travel advisories are subject to reissue, change, and cancellation at any time. Current travel advisory information is available by calling the U.S. Department of State Travel Advisory Hotline at (202) 647-5225. The current travel advisory status is also available from the Herchmer Database update system (see Chapter 2.8).

SECSTATE WSH
JANUARY 4, 1990
IRAQ—CAUTION
THE DEPARTMENT OF STATE ADVISES AMERICAN CITZENS THAT,
WITH THE ADVENT OF THE CEASEFIRE BETWEEN IRAN AND IRAQ,
WARTIME CONDITIONS NO LONGER PREVAIL IN IRAQ.
NONETHELESS, BECAUSE OF THE CONTINUING TENSION BE-
TWEEN IRAN AND IRAQ, TRAVEL IS NOT RECOMMENDED TO AR-
EAS NORTH AND EAST OF MOSUL AND ALONG BORDER AREAS
WITH IRAN. VISITORS TO IRAQ SHOULD ALSO BE ADVISED THAT
BANS ON TRAVEL TO THE NORTH OF MOSUL ARE PERIODICALLY
IMPOSED.
ALL U.S. CITIZENS ARE STRONGLY URGED TO REGISTER WITH
THE U.S. EMBASSY AFTER ARRIVAL IN IRAQ. THE EMBASSY IS LO-
CATED ACROSS FROM THE FOREIGN MINISTRY CLUB IN THE MAS-
BAH QUARTER OF BAGHDAD. THE TELEPHONE NUMBERS ARE
719-6138 AND 719-6139. THE TELEX NUMBER IS 212287 USINT IK.
AN ALTERNATE TELEX IS THE COMMERICAL SECTION TELEX,
NUMBER 213966 USFCS IK.
EXPIRATION : DECEMBER 31, 1990

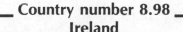

Country number 8.98
Ireland

INFECTIOUS DISEASE RISK

Malaria Risk
There is no malaria risk in this country.

Diseases of Special Risk

Food/Water Safety
Local water is considered safe without further treatment. Milk is pasteurized and safe to drink. Butter, cheese, yogurt and ice-cream are safe. Local
meat, poultry, seafood, vegetables, and fruits are safe to eat.

VACCINATIONS

Routine immunizations should be current. For infants and children
through 16 years of age, refer to Chapter 4.3. A rubeola (measles) booster
should be considered. Persons age 16 to 65 should receive a booster of tetanus
and diphtheria every ten years. Healthy adults under age 65 do not require
pneumococcal vaccine, but it is appropriate for those with chronic medical
conditions. Influenza vaccine may be considered for those providing essential

community services, health care workers, and those wishing to reduce the likelihood of becoming ill with influenza. Adults over 65 years of age are urged to obtain yearly influenza immunization and to insure that their tetanus and diphtheria immunizations are current. Pneumococcal vaccination is also suggested for this age group.

No vaccinations are required to enter this country.

U.S. Foreign Service:
42 Elgin Rd; Ballsbridge
Dublin, Telephone 688-777

Canadian High Commission/Embassy Office:
65 St. Stephen's Green
Dublin, Telephone 781-988

Country number 8.99
Isle of Man (UK)

INFECTIOUS DISEASE RISK

Malaria Risk
There is no malaria risk in this country.

Diseases of Special Risk

Food/Water Safety
Local water is considered safe without further treatment. Milk is pasteurized and safe to drink. Butter, cheese, yogurt and ice-cream are safe. Local meat, poultry, seafood, vegetables, and fruits are safe to eat.

VACCINATIONS
Routine immunizations should be current. For infants and children through 16 years of age, refer to Chapter 4.3. A rubeola (measles) booster should be considered. Persons age 16 to 65 should receive a booster of tetanus and diphtheria every ten years. Healthy adults under age 65 do not require pneumococcal vaccine, but it is appropriate for those with chronic medical conditions. Influenza vaccine may be considered for those providing essential community services, health care workers, and those wishing to reduce the likelihood of becoming ill with influenza. Adults over 65 years of age are urged to obtain yearly influenza immunization and to insure that their tetanus and diphtheria immunizations are current. Pneumococcal vaccination is also suggested for this age group.

No vaccinations are required to enter this country.

_____ **Country number 8.100** _____
Israel

INFECTIOUS DISEASE RISK

Malaria Risk
There is no malaria risk in this country.

Diseases of Special Risk
In addition to the worldwide hazard of tetanus and the routine and any special immunizations recommended below, the traveler should be aware that risk of exposure to the following diseases exists in this country. This list is not all inclusive, but it is a caution concerning the more likely endemic disease risks.

A recent polio epidemic makes it advisable for eveyone traveling to Israel to be current on polio immunization.

DISEASE RISK PROFILE

Disease	endemic	risk	hazard
Brucellosis			x
Cholera	x		
Diarrheal Diseases		x	
Dracunculiasis/Guinea Worm	x		
Echinococcosis	x		
Hepatitis, Viral		x	
Leishmaniasis			
Cutaneous		x	
Visceral		x	
Rabies	x		
Relapsing Fever	x		
Tapeworms	x		
Trachoma	x		
Typhoid Fever		x	
Typhus, Endemic Flea-Borne	x		
Typhus, Scrub	x		

Food/Water Safety
Water is probably safe, but due to local variations in bacterial counts, using bottled water for the first few weeks will help the traveler adjust and decrease the chance of traveler's diarrhea. There has been a steady increase in infectious hepatitis in recent years. Milk is pasteurized and safe to drink. Butter, cheese, yogurt and ice-cream are generally safe. Local meat, poultry, seafood, vegetables, and fruits are safe to eat with caution as to the source.

VACCINATIONS

Routine immunizations should be current. For infants and children through 16 years of age, refer to Chapter 4.3. A rubeola (measles) booster should be considered. Persons age 16 to 65 should receive a booster of tetanus and diphtheria every ten years. Healthy adults under age 65 do not require pneumococcal vaccine, but it is appropriate for those with chronic medical conditions. Influenza vaccine may be considered for those providing essential community services, health care workers, and those wishing to reduce the likelihood of becoming ill with influenza. Adults over 65 years of age are urged to obtain yearly influenza immunization and to insure that their tetanus and diphtheria immunizations are current. Pneumococcal vaccination is also suggested for this age group.

No vaccinations are required to enter this country.

U.S. Foreign Service:
71 Hayarkon St.
Tel Aviv, Telephone (03) 654338

Canadian High Commission/Embassy Office:
220 Hayarkon St.
Tel Aviv, Telephone (03) 228122/3/4/5/6

TRAVEL ADVISORY

A U.S. Department of State Travel Advisory was in effect on 4 May 1990 when this book went to press. The entire text is included below. Travel advisories are subject to reissue, change, and cancellation at any time. Current travel advisory information is available by calling the U.S. Department of State Travel Advisory Hotline at (202) 647-5225. The current travel advisory status is also available from the Herchmer Database update system (see Chapter 2.8).

UNITED STATES DEPARTMENT OF STATE TRAVEL ADVISORY 13 SEP 1989
WEST BANK AND GAZA (JERUSALEM)—WARNING
DUE TO CONTINUING DISTURBANCES IN THE WEST BANK AND GAZA, THE DEPARTMENT OF STATE ADVISES ALL U.S. CITIZENS TO AVOID TRAVEL TO THESE AREAS UNTIL FURTHER NOTICE. AMERICANS RESIDING IN THESE AREAS SHOULD EXERCISE PARTICULAR CAUTION. U.S. CITIZENS WHO MUST TRAVEL TO THE WEST BANK SHOULD AVOID ALL TOWN CENTERS UNTIL FURTHER NOTICE DUE TO INCREASED THREATS OF VIOLENCE AGAINST ALL FOREIGNERS. IF TRAVEL TO THE WEST BANK IS UNAVOIDABLE, TRAVELERS SHOULD CONSULT WITH THE CONSULATE GENERAL IN JERUSALEM, AND IN THE CASE OF TRAVEL TO GAZA, WITH THE U.S. EMBASSY IN TEL AVIV.

ALTHOUGH THE SITUATION IN EAST JERUSALEM IS SUBJECT TO CHANGE, TOURISTS OF ALL NATIONS CONTINUE TO VISIT THERE (INCLUDING THE OLD CITY) WITHOUT SIGNIFICANT PROBLEMS. AMERICANS WHO DESIRE CURRENT INFORMATION SHOULD CONTACT THE CONSULATE GENERAL IN JERUSALEM BEFORE ENTERING THIS AREA.

UNDER ALL CIRCUMSTANCES, AMERICANS SHOULD AVOID DEMONSTRATIONS AND OTHER SITUATIONS THAT HAVE THE POTENTIAL TO LEAD TO VIOLENCE. AMERICAN TRAVELERS SHOULD CARRY THEIR U.S. PASSPORTS AT ALL TIMES.

ANY AMERICAN WHO WISHES FURTHER INFORMATION ON THE CURRENT SECURITY SITUATION SHOULD CONSULT THE AMERICAN EMBASSY IN TEL AVIV (TELEPHONE NUMBER 654-338) OR THE AMERICAN CONSULATE GENERAL IN JERUSALEM (TELEPHONE NUMBER 234-271).

EXPIRATION DATE: INDEFINITE

Country number 8.101
Italy

INFECTIOUS DISEASE RISK

Malaria Risk

There is no malaria risk in this country.

Diseases of Special Risk

In addition to the worldwide hazard of tetanus and the routine and any special immunizations recommended below, the traveler should be aware that risk of exposure to the following diseases exists in this country. This list is not all inclusive, but it is a caution concerning the more likely endemic disease risks.

DISEASE RISK PROFILE

Disease	endemic	risk	hazard
Brucellosis	x		
Diarrheal Diseases	x		
Dysentery, Bacillary	x		
Echinococcosis	x		
Hepatitis, Viral	x		
Leishmaniasis			
Cutaneous	x		
Visceral	x		
Sandfly Fever	x		
Typhoid Fever	x		

Disease	endemic	risk	hazard
Typhus, Endemic Flea-Borne	x		
Typhus, Scrub	x		
West Nile Fever	x		

Food/Water Safety

Water is probably safe, but due to local variations in bacterial counts, using bottled water for the first few weeks will help the traveler adjust and decrease the chance of traveler's diarrhea. This problem is more common in the summer months in the southern portion of the country. Water in the Adige River in northeastern Italy is contaminated with toxic chemicals and should not be drunk. Milk is pasteurized and safe to drink. Butter, cheese, yogurt and ice-cream are safe. Local meat, poultry, seafood, vegetables, and fruits are safe to eat.

VACCINATIONS

Routine immunizations should be current. For infants and children through 16 years of age, refer to Chapter 4.3. A rubeola (measles) booster should be considered. Persons age 16 to 65 should receive a booster of tetanus and diphtheria every ten years. Healthy adults under age 65 do not require pneumococcal vaccine, but it is appropriate for those with chronic medical conditions. Influenza vaccine may be considered for those providing essential community services, health care workers, and those wishing to reduce the likelihood of becoming ill with influenza. Adults over 65 years of age are urged to obtain yearly influenza immunization and to insure that their tetanus and diphtheria immunizations are current. Pneumococcal vaccination is also suggested for this age group.

No vaccinations are required to enter this country.

The vaccinations listed are recommended for the traveler's protection.

Hepatitis A is found with increasing risk in this country, therefore gamma globulin injection is recommended.

U.S. Foreign Service:

Via Veneto 119/A
Rome, telephone (010)282-741 thru 5

Piazza Republica 32
Milan, Telephone (02) 652-841 thru 5

Piazza della Repubblica
Naples, Telephone (081) 660966

Via Baccarini 1
Palermo, Telephone (091) 291532-35

Lungarmo Amerigo Vespucci 38
Florence, Telephone (055) 298-276

Via Roma 9
4th Fl.
Trieste, Telephone (040) 68728/29

Via Pomba 23
2nd Fl.
Turin, Telephone (11) 517-4378

Canadian High Commission/Embassy Office:
Via G.B. de Rossi 27
Rome, Telephone (010) 855-341/342/343

Via Vittor Pisani 19
Milan, Telephone (02) 657-0451/2/3/4/5

_____ Country number 8.102 _____
Ivory Coast
Cote D' Ivoire

INFECTIOUS DISEASE RISK

Malaria Risk

Malaria is present in this entire country, all year, to include urban areas. The malaria in this country is resistant to chloroquine. The CDC recommends the use of mefloquine (Lariam) as described in Chapter 6.31 for chemical prophylaxis.

Falciparum malaria represents 88% of malaria, therefore there is a slight risk of p. vivax malaria exposure. Consider use of Primaquine upon return home.

Diseases of Special Risk

In addition to the worldwide hazard of tetanus and the routine and any special immunizations recommended below, the traveler should be aware that risk of exposure to the following diseases exists in this country. This list is not all inclusive, but it is a caution concerning the more likely endemic disease risks.

This country must be considered receptive to dengue fever. Intermittent epidemics in the past make renewed activity or reintroduction of the virus possible.

Schistosomiasis may be found in this country. Avoid contact with contaminated fresh water lakes, ponds, or streams.

Meningococcal meningitis may occur in the Sahelian savannah areas during the dry season from December until June.

DISEASE RISK PROFILE

Disease	endemic	risk	hazard
Cholera	x		
Dracunculiasis/Guinea Worm	x		
Diarrheal Disease Risk			x
Dysentery, Amoebic/Bacillary			x
Echinococcosis		x	
Filariasis			x
Giardiasis			x
Helminthic Diseases (see Chapter 6.21)			x
Hepatitis, Viral			x
Leishmaniasis			
Cutaneous	x		
Visceral	x		
Loiasis			x
Onchocerciasis			x
Rabies	x		
Relapsing Fever	x		
Trachoma			x
Trypanosomiasis, African Sleeping Sickness	x		
Tungiasis			x
Typhoid Fever			x
Typhus, Endemic Flea-Borne	x		
Typhus, Epidemic Louse-Borne	x		
Typhus, Scrub	x		

Food/Water Safety

All tap water used for drinking, brushing teeth, and making ice cubes should be boiled prior to use. Insure that bottled water is uncapped in your presence. Milk should be boiled to insure safety. Powdered and evaporated milk are available and safe. Avoid butter and other dairy products. All meat, poultry and seafood must be well cooked and served while hot. Pork is best avoided. Vegetables should be well cooked and served hot. Salads and mayonnaise are best avoided. Fruits with intact skins should be peeled by you just prior to consumption. Avoid cold buffets, custards, and any frozen dessert. First class hotels and restaurants in Abidjan serve purified drinking water and reliable food. However, the hazard is left to your judgement.

VACCINATIONS

Yellow fever—A vaccination certificate is required on arrival from all countries. A vaccination certificate is required for children over one year of age. CDC recommends vaccination for all travelers over 9 months of age who will travel outside of urban areas.

Routine immunizations should be current. For infants and children through 16 years of age, refer to Chapter 4.3. A rubeola (measles) booster should be considered. Persons age 16 to 65 should receive a booster of tetanus and diphtheria every ten years. Healthy adults under age 65 do not require pneumococcal vaccine, but it is appropriate for those with chronic medical conditions. Influenza vaccine may be considered for those providing essential community services, health care workers, and those wishing to reduce the likelihood of becoming ill with influenza. Adults over 65 years of age are urged to obtain yearly influenza immunization and to insure that their tetanus and diphtheria immunizations are current. Pneumococcal vaccination is also suggested for this age group.

The vaccinations listed are recommended for the traveler's protection.
Poliomyelitis—A poliomyelitis booster is indicated for this country.
Cholera—Cholera is present in this country. Risk to western travelers is low. Immunization is not required or recommended for travel to this country due to its low effectiveness. Avoid uncooked foods and untreated water. Vaccination is advised only for persons living or working under inadequate sanitary conditions and for those with impaired defense mechanisms.
Viral Hepatitis A—Vaccination is recommended for all travelers for their protection.
Typhoid fever—Vaccination is recommended for all travelers for their protection.

Selective vaccinations—These apply only to specific groups of travelers or persons on specific working assignments:
Viral Hepatitis B—Because of the high rate of healthy carriers of hepatitis B in this country, vaccination is recommended for persons on working assignments in the health care field (dentists, physicians, nurses, laboratory technicians), or working in close contact with the local population (teachers, missionaries, Peace Corps), or persons foreseeing sexual relations with local inhabitants.

U.S. Foreign Service:
5, Rue Jesse Owens
Abidjan, Telephone 32-09-79

Canadian High Commission/Embassy Office:
Immeuble "Trade Center"
23, Ave. Nogues
Abidjan, Telephone 32-20-09

_____ **Country number 8.103** _____
Jamaica

INFECTIOUS DISEASE RISK

Malaria Risk
There is no malaria risk in this country.

Diseases of Special Risk
In addition to the worldwide hazard of tetanus and the routine and any special immunizations recommended below, the traveler should be aware that risk of exposure to the following diseases exists in this country. This list is not all inclusive, but it is a caution concerning the more likely endemic disease risks.

Potential risk of dengue fever exists. The virus is present in this country at all times and may give rise to major outbreaks. Scabies and head lice are frequent problems amongst the lower class native population.

Dumping of raw sewage into the ocean at major resort areas and in Kingston Bay are potential health problems that may grow as the tourist business increases.

DISEASE RISK PROFILE

Disease	endemic	risk	hazard
Diarrheal Disease Risk		x	
Dysentery, Amoebic/Bacillary		x	
Hepatitis, Viral	x		
Leptospirosis	x		
Rabies (esp in mongoose)	x		
Typhoid Fever	x		

Food/Water Safety
Water is probably safe, but due to local variations in bacterial counts, using bottled water for the first few weeks will help the traveler adjust and decrease the chance of traveler's diarrhea. Milk is pasteurized and safe to drink. Butter, cheese, yogurt and ice-cream are safe. Local meat, poultry, seafood, vegetables, and fruits are safe to eat.

VACCINATIONS

Yellow fever—A vaccination certificate is required for travelers coming from infected areas and from or in transit through countries with active infection. A vaccination certificate is required for children over one year of age.

Routine immunizations should be current. For infants and children through 16 years of age, refer to Chapter 4.3. A rubeola (measles) booster should be considered. Persons age 16 to 65 should receive a booster of tetanus

and diphtheria every ten years. Healthy adults under age 65 do not require pneumococcal vaccine, but it is appropriate for those with chronic medical conditions. Influenza vaccine may be considered for those providing essential community services, health care workers, and those wishing to reduce the likelihood of becoming ill with influenza. Adults over 65 years of age are urged to obtain yearly influenza immunization and to insure that their tetanus and diphtheria immunizations are current. Pneumococcal vaccination is also suggested for this age group.

U.S. Foreign Service:
Jamaica Mutual Life Center
2 Oxford Rd., 3d Fl.
Kingston, Telephone (809) 929-4850

Canadian High Commission/Embassy Office:

Royal Bank Building
30-36 Knutsford Blvd.
Kingston, Telephone (809) 926-1500/1/2/3/4

Country number 8.104
Japan

INFECTIOUS DISEASE RISK

Malaria Risk
There is no malaria risk in this country.

Diseases of Special Risk
In addition to the worldwide hazard of tetanus and the routine and any special immunizations recommended below, the traveler should be aware that risk of exposure to the following diseases exists in this country. This list is not all inclusive, but it is a caution concerning the more likely endemic disease risks.

Schistosomiasis is reported in this country. Check with local authorities prior to swimming in fresh water pounds, rivers or lakes.

DISEASE RISK PROFILE

Disease	endemic	risk	hazard
Clonorchiasis	x		
Dengue Fever	x		
Paragonimiasis	x		
Typhoid Fever (Okinawa)	x		
Typhus, Scrub	x		

Food/Water Safety

Local water is considered safe without further treatment. Milk is pasteurized and safe to drink. Butter, cheese, yogurt and ice-cream are safe. Local meat, poultry, seafood, vegetables, and fruits are safe to eat.

VACCINATIONS

Routine immunizations should be current. For infants and children through 16 years of age, refer to Chapter 4.3. A rubeola (measles) booster should be considered. Persons age 16 to 65 should receive a booster of tetanus and diphtheria every ten years. Healthy adults under age 65 do not require pneumococcal vaccine, but it is appropriate for those with chronic medical conditions. Influenza vaccine may be considered for those providing essential community services, health care workers, and those wishing to reduce the likelihood of becoming ill with influenza. Adults over 65 years of age are urged to obtain yearly influenza immunization and to insure that their tetanus and diphtheria immunizations are current. Pneumococcal vaccination is also suggested for this age group.

No vaccinations are required to enter this country.

The vaccination listed is recommended for the traveler's protection.

Japanese encephalitis—Vaccination is indicated for persons traveling extensively in rual areas or living and working near rice growing rural and suburban areas and other irrigated land, when exposure to the disease carrying mosquitoes is high. Children are especially susceptible to the infection. Outbreaks occur in western and southern Japan, especially on the islands of Kyushu and Okinawa. Period of transmission is June through October, with the elederly being at the highest risk.

U.S. Foreign Service:

10-5, Akasaka 1-chome, Minato-ku
Tokyo, Telephone 583-7141

No. 2129, Gusukuma, Urasoe City
Naha, Okinawa, Telephone (0988) 77-8142/8627

5-26 Ohori 2-chome, Chuo-ku
Fukuoka, Telephone (092) 751-9331/4

Kita 1-Jyo Nishi 28-chome, Chuo-ku
Sapporo, Telephone (011) 641-1115/7

Canadian High Commission/Embassy Office:

3-38 Akasaka 7-chome, Minato-ku
Tokyo, Telephone 408-2101

_____ **Country number 8.105** _____
Jersey (UK)

INFECTIOUS DISEASE RISK

Malaria Risk
There is no malaria risk in this country.

Diseases of Special Risk

Food/Water Safety
Local water is considered safe without further treatment. Milk is pasteurized and safe to drink. Butter, cheese, yogurt and ice-cream are safe. Local meat, poultry, seafood, vegetables, and fruits are safe to eat.

VACCINATIONS
Routine immunizations should be current. For infants and children through 16 years of age, refer to Chapter 4.3. A rubeola (measles) booster should be considered. Persons age 16 to 65 should receive a booster of tetanus and diphtheria every ten years. Healthy adults under age 65 do not require pneumococcal vaccine, but it is appropriate for those with chronic medical conditions. Influenza vaccine may be considered for those providing essential community services, health care workers, and those wishing to reduce the likelihood of becoming ill with influenza. Adults over 65 years of age are urged to obtain yearly influenza immunization and to insure that their tetanus and diphtheria immunizations are current. Pneumococcal vaccination is also suggested for this age group.

No vaccinations are required to enter this country.

_____ **Country number 8.106** _____
Jordan

INFECTIOUS DISEASE RISK

Malaria Risk
There is no malaria risk in this country.

Diseases of Special Risk
In addition to the worldwide hazard of tetanus and the routine and any special immunizations recommended below, the traveler should be aware that risk of exposure to the following diseases exists in this country. This list is not all inclusive, but it is a caution concerning the more likely endemic disease risks.

The Department of State recommends meningococcal meningitis immunization for travel to this country, but the CDC does not.

DISEASE RISK PROFILE

Disease	endemic	risk	hazard
Brucellosis			x
Cholera	x		
Diarrheal Diseases		x	
Dracunculiasis/Guinea Worm	x		
Dysentery, Amoebic	x		
Echinococcosis	x		
Giardiasis	x		
Hepatitis, Viral		x	
Leishmaniasis			
Cutaneous	x		
Visceral	x		
Rabies	x		
Relapsing Fever	x		
Tapeworms	x		
Trachoma	x		
Typhoid Fever		x	
Typhus, Endemic Flea-Borne	x		
Typhus, Scrub	x		

Food/Water Safety

All tap water used for drinking, brushing teeth, and making ice cubes should be boiled prior to use. Insure that bottled water is uncapped in your presence. Milk should be boiled to insure safety. Powdered and evaporated milk are available and safe. Avoid butter and other dairy products. All meat, poultry and seafood must be well cooked and served while hot. Pork is best avoided. Vegetables should be well cooked and served hot. Salads and mayonnaise are best avoided. Fruits with intact skins should be peeled by you just prior to consumption. Avoid cold buffets, custards, and any frozen dessert. First class hotels and restaurants in Amman serve purified drinking water and reliable food. However, the hazard is left to your judgement.

VACCINATIONS

Routine immunizations should be current. For infants and children through 16 years of age, refer to Chapter 4.3. A rubeola (measles) booster should be considered. Persons age 16 to 65 should receive a booster of tetanus and diphtheria every ten years. Healthy adults under age 65 do not require pneumococcal vaccine, but it is appropriate for those with chronic medical conditions. Influenza vaccine may be considered for those providing essential community services, health care workers, and those wishing to reduce the likelihood of becoming ill with influenza. Adults over 65 years of age are urged to obtain yearly influenza immunization and to insure that their tetanus and diph-

theria immunizations are current. Pneumococcal vaccination is also suggested for this age group.

No vaccinations are required to enter this country.

The vaccinations listed are recommended for the traveler's protection.
Viral Hepatitis A—Vaccination is recommended for all travelers for their protection.
Typhoid fever—Vaccination is recommended for all travelers for their protection.

Selective vaccinations—These apply only to specific groups of travelers or persons on specific working assignments:
Viral Hepatitis B—Because of the high rate of healthy carriers of hepatitis B in this country, vaccination is recommended for persons on working assignments in the health care field (dentists, physicians, nurses, laboratory technicians), or working in close contact with the local population (teachers, missionaries, Peace Corps), or persons foreseeing sexual relations with local inhabitants.
Rabies—In this country, where rabies is a constant threat, a pre-exposure rabies vaccination is advised for persons planning an extended stay or on working assignments (naturalists, agricultural advisors, archeologists, geologists, etc.). Although this provides adequate initial protection, a person bitten by a potentially rabid animal would still require post exposure immunization (see Chapter 6.40). Children should be cautioned not to pet dogs, cats, or other mammals.

U.S. Foreign Service:
Jebel Amman
Amman, Telephone 443716
(Workweek: Sunday—Thursday

Canadian High Commission/Embassy Office:
Pearl of Shmeisani Building
SH Shmeisani
Amman, Telephone 666124/5/6

_____ **Country number 8.107** _____
Kenya

INFECTIOUS DISEASE RISK

Malaria Risk
Malaria is present in all parts of this country, including urban areas. The risk exists all year, but only below 2500 meters. There is no risk of malaria in

Nairobi and the highlands above 2500 meters of the central, Rift Valley, Eastern, Nyanza and Western provinces. The malaria in this country is resistant to chloroquine. The CDC recommends the use of mefloquine (Lariam) as described in Chapter 6.31 for chemical prophylaxis.

Falciparum malaria represents 85% of malaria, therefore there is a slight risk of p. vivax malaria exposure. Consider use of primaquine upon return home.

Diseases of Special Risk

In addition to the worldwide hazard of tetanus and the routine and any special immunizations recommended below, the traveler should be aware that risk of exposure to the following diseases exists in this country. This list is not all inclusive, but it is a caution concerning the more likely endemic disease risks.

Schistosomiasis may be found in this country. Avoid contact with contaminated fresh water lakes, ponds, or streams. Risk of infection is present along the shore of Lake Victoria, in the area of Kisumu, the Kano Plain; in the area of machakos southeast of Nairobi and along the Tana River in the northeastern part of the country.

Meningococcal meningitis is at times epidemic in the savannah during the dry season from December until June.

DISEASE RISK PROFILE

Disease	endemic	risk	hazard
Dracunculiasis/Guinea Worm	x		
Diarrheal Disease Risk			x
Dysentery, Amoebic/Bacillary			x
Echinococcosis		x	
Filariasis			x
Giardiasis			x
Helminthic Diseases (see Chapter 6.21)			x
Hepatitis, Viral			x
Leishmaniasis			
Cutaneous	x		
Visceral	x		
Hemorrhagic Fever (Marburg)	x		
Plague	x		
Polio			x
Rabies	x		
Relapsing Fever	x		
Trachoma			x
Trypanosomiasis, African Sleeping Sickness	x		
Typhoid Fever			x
Typhus, Endemic Flea-Borne	x		
Typhus, Epidemic Louse-Borne	x		
Typhus, Scrub	x		

Food/Water Safety

All tap water used for drinking, brushing teeth, and making ice cubes should be boiled prior to use. Insure that bottled water is uncapped in your presence. Milk is pasteurized and safe to drink. Butter, cheese, yogurt and ice-cream are safe. All meat, poultry and seafood must be well cooked and served while hot. Pork is best avoided. Vegetables should be well cooked and served hot. Salads and mayonnaise are best avoided. Fruits with intact skins should be peeled by you just prior to consumption. Avoid cold buffets, custards, and any frozen dessert. First class hotels and restaurants in Malindi, Mombasa, Nanyuki, and Tsavo serve purified drinking water and reliable food. However, the hazard is left to your judgement.

VACCINATIONS

Yellow fever—A vaccination certificate is required for travelers coming from infected areas and from or in transit through countries in the endemic yellow fever zone, see Chapter 6.63. A vaccination certificate is required for children over one year of age. Vaccination is recommended for all travelers for their protection. CDC recommends vaccination for all travelers over 9 months of age who will travel outside of urban areas.

Routine immunizations should be current. For infants and children through 16 years of age, refer to Chapter 4.3. A rubeola (measles) booster should be considered. Persons age 16 to 65 should receive a booster of tetanus and diphtheria every ten years. Healthy adults under age 65 do not require pneumococcal vaccine, but it is appropriate for those with chronic medical conditions. Influenza vaccine may be considered for those providing essential community services, health care workers, and those wishing to reduce the likelihood of becoming ill with influenza. Adults over 65 years of age are urged to obtain yearly influenza immunization and to insure that their tetanus and diphtheria immunizations are current. Pneumococcal vaccination is also suggested for this age group.

The vaccinations listed are recommended for the traveler's protection.
Poliomyelitis—A poliomyelitis booster is indicated for this country.
Cholera—Cholera is present in this country. Risk to western travelers is low. Immunization is not required or recommended for travel to this country due to its low effectiveness. Avoid uncooked foods and untreated water. Vaccination is advised only for persons living or working under inadequate sanitary conditions and for those with impaired defense mechanisms.
Viral Hepatitis A—Vaccination is recommended for all travelers for their protection.
Typhoid fever—Vaccination is recommended for all travelers for their protection.

Selective vaccinations—These apply only to specific groups of travelers or persons on specific working assignments:

Viral Hepatitis B—Because of the high rate of healthy carriers of hepatitis B in this country, vaccination is recommended for persons on working assignments in the health care field (dentists, physicians, nurses, laboratory technicians), or working in close contact with the local population (teachers, missionaries, Peace Corps), or persons foreseeing sexual relations with local inhabitants.

Plague—Vaccination is recommended only for persons who may be occupationally exposed to wild rodents (anthropologists, geologists, medical personnel, missionaries, etc). The standard vaccination course must be completed before entering the plague infested area. Geographical distribution of the area of risk for this country is in the areas around Nairobi and along the border with Tanzania (eastern part).

U.S. Foreign Service:
Moi/Haile Selassie Avenue
Nairobi, Telephone 334-141

Paili House
Nyerere Avenue
Mombasa, Telephone 315-101

Canadian High Commission/Embassy Office:
Comcraft House
Haile Selassie Avenue
Nairobi, Telephone 334-033/4/5/6

TRAVEL ADVISORY

A U.S. Department of State Travel Advisory was in effect on 4 May 1990 when this book went to press. The entire text is included below. Travel advisories are subject to reissue, change, and cancellation at any time. Current travel advisory information is available by calling the U.S. Department of State Travel Advisory Hotline at (202) 647-5225. The current travel advisory status is also available from the Herchmer Database update system (see Chapter 2.8).

9FB DN37 3-1 1LA71 3 09/01/89 09:24 SECSTATE WSH SUBJECT: TRAVEL ADVISORY
KENYA—CAUTION
1. THE DEPARTMENT OF STATE ADVISES AMERICAN CITIZENS THAT WHEN VISITING KENYA, THE FOLLOWING BASIC PRECAUTIONS SHOULD BE TAKEN.
IN 1989, THERE HAS BEEN AN INCREASINGLY FREQUENT PATTERN OF ROBBERY-MOTIVATED ATTACKS ON TOURISTS ALONG

THE COAST SOUTH OF MOMBASA AND IN THE REMOTE AREAS OF THE COUNTRY, INCLUDING SOME NATIONAL PARKS. THE ATTACKS IN AND NEAR THE MERU, TSAVO, SHABA, MASAI MARA, AND KORA RESERVES/PARKS, SOME OF WHICH HAVE RESULTED IN THE DEATH OF VISITORS, HAVE BEEN ATTRIBUTED TO HEAVILY ARMED WILDLIFE POACHERS AND BANDITS.

2. THE GOVERNMENT OF KENYA IS MAKING EFFORTS TO insure THE SAFETY OF VISITORS. NEVERTHELESS, VISITORS SHOULD TAKE PRECAUTIONS:

—IN THE PARKS, ALWAYS TRAVEL WITH A GUIDE FROM A REPUTABLE SAFARI FIRM OR A GAME RANGER = SOLO TRAVEL IS NOT SAFE. TRAVELERS SHOULD CONSIDER ASKING TOUR OPERATORS TO BOOK AN ESCORTING GAME RANGER IN ADDITION TO A GUIDE.

—WHEN PLANNING AN OVERNIGHT STAY IN REMOTE AREAS (WHETHER CAMPING OR IN A LODGE), ASK THE TOUR OPERATOR ABOUT OVERNIGHT SECURITY ARRANGEMENTS IN ADVANCE. IF NOT ADEQUATE, CHOOSE ANOTHER LODGING.

—WHENEVER POSSIBLE, TRAVEL IN LARGE GROUPS. INSIST THAT GROUPS STICK TOGETHER. NORMALLY, THERE IS INCREASED SAFETY IN NUMBERS.

—VISITORS SHOULD ALSO BE AWARE THAT PURSE SNATCHERS AND PICKPOCKETS OPERATE HERE MUCH LIKE THEIR COUNTERPARTS IN OTHER LARGE CITIES OR AREAS HEAVILY FREQUENTED BY TOURISTS. VALUABLES, ESPECIALLY GOLD CHAINS AND EARRINGS, AND PASSPORTS SHOULD BE LEFT IN HOTEL SAFES.

—KENYA, AS IN MANY OTHER EAST AFRICAN COUNTRIES, HAS CHLOROQUINE-RESISTANT MALARIA AND TRAVELERS SHOULD CONSULT A KNOWLEDGEABLE PHYSICIAN REGARDING MEDICATION PRIOR TO TRAVELING IN THE AREA.

3. THE U.S. EMBASSY IN NAIROBI AND THE CONSULATE IN MOMBASA ARE PREPARED TO OFFER MORE SPECIFIC INFORMATION TO U.S. VISITORS, WHO ARE ENCOURAGED TO REGISTER WITH THE EMBASSY UPON ARRIVAL IN KENYA. THE EMBASSY IS LOCATED AT THE INTERSECTION OF MOI AND HAILE SELASSIE AVENUES IN NAIROBI = THE PHONE NUMBER IS 334141. IN MOMBASA THE CONSULATE IS LOCATED AT PALLI HOUSE ON NYERERE AVENUE = THE PHONE NUMBER IS 315101.

4. EXPIRATION DATE: SEPTEMBER 1, 1990.

5. THIS CANCELS TRAVEL ADVISORY CONTAINED IN STATE 241756 DATED JULY 29, 1989. BAKER DEPT OF STATE WASHDC 281661 / L0058 655

_____ **Country number 8.108** _____
Kiribati (Formerly Gilbert Islands)

INFECTIOUS DISEASE RISK

Malaria Risk
There is no malaria risk in this country.

Diseases of Special Risk
In addition to the worldwide hazard of tetanus and the routine and any special immunizations recommended below, the traveler should be aware that risk of exposure to the following diseases exists in this country. This list is not all inclusive, but it is a caution concerning the more likely endemic disease risks.

DISEASE RISK PROFILE

Disease	endemic	risk	hazard
Dengue Fever	x		
Diarrheal Diseases		x	
Encephalitis, Japanese	x		
Filariasis			x
Helminthic Diseases (see Chapter 6.21)		x	
Typhoid Fever		x	

Food/Water Safety
All tap water used for drinking, brushing teeth, and making ice cubes should be boiled prior to use. Insure that bottled water is uncapped in your presence. Milk should be boiled to insure safety. Powdered and evaporated milk are available and safe. Avoid butter and other dairy products. All meat, poultry and seafood must be well cooked and served while hot. Pork is best avoided. Vegetables should be well cooked and served hot. Salads and mayonnaise are best avoided. Fruits with intact skins should be peeled by you just prior to consumption. Avoid cold buffets, custards, and any frozen dessert.

VACCINATIONS
Yellow fever—A vaccination certificate is required for travelers coming from infected areas. A vaccination certificate is required for children over one year of age.

Routine immunizations should be current. For infants and children through 16 years of age, refer to Chapter 4.3. A rubeola (measles) booster should be considered. Persons age 16 to 65 should receive a booster of tetanus and diphtheria every ten years. Healthy adults under age 65 do not require pneumococcal vaccine, but it is appropriate for those with chronic medical conditions. Influenza vaccine may be considered for those providing essential

community services, health care workers, and those wishing to reduce the likelihood of becoming ill with influenza. Adults over 65 years of age are urged to obtain yearly influenza immunization and to insure that their tetanus and diphtheria immunizations are current. Pneumococcal vaccination is also suggested for this age group.

The vaccinations listed are recommended for the traveler's protection.
Viral Hepatitis A—Vaccination is recommended for all travelers for their protection.
Typhoid fever—Vaccination is recommended for all travelers for their protection.

Selective vaccinations—These apply only to specific groups of travelers or persons on specific working assignments:
Viral Hepatitis B—Because of the high rate of healthy carriers of hepatitis B in this country, vaccination is recommended for persons on working assignments in the health care field (dentists, physicians, nurses, laboratory technicians), or working in close contact with the local population (teachers, missionaries, Peace Corps), or persons foreseeing sexual relations with local inhabitants.

Country number 8.109
Korea, Democratic People's Republic (North Korea)

INFECTIOUS DISEASE RISK

Malaria Risk
There is no malaria risk in this country.

Diseases of Special Risk
In addition to the worldwide hazard of tetanus and the routine and any special immunizations recommended below, the traveler should be aware that risk of exposure to the following diseases exists in this country. This list is not all inclusive, but it is a caution concerning the more likely endemic disease risks.

DISEASE RISK PROFILE

Disease	endemic	risk	hazard
Dengue Fever	x		
Diarrheal Diseases		x	
Encephalitis, Japanese	x		
Encephalitis, Tick-Borne Hepatitis, Viral		x	

Food/Water Safety

All tap water used for drinking, brushing teeth, and making ice cubes should be boiled prior to use. Insure that bottled water is uncapped in your presence. Milk should be boiled to insure safety. Powdered and evaporated milk are available and safe. Avoid butter and other dairy products. All meat, poultry and seafood must be well cooked and served while hot. Pork is best avoided. Vegetables should be well cooked and served hot. Salads and mayonnaise are best avoided. Fruits with intact skins should be peeled by you just prior to consumption. Avoid cold buffets, custards, and any frozen dessert. First class hotels and restaurants in Pyongyang serve purified drinking water and reliable food. However, the hazard is left to your judgement.

VACCINATIONS

Routine immunizations should be current. For infants and children through 16 years of age, refer to Chapter 4.3. A rubeola (measles) booster should be considered. Persons age 16 to 65 should receive a booster of tetanus and diphtheria every ten years. Healthy adults under age 65 do not require pneumococcal vaccine, but it is appropriate for those with chronic medical conditions. Influenza vaccine may be considered for those providing essential community services, health care workers, and those wishing to reduce the likelihood of becoming ill with influenza. Adults over 65 years of age are urged to obtain yearly influenza immunization and to insure that their tetanus and diphtheria immunizations are current. Pneumococcal vaccination is also suggested for this age group.

No vaccinations are required to enter this country.

The vaccinations listed are recommended for the traveler's protection.

Viral Hepatitis A—Vaccination is recommended when traveling outside the areas usually visited by tourists, traveling extensively in the interior of the country (trekkers, hikers) and for persons on working assignments in remote areas.

Typhoid fever—Vaccination is recommended when traveling outside the areas usually visited by tourists, traveling extensively in the interior of the country (trekkers, hikers) and for persons on working assignments in remote areas.

Selective vaccinations—*These apply only to specific groups of travelers or persons on specific working assignments:*

Viral Hepatitis B—Because of the high rate of healthy carriers of hepatitis B in this country, vaccination is recommended for persons on working assignments in the health care field (dentists, physicians, nurses, laboratory technicians), or working in close contact with the local population (teachers, missionaries, Peace Corps), or persons foreseeing sexual relations with local inhabitants.

Japanese encephalitis—Vaccination is indicated for persons traveling extensively in rual areas or living and working near rice growing rural and suburban areas and other irrigated land, when exposure to the disease carrying mosquitoes is high. Children are especially susceptible to the infection. Outbreaks occur occasionally, with the period of transmission from June to October.

TRAVEL ADVISORY

A U.S. Department of State Travel Advisory was in effect on 4 May 1990 when this book went to press. The entire text is included below. Travel advisories are subject to reissue, change, and cancellation at any time. Current travel advisory information is available by calling the U.S. Department of State Travel Advisory Hotline at (202) 647-5225. The current travel advisory status is also available from the Herchmer Database update system (see Chapter 2.8).

MARCH 13, 1990
NORTH KOREA—WARNING
THE UNITED STATES DOES NOT RECOGNIZE THE GOVERNMENT OF NORTH KOREA AND DOES NOT MAINTAIN DIPLOMATIC OR CONSULAR RELATIONS WITH NORTH KOREAN AUTHORITIES. BECAUSE NO THIRD COUNTRY REPRESENTS UNITED STATES INTERESTS IN NORTH KOREA, THE UNITED STATES GOVERNMENT IS NOT IN A POSITION OT ACCORD NORMAL CONSULAR PROTECTIVE SERVICES TO U.S. CITIZENS IN NORTH KOREA.
U.S. PASSPORTS ARE VALID FOR TRAVEL TO NORTH KOREA. HOWEVER, IT IS THE TRAVELER'S RESPONSIBILITY TO APPLY FOR THE REQUIRED VISA.
FINANCIAL TRANSACTION BY U.S. INDIVIDUALS IN NORTH KOREA ARE RESTRICTED. UNDER THE FOREIGN ASSETS CONTROL REGULATION ADMINISTERED BY THE TREASURY DEPARTMENT, INDIVIDUALS MAY ONLY SPEND MONEY IN NORTH KOREA TO PURCHASE ITEMS RELATED TO TRAVEL, SUCH AS HOTEL ACCOMMODATIONS, MEALS, AND GOODS FOR PERSONAL CONSUMPTION BY THE TRAVELER IN NORTH KOREA. IN ADDITION, A TRAVELER RETUNING FROM NORTH KOREA MAY BRING BACK INTO THE UNITED STATES AS ACCOMPANIED BAGGAGE $100 U.S. DOLLARS WORTH OF MERCHANDISE IN NON-COMMERCIAL QUANTITIES, AS WELL AS INFORMATIONAL MATERIALS WITHOUT LIMITATION. HOWEVER, RECEIPTS SHOULD BE KEPT TO DOCUMENT ANY GOODS PURCHASED IN NORTH KOREA AND MADE AVAILABLE TO THE U.S. CUSTOMS SERVICE WHEN ENTRY IS MADE INTO THE UNITED STATES.
U.S. REGULATIONS PROHIBIT USE OF CREDIT AND OTHER CHARGE CARDS IN NORTH KOREA, EVEN FOR LIVING EXPENSES OR FOR THE PURCHASE OF GOODS USED BY THE TRAVELER.
IN GENERAL, U.S. TRAVEL SERVICE PROVIDERS ARE PROHIBITED FROM ARRANGING, PROMOTING OR FACILITATING TOURS TO

NORTH KOREA UNLESS SPECIFICALLY LICENSED BY THE U.S. TREASURY DEPARTMENT TO PROVIDE TRAVEL SERVICES TO GROUPS OR INDIVIDUALS INVOLVED IN ACADEMIC, SPORTS, CULTURAL, FAMILY REUNIONS OR CERTAIN OTHER NONCOMMERCIAL ACTIVITIES. THE ONLY TRANSACTION THAT A U.S. TRAVEL SERVICE PROVIDER IS PERMITTED TO PERFORM WITHOUT A SPECIFIC TREASURY LICENSE IS THE BOOKING OF PASSAGE FOR AN INDIVIDUAL TRAVELER TO NORTH KOREA ABOARD A "NONBLOCKED CARRIER." A NON-BLOCKED CARRIER IS ANY CARRIER OTHER THAN A LIBYAN, CUBAN, CAMBODIAN, VIETNAMESE, OR NORTH KOREA ARE AVAILABLE FROM OR AUTHORIZED FOR U.S. CARRIERS. TRAVELERS ARE CAUTIONED AGAINST SIGNING UP FOR A U.S. SPONSORED OR AFFILIATED TOUR GROUP DESTINED FOR NORTH KOREA WITHOUT FIRST CHECKING WITH THE OFFICE OF FOREIGN ASSETS CONTROL OF THE U.S. TREASURY DEPARTMENT.

THIS ADVISORY PROVIDES ONLY GENERAL GUIDANCE REGARDING APPLICABLE TREASURY REGULATIONS. INDIVIDUALS CONTEMPLATING TRAVEL TO NORTH KOREA ARE ENCOURAGED TO CONTACT THE DEPARTMENT OF THE TREASURY FOR FURTHER INFORMATION AT:

LICENSING SECTION
OFFICE OF FOREIGN ASSETS CONTROL
DEPARTMENT OF THE TREASURY
WASHINGTON, D.C. 20220
TEL: (202) 376-0236

DUAL CITIZENSHIP

U.S. CITIZENS WHO WERE BORN IN NORTH KOREA OR WHO WERE AT ONE TIME CITIZENS OF NORTH KOREA, AND THE CHILDREN OF SUCH PERSONS MAY BE CONSIDERED DUAL NATIONALS BY NORTH KOREAN AUTHORITIES AND MAY, THEREFORE, BE SUBJECTED TO NORTH KOREAN LAWS. THESE LAWS MAY IMPOSE SPECIAL OBLIGATIONS UPON NORTH KOREAN NATIONAL, E.G., MILITARY SERVICE, TAXES. THE STATE DEPARTMENT IS UNAWARE OF ANY SUCH CASES IN RECENT MEMORY.

U.S. CITIZENS CONTEMPLATING TRAVEL TO NORTH KOREA SHOULD ONLY CARRY U.S. PASSPORTS WITH THE PROPER VISA AFFIXED. UNDER NO CONDITIONS SHOULD U.S. CITIZENS ACCEPT TRAVEL DOCUMENTS THAT IDENTIFY THEM AS CITIZENS OF NORTH KOREA.

SPECIFIC QUESTIONS ON DUAL NATIONALITY MAY BE DIRECTED TO THE OFFICE OF CITIZENS CONSULAR SERVICES, DEPARTMENT OF STATE, WASHINGTON, D.C. 20520.(PHONE:202-647-3675)

EXPIRATION: INDEFINITE

Country number 8.110
Republic of Korea
(South Korea)

INFECTIOUS DISEASE RISK

Malaria Risk
There is no malaria risk in this country.

Diseases of Special Risk
In addition to the worldwide hazard of tetanus and the routine and any special immunizations recommended below, the traveler should be aware that risk of exposure to the following diseases exists in this country. This list is not all inclusive, but it is a caution concerning the more likely endemic disease risks.

DISEASE RISK PROFILE

Disease	endemic	risk	hazard
Clonorchiasis	x		
Dengue Fever	x		
Diarrheal Diseases		x	
Encephalitis, Japanese	x		
Encephalitis, Tick-Borne	x		
Filariasis	x		
Hepatitis, Viral			x
Paragonimiasis	x		
Typhus, Scrub	x		

Food/Water Safety
All tap water used for drinking, brushing teeth, and making ice cubes should be boiled prior to use. Insure that bottled water is uncapped in your presence. Milk should be boiled to insure safety. Powdered and evaporated milk are available and safe. Avoid butter and other dairy products. All meat, poultry and seafood must be well cooked and served while hot. Pork is best avoided. Vegetables should be well cooked and served hot. Salads and mayonnaise are best avoided. Fruits with intact skins should be peeled by you just prior to consumption. Avoid cold buffets, custards, and any frozen dessert. First class hotels and restaurants in Pusan and Soul (Seoul) serve purified drinking water and reliable food. However, the hazard is left to your judgement.

VACCINATIONS
Routine immunizations should be current. For infants and children through 16 years of age, refer to Chapter 4.3. A rubeola (measles) booster should be considered. Persons age 16 to 65 should receive a booster of tetanus

and diphtheria every ten years. Healthy adults under age 65 do not require pneumococcal vaccine, but it is appropriate for those with chronic medical conditions. Influenza vaccine may be considered for those providing essential community services, health care workers, and those wishing to reduce the likelihood of becoming ill with influenza. Adults over 65 years of age are urged to obtain yearly influenza immunization and to insure that their tetanus and diphtheria immunizations are current. Pneumococcal vaccination is also suggested for this age group.

No vaccinations are required to enter this country.

The vaccinations listed are recommended for the traveler's protection.

Viral Hepatitis A—Vaccination is recommended when traveling outside the areas usually visited by tourists, traveling extensively in the interior of the country (trekkers, hikers) and for persons on working assignments in remote areas.

Typhoid fever—Vaccination is recommended when traveling outside the areas usually visited by tourists, traveling extensively in the interior of the country (trekkers, hikers) and for persons on working assignments in remote areas.

Selective vaccinations—These apply only to specific groups of travelers or persons on specific working assignments:

Viral Hepatitis B—Because of the high rate of healthy carriers of hepatitis B in this country, vaccination is recommended for persons on working assignments in the health care field (dentists, physicians, nurses, laboratory technicians), or working in close contact with the local population (teachers, missionaries, Peace Corps), or persons foreseeing sexual relations with local inhabitants.

Japanese encephalitis—Vaccination is indicated for persons traveling extensively in rual areas or living and working near rice growing rural and suburban areas and other irrigated land, when exposure to the disease carrying mosquitoes is high. Children are especially susceptible to the infection. Outbreaks reported from all provinces, especially the southwest, with the period of transmission from June to October. High risk groups are children and young adults.

U.S. Foreign Service:
    82 Sejong-Ro
    Chongro-ku
    Seoul, Telephone 732-2601/18

Canadian High Commission/Embassy Office:
    Kolon Building
    10th Floor
    45 Mugyo-Dong; Jung-Ku
    Seoul, Telephone 776-4062/68/69

_____ **Country number 8.111** _____
Kuwait

INFECTIOUS DISEASE RISK

Malaria Risk
There is no malaria risk in this country.

Diseases of Special Risk
In addition to the worldwide hazard of tetanus and the routine and any special immunizations recommended below, the traveler should be aware that risk of exposure to the following diseases exists in this country. This list is not all inclusive, but it is a caution concerning the more likely endemic disease risks.

DISEASE RISK PROFILE

Disease	endemic	risk	hazard
Brucellosis			x
Cholera	x		
Diarrheal Diseases			x
Dracunculiasis/Guinea Worm	x		
Echinococcosis	x		
Hepatitis, Viral		x	
Leishmaniasis			
Cutaneous	x		
Visceral	x		
Rabies	x		
Relapsing Fever	x		
Tapeworms	x		
Trachoma	x		
Typhoid Fever		x	
Typhus, Endemic Flea-Borne	x		
Typhus, Scrub	x		

Food/Water Safety
Water is probably safe, but due to local variations in bacterial counts, using bottled water for the first few weeks will help the traveler adjust and decrease the chance of traveler's diarrhea. Milk is pasteurized and safe to drink. Butter, cheese, yogurt and ice-cream are safe. Local meat, poultry, seafood, vegetables, and fruits are safe to eat.

VACCINATIONS

Routine immunizations should be current. For infants and children through 16 years of age, refer to Chapter 4.3. A rubeola (measles) booster should be considered. Persons age 16 to 65 should receive a booster of tetanus and diphtheria every ten years. Healthy adults under age 65 do not require

pneumococcal vaccine, but it is appropriate for those with chronic medical conditions. Influenza vaccine may be considered for those providing essential community services, health care workers, and those wishing to reduce the likelihood of becoming ill with influenza. Adults over 65 years of age are urged to obtain yearly influenza immunization and to insure that their tetanus and diphtheria immunizations are current. Pneumococcal vaccination is also suggested for this age group.

No vaccinations are required to enter this country.

The vaccinations listed are recommended for the traveler's protection.

Viral Hepatitis A—Vaccination is recommended for all travelers for their protection.

Typhoid fever—Vaccination is recommended for all travelers for their protection.

U.S. Foreign Service:
P.O. Box 77 SAFAT
Kuwait, Telephone 424-151/2/3/4/5
(Workweek: Saturday-Wednesday)

Canadian High Commission/Embassy Office:
28 Quaraish Street
Nuzha District
Kuwait City, Telephone 255-5754, 256-3025,
256-3078

TRAVEL ADVISORY

A U.S. Department of State Travel Advisory was in effect on 4 May 1990 when this book went to press. The entire text is included below. Travel advisories are subject to reissue, change, and cancellation at any time. Current travel advisory information is available by calling the U.S. Department of State Travel Advisory Hotline at (202) 647-5225. The current travel advisory status is also available from the Herchmer Database update system (see Chapter 2.8).

SECSTATE WSH TRAVEL ADVISORY 11 FEB 1989
KUWAIT—CAUTION
THE DEPARTMENT OF STATE ADVISES TRAVELERS TO KUWAIT THAT EVEN THOUGH HOSTILITIES BETWEEN IRAN AND IRAQ HAVE CEASED, NO FORMAL PEACE TREATY HAS YET BEEN SIGNED. TRAVELERS SHOULD BE AWARE THAT THE POTENTIAL FOR TERRORIST ACTIVITY EXISTS. ALL AMERICAN CITIZENS PLANNING TO REMAIN IN KUWAIT FOR AN EXTENDED PERIOD ARE URGED TO REGISTER WITH THE U.S. EMBASSY (TELEPHONE 242-4151).
EXPIRATION: INDEFINITE

_____ **Country number 8.112** _____
Lao People's Democratic Republic
(Laos)

INFECTIOUS DISEASE RISK

Malaria Risk

Diseases of Special Risk

In addition to the worldwide hazard of tetanus and the routine and any special immunizations recommended below, the traveler should be aware that risk of exposure to the following diseases exists in this country. This list is not all inclusive, but it is a caution concerning the more likely endemic disease risks.

Potential risk of dengue fever exists. The virus is present in this country at all times and may give rise to major outbreaks.

Schistosomiasis may be found in this country. Avoid contact with contaminated fresh water lakes, ponds, or streams. The only known area of infection is the Khong Island in the Mekong River, in the southwest on the border with Kampuchea (Cambodia).

DISEASE RISK PROFILE

Disease	endemic	risk	hazard
Chikungunya Fever	x		
Cholera	x		
Clonorchiasis/Opisthorchiasis	x		
Dengue Fever	x		
Diarrheal Disease Risk			x
Dysentery, Amoebic/Bacillary		x	
Encephalitis, Japanese	x		
Fasciolopsiasis	x		
Filariasis			x
Helminthic Diseases (see Chapter 6.21)	x		
Hepatitis, Viral	x		
Melioidosis	x		
Rabies	x		
Typhoid Fever	x		
Typhus, Scrub	x		

Food/Water Safety

All tap water used for drinking, brushing teeth, and making ice cubes should be boiled prior to use. Insure that bottled water is uncapped in your presence. Milk should be boiled to insure safety. Powdered and evaporated milk are available and safe. Avoid butter and other dairy products. All meat, poultry and seafood must be well cooked and served while hot. Pork is best avoided.

Vegetables should be well cooked and served hot. Salads and mayonnaise are best avoided. Fruits with intact skins should be peeled by you just prior to consumption. Avoid cold buffets, custards, and any frozen dessert. First class hotels and restaurants in Vientiane serve purified drinking water and reliable food. However, the hazard is left to your judgement.

VACCINATIONS

Yellow fever—A vaccination certificate is required for travelers coming from infected areas. A vaccination is required for children of all ages. Children under nine months of age should not be vaccinated due to health considerations. Please refer to the discussion in Chapter 6.63 on avoiding yellow fever vaccination in this age group.

Routine immunizations should be current. For infants and children through 16 years of age, refer to Chapter 4.3. A rubeola (measles) booster should be considered. Persons age 16 to 65 should receive a booster of tetanus and diphtheria every ten years. Healthy adults under age 65 do not require pneumococcal vaccine, but it is appropriate for those with chronic medical conditions. Influenza vaccine may be considered for those providing essential community services, health care workers, and those wishing to reduce the likelihood of becoming ill with influenza. Adults over 65 years of age are urged to obtain yearly influenza immunization and to insure that their tetanus and diphtheria immunizations are current. Pneumococcal vaccination is also suggested for this age group.

The vaccinations listed are recommended for the traveler's protection.
Poliomyelitis—A poliomyelitis booster is indicated for this country.
Viral Hepatitis A—Vaccination is recommended for all travelers for their protection.
Typhoid fever—Vaccination is recommended for all travelers for their protection.

Selective vaccinations—These apply only to specific groups of travelers or persons on specific working assignments:
Viral Hepatitis B—Because of the high rate of healthy carriers of hepatitis B in this country, vaccination is recommended for persons on working assignments in the health care field (dentists, physicians, nurses, laboratory technicians), or working in close contact with the local population (teachers, missionaries, Peace Corps), or persons foreseeing sexual relations with local inhabitants.
Japanese encephalitis—Vaccination is indicated for persons traveling extensively in rual areas or living and working near rice growing rural and suburban areas and other irrigated land, when exposure to the disease carrying mosquitoes is high. Children are especially susceptible to the infection. The disease is endemic throughout the year. Period of transmission is all year.

U.S. Foreign Service:
Rue Bartholoni
Vientiane, Telephone 2220, 2357, 2384, 3570

Country number 8.113
Lebanon

INFECTIOUS DISEASE RISK

Malaria Risk
There is no malaria risk in this country.

Diseases of Special Risk
In addition to the worldwide hazard of tetanus and the routine and any special immunizations recommended below, the traveler should be aware that risk of exposure to the following diseases exists in this country. This list is not all inclusive, but it is a caution concerning the more likely endemic disease risks.

DISEASE RISK PROFILE

Disease	endemic	risk	hazard
Brucellosis			x
Cholera	x		
Diarrheal Diseases			x
Dracunculiasis/Guinea Worm	x		
Echinococcosis	x		
Hepatitis, Viral	x		
Leishmaniasis			
Cutaneous	x		
Visceral	x		
Polio			x
Rabies	x		
Relapsing Fever	x		
Tapeworms	x		
Trachoma	x		
Typhoid Fever		x	
Typhus, Endemic Flea-Borne	x		
Typhus, Scrub	x		

Food/Water Safety
All tap water used for drinking, brushing teeth, and making ice cubes should be boiled prior to use. Insure that bottled water is uncapped in your presence. Milk should be boiled to insure safety. Powdered and evaporated milk are available and safe. Avoid butter and other dairy products. All meat, poultry and seafood must be well cooked and served while hot. Pork is best avoided.

Vegetables should be well cooked and served hot. Salads and mayonnaise are best avoided. Fruits with intact skins should be peeled by you just prior to consumption. Avoid cold buffets, custards, and any frozen dessert.

VACCINATIONS

Yellow fever—A vaccination certificate is required for travelers coming from infected areas. Children under nine months of age should not be vaccinated due to health considerations. Please refer to the discussion in Chapter 6.63 on avoiding yellow fever vaccination in this age group.

Routine immunizations should be current. For infants and children through 16 years of age, refer to Chapter 4.3. A rubeola (measles) booster should be considered. Persons age 16 to 65 should receive a booster of tetanus and diphtheria every ten years. Healthy adults under age 65 do not require pneumococcal vaccine, but it is appropriate for those with chronic medical conditions. Influenza vaccine may be considered for those providing essential community services, health care workers, and those wishing to reduce the likelihood of becoming ill with influenza. Adults over 65 years of age are urged to obtain yearly influenza immunization and to insure that their tetanus and diphtheria immunizations are current. Pneumococcal vaccination is also suggested for this age group.

The vaccinations listed are recommended for the traveler's protection.
Poliomyelitis—A poliomyelitis booster is indicated for this country.
Viral Hepatitis A—Vaccination is recommended for all travelers for their protection.
Typhoid fever—Vaccination is recommended for all travelers for their protection.

Selective vaccinations—These apply only to specific groups of travelers or persons on specific working assignments:
Viral Hepatitis B—Because of the high rate of healthy carriers of hepatitis B in this country, vaccination is recommended for persons on working assignments in the health care field (dentists, physicians, nurses, laboratory technicians), or working in close contact with the local population (teachers, missionaries, Peace Corps), or persons foreseeing sexual relations with local inhabitants.

U.S. Foreign Service:
  Avenue de Paris
  Beirut, Telephone 361-800/964

Canadian High Commission/Embassy Office:
  Immeuble Sabbagh
  Rue Hamra
  Beirut, Telephone 350-660/662/663

TRAVEL ADVISORY

A U.S. Department of State Travel Advisory was in effect on 4 May 1990 when this book went to press. The entire text is included below. Travel advisories are subject to reissue, change, and cancellation at any time. Current travel advisory information is available by calling the U.S. Department of State Travel Advisory Hotline at (202) 647-5225. The current travel advisory status is also available from the Herchmer Database update system (see Chapter 2.8).

9FB DN37 1-1 1LA71 1 09/14/89 02:28
SECSTATE WSH
SUBJECT: TRAVEL ADVISORY— LEBANON— WARNING
1. THE DEPARTMENT OF STATE CONTINUES TO BELIEVE THAT THE SITUATION IN LEBANON IS SO DANGEROUS FOR AMERICANS THAT NO U.S. CITIZEN CAN BE CONSIDERED SAFE FROM TERRORIST ACTS. ON SEPTEMBER 6, 1989 ALL AMERICAN PERSONNEL AT THE U.S. EMBASSY IN BEIRUT WERE EVACUATED, AND THEREFORE THE U.S. EMBASSY CANNOT PROVIDE SERVICES TO AMERICAN CITIZENS.
2. U.S. PASSPORTS REMAIN INVALID FOR TRAVEL TO, IN, OR THROUGH LEBANON AND MAY NOT BE USED FOR THAT PURPOSE UNLESS A SPECIAL VALIDATION HAS BEEN OBTAINED. USE OF A U.S. PASSPORT FOR TRAVEL TO, IN, OR THROUGH LEBANON MAY CONSTITUTE A VIOLATION OF 18 U.S.C. 1544, AND BE PUNISHABLE BY A FINE AND/OR IMPRISONMENT.
3. EXCEPTIONS TO THIS RESTRICTION ARE BEING REVIEWED CAREFULLY ON A CASE-BY-CASE BASIS. THE CATEGORIES OF INDIVIDUALS ELIGIBLE FOR CONSIDERATION FOR A SPECIAL VALIDATION ARE SET FORTH IN 22 C.F.R. 51.74. PASSPORT VALIDATION REQUESTS FOR LEBANON SHOULD BE FORWARDED IN WRITING TO THE FOLLOWING ADDRESS:
MR. HARRY L. COBURN DEPUTY ASSISTANT SECRETARY FOR PASSPORT SERVICES U.S. DEPARTMENT OF STATE 1425 K STREET, N.W. WASHINGTON, D.C. 20522-1705 ATTN: OFFICE OF CITIZENSHIP APPEALS AND LEGAL ASSISTANCE (RM 300)
THE REQUEST MUST BE ACCOMPANIED BY SUBSTANTIATING DOCUMENTATION ACCORDING TO THE CATEGORY UNDER WHICH VALIDATION IS SOUGHT. THE FOUR REGULATORY CATEGORIES ARE AS FOLLOWS:
(1) PROFESSIONAL REPORTER: INCLUDES FULL-TIME MEMBERS OF THE REPORTING OR WRITING STAFF OF A NEWSPAPER, MAGAZINE OR BROADCASTING NETWORK WHOSE PURPOSE FOR TRAVEL IS TO GATHER INFORMATION ABOUT LEBANON FOR DISSEMINATION TO THE GENERAL PUBLIC. THE REQUEST MUST COME FROM THE APPLICANT'S EMPLOYER, AND CONTAIN INFORMATION ATTESTING TO

THE REPORTER'S STATUS WITH THA ORGANIZATION.

(2) AMERICAN RED CROSS: APPLICANT ESTABLISHES THAT HE OR SHE IS A REPRESENTATIVE OF THE AMERICAN RED CROSS OR INTERNATIONAL RED CROSS TRAVELING PURSUANT TO AN OFFICIALLY SPONSORED RED CROSS MISSION.

(3) HUMANITARIAN CONSIDERATIONS: APPLICANT MUST ESTABLISH THAT HIS OR HER TRIP IS JUSTIFIED BY COMPELLING HUMANITARIAN CONSIDERATIONS. AT THIS TIME, +COMPELLING HUMANITARIAN CONSIDERATIONS + ARE BEING INTERPRETED AS EITHER THOSE SITUATIONS WHERE THE APPLICANT CAN DOCUMENT THAT AN IMMEDIATE FAMILY MEMBER IS CRITICALLY ILL IN LEBANON, OR +FAMILY UNIFICATION+ CASES WHERE SPOUSES OR MINOR CHILDREN ARE RESIDING IN LEBANON, WITH AND DEPENDENT ON, A LEBANESE NATIONAL SPOUSE OR PARENT FOR THEIR SUPPORT. DOCUMENTATION CONCERNING FAMILY ILLNESS MUST INCLUDE THE NAME AND ADDRESS OF THE RELATIVE, AND BE FROM THAT RELATIVE'S PHYSICIAN ATTESTING TO THE NATURE AND GRAVITY OF THE ILLNESS.

(4) NATIONAL INTEREST: THE APPLICANT'S REQUEST IS OTHERWISE FOUND TO BE IN THE NATIONAL INTEREST. IN ALL REQUESTS FOR PASSPORT VALIDATION FOR TRAVEL TO LEBANON, THE NAME, DATE AND PLACE OF BIRTH FOR ALL CONCERNED PERSONS MUST BE GIVEN, AS WELL AS THE U.S. PASSPORT NUMBERS, IF ANY EXIST. DOCUMENTATION AS OUTLINED ABOVE SHOULD ACCOMPANY ALL REQUESTS. ADDITIONAL INFORMATION MAY BE OBTAINED BY WRITING TO THE ABOVE ADDRESS OR BY CALLING THE OFFICE OF CITIZENSHIP APPEALS AND LEGAL ASSISTANCE AT (202) 326-6178 OR 326-6168.

4. EXPIRATION DATE: INDEFINITE.

5. THIS CANCELS TRAVEL ADVISORY DATED JANUARY 31, 1987 CONTAINED IN 87 STATE 027056.

DEPARTMENT OF STATE WASHINGTON, D.C. 20520 293313/0983L

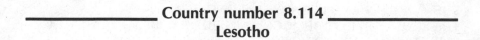

_____ **Country number 8.114** _____
Lesotho

INFECTIOUS DISEASE RISK

Malaria Risk

There is no malaria risk in this country.

Diseases of Special Risk

In addition to the worldwide hazard of tetanus and the routine and any special immunizations recommended below, the traveler should be aware that

risk of exposure to the following diseases exists in this country. This list is not all inclusive, but it is a caution concerning the more likely endemic disease risks.

Schistosomiasis may be found in this country. Avoid contact with contaminated fresh water lakes, ponds, or streams. Locations of infection are not confirmed.

DISEASE RISK PROFILE

Disease	endemic	risk	hazard
Diarrheal Disease Risk		x	
Dysentery, Amoebic		x	
Plague	x		
Rabies		x	
Relapsing Fever	x		
Rift Valley Fever	x		
Trypanosomiasis, African Sleeping Sickness	x		
Typhoid Fever		x	
Typhus, Scrub	x		

Food/Water Safety

Water, milk, and food is safe in Maseru, but precautions should be taken in other areas of the country.

VACCINATIONS

Yellow fever—A vaccination certificate is required for travelers coming from infected areas. Children under nine months of age should not be vaccinated due to health considerations. The U.S. Embassy reports that the yellow fever certificate is generally not checked by officials upon entry to this countyr.

Routine immunizations should be current. For infants and children through 16 years of age, refer to Chapter 4.3. A rubeola (measles) booster should be considered. Persons age 16 to 65 should receive a booster of tetanus and diphtheria every ten years. Healthy adults under age 65 do not require pneumococcal vaccine, but it is appropriate for those with chronic medical conditions. Influenza vaccine may be considered for those providing essential community services, health care workers, and those wishing to reduce the likelihood of becoming ill with influenza. Adults over 65 years of age are urged to obtain yearly influenza immunization and to insure that their tetanus and diphtheria immunizations are current. Pneumococcal vaccination is also suggested for this age group.

The vaccinations listed are recommended for the traveler's protection.
Poliomyelitis—A poliomyelitis booster is indicated for this country.
Viral Hepatitis A—Vaccination is recommended for all travelers for their protection.

Typhoid fever—Vaccination is recommended for all travelers for their protection.

Selective vaccinations—These apply only to specific groups of travelers or persons on specific working assignments:

Viral Hepatitis B—Because of the high rate of healthy carriers of hepatitis B in this country, vaccination is recommended for persons on working assignments in the health care field (dentists, physicians, nurses, laboratory technicians), or working in close contact with the local population (teachers, missionaries, Peace Corps), or persons foreseeing sexual relations with local inhabitants.

Plague—Vaccination is recommended only for persons who may be occupationally exposed to wild rodents (anthropologists, geologists, medical personnel, missionaries, etc). The standard vaccination course must be completed before entering the plague infested area. Geographical distribution of the area of risk for this country is the western half of the country.

Rabies—In this country, where rabies is a constant threat, a pre-exposure rabies vaccination is advised for persons planning an extended stay or on working assignments (naturalists, agricultural advisors, archeologists, geologists, etc.). Although this provides adequate initial protection, a person bitten by a potentially rabid animal would still require post exposure immunization (see Chapter 6.40). Children should be cautioned not to pet dogs, cats, or other mammals.

U.S. Foreign Service:
P.O. Box MS 333, Maseru 100
Maseru, Telephone 22666/7, 313892

Country number 8.115
Liberia

INFECTIOUS DISEASE RISK

Malaria Risk
Malaria is present in all parts of this country, including urban areas. The risk exists all year. The malaria in this country is resistant to chloroquine. The CDC recommends the use of mefloquine (Lariam) as described in Chapter 6.31 for chemical prophylaxis.

Falciparum malaria represents 90% of malaria, therefore there is a 10% risk of p. vivax malaria exposure. Consider use of primaquine upon return home.

Diseases of Special Risk

In addition to the worldwide hazard of tetanus and the routine and any special immunizations recommended below, the traveler should be aware that risk of exposure to the following diseases exists in this country. This list is not all inclusive, but it is a caution concerning the more likely endemic disease risks.

Potential risk of dengue fever exists. The virus is present in this country at all times and may give rise to major outbreaks.

Schistosomiasis may be found in this country. Avoid contact with contaminated fresh water lakes, ponds, or streams. The coastal regions of Liberia are free of infection.

DISEASE RISK PROFILE

Disease	endemic	risk	hazard
Diarrheal Disease Risk			x
Dysentery, Amoebic/Bacillary			x
Echinococcosis		x	
Filariasis			x
Helminthic Diseases (see Chapter 6.21)			x
Hepatitis, Viral			x
Lassa Fever	x		
Loiasis			x
Onchocerciasis			x
Polio			x
Rabies	x		
Relapsing Fever	x		
Trachoma			x
Trypanosomiasis, African Sleeping Sickness	x		
Tungiasis			x
Typhoid Fever			x

Food/Water Safety

All tap water used for drinking, brushing teeth, and making ice cubes should be boiled prior to use. Insure that bottled water is uncapped in your presence. Milk should be boiled to insure safety. Powdered and evaporated milk are available and safe. Avoid butter and other dairy products. All meat, poultry and seafood must be well cooked and served while hot. Pork is best avoided. Vegetables should be well cooked and served hot. Salads and mayonnaise are best avoided. Fruits with intact skins should be peeled by you just prior to consumption. Avoid cold buffets, custards, and any frozen dessert.

VACCINATIONS

Yellow fever—A vaccination certificate is required for travelers coming from all countries. A vaccination certificate is required for children over one year of age. CDC recommends vaccination for all travelers over 9 months of age, but see also Chapter 6.63.

Routine immunizations should be current. For infants and children through 16 years of age, refer to Chapter 4.3. A rubeola (measles) booster should be considered. Persons age 16 to 65 should receive a booster of tetanus and diphtheria every ten years. Healthy adults under age 65 do not require pneumococcal vaccine, but it is appropriate for those with chronic medical conditions. Influenza vaccine may be considered for those providing essential community services, health care workers, and those wishing to reduce the likelihood of becoming ill with influenza. Adults over 65 years of age are urged to obtain yearly influenza immunization and to insure that their tetanus and diphtheria immunizations are current. Pneumococcal vaccination is also suggested for this age group.

The vaccinations listed are recommended for the traveler's protection.
Poliomyelitis—A poliomyelitis booster is indicated for this country.
Cholera—Cholera is present in this country. Risk to western travelers is low. Immunization is not required or recommended for travel to this country due to its low effectiveness. Avoid uncooked foods and untreated water. Vaccination is advised only for persons living or working under inadequate sanitary conditions and for those with impaired defense mechanisms.
Viral Hepatitis A—Vaccination is recommended for all travelers for their protection.
Typhoid fever—Vaccination is recommended for all travelers for their protection.

Selective vaccinations—*These apply only to specific groups of travelers or persons on specific working assignments:*
Viral Hepatitis B—Because of the high rate of healthy carriers of hepatitis B in this country, vaccination is recommended for persons on working assignments in the health care field (dentists, physicians, nurses, laboratory technicians), or working in close contact with the local population (teachers, missionaries, Peace Corps), or persons foreseeing sexual relations with local inhabitants.
Rabies—In this country, where rabies is a constant threat, a pre-exposure rabies vaccination is advised for persons planning an extended stay or on working assignments (naturalists, agricultural advisors, archeologists, geologists, etc.). Although this provides adequate initial protection, a person bitten by a potentially rabid animal would still require post exposure immunization (see Chapter 6.40). Children should be cautioned not to pet dogs, cats, or other mammals.

U.S. Foreign Service:
111 United Nations Dr.
Monrovia, Telephone 22991/2/3/4

TRAVEL ADVISORY

A U.S. Department of State Travel Advisory was in effect on 4 May 1990 when this book went to press. The entire text is included below. Travel advisories are subject to reissue, change, and cancellation at any time. Current travel advisory information is available by calling the U.S. Department of State Travel Advisory Hotline at (202) 647-5225. The current travel advisory status is also available from the Herchmer Database update system (see Chapter 2.8).

APRIL 24, 1990
LIBERIA—WARNING
THE U.S. DEPARTMENT OF STATE ADVISES U.S. CITIZENS TO DE-FER ALL NON-ESSENTIAL TRAVEL TO LIBERIA UNTIL FURTHER NO-TICE DUE TO CONTINUED FIGHTING BETWEEN REBELS AND GOVERNMENT FORCES IN THE INTERIOR.
EXPIRATION: INDEFINITE

_____ Country number 8.116 _____
Libyan Arab Jamahiriya (Republic)
Libya

INFECTIOUS DISEASE RISK

Malaria Risk

There is no malaria risk in this country exceot in two small areas in the south of the country. The CDC does not recommend taking any preventative medication for travel to this country.

Falciparum malaria represents 1% of malaria, therefore the risk of exposure is limited to p. vivax malaria in the infected areas. Consider use of Primaquine upon return home (see Chapter 6.31), if travel and exposure in southwest Libia has occurred.

Diseases of Special Risk

In addition to the worldwide hazard of tetanus and the routine and any special immunizations recommended below, the traveler should be aware that risk of exposure to the following diseases exists in this country. This list is not all inclusive, but it is a caution concerning the more likely endemic disease risks.

Schistosomiasis may be found in this country. Avoid contact with contaminated fresh water lakes, ponds, or streams. Infection exists in the coastal areas of Dabusia and Lathrum west of Darnah (Derna), and in a restricted focus in Taurorga west of Misratah; risk is also present in the southwestern part of the country in the valleys of Fezzan including the area of Al Birkah on the Algerian border.

DISEASE RISK PROFILE

Disease	endemic	risk	hazard
Brucellosis		x	
Dengue Fever	x		
Diarrheal Disease Risk		x	
Echinococcosis	x		
Giardiasis		x	
Helminthic Diseases (see Chapter 6.21)		x	
Hepatitis, Viral		x	
Leishmaniasis	x		
Polio	x		
Rabies	x		
Relapsing Fever	x		
Rift Valley Fever	x		
Sandfly Fever	x		
Trachoma	x		
Typhoid Fever		x	
Typhus	x		

Food/Water Safety

All tap water used for drinking, brushing teeth, and making ice cubes should be boiled prior to use. Insure that bottled water is uncapped in your presence. Milk should be boiled to insure safety. Powdered and evaporated milk are available and safe. Avoid butter and other dairy products. All meat, poultry and seafood must be well cooked and served while hot. Pork is best avoided. Vegetables should be well cooked and served hot. Salads and mayonnaise are best avoided. Fruits with intact skins should be peeled by you just prior to consumption. Avoid cold buffets, custards, and any frozen dessert. First class hotels and restaurants in Al Jaghbub, Banghazi (Benghazi), and Tarabulus (Tripoli) serve purified drinking water and reliable food. However, the hazard is left to your judgement.

VACCINATIONS

Yellow fever—A vaccination certificate is required for travelers coming from infected areas. A vaccination certificate is required for children over one year of age.

Routine immunizations should be current. For infants and children through 16 years of age, refer to Chapter 4.3. A rubeola (measles) booster should be considered. Persons age 16 to 65 should receive a booster of tetanus and diphtheria every ten years. Healthy adults under age 65 do not require pneumococcal vaccine, but it is appropriate for those with chronic medical conditions. Influenza vaccine may be considered for those providing essential community services, health care workers, and those wishing to reduce the likelihood of becoming ill with influenza. Adults over 65 years of age are urged to obtain yearly influenza immunization and to insure that their tetanus and diphtheria immunizations are current. Pneumococcal vaccination is also suggested for this age group.

The vaccinations listed are recommended for the traveler's protection.
Poliomyelitis—A poliomyelitis booster is indicated for this country.
Viral Hepatitis A—Vaccination is recommended for all travelers for their protection.
Typhoid fever—Vaccination is recommended for all travelers for their protection.

Selective vaccinations—*These apply only to specific groups of travelers or persons on specific working assignments:*
Plague—Vaccination is recommended only for persons who may be occupationally exposed to wild rodents (anthropologists, geologists, medical personnel, missionaries, etc). The standard vaccination course must be completed before entering the plague infested area. Geographical distribution of the area of risk for this country is around Tobruk (northeastern part of the country) and the areas around Sidra.
Rabies—In this country, where rabies is a constant threat, a pre-exposure rabies vaccination is advised for persons planning an extended stay or on working assignments (naturalists, agricultural advisors, archeologists, geologists, etc.). Although this provides adequate initial protection, a person bitten by a potentially rabid animal would still require post exposure immunization (see Chapter 6.40). Children should be cautioned not to pet dogs, cats, or other mammals.

TRAVEL ADVISORY
A U.S. Department of State Travel Advisory was in effect on 4 May 1990 when this book went to press. The entire text is included below. Travel advisories are subject to reissue, change, and cancellation at any time. Current travel advisory information is available by calling the U.S. Department of State Travel Advisory Hotline at (202) 647-5225. The current travel advisory status is also available from the Herchmer Database update system (see Chapter 2.8).

9FB DN37 2-1 1LA71 2 09/06/89 08:57
SECSTATE WSH
SUBJECT: TRAVEL ADVISORY— LIBYA— WARNING 1. ON DECEMBER 11, 1981, U.S. PASSPORTS CEASED TO BE VALID FOR TRAVEL TO, IN OR THROUGH LIBYA AND MAY NOT BE USED FOR THAT PURPOSE UNLESS A SPECIAL VALIDATION HAS BEEN OBTAINED. USE OF A U.S. PASSPORT FOR TRAVEL TO, IN OR THROUGH LIBYA MAY CONSTITUTE A VIOLATION OF 18 U.S.C. 1544, AND BE PUNISHABLE BY A FINE AND/OR IMPRISONMENT.
2. THE CATEGORIES OF INDIVIDUALS ELIGIBLE FOR CONSIDERATION FOR A SPECIAL VALIDATION ARE SET FORTH IN 22 C.F.R. 51.74. PASSPORT VALIDATION REQUESTS FOR LIBYA SHOULD BE FORWARDED IN WRITING TO THE FOLLOWING ADDRESS:

MR. HARRY L. COBURN DEPUTY ASSISTANT SECRETARY FOR PASSPORT SERVICES U.S. DEPARTMENT OF STATE 1425 K STREET, N.W. WASHINGTON, D.C. 20522-1705 ATTN: OFFICE OF CITIZENSHIP APPEALS AND LEGAL ASSISTANCE (RM 300)

THE REQUEST MUST BE ACCOMPANIED BY SUBSTANTIATING DOCUMENTATION ACCORDING TO THE CATEGORY UNDER WHICH VALIDATION IS SOUGHT. CURRENTLY, THE FOUR CATEGORIES OF PERSONS BEING CONSIDERED ARE AS FOLLOWS:

(1) PROFESSIONAL REPORTER: INCLUDES FULL-TIME MEMBERS OF THE REPORTING OR WRITING STAFF OF A NEWSPAPER, MAGAZINE OR BROADCASTING NETWORK WHOSE PURPOSE FOR TRAVEL IS TO GATHER INFORMATION ABOUT LIBYA FOR DISSEMINATION TO THE GENERAL PUBLIC. THE REQUEST MUST COME FROM THE APPLICANT'S EMPLOYER, AND CONTAIN INFORMATION ATTESTING TO THE REPORTER'S STATUS WITH THAT ORGANIZATION.

(2) AMERICAN RED CROSS: APPLICANT ESTABLISHES THAT HE OR SHE IS A REPRESENTATIVE OF THE AMERICAN RED CROSS OR INTERNATIONAL RED CROSS TRAVELING PURSUANT TO AN OFFICIALLY SPONSORED RED CROSS MISSION.

(3) HUMANITARIAN CONSIDERATIONS: APPLICANT MUST ESTABLISH THAT HIS OR HER TRIP IS JUSTIFIED BY COMPELLING HUMANITARIAN CONSIDERATIONS. AT THIS TIME, +COMPELLING HUMANITARIAN CONSIDERATIONS+ ARaE BEING INTERPRETED AS EITHER THOSE SITUATIONS WHERE THE APPLICANT CAN DOCUMENT THAT AN IMMEDIATE FAMILY MEMBER IS CRITICALLY ILL IN LIBYA, OR +FAMILY UNIFICATION+ CASES WHERE SPOUSES OR MINOR CHILDREN ARE RESIDING IN LIBYA, WITH AND DEPENDENT;OR ON, A LIBYAN NATIONAL SPOUSE OR PARENT FOR THEIR SUPPORT. DOCUMENTATION CONCERNING FAMILY ILLNESS MUST INCLUDE THE NAME AND ADDRESS OF THE RELATIVE, AND BE FROM THAT RELATIVE'S PHYSICIAN ATTESTING TO THE NATURE AND GRAVITY OF THE ILLNESS.

(4) NATIONAL INTEREST: THE APPLICANT'S REQUEST IS OTHERWISE FOUND TO BE IN THE NATIONAL INTEREST.

IN ALL REQUESTS FOR PASSPORT VALIDATION FOR TRAVEL TO LIBYA, THE NAME, DATE AND PLACE OF BIRTH FOR ALL CONCERNED PERSONS MUST BE GIVEN, AS WELL AS THE U.S. PASSPORT NUMBERS, IF ANY EXIST. DOCUMENTATION AS OUTLINED ABOVE SHOULD ACCOMPANY ALL REQUESTS. ADDITIONAL INFORMATION MAY BE OBTAINED BY WRITING TO THE ABOVE ADDRESS OR BY CALLING THE OFFICE OF CITIZENSHIP APPEALS AND LEGAL ASSISTANCE AT (202) 326-6168 OR 6178.

4. PERSONS CONTEMPLATING TRAVEL TO LIBYA ALSO SHOULD BE AWARE THAT THERE IS NO U.S. MISSION IN LIBYA AND THAT OUR

INTERESTS ARE BEING PROTECTED AND REPRESENTED BY THE GOVERNMENT OF BELGIUM. THIS PROTECTING POWER CAN PRO-VIDE ONLY LIMITED EMERGENCY SERVICES, AND THE NORMAL PROTECTION OF U.S. DIPLOMATIC AND CONSULAR REPRESENTA-TIVES CANNOT BE PROVIDED TO AMERICANS TRAVELING IN LIBYA. 5. U.S. TREASURY RESTRICTIONS: THE U.S. DEPARTMENT OF TREASURY (OFFICE OF FOREIGN ASSETS CONTROL), ALSO HAS IMPOSED RESTRICTIONS UPON U.S. CITIZENS WHO WISH TO TRA-VEL TO LIBYA. QUESTIONS CONCERNING THESE RESTRICTIONS, AND ANY EXCEPTIONS TO THE RESTRICTIONS, MUST BE AD-DRESSED DIREdCTLY TO THAT AGENCY. THE ADDRESS AND TELE-PHONE NUMBER ARE U.S. DEPARTMENT OF THE TREASURY, OFFICE OF FOREIGN ASSETS CONTROL, 1331 G STREET, N.W., WASHINGTON, D.C. 20220, (202) 376-0408.
6. EXPIRATION DATE: INDEFINITE.
7. THIS WARNING CANCELS PREVIOUS TRAVEL WARNING FOR LIBYA WHICH WAS ISSUED ON DECEMBER 1, 1984.
BAKER DEPT OF STATE WASHDC 285250 / L0406 655

Country number 8.117
Liechtenstein

INFECTIOUS DISEASE RISK

Malaria Risk
There is no malaria risk in this country.

Diseases of Special Risk
The traveler should be aware that risk of exposure to rabies occus in wild animals in this country.

Food/Water Safety
Local water is considered safe without further treatment. Milk is pasteur-ized and safe to drink. Butter, cheese, yogurt and ice-cream are safe. Local meat, poultry, seafood, vegetables, and fruits are safe to eat.

VACCINATIONS
Routine immunizations should be current. For infants and children through 16 years of age, refer to Chapter 4.3. A rubeola (measles) booster should be considered. Persons age 16 to 65 should receive a booster of tetanus and diphtheria every ten years. Healthy adults under age 65 do not require pneumococcal vaccine, but it is appropriate for those with chronic medical conditions. Influenza vaccine may be considered for those providing essential

community services, health care workers, and those wishing to reduce the likelihood of becoming ill with influenza. Adults over 65 years of age are urged to obtain yearly influenza immunization and to insure that their tetanus and diphtheria immunizations are current. Pneumococcal vaccination is also suggested for this age group.

No vaccinations are required to enter this country.

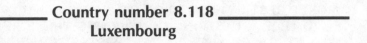

Country number 8.118
Luxembourg

INFECTIOUS DISEASE RISK

Malaria Risk
There is no malaria risk in this country.

Diseases of Special Risk
The traveler should be aware that risk of exposure to rabies occus in wild animals, especially foxes, in this country.

Food/Water Safety
Local water is considered safe without further treatment. Milk is pasteurized and safe to drink. Butter, cheese, yogurt and ice-cream are safe. Local meat, poultry, seafood, vegetables, and fruits are safe to eat.

VACCINATIONS
Routine immunizations should be current. For infants and children through 16 years of age, refer to Chapter 4.3. A rubeola (measles) booster should be considered. Persons age 16 to 65 should receive a booster of tetanus and diphtheria every ten years. Healthy adults under age 65 do not require pneumococcal vaccine, but it is appropriate for those with chronic medical conditions. Influenza vaccine may be considered for those providing essential community services, health care workers, and those wishing to reduce the likelihood of becoming ill with influenza. Adults over 65 years of age are urged to obtain yearly influenza immunization and to insure that their tetanus and diphtheria immunizations are current. Pneumococcal vaccination is also suggested for this age group.

No vaccinations are required to enter this country.

U.S. Foreign Service:
22 Blvd. Emmanuel-Servais
Luxembourg, Telephone 40123/4/5/6/7

_____ **Country number 8.119** _____
Macao

INFECTIOUS DISEASE RISK

Malaria Risk
There is no malaria risk in this country.

Diseases of Special Risk
In addition to the worldwide hazard of tetanus and the routine and any special immunizations recommended below, the traveler should be aware that risk of exposure to the following diseases exists in this country. This list is not all inclusive, but it is a caution concerning the more likely endemic disease risks.

DISEASE RISK PROFILE

Disease	endemic	risk	hazard
Dengue Fever	x		
Diarrheal Diseases		x	
Encephalitis, Japanese	x		
Helminthic Diseases (see Chapter 6.21)	x		
Hepatitis, Viral		x	

Food/Water Safety
First class hotels and restaurants serve purified drinking water and reliable food. However, the hazard is left to your judgement.

VACCINATIONS
Routine immunizations should be current. For infants and children through 16 years of age, refer to Chapter 4.3. A rubeola (measles) booster should be considered. Persons age 16 to 65 should receive a booster of tetanus and diphtheria every ten years. Healthy adults under age 65 do not require pneumococcal vaccine, but it is appropriate for those with chronic medical conditions. Influenza vaccine may be considered for those providing essential community services, health care workers, and those wishing to reduce the likelihood of becoming ill with influenza. Adults over 65 years of age are urged to obtain yearly influenza immunization and to insure that their tetanus and diphtheria immunizations are current. Pneumococcal vaccination is also suggested for this age group.
No vaccinations are required to enter this country.

Selective vaccinations—These apply only to specific groups of travelers or persons on specific working assignments:
Viral Hepatitis B—Because of the high rate of healthy carriers of hepatitis

B in this country, vaccination is recommended for persons on working assignments in the health care field (dentists, physicians, nurses, laboratory technicians), or working in close contact with the local population (teachers, missionaries, Peace Corps), or persons foreseeing sexual relations with local inhabitants.

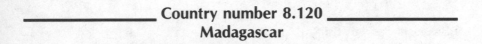

Country number 8.120
Madagascar

INFECTIOUS DISEASE RISK

Malaria Risk

Malaria is present in all parts of this country, below 1700 meters, including most urban areas. The risk exists all year. There is almost no risk of malaria in the town of Antananarivo and minimal risk in the outskirts. There is minimal risk in the towns of Antsirabe, Manjakandriana, and Anramasina. The malaria in this country is resistant to chloroquine. The CDC recommends the use of mefloquine (Lariam) as described in Chapter 6.31 for chemical prophylaxis.

Falciparum malaria represents 85% of malaria, therefore there is a slight risk of p. vivax malaria exposure. Consider use of primaquine upon return home.

Diseases of Special Risk

In addition to the worldwide hazard of tetanus and the routine and any special immunizations recommended below, the traveler should be aware that risk of exposure to the following diseases exists in this country. This list is not all inclusive, but it is a caution concerning the more likely endemic disease risks.

Schistosomiasis may be found in this country. Avoid contact with contaminated fresh water lakes, ponds, or streams. The following areas are not infected: the area of Diego Suarez on the extreme north tip of the island, the area of Antananarivo in the central part of the island, the peninsula Presqu'ile including the areas of Maroantsetra and Antalaha. S. haematobium is prevalent on the western part of the island, while S. mansoni is predominant in the eastern part.

DISEASE RISK PROFILE

Disease	endemic	risk	hazard
Dracunculiasis/Guinea Worm	x		
Diarrheal Disease Risk			x
Dysentery, Amoebic/Bacillary			x
Filariasis			x
Giardiasis			x

Disease	endemic	risk	hazard
Helminthic Diseases (see Chapter 6.21)			x
Hepatitis, Viral			x
Leishmaniasis			
Cutaneous	x		
Visceral	x		
Plague	x		
Polio	x		
Rabies	x		
Relapsing Fever	x		
Trachoma			x
Typhoid Fever			x
Typhus, Endemic Flea-Borne	x		
Typhus, Epidemic Louse-Borne	x		
Typhus, Scrub	x		

Food/Water Safety

All tap water used for drinking, brushing teeth, and making ice cubes should be boiled prior to use. Insure that bottled water is uncapped in your presence. Milk should be boiled to insure safety. Powdered and evaporated milk are available and safe. Avoid butter and other dairy products. All meat, poultry and seafood must be well cooked and served while hot. Pork is best avoided. Vegetables should be well cooked and served hot. Salads and mayonnaise are best avoided. Fruits with intact skins should be peeled by you just prior to consumption. Avoid cold buffets, custards, and any frozen dessert. First class hotels and restaurants in Antananarivo (Tananarive) and Tamatave serve purified drinking water and reliable food. However, the hazard is left to your judgement.

VACCINATIONS

Cholera—A cholera vaccination certificate is recommended for travelers coming from or having been in transit through areas considered infected. Local officials frequently demand, however, that travelers show proof of cholera immunization, even though they have not been in infected areas.

Yellow fever—A vaccination certificate is required for travelers coming from infected areas and sometimes from or in transit through countries in the endemic yellow fever zone, see Chapter 6.63. A vaccination is required for children of all ages. Children under 9 months of age should not be vaccinated due to health considerations. Please refer to the discussion in Chapter 6.63 on avoiding yellow fever vaccination in this age group.

Routine immunizations should be current. For infants and children through 16 years of age, refer to Chapter 4.3. A rubeola (measles) booster should be considered. Persons age 16 to 65 should receive a booster of tetanus and diphtheria every ten years. Healthy adults under age 65 do not require pneumococcal vaccine, but it is appropriate for those with chronic medical conditions. Influenza vaccine may be considered for those providing essential community services, health care workers, and those wishing to reduce the likelihood of becoming ill with influenza. Adults over 65 years of age are urged to

obtain yearly influenza immunization and to insure that their tetanus and diphtheria immunizations are current. Pneumococcal vaccination is also suggested for this age group.

The vaccinations listed are recommended for the traveler's protection.
Poliomyelitis—A poliomyelitis booster is indicated for this country.
Viral Hepatitis A—Vaccination is recommended for all travelers for their protection.
Typhoid fever—Vaccination is recommended for all travelers for their protection.

Selective vaccinations—These apply only to specific groups of travelers or persons on specific working assignments:
Viral Hepatitis B—Because of the high rate of healthy carriers of hepatitis B in this country, vaccination is recommended for persons on working assignments in the health care field (dentists, physicians, nurses, laboratory technicians), or working in close contact with the local population (teachers, missionaries, Peace Corps), or persons foreseeing sexual relations with local inhabitants.
Plague—Vaccination is recommended only for persons who may be occupationally exposed to wild rodents (anthropologists, geologists, medical personnel, missionaries, etc). The standard vaccination course must be completed before entering the plague infested area. Geographical distribution of the area of risk for this country is in the central highlands (Antananarivo and Fianarantsoa provinces).
Rabies—In this country, where rabies is a constant threat, a pre-exposure rabies vaccination is advised for persons planning an extended stay or on working assignments (naturalists, agricultural advisors, archeologists, geologists, etc.). Although this provides adequate initial protection, a person bitten by a potentially rabid animal would still require post exposure immunization (see Chapter 6.40). Children should be cautioned not to pet dogs, cats, or other mammals.

U.S. Foreign Service:
14 and 16 Rue Rainitovo, Antsohavola
Antananarivo, Telephone 212-57, 209-56

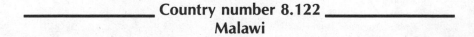

Country number 8.121
Madeira

INFECTIOUS DISEASE RISK

Malaria Risk
There is no malaria risk in this country.

Food/Water Safety
Local water is considered safe without further treatment. Milk is pasteurized and safe to drink. Butter, cheese, yogurt and ice-cream are safe. Local meat, poultry, seafood, vegetables, and fruits are safe to eat.

VACCINATIONS
Yellow fever—A vaccination certificate is required for travelers coming from infected areas and from or in transit through countries with active infection. A vaccination certificate is required for children over one year of age. The requirement applies only to travelers arriving in or destined for the Azores and Madeira. No certificate is, however, required from transit passengers at Funchal, Porto Santo, and Santa Maria.

Routine immunizations should be current. For infants and children through 16 years of age, refer to Chapter 4.3. A rubeola (measles) booster should be considered. Persons age 16 to 65 should receive a booster of tetanus and diphtheria every ten years. Healthy adults under age 65 do not require pneumococcal vaccine, but it is appropriate for those with chronic medical conditions. Influenza vaccine may be considered for those providing essential community services, health care workers, and those wishing to reduce the likelihood of becoming ill with influenza. Adults over 65 years of age are urged to obtain yearly influenza immunization and to insure that their tetanus and diphtheria immunizations are current. Pneumococcal vaccination is also suggested for this age group.

Country number 8.122
Malawi

INFECTIOUS DISEASE RISK

Malaria Risk
Malaria is present in all parts of this country, including urban areas. The risk exists all year. The malaria in this country is resistant to chloroquine. The CDC recommends the use of mefloquine (Lariam) as described in Chapter 6.31 for chemical prophylaxis.

Falciparum malaria represents 90% of malaria, therefore there is a slight risk of p. vivax malaria exposure. Consider use of primaquine upon return home.

Diseases of Special Risk

In addition to the worldwide hazard of tetanus and the routine and any special immunizations recommended below, the traveler should be aware that risk of exposure to the following diseases exists in this country. This list is not all inclusive, but it is a caution concerning the more likely endemic disease risks.

Schistosomiasis may be found in this country in all areas, including urban settlements. Avoid contact with contaminated fresh water lakes, ponds, or streams.

DISEASE RISK PROFILE

Disease	endemic	risk	hazard
Dracunculiasis/Guinea Worm	x		
Diarrheal Disease Risk			x
Dysentery, Amoebic/Bacillary			x
Echinococcosis		x	
Filariasis			x
Giardiasis			x
Helminthic Diseases (see Chapter 6.21)			x
Hepatitis, Viral			x
Leishmaniasis			
Cutaneous	x		
Visceral	x		
Meningitis	x		
Onchocerciasis			x
Polio			x
Rabies		x	
Relapsing Fever	x		
Trachoma			x
Trypanosomiasis, African Sleeping Sickness	x		
Typhoid Fever			x
Typhus, Endemic Flea-Borne	x		
Typhus, Epidemic Louse-Borne	x		
Typhus, Scrub	x		

Food/Water Safety

All tap water used for drinking, brushing teeth, and making ice cubes should be boiled prior to use. Insure that bottled water is uncapped in your presence. Milk should be boiled to insure safety. Powdered and evaporated milk are available and safe. Avoid butter and other dairy products. All meat, poultry and seafood must be well cooked and served while hot. Pork is best avoided. Vegetables should be well cooked and served hot. Salads and mayonnaise are

best avoided. Fruits with intact skins should be peeled by you just prior to consumption. Avoid cold buffets, custards, and any frozen dessert. First class hotels and restaurants in Blantyre serve purified drinking water and reliable food. However, the hazard is left to your judgement.

VACCINATIONS

Yellow fever—A vaccination certificate is required for travelers coming from infected areas and from or in transit through countries in the endemic yellow fever zone, see Chapter 6.63. A vaccination is required for children of all ages. Children under nine months of age should not be vaccinated due to health considerations. Please refer to the discussion in Chapter 6.63 on avoiding yellow fever vaccination in this age group. Vaccination is recommended for all travelers for their protection. Vaccination is not advised for children under nine months of age.

Routine immunizations should be current. For infants and children through 16 years of age, refer to Chapter 4.3. A rubeola (measles) booster should be considered. Persons age 16 to 65 should receive a booster of tetanus and diphtheria every ten years. Healthy adults under age 65 do not require pneumococcal vaccine, but it is appropriate for those with chronic medical conditions. Influenza vaccine may be considered for those providing essential community services, health care workers, and those wishing to reduce the likelihood of becoming ill with influenza. Adults over 65 years of age are urged to obtain yearly influenza immunization and to insure that their tetanus and diphtheria immunizations are current. Pneumococcal vaccination is also suggested for this age group.

The vaccinations listed are recommended for the traveler's protection.
Poliomyelitis—A poliomyelitis booster is indicated for this country.
Viral Hepatitis A—Vaccination is recommended for all travelers for their protection.
Typhoid fever—Vaccination is recommended for all travelers for their protection.

Selective vaccinations—*These apply only to specific groups of travelers or persons on specific working assignments:*
Viral Hepatitis B—Because of the high rate of healthy carriers of hepatitis B in this country, vaccination is recommended for persons on working assignments in the health care field (dentists, physicians, nurses, laboratory technicians), or working in close contact with the local population (teachers, missionaries, Peace Corps), or persons foreseeing sexual relations with local inhabitants.
Plague—Vaccination is recommended only for persons who may be occupationally exposed to wild rodents (anthropologists, geologists, medical personnel, missionaries, etc). The standard vaccination course must be completed

before entering the plague infested area. Geographical distribution of the area of risk for this country is the southern half of the country.

Rabies—In this country, where rabies is a constant threat, a pre-exposure rabies vaccination is advised for persons planning an extended stay or on working assignments (naturalists, agricultural advisors, archeologists, geologists, etc.). Although this provides adequate initial protection, a person bitten by a potentially rabid animal would still require post exposure immunization (see Chapter 6.40). Children should be cautioned not to pet dogs, cats, or other mammals.

U.S. Foreign Service:
P.O. Box 30016
Lilongwe, Telephone 730-166
Kanabar House
2nd Fl., Victoria Ave.
Blantyre, Telephone 635-721

Country number 8.123
Malaysia

INFECTIOUS DISEASE RISK

Malaria Risk
Malaria is present only below 1700 meters this country, in rural areas only. Urban and coastal areas are free of malaria, except in Sabah. The risk exists all year. The malaria in this country is resistant to chloroquine. The CDC recommends the use of mefloquine (Lariam) as described in Chapter 6.31 for chemical prophylaxis.

Falciparum malaria represents 22% of malaria, therefore there is a risk of p. vivax malaria exposure. Consider use of Primaquine upon return home.

Diseases of Special Risk
In addition to the worldwide hazard of tetanus and the routine and any special immunizations recommended below, the traveler should be aware that risk of exposure to the following diseases exists in this country. This list is not all inclusive, but it is a caution concerning the more likely endemic disease risks.

Potential risk of dengue fever exists. The virus is present in this country at all times and may give rise to major outbreaks. Dengue fever is on an increase in this country and may be a particular hazard during 1990 and 1991.

Schistosomiasis may be found in this country. Avoid contact with contaminated fresh water lakes, ponds, or streams. Foci of infection are present along the Kapor River system, tributary of the Pahang River (central Malaysia, east of

Kuala Lumpur). Foci of infection in Sabah (northeastern part of the island of Borneo) have not been ruled out.

Due to the high incidence of tuberculosis in this country, and pre-travel and post-travel TB test is recommended when traveling to this country.

DISEASE RISK PROFILE

Disease	endemic	risk	hazard
Cholera		x	
Opisthorchiasis	x		
Dengue Fever	x		
Diarrheal Disease Risk		x	
Dysentery, Amoebic/Bacillary		x	
Encephalitis, Japanese	x		
Fasciolopsiasis	x		
Filariasis			x
Hepatitis, Viral	x		
Melioidosis	x		
Polio	x		
Rabies	x		
Typhoid Fever	x		
Typhus, Scrub	x		

Food/Water Safety

All tap water used for drinking, brushing teeth, and making ice cubes should be boiled prior to use. Insure that bottled water is uncapped in your presence. Milk should be boiled to insure safety. Powdered and evaporated milk are available and safe. Avoid butter and other dairy products. All meat, poultry and seafood must be well cooked and served while hot. Pork is best avoided. Vegetables should be well cooked and served hot. Salads and mayonnaise are best avoided. Fruits with intact skins should be peeled by you just prior to consumption. Avoid cold buffets, custards, and any frozen dessert. First class hotels and restaurants in Kuala Lumpur and Pinang (George Town) serve purified drinking water and reliable food. However, the hazard is left to your judgement.

VACCINATIONS

Yellow fever—A vaccination certificate is required for travelers coming from infected areas and from or in transit through countries in the endemic yellow fever zone, see Chapter 6.63. A vaccination certificate is required for children over one year of age.

Routine immunizations should be current. For infants and children through 16 years of age, refer to Chapter 4.3. A rubeola (measles) booster should be considered. Persons age 16 to 65 should receive a booster of tetanus and diphtheria every ten years. Healthy adults under age 65 do not require pneumococcal vaccine, but it is appropriate for those with chronic medical conditions. Influenza vaccine may be considered for those providing essential

community services, health care workers, and those wishing to reduce the likelihood of becoming ill with influenza. Adults over 65 years of age are urged to obtain yearly influenza immunization and to insure that their tetanus and diphtheria immunizations are current. Pneumococcal vaccination is also suggested for this age group.

The vaccinations listed are recommended for the traveler's protection.
Poliomyelitis—A poliomyelitis booster is indicated for this country.
Cholera—Cholera is present in this country. Risk to western travelers is low. Immunization is generally not recommended for travel due to its low level of effectiveness, but this vaccine is considered appropriate when traveling to this country due to the significant exposure risk here. Avoid uncooked foods and untreated water. Vaccination is advised particularly for persons living or working under inadequate sanitary conditions and for those with impaired defense mechanisms.
Viral Hepatitis A—Vaccination is recommended when traveling outside the areas usually visited by tourists, traveling extensively in the interior of the country (trekkers, hikers) and for persons on working assignments in remote areas.
Typhoid fever—Vaccination is recommended when traveling outside the areas usually visited by tourists, traveling extensively in the interior of the country (trekkers, hikers) and for persons on working assignments in remote areas.

Selective vaccinations—These apply only to specific groups of travelers or persons on specific working assignments:
Viral Hepatitis B—Because of the high rate of healthy carriers of hepatitis B in this country, vaccination is recommended for persons on working assignments in the health care field (dentists, physicians, nurses, laboratory technicians), or working in close contact with the local population (teachers, missionaries, Peace Corps), or persons foreseeing sexual relations with local inhabitants.
Japanese encephalitis—Vaccination is indicated for persons traveling extensively in rual areas or living and working near rice growing rural and suburban areas and other irrigated land, when exposure to the disease carrying mosquitoes is high. Children are especially susceptible to the infection. Sporadic cases are reported throughout the country, throughout the year.

U.S. Foreign Service:
A.I.A. Bldg., Jalan Tun Razak
Kuala Lumpur, Telephone 489011

Canadian High Commission/Embassy Office:
A.I.A Bldg., 99 Jalan Ampang
5th Floor
Kuala Lumpur, 289722/3/4/5

TRAVEL ADVISORY

A U.S. Department of State Travel Advisory was in effect on 4 May 1990 when this book went to press. The entire text is included below. Travel advisories are subject to reissue, change, and cancellation at any time. Current travel advisory information is available by calling the U.S. Department of State Travel Advisory Hotline at (202) 647-5225. The current travel advisory status is also available from the Herchmer Database update system (see Chapter 2.8).

MALAYSIA
SUBJECT: TRAVEL ADVISOR—MALAYSIA
REF: KUALA LUMPUR 2676
1. THE DEPARTMENT OF STATE ADVISES ALL U.S. CITIZENS TRAVELING TO MALAYSIA THAT THE MALAYSIAN GOVERNMENT HAS RECENTLY ENACTED NEW LEGISLATION WHICH PROVIDES FOR A MANDATORY DEATH PENALTY FOR CONVICTED DRUG TRAFFICKERS: ANY PERSON, WHO IS ARRESTED AS A TRAFFICKER, WILL BE SUBJECT TO THE DEATH PENALTY REGARDLESS OF THE AMOUNT OF DRUGS IN THAT PERSON'S POSSESSION. IN ADDITION, ANY PERSON, MALAYSIAN OR FOREIGN NATIONAL, FOUND IN POSSESSION OF 15 GRAMS OR MORE OF HEROIN WILL BE A DRUG TRAFFICKER BY DEFINITION. THE SAME DEFINITION WILL BE APPLIED FOR OTHER DRUGS, INCLUDING MARIJUANA, THOUGH WITH SOMEWHAT HIGHER MINIMUMS.
2. ANYONE WHO ENTERS A FOREIGN COUNTRY BECOMES SUBJECT TO THE LAWS OF THAT COUNTRY. WHILE THE DEPARTMENT OF STATE AND OUR CONSULAR OFFICERS OVERSEAS ARE CONCERNED ABOUT ALL AMERICAN CITIZENS ARRESTED ABROAD, WE CANNOT INTERVENE IN THE LEGAL PROCESS OF ANOTHER COUNTRY OR ACT AS LEGAL COUNSEL ON BEHALF OF THE IMPRISONED AMERICAN CITIZEN. UNDER PRESENT STANDARDS OF INTERNATIONAL LAW, CUSTOM, AND TREATY, THE UNITED STATES CANNOT DEMAND THAT AMERICANS BE GIVEN PREFERENTIAL TREATMENT OR RIGHTS NOT AFFORDED TO NATIONALS OF OTHER COUNTRIES.
3. EXPIRATION DATE: INDEFINITE. SHULTZ

_____ **Country number 8.124** _____
Maldives

INFECTIOUS DISEASE RISK

Malaria Risk

There is no risk of malaria in Male Island, Kaafu Atoll and resort areas. The CDC recommends a weekly dose of chloroquine when traveling to areas of risk in this country. Malaria in other areas is only 1% falciparum. Consider use of Primaquine therapy upon return home if heavy exposure occurs (see Chapter 6.31).

Diseases of Special Risk

In addition to the worldwide hazard of tetanus and the routine and any special immunizations recommended below, the traveler should be aware that risk of exposure to the following diseases exists in this country. This list is not all inclusive, but it is a caution concerning the more likely endemic disease risks.

Potential risk of dengue fever exists. The virus is present in this country at all times and may give rise to major outbreaks.

DISEASE RISK PROFILE

Disease	endemic	risk	hazard
Brucellosis		x	
Cholera		x	
Diarrheal Disease Risk		x	
Dysentery, Amoebic/Bacillary		x	
Echinococcosis		x	
Helminthic Diseases (see Chapter 6.21)		x	
Hemorrhagic Fever, Crimea-Congo	x		
Hepatitis, Viral		x	
Leishmaniasis Visceral			x
Polio			x
Rabies		x	
Sandfly Fever			x
Typhoid Fever		x	

Food/Water Safety

All tap water used for drinking, brushing teeth, and making ice cubes should be boiled prior to use. Insure that bottled water is uncapped in your presence. Milk should be boiled to insure safety. Powdered and evaporated milk are available and safe. Avoid butter and other dairy products. All meat, poultry and seafood must be well cooked and served while hot. Pork is best avoided. Vegetables should be well cooked and served hot. Salads and mayonnaise are

best avoided. Fruits with intact skins should be peeled by you just prior to consumption. Avoid cold buffets, custards, and any frozen dessert.

VACCINATIONS

Yellow fever—A vaccination certificate is required for travelers coming from infected areas. A vaccination is required for children of all ages. Children under nine months of age should not be vaccinated due to health considerations. Please refer to the discussion in Chapter 6.63 on avoiding yellow fever vaccination in this age group.

Routine immunizations should be current. For infants and children through 16 years of age, refer to Chapter 4.3. A rubeola (measles) booster should be considered. Persons age 16 to 65 should receive a booster of tetanus and diphtheria every ten years. Healthy adults under age 65 do not require pneumococcal vaccine, but it is appropriate for those with chronic medical conditions. Influenza vaccine may be considered for those providing essential community services, health care workers, and those wishing to reduce the likelihood of becoming ill with influenza. Adults over 65 years of age are urged to obtain yearly influenza immunization and to insure that their tetanus and diphtheria immunizations are current. Pneumococcal vaccination is also suggested for this age group.

The vaccinations listed are recommended for the traveler's protection.

Poliomyelitis—A poliomyelitis booster is indicated for this country.

Viral Hepatitis A—Vaccination is recommended for all travelers for their protection.

Typhoid fever—Vaccination is recommended for all travelers for their protection.

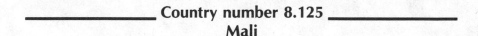

Country number 8.125
Mali

INFECTIOUS DISEASE RISK

Malaria Risk

Malaria is present in all parts of this country, including urban areas. The risk exists all year. The malaria in this country is resistant to chloroquine. The CDC recommends the use of mefloquine (Lariam) as described in Chapter 6.31 for chemical prophylaxis.

Falciparum malaria represents 85% of malaria, therefore there is a risk of p. vivax malaria exposure. Consider the use of primaquine upon return home.

Diseases of Special Risk

In addition to the worldwide hazard of tetanus and the routine and any special immunizations recommended below, the traveler should be aware that

risk of exposure to the following diseases exists in this country. This list is not all inclusive, but it is a caution concerning the more likely endemic disease risks.

Schistosomiasis may be found throughout this country, including urban areas. Avoid contact with contaminated fresh water lakes, ponds, or streams.

Cholera is present in this country. Risk to western travelers is low. Immunization is not required or recommended for travel to this country due to its low effectiveness. Avoid uncooked foods and untreated water.

DISEASE RISK PROFILE

Disease	endemic	risk	hazard
Dracunculiasis/Guinea Worm	x		
Diarrheal Disease Risk			x
Dysentery, Amoebic/Bacillary			x
Echinococcosis		x	
Filariasis			x
Giardiasis			x
Helminthic Diseases (see Chapter 6.21)			x
Hepatitis, Viral			x
Lassa Fever	x		
Leishmaniasis			
Cutaneous	x		
Visceral	x		
Loiasis			x
Onchocerciasis			x
Rabies	x		
Relapsing Fever	x		
Trachoma			x
Trypanosomiasis, African	x		
Sleeping Sickness			
Tungiasis			x
Typhoid Fever			x
Typhus, Endemic Flea-Borne	x		
Typhus, Epidemic Louse-Borne	x		
Typhus, Scrub	x		

Food/Water Safety

All tap water used for drinking, brushing teeth, and making ice cubes should be boiled prior to use. Insure that bottled water is uncapped in your presence. Milk should be boiled to insure safety. Powdered and evaporated milk are available and safe. Avoid butter and other dairy products. All meat, poultry and seafood must be well cooked and served while hot. Pork is best avoided. Vegetables should be well cooked and served hot. Salads and mayonnaise are best avoided. Fruits with intact skins should be peeled by you just prior to consumption. Avoid cold buffets, custards, and any frozen dessert.

VACCINATIONS

Yellow fever—A vaccination certificate is required on arrival from all countries. Except: travelers arriving from a non-infected area and staying less than two weeks in the country. Vaccination is recommended for all travelers for their protection, including those visiting the capital Bamako. This disease is active in this country at this time. CDC recommends vaccination for all travelers over 9 months of age.

Routine immunizations should be current. For infants and children through 16 years of age, refer to Chapter 4.3. A rubeola (measles) booster should be considered. Persons age 16 to 65 should receive a booster of tetanus and diphtheria every ten years. Healthy adults under age 65 do not require pneumococcal vaccine, but it is appropriate for those with chronic medical conditions. Influenza vaccine may be considered for those providing essential community services, health care workers, and those wishing to reduce the likelihood of becoming ill with influenza. Adults over 65 years of age are urged to obtain yearly influenza immunization and to insure that their tetanus and diphtheria immunizations are current. Pneumococcal vaccination is also suggested for this age group.

The vaccinations listed are recommended for the traveler's protection.
Poliomyelitis—A poliomyelitis booster is indicated for this country.
Viral Hepatitis A—Vaccination is recommended for all travelers for their protection.
Typhoid fever—Vaccination is recommended for all travelers for their protection.

Selective vaccinations—These apply only to specific groups of travelers or persons on specific working assignments:
Viral Hepatitis B—Because of the high rate of healthy carriers of hepatitis B in this country, vaccination is recommended for persons on working assignments in the health care field (dentists, physicians, nurses, laboratory technicians), or working in close contact with the local population (teachers, missionaries, Peace Corps), or persons foreseeing sexual relations with local inhabitants.
Meningococcal meningitis—Vaccination is advised for persons traveling extensively or on working assignements in the meningitis belt of Africa's northern savannah, which stretches from the Red Sea to the Atlantic Ocean. Peak season is March and April. Local area of greatest danger in the southern half of the country.
Rabies—In this country, where rabies is a constant threat, a pre-exposure rabies vaccination is advised for persons planning an extended stay or on working assignments (naturalists, agricultural advisors, archeologists, geologists, etc.). Although this provides adequate initial protection, a person bitten by a potentially rabid animal would still require post exposure immunization (see

Chapter 6.40). Children should be cautioned not to pet dogs, cats, or other mammals.

U.S. Foreign Service:
Rue Testard and Rue Mohamed V
Bamako, Telephone 225834, 225663

_____ Country number 8.126 _____
Malta

INFECTIOUS DISEASE RISK

Malaria Risk
There is no malaria risk in this country.

Diseases of Special Risk
In addition to the worldwide hazard of tetanus and the routine and any special immunizations recommended below, the traveler should be aware that risk of exposure to the following diseases exists in this country. This list is not all inclusive, but it is a caution concerning the more likely endemic disease risks.

DISEASE RISK PROFILE

Disease	endemic	risk	hazard
Brucellosis	x		
Diarrheal Diseases	x		
Dysentery, Bacillary	x		
Echinococcosis	x		
Leishmaniasis			
Cutaneous	x		
Visceral	x		
Sandfly Fever	x		
Typhoid Fever	x		
Typhus, Endemic Flea-Borne	x		
Typhus, Scrub	x		
West Nile Fever	x		

Food/Water Safety
Water is probably safe, but due to local variations in bacterial counts, using bottled water for the first few weeks will help the traveler adjust and decrease the chance of traveler's diarrhea. Milk is pasteurized and safe to drink. Butter, cheese, yogurt and ice-cream are safe. Local meat, poultry, seafood, vegetables, and fruits are safe to eat.

VACCINATIONS

Yellow fever—A vaccination certificate is required for travelers coming from infected areas. A vaccination certificate is required for children over six months of age. Children under nine months of age should not be vaccinated due to health considerations. Please refer to the discussion in Chapter 6.63 on avoiding yellow fever vaccination in this age group. If indicated on epidemiological grounds, infants under six months of age are subject to isolation or surveillance if coming from an infected area.

Routine immunizations should be current. For infants and children through 16 years of age, refer to Chapter 4.3. A rubeola (measles) booster should be considered. Persons age 16 to 65 should receive a booster of tetanus and diphtheria every ten years. Healthy adults under age 65 do not require pneumococcal vaccine, but it is appropriate for those with chronic medical conditions. Influenza vaccine may be considered for those providing essential community services, health care workers, and those wishing to reduce the likelihood of becoming ill with influenza. Adults over 65 years of age are urged to obtain yearly influenza immunization and to insure that their tetanus and diphtheria immunizations are current. Pneumococcal vaccination is also suggested for this age group.

U.S. Foreign Service:
2nd FL.
Development House
St. Anne St., Floriana
Valleta, Telephone 623653, 620424, 623216

Country number 8.127
Martinique

INFECTIOUS DISEASE RISK

Malaria Risk
There is no malaria risk in this country.

Diseases of Special Risk
In addition to the worldwide hazard of tetanus and the routine and any special immunizations recommended below, the traveler should be aware that risk of exposure to the following diseases exists in this country. This list is not all inclusive, but it is a caution concerning the more likely endemic disease risks.

Potential risk of dengue fever exists. The virus is present in this country at all times and may give rise to major outbreaks.

Schistosomiasis may be found throughout this country, including urban areas. Avoid contact with contaminated fresh water lakes, ponds, or streams.

DISEASE RISK PROFILE

Disease	endemic	risk	hazard
Diarrheal Disease Risk		x	
Dysentery, Amoebic/Bacillary		x	
Hepatitis, Viral	x		
Typhoid Fever	x		

Food/Water Safety

All tap water used for drinking, brushing teeth, and making ice cubes should be boiled prior to use. Insure that bottled water is uncapped in your presence. Milk should be boiled to insure safety. Powdered and evaporated milk are available and safe. Avoid butter and other dairy products. All meat, poultry and seafood must be well cooked and served while hot. Pork is best avoided. Vegetables should be well cooked and served hot. Salads and mayonnaise are best avoided. Fruits with intact skins should be peeled by you just prior to consumption. Avoid cold buffets, custards, and any frozen dessert. Water, milk, and food in Forte-de-France are considered safe, however, the hazard is left to your judgement.

VACCINATIONS

Yellow fever—A vaccination certificate is required for travelers coming from infected areas. A vaccination certificate is required for children over one year of age.

Routine immunizations should be current. For infants and children through 16 years of age, refer to Chapter 4.3. A rubeola (measles) booster should be considered. Persons age 16 to 65 should receive a booster of tetanus and diphtheria every ten years. Healthy adults under age 65 do not require pneumococcal vaccine, but it is appropriate for those with chronic medical conditions. Influenza vaccine may be considered for those providing essential community services, health care workers, and those wishing to reduce the likelihood of becoming ill with influenza. Adults over 65 years of age are urged to obtain yearly influenza immunization and to insure that their tetanus and diphtheria immunizations are current. Pneumococcal vaccination is also suggested for this age group.

The vaccinations listed are recommended for the traveler's protection.

Typhoid fever—Vaccination is recommended for all travelers for their protection.

Country number 8.128
Mauritania

INFECTIOUS DISEASE RISK

Malaria Risk

There is no risk of malaria in Dakhlet-Nouadhibou, Inchiri, Adrar, and Tiris-Zemour. Malaria is present all year, throughout the country, except as noted. The malaria in this country is resistant to chloroquine. The CDC recommends the use of mefloquine (Lariam) as described in Chapter 6.31 for chemical prophylaxis.

Falciparum malaria represents 8% of malaria, therefore there is a significant risk of p. vivax malaria exposure. Consider use of Primaquine upon return home.

Diseases of Special Risk

In addition to the worldwide hazard of tetanus and the routine and any special immunizations recommended below, the traveler should be aware that risk of exposure to the following diseases exists in this country. This list is not all inclusive, but it is a caution concerning the more likely endemic disease risks.

Schistosomiasis may be found in this country. Avoid contact with contaminated fresh water lakes, ponds, or streams.

Rift Valley fever is a risk to persons working with domestic animals and livestock, and from mosquito exposure, in the Tarza Region, especially in the Departments of Rosso and Keur Macene.

DISEASE RISK PROFILE

Disease	endemic	risk	hazard
Dracunculiasis/Guinea Worm	x		
Diarrheal Disease Risk			x
Dysentery, Amoebic/Bacillary			x
Echinococcosis		x	
Filariasis			x
Giardiasis			x
Helminthic Diseases (see Chapter 6.21)			x
Hepatitis, Viral			x
Lassa Fever	x		
Leishmaniasis			
Cutaneous	x		
Visceral	x		
Loiasis			x
Rabies	x		
Relapsing Fever	x		
Rift Valley Fever	x		
Trachoma			x

Disease	endemic	risk	hazard
Tungiasis			x
Typhoid Fever			x
Typhus, Endemic Flea-Borne	x		
Typhus, Epidemic Louse-Borne	x		
Typhus, Scrub	x		

Food/Water Safety

All tap water used for drinking, brushing teeth, and making ice cubes should be boiled prior to use. Insure that bottled water is uncapped in your presence. Milk should be boiled to insure safety. Powdered and evaporated milk are available and safe. Avoid butter and other dairy products. All meat, poultry and seafood must be well cooked and served while hot. Pork is best avoided. Vegetables should be well cooked and served hot. Salads and mayonnaise are best avoided. Fruits with intact skins should be peeled by you just prior to consumption. Avoid cold buffets, custards, and any frozen dessert.

VACCINATIONS

Yellow fever—A vaccination certificate is required on arrival from all countries. A vaccination certificate is required for children over one year of age. Except: travelers arriving from a non-infected area and staying less than two weeks in the country. CDC recommends vaccination for all travelers over 9 months of age.

Routine immunizations should be current. For infants and children through 16 years of age, refer to Chapter 4.3. A rubeola (measles) booster should be considered. Persons age 16 to 65 should receive a booster of tetanus and diphtheria every ten years. Healthy adults under age 65 do not require pneumococcal vaccine, but it is appropriate for those with chronic medical conditions. Influenza vaccine may be considered for those providing essential community services, health care workers, and those wishing to reduce the likelihood of becoming ill with influenza. Adults over 65 years of age are urged to obtain yearly influenza immunization and to insure that their tetanus and diphtheria immunizations are current. Pneumococcal vaccination is also suggested for this age group.

The vaccinations listed are recommended for the traveler's protection.

Poliomyelitis—A poliomyelitis booster is indicated for this country.

Cholera—Cholera is present in this country. Risk to western travelers is low. Immunization is not required or recommended for travel to this country due to its low effectiveness. Avoid uncooked foods and untreated water. Vaccination is advised only for persons living or working under inadequate sanitary conditions and for those with impaired defense mechanisms (see Chapter 6.5).

Hepatitis A—Vaccination is recommended for all travelers for their protection.

Typhoid fever—Vaccination is recommended for all travelers for their protection.

Selective vaccinations—These apply only to specific groups of travelers or persons on specific working assignments:

Viral Hepatitis B—Because of the high rate of healthy carriers of hepatitis B in this country, vaccination is recommended for persons on working assignments in the health care field (dentists, physicians, nurses, laboratory technicians), or working in close contact with the local population (teachers, missionaries, Peace Corps), or persons foreseeing sexual relations with local inhabitants.

Meningococcal meningitis—Vaccination is advised for persons traveling extensively or on working assignements in the meningitis belt of Africa's northern savannah, which stretches from the Red Sea to the Atlantic Ocean. Peak season is March and April. Local area of greatest danger in the southern third of the country.

Plague—Vaccination is recommended only for persons who may be occupationally exposed to wild rodents (anthropologists, geologists, medical personnel, missionaries, etc). The standard vaccination course must be completed before entering the plague infested area. Geographical distribution of the area of risk for this country is the northwestern corner of the country along the border with Morocco.

Rabies—In this country, where rabies is a constant threat, a pre-exposure rabies vaccination is advised for persons planning an extended stay or on working assignments (naturalists, agricultural advisors, archeologists, geologists, etc.). Although this provides adequate initial protection, a person bitten by a potentially rabid animal would still require post exposure immunization (see Chapter 6.40). Children should be cautioned not to pet dogs, cats, or other mammals.

U.S. Foreign Service:
P.O. Box 222
Nouakchott, Telephone 52660/3

TRAVEL ADVISORY

A U.S. Department of State Travel Advisory was in effect on 4 May 1990 when this book went to press. The entire text is included below. Travel advisories are subject to reissue, change, and cancellation at any time. Current travel advisory information is available by calling the U.S. Department of State Travel Advisory Hotline at (202) 647-5225. The current travel advisory status is also available from the Herchmer Database update system (see Chapter 2.8).

JANUARY 12, 1990
MAURITANIA—CAUTION
THE DEPARTMENT OF STATE ADVISES U.S. CITIZENS VISITING MAURITANIA TO AVOID UNNECESSARY TRAVEL IN HE REGION OF THE MAURITANIA/SENEGAL BORDER DUE TO UNSETTLED CONDI-

TIONS IN THAT AREA. FOR THE SAME REASON, TRAVEL IS NOT RECOMMENDED ON OR NEAR THE SENEGAL RIVER FROM THE ATLANTIC OCEAN TO THE MALIAN BORDER SOUTH OF SELIBABI. DUE TO THE RUPTURE IN DIPLOMATIC RELATIONS BETWEEN MAURITANIA AND SENEGAL, ALL LAND AND AIR ROUTES BE-TWEEN MAURITANIA AND SENEGAL HAVE BEEN CLOSED. IT IS NOT POSSIBLE TO TRAVEL DIRECTLY FROM MAURITANIA TO SENE-GAL, NOR IS IT POSSIBLE TO OBTAIN A SENEGALESE VISA IN MAURITANIA.
EXPIRATION: JULY 1, 1990.

——————— Country number 8.129 ———————
Mauritius

INFECTIOUS DISEASE RISK

Malaria Risk

Malaria is present in the country in rural areas only. No malaria is found on Rodiguez Island. Consider the use of chloroquine (Chapter 6.31). Falci-parum malaria represents 0% of malaria, therefore there is a risk of p. vivax malaria exposure. Consider use of Primaquine upon return home.

Diseases of Special Risk

In addition to the worldwide hazard of tetanus and the routine and any special immunizations recommended below, the traveler should be aware that risk of exposure to the following diseases exists in this country. This list is not all inclusive, but it is a caution concerning the more likely endemic disease risks.

Schistosomiasis may be found throughout this country. Avoid contact with contaminated fresh water lakes, ponds, or streams. Tuberculosis would be a risk if the traveler is in intimate contact with the native population over a period of time. Pre- and post-trip tuberculosis skin tests are advised under the above circu,stance.

DISEASE RISK PROFILE

Disease	endemic	risk	hazard
Dracunculiasis/Guinea Worm	x		
Diarrheal Disease Risk			x
Dysentery, Amoebic/Bacillary			x
Echinococcosis		x	
Filariasis			x
Giardiasis			x
Helminthic Diseases (see Chapter 6.21)			x
Hepatitis, Viral			x

Disease	endemic	risk	hazard
Leishmaniasis			
Cutaneous	x		
Visceral	x		
Rabies	x		
Relapsing Fever	x		
Trachoma			x
Typhoid Fever			x
Typhus, Endemic Flea-Borne	x		
Typhus, Epidemic Louse-Borne	x		
Typhus, Scrub	x		

Food/Water Safety

All tap water used for drinking, brushing teeth, and making ice cubes should be boiled prior to use. Insure that bottled water is uncapped in your presence. Milk should be boiled to insure safety. Powdered and evaporated milk are available and safe. Avoid butter and other dairy products. All meat, poultry and seafood must be well cooked and served while hot. Pork is best avoided. Vegetables should be well cooked and served hot. Salads and mayonnaise are best avoided. Fruits with intact skins should be peeled by you just prior to consumption. Avoid cold buffets, custards, and any frozen dessert.

VACCINATIONS

Yellow fever—A vaccination certificate is required for travelers coming from infected areas and from or in transit through countries in the endemic yellow fever zone, see Chapter 6.63. A vaccination certificate is required for children over one year of age.

Routine immunizations should be current. For infants and children through 16 years of age, refer to Chapter 4.3. A rubeola (measles) booster should be considered. Persons age 16 to 65 should receive a booster of tetanus and diphtheria every ten years. Healthy adults under age 65 do not require pneumococcal vaccine, but it is appropriate for those with chronic medical conditions. Influenza vaccine may be considered for those providing essential community services, health care workers, and those wishing to reduce the likelihood of becoming ill with influenza. Adults over 65 years of age are urged to obtain yearly influenza immunization and to insure that their tetanus and diphtheria immunizations are current. Pneumococcal vaccination is also suggested for this age group.

U.S. Foreign Service:

Rogers Bldg.
4th Fl.
John Kennedy St.
Port-Louis, Telephone 2-3218/9

_____ **Country number 8.130** _____
Mexico

INFECTIOUS DISEASE RISK

Malaria Risk

Malaria risk in Mexico has been increasing in recent years, doubling from 42,104 in 1980 to 85,501 in 1984 (the last year of current statistics). There is only limited risk of malaria in the major tourist developments of the Pacific and Gulf coasts. There is no risk of malaria in urban areas. It is only found below 1000 meters. Malaria risk is from May through October in Aquascalientes, Baja California Sur, Colima, Durango, Morelos, Nuevo Leon, San Luis Potosi, Tamaulipas and Zacatecas States. It is found all year in the provinces of Campeche, Chiapas, Chihuahua, Guerrero, Jalisco, Mexico, Michoacan, Nayarit, Daxaca, Puebla Quintana Roo, Sinaloa, Tabasco, Veracruz (eastern part) and Yucatan. There is no risk in the Distrito Federal and the states directly north and northeast of the capital (Guanajuato, Hidalgo, Queretaro, Tiaxcala) and the US border states of Baja California Norte, Sonora, and Coahuila. A weekly dose of chloroquine is recommeded for travelers in areas of malaria risk (see Chapter 6.31).

Falciparum malaria represents 1% of malaria, therefore there is a risk of p. vivax malaria exposure. Consider use of Primaquine upon return home if significant exposure in the areas at risk has been encountered.

Diseases of Special Risk

In addition to the worldwide hazard of tetanus and the routine and any special immunizations recommended below, the traveler should be aware that risk of exposure to the following diseases exists in this country. This list is not all inclusive, but it is a caution concerning the more likely endemic disease risks.

Chaga's Disease risk is present below 1500 meters in the followign states: Pacific Coast: Sonora, Sinola, Nayarit, Jalisco, Colima, Michoacan, Guerrero, Oaxaca, Chiapas; Gulf of Mexico and Caribbean coast: Veracruz, Tabasco, Campeche, Yucatan, Quintana Roo; Central Mexico: Durango, Zacatecas, San Luis Potosi, Mexico, Morelos, and Puebla.

This country must be considered receptive to dengue fever. Intermittent epidemics in the past make renewed activity or reintroduction of the virus possible.

DISEASE RISK PROFILE

Disease	endemic	risk	hazard
Diarrheal Disease Risk		x	
Dysentery, Amoebic/Bacillary		x	
Encephalitis, Venezuelan Equine	x		

Disease	endemic	risk	hazard
Helminthic Diseases (see Chapter 6.21)		x	
Hepatitis, Viral		x	
Leishmaniasis	x		
Onchocerciasis	x		
Rabies (esp dogs and bats)			x
Trypanosomiasis, American Chaga's Disease	x		

Food/Water Safety

All tap water used for drinking, brushing teeth, and making ice cubes should be boiled prior to use. Insure that bottled water is uncapped in your presence. Milk should be boiled to insure safety. Powdered and evaporated milk are available and safe. Avoid butter and other dairy products. All meat, poultry and seafood must be well cooked and served while hot. Pork is best avoided. Vegetables should be well cooked and served hot. Salads and mayonnaise are best avoided. Fruits with intact skins should be peeled by you just prior to consumption. Avoid cold buffets, custards, and any frozen dessert. First class hotels and restaurants serve purified drinking water and reliable food. However, the hazard is left to your judgement.

VACCINATIONS

Yellow fever—A vaccination certificate is required for travelers coming from infected areas. A vaccination certificate is required for children over six months of age. Children under nine months of age should not be vaccinated due to health considerations. Please refer to the discussion in Chapter 6.63 on avoiding yellow fever vaccination in this age group.

Routine immunizations should be current. For infants and children through 16 years of age, refer to Chapter 4.3. A rubeola (measles) booster should be considered. Persons age 16 to 65 should receive a booster of tetanus and diphtheria every ten years. Healthy adults under age 65 do not require pneumococcal vaccine, but it is appropriate for those with chronic medical conditions. Influenza vaccine may be considered for those providing essential community services, health care workers, and those wishing to reduce the likelihood of becoming ill with influenza. Adults over 65 years of age are urged to obtain yearly influenza immunization and to insure that their tetanus and diphtheria immunizations are current. Pneumococcal vaccination is also suggested for this age group.

The vaccinations listed are recommended for the traveler's protection.

Poliomyelitis—Vaccination is recommended when traveling outside the areas usually visited by tourists, traveling extensively in the interior of the country (trekkers, hikers) and for persons on working assignments in remote areas.

Viral Hepatitis A—Vaccination is recommended when traveling outside the areas usually visited by tourists, traveling extensively in the interior of the country (trekkers, hikers) and for persons on working assignments in remote areas.

Typhoid fever—Vaccination is recommended when traveling outside the areas usually visited by tourists, traveling extensively in the interior of the country (trekkers, hikers) and for persons on working assignments in remote areas.

Selective vaccinations—These apply only to specific groups of travelers or persons on specific working assignments:

Rabies—In this country, where rabies is a constant threat, a pre-exposure rabies vaccination is advised for persons planning an extended stay or on working assignments (naturalists, agricultural advisors, archeologists, geologists, etc.). Although this provides adequate initial protection, a person bitten by a potentially rabid animal would still require post exposure immunization (see Chapter 6.40). Children should be cautioned not to pet dogs, cats, or other mammals.

U.S. Foreign Service:
Paseo de la Reforma 305
Mexico City, Telephone 211-00-42

Progreso 175
Guadalajara, Telephone 25-29-98, 25-27-00

No. 139 Morelia
Hermosillo, Telephone 3-89-23-(25)

Avenida Constitucion 411 Poniente
Monterrey, Telephone 4306 50/59

Tapachula 96
Tijuana, Telephone 86-10-01/5

924 Avenue Lopez Mateos
Ciudad Juarez, Telephone 34048

Ave. Primera No. 232
Matamoros, Telephone 2-52-50/1/2

6 Circonvalacion No. 6 (at Venustiana Carranza)
Mazatlan, Telephone 1-29-05

Paseo Montejo 453
Merida, Telephone 5-54-09, 5-50-11

Avenida Allende 3330, Col. Jardin
Nuevo Laredo, Telephone 4-05-12, 4-06-18

Canadian High Commission/Embassy Office:
Calle Schiller 529 (Rincon del Bosque)
Colonia Polanco
Mexico City, Telephone 254-32-88

Hotel Club del Sol
Mezzanine Floor
Costera Miguel Aleman
Acapulco, Telephone 5-66-21

Avenida Albatros 52(705)
Mazatlan, Telephone 3-73-20

Calle 1-F 249 (X36)
Fracc. Campestre
Merida, Telephone 7-04-60

German Gedovious 5, Desp. 201
Condominio del Parque
Tijuana, Telephone 84-04-61

TRAVEL ADVISORY

A U.S. Department of State Travel Advisory was in effect on 4 May 1990 when this book went to press. The text for this advisory was printed in Chapter 2.2. Travel advisories are subject to reissue, change, and cancellation at any time. Current travel advisory information is available by calling the U.S. Department of State Travel Advisory Hotline at (202) 647-5225. The current travel advisory status is also available from the Herchmer Database update system (see Chapter 2.8).

Further travel advisory information is also posted:

Americans driving in Mexico are urged to avoid driving alone and at night and should never sleep in their vehicles at roadside. Particular caution should be exercised when traveling in areas where Americans have been assaulted. These areas include highway 40 west from the city of Durango to the Pacific coast, highway 15 in the State of Sinaloa, highway 2 in the vacinity of Caborca, Sonora, highway 57 between Matehuala and San Luis Potosi and the highway between Palomares and Tuxtepac in the State of Oaxaca.

Visitors to Mexico should use common sense in assessing the inherent risk in certain activities and be cautious in swimming pools and at beaches without life guards. They should be aware that some of the newer resorts lack well-developed medical facilities.

_____ **Country number 8.131** _____
Monaco

INFECTIOUS DISEASE RISK

Malaria Risk
There is no malaria risk in this country.

Diseases of Special Risk
In addition to the worldwide hazard of tetanus and the routine and any special immunizations recommended below, the traveler should be aware that risk of exposure to the following diseases exists in this country. This list is not all inclusive, but it is a caution concerning the more likely endemic disease risks.

DISEASE RISK PROFILE

Disease	endemic	risk	hazard
Diarrheal Diseases	x		
Dysentery, Bacillary	x		
Leishmaniasis			
Cutaneous	x		
Visceral	x		
Rabies	x		
Sandfly Fever	x		
Typhus, Endemic Flea-Borne	x		
Typhus, Scrub	x		
West Nile Fever	x		

Food/Water Safety
Water is probably safe, but due to local variations in bacterial counts, using bottled water for the first few weeks will help the traveler adjust and decrease the chance of traveler's diarrhea. Milk is pasteurized and safe to drink. Butter, cheese, yogurt and ice-cream are safe. Local meat, poultry, seafood, vegetables, and fruits are safe to eat.

VACCINATIONS
Routine immunizations should be current. For infants and children through 16 years of age, refer to Chapter 4.3. A rubeola (measles) booster should be considered. Persons age 16 to 65 should receive a booster of tetanus and diphtheria every ten years. Healthy adults under age 65 do not require pneumococcal vaccine, but it is appropriate for those with chronic medical conditions. Influenza vaccine may be considered for those providing essential community services, health care workers, and those wishing to reduce the likelihood of becoming ill with influenza. Adults over 65 years of age are urged to obtain yearly influenza immunization and to insure that their tetanus and diph-

theria immunizations are current. Pneumococcal vaccination is also suggested for this age group.

No vaccinations are required to enter this country.

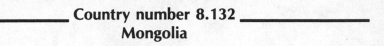

Country number 8.132
Mongolia

INFECTIOUS DISEASE RISK

Malaria Risk
There is no malaria risk in this country.

Diseases of Special Risk
In addition to the worldwide hazard of tetanus and the routine and any special immunizations recommended below, the traveler should be aware that risk of exposure to the following diseases exists in this country. This list is not all inclusive, but it is a caution concerning the more likely endemic disease risks.

DISEASE RISK PROFILE

Disease	endemic	risk	hazard
Dengue Fever	x		
Diarrheal Diseases		x	
Encephalitis, Japanese	x		
Hemorrhagic Fever	x		
Hepatitis, Viral			x

Food/Water Safety
All tap water used for drinking, brushing teeth, and making ice cubes should be boiled prior to use. Insure that bottled water is uncapped in your presence. Milk should be boiled to insure safety. Powdered and evaporated milk are available and safe. Avoid butter and other dairy products. All meat, poultry and seafood must be well cooked and served while hot. Pork is best avoided. Vegetables should be well cooked and served hot. Salads and mayonnaise are best avoided. Fruits with intact skins should be peeled by you just prior to consumption. Avoid cold buffets, custards, and any frozen dessert.

VACCINATIONS

Routine immunizations should be current. For infants and children through 16 years of age, refer to Chapter 4.3. A rubeola (measles) booster should be considered. Persons age 16 to 65 should receive a booster of tetanus and diphtheria every ten years. Healthy adults under age 65 do not require pneumococcal vaccine, but it is appropriate for those with chronic medical conditions. Influenza vaccine may be considered for those providing essential

community services, health care workers, and those wishing to reduce the likelihood of becoming ill with influenza. Adults over 65 years of age are urged to obtain yearly influenza immunization and to insure that their tetanus and diphtheria immunizations are current. Pneumococcal vaccination is also suggested for this age group.

No vaccinations are required to enter this country.

The vaccinations listed are recommended for the traveler's protection.
Viral Hepatitis A—Vaccination is recommended when traveling outside the areas usually visited by tourists, traveling extensively in the interior of the country (trekkers, hikers) and for persons on working assignments in remote areas.
Typhoid fever—Vaccination is recommended when traveling outside the areas usually visited by tourists, traveling extensively in the interior of the country (trekkers, hikers) and for persons on working assignments in remote areas.

Selective vaccinations—*These apply only to specific groups of travelers or persons on specific working assignments:*
Viral Hepatitis B—Because of the high rate of healthy carriers of hepatitis B in this country, vaccination is recommended for persons on working assignments in the health care field (dentists, physicians, nurses, laboratory technicians), or working in close contact with the local population (teachers, missionaries, Peace Corps), or persons foreseeing sexual relations with local inhabitants.
Plague—Vaccination is recommended only for persons who may be occupationally exposed to wild rodents (anthropologists, geologists, medical personnel, missionaries, etc). The standard vaccination course must be completed before entering the plague infested area. Geographical distribution of the area of risk is scattered throughout the country.

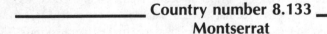

Country number 8.133
Montserrat

INFECTIOUS DISEASE RISK

Malaria Risk
There is no malaria risk in this country.

Diseases of Special Risk
In addition to the worldwide hazard of tetanus and the routine and any special immunizations recommended below, the traveler should be aware that risk of exposure to the following diseases exists in this country. This list is not all inclusive, but it is a caution concerning the more likely endemic disease risks.

DISEASE RISK PROFILE

Disease	endemic	risk	hazard
Dengue	x		
Diarrheal Disease Risk		x	
Dysentery, Amoebic/Bacillary		x	
Hepatitis, Viral	x		
Rabies (esp mongoose)	x		

Food/Water Safety

Water is probably safe, but due to local variations in bacterial counts, using bottled water for the first few weeks will help the traveler adjust and decrease the chance of traveler's diarrhea. Milk is pasteurized and safe to drink. Butter, cheese, yogurt and ice-cream are safe. Local meat, poultry, seafood, vegetables, and fruits are safe to eat.

VACCINATIONS

Yellow fever—A vaccination certificate is required for travelers coming from infected areas and from or in transit through countries with active disease. A vaccination certificate is required for children over one year of age.

Routine immunizations should be current. For infants and children through 16 years of age, refer to Chapter 4.3. A rubeola (measles) booster should be considered. Persons age 16 to 65 should receive a booster of tetanus and diphtheria every ten years. Healthy adults under age 65 do not require pneumococcal vaccine, but it is appropriate for those with chronic medical conditions. Influenza vaccine may be considered for those providing essential community services, health care workers, and those wishing to reduce the likelihood of becoming ill with influenza. Adults over 65 years of age are urged to obtain yearly influenza immunization and to insure that their tetanus and diphtheria immunizations are current. Pneumococcal vaccination is also suggested for this age group.

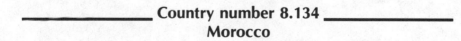

Country number 8.134

Morocco

INFECTIOUS DISEASE RISK

Malaria Risk

Malaria risk is present from May through October in the rural areas of coastal provinces. There is no risk in urban areas. CDC recommends mosquito protection for prevention of malaria in this country.

Falciparum malaria represents 1% of malaria, therefore there is a risk of p. vivax malaria exposure. Consider use of primaquine upon return home only if considerable mosquito exposure has occurred.

Diseases of Special Risk

In addition to the worldwide hazard of tetanus and the routine and any special immunizations recommended below, the traveler should be aware that risk of exposure to the following diseases exists in this country. This list is not all inclusive, but it is a caution concerning the more likely endemic disease risks.

Schistosomiasis may be found in this country. Avoid contact with contaminated fresh water lakes, ponds, or streams. Risk is present:

—North of Rabat, in the region of the Gharb; and northeast of Larache, in the area of Tleta Rissana.

—In the District of Marrakech, in all towns and villages of the Tensift River valley.

—In the District of Meknes, the valleys of the rivers of Guir and Rheris and their tributaries, south of the Atlas Range.

—In the areas of Ouarzazate, Agdz, M'hamid, Tamgrout, Zagora and the surrounding villages along the Draa River.

—South of Agadir, in the region between the river Sous and the western part of the Antiatlas Range, affecting Ait Baha and Anezi.

—In the region south of the Antiatlas Range, affecting Assa, Akka, Tata and the surrounding communities.

DISEASE RISK PROFILE

Disease	endemic	risk	hazard
Brucellosis		x	
Dengue Fever	x		
Diarrheal Disease Risk		x	
Dysentery, Amoebic/Bacillary		x	
Echinococcosis	x		
Giardiasis		x	
Helminthic Diseases (see Chapter 6.21)		x	
Hepatitis, Viral		x	
Lassa Fever	x		
Leishmaniasis	x		
Rabies	x		
Relapsing Fever	x		
Trachoma	x		
Tungiasis			x
Typhoid Fever		x	
Typhus	x		

Food/Water Safety

All tap water used for drinking, brushing teeth, and making ice cubes should be boiled prior to use. Insure that bottled water is uncapped in your presence. Milk should be boiled to insure safety. Powdered and evaporated milk are available and safe. Avoid butter and other dairy products. All meat, poultry and seafood must be well cooked and served while hot. Pork is best avoided.

Vegetables should be well cooked and served hot. Salads and mayonnaise are best avoided. Fruits with intact skins should be peeled by you just prior to consumption. Avoid cold buffets, custards, and any frozen dessert. First class hotels and restaurants in Agadir, Al Hoceima, Casablanca, Essaouira (Mogador), Fes (Fez), Ketama, Marrakech, Meknes, Rabat, Safi, Tanger (Tangier) serve purified drinking water and reliable food. However, the hazard is left to your judgement.

VACCINATIONS

Routine immunizations should be current. For infants and children through 16 years of age, refer to Chapter 4.3. A rubeola (measles) booster should be considered. Persons age 16 to 65 should receive a booster of tetanus and diphtheria every ten years. Healthy adults under age 65 do not require pneumococcal vaccine, but it is appropriate for those with chronic medical conditions. Influenza vaccine may be considered for those providing essential community services, health care workers, and those wishing to reduce the likelihood of becoming ill with influenza. Adults over 65 years of age are urged to obtain yearly influenza immunization and to insure that their tetanus and diphtheria immunizations are current. Pneumococcal vaccination is also suggested for this age group.

No vaccinations are required to enter this country.

The vaccinations listed are recommended for the traveler's protection.
Poliomyelitis—A poliomyelitis booster is indicated for this country.
Viral Hepatitis A—Vaccination is recommended for all travelers for their protection.
Typhoid fever—Vaccination is recommended for all travelers for their protection.

Selective vaccinations—These apply only to specific groups of travelers or persons on specific working assignments:
Plague—Vaccination is recommended only for persons who may be occupationally exposed to wild rodents (anthropologists, geologists, medical personnel, missionaries, etc). The standard vaccination course must be completed before entering the plague infested area. Geographical distribution of the area of risk for this country is in the southern part of the country (areas of former Spanish Sahara).
Rabies—In this country, where rabies is a constant threat, a pre-exposure rabies vaccination is advised for persons planning an extended stay or on working assignments (naturalists, agricultural advisors, archeologists, geologists, etc.). Although this provides adequate initial protection, a person bitten by a potentially rabid animal would still require post exposure immunization (see Chapter 6.40). Children should be cautioned not to pet dogs, cats, or other mammals.

U.S. Foreign Service:
2 Ave. de Marrakech; P.O. Box 120
Rabat-Agdal, Telephone 622-65

8 Blvd. Moulay Youssef
Casablanca, Telephone 22-41-49

Chemin des Amoureux
Tangier, Telephone 359-05

Canadian High Commission/Embassy Office:
13 Bis, Rue Jaafar As-Sadik
Rabat-Agdal, Telephone 713-75/76/77

_____ Country number 8.135 _____
Mozambique

INFECTIOUS DISEASE RISK

Malaria Risk
Malaria is present in all parts of this country, including urban areas. The risk exists all year. The malaria in this country is resistant to chloroquine. The CDC recommends the use of mefloquine (Lariam) as described in Chapter 6.31 for chemical prophylaxis.

Falciparum malaria represents 95% of malaria, therefore there is a slight risk of p. vivax malaria exposure. Consider use of primaquine upon return home.

Diseases of Special Risk
In addition to the worldwide hazard of tetanus and the routine and any special immunizations recommended below, the traveler should be aware that risk of exposure to the following diseases exists in this country. This list is not all inclusive, but it is a caution concerning the more likely endemic disease risks.

Schistosomiasis is found throughout this country. Avoid contact with contaminated fresh water lakes, ponds, or streams.

Louse-borne typhus is cosmopolitan in distribution and is present wherever groups of persons are crowded together under conditions of poor sanitation and malnutrition. Risk exists for persons living or working in remote areas of the country (anthropologists, archeologists, geologists, medical personnel, missionaries, etc.). Freedom from louse infestation is the most effective protection against typhus.

DISEASE RISK PROFILE

Disease	endemic	risk	hazard
Dracunculiasis/Guinea Worm	x		
Diarrheal Disease Risk			x
Dysentery, Amoebic/Bacillary			x
Echinococcosis		x	
Filariasis			x
Giardiasis			x
Helminthic Diseases (see Chapter 6.21)			x
Hepatitis, Viral			x
Leishmaniasis			
Cutaneous	x		
Visceral	x		
Plague	x		
Rabies	x		
Relapsing Fever	x		
Trachoma			x
Trypanosomiasis, African	x		
Sleeping Sickness			
Typhoid Fever			x
Typhus, Endemic Flea-Borne	x		
Typhus, Epidemic Louse-Borne	x		
Typhus, Scrub	x		

Food/Water Safety

All tap water used for drinking, brushing teeth, and making ice cubes should be boiled prior to use. Insure that bottled water is uncapped in your presence. Milk should be boiled to insure safety. Powdered and evaporated milk are available and safe. Avoid butter and other dairy products. All meat, poultry and seafood must be well cooked and served while hot. Pork is best avoided. Vegetables should be well cooked and served hot. Salads and mayonnaise are best avoided. Fruits with intact skins should be peeled by you just prior to consumption. Avoid cold buffets, custards, and any frozen dessert. First class hotels and restaurants in Beira and Maputo (Lourenco Marques) serve purified drinking water and reliable food. However, the hazard is left to your judgement.

VACCINATIONS

Yellow fever—A vaccination certificate is required for travelers coming from infected areas and from or in transit through countries with active disease. A vaccination certificate is required for children over one year of age.

Routine immunizations should be current. For infants and children through 16 years of age, refer to Chapter 4.3. A rubeola (measles) booster should be considered. Persons age 16 to 65 should receive a booster of tetanus and diphtheria every ten years. Healthy adults under age 65 do not require pneumococcal vaccine, but it is appropriate for those with chronic medical conditions. Influenza vaccine may be considered for those providing essential community services, health care workers, and those wishing to reduce the likeli-

hood of becoming ill with influenza. Adults over 65 years of age are urged to obtain yearly influenza immunization and to insure that their tetanus and diphtheria immunizations are current. Pneumococcal vaccination is also suggested for this age group.

The vaccinations listed are recommended for the traveler's protection.
Poliomyelitis—A poliomyelitis booster is indicated for this country.
Cholera—Cholera is present in this country. Risk to western travelers is low. Immunization is not required or recommended for travel to this country due to its low effectiveness. Avoid uncooked foods and untreated water. Vaccination is advised only for persons living or working under inadequate sanitary conditions and for those with impaired defense mechanisms.
Viral Hepatitis A—Vaccination is recommended for all travelers for their protection.
Typhoid fever—Vaccination is recommended for all travelers for their protection.

Selective vaccinations—*These apply only to specific groups of travelers or persons on specific working assignments:*
Viral Hepatitis B—Because of the high rate of healthy carriers of hepatitis B in this country, vaccination is recommended for persons on working assignments in the health care field (dentists, physicians, nurses, laboratory technicians), or working in close contact with the local population (teachers, missionaries, Peace Corps), or persons foreseeing sexual relations with local inhabitants.
Plague—Vaccination is recommended only for persons who may be occupationally exposed to wild rodents (anthropologists, geologists, medical personnel, missionaries, etc). The standard vaccination course must be completed before entering the plague infested area. Geographical distribution of the area of risk for this country is in the north of the country (all of Niassa province and the western part of Tete province).
Rabies—In this country, where rabies is a constant threat, a pre-exposure rabies vaccination is advised for persons planning an extended stay or on working assignments (naturalists, agricultural advisors, archeologists, geologists, etc.). Although this provides adequate initial protection, a person bitten by a potentially rabid animal would still require post exposure immunization (see Chapter 6.40). Children should be cautioned not to pet dogs, cats, or other mammals.

U.S. Foreign Service:
35 rua da Mesquita
3rd Fl.
Maputo, Telephone 26051/2/3

TRAVEL ADVISORY

A U.S. Department of State Travel Advisory was in effect on 4 May 1990 when this book went to press. The entire text is included below. Travel advisories are subject to reissue, change, and cancellation at any time. Current travel advisory information is available by calling the U.S. Department of State Travel Advisory Hotline at (202) 647-5225. The current travel advisory status is also available from the Herchmer Database update system (see Chapter 2.8).

9FB DN37 1-1 1LA71 1 07/13/89 17:28
SECSTATE WSH
SUBJECT:
TRAVEL ADVISORY— MOZAMBIQUE— WARNING
1. THE DEPARTMENT OF STATE WARNS AMERICAN TRAVELERS THAT THE INSURGENT GUERRILLA WAR AGAINST THE MOZAMBICAN GOVERNMENT BY THE MOZAMBICAN NATIONAL RESISTANCE (RENAMO) HAS INTENSIFIED AND IS ACTIVE IN ALL OF THE COUNTRY'S TEN PROVINCES. DUE TO RANDOM AND CONTINUOUS ATTACKS ON CIVILIAN AND ECONOMIC TARGETS, ROAD AND RAIL TRAVEL OUTSIDE OF PROVINCIAL CAPITALS IS HAZARDOUS. THE DEFENSE PERIMETER AROUND PROVINCIAL CAPITALS AND THE CAPITAL CITY OF MAPUTO IS LIMITED AN[D WEAK, RARELY EXTENDING BEYOND 15 MILES. TRAVEL AT NIGHT OUTSIDE MAJOR CITIES IS EXTREMELY HAZARDOUS AND SHOULD BE AVOIDED. TRAVEL ON THE NATIONAL HIGHWAYS BETWEEN SWAZILAND AND MAPUTO OR SOUTH AFRICA IS NOT SAFE. ATTACKS HAVE CONTINUED ON THESE HIGHWAYS DESPITE INCREASED SECURITY MEASURES BY GOVERNMENT FORCES.
2. THERE ARE FOOD SHORTAGES IN RURAL AREAS AND MANY DISTRICT CAPITALS. TRAVELERS SHOULD BE PREPARED TO PAY MOST BILLS IN DOLLARS OR TRAVELERS CHECKS. CURRENCY SHOULD NOT BE CONVERTED EXCEPT AT LOCATIONS AUTHORIZED BY THE MOZAMBICAN GOVERNMENT.
3. PROPERTY CRIME HAS INCREASED DRAMATICALLY IN URBAN CENTERS DURING THE LAST YEAR. THERE IS A VERY HIGH LEVEL OF AUTOMOBILE THEFTS ESPECIALLY IN THE CAPITAL CITY, MAPUTO. THERE ALSO HAVE BEEN REPORTS OF A SLIGHT INCREASE OF VIOLENT CRIMES IN URBAN AREAS. CITY STREETS ARE HEAVILY PATROLLED BY POLICE AND SOLDIERS. SOLDIERS NORMALLY CARRY AUTOMATIC WEAPONS, AND THEIR AUTHORITY SHOULD NOT BE CHALLENGED.
4. U.S. CITIZENS WHO VISIT OR LIVE IN MOZAMBIQUE SHOULD REGISTER UPON ARRIVAL AT THE U.S. EMBASSY IN MAPUTO. ADDRESS: AV. KENNETH KAUNDA, 193, TELEPHONE NUM2ER 492797 AND 490350. THE EMBASSY IS THE BEST SOURCE FOR THE MOST

CURRENT INFORMATION.
5. EXPIRATION DATE: JULY 30, 1990.
6. THIS CANCELS TRAVEL ADVISORY DATED JULY 23, 1988, CONTAINED IN 88 STATE 238354. DEPT OF STATE WASHDC 221781/L761

Country number 8.136
Namibia
(South-West Africa)

INFECTIOUS DISEASE RISK

Malaria Risk
　　Malaria risk in Ovamboland and Caprivi Strip is from November through May. The malaria in this country is resistant to chloroquine. The CDC recommends the use of mefloquine (Lariam) as described in Chapter 6.31 for chemical prophylaxis.
　　Falciparum malaria represents 90% of malaria, therefore there is only a slight risk of p. vivax malaria exposure. Consider use of Primaquine upon return home.

Diseases of Special Risk
　　In addition to the worldwide hazard of tetanus and the routine and any special immunizations recommended below, the traveler should be aware that risk of exposure to the following diseases exists in this country. This list is not all inclusive, but it is a caution concerning the more likely endemic disease risks.
　　Schistosomiasis may be found in this country. Avoid contact with contaminated fresh water lakes, ponds, or streams. Risk is only present in the north of the country in a thin strip along the border with Angola extending into the Caprivi Strip between Zambia and Botswana.

DISEASE RISK PROFILE

Disease	endemic	risk	hazard
Diarrheal Disease Risk	x		
Dysentery, Amoebic	x		
Plague	x		
Relapsing Fever	x		
Rift Valley Fever	x		
Trypanosomiasis, African Sleeping Sickness	x		
Typhoid Fever	x		
Typhus, Scrub	x		

Food/Water Safety

Water, milk, and food is considered safe in Swakopmund, Walvis Bay, and Windhoek. Elsewhere all tap water used for drinking, brushing teeth, and making ice cubes should be boiled prior to use. Insure that bottled water is uncapped in your presence. Milk should be boiled to insure safety. Powdered and evaporated milk are available and safe. Avoid butter and other dairy products. All meat, poultry and seafood must be well cooked and served while hot. Pork is best avoided. Vegetables should be well cooked and served hot. Salads and mayonnaise are best avoided. Fruits with intact skins should be peeled by you just prior to consumption. Avoid cold buffets, custards, and any frozen dessert.

TRAVEL ADVISORY

A U.S. Department of State Travel Advisory was in effect on 4 May 1990 when this book went to press. The entire text is included below. Travel advisories are subject to reissue, change, and cancellation at any time. Current travel advisory information is available by calling the U.S. Department of State Travel Advisory Hotline at (202) 647-5225. The current travel advisory status is also available from the Herchmer Database update system (see Chapter 2.8).

9FB DN37 1-1 1LA71 1 04/14/89 00:52
SECSTATE WSH
SUBJECT: TRAVEL ADVISORY—NAMIBIA—CAUTION
1. DUE TO ONGOING HOSTILITIES IN THE NAMIBIA/ANGOLA BORDER REGION THE DEPARTMENT OF STATE ADVISES U.S. CITIZENS AGAINST TRAVEL TO THIS AREA UNTIL FURTHER NOTICE. ALTHOUGH MOST TOURIST DESTINATIONS INCLUDING ETOSHA NATIONAL PARK CONTINUE TO BE SAFE, MOST OF NORTHERN NAMIBIA INCLUDING KAKOLAND, OWAMBO AND KAVANGO SHOULD BE AVOIDED.
2. TRAVELERS PLANNING TO VISIT THIS AREA SHOULD CONSULT THE DEPARTMENT OF STATE OR THE AMERICAN CONSULATE GENERA IN CAPE TOWN,BROADWAY INDUSTRIES CENTER, HEERENGRACHT, FORESHORE. TEL. (27) (21) 214-280/7 FOR THE LATEST INFORMATION.
3. EXPIRATION DATE: APRIL 5, 1990.

Country number 8.137
Nauru

INFECTIOUS DISEASE RISK

Malaria Risk
There is no malaria risk in this country.

Diseases of Special Risk
In addition to the worldwide hazard of tetanus and the routine and any special immunizations recommended below, the traveler should be aware that risk of exposure to the following diseases exists in this country. This list is not all inclusive, but it is a caution concerning the more likely endemic disease risks.

This country must be considered receptive to dengue fever. Intermittent epidemics in the past make renewed activity or reintroduction of the virus possible.

DISEASE RISK PROFILE

Disease	endemic	risk	hazard
Diarrheal Disease Risk		x	
Encephalitis, Japanese	x		
Filariasis			x
Helminthic Diseases (see Chapter 6.21)		x	
Typhoid Fever		x	

Food/Water Safety
All tap water used for drinking, brushing teeth, and making ice cubes should be boiled prior to use. Insure that bottled water is uncapped in your presence. Milk should be boiled to insure safety. Powdered and evaporated milk are available and safe. Avoid butter and other dairy products. All meat, poultry and seafood must be well cooked and served while hot. Pork is best avoided. Vegetables should be well cooked and served hot. Salads and mayonnaise are best avoided. Fruits with intact skins should be peeled by you just prior to consumption. Avoid cold buffets, custards, and any frozen dessert.

VACCINATIONS

Yellow fever—A vaccination certificate is required for travelers coming from infected areas. A vaccination certificate is required for children over one year of age.

Routine immunizations should be current. For infants and children through 16 years of age, refer to Chapter 4.3. A rubeola (measles) booster should be considered. Persons age 16 to 65 should receive a booster of tetanus and diphtheria every ten years. Healthy adults under age 65 do not require pneumococcal vaccine, but it is appropriate for those with chronic medical

conditions. Influenza vaccine may be considered for those providing essential community services, health care workers, and those wishing to reduce the likelihood of becoming ill with influenza. Adults over 65 years of age are urged to obtain yearly influenza immunization and to insure that their tetanus and diphtheria immunizations are current. Pneumococcal vaccination is also suggested for this age group.

The vaccinations listed are recommended for the traveler's protection.
Viral Hepatitis A—Vaccination is recommended for all travelers for their protection.
Typhoid fever—Vaccination is recommended for all travelers for their protection.

Selective vaccinations—These apply only to specific groups of travelers or persons on specific working assignments:
Viral Hepatitis B—Because of the high rate of healthy carriers of hepatitis B in this country, vaccination is recommended for persons on working assignments in the health care field (dentists, physicians, nurses, laboratory technicians), or working in close contact with the local population (teachers, missionaries, Peace Corps), or persons foreseeing sexual relations with local inhabitants.

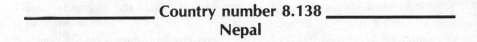

Country number 8.138
Nepal

INFECTIOUS DISEASE RISK

Malaria Risk
Malaria risk is primarily in Terai district and hill districts below 1200 meters. The risk exists all year. There is no risk of malaria in urban areas. The malaria in this country is resistant to chloroquine. The CDC recommends the use of mefloquine (Lariam) as described in Chapter 6.31 for chemical prophylaxis.
Falciparum malaria represents 15% of malaria, therefore there is a risk of p. vivax malaria exposure. Consider use of Primaquine upon return home.

Diseases of Special Risk
In addition to the worldwide hazard of tetanus and the routine and any special immunizations recommended below, the traveler should be aware that risk of exposure to the following diseases exists in this country. This list is not all inclusive, but it is a caution concerning the more likely endemic disease risks.

DISEASE RISK PROFILE

Disease	endemic	risk	hazard
Brucellosis		x	
Diarrheal Diseases		x	
Dysentery, Amoebic/Bacillary		x	
Echinococcosis		x	
Encephalitis, Japanese	x		
Helminthic Diseases (see Chapter 6.21)		x	
Hepatitis, Viral		x	
Leishmaniasis			
Visceral			x
Meningococcus		x	
Polio			x
Sandfly Fever			x
Tapeworms		x	
Trachoma		x	
Typhoid Fever		x	

Food/Water Safety

All tap water used for drinking, brushing teeth, and making ice cubes should be boiled prior to use. Insure that bottled water is uncapped in your presence. Milk should be boiled to insure safety. Powdered and evaporated milk are available and safe. Avoid butter and other dairy products. All meat, poultry and seafood must be well cooked and served while hot. Pork is best avoided. Vegetables should be well cooked and served hot. Salads and mayonnaise are best avoided. Fruits with intact skins should be peeled by you just prior to consumption. Avoid cold buffets, custards, and any frozen dessert. First class hotels and restaurants in Kathmandu serve purified drinking water and reliable food. However, the hazard is left to your judgement.

VACCINATIONS

Yellow fever—A vaccination certificate is required for travelers coming from infected areas. A vaccination is required for children of all ages. Children under nine months of age should not be vaccinated due to health considerations. Please refer to the discussion in Chapter 6.63 on avoiding yellow fever vaccination in this age group.

Routine immunizations should be current. For infants and children through 16 years of age, refer to Chapter 4.3. A rubeola (measles) booster should be considered. Persons age 16 to 65 should receive a booster of tetanus and diphtheria every ten years. Healthy adults under age 65 do not require pneumococcal vaccine, but it is appropriate for those with chronic medical conditions. Influenza vaccine may be considered for those providing essential community services, health care workers, and those wishing to reduce the likelihood of becoming ill with influenza. Adults over 65 years of age are urged to obtain yearly influenza immunization and to insure that their tetanus and diph-

theria immunizations are current. Pneumococcal vaccination is also suggested for this age group.

The vaccinations listed are recommended for the traveler's protection.
Poliomyelitis—A poliomyelitis booster is indicated for this country.
Viral Hepatitis A—Vaccination is recommended for all travelers for their protection.
Meningococcal meningitis—Vaccination is recommended when traveling outside the areas usually visited by tourists, traveling extensively in the interior of the country (trekkers, hikers) and for persons on working assignments in remote areas. All persons planning treks outside the Kathmandu Valley should receive the vaccine.
Typhoid fever—Vaccination is recommended for all travelers for their protection.

Selective vaccinations—*These apply only to specific groups of travelers or persons on specific working assignments:*
Viral Hepatitis B—Because of the high rate of healthy carriers of hepatitis B in this country, vaccination is recommended for persons on working assignments in the health care field (dentists, physicians, nurses, laboratory technicians), or working in close contact with the local population (teachers, missionaries, Peace Corps), or persons foreseeing sexual relations with local inhabitants.
Japanese encephalitis—Vaccination is indicated for persons traveling extensively in rual areas or living and working near rice growing rural and suburban areas and other irrigated land, when exposure to the disease carrying mosquitoes is high. Children are especially susceptible to the infection. Outbreaks occur occasionally in the southern plains bordering India (Terai Districts). Period of transmission is June to October. High risk groups are all ages.
Plague—Vaccination is recommended only for persons who may be occupationally exposed to wild rodents (anthropologists, geologists, medical personnel, missionaries, etc). The standard vaccination course must be completed before entering the plague infested area. Geographical distribution of the area of risk for this country is the western half of the country.
Rabies—In this country, where rabies is a constant threat, a pre-exposure rabies vaccination is advised for persons planning an extended stay or on working assignments (naturalists, agricultural advisors, archeologists, geologists, etc.). Although this provides adequate initial protection, a person bitten by a potentially rabid animal would still require post exposure immunization (see Chapter 6.40). Children should be cautioned not to pet dogs, cats, or other mammals.

U.S. Foreign Service:
Pani Pokhari
Kathmandu, Telephone 211199, 212718, 211601, 211603/4, 213158

TRAVEL ADVISORY

A U.S. Department of State Travel Advisory was in effect on 4 May 1990 when this book went to press. The entire text is included below. Travel advisories are subject to reissue, change, and cancellation at any time. Current travel advisory information is available by calling the U.S. Department of State Travel Advisory Hotline at (202) 647-5225. The current travel advisory status is also available from the Herchmer Database update system (see Chapter 2.8).

APRIL 24, 1990
NEPAL—WARNING
THE DEPARTMENT OF STATE ADVISES U.S. CITIZENS TO DEFER TRAVEL TO NEPAL AT THE PRESENT TIME DUE TO UNSETTLED SECURITY CONDITIONS. VIOLENCE, WHICH HAS BEEN LIMITED TO KATHMANDU, HAS NOT BEEN DIRECTED AGAINST FOREIGNERS, BUT THE SITUATIONS REMAIN VOLATILE. AMERICAN CITIZENS ALREADY IN NEPAL SHOULD CLOSELY MONITOR LOCAL CONDITIONS AND ARE URGED TO REGISTER AT THE AMERICAN EMBASSY IN KATHMANDU.
EXPIRATION: INDEFINITE

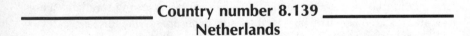

Country number 8.139
Netherlands

INFECTIOUS DISEASE RISK

Malaria Risk
There is no malaria risk in this country.

Diseases of Special Risk
In addition to the worldwide hazard of tetanus and the other routine immunizations recommended above, the traveler should be aware that risk of exposure to rabies, primarily found in foxes, exists in this country.

Food/Water Safety
Water is probably safe, but due to local variations in bacterial counts, using bottled water for the first few weeks will help the traveler adjust and decrease the chance of traveler's diarrhea. Milk is pasteurized and safe to drink. Butter, cheese, yogurt and ice-cream are safe. Local meat, poultry, seafood, vegetables, and fruits are safe to eat.

VACCINATIONS

Routine immunizations should be current. For infants and children through 16 years of age, refer to Chapter 4.3. A rubeola (measles) booster should be considered. Persons age 16 to 65 should receive a booster of tetanus and diphtheria every ten years. Healthy adults under age 65 do not require pneumococcal vaccine, but it is appropriate for those with chronic medical conditions. Influenza vaccine may be considered for those providing essential community services, health care workers, and those wishing to reduce the likelihood of becoming ill with influenza. Adults over 65 years of age are urged to obtain yearly influenza immunization and to insure that their tetanus and diphtheria immunizations are current. Pneumococcal vaccination is also suggested for this age group.

No vaccinations are required to enter this country.

U.S. Foreign Service:
Lang Voorhout 102
The Hague, Telephone 62-49-11

Museumplein 19
Amsterdam, Telephone 790321
Baan 50
Rotterdam, Telephone 117560

Canadian High Commission/Embassy Office:
Sophialaan 7
The Hague, Telephone 614111

Country number 8.140
Netherland Antilles

INFECTIOUS DISEASE RISK

Malaria Risk
There is no malaria risk in this country.

Diseases of Special Risk
In addition to the worldwide hazard of tetanus and the routine and any special immunizations recommended below, the traveler should be aware that risk of exposure to the following diseases exists in this country. This list is not all inclusive, but it is a caution concerning the more likely endemic disease risks.

Potential risk of dengue fever exists. The virus is present in this country at all times and may give rise to major outbreaks.

DISEASE RISK PROFILE

Disease	endemic	risk	hazard
Dysentery, Amoebic/Bacillary	x		
Hepatitis, Viral	x		
Rabies (esp mongoose)	x		

Food/Water Safety

Water is probably safe, but due to local variations in bacterial counts, using bottled water for the first few weeks will help the traveler adjust and decrease the chance of traveler's diarrhea. Milk is pasteurized and safe to drink. Butter, cheese, yogurt and ice-cream are safe. Local meat, poultry, seafood, vegetables, and fruits are safe to eat.

VACCINATIONS

Yellow fever—A vaccination certificate is required for travelers coming from infected areas and from or in transit through countries with active infection. A vaccination certificate is required for children over one year of age.

Routine immunizations should be current. For infants and children through 16 years of age, refer to Chapter 4.3. A rubeola (measles) booster should be considered. Persons age 16 to 65 should receive a booster of tetanus and diphtheria every ten years. Healthy adults under age 65 do not require pneumococcal vaccine, but it is appropriate for those with chronic medical conditions. Influenza vaccine may be considered for those providing essential community services, health care workers, and those wishing to reduce the likelihood of becoming ill with influenza. Adults over 65 years of age are urged to obtain yearly influenza immunization and to insure that their tetanus and diphtheria immunizations are current. Pneumococcal vaccination is also suggested for this age group.

U.S. Foreign Service:

St. Anna Blvd. 19
Willemstad, Curacao Telephone 613066, 613350, 613441

Canadian High Commission/Embassy Office:

Maduro and Curiels Bank, N.V.
Plaza JoJo Correa 2-4
Willemstad,
Curacao Telephone 613515, 611100,
Ext. 116

Country number 8.141
New Caledonia and Dependencies

INFECTIOUS DISEASE RISK

Malaria Risk
There is no malaria risk in this country.

Diseases of Special Risk
In addition to the worldwide hazard of tetanus and the routine and any special immunizations recommended below, the traveler should be aware that risk of exposure to the following diseases exists in this country. This list is not all inclusive, but it is a caution concerning the more likely endemic disease risks.

Potential risk of dengue fever exists. The virus is present in this country at all times and may give rise to major outbreaks.

DISEASE RISK PROFILE

Disease	endemic	risk	hazard
Diarrheal Disease Risk	x		
Encephalitis, Japanese	x		
Filariasis			x
Helminthic Diseases (see Chapter 6.21)	x		
Typhoid Fever	x		

Food/Water Safety
Water is probably safe, but due to local variations in bacterial counts, using bottled water for the first few weeks will help the traveler adjust and decrease the chance of traveler's diarrhea. Milk is pasteurized and safe to drink. Butter, cheese, yogurt and ice-cream are safe. Local meat, poultry, seafood, vegetables, and fruits are safe to eat.

VACCINATIONS
Cholera—Travelers from infected areas must complete a form for the Health Service. No immunization required.

Yellow fever—A vaccination certificate is required for travelers coming from infected areas and from or in transit through countries with active disease. A vaccination certificate is required for children over one year of age.

Routine immunizations should be current. For infants and children through 16 years of age, refer to Chapter 4.3. A rubeola (measles) booster should be considered. Persons age 16 to 65 should receive a booster of tetanus and diphtheria every ten years. Healthy adults under age 65 do not require pneumococcal vaccine, but it is appropriate for those with chronic medical conditions. Influenza vaccine may be considered for those providing essential

community services, health care workers, and those wishing to reduce the likelihood of becoming ill with influenza. Adults over 65 years of age are urged to obtain yearly influenza immunization and to insure that their tetanus and diphtheria immunizations are current. Pneumococcal vaccination is also suggested for this age group.

The vaccinations listed are recommended for the traveler's protection.
*Poliomyelitis—*A poliomyelitis booster is indicated for this country.
*Viral Hepatitis A—*Vaccination is recommended for all travelers for their protection.
*Typhoid fever—*Vaccination is recommended for all travelers for their protection.

*Selective vaccinations—*These apply only to specific groups of travelers or persons on specific working assignments:
*Viral Hepatitis B—*Because of the high rate of healthy carriers of hepatitis B in this country, vaccination is recommended for persons on working assignments in the health care field (dentists, physicians, nurses, laboratory technicians), or working in close contact with the local population (teachers, missionaries, Peace Corps), or persons foreseeing sexual relations with local inhabitants.

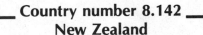

Country number 8.142
New Zealand

INFECTIOUS DISEASE RISK

Malaria Risk
There is no malaria risk in this country.

Diseases of Special Risk

Food/Water Safety
Local water is considered safe without further treatment. Milk is pasteurized and safe to drink. Butter, cheese, yogurt and ice-cream are safe. Local meat, poultry, seafood, vegetables, and fruits are safe to eat. Hydatid tapeworm infections can occur, but likelihood of infection is low.

VACCINATIONS
Routine immunizations should be current. For infants and children through 16 years of age, refer to Chapter 4.3. A rubeola (measles) booster should be considered. Persons age 16 to 65 should receive a booster of tetanus and diphtheria every ten years. Healthy adults under age 65 do not require

pneumococcal vaccine, but it is appropriate for those with chronic medical conditions. Influenza vaccine may be considered for those providing essential community services, health care workers, and those wishing to reduce the likelihood of becoming ill with influenza. Adults over 65 years of age are urged to obtain yearly influenza immunization and to insure that their tetanus and diphtheria immunizations are current. Pneumococcal vaccination is also suggested for this age group.

No vaccinations are required to enter this country.

Selective vaccinations—These apply only to specific groups of travelers or persons on specific working assignments:

Viral Hepatitis B—Because of the high rate of healthy carriers of hepatitis B among Maori, vaccination is recommended for persons working in health care, education, or in close contact with them.

U.S. Foreign Service:
29 Fitzherbert Ter., Thorndon,
Wellington, Telephone 722-068

4th Fl.
Yorkshire General Bldg.
Shortland and O'Connell Sts.
Auckland, Telephone 32-724

Canadian High Commission/Embassy Office:
I.C.I. Building
Molesworth Street
Wellington, Telephone 739-577

61 Wakefield Street
Auckland, Telephone 308-516

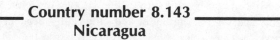

Country number 8.143
Nicaragua

INFECTIOUS DISEASE RISK

Malaria Risk
Malaria exists in rural areas below 1000 meters from May through December. There is some risk in the outskirt towns of Chinandega, Leon, Granada, Managua, Nandaime, and Tipitapa. Prophylaxis may not be needed if trips are restricted to urban areas. See Chapter 6.31 for use of chloroquine.

Falciparum malaria represents 14% of malaria, therefore there is a risk of p. vivax malaria exposure. Consider use of primaquine upon return home if heavy mosquito exposure was encountered.

Diseases of Special Risk

In addition to the worldwide hazard of tetanus and the routine and any special immunizations recommended below, the traveler should be aware that risk of exposure to the following diseases exists in this country. This list is not all inclusive, but it is a caution concerning the more likely endemic disease risks.

Chaga's Disease is present in rural areas below 1500 meters in the following departments: Esteli, Jinotega, Leon, Madriz, Managua, Masaya, Matagalpa, Nueva Segovia, and Rivas.

This country must be considered receptive to dengue fever. Intermittent epidemics in the past make renewed activity or reintroduction of the virus possible.

DISEASE RISK PROFILE

Disease	endemic	risk	hazard
Brucellosis	x		
Diarrheal Disease Risk		x	
Dysentery, Amoebic/Bacillary		x	
Encephalitis, Venezuelan Equine	x		
Helminthic Diseases (see Chapter 6.21)		x	
Hepatitis, Viral	x		
Leishmaniasis	x		
Polio		x	
Rabies (esp dogs and bats)			x
Trypanosomiasis, American	x		
Chaga's Disease			
Typhoid Fever		x	

Food/Water Safety

All tap water used for drinking, brushing teeth, and making ice cubes should be boiled prior to use. Insure that bottled water is uncapped in your presence. Milk should be boiled to insure safety. Powdered and evaporated milk are available and safe. Avoid butter and other dairy products. All meat, poultry and seafood must be well cooked and served while hot. Pork is best avoided. Vegetables should be well cooked and served hot. Salads and mayonnaise are best avoided. Fruits with intact skins should be peeled by you just prior to consumption. Avoid cold buffets, custards, and any frozen dessert. First class hotels and restaurants in Managua serve purified drinking water and reliable food. However, the hazard is left to your judgement.

VACCINATIONS

Yellow fever vaccination is required of any traveler older than 1 year of age arriving from areas infected with this disease.

Routine immunizations should be current. For infants and children through 16 years of age, refer to Chapter 4.3. A rubeola (measles) booster should be considered. Persons age 16 to 65 should receive a booster of tetanus and diphtheria every ten years. Healthy adults under age 65 do not require pneumococcal vaccine, but it is appropriate for those with chronic medical conditions. Influenza vaccine may be considered for those providing essential community services, health care workers, and those wishing to reduce the likelihood of becoming ill with influenza. Adults over 65 years of age are urged to obtain yearly influenza immunization and to insure that their tetanus and diphtheria immunizations are current. Pneumococcal vaccination is also suggested for this age group.

The vaccinations listed are recommended for the traveler's protection.

Viral Hepatitis A—Vaccination is recommended for all travelers for their protection.

Typhoid fever—Vaccination is recommended for all travelers for their protection.

U.S. Foreign Service:
Kilometer 4 1/2, Carretera Sur.
Managua, Telephone 666-010
alternate telephone numbers 66013,66015/8

British Embassy
Managua, Telephone 70034

TRAVEL ADVISORY

A U.S. Department of State Travel Advisory was in effect on 4 May 1990 when this book went to press. The entire text is included below. Travel advisories are subject to reissue, change, and cancellation at any time. Current travel advisory information is available by calling the U.S. Department of State Travel Advisory Hotline at (202) 647-5225. The current travel advisory status is also available from the Herchmer Database update system (see Chapter 2.8).

9FB DN37 19-1 1LA71 1 05/16/89 04:12
SECSTATE WSH
SUBJECT: TRAVEL ADVISORY—NICARAGUA—WARNING
1. SUMMARY: THE DEPARTMENT OF STATE WARNS U.S. CITIZENS TO EXERCISE EXTREME CAUTION WHEN TRAVELING TO NICARAGUA. POOR RELATIONS BETWEEN NICARAGUA AND THE UNITED STATES HAVE MADE MORE DIFFICULT THE EMBASSY'S EFFORTS TO

PROVIDE PROTECTIVE SERVICE TO AMERICAN CITIZENS IN NICARA-
GUA. DESPITE THE CEASE-FIRE BETWEEN THE SANDINISTA GOV-
ERNMENT AND THE NICARAGUAN RESISTANCE, OCCASIONAL
FIGHTING CONTINUES, MAKING OVERLAND TRAVEL HAZARDOUS
IN MANY REGIONS OF THE COUNTRY. TRAVELERS SHOULD AR-
RIVE BY AIR AT SANDINO INTERNATIONAL AIRPORT IN MANAGUA.
OVERLAND TRAVELERS SHOULD BE AWARE THAT THE ONLY OPEN
BORDER CROSSING FROM HONDURAS INTO NICARAGUA IS EL ES-
PINO ON THE PAN AMERICAN HIGHWAY. IN THE SOUTH, PENAS
BLANCA BORDER CROSSING IS OPEN FOR TRAVEL TO AND FROM
COSTA RICA. AMERICAN CITIZENS ARE STRONGLY URGED TO
AVOID ATTEMPTING TO ENTER NICARAGUA BY CROSSING THE
GULF OF FONSECA BY FERRY FROM UNION, EL SALVADOR TO PO-
TOSI, NICARAGUA.
2. DUAL NATIONALS, ESPECIALLY MALES OF MILITARY AGE,
SHOULD ESPECIALLY CONSIDER CAREFULLY ANY PLANS TO TRA-
VEL TO NICARAGUA BECAUSE THE GOVERNMENT OF NICARAGUA
NOW STRICTLY ENFORCES ITS NATIONALITY LAW. THIS LAW PRO-
VIDES THAT ALL PERSONS BORN IN NICARAGUA, EXCEPT CHIL-
DREN OF DIPLOMATS ACCREDITED TO NICARAGUA AT THE TIME
OF THE CHILD'S BIRTH, ARE NICARAGUAN CITIZENS. ALL AMERI-
CAN TRAVELERS TO NICARAGUA ARE URGED TO REGISTER WITH
THE CONSULAR SECTION OF THE U.S. EMBASSY AT KILOMETER 4
1/2, CARRETERA SUR, MANAGUA AT TEL: 666-010.
3. AMERICANS SHOULD BE AWARE THAT POOR RELATIONS BE-
TWEEN THE U.S. AND NICARAGUA HAVE COMPLICATED THE PRO-
VISION OF CONSULAR SERVICES TO AMERICANS, ESPECIALLY IN
ARREST CASES. IN SEVERAL CASES, THE NICARAGUAN AUTHORI-
TIES HAVE FAILED TO NOTIFY THE EMBASSY OF THE ARREST/
DETENTION OF AMERICANS AND/OR HAVE REFUSED TO ALLOW
PRIVATE CONSULAR VISITS WITH AMERICAN PRISONERS.
4. SENSITIVE AND DANGEROUS AREAS: DESPITE THE TRUCE
AGREED TO BY THE SANDINISTA GOVERNMENT AND THE NICARA-
GUAN RESISTANCE IN MARCH, 1988, FIGHTING BETWEEN GOV-
ERNMENT AND OPPOSITION FORCES REMAINS UNPREDICTABLE,
SPORADIC, AND OCCASIONALLY INTENSE ALONG THE NORTHERN
AND SOUTHERN BORDERS OF NICARAGUA, THE CENTRAL HIGH-
LANDS AND IN THE ATLANTIC COASTAL DEPARTMENT OF ZELAYA.
LAND TRAVEL IN MUCH OF NICARAGUA OUTSIDE THE MAJOR CIT-
IES IS DANGEROUS DUE TO UNEXPLODED LANDMINES AFFECT-
ING ROADS, TRAILS, AND PATHS. TRAVELERS SHOULD NOT
TRAVEL OUTSIDE CITIES AT NIGHT AND SHOULD AVOID BORDER
AREAS AT ALL TIMES. TRAVELERS ARE URGED TO CONSULT WITH
THE AMERICAN EMBASSY BEFORE ATTEMPTING TRAVEL INTO RU-

RAL AREAS.

5. FOREIGNERS MAY NOT TRAVEL TO THE ATLANTIC/CARIBBEAN COAST WITHOUT PERMISSION FROM THE MINISTRY OF INTERIOR. AS CONSULAR ACCESS TO THE REGION IS ALSO RESTRICTED, THE EMBASSY MAY BE UNABLE TO PROVIDE CONSULAR SERVICES TO U.S. CITIZENS TRAVELING IN THE REGION. TRAVEL IS ALSO PROHIBITED IN THE VICINITY OF MILITARY OPERATIONS. TOURISTS FOUND IN SUCH AREAS MAY BE SEARCHED AND DETAINED. FATIGUES OR MILITARY-STYLE CLOTHING WORN ANYWHERE IN NICARAGUA MAY BE CONFISCATED. PHOTOGRAPHY OF MILITARY INSTALLATIONS, EQUIPMENT, VEHICLES, AND ACTIVITY IS PROHIBITED.

6. PRIVATE VESSELS: SAILORS SHOULD AVOID NICARAGUAN TERRITORIAL WATERS. PRIVATE VESSELS WHICH ENTER NICARAGUAN WATERS WITHOUT AUTHORIZATION MAY BE SEIZED, HELD, AND FINED BY NICARAGUAN NAVAL AUTHORITIES. THERE HAS BEEN A CREDIBLE REPORT OF NICARAGUAN NAVY VESSELS BEING USED IN THE COMMISSION OF CRIMES AGAINST A PRIVATE VESSEL NEAR THE NICARAGUAN COAST.

7. CURRENCY CONTROLS: ALL VISITORS MUST EXCHANGE U.S. SIXTY DOLLARS INTO LOCAL CURRENCY AT THE PREVAILING OFFICIAL EXCHANGE RATE AT THE PORT OF ENTRY. SUBSEQUENT CONVERSIONS OF CASH OR TRAVELER'S CHECKS MAY BE MADE AT AN AUTHORIZED CURRENCY EXCHANGE FACILITY (CASA DE CAMBIO) IN MANAGUA. TRAVELERS CHECKS WILL NOT BE EXCHANGED FOR U.S. DOLLARS. THE INTERCONTINENTAL AND CAMINO REAL HOTELS IN MANAGUA ALSO PROVIDE AUTHORIZED CURRENCY EXCHANGE FACILITIES. THE UNOFFICIAL SALE OR PURCHASE OF LOCAL CURRENCY IS A VIOLATION OF NICARAGUAN LAW AND MAY RESULT IN PROSECUTION.

8. MAJOR HOTELS IN MANAGUA, ALONG WITH A NUMBER OF SMALLER HOTELS AND HOSTELS, CHARGE FOREIGNERS IN U.S. DOLLARS AND MANY WILL NOT ACCEPT TRAVELERS CHECKS. VISITORS SHOULD TAKE TO NICARAGUA SUFFICIENT CASH TO COVER THEIR EXPENSES. CREDIT CARDS, PERSONAL CHECKS AND OTHER FINANCIAL INSTRUMENTS ARE NOT RECOGNIZED OR ACCEPTED AT MOST HOTELS, RESTAURANTS OR BANKS IN NICARAGUA. CREDIT CARD PURCHASES WRITTEN IN NICARAGUAN CORDOBAS MAY BE CHARGED IN U.S. DOLLARS USING A DISADVANTAGEOUS EXCHANGE RATE, GREATLY INCREASING THE FINAL COST TO THE PURCHASER. THE U.S. EMBASSY CANNOT EXCHANGE TRAVELERS CHECKS FOR TRAVELERS.

9. WHILE COMMERCIAL BANK TRANSFERS FOR PAYMENT IN DOLLARS ARE VIRTUALLY IMPOSSIBLE TO ARRANGE, THE

GOVERNMENT-AFFILIATED EXCHANGE FACILITY IN MANAGUA WILL ACCEPT TRANSFERS FOR DISBURSEMENT AT 90 PERCENT IN DOLLARS AND 10 PERCENT IN LOCAL CURRENCY.

10. CRIME: THE COLLAPSE OF THE NICARAGUAN ECONOMY DURING RECENT YEARS HAS CONTRIBUTED TO A RISE IN CRIME, ESPECIALLY PETTY THEFT. GREAT CARE SHOULD BE TAKEN IN PROTECTING PERSONAL EFFECTS, ESPECIALLY ON MANAGUA'S OVERCROWDED PUBLIC BUSES, WHERE PICKPOCKETS ABOUND.

11. DUAL NATIONALS: THE GOVERNMENT OF NICARAGUA NOW STRICTLY ENFORCES THE 1981 NICARAGUAN NATIONALITY LAW, WHICH PROVIDES THAT ALL PERSONS BORN IN NICARAGUA, EXCEPT THE CHILDREN OF DIPLOMATS ACCREDITED TO NICARAGUA AT THE TIME OF THE CHILD'S BIRTH, ARE NICARAGUAN CITIZENS. IN ADDITION, PERSONS BORN OUTSIDE NICARAGUA TO AT LEAST ONE NICARAGUAN PARENT MAY ALSO BE CONSIDERED TO BE CITIZENS OF NICARAGUA. NICARAGUAN IMMIGRATION AUTHORITIES OFTEN REQUIRE PERSONS WITH NICARAGUAN CITIZENSHIP, REGARDLESS OF WHETHER THEY ENTERED NICARAGUA WITH A U.S. PASSPORT, TO OBTAIN NICARAGUAN PASSPORTS BEFORE LEAVING THE COUNTRY. THIS APPLICATION PROCESS MAY TAKE SEVERAL MONTHS. YOUNG MEN MUST USUALLY REGISTER WITH THEIR LOCAL DRAFT BOARDS BEFORE THEY APPLY FOR THEIR NICARAGUAN PASSPORT. ONCE THE PASSPORT IS ISSUED, THE DUAL NATIONAL MUST OBTAIN AN EXIT VISA.

12. MALE DUAL NATIONALS OF MILITARY AGE: AMERICAN CITIZENS WHO MAY ALSO HAVE NICARAGUAN NATIONALITY, ESPECIALLY MALES 14 YEARS OF AGE OR OLDER, SHOULD CONSIDER VERY CAREFULLY ANY PLANS TO TRAVEL TO NICARAGUA. AT PRESENT, DUAL NATIONALS OF MILITARY AGE WHO RESIDE OUTSIDE OF NICARAGUA ARE EXEMPT FROM ACTIVE MILITARY SERVICE. DUAL NATIONALS WHO REMAIN IN NICARAGUA BEYOND THE NINETY-DAY PERIOD OF STAY AUTHORIZED FOR FOREIGNERS MAY BE CONSIDERED RESIDENTS OF NICARAGUA AND CALLED FOR ACTIVE MILITARY SERVICE. THERE HAVE BEEN UNFORTUNATE CASES OF MILITARY AGE DUAL NATIONAL MALES VISITING NICARAGUA WHO HAVE BEEN REQUIRED TO ACQUIRE A NICARAGUAN PASSPORT TO DEPART AND WHOSE DEPARTURE HAS BEEN DELAYED.

13. RENUNCIATION OF NICARAGUAN CITIZENSHIP IS NOT EFFECTIVE UNTIL THE RENUNCIATION IS ACCEPTED BY THE COMPETENT AUTHORITIES IN MANAGUA. FURTHER INFORMATION CONCERNING NICARAGUAN CITIZENSHIP LAWS AND MILITARY SERVICE REQUIREMENTS MAY BE OBTAINED FROM THE EMBASSY OF NICARAGUA IN WASHINGTON D.C.

14. TRAVEL ADVISORY CONTAINED IN 88 STATE 348540 DATED OCT. 25,1988 IS HEREBY CANCELLED.
EXPIRATION DATE: MAY 1 1990.
U.S. DEPARTMENT OF STATE WASHINGTON D.C. 20520

_____ **Country number 8.144** _____
Niger

INFECTIOUS DISEASE RISK

Malaria Risk

Malaria is present in all parts of this country, including urban areas. The risk exists all year. The malaria in this country is resistant to chloroquine. The CDC recommends the use of mefloquine (Lariam) as described in Chapter 6.31 for chemical prophylaxis.

Falciparum malaria represents 82% of malaria, therefore there is a risk of p. vivax malaria exposure. Consider use of primaquine upon return home.

Diseases of Special Risk

In addition to the worldwide hazard of tetanus and the routine and any special immunizations recommended below, the traveler should be aware that risk of exposure to the following diseases exists in this country. This list is not all inclusive, but it is a caution concerning the more likely endemic disease risks.

Schistosomiasis may be found in this country. Avoid contact with contaminated fresh water lakes, ponds, or streams. Known endemic areas exist along the Niger River, including the capital Niamey, the regions of Zinder, Maradi and Tanout.

DISEASE RISK PROFILE

Disease	endemic	risk	hazard
Dracunculiasis/Guinea Worm	x		
Diarrheal Disease Risk			x
Dysentery, Amoebic/Bacillary			x
Echinococcosis		x	
Filariasis			x
Giardiasis			x
Helminthic Diseases (see Chapter 6.21)			x
Hepatitis, Viral			x
Lassa Fever	x		
Leishmaniasis			
Cutaneous	x		
Visceral	x		
Onchocerciasis			x
Polio			x

Disease	endemic	risk	hazard
Rabies	x		
Relapsing Fever	x		
Trachoma			x
Trypanosomiasis, African Sleeping Sickness	x		
Tungiasis			x
Typhoid Fever			x
Typhus, Endemic Flea-Borne	x		
Typhus, Epidemic Louse-Borne	x		
Typhus, Scrub	x		

Food/Water Safety

All tap water used for drinking, brushing teeth, and making ice cubes should be boiled prior to use. Insure that bottled water is uncapped in your presence. Milk should be boiled to insure safety. Powdered and evaporated milk are available and safe. Avoid butter and other dairy products. All meat, poultry and seafood must be well cooked and served while hot. Pork is best avoided. Vegetables should be well cooked and served hot. Salads and mayonnaise are best avoided. Fruits with intact skins should be peeled by you just prior to consumption. Avoid cold buffets, custards, and any frozen dessert.

VACCINATIONS

Yellow fever—A vaccination certificate is required on arrival from all countries. A vaccination certificate is required for children over one year of age. CDC recommends vaccination for all travelers over 9 months of age who will be traveling outside of urban areas.

Routine immunizations should be current. For infants and children through 16 years of age, refer to Chapter 4.3. A rubeola (measles) booster should be considered. Persons age 16 to 65 should receive a booster of tetanus and diphtheria every ten years. Healthy adults under age 65 do not require pneumococcal vaccine, but it is appropriate for those with chronic medical conditions. Influenza vaccine may be considered for those providing essential community services, health care workers, and those wishing to reduce the likelihood of becoming ill with influenza. Adults over 65 years of age are urged to obtain yearly influenza immunization and to insure that their tetanus and diphtheria immunizations are current. Pneumococcal vaccination is also suggested for this age group.

The vaccinations listed are recommended for the traveler's protection.
Poliomyelitis—A poliomyelitis booster is indicated for this country.
Cholera—Cholera is present in this country. Risk to western travelers is low. Immunization is not required or recommended for travel to this country due to its low effectiveness. Avoid uncooked foods and untreated water. Vaccination is advised only for persons living or working under inadequate sanitary conditions and for those with impaired defense mechanisms.

Viral Hepatitis A—Vaccination is recommended for all travelers for their protection.

Meningococcal meningitis—Vaccination is advised for persons traveling extensively or on working assignements in the meningitis belt of Africa's northern savannah, which stretches from the Red Sea to the Atlantic Ocean. Peak season is March and April. Local area of greatest danger is in the southern third of the country.

Typhoid fever—Vaccination is recommended for all travelers for their protection.

Selective vaccinations—These apply only to specific groups of travelers or persons on specific working assignments:

Viral Hepatitis B—Because of the high rate of healthy carriers of hepatitis B in this country, vaccination is recommended for persons on working assignments in the health care field (dentists, physicians, nurses, laboratory technicians), or working in close contact with the local population (teachers, missionaries, Peace Corps), or persons foreseeing sexual relations with local inhabitants.

Rabies—In this country, where rabies is a constant threat, a pre-exposure rabies vaccination is advised for persons planning an extended stay or on working assignments (naturalists, agricultural advisors, archeologists, geologists, etc.). Although this provides adequate initial protection, a person bitten by a potentially rabid animal would still require post exposure immunization (see Chapter 6.40). Children should be cautioned not to pet dogs, cats, or other mammals.

U.S. Foreign Service:
P.O. Box 11201
Niamey, Telephone 72-26-61/2/3/4, 72-26-70

_____ **Country number 8.145** _____
Nigeria

INFECTIOUS DISEASE RISK

Malaria Risk

Malaria is present in all parts of this country, including urban areas. The risk exists all year. The malaria in this country is resistant to chloroquine. The CDC recommends the use of mefloquine (Lariam) as described in Chapter 6.31 for chemical prophylaxis.

Falciparum malaria represents 83% of malaria, therefore there is a risk of p. vivax malaria exposure. Consider use of primaquine upon return home.

Diseases of Special Risk

In addition to the worldwide hazard of tetanus and the routine and any special immunizations recommended below, the traveler should be aware that risk of exposure to the following diseases exists in this country. This list is not all inclusive, but it is a caution concerning the more likely endemic disease risks.

This country must be considered receptive to dengue fever. Intermittent epidemics in the past make renewed activity or reintroduction of the virus possible.

Schistosomiasis may be found throughout this country, including urban areas. Avoid contact with contaminated fresh water lakes, ponds, or streams.

Louse-borne typhus is cosmopolitan in distribution and is present wherever groups of persons are crowded together under conditions of poor sanitation and malnutrition. Risk exists for persons living or working in remote areas of the country (anthropologists, archeologists, geologists, medical personnel, missionaries, etc.). Freedom from louse infestation is the most effective protection against typhus.

DISEASE RISK PROFILE

Disease	endemic	risk	hazard
Dracunculiasis/Guinea Worm	x		
Diarrheal Disease Risk			x
Dysentery, Amoebic/Bacillary			x
Echinococcosis		x	
Filariasis			x
Giardiasis			x
Helminthic Diseases (see Chapter 6.21)			x
Hepatitis, Viral			x
Lassa Fever	x		
Leishmaniasis			
Cutaneous	x		
Visceral	x		
Loiasis			x
Onchocerciasis			x
Polio			x
Rabies	x		
Relapsing Fever	x		
Trachoma			x
Trypanosomiasis, African Sleeping Sickness	x		
Tungiasis			x
Typhoid Fever			x
Typhus, Endemic Flea-Borne	x		
Typhus, Epidemic Louse-Borne	x		
Typhus, Scrub	x		

Food/Water Safety

All tap water used for drinking, brushing teeth, and making ice cubes should be boiled prior to use. Insure that bottled water is uncapped in your

presence. Milk should be boiled to insure safety. Powdered and evaporated milk are available and safe. Avoid butter and other dairy products. All meat, poultry and seafood must be well cooked and served while hot. Pork is best avoided. Vegetables should be well cooked and served hot. Salads and mayonnaise are best avoided. Fruits with intact skins should be peeled by you just prior to consumption. Avoid cold buffets, custards, and any frozen dessert. First class hotels and restaurants in Enugu, Ibadan, Kano, and Lagos serve purified drinking water and reliable food. However, the hazard is left to your judgement.

VACCINATIONS

Cholera—Cholera is present in this country. Risk to western travelers is low. Immunization is not required or recommended for travel to this country due to its low effectiveness. Avoid uncooked foods and untreated water. Vaccination is advised only for persons living or working under inadequate sanitary conditions and for those with impaired defense mechanisms. Travelers leaving this country are required to possess a vaccination certificate on their departure to an infected area or to countries which still demand such a certificate.

Yellow fever—A vaccination certificate is required on arrival from all countries. A vaccination certificate is required for children over one year of age. The CDC recommends vaccination of all travelers older than 9 months of age who will be traveling outside of urban areas. Yellow fever is currently active in this country in Benuc, Cross River, Kaduna, Kwara, Ogum, Ondo, Dyo, and Lagos States. 1,320 deaths from yellow fever were reported in 1987. In 1989 49 deaths were reported from Imo State.

Routine immunizations should be current. For infants and children through 16 years of age, refer to Chapter 4.3. A rubeola (measles) booster should be considered. Persons age 16 to 65 should receive a booster of tetanus and diphtheria every ten years. Healthy adults under age 65 do not require pneumococcal vaccine, but it is appropriate for those with chronic medical conditions. Influenza vaccine may be considered for those providing essential community services, health care workers, and those wishing to reduce the likelihood of becoming ill with influenza. Adults over 65 years of age are urged to obtain yearly influenza immunization and to insure that their tetanus and diphtheria immunizations are current. Pneumococcal vaccination is also suggested for this age group.

The vaccinations listed are recommended for the traveler's protection.

Poliomyelitis—A poliomyelitis booster is indicated for this country.

Viral Hepatitis A—Vaccination is recommended for all travelers for their protection.

Meningococcal meningitis—Vaccination is advised for persons traveling extensively or on working assignements in the meningitis belt of Africa's northern savannah, which stretches from the Red Sea to the Atlantic Ocean. Peak season is March and April. Local area of greatest danger is the northern half of the country.

Typhoid fever—Vaccination is recommended for all travelers for their protection.

Selective vaccinations—These apply only to specific groups of travelers or persons on specific working assignments:
Viral Hepatitis B—Because of the high rate of healthy carriers of hepatitis B in this country, vaccination is recommended for persons on working assignments in the health care field (dentists, physicians, nurses, laboratory technicians), or working in close contact with the local population (teachers, missionaries, Peace Corps), or persons foreseeing sexual relations with local inhabitants.

Rabies—In this country, where rabies is a constant threat, a pre-exposure rabies vaccination is advised for persons planning an extended stay or on working assignments (naturalists, agricultural advisors, archeologists, geologists, etc.). Although this provides adequate initial protection, a person bitten by a potentially rabid animal would still require post exposure immunization (see Chapter 6.40). Children should be cautioned not to pet dogs, cats, or other mammals.

U.S. Foreign Service:
2 Eleke Crescent
Lagos, Telephone 610097

2 Maska Road
Kaduna, Telephone (062) 213-043, 312-074, 213-175

Canadian High Commission/Embassy Office:
Committee of Vice-Chancellors Building
Plot 8A
4 Idowu-Taylor St.
Victoria Island, Telephone 612-382/383/384/385

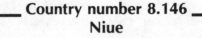

Country number 8.146
Niue

INFECTIOUS DISEASE RISK

Malaria Risk
There is no malaria risk in this country.

Diseases of Special Risk
In addition to the worldwide hazard of tetanus and the routine and any special immunizations recommended below, the traveler should be aware that

risk of exposure to the following diseases exists in this country. This list is not all inclusive, but it is a caution concerning the more likely endemic disease risks.

This country must be considered receptive to dengue fever. Intermittent epidemics in the past make renewed activity or reintroduction of the virus possible.

DISEASE RISK PROFILE

Disease	endemic	risk	hazard
Diarrheal Disease Risk		x	
Encephalitis, Japanese	x		
Filariasis			x
Helminthic Diseases (see Chapter 6.21)		x	
Typhoid Fever		x	

Food/Water Safety

Water is probably safe, but due to local variations in bacterial counts, using bottled water for the first few weeks will help the traveler adjust and decrease the chance of traveler's diarrhea. Milk is pasteurized and safe to drink. Butter, cheese, yogurt and ice-cream are usually safe. Local meat, poultry, seafood, vegetables, and fruits are generally safe to eat.

VACCINATIONS

Yellow fever—A vaccination certificate is required for travelers coming from infected areas. A vaccination certificate is required for children over one year of age.

Routine immunizations should be current. For infants and children through 16 years of age, refer to Chapter 4.3. A rubeola (measles) booster should be considered. Persons age 16 to 65 should receive a booster of tetanus and diphtheria every ten years. Healthy adults under age 65 do not require pneumococcal vaccine, but it is appropriate for those with chronic medical conditions. Influenza vaccine may be considered for those providing essential community services, health care workers, and those wishing to reduce the likelihood of becoming ill with influenza. Adults over 65 years of age are urged to obtain yearly influenza immunization and to insure that their tetanus and diphtheria immunizations are current. Pneumococcal vaccination is also suggested for this age group.

Country number 8.147
Norfolk Island

INFECTIOUS DISEASE RISK

Malaria Risk

There is no malaria risk in this country.

Food/Water Safety
Local water is considered safe without further treatment. Milk is pasteurized and safe to drink. Butter, cheese, yogurt and ice-cream are safe. Local meat, poultry, seafood, vegetables, and fruits are safe to eat.

VACCINATIONS
Routine immunizations should be current. For infants and children through 16 years of age, refer to Chapter 4.3. A rubeola (measles) booster should be considered. Persons age 16 to 65 should receive a booster of tetanus and diphtheria every ten years. Healthy adults under age 65 do not require pneumococcal vaccine, but it is appropriate for those with chronic medical conditions. Influenza vaccine may be considered for those providing essential community services, health care workers, and those wishing to reduce the likelihood of becoming ill with influenza. Adults over 65 years of age are urged to obtain yearly influenza immunization and to insure that their tetanus and diphtheria immunizations are current. Pneumococcal vaccination is also suggested for this age group.
No vaccinations are required to enter this country.

Country number 8.148
Norway

INFECTIOUS DISEASE RISK

Malaria Risk
There is no malaria risk in this country.

Diseases of Special Risk
Rabies is a risk in rural areas in wild animals, especially foxes.

Food/Water Safety
Local water is considered safe without further treatment. Milk is pasteurized and safe to drink. Butter, cheese, yogurt and ice-cream are safe. Local meat, poultry, seafood, vegetables, and fruits are safe to eat.

VACCINATIONS
Routine immunizations should be current. For infants and children through 16 years of age, refer to Chapter 4.3. A rubeola (measles) booster should be considered. Persons age 16 to 65 should receive a booster of tetanus and diphtheria every ten years. Healthy adults under age 65 do not require pneumococcal vaccine, but it is appropriate for those with chronic medical conditions. Influenza vaccine may be considered for those providing essential community services, health care workers, and those wishing to reduce the likeli-

hood of becoming ill with influenza. Adults over 65 years of age are urged to obtain yearly influenza immunization and to insure that their tetanus and diphtheria immunizations are current. Pneumococcal vaccination is also suggested for this age group.

No vaccinations are required to enter this country.

The vaccinations listed are recommended for the traveler's protection.

Tick-borne encephalitis—(Central European encephalitis) Vaccination is recommended for persons involved in recreational activities in forested areas (camping, hiking) or working in forestry occupations. Risk season: March to November. Risk is present in scattered areas around Bergen.

Rabies—This disease is common in wild animals, primarily foxes, in rural areas. See Chapter 6.40 for discussion of immunization and post exposure treatment.

U.S. Foreign Service:
Drammensveien 18, Oslo 1
Oslo, Telephone 56-68-80

Canadian High Commission/Embassy Office:
Oscar's Gate 20
Oslo, Telephone 46-69-55

_____ Country number 8.149 _____
Oman

INFECTIOUS DISEASE RISK

Malaria Risk

Malaria is present in all parts of this country, including urban areas. The risk exists all year. See page EEE for use of Chloroquine.

Falciparum malaria represents 86% of malaria, therefore there is a risk of p. vivax malaria exposure. Consider use of primaquine upon return home.

Diseases of Special Risk

In addition to the worldwide hazard of tetanus and the routine and any special immunizations recommended below, the traveler should be aware that risk of exposure to the following diseases exists in this country. This list is not all inclusive, but it is a caution concerning the more likely endemic disease risks.

DISEASE RISK PROFILE

Disease	endemic	risk	hazard
Brucellosis			x
Cholera	x		
Dracunculiasis/Guinea Worm	x		
Echinococcosis	x		
Hepatitis, Viral		x	
Leishmaniasis			
Cutaneous	x		
Visceral	x		
Polio			x
Rabies	x		
Relapsing Fever	x		
Tapeworms	x		
Trachoma	x		
Typhoid Fever		x	
Typhus, Endemic Flea-Borne	x		
Typhus, Scrub	x		

Food/Water Safety

All tap water used for drinking, brushing teeth, and making ice cubes should be boiled prior to use. Insure that bottled water is uncapped in your presence. Milk should be boiled to insure safety. Powdered and evaporated milk are available and safe. Avoid butter and other dairy products. All meat, poultry and seafood must be well cooked and served while hot. Pork is best avoided. Vegetables should be well cooked and served hot. Salads and mayonnaise are best avoided. Fruits with intact skins should be peeled by you just prior to consumption. Avoid cold buffets, custards, and any frozen dessert.

VACCINATIONS

Yellow fever—A vaccination certificate is required for travelers coming from infected areas. A vaccination is required for children of all ages. Children under nine months of age should not be vaccinated due to health considerations. Please refer to the discussion in Chapter 6.63 on avoiding yellow fever vaccination in this age group.

Routine immunizations should be current. For infants and children through 16 years of age, refer to Chapter 4.3. A rubeola (measles) booster should be considered. Persons age 16 to 65 should receive a booster of tetanus and diphtheria every ten years. Healthy adults under age 65 do not require pneumococcal vaccine, but it is appropriate for those with chronic medical conditions. Influenza vaccine may be considered for those providing essential community services, health care workers, and those wishing to reduce the likelihood of becoming ill with influenza. Adults over 65 years of age are urged to obtain yearly influenza immunization and to insure that their tetanus and diphtheria immunizations are current. Pneumococcal vaccination is also suggested for this age group.

The vaccinations listed are recommended for the traveler's protection.

Poliomyelitis—A poliomyelitis booster is indicated for this country. In 1988 an outbreak of polio resulted in at least 80 cases centered around the western towns of Rostaq and Jalan on the Batinah coast.

Viral Hepatitis A—Vaccination is recommended for all travelers for their protection.

Typhoid fever—Vaccination is recommended for all travelers for their protection.

Selective vaccinations—These apply only to specific groups of travelers or persons on specific working assignments:

Viral Hepatitis B—Because of the high rate of healthy carriers of hepatitis B in this country, vaccination is recommended for persons on working assignments in the health care field (dentists, physicians, nurses, laboratory technicians), or working in close contact with the local population (teachers, missionaries, Peace Corps), or persons foreseeing sexual relations with local inhabitants.

U.S. Foreign Service:
P.O. Box 966
Muscat, Telephone 745-231
(Workweek:Saturday-Wednesday)

Country number 8.150
Pakistan

INFECTIOUS DISEASE RISK

Malaria Risk

Malaria is present in all parts of this country, including urban areas. The risk exists all year. The malaria in this country is resistant to chloroquine. The CDC recommends the use of mefloquine (Lariam) as described in Chapter 6.31 for chemical prophylaxis.

Falciparum malaria represents 23% of malaria, therefore there is a risk of p. vivax malaria exposure. Consider use of primaquine upon return home.

Diseases of Special Risk

In addition to the worldwide hazard of tetanus and the routine and any special immunizations recommended below, the traveler should be aware that risk of exposure to the following diseases exists in this country. This list is not all inclusive, but it is a caution concerning the more likely endemic disease risks.

Leprosy and tuberculosis are present in this country. Risk to travelers is quite low, but pre- and post-trip TB tests are recommended if contact with the local population has been extensive.

DISEASE RISK PROFILE

Disease	endemic	risk	hazard
Brucellosis		x	
Diarrheal Diseases			x
Dysentery, Amoebic/Bacillary			x
Echinococcosis		x	
Giardiasis			x
Helminthic Diseases (see Chapter 6.21)			x
Hepatitis, Viral			x
Polio			x
Rabies		x	
Trachoma		x	
Typhoid Fever		x	

Food/Water Safety

All tap water used for drinking, brushing teeth, and making ice cubes should be boiled prior to use. Insure that bottled water is uncapped in your presence. Milk should be boiled to insure safety. Powdered and evaporated milk are available and safe. Avoid butter and other dairy products. All meat, poultry and seafood must be well cooked and served while hot. Pork is best avoided. Vegetables should be well cooked and served hot. Salads and mayonnaise are best avoided. Fruits with intact skins should be peeled by you just prior to consumption. Avoid cold buffets, custards, and any frozen dessert. First class hotels and restaurants in Karachi, Lahore, and Rawalpindi serve purified drinking water and reliable food. However, the hazard is left to your judgement.

VACCINATIONS

Cholera—A cholera vaccination certificate is required when coming from an infected area.

Yellow fever—A vaccination certificate is required for travelers coming from infected areas and from or in transit through countries in the endemic yellow fever zone, see Chapter 6.63. A vaccination certificate is required for children over six months of age. However, children under nine months of age should not be vaccinated due to health considerations. Please refer to the discussion in Chapter 6.63 on avoiding yellow fever vaccination in this age group.

Routine immunizations should be current. For infants and children through 16 years of age, refer to Chapter 4.3. A rubeola (measles) booster should be considered. Persons age 16 to 65 should receive a booster of tetanus and diphtheria every ten years. Healthy adults under age 65 do not require pneumococcal vaccine, but it is appropriate for those with chronic medical conditions. Influenza vaccine may be considered for those providing essential

community services, health care workers, and those wishing to reduce the likelihood of becoming ill with influenza. Adults over 65 years of age are urged to obtain yearly influenza immunization and to insure that their tetanus and diphtheria immunizations are current. Pneumococcal vaccination is also suggested for this age group.

The vaccinations listed are recommended for the traveler's protection.
Poliomyelitis—A poliomyelitis booster is indicated for this country.
Viral Hepatitis A—Vaccination is recommended for all travelers for their protection.
Typhoid fever—Vaccination is recommended for all travelers for their protection.

Selective vaccinations—*These apply only to specific groups of travelers or persons on specific working assignments:*
Viral Hepatitis B—Because of the high rate of healthy carriers of hepatitis B in this country, vaccination is recommended for persons on working assignments in the health care field (dentists, physicians, nurses, laboratory technicians), or working in close contact with the local population (teachers, missionaries, Peace Corps), or persons foreseeing sexual relations with local inhabitants.
Plague—Vaccination is recommended only for persons who may be occupationally exposed to wild rodents (anthropologists, geologists, medical personnel, missionaries, etc). The standard vaccination course must be completed before entering the plague infested area. Geographical distribution of the area of risk for this country is northern Kashmir.
Rabies—In this country, where rabies is a constant threat, a pre-exposure rabies vaccination is advised for persons planning an extended stay or on working assignments (naturalists, agricultural advisors, archeologists, geologists, etc.). Although this provides adequate initial protection, a person bitten by a potentially rabid animal would still require post exposure immunization (see Chapter 6.40). Children should be cautioned not to pet dogs, cats, or other mammals.

U. S. Foreign Service:
P.O. Box 1048
Isamabad, Telephone 24071

8 Abdullah Haroon Rd
Karachi, Telephone 515081

50 Zafar Ali Rd.
Gulberg 5
Lahore, Telephone 870221 thru 5

11 Hospital Road
Peshawar, Telephone 73361, 73405

(Workweek:Sunday-Thursday)

Canadian High Commission/Embassy Office:
Diplomatic Enclave
Sector G-5
Islamabad, Telephone 821101/2/3/4

TRAVEL ADVISORY

A U. S. Department of State Travel Advisory was in effect on 4 May 1990 when this book went to press. The entire text is included below. Travel advisories are subject to reissue, change, and cancellation at any time. Current travel advisory information is available by calling the U. S. Department of State Travel Advisory Hotline at (202) 647-5225. The current travel advisory status is also available from the Herchmer Database update system (see Chapter 2.8).

9 NOVEMBER 1989
SECSTATE WSH SUBJECT: TRAVEL ADVISORY—PAKISTAN—WARNING
THE DEPARTMENT OF STATE ADVISES U.S. CITIZENS TRAVELING TO PAKISTAN OF THE FOLLOWING:
SUMMARY: DEMONSTRATIONS, RALLIES AND PROCESSIONS FREQUENTLY OCCUR THROUGHOUT PAKISTAN ON VERY SHORT NOTICE. SUCH OCCURRENCES MAY MAKE IT PREFERABLE FOR AMERICANS TO AVOID PARTICULAR AREAS OF PAKISTAN, OR PARTICULAR AREAS WITHIN A PAKISTANI CITY, FOR A SPECIFIC TIME PERIOD. GIVEN THE RAPIDITY WITH WHICH A LOCAL SITUATION CAN CHANGE, IT IS RECOMMENDED THAT TRAVELERS TO PAKISTAN READ THE LOCAL ENGLISH NEWSPAPERS AND CHECK WITH THE AMERICAN EMBASSY'S CONSULAR SECTION (OR APPROPRIATE AMERICAN CONSULATE) TO ASCERTAIN WHETHER THERE IS ANY SITUATION TO WHICH THEY SHOULD BE ALERT. OTHER TRAVEL PRECAUTIONS FOLLOW.
TRAVEL IN BALUCHISTAN PROVINCE: DUE TO ONLY A LIMITED PROVINCIAL POLICE PRESENCE AND INFLUENCE, THOSE PERSONS CONSIDERING A TRIP THROUGH RURAL AREAS, PARTICULARLY THOSE DISTRICTS BORDERING AFGHANISTAN, ARE ADVISED TO INFORM THE HOME SECRETARY OF THE PROVINCE PRIOR TO THEIR TRAVEL. AMERICANS PLANNING TO TRAVEL IN BALUCHISTAN OUTSIDE THE CITY OF QUETTA SHOULD EXERCISE PRUDENCE AND TRAVEL ONLY IN A GROUP AND TRAVEL ONLY DURING DAYLIGHT HOURS.

TRAVEL IN SINDH PROVINCE: THE CITIES OF HYDERABAD AND KARACHI HAVE EXPERIENCED PERIODIC INCIDENTS OF ETHNIC AND SECTARIAN VIOLENCE WHICH HAS ON OCCASION RESULTED IN THE IMPOSITION OF A CURFEW OVER THE LAST SEVERAL YEARS. SUCH INCIDENTS DO NOT NORMALLY AFFECT THE AREAS FREQUENTED BY AMERICANS, ALTHOUGH THERE HAVE BEEN INCIDENTS OF KIDNAPPING FOR RANSOM IN KARACHI, THEY HAVE SO FAR NOT INVOLVED THE FOREIGN COMMUNITY. TRAVELERS SHOULD CONSULT WITH THE U.S. CONSULATE IN KARACHI BEFORE PLANNING TRIPS TO RURAL AREAS IN SINDH PROVINCE. DUE TO THE HIGH INCIDENCE OF HIGHWAY ROBBERY, THERE SHOULD BE NO TRAVEL AFTER DARK. IN ADDITION, DAYTIME ROAD TRAVEL IN DADU AND LARKANA DISTRICTS (LATTER IS SITE OF THE MOENJODARO ARCHEOLOGICAL RUINS), ON THE WEST BANK OF THE INDUS RIVER, SHOULD BE AVOIDED UNTIL FURTHER NOTICE. TRAVELERS BY ROAD HAVE BEEN THE VICTIMS OF ROBBERIES, ABDUCTIONS, AND SHOOTINGS IN DAYLIGHT HOURS. ALTHOUGH NO FOREIGNERS HAVE YET BEEN VICTIMIZED, PRUDENCE SHOULD BE EXERCISED IN DAYTIME TRAVEL BY ROAD IN ALL DISTRICTS OF RURAL SINDH. INTERCITY BUSES AND TRAINS IN THE PROVINCE OF SINDH HAVE ALSO BEEN THE OCCASIONAL TARGET OF ARMED ROBBERS.

TRAVEL TO NORTHWEST FRONTIER TRIBAL AREAS: THE GOVERNMENT OF PAKISTAN MAINTAINS A VERY LIMITED PRESENCE IN THE TRIBAL AREAS AND, THEREFORE, CANNOT GUARANTEE THE SAFETY OF UNAUTHORIZED TRAVELERS. THE GOVERNMENT OF PAKISTAN REQUIRES THAT FOREIGN NATIONALS OBTAIN A SPECIAL PERMIT IN ORDER TO VISIT THE FEDERALLY ADMINISTRATED TRIBAL AREAS BORDERING AFGHANISTAN. THESE AREAS ARE BAJAUR, MOHMAND, KHYBER, ORAKZAI, KURRAM, NORTH WAZIRISTAN, AND SOUTH WAZIRISTAN. A SPECIAL PERMIT IS ALSO REQUIRED TO VISIT THE PROVINCIALLY ADMINISTERED TRIBAL AREA OF DARRA ADAM KHEL BETWEEN THE CITIES OF PESHAWAR AND KOHAT. THE GOVERNMENT OF PAKISTAN RARELY GRANTS PERMITS TO THE KHYBER PASS. PERSONS WHO DO OBTAIN A PERMIT TO GO TO DARRA ADAM KHEL SHOULD BE ADVISED THAT WHILE WEAPONS, INCLUDING PEN GUNS, ARE EASILY OBTAINED, IT IS ILLEGAL, OR EXTREMELY DIFFICULT TO EXPORT SOME OF THEM, DEPENDING UPON THE WEAPON. PERSONS TRAVELING TO THIS AREA WITHOUT PERMITS OR IN VIOLATION OF THE TERMS OF THE PERMIT, ARE SUBJECT TO ARREST.

TRAVEL TO OTHER PARTS OF THE NORTHWEST FRONTIER PROVINCE: TRAVELERS ARE ALSO URGED TO EXERCISE CAUTION IN VISITS TO THE OTHER AREAS OF THE NORTHWEST FRONTIER

PROVINCE DUE TO OCCASIONAL EXPLOSIONS, BANDITRY, AND KIDNAPPINGS. DUE TO HIGH INCIDENCE OF HIGHWAY ROBBERY, THERE SHOULD BE NO TRAVEL AFTER DARK IN RURAL AREAS. VISITORS ARE URGED TO STAY IN TOUCH WITH THE U.S. CONSULATE IN PESHAWAR, AS THE SECURITY SITUATION CAN CHANGE WITH LITTLE WARNING.

MOUNTAIN CLIMBING IN THE KARAKORAM MOUNTAIN RANGE: BOTH INDIA AND PAKISTAN LAY CLAIM TO AN AREA OF THE KAROKORAM MOUNTAIN RANGE WHICH INCLUDES THE SIACHEN GLACIER. BECAUSE OF PAST MILITARY CLASHES THERE, THE DEPARTMENT OF STATE WARNS AMERICANS AGAINST TRAVELING TO OR CLIMBING PEAKS ANYWHERE IN THE DISPUTED AREAS OF THE MOUNTAINS IN THE EAST KARAKORAM RANGE, AND ESPECIALLY AGAINST VENTURING ON OR NEAR THE SIACHEN GLACIER. IN PARTICULAR, CLIMBERS SHOULD AVOID THE FOLLOWING PEAKS WHICH LIE WITHIN THE DISPUTED AREAS CLAIMED BY BOTH INDIA AND PAKISTAN: RIMO PEAK APSARASAS-I,II,AND III; TERM KANGRI-I, II AND III; SINGHI KANGRI, FHAINTI I AND II; INDIRA COL; AND SIA KANGRI.

INDIA-PAKISTAN BORDER: THE ONLY OFFICIAL BORDER CROSSING POINT FOR FOREIGNERS IS AT WAGAH, PAKISTAN/ATTARI, INDIA. FOREIGNERS TRAVELING BY LAND BETWEEN PAKISTAN AND INDIA BY BUS, TRAIN, OR PRIVATE VEHICLE ARE PERMITTED TO CROSS ANY DAY OF THE WEEK BETWEEN 0930 AND 1700 HOURS. INDIAN VISAS NO LONGER NEED TO BE SPECIFICALLY ANNOTATED FOR THE MODE OF TRAVEL USED. A PAKISTANI EXIT PERMIT IS REQUIRED.

REGISTRATION: AMERICANS RESIDENT IN OR VISITING PAKISTAN ARE ENCOURAGED TO REGISTER WITH THE U.S. EMBASSY IN ISLAMABAD, DIPLOMATIC ENCLAVE, RAMA 5, TELEPHONE NUMBER 92-51-826161; WITH THE U.S. CONSULATE IN EITHER KARACHI, 8 ABDULLAH HAROON RD., TELEPHONE NUMBER 92-21-515081; LAHORE, 50 ZAFAR ALI RD., GULBERG 5, TELEPHONE NUMBER 92-42-870221; OR PESHAWAR, 11 HOSPITAL ROAD, TELEPHONE NUMBER 92-521-79801, 79802, 79803.

EXPIRATION: NOVEMBER 1, 1990.

_____ **Country number 8.151** _____
Panama

INFECTIOUS DISEASE RISK

Malaria Risk

Malaria is present in rural areas of the eastern provinces (Darien and San Blas) and the northwestern provinces (Bocas Del Toro and Veraguas). The risk exists all year. Chloroquine resistant malaria has developed in all malarious areas east of the Canal Zone, including the San Blas Islands. The malaria in this country is resistant to chloroquine. The CDC recommends the use of mefloquine (Lariam) as described in Chapter 6.31 for chemical prophylaxis.

Falciparum malaria represents 16% of the malaria encountered, therefore there is a risk of vivax exposure. Consider the use of primaquine upon return home if prolonged mosquito exposure was encountered.

Diseases of Special Risk

In addition to the worldwide hazard of tetanus and the routine and any special immunizations recommended below, the traveler should be aware that risk of exposure to the following diseases exists in this country. This list is not all inclusive, but it is a caution concerning the more likely endemic disease risks.

Chaga's Disease is present in the rural areas of the province of Chiriqui (bordering Costa Rica) and the in the valley of the Rio Chagres (in central Panama) and the areas of the Canal Zone adjacent to Rio Chagres.

Tuberculosis is endemic in this country. If the traveler will experience close contact with the native population, a pre- and post-trip TB skin test is advised.

This country must be considered receptive to dengue fever. Intermittent epidemics in the past make renewed activity or reintroduction of the virus possible.

DISEASE RISK PROFILE

Disease	endemic	risk	hazard
Diarrheal Disease Risk		x	
Dysentery, Amoebic		x	
Encephalitis, Venezuelan Equine	x		
Helminthic Diseases (see Chapter 6.21)		x	
Hepatitis, Viral	x		
Leishmaniasis	x		
Paragonimiasis	x		
Rabies (esp dogs and bats)			x
Trypanosomiasis, American Chaga's Disease	x		
Typhoid Fever		x	

Food/Water Safety

All tap water used for drinking, brushing teeth, and making ice cubes should be boiled prior to use. Insure that bottled water is uncapped in your presence. Milk should be boiled to insure safety. Powdered and evaporated milk are available and safe. Avoid butter and other dairy products. All meat, poultry and seafood must be well cooked and served while hot. Pork is best avoided. Vegetables should be well cooked and served hot. Salads and mayonnaise are best avoided. Fruits with intact skins should be peeled by you just prior to consumption. Avoid cold buffets, custards, and any frozen dessert. Water, milk, and food in Panama City is safe.

VACCINATIONS

Routine immunizations should be current. For infants and children through 16 years of age, refer to Chapter 4.3. A rubeola (measles) booster should be considered. Persons age 16 to 65 should receive a booster of tetanus and diphtheria every ten years. Healthy adults under age 65 do not require pneumococcal vaccine, but it is appropriate for those with chronic medical conditions. Influenza vaccine may be considered for those providing essential community services, health care workers, and those wishing to reduce the likelihood of becoming ill with influenza. Adults over 65 years of age are urged to obtain yearly influenza immunization and to insure that their tetanus and diphtheria immunizations are current. Pneumococcal vaccination is also suggested for this age group.

No vaccinations are required to enter this country.

The vaccinations listed are recommended for the traveler's protection.

Yellow fever—A yellow fever vaccination certificate is recommended for all travelers going to the provinces of Bocas del Toro and Darien. Vaccination is recommended when traveling outside the areas usually visited by tourists, traveling extensively in the interior of the country (trekkers, hikers) and for persons on working assignments in remote areas. CDC recommends vaccination for all travelers over 9 months of age, but see also Chapter 6.63.

Poliomyelitis—Vaccination is recommended when traveling outside the areas usually visited by tourists, traveling extensively in the interior of the country (trekkers, hikers) and for persons on working assignments in remote areas.

Viral Hepatitis A—Vaccination is recommended when traveling outside the areas usually visited by tourists, traveling extensively in the interior of the country (trekkers, hikers) and for persons on working assignments in remote areas.

Typhoid fever—Vaccination is recommended when traveling outside the areas usually visited by tourists, traveling extensively in the interior of the country (trekkers, hikers) and for persons on working assignments in remote areas.

U. S. Foreign Service:
Avenida Balboa y Calle 38
Panama City, Telephone Panama 27-1777

TRAVEL ADVISORY

A U. S. Department of State Travel Advisory was in effect just prior to this book going to press. The entire text is included below. Travel advisories are subject to reissue, change, and cancellation at any time. Current travel advisory information is available by calling the U. S. Department of State Travel Advisory Hotline at (202) 647-5225. The current travel advisory status is also available from the Herchmer Database update system (see Chapter 2.8).

JANUARY 25, 1990
PANAMA— CAUTION
THE DEPARTMENT OF STATE ADVISES U.S. CITIZENS TRAVELING TO PANAMA THAT THE SITUATION IN THE COUNTRY HAS LARGELY STABILIZED. THE POLICE FORCES ARE BEING REORGANIZED BY THE NEW ENDARA GOVERNMENT WITH HELP FROM THE UNITED STATES. HOWEVER, CRIMINAL ACTIVITY REMAINS A PROBLEM, ESPECIALLY IN COLON. SOME ELEMENTS PRONE TO VIOLENCE REMAIN AT LARGE, AND A CURFEW REMAINS IN EFFECT FROM 12:00 A.M. UNTIL 5:00 A.M. THE OPERATION OF THE PANAMA CANAL CONTINUES IN A NORMAL AND EFFICIENT MANNER. THE U.S. EMBASSY IS OPEN TO ASSIST U.S. CITIZENS. FOR INFORMATION AND ASSISTANCE, U.S. CITIZENS SHOULD CONTACT THE CONSULAR SECTION OF THE EMBASSY AT 271-777.
EXPIRATION: APRIL 25, 1990

Country number 8.152
Papau New Guinea

INFECTIOUS DISEASE RISK

Malaria Risk

Malaria is present in all parts of this country, including urban areas. The risk exists all year. The malaria in this country is resistant to chloroquine. The CDC recommends the use of mefloquine (Lariam) as described in Chapter 6.31 for chemical prophylaxis.

Falciparum malaria represents 73% of malaria, therefore there is a risk of p. vivax malaria exposure. Consider use of primaquine upon return home.

Diseases of Special Risk

In addition to the worldwide hazard of tetanus and the routine and any special immunizations recommended below, the traveler should be aware that risk of exposure to the following diseases exists in this country. This list is not all inclusive, but it is a caution concerning the more likely endemic disease risks.

Potential risk of dengue fever exists. The virus is present in this country at all times and may give rise to major outbreaks.

DISEASE RISK PROFILE

Disease	endemic	risk	hazard
Diarrheal Disease Risk		x	
Encephalitis, Japanese	x		
Filariasis			x
Helminthic Diseases (see Chapter 6.21)		x	
Typhoid Fever		x	
Typhus, Scrub	x		

Food/Water Safety

All tap water used for drinking, brushing teeth, and making ice cubes should be boiled prior to use. Insure that bottled water is uncapped in your presence. All meat, poultry and seafood must be well cooked and served while hot. Pork is best avoided. Vegetables should be well cooked and served hot. Salads and mayonnaise are best avoided. Fruits with intact skins should be peeled by you just prior to consumption. Avoid cold buffets, custards, and any frozen dessert. Milk is pasteurized and safe to drink. Butter, cheese, yogurt and ice-cream are safe.

VACCINATIONS

Yellow fever—A vaccination certificate is required for travelers coming from infected areas and from or in transit through countries with active disease. A vaccination certificate is required for children over one year of age.

Routine immunizations should be current. For infants and children through 16 years of age, refer to Chapter 4.3. A rubeola (measles) booster should be considered. Persons age 16 to 65 should receive a booster of tetanus and diphtheria every ten years. Healthy adults under age 65 do not require pneumococcal vaccine, but it is appropriate for those with chronic medical conditions. Influenza vaccine may be considered for those providing essential community services, health care workers, and those wishing to reduce the likelihood of becoming ill with influenza. Adults over 65 years of age are urged to obtain yearly influenza immunization and to insure that their tetanus and diphtheria immunizations are current. Pneumococcal vaccination is also suggested for this age group.

The vaccinations listed are recommended for the traveler's protection.
Poliomyelitis—A poliomyelitis booster is indicated for this country.
Viral Hepatitis A—Vaccination is recommended for all travelers for their protection.
Typhoid fever—Vaccination is recommended for all travelers for their protection.

Selective vaccinations—These apply only to specific groups of travelers or persons on specific working assignments:

Viral Hepatitis B—Because of the high rate of healthy carriers of hepatitis B in this country, vaccination is recommended for persons on working assignments in the health care field (dentists, physicians, nurses, laboratory technicians), or working in close contact with the local population (teachers, missionaries, Peace Corps), or persons foreseeing sexual relations with local inhabitants.

U. S. Foreign Service:
Armit St.
Port Moresby, Telephone 211455/594/654

TRAVEL ADVISORY

A U. S. Department of State Travel Advisory was in effect on 4 May 1990 when this book went to press. The entire text is included below. Travel advisories are subject to reissue, change, and cancellation at any time. Current travel advisory information is available by calling the U. S. Department of State Travel Advisory Hotline at (202) 647-5225. The current travel advisory status is also available from the Herchmer Database update system (see Chapter 2.8).

JANUARY 31, 1990
PAPUA NEW GUINEA— CAUTION
THE DEPARTMENT OF STATE ADVISES U.S. CITIZENS THAT A STATE OF EMERGENCY EXISTS ON BOUGAINVILLE ISLAND, WHERE AN ARMED INSURGENCY HAS RECENTLY INTENSIFIED. TRAVEL TO BOUGAINVILE IS UNSAFE AND SHOULD BE AVOIDED UNTIL FURTHER NOTICE.
IN ADDITION, CIVIL DISTURBANCES AND VIOLENT CRIME CONTINUE TO BE A SERIOUS PROBLEM IN RURAL AND URBAN AREAS OF PAPUA NEW GUINEA. INDIVIDUALS ARE ADVISED NOT TO TRAVEL ALONE. TOURISTS SHOULD VISIT ONLY UNDER THE AUSPICES OF ESTABLISHED AGENCIES.
TRAVELERS TO PORT MORESBY, LAE AND OTHER URBAN AREAS SHOULD EXERCISE CAUTION, PARTICULARLY AFTER DARK. MT. HAGEN AND THE DAIVER RIVER AREA IN THE WESTERN HIGHLANDS SHOULD BE AVOIDED.
AMERICAN CITIZENS SHOULD INQUIRE AT THE CONSULAR SECTION OF THE U.S. EMBASSY AT PORT MORESBY FOR UP-TO-DATE INFORMATION. VISITORS ARE ALSO ENCOURAGED TO REGISTER WITH THE EMBASSY UPON ARRIVAL. EMBASSY TELEPHONE IS 211-455.
EXPIRATION: DECEMBER 1, 1990.

_____ **Country number 8.153** _____
Paraguay

INFECTIOUS DISEASE RISK

Malaria Risk

Malaria risk is present from October through May in areas bordering Brazil, rural parts of Amambay, Canendiyu and Alto Parana Departments. There is no risk of malaria in urban areas. See Chapter 6.31 reguarding the use of chloroquine.

Falciparum malaria represents 6% of malaria, therefore there is a risk of p. vivax malaria exposure. Consider use of primaquine upon return home.

Diseases of Special Risk

In addition to the worldwide hazard of tetanus and the routine and any special immunizations recommended below, the traveler should be aware that risk of exposure to the following diseases exists in this country. This list is not all inclusive, but it is a caution concerning the more likely endemic disease risks.

Chaga's Disease is present in rural areas of the following departments: Boqueron, Caaguazu, Central, Concepcion, Cordillera, Guaira, Neembucu, Paraguari, San Pedro, Villa Hayes.

DISEASE RISK PROFILE

Disease	endemic	risk	hazard
Brucellosis		x	
Diarrheal Disease Risk		x	
Dysentery, Amoebic		x	
Echinococcosis	x		
Helminthic Diseases (see Chapter 6.21)		x	
Hepatitis, Viral	x		
Leishmaniasis			
Cutaneous		x	
Mucocutaneous		x	
Visceral		x	
Polio	x		
Rabies	x		
Trypanosomiasis, American	x		
Chaga's Disease			

Food/Water Safety

All tap water used for drinking, brushing teeth, and making ice cubes should be boiled prior to use. Insure that bottled water is uncapped in your presence. Milk should be boiled to insure safety. Powdered and evaporated milk are available and safe. Avoid butter and other dairy products. All meat, poultry

and seafood must be well cooked and served while hot. Pork is best avoided. Vegetables should be well cooked and served hot. Salads and mayonnaise are best avoided. Fruits with intact skins should be peeled by you just prior to consumption. Avoid cold buffets, custards, and any frozen dessert. First class hotels and restaurants in Asuncion serve purified drinking water and reliable food. However, the hazard is left to your judgement.

VACCINATIONS

Yellow fever—A vaccination certificate is required for travelers coming from infected areas and from or in transit through countries with active disease. A vaccination certificate is required for children over six months of age. CDC recommends vaccination for all travelers over 9 months of age. See Chapter 6.63 on avoiding this vaccine in children younger than 9 months due to a higher complication rate.

Routine immunizations should be current. For infants and children through 16 years of age, refer to Chapter 4.3. A rubeola (measles) booster should be considered. Persons age 16 to 65 should receive a booster of tetanus and diphtheria every ten years. Healthy adults under age 65 do not require pneumococcal vaccine, but it is appropriate for those with chronic medical conditions. Influenza vaccine may be considered for those providing essential community services, health care workers, and those wishing to reduce the likelihood of becoming ill with influenza. Adults over 65 years of age are urged to obtain yearly influenza immunization and to insure that their tetanus and diphtheria immunizations are current. Pneumococcal vaccination is also suggested for this age group.

The vaccinations listed are recommended for the traveler's protection.

Viral Hepatitis A—Vaccination is recommended when traveling outside the areas usually visited by tourists, traveling extensively in the interior of the country (trekkers, hikers) and for persons on working assignments in remote areas.

Typhoid fever—Vaccination is recommended when traveling outside the areas usually visited by tourists, traveling extensively in the interior of the country (trekkers, hikers) and for persons on working assignments in remote areas.

Selective vaccinations—These apply only to specific groups of travelers or persons on specific working assignments:

Rabies—In this country, where rabies is a constant threat, a pre-exposure rabies vaccination is advised for persons planning an extended stay or on working assignments (naturalists, agricultural advisors, archeologists, geologists, etc.). Although this provides adequate initial protection, a person bitten by a potentially rabid animal would still require post exposure immunization (see Chapter 6.40). Children should be cautioned not to pet dogs, cats, or other mammals.

U. S. Foreign Service:
1776 Mariscal Lopez Ave.
Asuncion, Telephone 201-041

_____ **Country number 8.154** _____
Peru

INFECTIOUS DISEASE RISK

Malaria Risk
Malaria risk exists in rural areas of Departments of Amazonas, Cajamarca (except Hualgayoc Province), La Libertad (except Otuzco, Santiago de Choco Provs.), Lambayeque, Loreto, Piur (except Talara Prov.), San Martin and Tumbes; parts fo La Convencion (Cuzco Dept), Tauacaja (Huancavelcia Dept), Satipo (Junin Dept). See Chapter 6.63 with regard to Chloroquine use. Malaria risk exists all year, but only below 1500 meters. Chloroquine resistance has developed in malaria in the nothern provinces bordering Brazil. See Chapter 6.63 for the use of mefloquine for travel to this area. Travelers who will visit only Lima and highland tourist areas (Cuzco and Machu Picchu) are not at risk and need no prophylaxis.

Falciparum malaria represents 1% of malaria, therefore there is a risk of p. vivax malaria exposure. Consider use of primaquine upon return home.

Diseases of Special Risk
In addition to the worldwide hazard of tetanus and the routine and any special immunizations recommended below, the traveler should be aware that risk of exposure to the following diseases exists in this country. This list is not all inclusive, but it is a caution concerning the more likely endemic disease risks.

Chaga's Disease is present in two seperate geographical areas: 1) Rural and suburban areas of the states of Tumbes and Amazonas in the northwestern part of the country bordering Ecuador; 2) Rural and suburban areas under 3500 meters of the costal states of Tacna, Moquegua, Arequipa, and the southern part of Ica (the area of the city of Nazca).

Louse-borne typhus is cosmopolitan in distribution and is present wherever groups of persons are crowded together under conditions of poor sanitation and malnutrition. Risk exists for persons living or working in remote areas of the country (anthropologists, archeologists, geologists, medical personnel, missionaries, etc.). Freedom from louse infestation is the most effective protection against typhus.

DISEASE RISK PROFILE

Disease	endemic	risk	hazard
Bartonellosis	x		
Diarrheal Disease Risk		x	
Dysentery, Amoebic		x	
Echinococcosis	x		
Helminthic Diseases (see Chapter 6.21)		x	
Hepatitis, Viral		x	
Leishmaniasis			
Cutaneous	x		
Mucocutaneous	x		
Visceral	x		
Polio		x	
Rabies (esp bats)			x
Trypanosomiasis, American	x		
Chaga's Disease			
Typhus, Scrub (in mountains)	x		

Food/Water Safety

All tap water used for drinking, brushing teeth, and making ice cubes should be boiled prior to use. Insure that bottled water is uncapped in your presence. Milk should be boiled to insure safety. Powdered and evaporated milk are available and safe. Avoid butter and other dairy products. All meat, poultry and seafood must be well cooked and served while hot. Pork is best avoided. Vegetables should be well cooked and served hot. Salads and mayonnaise are best avoided. Fruits with intact skins should be peeled by you just prior to consumption. Avoid cold buffets, custards, and any frozen dessert. First class hotels and restaurants in Cuzco, Iquitos, and Lima serve purified drinking water and reliable food. However, the hazard is left to your judgement.

VACCINATIONS

Yellow fever—A vaccination certificate is required for travelers coming from infected areas and from or in transit through countries in the endemic yellow fever zone. A vaccination certificate is required for children over six months of age. CDC recommends vaccination for all travelers over 9 months of age, but see also Chapter 6.63 on avoiding vaccination in infants younger than 9 months of age due to a significant increase in side effects of the vaccine in that age group.

Routine immunizations should be current. For infants and children through 16 years of age, refer to Chapter 4.3. A rubeola (measles) booster should be considered. Persons age 16 to 65 should receive a booster of tetanus and diphtheria every ten years. Healthy adults under age 65 do not require pneumococcal vaccine, but it is appropriate for those with chronic medical conditions. Influenza vaccine may be considered for those providing essential community services, health care workers, and those wishing to reduce the likelihood of becoming ill with influenza. Adults over 65 years of age are urged to

obtain yearly influenza immunization and to insure that their tetanus and diphtheria immunizations are current. Pneumococcal vaccination is also suggested for this age group.

The vaccinations listed are recommended for the traveler's protection.
Poliomyelitis—A poliomyelitis booster is indicated for this country.
Viral Hepatitis A—Vaccination is recommended for all travelers for their protection.
Typhoid fever—Vaccination is recommended for all travelers for their protection.

Selective vaccinations—These apply only to specific groups of travelers or persons on specific working assignments:
Plague—Vaccination is recommended only for persons who may be occupationally exposed to wild rodents (anthropologists, geologists, medical personnel, missionaries, etc). The standard vaccination course must be completed before entering the plague infested area. Geographical distribution of the area of risk for this country is: the north of thr country; western part of Piura Department (Huancabama provine), all of Cajamarca Department, and the southern part of Ancash Department.

U. S. Foreign Service:
Corner Avenidas Inca Garcilaso de la Vega and Espana
Lima, Telephone 28-60-00

Canadian High Commission/Embassy Office:
Federico Gerdes 130
(Ante Calle Libertad)
Miraflores, Telephone 46-38-90, 46-11-35

TRAVEL ADVISORY

A U. S. Department of State Travel Advisory was in effect on 4 May 1990 when this book went to press. The entire text is included below. Travel advisories are subject to reissue, change, and cancellation at any time. Current travel advisory information is available by calling the U. S. Department of State Travel Advisory Hotline at (202) 647-5225. The current travel advisory status is also available from the Herchmer Database update system (see Chapter 2.8).

NOVEMBER 15, 1989
SECSTATE WSH SUBJECT: TRAVEL ADVISORY—PERU—WARNING
SUMMARY: THE DEPARTMENT OF STATE ADVISES U.S. CITIZENS THAT BOTH TERRORISM AND CRIME ARE SERIOUS PROBLEMS THROUGHOUT PERU. SINCE 1983 TWO TERRORIST GROUPS, SENDERO LUMINOSO (SHINING PATH) AND THE TUPAC AMARU REVO-

LUTIONARY MOVEMENT (MRTA), HAVE USED VIOLENT TACTICS IN AN ATTEMPT TO DESTABILIZE THE GOVERNMENT. OVER A PERIOD OF SEVERAL YEARS, THE PERUVIAN GOVERNMENT HAS DE-CLARED MOST OF THE CENTRAL ANDEAN REGION AS AN EMER-GENCY ZONE UNDER MILITARY CONTROL. TRAVEL TO ALL EMERGENCY ZONES, HUARAZ AND THE CORDILLERA BLANCA, THE HUAYHUASH AREA, THE UPPER HUALLAGA VALLEY, PU-CALLPA, AND ALONG THE INCA TRAIL SHOULD BE AVOIDED. IN ADDITION, A DIFFICULT ECONOMIC SITUATION HAS LED TO IN-CREASED CRIME IN TOURIST AREAS. WHILE CRIMINAL VIOLENCE IS RANDOM, AND POLITICAL VIOLENCE USUALLY IS TARGETED AT PERUVIAN CIVIC LEADERS AND INFRASTRUCTURE, VISITORS MUST EXERCISE CAUTION. OVER THE PAST SEVERAL YEARS, SEVERAL TOURISTS HAVE BEEN INJURED OR KILLED IN TERROR-IST AND CRIMINAL INCIDENTS. TRAVEL BY PUBLIC BUS IS NOT RECOMMENDED BECAUSE OF TERRORISM, BANDITRY AND POOR ROAD CONDITIONS. VISITORS SHOULD BE AWARE THAT CONDI-TIONS IN PERU CAN CHANGE AT ANY TIME. ALTHOUGH THIS ADVI-SORY IDENTIFIES SPECIFIC AREAS TO AVOID AND SUGGESTS PRECAUTIONS TO TAKE, TRAVELERS ARE URGED TO SEEK THE LATEST TRAVEL INFORMATION UPON ARRIVAL IN PERU FROM THE EMBASSY'S CONSULAR SECTION.

LIMA: IN LIMA, TERRORIST ATTACKS ARE UNPREDICTABLE. AT-TACKS HAVE BEEN DIRECTED PRIMARILY AGAINST PERUVIAN GOVERNMENT PERSONNEL AND INSTALLATIONS, BANKS, BUSI-NESSES, AND FOREIGN DIPLOMATIC MISSIONS, INCLUDING U.S. GOVERNMENT BUILDINGS. LABOR STRIKES ARE FREQUENT AND MAY GENERATE POLICE ACTION AND/OR MASK TERRORIST ACTIV-ITY. STREET CRIME IS ALSO PREVALENT.

CUSCO/MACHU PICCHU:

DAY TRIPS FROM CUSCO: BECAUSE OF THE POSSIBILITY OF VIO-LENT CRIME, VISITORS TO THE RUINS NEAR CUSCO AND IN THE SACRED VALLEY SHOULD NOT WANDER AWAY FROM WELL-TRAVELED ROADS. TOURISTS HAVE BEEN ROBBED IN CUSCO AND ON THE TRAINS FROM, CUSCO TO MACHU PICCHU AND PUNO.

TRAIN TRAVEL TO MACHU PICCHU: SINCE JUNE OF 1986 THERE HAVE BEEN SEVERAL INSTANCES OF SABOTAGE AGAINST TRAINS ON THE CUSCO-MACHU PICCHU LINE. TWO PARTICULAR IN-STANCES RESULTED IN THE INJURY AND DEATH OF U.S. CITIZENS. ALTHOUGH THOUSANDS OF TOURISTS TRAVEL SAFELY EACH YEAR, NO SECURITY IS PROVIDED ALONG THE ROUTE.

INCA TRAIL: HIKERS ARE ADVISED TO AVOID THE INCA TRAIL. THOSE WHO DO HIKE THE TRAIL ARE ADVISED TO TRAVEL IN LARGE GROUPS WITH GUIDES. ROBBERIES ARE FREQUENT,

SOMETIMES RESULTING IN SERIOUS INJURY. THERE HAVE BEEN TWO RECENT DEATHS.

HURAZ/CALLEJON DE HUAYLAS (DEPARTMENT OF ANCASH): AVOID THE CALLEJON DE HUAYLAS AS SENDERO LUMINOSO IS PRESENT THROUGHOUT THE AREA. SENDERO HAS COMMITTED MURDERS CLOSE TO HUARAZ, INCLUDING THAT OF A TOURIST IN MAY 1989. HOTELS AND TOURIST AGENCIES IN HUARAZ ITSELF HAVE BEEN TERRORIST TARGETS. SIZEABLE SENDERO LUMINOSO COLUMNS HAVE BEEN ENCOUNTERED BY HIKERS IN THE HUAYHUASH, A HIKING AREA 70 MILES SOUTH OR HUARAZ. MOUNTAIN CLIMBERS HAVE ALSO RECEIVED DEATH THREATS.

UPPER HUALLAGA VALLEY: AVOID THE UPPER HUALLAGA RIVER VALLEY, INCLUDING THE CITIES OF TINGO MARIA AND UCHIZA, AS IT IS AN EXTREMELY DANGEROUS ZONE. IT IS THE CENTER OF NARCOTICS TRAFFICKING, AND MUCH OF THE RURAL PORTION IS CONTROLLED BY SENDERO LUMINOSO.

AREQUIPA/COLCA CANYON: ALTHOUGH THE CITY OF AREQUIPA HAS BEEN RELATIVELY FREE OF PROBLEMS, THE NEARBY COLCA CANYON HAS BEEN THE SITE OF NUMEROUS ROBBERIES AGAINST TOURISTS. TRAVELERS SHOULD AVOID TRAVEL TO THE CANYON. THOSE WHO DO VISIT THE CANYON SHOULD TRAVEL IN LARGE GROUPS WITH REPUTABLE TOURIST OPERATORS.

PUCALLPA: AVOID THE CITY OF PUCALLPA AND THE SURROUND-ING AREA AS THEY ARE EXPERIENCING HEAVY MRTA ACTIVITY. MRTA COLUMNS ARE PRESENT THROUGHOUT THE AREA AND THE CITY ITSELF HAS EXPERIENCED INCREASED VIOLENCE, IN-CLUDING MURDERS AND THREATS TO LOCAL RESIDENTS.

OTHER JUNGLE AREAS: TOURISTS SHOULD NOT TRAVEL THROUGH ANY REMOTE JUNGLE AREAS ALONE OR IN SMALL GROUPS. THE MAJOR JUNGLE TOURIST AREAS OF IQUITOS AND PUERTO MALDONADO HAVE BEEN AFFECTED BY TERRORISM OR NARCOTICS-RELATED VIOLENCE.

RURAL EMERGENCY ZONES: A LARGE AREA OF CENTRAL PERU, EXTENDING FROM THE DEPARTMENT OF SAN MARTIN IN THE NORTH THROUGH AYACUCHO IN THE SOUTH, HAS BEEN DE-CLARED AN EMERGENCY ZONE DUE TO TERRORIST ACTIVITY. THE AREA INCLUDES THE DEPARTMENTS OF SAN MARTIN, JUNIN, AYACUCHO, HUANCAVELICA, UCAYALI, THE PROVINCE OF CONTA-MANA IN THE DEPARTMENT OF LORETO, THE WESTERN AND CEN-TRAL PROVINCES OF THE DEPARTMENT OF HUANUCO, AND MOST OF THE DEPARTMENTS OF PASCO AND APURIMAC. THESE ZONES ARE UNDER MILITARY CONTROL, AND PERUVIAN CONSTITU-TIONAL GUARANTEES HAVE BEEN SUSPENDED. THE EMER-GENCY ZONES ARE NOT AREAS NORMALLY FREQUENTED BY

TOURISTS, BUT THE ROAD BETWEEN HUARAZ AND LA UNION, THE ROAD BETWEEN CUSCO AND NAZCA AND THE CENTRAL HIGHWAY FROM LIMA TO THE HUANCAYO AREA CROSS THESE ZONES.
ROAD TRAVEL: IN GENERAL, ROAD TRAVEL IN PERU IS NOT REC-OMMENDED BECAUSE OF TERRORISM, BANDITRY AND POOR ROAD CONDITIONS. CITIZENS ARE ADVISED NOT TO TRAVEL BY ROAD AT NIGHT, AND SHOULD AVOID TRAVEL BY PUBLIC BUS NOT ONLY DUE TO THE POSSIBILITY OF ROBBERY BUT ALSO BECAUSE OF THE LACK OF MAINTENANCE AND GENERAL SAFETY CONSID-ERATIONS.
OTHER AREAS: AREAS NOT SPECIFICALLY MENTIONED IN THIS ADVISORY ARE CONSIDERED RELATIVELY SAFE; HOWEVER, CITI-ZENS SHOULD BE AWARE THAT CONDITIONS MAY CHANGE AT ANY TIME. U.S. CITIZENS SHOULD SEEK THE LATEST TRAVEL IN-FORMATION AND REGISTER WITH THE CONSULAR SECTION OF THE AMERICAN EMBASSY AT 346 GRIMALDO DEL SOLAR, MIRA-FLORES, LIMA. TEL: 44-36-21 OR 44-39-21.
EXPIRATION DATE: NOVEMBER 15, 1990

_____ Country number 8.155 _____
Philippine Islands

INFECTIOUS DISEASE RISK

Malaria Risk

Malaria is found only in rural areas below 600 meters. There is no risk of malaria in Bohol, Catanduanes, Cebu, Leyte, Misamis Occidental. Use of Chloroquine is recommended only for those travelers who will have outdoor exposure in rural areas during evening and nightime hours. See Chapter 6.63 for use of chloroquine.

Chloroquine resistant malaria is found on the islands of Luzon, Basilan, Mindoro, Palawan, Mindano and the Sulu Archipelago. See Chapter 6.63 for use of mefloquine in these areas.

Falciparum malaria represents 69% of malaria, therefore there is a risk of p. vivax malaria exposure. Consider use of primaquine upon return home.

Diseases of Special Risk

In addition to the worldwide hazard of tetanus and the routine and any special immunizations recommended below, the traveler should be aware that risk of exposure to the following diseases exists in this country. This list is not all inclusive, but it is a caution concerning the more likely endemic disease risks.

Potential risk of dengue fever exists. The virus is present in this country at all times and may give rise to major outbreaks.

Schistosomiasis may be found in this country. Avoid contact with contaminated fresh water lakes, ponds, or streams. Known ares of infection are present in Luzon: the area of Sorsogon in the Irosin-Juban Valley on the southeastern tip of the island. Mindoro: the area surrounding Lake Naujan, including the villages of Pola, Victoria, and Naujan. Samar: the main island of Samar Province in infected. Leyte: the northeastern plain of the island from Carigara to Abuyog is infected. Bohol: the whole island, located southeast of Leyte is infected. Mindanao: the infection is present throughout the island with the exception of the District of East Misamis.

Penicillin resistant gonorrhea is common in the Phillipines.

The local population has a high incidence of tuberculosis. Persons in close contact with the native population should consider a pre- and post-trip TB skin test.

DISEASE RISK PROFILE

Disease	endemic	risk	hazard
Chikungunya Fever	x		
Cholera	x		
Dengue Fever	x		
Diarrheal Disease Risk		x	
Dysentery, Amoebic/Bacillary		x	
Encephalitis, Japanese	x		
Fasciolopsiasis	x		
Filariasis			x
Helminthic Diseases (see Chapter 6.21)		x	
Hepatitis, Viral		x	
Melioidosis	x		
Opisthorchiasis	x		
Paragonimiasis	x		
Polio	x		
Rabies	x		
Typhoid Fever	x		
Typhus, Scrub	x		

Food/Water Safety

All tap water used for drinking, brushing teeth, and making ice cubes should be boiled prior to use. Insure that bottled water is uncapped in your presence. Milk should be boiled to insure safety. Powdered and evaporated milk are available and safe. Avoid butter and other dairy products. All meat, poultry and seafood must be well cooked and served while hot. Pork is best avoided. Vegetables should be well cooked and served hot. Salads and mayonnaise are best avoided. Fruits with intact skins should be peeled by you just prior to consumption. Avoid cold buffets, custards, and any frozen dessert. First class hotels and restaurants serve purified drinking water and reliable food. However, the hazard is left to your judgement.

VACCINATIONS

Yellow fever—A vaccination certificate is required for travelers coming from infected areas and from or in transit through countries with active disease. A vaccination certificate is required for children over one year of age. Children under one year of age are subject to isolation or surveillance, if indicated.

Routine immunizations should be current. For infants and children through 16 years of age, refer to Chapter 4.3. A rubeola (measles) booster should be considered. Persons age 16 to 65 should receive a booster of tetanus and diphtheria every ten years. Healthy adults under age 65 do not require pneumococcal vaccine, but it is appropriate for those with chronic medical conditions. Influenza vaccine may be considered for those providing essential community services, health care workers, and those wishing to reduce the likelihood of becoming ill with influenza. Adults over 65 years of age are urged to obtain yearly influenza immunization and to insure that their tetanus and diphtheria immunizations are current. Pneumococcal vaccination is also suggested for this age group.

Selective vaccinations—These apply only to specific groups of travelers or persons on specific working assignments:

Poliomyelitis—Vaccination is recommended when traveling outside the areas usually visited by tourists, traveling extensively in the interior of the country (trekkers, hikers) and for persons on working assignments in remote areas.

Viral Hepatitis A—Vaccination is recommended when traveling outside the areas usually visited by tourists, traveling extensively in the interior of the country (trekkers, hikers) and for persons on working assignments in remote areas.

Typhoid fever—Vaccination is recommended when traveling outside the areas usually visited by tourists, traveling extensively in the interior of the country (trekkers, hikers) and for persons on working assignments in remote areas.

Viral Hepatitis B—Because of the high rate of healthy carriers of hepatitis B in this country, vaccination is recommended for persons on working assignments in the health care field (dentists, physicians, nurses, laboratory technicians), or working in close contact with the local population (teachers, missionaries, Peace Corps), or persons foreseeing sexual relations with local inhabitants.

Japanese encephalitis—Vaccination is indicated for persons traveling extensively in rual areas or living and working near rice growing rural and suburban areas and other irrigated land, when exposure to the disease carrying mosquitoes is high. Children are especially susceptible to the infection. Sporadic cases are reported throuhgout the country. Period of transmission is all year.

Rabies—In this country, where rabies is a constant threat, a pre-exposure rabies vaccination is advised for persons planning an extended stay or on working assignments (naturalists, agricultural advisors, archeologists, geologists, etc.). Although this provides adequate initial protection, a person bitten by a potentially rabid animal would still require post exposure immunization (see Chapter 6.40). Children should be cautioned not to pet dogs, cats, or other mammals.

U. S. Foreign Service:
1201 Roxas Blvd.
Manila, Telephone 521-71-16

3rd Fl., Philippine American Life Insurance Bldg.
Jones Ave.
Cebu, Telephone 7-95-10/24

Canadian High Commission/Embassy Office:
Allied Bank Center
9th Floor
6754 Ayala Avenue
Makati, Metro Manila Telephone 815-95-36

TRAVEL ADVISORY
A U. S. Department of State Travel Advisory was in effect on 4 May 1990 when this book went to press. The entire text is included below. Travel advisories are subject to reissue, change, and cancellation at any time. Current travel advisory information is available by calling the U. S. Department of State Travel Advisory Hotline at (202) 647-5225. The current travel advisory status is also available from the Herchmer Database update system (see Chapter 2.8).

UNITED STATES DEPARTMENT OF STATE TRAVEL ADVISORY APRIL 24, 1990 PHILIPPINES — CAUTION
THIS REPLACES THE ADVISORY OF FEBRUARY 14, 1990.
THE DEPARTMENT OF STATE ADVISES THAT DUE TO ONGOING COMMUNIST INSURGENCY AND CRIMINAL ACTIVITY, AMERICANS ARE URGED NOT TO TRAVEL TO THE FOLLOWING AREAS: —
SAMAR ISLAND;
— BASILAN ISLAND;
— MASBATE PROVINCE;
— SULU PROVINCE;
— LANAO DEL SUR PROVINCE (INCLUDING MARAWI CITY);
— KALINGA APAYAO PROVINCE;
— THE CAGAYAN VALLEY LOCATED IN CAGAYAN;
HOWEVER, MOST OF THE MAJOR TOURIST DESTINATIONS AND

MOST URBAN AREAS IN GENERAL HAVE NOT EXPERIENCED THE TYPE OF CIVIL DISORDER NOTED ELSEWHERE IN THIS ADVISORY. THESE AREAS INCLUDE MANILA AND BAGUIO, THE BATANGAS AREA, PUERTO GALERA, DIPOLOG (DAKAK), AND THE ISLANDS OF PALAWAN, BORACAY, CAMIGUIN, MARINDUQUE AND CEBU.

WHILE TRAFFIC TO AND FROM U.S. GOVERNMENT INSTALLATIONS FLOWS NORMALLY, PEOPLE SHOULD BE AWARE THAT A THREAT EXISTS AGAINST U.S. OFFICIAL PERSONNEL AND FACILITIES, AND TRAVELERS SHOULD TAKE APPROPRIATE PRECAUTIONS.

BECAUSE OF CRIMINAL ACTIVITIES, TRAVELERS SHOULD EXERCISE CAUTION AT NIGHT IN THE DOWNTOWN ENTERTAINMENT DISTRICTS OF MAJOR CITIES AND SHOULD AVOID TRAVEL TO REMOTE MOUNTAINOUS AREAS.

SPECIAL CARE SHOULD BE EXERCISED WHEN TRAVELING BY PUBLIC CONVEYANCES AS WELL AS PRIVATE VEHICLES. UNSETTLED CONDTIONS MAY OCCUR AT ANY TIME OR PLACE. ONLY NATIONAL HIGHWAYS AND PAVED ROADS SHOULD BE USED. EXCEPT FOR MAJOR URBAN AREAS ROAD TRAVEL AT NIGHT SHOULD BE AVOIDED.

SPECIAL CARE SHOULD BE EXERCISED WHEN TRAVELING TO SOME AREAS OF LUZON, PRINCIPALLY ARBA, IFUGAO, AND MOUNTAIN PROVINCES (INCLUDING BANAUE AND SAGADA), QUEZON PROVINCE, AURORA PROVINCE, SOUTHERN LAGUNA PROVINCE, AND ALL OF LUZON SOUTH OF LUCENA CITY EXCEPT FOR LEGASPI AND NAGA CITIES. VISITORS SHOULD CHECK WITH THE EMBASSY OR LOCAL AUTHORITIES BEFORE TRAVELING.

BECAUSE OF CONTINUED CRIME AND INSURGENCY, TRAVEL ON THE ISLAND OF MINDANAO SHOULD BE LIMITED TO BUKIDNON PROVINCE AND THE CITIES O BUTUAN, CAGAYAN DE ORO, COTABATO, DIPILOG, ILIGAN, GENERAL SANTOS, PAGADIAN, DAPITAN, GINGOOG, SURIGAO CITY, AND THE "DOWNTOWN CENTERS" OF DAVAO AND ZAMBOANGA CITIES. ON PANAY ISLAND, CAUTION IS ADVISED IN AKLAN PROVINCE (EXCLUDING BORACAY) DUE TO AN INCREASE IN CRIME, INCLUDING THE ROBBERY OF NUMBEROUS TOURISTS. TRAVEL TO ANTIQUE SHOULD BE LIMITED TO THE ROAD BETWEEN ILOILO AND SAN JOSE.

AMERICANS ARE URGED TO CONFINE TRAVEL ON THE ISLAND OF NEGROS TO THE URBAN AREAS OF BACOLOD AND DUMAGUETE. CAUTION IS ALSO ADVISED IN THE RURAL AREAS OF BOHOL ISLAND.

U.S. CITIZENS ARE ADVISED TO REGISTER AT THE U.S. EMBASSY IN MANILA AND CONSULATE IN CEBU. FOR FURTHER INFORMATION, AMERICANS MAY CONSULT WITH THE CONSULAR SECTION OF THE EMBASSY IN MANILA, TEL: 521-7116, EXT. 2567 OR 2246;

THE CONSULATE IN CEBU, TEL: 73486; OR THE FOREIGN LIAISON OFFICE OF THE PHILIPPINE CONSTABULARY IN MANILA, TEL: 79-38-49; 79-40-89. UPDATES ABOUT CONDITIONS MAY BE HEARD BY TELEPHONING 521-9261 IN MANILA. IN MANY PHILIPPINE CITIES AND PROVINCIAL CAPITALS AN UPDATE CAN BE OBTAINED BY LOCAL AUTHORITIES.

Country number 8.156
Pitcairn Island

INFECTIOUS DISEASE RISK

Malaria Risk
There is no malaria risk in this country.

Diseases of Special Risk

Food/Water Safety
Water is probably safe, but due to local variations in bacterial counts, using bottled water for the first few weeks will help the traveler adjust and decrease the chance of traveler's diarrhea. Safety of milk and dairy products unknown. Local meat, poultry, seafood, vegetables, and fruits are safe to eat.

VACCINATIONS
Cholera—A cholera vaccination certificate is required when coming from an infected area.

Yellow fever—A vaccination certificate is required for travelers coming from infected areas and from or in transit through countries with active disease. A vaccination certificate is required for children over one year of age.

Routine immunizations should be current. For infants and children through 16 years of age, refer to Chapter 4.3. A rubeola (measles) booster should be considered. Persons age 16 to 65 should receive a booster of tetanus and diphtheria every ten years. Healthy adults under age 65 do not require pneumococcal vaccine, but it is appropriate for those with chronic medical conditions. Influenza vaccine may be considered for those providing essential community services, health care workers, and those wishing to reduce the likelihood of becoming ill with influenza. Adults over 65 years of age are urged to obtain yearly influenza immunization and to insure that their tetanus and diphtheria immunizations are current. Pneumococcal vaccination is also suggested for this age group.

_____ **Country number 8.157** _____
Poland

INFECTIOUS DISEASE RISK

Malaria Risk

There is no malaria risk in this country.

Diseases of Special Risk

Rabies is frequent in wild animals in rural areas, especially in foxes.

For those traveling into rural areas, there is risk of typhoid and hepatitis A from contaminate water supplies. Immunizations against these diseases is advisable.

The fish tapeworm (diphyllobothriasis) is found in the Baltic Sea area.

Food/Water Safety

Water is probably safe, but due to local variations in bacterial counts, using bottled water for the first few weeks will help the traveler adjust and decrease the chance of traveler's diarrhea. Milk is pasteurized and safe to drink. Butter, cheese, yogurt and ice-cream are safe. Local meat, poultry, seafood, vegetables, and fruits are safe to eat.

VACCINATIONS

Routine immunizations should be current. For infants and children through 16 years of age, refer to Chapter 4.3. A rubeola (measles) booster should be considered. Persons age 16 to 65 should receive a booster of tetanus and diphtheria every ten years. Healthy adults under age 65 do not require pneumococcal vaccine, but it is appropriate for those with chronic medical conditions. Influenza vaccine may be considered for those providing essential community services, health care workers, and those wishing to reduce the likelihood of becoming ill with influenza. Adults over 65 years of age are urged to obtain yearly influenza immunization and to insure that their tetanus and diphtheria immunizations are current. Pneumococcal vaccination is also suggested for this age group.

Selective vaccinations—These apply only to specific groups of travelers or persons on specific working assignments:

Tick-borne encephalitis—(Central European encephalitis) Vaccination is recommended for persons involved in recreational activities in forested areas (camping, hiking) or working in forestry occupations. Risk season: March to November. Risk is present in the northern part of the country extending from the forested areas around Gdansk south and eastward to the Russian border, including the areas around Bialystock. Other areas of risk are forested lands around

Warsaw, Lodz and Lukow, and along the border with Czechoslovakia south of Wroclaw.

U. S. Foreign Service:
Aleje Ujazdowskie 29/31
Warsaw, Telephone 28-30-41/9

Ulica Stolarska 9, 31043 Krakow
Krakow, Telephone 22-97-64, 22-14-00, 22-60-40, 22-77-93
Ulica Chopina 4
Poznan, Telephone 595-86/87, 598-74

Canadian High Commission/Embassy Office:
Ulica Matejki 1/5
Warsaw, Telephone 29-80-51

Country number 8.158
Portugal

INFECTIOUS DISEASE RISK

Malaria Risk
There is no malaria risk in this country.

Diseases of Special Risk
In addition to the worldwide hazard of tetanus and the routine and any special immunizations recommended below, the traveler should be aware that risk of exposure to the following diseases exists in this country. This list is not all inclusive, but it is a caution concerning the more likely endemic disease risks.

Due to a high incidence of tuberculosis amongst the local population, the traveler may need to consider a pre- and post-trip TB skin test.

DISEASE RISK PROFILE

Disease	endemic	risk	hazard
Brucellosis	x		
Diarrheal Diseases	x		
Dysentery, Bacillary	x		
Typhoid Fever	x		

Food/Water Safety
Water is probably safe, but due to local variations in bacterial counts, using bottled water for the first few weeks will help the traveler adjust and

decrease the chance of traveler's diarrhea. Milk is pasteurized and safe to drink. Butter, cheese, yogurt and ice-cream are safe. Local meat, poultry, seafood, vegetables, and fruits are safe to eat.

VACCINATIONS

Yellow fever—A vaccination certificate is required only for travelers coming from infected areas and from or in transit through countries with active infection arriving in or destined for the Azores and Madeira. A vaccination certificate is required for children over one year of age. No certificate is, however, required from transit passengers at Funchal, Porto Santo, and Santa Maria.

Routine immunizations should be current. For infants and children through 16 years of age, refer to Chapter 4.3. A rubeola (measles) booster should be considered. Persons age 16 to 65 should receive a booster of tetanus and diphtheria every ten years. Healthy adults under age 65 do not require pneumococcal vaccine, but it is appropriate for those with chronic medical conditions. Influenza vaccine may be considered for those providing essential community services, health care workers, and those wishing to reduce the likelihood of becoming ill with influenza. Adults over 65 years of age are urged to obtain yearly influenza immunization and to insure that their tetanus and diphtheria immunizations are current. Pneumococcal vaccination is also suggested for this age group.

The vaccinations listed are recommended for the traveler's protection.
Viral Hepatitis A—Vaccination is recommended when traveling outside the areas usually visited by tourists, traveling extensively in the interior of the country (trekkers, hikers) and for persons on working assignments in remote areas.
Poliomyelitis—Vaccination is recommended when traveling outside the areas usually visited by tourists, traveling extensively in the interior of the country (trekkers, hikers) and for persons on working assignments in remote areas.
Typhoid fever—Vaccination is recommended when traveling outside the areas usually visited by tourists, traveling extensively in the interior of the country (trekkers, hikers) and for persons on working assignments in remote areas.

U. S. Foreign Service:
Avenida das Forcas Armadas, 1600
Lisbon, Telephone 72-56-00

Rua Julio Dinis 826-30
Oporto, Telephone 6-3094/5/6

Canadian High Commission/Embassy Office:
Rua Rosa Araujo 2
6th Floor
Lisbon, Telephone 56-38-21

Country number 8.159
Puerto Rico

INFECTIOUS DISEASE RISK

Malaria Risk
There is no malaria risk in this country.

Diseases of Special Risk
In addition to the worldwide hazard of tetanus and the routine and any special immunizations recommended below, the traveler should be aware that risk of exposure to the following diseases exists in this country. This list is not all inclusive, but it is a caution concerning the more likely endemic disease risks.

Potential risk of dengue fever exists. The virus is present in this country at all times and may give rise to major outbreaks.

Schistosomiasis may be found in this country. Avoid contact with contaminated fresh water lakes, ponds, or streams. Low infection rates have been reported from all parts of the island. Infection also occurs on the islands of Vieques and Culebra, both located off the eastern coast of Puerto Rico.

DISEASE RISK PROFILE

Disease	endemic	risk	hazard
Diarrheal Disease Risk		x	
Dysentery, Amoebic/Bacillary		x	
Filariasis (Bancroftian)	x		
Hepatitis	x		
Rabies	x		

Food/Water Safety
Local water is considered safe without further treatment. Milk is pasteurized and safe to drink. Butter, cheese, yogurt and ice-cream are safe. Local meat, poultry, seafood, vegetables, and fruits are safe to eat.

VACCINATIONS

Routine immunizations should be current. For infants and children through 16 years of age, refer to Chapter 4.3. A rubeola (measles) booster should be considered. Persons age 16 to 65 should receive a booster of tetanus and diphtheria every ten years. Healthy adults under age 65 do not require pneumococcal vaccine, but it is appropriate for those with chronic medical conditions. Influenza vaccine may be considered for those providing essential community services, health care workers, and those wishing to reduce the likelihood of becoming ill with influenza. Adults over 65 years of age are urged to obtain yearly influenza immunization and to insure that their tetanus and diph-

theria immunizations are current. Pneumococcal vaccination is also suggested for this age group.

No vaccinations are required to enter this country.

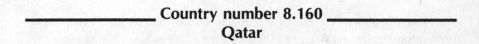

Country number 8.160
Qatar

INFECTIOUS DISEASE RISK

Malaria Risk

There is no malaria risk in this country.

Diseases of Special Risk

In addition to the worldwide hazard of tetanus and the routine and any special immunizations recommended below, the traveler should be aware that risk of exposure to the following diseases exists in this country. This list is not all inclusive, but it is a caution concerning the more likely endemic disease risks.

DISEASE RISK PROFILE

Disease	endemic	risk	hazard
Brucellosis			x
Cholera	x		
Diarrheal Diseases		x	
Echinococcosis	x		
Hepatitis, Viral		x	
Leishmaniasis			
Cutaneous	x		
Visceral	x		
Rabies	x		
Relapsing Fever	x		
Tapeworms	x		
Trachoma	x		
Typhoid Fever		x	
Typhus, Endemic Flea-Borne	x		
Typhus, Scrub	x		

Food/Water Safety

All tap water used for drinking, brushing teeth, and making ice cubes should be boiled prior to use. Insure that bottled water is uncapped in your presence. Milk should be boiled to insure safety. Powdered and evaporated milk are available and safe. Avoid butter and other dairy products. All meat, poultry and seafood must be well cooked and served while hot. Pork is best avoided.

Vegetables should be well cooked and served hot. Salads and mayonnaise are best avoided. Fruits with intact skins should be peeled by you just prior to consumption. Avoid cold buffets, custards, and any frozen dessert. First class hotels and restaurants in Ad Dawhah (Doha) serve purified drinking water and reliable food. However, the hazard is left to your judgement.

VACCINATIONS

Yellow fever—A vaccination certificate is required for travelers coming from infected areas and from or in transit through countries with active infections. A vaccination certificate is required for children over one year of age.

Routine immunizations should be current. For infants and children through 16 years of age, refer to Chapter 4.3. A rubeola (measles) booster should be considered. Persons age 16 to 65 should receive a booster of tetanus and diphtheria every ten years. Healthy adults under age 65 do not require pneumococcal vaccine, but it is appropriate for those with chronic medical conditions. Influenza vaccine may be considered for those providing essential community services, health care workers, and those wishing to reduce the likelihood of becoming ill with influenza. Adults over 65 years of age are urged to obtain yearly influenza immunization and to insure that their tetanus and diphtheria immunizations are current. Pneumococcal vaccination is also suggested for this age group.

The vaccinations listed are recommended for the traveler's protection.
Poliomyelitis—A poliomyelitis booster is indicated for this country.
Viral Hepatitis A—Vaccination is recommended for all travelers for their protection.
Typhoid fever—Vaccination is recommended for all travelers for their protection.

Selective vaccinations—These apply only to specific groups of travelers or persons on specific working assignments:
Viral Hepatitis B—Because of the high rate of healthy carriers of hepatitis B in this country, vaccination is recommended for persons on working assignments in the health care field (dentists, physicians, nurses, laboratory technicians), or working in close contact with the local population (teachers, missionaries, Peace Corps), or persons foreseeing sexual relations with local inhabitants.

_____ **Country number 8.161** _____
Reunion

INFECTIOUS DISEASE RISK

Malaria Risk

There is no malaria risk in this country.

Diseases of Special Risk

In addition to the worldwide hazard of tetanus and the routine and any special immunizations recommended below, the traveler should be aware that risk of exposure to the following diseases exists in this country. This list is not all inclusive, but it is a caution concerning the more likely endemic disease risks.

DISEASE RISK PROFILE

Disease	endemic	risk	hazard
Diarrheal Diseases			x
Dysentery, Amoebic/Bacillary			x
Echinococcosis		x	
Filariasis			x
Helminthic Diseases (see Chapter 6.21)			x
Hepatitis, Viral			x
Leishmaniasis			
Cutaneous	x		
Visceral	x		
Rabies	x		
Relapsing Fever	x		
Trachoma			x
Typhoid Fever			x
Typhus, Endemic Flea-Borne	x		
Typhus, Epidemic Louse-Borne	x		
Typhus, Scrub	x		

Food/Water Safety

All tap water used for drinking, brushing teeth, and making ice cubes should be boiled prior to use. Insure that bottled water is uncapped in your presence. Milk should be boiled to insure safety. Powdered and evaporated milk are available and safe. Avoid butter and other dairy products. All meat, poultry and seafood must be well cooked and served while hot. Pork is best avoided. Vegetables should be well cooked and served hot. Salads and mayonnaise are best avoided. Fruits with intact skins should be peeled by you just prior to consumption. Avoid cold buffets, custards, and any frozen dessert.

VACCINATIONS

Yellow fever—A vaccination certificate is required for travelers coming from infected areas. A vaccination certificate is required for children over one year of age.

Routine immunizations should be current. For infants and children through 16 years of age, refer to Chapter 4.3. A rubeola (measles) booster should be considered. Persons age 16 to 65 should receive a booster of tetanus and diphtheria every ten years. Healthy adults under age 65 do not require pneumococcal vaccine, but it is appropriate for those with chronic medical conditions. Influenza vaccine may be considered for those providing essential community services, health care workers, and those wishing to reduce the likelihood of becoming ill with influenza. Adults over 65 years of age are urged to obtain yearly influenza immunization and to insure that their tetanus and diphtheria immunizations are current. Pneumococcal vaccination is also suggested for this age group.

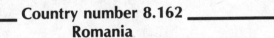

Country number 8.162
Romania

INFECTIOUS DISEASE RISK

Malaria Risk

There is no malaria risk in this country.

Diseases of Special Risk

In addition to the worldwide hazard of tetanus and the routine and any special immunizations recommended below, the traveler should be aware that risk of exposure to the following diseases exists in this country. This list is not all inclusive, but it is a caution concerning the more likely endemic disease risks.

DISEASE RISK PROFILE

Disease	endemic	risk	hazard
Brucellosis	x		
Diarrheal Diseases	x		
Hepatitis, Viral	x		
Rabies	x		

Food/Water Safety

Water is probably safe, but due to local variations in bacterial counts, using bottled water for the first few weeks will help the traveler adjust and decrease the chance of traveler's diarrhea. Milk is pasteurized and safe to drink. Butter, cheese, yogurt and ice-cream are safe. Local meat, poultry, seafood, vegetables, and fruits are safe to eat.

VACCINATIONS

Routine immunizations should be current. For infants and children through 16 years of age, refer to Chapter 4.3. A rubeola (measles) booster should be considered. Persons age 16 to 65 should receive a booster of tetanus and diphtheria every ten years. Healthy adults under age 65 do not require pneumococcal vaccine, but it is appropriate for those with chronic medical conditions. Influenza vaccine may be considered for those providing essential community services, health care workers, and those wishing to reduce the likelihood of becoming ill with influenza. Adults over 65 years of age are urged to obtain yearly influenza immunization and to insure that their tetanus and diphtheria immunizations are current. Pneumococcal vaccination is also suggested for this age group.

No vaccinations are required to enter this country.

Selective vaccinations—These apply only to specific groups of travelers or persons on specific working assignments:

Viral Hepatitis B—Because of the high rate of healthy carriers of hepatitis B in this country, vaccination is recommended for persons on working assignments in the health care field (dentists, physicians, nurses, laboratory technicians), or working in close contact with the local population (teachers, missionaries, Peace Corps), or persons foreseeing sexual relations with local inhabitants.

Tick-borne encephalitis—(Central European encephalitis) Vaccination is recommended for persons involved in recreational activities in forested areas (camping, hiking) or working in forestry occupations. Risk season: March to November. Risk is present in the forested areas in the western part of the country.

U. S. Foreign Service:
Strada Tudor Arghezi 7-9
Bucharest, Telephone 12-40-40

Canadian High Commission/Embassy Office:
36 Nicolae Iorga
Bucharest, Telephone 50-65-80, 50-62-90, 50-63-30, 50-61-40

TRAVEL ADVISORY

A U. S. Department of State Travel Advisory was in effect on 4 May 1990 when this book went to press. The entire text is included below. Travel advisories are subject to reissue, change, and cancellation at any time. Current travel advisory information is available by calling the U. S. Department of State Travel Advisory Hotline at (202) 647-5225. The current travel advisory status is also available from the Herchmer Database update system (see Chapter 2.8).

JANUARY 12, 1990
ROMANIA—CAUTION
THE DEPARTMENT OF STATE ADVISES U.S. CITIZENS TO EXERCISE
CAUTION IN TRAVELING TO ROMANIA. SINCE THE RECENT
CHANGES IN THE ROMANIAN GOVERNMENT, THE SECURITY SITU-
ATION HAS STABILIZED THROUGHOUT THE COUNTRY, ALTHOUGH
THE POTENTIAL FOR RANDOM VIOLENCE REMAINS. THERE HAS
BEEN NO DIRECT THREAT TO U.S. CITIZENS.
BECAUSE OF THESE DEVELOPMENTS, ALL AMERICAN EMBASSY
PERSONNEL AND DEPENDENTS SUBJECT TO THE EVACUTION OR-
DER ARE RETURNING TO BUCHAREST BEGINNING JANUARY 15.
U.S. CITIZENS IN ROMANIA SHOULD CONTACT THE U.S. EMBASSY
IN BUCHAREST, STRADA TUDOR ARGHEZI 7-9, TELEPHONE 10-40-
40 FOR INFORMATION.
EXPIRATION: INDEFINITE.

————————————— **Country number 8.163** —————————————
Rwanda

INFECTIOUS DISEASE RISK

Malaria Risk

Malaria is present in all parts of this country, including urban areas. The
risk exists all year. The malaria in this country is resistant to chloroquine. The
CDC recommends the use of mefloquine (Lariam) as described in Chapter 6.31
for chemical prophylaxis.

Falciparum malaria represents 90% of malaria, therefore there is a risk of
p. vivax malaria exposure. Consider use of primaquine upon return home.

Diseases of Special Risk

In addition to the worldwide hazard of tetanus and the routine and any
special immunizations recommended below, the traveler should be aware that
risk of exposure to the following diseases exists in this country. This list is not
all inclusive, but it is a caution concerning the more likely endemic disease
risks.

Louse-borne typhus is cosmopolitan in distribution and is present wherever groups of persons are crowded together under conditions of poor sanitation
and malnutrition. Risk exists for persons living or working in remote areas of
the country (anthropologists, archeologists, geologists, medical personnel, missionaries, etc.). Freedom from louse infestation is the most effective protection
against typhus.

DISEASE RISK PROFILE

Disease	endemic	risk	hazard
Diarrheal Diseases			x
Dracunculiasis/Guinea Worm	x		
Dysentery, Amoebic/Bacillary			x
Echinococcosis		x	
Filariasis			x
Giardiasis			x
Helminthic Diseases (see Chapter 6.21)			x
Hepatitis, Viral			x
Leishmaniasis			
Cutaneous	x		
Visceral	x		
Onchocerciasis			x
Polio			x
Rabies	x		
Relapsing Fever	x		
Trachoma			x
Trypanosomiasis, African	x		
Sleeping Sickness			
Typhoid Fever			x
Typhus, Endemic Flea-Borne	x		
Typhus, Epidemic Louse-Borne	x		
Typhus, Scrub	x		

Food/Water Safety

All tap water used for drinking, brushing teeth, and making ice cubes should be boiled prior to use. Insure that bottled water is uncapped in your presence. Milk should be boiled to insure safety. Powdered and evaporated milk are available and safe. Avoid butter and other dairy products. All meat, poultry and seafood must be well cooked and served while hot. Pork is best avoided. Vegetables should be well cooked and served hot. Salads and mayonnaise are best avoided. Fruits with intact skins should be peeled by you just prior to consumption. Avoid cold buffets, custards, and any frozen dessert. First class hotels and restaurants in Kigali serve purified drinking water and reliable food. However, the hazard is left to your judgement.

VACCINATIONS

Cholera—Risk to western travelers is low. Avoid uncooked foods and untreated water. WHILE CHOLERA VACCINE IS NOT OFFICIALLY REQUIRED FOR ENTRY TO THIS COUNTRY, ACCORDING TO RECENT REPORTS BORDER OFFICIALS ARE INSISTING ON CHOLERA VACCINATION FOR ENTRY. Travelers arriving without a current cholera vaccination are having tickets for forward travel impounded until they obtain vaccination in country. This means that they must buy their own needle and syringe and report to a local hospital for vaccination.

Yellow fever—A vaccination certificate is required on arrival from all countries, except passengers in transit who do not leave the airport. A vaccination certificate is required for children over one year of age. CDC recommends vaccination for all travelers over 9 months of age who will travel outside of urban areas.

Routine immunizations should be current. For infants and children through 16 years of age, refer to Chapter 4.3. A rubeola (measles) booster should be considered. Persons age 16 to 65 should receive a booster of tetanus and diphtheria every ten years. Healthy adults under age 65 do not require pneumococcal vaccine, but it is appropriate for those with chronic medical conditions. Influenza vaccine may be considered for those providing essential community services, health care workers, and those wishing to reduce the likelihood of becoming ill with influenza. Adults over 65 years of age are urged to obtain yearly influenza immunization and to insure that their tetanus and diphtheria immunizations are current. Pneumococcal vaccination is also suggested for this age group.

The vaccinations listed are recommended for the traveler's protection.
Poliomyelitis—A poliomyelitis booster is indicated for this country.
Viral Hepatitis A—Vaccination is recommended for all travelers for their protection.
Typhoid fever—Vaccination is recommended for all travelers for their protection.

Selective vaccinations—*These apply only to specific groups of travelers or persons on specific working assignments:*
Viral Hepatitis B—Because of the high rate of healthy carriers of hepatitis B in this country, vaccination is recommended for persons on working assignments in the health care field (dentists, physicians, nurses, laboratory technicians), or working in close contact with the local population (teachers, missionaries, Peace Corps), or persons foreseeing sexual relations with local inhabitants.
Rabies—In this country, where rabies is a constant threat, a pre-exposure rabies vaccination is advised for persons planning an extended stay or on working assignments (naturalists, agricultural advisors, archeologists, geologists, etc.). Although this provides adequate initial protection, a person bitten by a potentially rabid animal would still require post exposure immunization (see Chapter 6.40). Children should be cautioned not to pet dogs, cats, or other mammals.

U. S. Foreign Service:
Blvd. de la Revolution
Kigali, Telephone 5601

Country number 8.164
Ryukyu Islands
(Okinawa)

INFECTIOUS DISEASE RISK

Malaria Risk

There is no malaria risk in this country.

Diseases of Special Risk

In addition to the worldwide hazard of tetanus and the routine and any special immunizations recommended below, the traveler should be aware that risk of exposure to the following diseases exists in this country. This list is not all inclusive, but it is a caution concerning the more likely endemic disease risks.

DISEASE RISK PROFILE

Disease	endemic	risk	hazard
Clonorchiasis	x		
Dengue Fever	x		
Paragonimiasis	x		
Typhoid Fever	x		
Typhus, Scrub	x		

Food/Water Safety

Local water is considered safe without further treatment. Milk is pasteurized and safe to drink. Butter, cheese, yogurt and ice-cream are safe. Local meat, poultry, seafood, vegetables, and fruits are safe to eat.

VACCINATIONS

Routine immunizations should be current. For infants and children through 16 years of age, refer to Chapter 4.3. A rubeola (measles) booster should be considered. Persons age 16 to 65 should receive a booster of tetanus and diphtheria every ten years. Healthy adults under age 65 do not require pneumococcal vaccine, but it is appropriate for those with chronic medical conditions. Influenza vaccine may be considered for those providing essential community services, health care workers, and those wishing to reduce the likelihood of becoming ill with influenza. Adults over 65 years of age are urged to obtain yearly influenza immunization and to insure that their tetanus and diphtheria immunizations are current. Pneumococcal vaccination is also suggested for this age group.

No vaccinations are required to enter this country.

The vaccinations listed are recommended for the traveler's protection.
Poliomyelitis—A poliomyelitis booster is indicated for this country.
Typhoid fever—Vaccination is recommended for all travelers for their protection.

Japanese encephalitis—Vaccination is indicated for persons traveling extensively in rual areas or living and working near rice growing rural and suburban areas and other irrigated land, when exposure to the disease carrying mosquitoes is high. Children are especially susceptible to the infection. Outbreaks occur in western and southern Japan, especially on the islands of Kyushu and Okinawa. Period of transmission is June through October, with the elederly being at the highest risk.

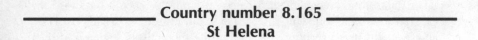

Country number 8.165
St Helena

INFECTIOUS DISEASE RISK

Malaria Risk
There is no malaria risk in this country.

Diseases of Special Risk
In addition to the worldwide hazard of tetanus and the routine and any special immunizations recommended below, the traveler should be aware that risk of exposure to the following diseases exists in this country. This list is not all inclusive, but it is a caution concerning the more likely endemic disease risks.

DISEASE RISK PROFILE

Disease	endemic	risk	hazard
Diarrheal Diseases		x	
Dysentery, Amoebic		x	
Typhoid		x	

Food/Water Safety
Water is probably safe, but due to local variations in bacterial counts, using bottled water for the first few weeks will help the traveler adjust and decrease the chance of traveler's diarrhea. Milk is pasteurized and safe to drink. Butter, cheese, yogurt and ice-cream are safe. Local meat, poultry, seafood, vegetables, and fruits are safe to eat.

VACCINATIONS
Routine immunizations should be current. For infants and children through 16 years of age, refer to Chapter 4.3. A rubeola (measles) booster

should be considered. Persons age 16 to 65 should receive a booster of tetanus and diphtheria every ten years. Healthy adults under age 65 do not require pneumococcal vaccine, but it is appropriate for those with chronic medical conditions. Influenza vaccine may be considered for those providing essential community services, health care workers, and those wishing to reduce the likelihood of becoming ill with influenza. Adults over 65 years of age are urged to obtain yearly influenza immunization and to insure that their tetanus and diphtheria immunizations are current. Pneumococcal vaccination is also suggested for this age group.

Country number 8.166
Saint Christopher and Nevis
formerly St. Kitts

INFECTIOUS DISEASE RISK

Malaria Risk
There is no malaria risk in this country.

Diseases of Special Risk
In addition to the worldwide hazard of tetanus and the routine and any special immunizations recommended below, the traveler should be aware that risk of exposure to the following diseases exists in this country. This list is not all inclusive, but it is a caution concerning the more likely endemic disease risks.
Potential risk of dengue fever exists. The virus is present in this country at all times and may give rise to major outbreaks.

DISEASE RISK PROFILE

Disease	endemic	risk	hazard
Diarrheal Disease Risk		x	
Dysentery, Amoebic/Bacillary		x	
Hepatitis, Viral	x		
Rabies (esp mongoose)	x		

Food/Water Safety
Water is probably safe, but due to local variations in bacterial counts, using bottled water for the first few weeks will help the traveler adjust and decrease the chance of traveler's diarrhea. Local meat, poultry, seafood, vegetables, and fruits are safe to eat. Milk is pasteurized and safe to drink. Butter, cheese, yogurt and ice-cream are safe.

VACCINATIONS

Yellow fever—A vaccination certificate is required for travelers coming from infected areas and from or in transit through countries with active infection. A vaccination certificate is required for children over one year of age.

Routine immunizations should be current. For infants and children through 16 years of age, refer to Chapter 4.3. A rubeola (measles) booster should be considered. Persons age 16 to 65 should receive a booster of tetanus and diphtheria every ten years. Healthy adults under age 65 do not require pneumococcal vaccine, but it is appropriate for those with chronic medical conditions. Influenza vaccine may be considered for those providing essential community services, health care workers, and those wishing to reduce the likelihood of becoming ill with influenza. Adults over 65 years of age are urged to obtain yearly influenza immunization and to insure that their tetanus and diphtheria immunizations are current. Pneumococcal vaccination is also suggested for this age group.

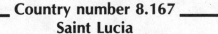

Country number 8.167
Saint Lucia

INFECTIOUS DISEASE RISK

Malaria Risk

There is no malaria risk in this country.

Diseases of Special Risk

In addition to the worldwide hazard of tetanus and the routine and any special immunizations recommended below, the traveler should be aware that risk of exposure to the following diseases exists in this country. This list is not all inclusive, but it is a caution concerning the more likely endemic disease risks.

Potential risk of dengue fever exists. The virus is present in this country at all times and may give rise to major outbreaks.

Schistosomiasis may be found in this country. Avoid contact with contaminated fresh water lakes, ponds, or streams. Known areas of infection are the Cul de Sac River valley south of Casties; the Roseau valley; and the areas of Soufriere and Riche Fond.

DISEASE RISK PROFILE

Disease	endemic	risk	hazard
Diarrheal Disease Risk		x	
Dysentery, Amoebic/Bacillary		x	
Hepatitis, Viral	x		

Food/Water Safety
    Water is probably safe, but due to local variations in bacterial counts, using bottled water for the first few weeks will help the traveler adjust and decrease the chance of traveler's diarrhea. Local meat, poultry, seafood, vegetables, and fruits are safe to eat. Milk is pasteurized and safe to drink. Butter, cheese, yogurt and ice-cream are safe.

VACCINATIONS
    Yellow fever—A vaccination certificate is required for travelers coming from infected areas and from or in transit through countries with active disease. A vaccination certificate is required for children over one year of age.
    Routine immunizations should be current. For infants and children through 16 years of age, refer to Chapter 4.3. A rubeola (measles) booster should be considered. Persons age 16 to 65 should receive a booster of tetanus and diphtheria every ten years. Healthy adults under age 65 do not require pneumococcal vaccine, but it is appropriate for those with chronic medical conditions. Influenza vaccine may be considered for those providing essential community services, health care workers, and those wishing to reduce the likelihood of becoming ill with influenza. Adults over 65 years of age are urged to obtain yearly influenza immunization and to insure that their tetanus and diphtheria immunizations are current. Pneumococcal vaccination is also suggested for this age group.

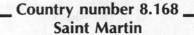

Country number 8.168
Saint Martin

INFECTIOUS DISEASE RISK

Malaria Risk
    There is no malaria risk in this country.

Food/Water Safety
    Water is probably safe, but due to local variations in bacterial counts, using bottled water for the first few weeks will help the traveler adjust and decrease the chance of traveler's diarrhea. Local meat, poultry, seafood, vegetables, and fruits are safe to eat. Milk is pasteurized and safe to drink. Butter, cheese, yogurt and ice-cream are safe.

VACCINATIONS
    Routine immunizations should be current. For infants and children through 16 years of age, refer to Chapter 4.3. A rubeola (measles) booster should be considered. Persons age 16 to 65 should receive a booster of tetanus and diphtheria every ten years. Healthy adults under age 65 do not require

pneumococcal vaccine, but it is appropriate for those with chronic medical conditions. Influenza vaccine may be considered for those providing essential community services, health care workers, and those wishing to reduce the likelihood of becoming ill with influenza. Adults over 65 years of age are urged to obtain yearly influenza immunization and to insure that their tetanus and diphtheria immunizations are current. Pneumococcal vaccination is also suggested for this age group.

Country number 8.169
Saint Pierre and Miquelon

INFECTIOUS DISEASE RISK

Malaria Risk
   There is no malaria risk in this country.

Diseases of Special Risk
   In addition to the worldwide hazard of tetanus and the routine and any special immunizations recommended below, the traveler should be aware that risk of exposure to the following diseases exists in this country. This list is not all inclusive, but it is a caution concerning the more likely endemic disease risks.

DISEASE RISK PROFILE

Disease	endemic	risk	hazard
Encephalitis	x		
Plague	x		
Rabies (esp bats)	x		
Rocky Mountain Spotted Fever	x		
Tularemia	x		

Food/Water Safety
   Water is probably safe, but due to local variations in bacterial counts, using bottled water for the first few weeks will help the traveler adjust and decrease the chance of traveler's diarrhea. Local meat, poultry, seafood, vegetables, and fruits are safe to eat. Milk is pasteurized and safe to drink. Butter, cheese, yogurt and ice-cream are safe.

VACCINATIONS
   Routine immunizations should be current. For infants and children through 16 years of age, refer to Chapter 4.3. A rubeola (measles) booster should be considered. Persons age 16 to 65 should receive a booster of tetanus and diphtheria every ten years. Healthy adults under age 65 do not require

pneumococcal vaccine, but it is appropriate for those with chronic medical conditions. Influenza vaccine may be considered for those providing essential community services, health care workers, and those wishing to reduce the likelihood of becoming ill with influenza. Adults over 65 years of age are urged to obtain yearly influenza immunization and to insure that their tetanus and diphtheria immunizations are current. Pneumococcal vaccination is also suggested for this age group.

No vaccinations are required to enter this country.

Country number 8.170
Saint Vincent and the Grenadines

INFECTIOUS DISEASE RISK

Malaria Risk

There is no malaria risk in this country.

Diseases of Special Risk

In addition to the worldwide hazard of tetanus and the routine and any special immunizations recommended below, the traveler should be aware that risk of exposure to the following diseases exists in this country. This list is not all inclusive, but it is a caution concerning the more likely endemic disease risks.

Potential risk of dengue fever exists. The virus is present in this country at all times and may give rise to major outbreaks.

DISEASE RISK PROFILE

Disease	endemic	risk	hazard
Diarrheal Disease Risk		x	
Dysentery, Amoebic/Bacillary		x	
Hepatitis, Viral	x		
Rabies (esp mongoose)	x		

Food/Water Safety

Water is probably safe, but due to local variations in bacterial counts, using bottled water for the first few weeks will help the traveler adjust and decrease the chance of traveler's diarrhea. Local meat, poultry, seafood, vegetables, and fruits are safe to eat. Milk is pasteurized and safe to drink. Butter, cheese, yogurt and ice-cream are safe.

VACCINATIONS

Yellow fever—A vaccination certificate is required for travelers coming from infected areas and from or in transit through countries with active disease.

A vaccination certificate is required for children over one year of age.

Routine immunizations should be current. For infants and children through 16 years of age, refer to Chapter 4.3. A rubeola (measles) booster should be considered. Persons age 16 to 65 should receive a booster of tetanus and diphtheria every ten years. Healthy adults under age 65 do not require pneumococcal vaccine, but it is appropriate for those with chronic medical conditions. Influenza vaccine may be considered for those providing essential community services, health care workers, and those wishing to reduce the likelihood of becoming ill with influenza. Adults over 65 years of age are urged to obtain yearly influenza immunization and to insure that their tetanus and diphtheria immunizations are current. Pneumococcal vaccination is also suggested for this age group.

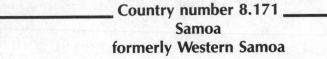

_____ Country number 8.171 _____
Samoa
formerly Western Samoa

INFECTIOUS DISEASE RISK

Malaria Risk
There is no malaria risk in this country.

Diseases of Special Risk
In addition to the worldwide hazard of tetanus and the routine and any special immunizations recommended below, the traveler should be aware that risk of exposure to the following diseases exists in this country. This list is not all inclusive, but it is a caution concerning the more likely endemic disease risks.

This country must be considered receptive to dengue fever. Intermittent epidemics in the past make renewed activity or reintroduction of the virus possible.

DISEASE RISK PROFILE

Disease	endemic	risk	hazard
Diarrheal Disease Risk		x	
Encephalitis, Japanese	x		
Filariasis			x
Helminthic Diseases (see Chapter 6.21)		x	
Typhoid Fever		x	

Food/Water Safety

Water is probably safe, but due to local variations in bacterial counts, using bottled water for the first few weeks will help the traveler adjust and decrease the chance of traveler's diarrhea. Local meat, poultry, seafood, vegetables, and fruits are safe to eat. Milk is pasteurized and safe to drink. Butter, cheese, yogurt and ice-cream are safe.

VACCINATIONS

Yellow fever—A vaccination certificate is required for travelers coming from infected areas and from or in transit through countries with active disease. A vaccination certificate is required for children over one year of age.

Routine immunizations should be current. For infants and children through 16 years of age, refer to Chapter 4.3. A rubeola (measles) booster should be considered. Persons age 16 to 65 should receive a booster of tetanus and diphtheria every ten years. Healthy adults under age 65 do not require pneumococcal vaccine, but it is appropriate for those with chronic medical conditions. Influenza vaccine may be considered for those providing essential community services, health care workers, and those wishing to reduce the likelihood of becoming ill with influenza. Adults over 65 years of age are urged to obtain yearly influenza immunization and to insure that their tetanus and diphtheria immunizations are current. Pneumococcal vaccination is also suggested for this age group.

The vaccinations listed are recommended for the traveler's protection.

Viral Hepatitis A—Vaccination is recommended for all travelers for their protection.

Typhoid fever—Vaccination is recommended for all travelers for their protection.

Selective vaccinations—These apply only to specific groups of travelers or persons on specific working assignments:

Viral Hepatitis B—Because of the high rate of healthy carriers of hepatitis B in this country, vaccination is recommended for persons on working assignments in the health care field (dentists, physicians, nurses, laboratory technicians), or working in close contact with the local population (teachers, missionaries, Peace Corps), or persons foreseeing sexual relations with local inhabitants.

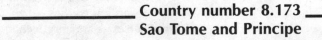

Country number 8.172
San Marino

INFECTIOUS DISEASE RISK

Malaria Risk
There is no malaria risk in this country.

Diseases of Special Risk

Food/Water Safety
Water is probably safe, but due to local variations in bacterial counts, using bottled water for the first few weeks will help the traveler adjust and decrease the chance of traveler's diarrhea. Local meat, poultry, seafood, vegetables, and fruits are safe to eat. Milk is pasteurized and safe to drink. Butter, cheese, yogurt and ice-cream are safe.

VACCINATIONS
Routine immunizations should be current. For infants and children through 16 years of age, refer to Chapter 4.3. A rubeola (measles) booster should be considered. Persons age 16 to 65 should receive a booster of tetanus and diphtheria every ten years. Healthy adults under age 65 do not require pneumococcal vaccine, but it is appropriate for those with chronic medical conditions. Influenza vaccine may be considered for those providing essential community services, health care workers, and those wishing to reduce the likelihood of becoming ill with influenza. Adults over 65 years of age are urged to obtain yearly influenza immunization and to insure that their tetanus and diphtheria immunizations are current. Pneumococcal vaccination is also suggested for this age group.
No vaccinations are required to enter this country.

Country number 8.173
Sao Tome and Principe

INFECTIOUS DISEASE RISK

Malaria Risk
Malaria is present in all parts of this country, including urban areas. The risk exists all year. See Chapter 6.31 for the weekly use of chloroquine for malaria prophylaxis for this country.

Diseases of Special Risk

In addition to the worldwide hazard of tetanus and the routine and any special immunizations recommended below, the traveler should be aware that risk of exposure to the following diseases exists in this country. This list is not all inclusive, but it is a caution concerning the more likely endemic disease risks.

DISEASE RISK PROFILE

Disease	endemic	risk	hazard
Diarrheal Diseases			x
Dracunculiasis/Guinea Worm	x		
Dysentery, Amoebic			x
Echinococcosis		x	
Filariasis			x
Giardiasis			x
Helminthic Diseases (see Chapter 6.21)			x
Hepatitis, Viral			x
Lassa Fever	x		
Leishmaniasis			
Cutaneous	x		
Visceral	x		
Polio			x
Rabies	x		
Relapsing Fever	x		
Trachoma			x
Tungiasis			x
Typhoid Fever			x
Typhus, Endemic Flea-Borne	x		
Typhus, Epidemic Louse-Borne	x		
Typhus, Scrub	x		

Food/Water Safety

All tap water used for drinking, brushing teeth, and making ice cubes should be boiled prior to use. Insure that bottled water is uncapped in your presence. Milk should be boiled to insure safety. Powdered and evaporated milk are available and safe. Avoid butter and other dairy products. All meat, poultry and seafood must be well cooked and served while hot. Pork is best avoided. Vegetables should be well cooked and served hot. Salads and mayonnaise are best avoided. Fruits with intact skins should be peeled by you just prior to consumption. Avoid cold buffets, custards, and any frozen dessert.

VACCINATIONS

Yellow fever—A vaccination certificate is required on arrival from all countries. A vaccination certificate is required for children over one year of age. Except: travelers arriving from a non-infected area and staying less than two weeks in the country. Vaccination is recommended for all travelers over one year of age for their protection.

Routine immunizations should be current. For infants and children through 16 years of age, refer to Chapter 4.3. A rubeola (measles) booster should be considered. Persons age 16 to 65 should receive a booster of tetanus and diphtheria every ten years. Healthy adults under age 65 do not require pneumococcal vaccine, but it is appropriate for those with chronic medical conditions. Influenza vaccine may be considered for those providing essential community services, health care workers, and those wishing to reduce the likelihood of becoming ill with influenza. Adults over 65 years of age are urged to obtain yearly influenza immunization and to insure that their tetanus and diphtheria immunizations are current. Pneumococcal vaccination is also suggested for this age group.

The vaccinations listed are recommended for the traveler's protection.
Poliomyelitis—A poliomyelitis booster is indicated for this country.
Viral Hepatitis A—Vaccination is recommended for all travelers for their protection.
Typhoid fever—Vaccination is recommended for all travelers for their protection.

Selective vaccinations—These apply only to specific groups of travelers or persons on specific working assignments:
Viral Hepatitis B—Because of the high rate of healthy carriers of hepatitis B in this country, vaccination is recommended for persons on working assignments in the health care field (dentists, physicians, nurses, laboratory technicians), or working in close contact with the local population (teachers, missionaries, Peace Corps), or persons foreseeing sexual relations with local inhabitants.

—————————— **Country number 8.174** ——————————
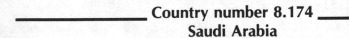
Saudi Arabia

INFECTIOUS DISEASE RISK

Malaria Risk
No malaria risk in the Eastern, Northern and Central Provinces; the high altitude areas of Asir Province and the urban areas of Jeddah, Mecca, Medina, and Taif. In other areas, including urban regions, malaria exists all year. See Chapter 6.31 with regard to the weekly use of chloroquine for malria prophylaxis.
Falciparum malaria represents 51% of malaria, therefore there is a risk of p. vivax malaria exposure. Consider use of primaquine upon return home.

Diseases of Special Risk

In addition to the worldwide hazard of tetanus and the routine and any special immunizations recommended below, the traveler should be aware that risk of exposure to the following diseases exists in this country. This list is not all inclusive, but it is a caution concerning the more likely endemic disease risks.

Schistosomiasis may be found in this country. Avoid contact with contaminated fresh water lakes, ponds, or streams. The city centers of Juddah, Mecca, Riyadh, Tabuk, Taif and the coastal areas of the Persian Gulf are risk free. Foci of infection are scattered throughout the country including the areas surrounding the above cities.

DISEASE RISK PROFILE

Disease	endemic	risk	hazard
Brucellosis			x
Cholera	x		
Dracunculiasis/Guinea Worm	x		
Diarrheal Disease Risk		x	
Echinococcosis	x		
Hepatitis, Viral	x		
Leishmaniasis			
Cutaneous	x		
Visceral	x		
Polio			x
Rabies	x		
Relapsing Fever (Tick Borne)	x		
Tapeworms	x		
Trachoma	x		
Typhoid Fever		x	
Typhus, Endemic Flea-Borne	x		
Typhus, Epidemic Louse-Borne	x		
Typhus, Scrub	x		

Food/Water Safety

All tap water used for drinking, brushing teeth, and making ice cubes should be boiled prior to use. Insure that bottled water is uncapped in your presence. Milk should be boiled to insure safety. Powdered and evaporated milk are available and safe. Avoid butter and other dairy products. All meat, poultry and seafood must be well cooked and served while hot. Pork is best avoided. Vegetables should be well cooked and served hot. Salads and mayonnaise are best avoided. Fruits with intact skins should be peeled by you just prior to consumption. Avoid cold buffets, custards, and any frozen dessert. First class hotels and restaurants in Ar Riyad (Riyadh), Az Zahran (Dhahran), and Juddah (Jidda) serve purified drinking water and reliable food. However, the hazard is left to your judgement.

VACCINATIONS

Yellow fever—A vaccination certificate is required for travelers coming from infected areas and from or in transit through countries any part of which is infected. A vaccination is required for children of all ages. Children under nine months of age should not be vaccinated due to health considerations. Please refer to the discussion in Chapter 6.63 on avoiding yellow fever vaccination in this age group.

Meningococcal meningitis—CDC and State Depertment confirmed active cases of meningococcal meningitis in Aug 1987 in this country. Active strains of menigitis serogroup A are most likely circulating among the population of this country. According to CDC comments "it would be prudent for future travelers to Saudi Arabia to receive meningococcal vaccine at least 10 days prior to departure." Vaccination may not be received more than 2 years prior to the arrival. Receipt of this vaccine is mandatory if arriving from Benin, Burkina Faso, Cameroon, Chad, Cote d' Ivoire, Egypt, Mautitania, Niger, Nigeria, Pakistan, Senegal, Sudan, Togo, Yemen, Ethiopia, India, Morocco, and the Syrian Arab Republic.

Routine immunizations should be current. For infants and children through 16 years of age, refer to Chapter 4.3. A rubeola (measles) booster should be considered. Persons age 16 to 65 should receive a booster of tetanus and diphtheria every ten years. Healthy adults under age 65 do not require pneumococcal vaccine, but it is appropriate for those with chronic medical conditions. Influenza vaccine may be considered for those providing essential community services, health care workers, and those wishing to reduce the likelihood of becoming ill with influenza. Adults over 65 years of age are urged to obtain yearly influenza immunization and to insure that their tetanus and diphtheria immunizations are current. Pneumococcal vaccination is also suggested for this age group.

The vaccinations listed are recommended for the traveler's protection.
Viral Hepatitis A—Vaccination is recommended for all travelers for their protection.
Typhoid fever—Vaccination is recommended for all travelers for their protection.

Selective vaccinations—These apply only to specific groups of travelers or persons on specific working assignments:
Viral Hepatitis B—Because of the high rate of healthy carriers of hepatitis B in this country, vaccination is recommended for persons on working assignments in the health care field (dentists, physicians, nurses, laboratory technicians), or working in close contact with the local population (teachers, missionaries, Peace Corps), or persons foreseeing sexual relations with local inhabitants.
Rabies—In this country, where rabies is a constant threat, a pre-exposure

rabies vaccination is advised for persons planning an extended stay or on working assignments (naturalists, agricultural advisors, archeologists, geologists, etc.). Although this provides adequate initial protection, a person bitten by a potentially rabid animal would still require post exposure immunization (see Chapter 6.40). Children should be cautioned not to pet dogs, cats, or other mammals.

U. S. Foreign Service:
Palestine Rd., Ruwais
Jeddah, Telephone (02) 667-0080

Between Aramco Headquarters and
Dhahran International Airport
Dahran, Telephone (03) 891-3200

Sulaimaniah District
Riyadh, Telephone (01) 464-0012
(Workweek:Saturday-Wednesday)

Canadian High Commission/Embassy Office:
6th Floor
Office Tower
Commercial and Residential Center
King Abdul Aziz St.
Jeddah, Telephone (02) 643-4900/4597/4598

Country number 8.175
Senegal

INFECTIOUS DISEASE RISK

Malaria Risk

Malaria is present in all parts of this country, including urban areas. The risk exists all year. The malaria in this country is resistant to chloroquine. The CDC recommends the use of mefloquine (Lariam) as described in Chapter 6.31 for chemical prophylaxis.

Falciparum malaria represents 85% of malaria, therefore there is a risk of p. vivax malaria exposure. Consider use of primaquine upon return home only if considerable mosquito exposure has occurred.

Diseases of Special Risk

In addition to the worldwide hazard of tetanus and the routine and any special immunizations recommended below, the traveler should be aware that

risk of exposure to the following diseases exists in this country. This list is not all inclusive, but it is a caution concerning the more likely endemic disease risks.

Schistosomiasis may be found in this country. Avoid contact with contaminated fresh water lakes, ponds, or streams.

DISEASE RISK PROFILE

Disease	endemic	risk	hazard
Dracunculiasis/Guinea Worm	x		
Diarrheal Disease Risk			x
Dysentery, Amoebic/Bacillary			x
Echinococcosis		x	
Filariasis			x
Giardiasis			x
Helminthic Diseases (see Chapter 6.21)			x
Hepatitis, Viral			x
Lassa Fever	x		
Leishmaniasis			
Cutaneous	x		
Visceral	x		
Loiasis			x
Onchocerciasis			x
Polio			x
Rabies	x		
Relapsing Fever	x		
Rift Valley Fever (in Northwest)	x		
Tapeworms			x
Trachoma			x
Trypanosomiasis, African	x		
Sleeping Sickness			
Tungiasis			x
Typhoid Fever	x		
Typhus, Endemic Flea-Borne	x		
Typhus, Epidemic Louse-Borne	x		
Typhus, Scrub	x		
Yellow Fever	x		

Food/Water Safety

All tap water used for drinking, brushing teeth, and making ice cubes should be boiled prior to use. Insure that bottled water is uncapped in your presence. Milk should be boiled to insure safety. Powdered and evaporated milk are available and safe. Avoid butter and other dairy products. All meat, poultry and seafood must be well cooked and served while hot. Pork is best avoided. Vegetables should be well cooked and served hot. Salads and mayonnaise are best avoided. Fruits with intact skins should be peeled by you just prior to consumption. Avoid cold buffets, custards, and any frozen dessert. First class hotels and restaurants in Dakar and St Louis serve purified drinking water and reliable food. However, the hazard is left to your judgement.

VACCINATIONS

Yellow fever—Vaccination is required for all travelers over 1 year of age coming from the endemic zones or infected areas. CDC recommends vaccination for all travelers over 9 months of age who will travel outside of urban areas.

Routine immunizations should be current. For infants and children through 16 years of age, refer to Chapter 4.3. A rubeola (measles) booster should be considered. Persons age 16 to 65 should receive a booster of tetanus and diphtheria every ten years. Healthy adults under age 65 do not require pneumococcal vaccine, but it is appropriate for those with chronic medical conditions. Influenza vaccine may be considered for those providing essential community services, health care workers, and those wishing to reduce the likelihood of becoming ill with influenza. Adults over 65 years of age are urged to obtain yearly influenza immunization and to insure that their tetanus and diphtheria immunizations are current. Pneumococcal vaccination is also suggested for this age group.

The vaccinations listed are recommended for the traveler's protection.

Poliomyelitis—A poliomyelitis booster is indicated for this country.

Cholera—Cholera is present in this country. Risk to western travelers is low. Immunization is not required or recommended for travel to this country due to its low effectiveness. Avoid uncooked foods and untreated water. Vaccination is advised only for persons living or working under inadequate sanitary conditions and for those with impaired defense mechanisms (see cholera disease chapter).

Viral Hepatitis A—Vaccination is recommended for all travelers for their protection.

Meningococcal meningitis—Vaccination is advised for persons traveling extensively or on working assignements in the meningitis belt of Africa's northern savannah, which stretches from the Red Sea to the Atlantic Ocean. Peak season is March and April, with risk being possible from December until June. Local area of greatest danger in in the northern third of the country.

Typhoid fever—Vaccination is recommended for all travelers for their protection.

Selective vaccinations—These apply only to specific groups of travelers or persons on specific working assignments:

Viral Hepatitis B—Because of the high rate of healthy carriers of hepatitis B in this country, vaccination is recommended for persons on working assignments in the health care field (dentists, physicians, nurses, laboratory technicians), or working in close contact with the local population (teachers, missionaries, Peace Corps), or persons foreseeing sexual relations with local inhabitants.

U. S. Foreign Service:
Avenue Jean XXIII
Dakar, Telephone 214296

Canadian High Commission/Embassy Office:
45 Ave. de la Republique
Dakar, Telephone 210290

TRAVEL ADVISORY

A U. S. Department of State Travel Advisory was in effect on 4 May 1990 when this book went to press. The entire text is included below. Travel advisories are subject to reissue, change, and cancellation at any time. Current travel advisory information is available by calling the U. S. Department of State Travel Advisory Hotline at (202) 647-5225. The current travel advisory status is also available from the Herchmer Database update system (see Chapter 2.8).

SECSTATE WSH JANUARY 4, 1990
SENEGAL—CAUTION
THE DEPARTMENT OF STATE ADVISES U.S. CITIZENS TO AVOID ANY UNNECESSARY TRAVEL IN THE NORTHERN REGION OF SEN-EGAL DUE TO UNSETTLED CONDITIONS, INCLUDING SHOOTING INCIDENTS ALONG THE SENEGAL—MAURITANIA FRONTIER. SPE-CIFICALLY, U.S. CITIZENS ARE ADVISED TO AVOID THE AREA IN THE SENEGAL RIVER REGION FROM ROSSO TO THE MALIAN BOR-DER SOUTH OF BAKEL.
DUE TO THE RUPTURE IN DIPLOMATIC RELATIONS BETWEEN SEN-EGAL AND MAURITANIA, ALL LAND AND AIR ROUTES BETWEEN SENEGAL AND MAURITANIA HAVE BEEN CLOSED. IT IS NOT POSSI-BLE TO TRAVEL DIRECTLY FROM SENEGAL TO MAURITANIA, NOR IS IT POSSIBLE TO OBTAIN A MAURITANIAN VISA IN SENEGAL.
EXPIRATION: JUNE 30, 1990

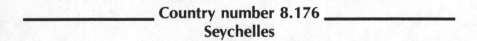

_____ **Country number 8.176** _____
Seychelles

INFECTIOUS DISEASE RISK

Malaria Risk
There is no malaria risk in this country.

Diseases of Special Risk
In addition to the worldwide hazard of tetanus and the routine and any special immunizations recommended below, the traveler should be aware that

risk of exposure to the following diseases exists in this country. This list is not all inclusive, but it is a caution concerning the more likely endemic disease risks.

This country must be considered receptive to dengue fever. Intermittent epidemics in the past make renewed activity or reintroduction of the virus possible.

DISEASE RISK PROFILE

Disease	endemic	risk	hazard
Diarrheal Disease Risk			x
Dysentery, Amoebic/Bacillary			x
Echinococcosis		x	
Filariasis			x
Giardiasis			x
Helminthic Diseases (see Chapter 6.21)			x
Hepatitis, Viral			x
Leishmaniasis			
Cutaneous	x		
Visceral	x		
Rabies	x		
Relapsing Fever	x		
Tapeworms			x
Trachoma			x
Typhoid Fever			x
Typhus, Endemic Flea-Borne	x		
Typhus, Epidemic Louse-Borne	x		
Typhus, Scrub	x		

Food/Water Safety

Water is probably safe, but due to local variations in bacterial counts, using bottled water for the first few weeks will help the traveler adjust and decrease the chance of traveler's diarrhea. Local meat, poultry, seafood, vegetables, and fruits are safe to eat. Milk is pasteurized and safe to drink. Butter, cheese, yogurt and ice-cream are safe.

VACCINATIONS

Routine immunizations should be current. For infants and children through 16 years of age, refer to Chapter 4.3. A rubeola (measles) booster should be considered. Persons age 16 to 65 should receive a booster of tetanus and diphtheria every ten years. Healthy adults under age 65 do not require pneumococcal vaccine, but it is appropriate for those with chronic medical conditions. Influenza vaccine may be considered for those providing essential community services, health care workers, and those wishing to reduce the likelihood of becoming ill with influenza. Adults over 65 years of age are urged to obtain yearly influenza immunization and to insure that their tetanus and diphtheria immunizations are current. Pneumococcal vaccination is also suggested for this age group.

No vaccinations are required to enter this country.

The vaccinations listed are recommended for the traveler's protection.

Typhoid fever—Vaccination is recommended for all travelers for their protection.

Viral Hepatitis A—Vaccination is recommended for all travelers for their protection.

U. S. Foreign Service:
Box 148
Victoria, Telephone 23921/2

Country number 8.177
Sierra Leone

INFECTIOUS DISEASE RISK

Malaria Risk

Malaria is present in all parts of this country, including urban areas. The risk exists all year. The malaria in this country is resistant to chloroquine. The CDC recommends the use of mefloquine (Lariam) as described in Chapter 6.31 for chemical prophylaxis.

Falciparum malaria represents 80% of malaria, therefore there is a risk of p. vivax malaria exposure. Consider use of primaquine upon return home.

Diseases of Special Risk

In addition to the worldwide hazard of tetanus and the routine and any special immunizations recommended below, the traveler should be aware that risk of exposure to the following diseases exists in this country. This list is not all inclusive, but it is a caution concerning the more likely endemic disease risks.

This country must be considered receptive to dengue fever. Intermittent epidemics in the past make renewed activity or reintroduction of the virus possible.

Schistosomiasis may be found in this country. Avoid contact with contaminated fresh water lakes, ponds, or streams. The coastal regions of Sierra Leone are free of infection.

DISEASE RISK PROFILE

Disease	endemic	risk	hazard
Dracunculiasis/Guinea Worm	x		
Diarrheal Disease Risk			x
Dysentery, Amoebic/Bacillary			x
Echinococcosis	x		
Filariasis			x
Giardiasis			x
Helminthic Diseases (see Chapter 6.21)			x

Disease	endemic	risk	hazard
Hepatitis, Viral			x
Lassa Fever	x		
Leishmaniasis			
Cutaneous	x		
Visceral	x		
Loiasis			x
Onchocerciasis			x
Polio			x
Rabies			x
Relapsing Fever	x		
Trachoma			x
Trypanosomiasis, African	x		
Sleeping Sickness			
Tungiasis			x
Typhoid Fever			x
Typhus, Endemic Flea-Borne	x		
Typhus, Epidemic Louse-Borne	x		
Typhus, Scrub	x		

Food/Water Safety

All tap water used for drinking, brushing teeth, and making ice cubes should be boiled prior to use. Insure that bottled water is uncapped in your presence. Milk should be boiled to insure safety. Powdered and evaporated milk are available and safe. Avoid butter and other dairy products. All meat, poultry and seafood must be well cooked and served while hot. Pork is best avoided. Vegetables should be well cooked and served hot. Salads and mayonnaise are best avoided. Fruits with intact skins should be peeled by you just prior to consumption. Avoid cold buffets, custards, and any frozen dessert.

VACCINATIONS

Yellow fever—A vaccination certificate is required for travelers coming from infected areas. A vaccination is required for children of all ages. CDC recommends vaccination for all travelers over 9 months of age who will be traveling outside of urban areas.

Routine immunizations should be current. For infants and children through 16 years of age, refer to Chapter 4.3. A rubeola (measles) booster should be considered. Persons age 16 to 65 should receive a booster of tetanus and diphtheria every ten years. Healthy adults under age 65 do not require pneumococcal vaccine, but it is appropriate for those with chronic medical conditions. Influenza vaccine may be considered for those providing essential community services, health care workers, and those wishing to reduce the likelihood of becoming ill with influenza. Adults over 65 years of age are urged to obtain yearly influenza immunization and to insure that their tetanus and diphtheria immunizations are current. Pneumococcal vaccination is also suggested for this age group.

The vaccinations listed are recommended for the traveler's protection.

Poliomyelitis—A poliomyelitis booster is indicated for this country.

Cholera—Cholera is present in this country. Risk to western travelers is low. Immunization is not required or recommended for travel to this country due to its low effectiveness. Avoid uncooked foods and untreated water. Vaccination is advised only for persons living or working under inadequate sanitary conditions and for those with impaired defense mechanisms (see chapter on cholera).

Viral Hepatitis A—Vaccination is recommended for all travelers for their protection.

Typhoid fever—Vaccination is recommended for all travelers for their protection.

Selective vaccinations—These apply only to specific groups of travelers or persons on specific working assignments:

Viral Hepatitis B—Because of the high rate of healthy carriers of hepatitis B in this country, vaccination is recommended for persons on working assignments in the health care field (dentists, physicians, nurses, laboratory technicians), or working in close contact with the local population (teachers, missionaries, Peace Corps), or persons foreseeing sexual relations with local inhabitants.

U. S. Foreign Service:
Corner Walpole and Siaka Stevens Sts.
Freetown, Telephone 26481

_____ **Country number 8.178** _____
Singapore

INFECTIOUS DISEASE RISK

Malaria Risk
There is no malaria risk in this country.

Diseases of Special Risk
In addition to the worldwide hazard of tetanus and the routine and any special immunizations recommended below, the traveler should be aware that risk of exposure to the following diseases exists in this country. This list is not all inclusive, but it is a caution concerning the more likely endemic disease risks.

Potential risk of dengue fever exists. The virus is present in this country at all times and may give rise to major outbreaks.

DISEASE RISK PROFILE

Disease	endemic	risk	hazard
Diarrheal Disease Risk	x		
Dysentery, Amoebic/Bacillary	x		
Encephalitis, Japanese	x		
Fasciolopsiasis	x		
Filariasis			x
Hepatitis, Viral	x		
Rabies	x		
Typhoid Fever	x		
Typhus, Scrub	x		

Food/Water Safety

Water is probably safe, but due to local variations in bacterial counts, using bottled water for the first few weeks will help the traveler adjust and decrease the chance of traveler's diarrhea. Milk is pasteurized and safe to drink. Butter, cheese, yogurt and ice-cream are safe. Local meat, poultry, seafood, vegetables, and fruits are safe to eat. Sinapore has been rated as one of the cleanest cities in Asia.

VACCINATIONS

Yellow fever—A vaccination certificate is required for travelers coming from infected areas and from or in transit through countries in the endemic yellow fever zone, see Chapter 6.63. A vaccination certificate is required for children over one year of age.

Routine immunizations should be current. For infants and children through 16 years of age, refer to Chapter 4.3. A rubeola (measles) booster should be considered. Persons age 16 to 65 should receive a booster of tetanus and diphtheria every ten years. Healthy adults under age 65 do not require pneumococcal vaccine, but it is appropriate for those with chronic medical conditions. Influenza vaccine may be considered for those providing essential community services, health care workers, and those wishing to reduce the likelihood of becoming ill with influenza. Adults over 65 years of age are urged to obtain yearly influenza immunization and to insure that their tetanus and diphtheria immunizations are current. Pneumococcal vaccination is also suggested for this age group.

The vaccinations listed are recommended for the traveler's protection.

Viral Hepatitis B—Because of the high rate of healthy carriers of hepatitis B in this country, vaccination is recommended for persons on working assignments in the health care field (dentists, physicians, nurses, laboratory technicians), or working in close contact with the local population (teachers, missionaries, Peace Corps), or persons foreseeing sexual relations with local inhabitants.

Japanese encephalitis—Vaccination is indicated for persons traveling extensively in rual areas or living and working near rice growing rural and suburban areas and other irrigated land, when exposure to the disease carrying mosquitoes is high. Children are especially susceptible to the infection. Sporadic cases occur on the island, all year.

Country number 8.179
Solomon Islands

INFECTIOUS DISEASE RISK

Malaria Risk

Malaria is present in all parts of this country below 400 meters, including urban areas. The risk exists all year. The malaria in this country is resistant to chloroquine. The CDC recommends the use of mefloquine (Lariam) as described in Chapter 6.31 for chemical prophylaxis.

Falciparum malaria represents 30% of malaria, therefore there is a risk of p. vivax malaria exposure. Consider use of primaquine upon return home.

Diseases of Special Risk

In addition to the worldwide hazard of tetanus and the routine and any special immunizations recommended below, the traveler should be aware that risk of exposure to the following diseases exists in this country. This list is not all inclusive, but it is a caution concerning the more likely endemic disease risks.

Potential risk of dengue fever exists. The virus is present in this country at all times and may give rise to major outbreaks.

DISEASE RISK PROFILE

Disease	endemic	risk	hazard
Diarrheal Disease Risk	x		
Encephalitis, Japanese	x		
Filariasis			x
Helminthic Diseases (see Chapter 6.21)		x	
Typhoid Fever		x	

Food/Water Safety

Water is probably safe, but due to local variations in bacterial counts, using bottled water for the first few weeks will help the traveler adjust and decrease the chance of traveler's diarrhea. Local meat, poultry, seafood, vegetables, and fruits are generally safe to eat. Milk is pasteurized and safe to drink. Butter, cheese, yogurt and ice-cream are safe.

VACCINATIONS

Yellow fever—A vaccination certificate is required for travelers coming from infected areas. A vaccination is required for children of all ages. Children under nine months of age should not be vaccinated due to health considerations. Please refer to the discussion in Chapter 6.63 on avoiding yellow fever vaccination in this age group.

Routine immunizations should be current. For infants and children through 16 years of age, refer to Chapter 4.3. A rubeola (measles) booster should be considered. Persons age 16 to 65 should receive a booster of tetanus and diphtheria every ten years. Healthy adults under age 65 do not require pneumococcal vaccine, but it is appropriate for those with chronic medical conditions. Influenza vaccine may be considered for those providing essential community services, health care workers, and those wishing to reduce the likelihood of becoming ill with influenza. Adults over 65 years of age are urged to obtain yearly influenza immunization and to insure that their tetanus and diphtheria immunizations are current. Pneumococcal vaccination is also suggested for this age group.

The vaccinations listed are recommended for the traveler's protection.
Viral Hepatitis A—Vaccination is recommended for all travelers for their protection.
Typhoid fever—Vaccination is recommended for all travelers for their protection.

Selective vaccinations—These apply only to specific groups of travelers or persons on specific working assignments:
Viral Hepatitis B—Because of the high rate of healthy carriers of hepatitis B in this country, vaccination is recommended for persons on working assignments in the health care field (dentists, physicians, nurses, laboratory technicians), or working in close contact with the local population (teachers, missionaries, Peace Corps), or persons foreseeing sexual relations with local inhabitants.

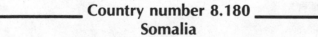

Country number 8.180
Somalia

INFECTIOUS DISEASE RISK

Malaria Risk

Malaria is present in all parts of this country, including urban areas. The risk exists all year. The malaria in this country is resistant to chloroquine. The CDC recommends the use of mefloquine (Lariam) as described in Chapter 6.31 for chemical prophylaxis.

Falciparum malaria represents 94% of malaria, therefore there is a 6% risk of p. vivax malaria exposure. Consider the use of primaquine upon return home only if considerable exposure to mosquitos has occurred.

Diseases of Special Risk

In addition to the worldwide hazard of tetanus and the routine and any special immunizations recommended below, the traveler should be aware that risk of exposure to the following diseases exists in this country. This list is not all inclusive, but it is a caution concerning the more likely endemic disease risks.

This country must be considered receptive to dengue fever. Intermittent epidemics in the past make renewed activity or reintroduction of the virus possible.

Schistosomiasis may be found in this country. Avoid contact with contaminated fresh water lakes, ponds, or streams. Well documented endemic areas are present in the southern part of the country, in the river basins of Scebeli, Juba, and Madagoi.

Meningitis is a risk during the dry season in the Savannah protion of this country, from December through March.

DISEASE RISK PROFILE

Disease	endemic	risk	hazard
Cholera	x		
Dracunculiasis/Guinea Worm	x		
Diarrheal Disease Risk			x
Dysentery, Amoebic/Bacillary			x
Echinococcosis		x	
Filariasis			x
Giardiasis			x
Helminthic Diseases (see Chapter 6.21)			x
Hepatitis, Viral			x
Leishmaniasis			
Cutaneous	x		
Visceral	x		
Polio			x
Rabies	x		
Relapsing Fever	x		
Trachoma			x
Typhoid Fever			x
Typhus, Endemic Flea-Borne	x		
Typhus, Epidemic Louse-Borne	x		
Typhus, Scrub	x		

Food/Water Safety

All tap water used for drinking, brushing teeth, and making ice cubes should be boiled prior to use. Insure that bottled water is uncapped in your presence. Milk should be boiled to insure safety. Powdered and evaporated milk are available and safe. Avoid butter and other dairy products. All meat, poultry

and seafood must be well cooked and served while hot. Pork is best avoided. Vegetables should be well cooked and served hot. Salads and mayonnaise are best avoided. Fruits with intact skins should be peeled by you just prior to consumption. Avoid cold buffets, custards, and any frozen dessert. First class hotels and restaurants in Mogadishu (Mogadiscio) serve purified drinking water and reliable food. However, the hazard is left to your judgement.

VACCINATIONS

Yellow fever—A vaccination certificate is required for all travelers coming from infected areas. A vaccination is required for children of all ages. Children under nine months of age should not be vaccinated due to health considerations. Please refer to the discussion in Chapter 6.63 on avoiding yellow fever vaccination in this age group. Vaccination is recommended for all travelers for their protection.

Routine immunizations should be current. For infants and children through 16 years of age, refer to Chapter 4.3. A rubeola (measles) booster should be considered. Persons age 16 to 65 should receive a booster of tetanus and diphtheria every ten years. Healthy adults under age 65 do not require pneumococcal vaccine, but it is appropriate for those with chronic medical conditions. Influenza vaccine may be considered for those providing essential community services, health care workers, and those wishing to reduce the likelihood of becoming ill with influenza. Adults over 65 years of age are urged to obtain yearly influenza immunization and to insure that their tetanus and diphtheria immunizations are current. Pneumococcal vaccination is also suggested for this age group.

The vaccinations listed are recommended for the traveler's protection.

Cholera—Cholera is possible in this country. Risk to western travelers is low. Immunization is not required or recommended for travel to this country due to its low effectiveness. Avoid uncooked foods and untreated water. Vaccination is advised only for persons living or working under inadequate sanitary conditions and for those with impaired defense mechanisms.

Poliomyelitis—A poliomyelitis booster is indicated for this country.

Viral Hepatitis A—Vaccination is recommended for all travelers for their protection.

Typhoid fever—Vaccination is recommended for all travelers for their protection.

Selective vaccinations—These apply only to specific groups of travelers or persons on specific working assignments:

Viral Hepatitis B—Because of the high rate of healthy carriers of hepatitis B in this country, vaccination is recommended for persons on working assignments in the health care field (dentists, physicians, nurses, laboratory technicians), or working in close contact with the local population (teachers, missionaries, Peace Corps), or persons foreseeing sexual relations with local inhabitants.

U. S. Foreign Service:
Corso Primo Luglio
Mogadishu, Telephone 28011
(Workweek:Sunday-Thursday)

TRAVEL ADVISORY

A U. S. Department of State Travel Advisory was in effect on 4 May 1990 when this book went to press. The entire text is included below. Travel advisories are subject to reissue, change, and cancellation at any time. Current travel advisory information is available by calling the U. S. Department of State Travel Advisory Hotline at (202) 647-5225. The current travel advisory status is also available from the Herchmer Database update system (see Chapter 2.8).

9FB DN37 1-1 1LA71 1 09/06/89 08:38 SECSTATE WSH SUBJECT: TRAVEL ADVISORY— SOMALIA— WARNING
1. THE DEPARTMENT OF STATE ADVISES U.S. CITIZENS TO DEFER ALL NONESSENTIAL TRAVEL TO SOMALIA AT THIS TIME DUE TO CONTINUED CIVIL STRIFE. THOSE AMERICAN CITIZENS WHO DO TRAVEL TO SOMALIA SHOULD CONTACT THE AMERICAN EMBASSY SOON AFTER ARRIVAL. THE EMBASSY IS LOCATED AT CORSO PRIMO LUGLIO IN MOGADISHU'S DOWNTOWN SHANGANI DISTRICT, TELEPHONE 20811/12/13/14.
2. THIS TRAVEL ADVISORY CANCELS THE ADVISORY DATED JULY 20, 1989 CONTAINED IN STATE 229481.
3. EXPIRATION DATE: INDEFINITE.
BAKER DEPT OF STATE WASHDC 285226 / L0400 655

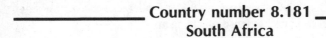

Country number 8.181
South Africa

INFECTIOUS DISEASE RISK

Malaria Risk

Malaria risk exists throughout the year in rural areas (including game parks) in the north, east, and western low altitude areas of Transvaal and in the Natal coastal areas north of 28 degrees south latitude. The malaria in this country is resistant to chloroquine. The CDC recommends the use of mefloquine (Lariam) as described in Chapter 6.31 for chemical prophylaxis.

Falciparum malaria represents 99% of malaria, therefore there is only a slight risk of p. vivax malaria exposure. There is little need to consider using primaquine upon returning home.

Diseases of Special Risk

In addition to the worldwide hazard of tetanus and the routine and any special immunizations recommended below, the traveler should be aware that risk of exposure to the following diseases exists in this country. This list is not all inclusive, but it is a caution concerning the more likely endemic disease risks.

Schistosomiasis may be found in this country. Avoid contact with contaminated fresh water lakes, ponds, or streams. Risk of infection is present in the northeastern and eastern parts of the country. In Transvaal endemic areas extend from the Limpopo River basin (on the border with Botswana, Zimbabwe and Mozambique) southwards to the northern part of the Witwatersrand mountain chain, including the Kruger National Park in the east. A small area of infection is present in Komatipoort and the Komati River basin, south of the Kruger National Park. In the east the infection extends over Natal and southwards along the coastal areas (east of Drakensberg) of Cape Province as far south as Humansdorp, about 80 km west of Port Elizabeth.

DISEASE RISK PROFILE

Disease	endemic	risk	hazard
Diarrheal Disease Risk		x	
Dysentery, Amoebic		x	
Plague	x		
Relapsing Fever	x		
Rift Valley Fever	x		
Trypanosomiasis, African Sleeping Sickness	x		
Typhoid Fever		x	
Typhus, Scrub	x		
West Nile Fever	x		

Food/Water Safety

Local water is considered safe without further treatment. Milk is pasteurized and safe to drink. Butter, cheese, yogurt and ice-cream are safe. Local meat, poultry, seafood, vegetables, and fruits are safe to eat.

VACCINATIONS

Yellow fever—A vaccination certificate is required for travelers coming from infected areas and from or in transit through countries in the endemic yellow fever zone in Africa, see Chapter 6.63. A vaccination certificate is required for children over one year of age. Travelers on scheduled airlines, whose flights have originated outside the areas regarded as infected and who are in transit through these areas, are not required to possess a certificate provided they have remained at the scheduled airport or in the adjacent town during transit. Children under one year of age are subject to isolation or surveillance, if indicated.

Routine immunizations should be current. For infants and children through 16 years of age, refer to Chapter 4.3. A rubeola (measles) booster should be considered. Persons age 16 to 65 should receive a booster of tetanus and diphtheria every ten years. Healthy adults under age 65 do not require pneumococcal vaccine, but it is appropriate for those with chronic medical conditions. Influenza vaccine may be considered for those providing essential community services, health care workers, and those wishing to reduce the likelihood of becoming ill with influenza. Adults over 65 years of age are urged to obtain yearly influenza immunization and to insure that their tetanus and diphtheria immunizations are current. Pneumococcal vaccination is also suggested for this age group.

The vaccinations listed are recommended for the traveler's protection.
Poliomyelitis—Vaccination is recommended when traveling outside the areas usually visited by tourists, traveling extensively in the interior of the country (trekkers, hikers) and for persons on working assignments in remote areas.
Cholera—Cholera is present in this country. Risk to western travelers is low. Immunization is not required or recommended for travel to this country due to its low effectiveness. Avoid uncooked foods and untreated water. Vaccination is advised only for persons living or working under inadequate sanitary conditions and for those with impaired defense mechanisms.
Viral Hepatitis A—Vaccination is recommended when traveling outside the areas usually visited by tourists, traveling extensively in the interior of the country (trekkers, hikers) and for persons on working assignments in remote areas.
Typhoid fever—Vaccination is recommended when traveling outside the areas usually visited by tourists, traveling extensively in the interior of the country (trekkers, hikers) and for persons on working assignments in remote areas.

Selective vaccinations—*These apply only to specific groups of travelers or persons on specific working assignments:*
Plague—Vaccination is recommended only for persons who may be occupationally exposed to wild rodents (anthropologists, geologists, medical personnel, missionaries, etc). The standard vaccination course must be completed before entering the plague infested area. Geographical distribution of the areas of risk for this country are present along the northern and western border with Lesotho and in Mountain Zebra National Park north of Port Elizabeth.

U. S. Foreign Service:
Thibault House
225 Pretorius St.
Pretoria, Telephone 28-4266

Broadway Industries Center
Heerengracht, Foreshore
Cape Town, Telephone 21-4280/7

Durban Bay House
29th Fl.
333 Smith St.
Durban, Telephone 32-4737

11th Fl., Kine Center
Commissioner and Kruis Sts.
Johannesburg, Telephone 33-11681

Canadian High Commission/Embassy Office:
Nedbank Plaza
5th Fl.
Corner Church and Beatrix Streets
Arcadia, Pretoria Telephone 28-7062
(mid-January to mid-June)

Reserve Bank Building
16th Floor
30 Hout Street
Capetown, Telephone 23-5240

TRAVEL ADVISORY

A U. S. Department of State Travel Advisory was in effect on 4 May 1990 when this book went to press. The entire text is included below. Travel advisories are subject to reissue, change, and cancellation at any time. Current travel advisory information is available by calling the U. S. Department of State Travel Advisory Hotline at (202) 647-5225. The current travel advisory status is also available from the Herchmer Database update system (see Chapter 2.8).

9FB DN37 2-1 1LA71 2 07/08/89 20:05
SECSTATE WSH SUBJECT:
TRAVEL ADVISORY— SOUTH AFRICA— CAUTION
1. THE DEPARTMENT OF STATE ADVISES U.S. CITIZENS THAT THE POLITICAL SITUATION IN SOUTH AFRICA REMAINS TENSE. A STATE OF EMERGENCY WITH SEVERE RESTRICTIONS ON THE ANTI-APARTHEID OPPOSITION AND THE MEDIA HAS BEEN IN EFFECT SINCE 1986. VISITORS SHOULD BE AWARE THAT ANTI-APARTHEID DEMONSTRATIONS ARE OFTEN MET WITH FORCE BY SECURITY OFFICIALS AND THE POTENTIAL FOR VIOLENT CLASHES ALWAYS EXISTS IN SUCH SITUATIONS. MANY FORMS OF POLITICAL GATH-

ERINGS AND OTHER EXPRESSIONS OF DISSENT ARE PROHIBITED OR ARE SUBJECT TO STRICT OFFICIAL CONTROLS.

2. STATE OF EMERGENCY REGULATIONS ALLOW SECURITY OFFICIALS TO DETAIN PERSONS WHOM THEY CONSIDER A THREAT TO PUBLIC ORDER AND HOLD THEM INDEFINITELY WITHOUT CHARGE. FOREIGN NATIONALS, INCLUDING U.S. CITIZENS, ARE NOT IMMUNE FROM SUCH DETENTION. SEVERE RESTRICTIONS HAVE BEEN PLACED ON THE REPORTING OR PHOTOGRAPHING OF ANTI-APARTHEID ACTIVITIES OR INCIDENTS OF UNREST. U.S. CITIZENS SHOULD EXERCISE EXTREME CAUTION IN PHOTO-GRAPHING OR FILMING ANY ASSEMBLY THAT COULD BE CON-STRUED AS ANTI-GOVERNMENT.

3. TRAVEL TO THE AREAS MOST FREQUENTED BY TOURISTS (SUCH AS CITY CENTERS, GAME PARKS, AND BEACHES) IS GEN-ERALLY SAFE. WHILE THERE HAVE BEEN NUMEROUS BOMB EX-PLOSIONS IN RECENT YEARS AGAINST CIVILIAN TARGETS, INCLUDING SHOPPING CENTERS AND BUS TERMINALS, THE FRE-QUENCY OF SUCH BOMBINGS APPEARS TO BE DIMINISHING.

4. TRAVEL TO THE SO-CALLED INDEPENDENT HOMELANDS OF BOPHUTHATSWANA, VENDA, CISKEI, AND TRANSKEI IS NOT EN-COURAGED. THE SOUTH AFRICAN GOVERNMENT CLAIMS THESE AREAS ARE INDEPENDENT COUNTRIES, BUT THE UNITED STATES AS WELL AS ALL OTHER COUNTRIES OF THE WORLD (EXCEPT SOUTH AFRICA) HAS REFUSED TO RECOGNIZE THEIR INDEPEN-DENCE. ACCESS BY U.S. CONSULAR OFFICIALS TO U.S. CITIZENS UNDER ARREST OR OTHERWISE IN DISTRESS IN THESE AREAS IS OFTEN DENIED OR SEVERELY LIMITED BY HOMELAND OFFICIALS. THESE OFFICIALS HAVE NOT CONSISTENTLY NOTIFIED U.S. CON-SULAR OFFICIALS WHEN AMERICAN CITIZENS HAVE BEEN AR-RESTED IN THE HOMELANDS.

5. DUE TO THE POTENTIAL FOR FAST-CHANGING POLITICAL DE-VELOPMENTS, U.S. CITIZENS WHO LIVE IN SOUTH AFRICA OR VISIT FOR AN EXTENDED PERIOD SHOULD REGISTER UPON AR-RIVAL AT THE U.S. CONSULATES GENERAL IN JOHANNESBURG, CAPE TOWN, OR DURBAN.

6. EXPIRATION DATE: JULY 1, 1990.

7. THIS CANCELS THE TRAVEL ADVISORY CONTAINED IN 88 STATE 199423 DATED JUNE 21, 1988. U S DEPARTMENT OF STATE WASH-INGTON D C 215719 L0482

_____ **Country number 8.182** _____
Spain

INFECTIOUS DISEASE RISK

Malaria Risk
There is no malaria risk in this country.

Diseases of Special Risk
In addition to the worldwide hazard of tetanus and the routine and any special immunizations recommended below, the traveler should be aware that risk of exposure to the following diseases exists in this country. This list is not all inclusive, but it is a caution concerning the more likely endemic disease risks.

Due to a high incidence of tuberculosis in the native population, persons with prolonged contact with local individuals should consider a pre- and post-trip tuberculosis skin tets.

DISEASE RISK PROFILE

Disease	endemic	risk	hazard
Brucellosis	x		
Diarrheal Diseases	x		
Dysentery, Amoebic	x		
Leishmaniasis			
Cutaneous	x		
Visceral	x		
Sandfly Fever	x		
Typhoid Fever	x		
Typhus, Endemic Flea-Borne	x		
Typhus, Scrub	x		
West Nile Fever	x		

Food/Water Safety
Water is probably safe, but due to local variations in bacterial counts, using bottled water for the first few weeks will help the traveler adjust and decrease the chance of traveler's diarrhea. Local meat, poultry, seafood, vegetables, and fruits are safe to eat. Milk is pasteurized and safe to drink. Butter, cheese, yogurt and ice-cream are safe.

VACCINATIONS

Routine immunizations should be current. For infants and children through 16 years of age, refer to Chapter 4.3. A rubeola (measles) booster should be considered. Persons age 16 to 65 should receive a booster of tetanus and diphtheria every ten years. Healthy adults under age 65 do not require pneumococcal vaccine, but it is appropriate for those with chronic medical

conditions. Influenza vaccine may be considered for those providing essential community services, health care workers, and those wishing to reduce the likelihood of becoming ill with influenza. Adults over 65 years of age are urged to obtain yearly influenza immunization and to insure that their tetanus and diphtheria immunizations are current. Pneumococcal vaccination is also suggested for this age group.

No vaccinations are required to enter this country.

U. S. Foreign Service:
Serrano 75
- Madrid, Telephone 276-3400/3600

Via Layetana 33; 09284
Barcelona, Telephone 319-9550

Paseo de las Delicias No. 7
Seville, Telephone 23-1885

Avenida del Ejercito, 11-3d Fl.,
Deusto-Bilbao 12
Bilbao, Telephone 435-8308/9

Canadian High Commission/Embassy Office:
Edificio Goya
Calle Nunez de Balboa 35
Madrid, Telephone 431-4300

Via Augusta 125
Atico 3A
Barcelona, Telephone 209-0634

Edificio Horizonte
Plaza de la Malagueta
Malaga, Telephone 22-3346

Country number 8.183
Western Sahara
formerly Spanish Sahara

INFECTIOUS DISEASE RISK

Malaria Risk
There is no malaria risk in this country.

VACCINATIONS

Routine immunizations should be current. For infants and children through 16 years of age, refer to Chapter 4.3. A rubeola (measles) booster should be considered. Persons age 16 to 65 should receive a booster of tetanus and diphtheria every ten years. Healthy adults under age 65 do not require pneumococcal vaccine, but it is appropriate for those with chronic medical conditions. Influenza vaccine may be considered for those providing essential community services, health care workers, and those wishing to reduce the likelihood of becoming ill with influenza. Adults over 65 years of age are urged to obtain yearly influenza immunization and to insure that their tetanus and diphtheria immunizations are current. Pneumococcal vaccination is also suggested for this age group.

No vaccinations are required to enter this country.

Country number 8.184
Sri Lanka
formerly Ceylon

INFECTIOUS DISEASE RISK

Malaria Risk

Malaria is present in all parts of this country below 800 meters, including urban areas, but excluding Colombo. The risk exists all year. The malaria in this country is resistant to chloroquine. The CDC recommends the use of mefloquine (Lariam) as described in Chapter 6.31 for chemical prophylaxis.

Falciparum malaria represents 27% of malaria, therefore there is a risk of p. vivax malaria exposure. Consider use of primaquine upon return home.

Diseases of Special Risk

In addition to the worldwide hazard of tetanus and the routine and any special immunizations recommended below, the traveler should be aware that risk of exposure to the following diseases exists in this country. This list is not all inclusive, but it is a caution concerning the more likely endemic disease risks.

Potential risk of dengue fever exists. The virus is present in this country at all times and may give rise to major outbreaks.

DISEASE RISK PROFILE

Disease	endemic	risk	hazard
Brucellosis		x	
Chikungunya Fever	x		
Cholera		x	
Diarrheal Disease Risk		x	

Disease	endemic	risk	hazard
Dysentery, Amoebic/Bacillary		x	
Echinococcosis		x	
Encephalitis, Japanese	x		
Helminthic Diseases (see Chapter 6.21)		x	
Hepatitis, Viral		x	
Leishmaniasis			
Visceral	x		
Polio			x
Rabies		x	
Sandfly Fever			x
Typhoid Fever		x	

Food/Water Safety

All tap water used for drinking, brushing teeth, and making ice cubes should be boiled prior to use. Insure that bottled water is uncapped in your presence. Milk should be boiled to insure safety. Powdered and evaporated milk are available and safe. Avoid butter and other dairy products. All meat, poultry and seafood must be well cooked and served while hot. Pork is best avoided. Vegetables should be well cooked and served hot. Salads and mayonnaise are best avoided. Fruits with intact skins should be peeled by you just prior to consumption. Avoid cold buffets, custards, and any frozen dessert. First class hotels and restaurants in Anuradhapura, Colombo, Kandy, Nuwara Eliya, and Trincomalee serve purified drinking water and reliable food. However, the hazard is left to your judgement.

VACCINATIONS

Yellow fever—A vaccination certificate is required for travelers coming from infected areas. A vaccination certificate is required for children over one year of age.

Routine immunizations should be current. For infants and children through 16 years of age, refer to Chapter 4.3. A rubeola (measles) booster should be considered. Persons age 16 to 65 should receive a booster of tetanus and diphtheria every ten years. Healthy adults under age 65 do not require pneumococcal vaccine, but it is appropriate for those with chronic medical conditions. Influenza vaccine may be considered for those providing essential community services, health care workers, and those wishing to reduce the likelihood of becoming ill with influenza. Adults over 65 years of age are urged to obtain yearly influenza immunization and to insure that their tetanus and diphtheria immunizations are current. Pneumococcal vaccination is also suggested for this age group.

The vaccinations listed are recommended for the traveler's protection.
Poliomyelitis—A poliomyelitis booster is indicated for this country.
Cholera—Risk to western travelers is low. Immunization is not required or recommended for travel to this country due to its low effectiveness. Avoid un-

cooked foods and untreated water. Vaccination is advised only for persons living or working under inadequate sanitary conditions and for those with impaired defense mechanisms.

Viral Hepatitis A—Vaccination is recommended for all travelers for their protection.

Typhoid fever—Vaccination is recommended for all travelers for their protection.

Selective vaccinations—These apply only to specific groups of travelers or persons on specific working assignments:

Viral Hepatitis B—Because of the high rate of healthy carriers of hepatitis B in this country, vaccination is recommended for persons on working assignments in the health care field (dentists, physicians, nurses, laboratory technicians), or working in close contact with the local population (teachers, missionaries, Peace Corps), or persons foreseeing sexual relations with local inhabitants.

Japanese encephalitis—Vaccination is indicated for persons traveling extensively in rual areas or living and working near rice growing rural and suburban areas and other irrigated land, when exposure to the disease carrying mosquitoes is high. Children are especially susceptible to the infection. Sporadic cases occur throughout the country with prevalence in the west. Period of transmission all year. High risk group is children under 15 years of age.

Rabies—In this country, where rabies is a constant threat, a pre-exposure rabies vaccination is advised for persons planning an extended stay or on working assignments (naturalists, agricultural advisors, archeologists, geologists, etc.). Although this provides adequate initial protection, a person bitten by a potentially rabid animal would still require post exposure immunization (see Chapter 6.40). Children should be cautioned not to pet dogs, cats, or other mammals.

U. S. Foreign Service:
201 Galle Road
Colombo 3
Colombo, Telephone 54-80-07

Canadian High Commission/Embassy Office:
6 Gregory's Road
Cinnamon Gardens
Colombo, Telephone 59-58-41/42/43/44

TRAVEL ADVISORY

A U. S. Department of State Travel Advisory was in effect on 4 May 1990 when this book went to press. The entire text is included below. Travel advisories are subject to reissue, change, and cancellation at any time. Current travel

advisory information is available by calling the U. S. Department of State Travel
Advisory Hotline at (202) 647-5225. The current travel advisory status is also
available from the Herchmer Database update system (see Chapter 2.8).

JANUARY 9, 1990
SRI LANKA—WARNING
THE DEPARTMENT OF STATE ADVISES PROSPECTIVE TRAVELERS
TO SRI LANKA THAT, THE SECURITY SITUATION REMAINS UNSET-
TLED AND VOLATILE. DISORDER AND ACTS OF VIOLENCE CON-
TINUE IN SOME PARTS OF THE COUNTRY. TRAVEL AT NIGHT,
PARTICULARLY OUTSIDE THE CITY OF COLOMBO, SHOULD BE
AVOIDED. WHILE THERE IS NO DIRECT THREAT TO AMERICANS AT
THIS TIME, A GENERAL RISK OF BEING INADVERTENTLY CAUGHT
UP IN OR NEAR ACTS OF VIOLENCE EXISTS.
ALL TRAVEL TO THE NORTH AND EAST SHOULD BE AVOIDED UN-
TIL FURTHER NOTICE. INDIAN TROOPS CONTINUE TO PULL OUT
OF THE AREA, LEAVING A SECURITY VOID IN VACATED AREAS
WHICH VARIOUS MILITANT GROUPS ARE TRYING TO FILL, OFTEN
WITH CONSIDERABLE VIOLENCE.
IN THE CENTER AND SOUTH OF THE ISLAND, THE TENSION HAS
EASED SOMEWHAT. HOWEVER, THE SINHALESE EXTREMIST
GROUP, THE JVP, AS WELL AS VARIOUS VAGILANTE GROUPS, ARE
CONTINUING TO ENGAGE IN ACTS OF VIOLENCE. TRAVELERS CAN
EXPECT TO ENCOUNTER POLICE AND MILITARY SECURITY
CHECKS AND ROAD BLOCKS AND SHOULD FOLLOW CLOSELY ANY
INSTRUCTIONS GIVEN. THE MAIN GAME PARK IN THE NORTH-
WEST, WILPATTU, REMAINS CLOSED TO TOURISTS, AND THE MAIN
PARK IN THE SOUTHEAST, RUHUNU (YALA), WHILE OPEN, IS IN A
REMOTE AREA AND EXTRA CAUTION IS URGED. VISITORS
SHOULD CHECK WITH THE EMBASSY AND THE TOURIST AUTHOR-
ITY BEFORE TRAVELING THERE OR TO THE ANCIENT CULTURAL
SITES OF POLONNARUWA AND ANURADHAPURA. TRAVELERS
SHOULD ALSO BE AWARE OF THREATS AGAINST INDIAN-OWNED
OR OPERATED ESTABLISHMENTS.
VIOLENCE, ALTHOUGH WIDESPREAD, VARIES IN INTENSITY BY
REGION AND FROM DAY TO DAY. BECAUSE THE SITUATION IN SRI
LANKA COULD CHANGE RAPIDLY, ALL AMERICAN VISITORS ARE
URGED TO REGISTER WITH THE EMBASSY UPON ARRIVAL. THE
EMBASSY IS LOCATED AT 210 GALLE ROAD, COLOMBO 3, TELE-
PHONE 548007.
EXPIRATION: JUNE 30, 1990

_____ **Country number 8.185** _____
Sudan

INFECTIOUS DISEASE RISK

Malaria Risk
Malaria is present in all parts of this country, including urban areas. The risk exists all year. The malaria in this country is resistant to chloroquine. The CDC recommends the use of mefloquine (Lariam) as described in Chapter 6.31 for chemical prophylaxis.

Falciparum malaria represents 99% of malaria, therefore there is only a slight risk of p. vivax malaria exposure. There is little need to consider use of primaquine upon return home.

Diseases of Special Risk
In addition to the worldwide hazard of tetanus and the routine and any special immunizations recommended below, the traveler should be aware that risk of exposure to the following diseases exists in this country. This list is not all inclusive, but it is a caution concerning the more likely endemic disease risks.

Schistosomiasis may be found throughout this country. Avoid contact with contaminated fresh water lakes, ponds, or streams. The exception is the swift flowing Blue Nile near Khartoum which is considered to be free of schistosomiasis.

DISEASE RISK PROFILE

Disease	endemic	risk	hazard
Dracunculiasis/Guinea Worm	x		
Diarrheal Disease Risk			x
Dysentery, Amoebic/Bacillary			x
Filariasis			x
Giardiasis			x
Helminthic Diseases (see Chapter 6.21)			x
Hepatitis, Viral			x
Leishmaniasis			
Cutaneous	x		
Visceral	x		
Onchocerciasis			x
Polio			x
Rabies	x		
Relapsing Fever	x		
Trachoma			x
Trypanosomiasis, African Sleeping Sickness	x		
Typhoid Fever			x

Disease	endemic	risk	hazard
Typhus, Endemic Flea-Borne	x		
Typhus, Epidemic Louse-Borne	x		
Typhus, Scrub	x		

Food/Water Safety

All tap water used for drinking, brushing teeth, and making ice cubes should be boiled prior to use. Insure that bottled water is uncapped in your presence. Milk should be boiled to insure safety. Powdered and evaporated milk are available and safe. Avoid butter and other dairy products. All meat, poultry and seafood must be well cooked and served while hot. Pork is best avoided. Vegetables should be well cooked and served hot. Salads and mayonnaise are best avoided. Fruits with intact skins should be peeled by you just prior to consumption. Avoid cold buffets, custards, and any frozen dessert. First class hotels and restaurants in Khartoum serve purified drinking water and reliable food. However, the hazard is left to your judgement.

VACCINATIONS

Cholera—A cholera vaccination certificate is required when coming from an infected area. Cholera is present in this country. Risk to western travelers is low. Immunization is not required or recommended for travel to this country due to its low effectiveness. Avoid uncooked foods and untreated water. Vaccination is advised only for persons living or working under inadequate sanitary conditions and for those with impaired defense mechanisms.

Yellow fever—A vaccination certificate is required for travelers coming from infected areas and from or in transit through countries in the endemic yellow fever zone, see Chapter 6.63. A vaccination certificate is required for children over one year of age. Travelers leaving this country are required to possess a vaccination certificate on their departure to an infected area or to countries which still demand such a certificate. Vaccination is recommended for all travelers for their protection. CDC recommends vaccination for all travelers over 9 months of age who will travel outside of urban areas.

Routine immunizations should be current. For infants and children through 16 years of age, refer to Chapter 4.3. A rubeola (measles) booster should be considered. Persons age 16 to 65 should receive a booster of tetanus and diphtheria every ten years. Healthy adults under age 65 do not require pneumococcal vaccine, but it is appropriate for those with chronic medical conditions. Influenza vaccine may be considered for those providing essential community services, health care workers, and those wishing to reduce the likelihood of becoming ill with influenza. Adults over 65 years of age are urged to obtain yearly influenza immunization and to insure that their tetanus and diphtheria immunizations are current. Pneumococcal vaccination is also suggested for this age group.

The vaccinations listed are recommended for the traveler's protection.

Poliomyelitis—A poliomyelitis booster is indicated for this country.

Viral Hepatitis A—Vaccination is recommended for all travelers for their protection.

Meningococcal meningitis—Vaccination is advised for persons traveling extensively or on working assignments in the meningitis belt of Africa's northern savannah, which stretches from the Red Sea to the Atlantic Ocean. Peak season is March and April. Local area of greatest danger is the southern two thirds of the country.

Typhoid fever—Vaccination is recommended for all travelers for their protection.

Selective vaccinations—These apply only to specific groups of travelers or persons on specific working assignments:

Viral Hepatitis B—Because of the high rate of healthy carriers of hepatitis B in this country, vaccination is recommended for persons on working assignments in the health care field (dentists, physicians, nurses, laboratory technicians), or working in close contact with the local population (teachers, missionaries, Peace Corps), or persons foreseeing sexual relations with local inhabitants.

Plague—Vaccination is recommended only for persons who may be occupationally exposed to wild rodents (anthropologists, geologists, medical personnel, missionaries, etc). The standard vaccination course must be completed before entering the plague infested area. Geographical distribution of areas of risk for this country are present in the southern part along the border with Zaire and Uganda.

Rabies—In this country, where rabies is a constant threat, a pre-exposure rabies vaccination is advised for persons planning an extended stay or on working assignments (naturalists, agricultural advisors, archeologists, geologists, etc.). Although this provides adequate initial protection, a person bitten by a potentially rabid animal would still require post exposure immunization (see Chapter 6.40). Children should be cautioned not to pet dogs, cats, or other mammals.

U. S. Foreign Service:
Sharia Ali Abdul Latif
Khartoum, Telephone 74700

TRAVEL ADVISORY

A U. S. Department of State Travel Advisory was in effect on 4 May 1990 when this book went to press. The entire text is included below. Travel advisories are subject to reissue, change, and cancellation at any time. Current travel advisory information is available by calling the U. S. Department of State Travel

Advisory Hotline at (202) 647-5225. The current travel advisory status is also available from the Herchmer Database update system (see Chapter 2.8).

UNITED STATES DEPARTMENT OF STATE TRAVEL ADVISORY 27 FEB 1990 SUDAN—WARNING
THE DEPARTMENT OF STATE WARNS U.S. CITIZENS TRAVELING TO SUDAN OF THE FOLLOWING:
KHARTOUM—A HIGH POTENTIAL FOR TERRORIST ACTS EXISTS IN KHARTOUM, THE CAPITAL OF SUDAN. WESTERN INTERESTS HAVE BEEN TARGETED SEVERAL TIMES IN RECENT YEARS WITH FATAL CONSEQUENCES.
SOUTHERN SUDAN: THE U.S. EMBASSY IN KHARTOUM HAS RE-PEATEDLY URGED ANY AMERI- CANS REMAINING IN THE SOUTH TO DEPART. DESPITE EXTENDED PERIODS OF VOLUNTARY CEASE-FIRES, THE CIVIL WAR IN SOUTHERN SUDAN PERSISTS AND PRI-VATE TRAVEL TO THE SOUTHERN PROVINCES OF UPPER NILE, BAHR EL-GHAZAL AND EQUATORIA REQUIRES SPECIAL PERMIS-SION FROM THE GOVERNMENT OF SUDAN. THE SAFETY OF AMERICANS RESIDING IN OR ATTEMPTING TO TRAVEL TO THESE AREAS CANNOT BE ASSURED. THE U.S. EMBASSY IS UNABLE TO PROVIDE NORMAL CONSULAR PROTECTION AND SERVICES IN SOUTHERN SUDAN.
WESTERN SUDAN: DUE TO UNSETTLED CONDITIONS INCLUDING HIGHWAY BANDITRY AND IN- CURSIONS BY SOUTHERN REBELS, TRAVELERS ARE ADVISED TO EXERCISE CAUTION IN WESTERN DARFUR PROVINCE (EXPECIALLY ALONG THE CHADIAN AND LIB-YAN BORDERS) AND SOUTHERN KORDOFAN PROVINCE.
CURFEW RULES—THE GOVERNMENT HAS ORDERED A CURFEW WHOSE RULES ARE STRICTLY ENFORCED. PERSONS FOUND OUT DURING CURFEW HOURS WITHOUT AUTHORIZATION ARE SUB-JECT TO ARREST. ALL ROAD BLOCKS MUST BE RESPECTED. U.S. TRAVELERS SHOULD CHECK WITH THE U.S. EMBASSY'S CON-SULAR SECTION, LOCATED AT SHARIA ALI ABDUL LATIF, TELE-PHONE NO. 74700 OR 74611, WITH THEIR HOTEL, OR WITH LOCAL POLICE TO DETERMINE THE CURRENT CURFEW HOURS IN EF-FECT (2300 TO 0430 AS OF OCTOBER 1989).
REGISTRATION WITH LOCAL POLICE—TRAVELERS ARE REQUIRED TO REGISTER WITH POLICE HEADQUARTERS WITHIN THREE DAYS OF ARRIVAL. TRAVELERS MUST OBTAIN POLICE PER-MISSION BE-FORE MOVING TO ANOTHER LOCATION IN SUDAN AND MUST REG-ISTER WITH POLICE WITHIN 24 HOURS OF ARRIVAL AT THE NEW LOCATION.
CURRENCY DECLARATION—TRAVELERS ARE REQUIRED TO DE-CLARE ALL CURRENCY AND TRAVELERS CHECKS BOTH ON AR-

RIVAL AND DEPARTURE FROM SUDAN. THE CURRENCY DE-
CLARATION, WHICH IS VALID FOR 60 DAYS, MUST BE STAMPED BY
CUSTOMS OFFICIALS UPON ARRIVAL. FUNDS CAN BE CON-
VERTED THROUGH AUTHORIZED OUTLETS SUCH AS BANKS AND
HOTELS ONLY ON PRESENTATION OF A VALID CURRENCY DECLA-
RATION. TRAVELERS ESTABLISHING TEMPORARY RESIDENCE IN
SUDAN (STAYING FOR MORE THAN 2 MONTHS) ARE REQUIRED TO
DEPOSIT THEIR FOREIGN FUNDS (INCLUDING TRAVELERS
CHECKS) IN FOREIGN CURRENCY ACCOUNTS. AMOUNTS LESS
THAN $5,000 US DOLLARS CAN BE RETRIEVED FROM THESE AC-
COUNTS IN TRAVELERS CHECKS UPON DEMAND. AMOUNTS IN
EXCESS OF $5,000 USD MUST BE REQUESTED THROUGH THE
BANK OF SUDAN.
EXPIRATION: NOVEMBER 1, 1990

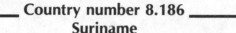

Country number 8.186
Suriname

INFECTIOUS DISEASE RISK

Malaria Risk

Malaria is present in all parts of this country, including urban areas,
except Paramaribo district and coastal areas north of 5 degrees North latitude.
The risk exists all year. The malaria in this country is resistant to chloroquine.
The CDC recommends the use of mefloquine (Lariam) as described in Chapter
6.31 for chemical prophylaxis.

Falciparum malaria represents 95% of malaria, therefore there is a slight
risk of p. vivax malaria exposure. Consider use of primaquine upon return
home only if considerable mosquito exposure has been experienced.

Diseases of Special Risk

In addition to the worldwide hazard of tetanus and the routine and any
special immunizations recommended below, the traveler should be aware that
risk of exposure to the following diseases exists in this country. This list is not
all inclusive, but it is a caution concerning the more likely endemic disease
risks.

Chaga's Disease is present in rural areas, but the exact extent is unknown.

Schistosomiasis may be found in this country. Avoid contact with contaminated fresh water lakes, ponds, or streams. Risk exists in the central part of the
coastal region, in the area surrounding the capital Paramaribo.

DISEASE RISK PROFILE

Disease	endemic	risk	hazard
Dengue Fever	x		
Diarrheal Disease Risk		x	
Dysentery, Amoebic		x	
Echinococcosis	x		
Encephalitis, Venezuelan Equine	x		
Filariasis (Bancroftian)			x
Helminthic Diseases (see Chapter 6.21)		x	
Hepatitis, Viral		x	
Leishmaniasis			
Cutaneous	x		
Mucocutaneous	x		
Polio			x
Rabies	x		
Trypanosomiasis, American	x		
Chaga's Disease			

Food/Water Safety

All tap water used for drinking, brushing teeth, and making ice cubes should be boiled prior to use. Insure that bottled water is uncapped in your presence. Milk should be boiled to insure safety. Powdered and evaporated milk are available and safe. Avoid butter and other dairy products. All meat, poultry and seafood must be well cooked and served while hot. Pork is best avoided. Vegetables should be well cooked and served hot. Salads and mayonnaise are best avoided. Fruits with intact skins should be peeled by you just prior to consumption. Avoid cold buffets, custards, and any frozen dessert. Water is safe to drink, food safe, but milk not safe without the above precautions in Paramaribo.

VACCINATIONS

Yellow fever—A vaccination certificate is required for travelers coming from infected areas. A vaccination is required for children of all ages. CDC recommends vaccination for all travelers over 9 months of age, who may travel beyond urban areas. See Chapter 6.63 concerning avoiding yellow fever vaccine in infants younger than 9 months due to increased side effects.

Routine immunizations should be current. For infants and children through 16 years of age, refer to Chapter 4.3. A rubeola (measles) booster should be considered. Persons age 16 to 65 should receive a booster of tetanus and diphtheria every ten years. Healthy adults under age 65 do not require pneumococcal vaccine, but it is appropriate for those with chronic medical conditions. Influenza vaccine may be considered for those providing essential community services, health care workers, and those wishing to reduce the likelihood of becoming ill with influenza. Adults over 65 years of age are urged to obtain yearly influenza immunization and to insure that their tetanus and diph-

theria immunizations are current. Pneumococcal vaccination is also suggested for this age group.

The vaccinations listed are recommended for the traveler's protection.
Viral Hepatitis A—Vaccination is recommended for all travelers for their protection.
Typhoid fever—Vaccination is recommended for all travelers for their protection.

U. S. Foreign Service:
Dr. Sophie Redmondstraat 120
Paramaribo, Telephone 76459, 76507

TRAVEL ADVISORY

A U. S. Department of State Travel Advisory was in effect on 4 May 1990 when this book went to press. The entire text is included below. Travel advisories are subject to reissue, change, and cancellation at any time. Current travel advisory information is available by calling the U. S. Department of State Travel Advisory Hotline at (202) 647-5225. The current travel advisory status is also available from the Herchmer Database update system (see Chapter 2.8).

JANUARY 23, 1990 SECSTATE WSH
SURINAME—CAUTION
DEPARTMENT OF STATE ADVISES U.S. CITIZENS CONSIDERING TRAVEL TO SURINAME THAT BECAUSE OF INSURGENCY IT IS DANGEROUS TO TRAVEL OUTSIDE THE CAPITAL CITY OF PARAMARIBO, ZANDERIJ AIRPORT AND THE CITY OF NIEUW NICKERIE IN WESTERN SURINAME. CAUTION SHOULD BE EXERCISED WHILE TRAVELING TO THE AREAS AROUND THE CAPITAL CITY AND NIEUW NICKERIE AND ON THE ROAD BETWEEN ZANDERIJ AIRPORT AND PARAMARIBO, PARTICULARLY AT NIGHT. IN ADDITION, ROAD TRAVEL BETWEEN PARAMARIBO AND NIEUW NICKERIE SHOULD BE AVOIDED BECAUSE OF THE REAL RISK THAT THE FERRY ACROSS THE COPPENAME RIVER COULD BE HIJACKED. AMERICANS WHO TRAVEL TO SURINAME ARE URGED TO SEEK THE LATEST TRAVEL INFORMATION AND TO REGISTER WITH THE CONSULAR SECTION OF THE AMERICAN EMBASSY AT DR. SOPHIE REDMONDSTRAAT 129, PARAMARIBO AT TEL: 72900. THE EMBASSY CAN ALSO BE REACHED ON EMERGENCY CASES AT 77881. EXPIRATION: JULY 31, 1990

Country number 8.187
Swaziland

INFECTIOUS DISEASE RISK

Malaria Risk

Malaria is present from December through March in the northern border areas of Bordergate, Lomahasha, Mhlume, and Tshaneni. The malaria in this country is resistant to chloroquine. The CDC recommends the use of mefloquine (Lariam) as described in Chapter 6.31 for chemical prophylaxis.

Falciparum malaria represents 99% of malaria, therefore there is very little risk of p. vivax malaria exposure. The traveler should probably not need to consider the use of primaquine upon return home.

Diseases of Special Risk

In addition to the worldwide hazard of tetanus and the routine and any special immunizations recommended below, the traveler should be aware that risk of exposure to the following diseases exists in this country. This list is not all inclusive, but it is a caution concerning the more likely endemic disease risks.

Schistosomiasis may be found in this country in all streams, pounds, and lakes below 4,000 feet. Avoid contact with contaminated fresh water lakes, ponds, or streams.

DISEASE RISK PROFILE

Disease	endemic	risk	hazard
Diarrheal Disease Risk		x	
Dysentery, Amoebic		x	
Hepatitis, Viral		x	
Plague	x		
Rabies			x
Relapsing Fever	x		
Rift Valley Fever	x		
Typhoid Fever		x	
Typhus, Scrub	x		

Food/Water Safety

All tap water used for drinking, brushing teeth, and making ice cubes should be boiled prior to use. Insure that bottled water is uncapped in your presence. Milk should be boiled to insure safety. Powdered and evaporated milk are available and safe. Avoid butter and other dairy products. All meat, poultry and seafood must be well cooked and served while hot. Pork is best avoided. Vegetables should be well cooked and served hot. Salads and mayonnaise are best avoided. Fruits with intact skins should be peeled by you just prior to consumption. Avoid cold buffets, custards, and any frozen dessert. Water, dairy products, and foods are safe in the city of Mbabane.

VACCINATIONS

Yellow fever—A vaccination certificate is required for travelers coming from infected areas. A vaccination is required for children of all ages. Children under nine months of age should not be vaccinated due to health considerations. Please refer to the discussion in Chapter 6.63 on avoiding yellow fever vaccination in this age group.

Routine immunizations should be current. For infants and children through 16 years of age, refer to Chapter 4.3. A rubeola (measles) booster should be considered. Persons age 16 to 65 should receive a booster of tetanus and diphtheria every ten years. Healthy adults under age 65 do not require pneumococcal vaccine, but it is appropriate for those with chronic medical conditions. Influenza vaccine may be considered for those providing essential community services, health care workers, and those wishing to reduce the likelihood of becoming ill with influenza. Adults over 65 years of age are urged to obtain yearly influenza immunization and to insure that their tetanus and diphtheria immunizations are current. Pneumococcal vaccination is also suggested for this age group.

The vaccinations listed are recommended for the traveler's protection.
Poliomyelitis—A poliomyelitis booster is indicated for this country.

Cholera—Cholera is present in this country. Risk to western travelers is low. Immunization is not required or recommended for travel to this country due to its low effectiveness. Avoid uncooked foods and untreated water. Vaccination is advised only for persons living or working under inadequate sanitary conditions and for those with impaired defense mechanisms.

Viral Hepatitis A—Vaccination is recommended for all travelers for their protection.

Typhoid fever—Vaccination is recommended for all travelers for their protection.

Selective vaccinations—These apply only to specific groups of travelers or persons on specific working assignments:
Viral Hepatitis B—Because of the high rate of healthy carriers of hepatitis B in this country, vaccination is recommended for persons on working assignments in the health care field (dentists, physicians, nurses, laboratory technicians), or working in close contact with the local population (teachers, missionaries, Peace Corps), or persons foreseeing sexual relations with local inhabitants.

U. S. Foreign Service:
Central Bank Bldg.
Warner Street
Mbabane, Telephone 22281/2/3/4/5

Country number 8.188
Sweden

INFECTIOUS DISEASE RISK

Malaria Risk
There is no malaria risk in this country.

Diseases of Special Risk
In addition to the worldwide hazard of tetanus and the routine and any special immunizations recommended below, the traveler should be aware that risk of exposure to the following diseases exists in this country. This list is not all inclusive, but it is a caution concerning the more likely endemic disease risks.

Fishing has been banned in Lake Opptjarn in central Sweden, due to high radiation levels detected in fish caught there, presumed to be due to the Chernobyl nuclear accident.

Diphyllobothrium, fish tapeworm, may contaminate the waters of the Baltic Sea area and caution is advised.

Food/Water Safety
Local water is considered safe without further treatment. Milk is pasteurized and safe to drink. Butter, cheese, yogurt and ice-cream are safe. Local meat, poultry, seafood, vegetables, and fruits are safe to eat.

VACCINATIONS

Routine immunizations should be current. For infants and children through 16 years of age, refer to Chapter 4.3. A rubeola (measles) booster should be considered. Persons age 16 to 65 should receive a booster of tetanus and diphtheria every ten years. Healthy adults under age 65 do not require pneumococcal vaccine, but it is appropriate for those with chronic medical conditions. Influenza vaccine may be considered for those providing essential community services, health care workers, and those wishing to reduce the likelihood of becoming ill with influenza. Adults over 65 years of age are urged to obtain yearly influenza immunization and to insure that their tetanus and diphtheria immunizations are current. Pneumococcal vaccination is also suggested for this age group.

No vaccinations are required to enter this country.

Selective vaccinations—These apply only to specific groups of travelers or persons on specific working assignments:

Tick-borne encephalitis—(Central European encephalitis) Vaccination is recommended for persons involved in recreational activities in forested areas (camping, hiking) or working in forestry occupations. Risk season: March to November. Risk is present in the forested areas around Uppsala down to Krisitanstad, including the islands of Gotland and Oland, and in the wooded areas around Goteborg.

U. S. Foreign Service:
Strandvagen 101
Stockholm, Telephone (08) 63-05-20

Canadian High Commission/Embassy Office:
7th Floor
Tegelbacken 4
Stockholm, Telephone 23-79-20

Country number 8.189
Switzerland

INFECTIOUS DISEASE RISK

Malaria Risk
There is no malaria risk in this country.

Food/Water Safety
Local water is considered safe without further treatment. Milk is pasteurized and safe to drink. Butter, cheese, yogurt and ice-cream are safe. Local meat, poultry, seafood, vegetables, and fruits are safe to eat.

VACCINATIONS

Routine immunizations should be current. For infants and children through 16 years of age, refer to Chapter 4.3. A rubeola (measles) booster should be considered. Persons age 16 to 65 should receive a booster of tetanus and diphtheria every ten years. Healthy adults under age 65 do not require pneumococcal vaccine, but it is appropriate for those with chronic medical conditions. Influenza vaccine may be considered for those providing essential community services, health care workers, and those wishing to reduce the likelihood of becoming ill with influenza. Adults over 65 years of age are urged to obtain yearly influenza immunization and to insure that their tetanus and diphtheria immunizations are current. Pneumococcal vaccination is also suggested for this age group.

No vaccinations are required to enter this country.

Selective vaccinations—These apply only to specific groups of travelers or persons on specific working assignments:

Tick-borne encephalitis—(Central European encephalitis) Vaccination is recommended for persons involved in recreational activities in forested areas (camping, hiking) or working in forestry occupations. Risk season: March to November. Risk is present in the wooded areas around Schaffhausen and north of Winterhur, and around the western shore of Lake Thun.

U. S. Foreign Service:
Jubilaeumstrasse 93
Bern, Telephone 43-70-11

Zollikerstrasse 141
Zurich, Telephone 55-25-66

11 Route de Pregny
Geneva, Telephone 34-60-31

Canadian High Commission/Embassy Office:
Kirchenfeldstrasse 88
Berne, Telephone 44-63-81/5

―――――――――― **Country number 8.190** ――――――――――
Syrian Arab Republic

INFECTIOUS DISEASE RISK

Malaria Risk
Malaria is present from May through October in this country below 600 meters, except Deir-es-Zor and Sweida. There is no risk of malaria in urban areas. The CDC recommends a weekly dose of Chloroquine for travels to areas of risk (see Chapter 6.31).

Falciparum malaria represents 1% of malaria, therefore there is a risk of p. vivax malaria exposure. Consider the use of primaquine upon return home if heavy exposure to mosquitos has been encountered.

Diseases of Special Risk
In addition to the worldwide hazard of tetanus and the routine and any special immunizations recommended below, the traveler should be aware that risk of exposure to the following diseases exists in this country. This list is not

all inclusive, but it is a caution concerning the more likely endemic disease risks.

Schistosomiasis may be found in this country. Avoid contact with contaminated fresh water lakes, ponds, or streams.Infection occurs in the northeastern part of the country. Contaminated areas include: The Balikh River basin from the town of Tall al Abyad to Ar Raqqah in the Governorate of Raqqah; Jaghjaghah, Jarah, Sublak and Ramila river systems, their tirbutaries and canals in the Governorate of Hasakah; the river Euphrates from the areas of Ar Raqqah to the Syrian border including its tributaries Khabur and Balikh.

Meningitis is a potential threat to travelers in this country. The CDC does not recommend this vaccine for travelers here at this time. The Department of State recommends that its personnel receive meningococcal meningitis vaccine. The WHO reports active disease.

DISEASE RISK PROFILE

Disease	endemic	risk	hazard
Brucellosis			x
Cholera	x		
Dracunculiasis/Guinea Worm	x		
Diarrheal Disease Risk			x
Dysentery, Amoebic/Bacillary			x
Echinococcosis	x		
Hepatitis, Viral		x	
Leishmaniasis			
Cutaneous	x		
Visceral	x		
Polio			x
Rabies	x		
Relapsing Fever	x		
Tapeworms	x		
Trachoma		x	
Typhoid Fever		x	
Typhus, Endemic Flea-Borne	x		
Typhus, Scrub	x		

Food/Water Safety

All tap water used for drinking, brushing teeth, and making ice cubes should be boiled prior to use. Insure that bottled water is uncapped in your presence. Milk should be boiled to insure safety. Powdered and evaporated milk are available and safe. Avoid butter and other dairy products. All meat, poultry and seafood must be well cooked and served while hot. Pork is best avoided. Vegetables should be well cooked and served hot. Salads and mayonnaise are best avoided. Fruits with intact skins should be peeled by you just prior to consumption. Avoid cold buffets, custards, and any frozen dessert. First class hotels and restaurants in Dimashq (Damascus) and Halab (Aleppo) serve purified drinking water and reliable food. However, the hazard is left to your judgement.

VACCINATIONS

Yellow fever—A vaccination certificate is required for travelers coming from infected areas. A vaccination is required for children of all ages. Children under nine months of age should not be vaccinated due to health considerations. Please refer to the discussion in Chapter 6.63 on avoiding yellow fever vaccination in this age group.

Routine immunizations should be current. For infants and children through 16 years of age, refer to Chapter 4.3. A rubeola (measles) booster should be considered. Persons age 16 to 65 should receive a booster of tetanus and diphtheria every ten years. Healthy adults under age 65 do not require pneumococcal vaccine, but it is appropriate for those with chronic medical conditions. Influenza vaccine may be considered for those providing essential community services, health care workers, and those wishing to reduce the likelihood of becoming ill with influenza. Adults over 65 years of age are urged to obtain yearly influenza immunization and to insure that their tetanus and diphtheria immunizations are current. Pneumococcal vaccination is also suggested for this age group.

The vaccinations listed are recommended for the traveler's protection.
Poliomyelitis—A poliomyelitis booster is indicated for this country.
Viral Hepatitis A—Vaccination is recommended for all travelers for their protection.
Typhoid fever—Vaccination is recommended for all travelers for their protection.

Selective vaccinations—These apply only to specific groups of travelers or persons on specific working assignments:
Viral Hepatitis B—Because of the high rate of healthy carriers of hepatitis B in this country, vaccination is recommended for persons on working assignments in the health care field (dentists, physicians, nurses, laboratory technicians), or working in close contact with the local population (teachers, missionaries, Peace Corps), or persons foreseeing sexual relations with local inhabitants.

Plague—Vaccination is recommended only for persons who may be occupationally exposed to wild rodents (anthropologists, geologists, medical personnel, missionaries, etc). The standard vaccination course must be completed before entering the plague infested area. Geographical distribution of the areas of risk for this country are present in the northern and eastern parts of the country bordering Iraq.

Rabies—In this country, where rabies is a constant threat, a pre-exposure rabies vaccination is advised for persons planning an extended stay or on working assignments (naturalists, agricultural advisors, archeologists, geologists, etc.). Although this provides adequate initial protection, a person bitten by a potentially rabid animal would still require post exposure immunization (see

Chapter 6.40). Children should be cautioned not to pet dogs, cats, or other mammals.

U. S. Foreign Service:
Abu Rumaneh, Al Mansur St., No. 2
Damascus, Telephone 333052/416, 332315/557/814

Country number 8.191
United Republic of Tanzania

INFECTIOUS DISEASE RISK

Malaria Risk
Malaria is present in all parts of this country, including urban areas. The risk exists all year. The malaria in this country is resistant to chloroquine. The CDC recommends the use of mefloquine (Lariam) as described in Chapter 6.31 for chemical prophylaxis.

Falciparum malaria represents 85% of malaria, therefore there is a risk of p. vivax malaria exposure. Consider use of primaquine upon return home if an unusual amount of mosquito exposure was encountered.

Diseases of Special Risk
In addition to the worldwide hazard of tetanus and the routine and any special immunizations recommended below, the traveler should be aware that risk of exposure to the following diseases exists in this country. This list is not all inclusive, but it is a caution concerning the more likely endemic disease risks.

Schistosomiasis may be found in this country. Avoid contact with contaminated fresh water lakes, ponds, or streams. Known areas of infection are present in the northern part of the country along the eastern and southern shore of Lake Victoria including the islands; and in the Tanga District in the northeastern part of the country. Infection has also been reported from the area of Kasulu, Kigoma District near the northern shore of Lake Tanganyika; the area of Lake Rukwa and the area of Songea in southwestern Tanzania; foci are present in Kidodi, Kitatu and Ruaha, northeast of Iringa. The islands of Zanzibar and Pemba are infected.

The Centers for Disease Control recommends travelers to the northern portions of this country receive meningococcal vaccine as an epidemic of meningitis occurred during late 1989 in the Arusha area. No cases of meningitis has been reported in travelers, but this area includes the most popular tourist destinations in the country.

DISEASE RISK PROFILE

Disease	endemic	risk	hazard
Dracunculiasis/Guinea Worm	x		
Diarrheal Disease Risk			x
Dysentery, Amoebic/Bacillary			x
Echinococcosis		x	
Filariasis			x
Giardiasis			x
Helminthic Diseases (see Chapter 6.21)			x
Hepatitis, Viral			x
Leishmaniasis			
Cutaneous	x		
Visceral	x		
Onchocerciasis			x
Plague	x		
Polio			x
Rabies	x		
Relapsing Fever	x		
Trachoma			x
Trypanosomiasis, African Sleeping Sickness	x		
Typhoid Fever			x
Typhus, Endemic Flea-Borne	x		
Typhus, Epidemic Louse-Borne	x		
Typhus, Scrub	x		

Food/Water Safety

All tap water used for drinking, brushing teeth, and making ice cubes should be boiled prior to use. Insure that bottled water is uncapped in your presence. Milk should be boiled to insure safety. Powdered and evaporated milk are available and safe. Avoid butter and other dairy products. All meat, poultry and seafood must be well cooked and served while hot. Pork is best avoided. Vegetables should be well cooked and served hot. Salads and mayonnaise are best avoided. Fruits with intact skins should be peeled by you just prior to consumption. Avoid cold buffets, custards, and any frozen dessert. First class hotels and restaurants in Arusha, Dar Es Salaam, Moshi, and Zanzibar serve purified drinking water and reliable food. However, the hazard is left to your judgement.

VACCINATIONS

Cholera—A cholera vaccination certificate is required for travelers intending to enter the islands of Pemba and Zanzibar. Although cholera vaccination certificate is not officially required for entering Tanzania, travelers may be asked to show proof of cholera vaccination upon arrival. (Complaints to that effect have been lodged by tourists.) To avoid harassment IAMAT suggests vaccination. One injection is sufficient to satisfy health officials, but it must be obtained 10 days prior to arrival.

Yellow fever—A vaccination certificate is required for travelers coming from infected areas and from or in transit through countries in the endemic yellow fever zone, see Chapter 6.63. A vaccination certificate is required for children over one year of age. Vaccination is recommended for all travelers for their protection. CDC recommends vaccination for all travelers over 9 months of age who are going to northwestern forest regions.

Routine immunizations should be current. For infants and children through 16 years of age, refer to Chapter 4.3. A rubeola (measles) booster should be considered. Persons age 16 to 65 should receive a booster of tetanus and diphtheria every ten years. Healthy adults under age 65 do not require pneumococcal vaccine, but it is appropriate for those with chronic medical conditions. Influenza vaccine may be considered for those providing essential community services, health care workers, and those wishing to reduce the likelihood of becoming ill with influenza. Adults over 65 years of age are urged to obtain yearly influenza immunization and to insure that their tetanus and diphtheria immunizations are current. Pneumococcal vaccination is also suggested for this age group.

The vaccinations listed are recommended for the traveler's protection.
Poliomyelitis—A poliomyelitis booster is indicated for this country.
Viral Hepatitis A—Vaccination is recommended for all travelers for their protection.
Typhoid fever—Vaccination is recommended for all travelers for their protection.

Selective vaccinations—*These apply only to specific groups of travelers or persons on specific working assignments:*
Viral Hepatitis B—Because of the high rate of healthy carriers of hepatitis B in this country, vaccination is recommended for persons on working assignments in the health care field (dentists, physicians, nurses, laboratory technicians), or working in close contact with the local population (teachers, missionaries, Peace Corps), or persons foreseeing sexual relations with local inhabitants.
Plague—Vaccination is recommended only for persons who may be occupationally exposed to wild rodents (anthropologists, geologists, medical personnel, missionaries, etc). The standard vaccination course must be completed before entering the plague infested area. Geographical distribution of the areas of risk for this country are present south of Lake Victoria and along the eastern part of the border with Kenya (Tanga Province).

TRAVEL ADVISORY

A U. S. Department of State Travel Advisory was in effect on 4 May 1990 when this book went to press. The entire text is included below. Travel advisories are subject to reissue, change, and cancellation at any time. Current travel advisory information is available by calling the U. S. Department of State Travel Advisory Hotline at (202) 647-5225. The current travel advisory status is also available from the Herchmer Database update system (see Chapter 2.8).

DECEMBER 26, 1989
TANZANIA—CAUTION
THE DEPARTMENT OF STATE ADVISES U.S. CITIZENS THAT WHEN TRAVELING IN TANZANIA THEY MAY ENCOUNTER PARTICULAR PROBLEMS. THESE INCLUDE:
—SPEEDY CONSULAR ASSISTANCE TO ARRESTED OR DETAINED AMERICAN CITIZENS CANNOT BE GUARANTEED, BECAUSE THE U.S. EMBASSY IS NOT ALWAYS PROMPTLY NOTIFIED OF SUCH INCIDENTS BY SECURITY OFFICIALS.
—SEVERE RESTRICTIONS ON PHOTOGRAPHY ARE ENFORCED THROUGHOUT THE COUNTRY.
—STREET CRIME CONTINUES TO BE A MAJOR PROBLEM IN URBAN AREAS.
—BEARERS OF PASSPORTS CONTAINING EVIDENCE OF TRAVEL TO SOUTH AFRICA WILL ENCOUNTER PROBLEMS UPON TRYING TO ENTER TANZANIA.
TANZANIAN POLICE AND PRISON OFFICIALS HAVE CONSISTENTLY FAILED TO INFORM IMMEDIATELY THE U.S. EMBASSY IN DAR ES SALAAM THAT AMERICAN CITIZENS WERE ARRESTED OR DETAINED, THUS IMPEDING THE ABILITY OF THE UNITED STATES GOVERNMENT TO PROVIDE TIMELY AND EFFECTIVE CONSULAR ASSISTANCE. TRAVEL TO OUT-OF-THE-WAY TOURIST ATTRACTIONS OR REMOTE REGIONS SHOULD BE UNDERTAKEN ONLY AFTER CONSULTATION WITH TANZANIAN AUTHORITIES.
THE PHOTOGRAPHING OF MILITARY INSTALLATIONS IS FORBIDDEN. PEOPLE HAVE BEEN DETAINED AND/OR HAD THEIR CAMERAS AND FILM CONFISCATED FOR TAKING PICTURES OF HOSPITALS, SCHOOLS, INDUSTRIAL SITES, AIRPORTS, HARBORS, RAILWAY STATIONS, BRIDGES, GOVERNMENT BUILDINGS AND OTHER SUCH FACILITIES, WHICH ARE NOT ALWAYS CLEARLY IDENTIFIED AS BEING OFF-LIMITS TO PHOTOGRAPHERS. THERE ARE NO RESTRICTIONS ON THE USE OF CAMERAS IN THE GAME PARKS.
VISITORS TO TANZANIA SHOULD HAVE A COMBINATION OF TWO ANTI-MALARIALS, WHICH SHOULD BE STARTED AT LEAST ONE WEEK PRIOR TO ENTRY AND CONTINUE FOR FOUR WEEKS AFTER DEPARTURE FROM TANZANIA. ALL VISITORS TO TANZANIA MUST HAVE VALID CHOLERA AND YELLOW FEVER INOCULATIONS STAMPED IN THEIR HEALTH CARDS 10 DAYS PRIOR TO ARRIVAL.
(Editors note: malaria prophylaxis has been changed since this bulletin

was posted to mefloquine as indicated above under the malaria section). INCIDENTS OF CRIME ARE ON THE INCREASE ALL OVER TANZANIA IN BOTH URBAN AND RURAL AREAS. MOST OF THE INCIDENTS ARE MUGGINGS, THEFTS OF AND FROM VEHICLES, AND BREAK-INS OF RESIDENCES. VISITORS SHOULD EXERCISE EXTREME CAUTION IN SAFEGUARDING DOCUMENTS AND VALUABLES SUCH AS PASSPORTS, TRAVELERS 'CHECKS, CAMERAS AND JEWELRY. TRAVEL BY NIGHT IN THE COUNTRYSIDE IS DANGEROUS DUE TO THE HAZARDOUS ROAD CONDITIONS AND INCREASING ATTACKS BY BANDITS WHO ARE FREQUENTLY ARMED. WALKING ALONE, EITHER BY DAY OR NIGHT, ALONG BEACHES IS NOT RECOMMENDED BECAUSE OF THE DANGER POSED BY PICKPOCKETS AND MUGGERS. VISITORS DRIVING IN THE VARIOUS GAME PARKS ARE ADVISED TO HAVE AN EXPERIENCED DRIVER OR GAME PARK OFFICIAL ACCOMPANY THEM, AS ATTACKS HAVE ALSO TAKEN PLACE IN SAFARI AREAS.

RECENTLY CONFIDENCE MEN POSING AS POLICEMEN HAVE STOPPED TOURISTS AND ASKED TO SEE THE CURRENCY DECLARATION FORMS WHICH EACH VISITOR OBTAINS UPON ARRIVAL IN TANZANIA. THIS FORM CONFIRMS THAT THE VISITOR IS IN POSSESSION OF CASH (AND HOW MUCH), AND THE CASH IS SEIZED—IN EFFECT STOLEN. VISITORS ARE STRONGLY ADVISED THAT CURRENCY EXCHANGE SHOULD BE TRANSACTED ONLY AT BANKS AND NOT ON THE STREET WITH BLACK MARKETEERS, PARTICULARLY SINCE POLICE POST AS MONEY EXCHANGERS FROM TIME TO TIME.

IN ADDITION, THERE ARE SOME VERY PARTICULAR RULES THAT APPLY REGARDING TRAVELERS WHO HAVE VISITED SOUTH AFRICA. TRAVELERS WITH SOUTH AFRICAN RESIDENCE PERMITS OR MULTIPLE ENTRY VISAS FOR SOUTH AFRICA ARE BARRED FROM ENTERING TANZANIA AND ARE OFTEN LABELED "PROHIBITED IMMIGRANTS" IF THEY ATTEMPT ENTRY. OTHER TRAVELERS CARRYING ANY EVIDENCE OF PRIOR OR FUTURE TRAVEL TO SOUTH AFRICA WILL ENCOUNTER PROBLEMS ON ARRIVAL AND MAY BE DENIED ENTRY. IN GENERAL, THE EMBASSY RECOMMENDS THAT TRAVELERS NOT PLAN TO VISIT TANZANIA AND SOUTH AFRICA ON THE SAME TRIP. TRAVELERS WHO HAVE SOUTH AFRICAN STAMPS IN THEIR PASSPORTS AND WHO WISH TO ATTEMPT TO ENTER TANZANIA MAY APPLY AT THE TANZANIAN EMBASSY, 2139 'R' NW, WASHINGTON, D.C. FOR A "REFERRED VISA."

ALL VISITORS, WHETHER BUSINESS PEOPLE OR TOURISTS, ARE URGED TO REGISTER AT THE AMERICAN EMBASSY, 30 LAIBON ROAD, DAR ES SALAAM, TELEPHONE NUMBER 37501-4.

OFFICE HOURS 8:30AM—3:30PM THOSE ENTERING THROUGH KI-LIMANJARO AIRPORT CAN REGISTER WITH THE CONSULAR AGENT, MRS. MARIE BENSON, ENGIRA ROAD, ARUSHA, TELE-PHONE NUMBER 2369.
EXPIRATION: JULY 30,1990

Country number 8.192
Thailand

INFECTIOUS DISEASE RISK

Malaria Risk

Malaria is present in all parts of this country, including urban areas. The risk exists all year. Resistance has developed in this country to chloroquine, Fansidar, and mefloquine—particularly in refugee camp areas. There is no risk of malaria in urban areas. Prophylaxis in not necessary if your trip is confined to these areas. Current prophylaxis recommendations can be obtained from Malaria Branch, Centers for Disease Control by your physician. Doxycycline 100 mg taken once daily has been a recent recommendation for prophylaxis in this area.

Falciparum malaria represents 70% of malaria, therefore there is a 30% risk of p. vivax malaria exposure. Consider use of primaquine upon return home.

Diseases of Special Risk

In addition to the worldwide hazard of tetanus and the routine and any special immunizations recommended below, the traveler should be aware that risk of exposure to the following diseases exists in this country. This list is not all inclusive, but it is a caution concerning the more likely endemic disease risks.

Schistosomiasis may be found in this country. Avoid contact with contaminated fresh water lakes, ponds, or streams. Infection has been reported from the following towns and adjacent areas:Phitsanulok and Phichit along the Yom River (about 480 km north of Bangkok); Ubon on the Mun River (443 km northeast of Bangkok); Surat Thani and Nakhon Si Thammarat in southern Thailand.

DISEASE RISK PROFILE

Disease	endemic	risk	hazard
Chikungunya Fever	x		
Cholera	x		
Opisthorchiasis	x		
Dengue Fever	x		
Diarrheal Disease Risk		x	

Disease	endemic	risk	hazard
Dysentery, Amoebic/Bacillary	x		
Encephalitis, Japanese	x		
Fasciolopsiasis	x		
Filariasis			x
Hepatitis, Viral	x		
Polio	x		
Rabies	x		
Trachoma	x		
Typhoid Fever	x		
Typhus, Scrub	x		

Food/Water Safety

All tap water used for drinking, brushing teeth, and making ice cubes should be boiled prior to use. Insure that bottled water is uncapped in your presence. Milk should be boiled to insure safety. Powdered and evaporated milk are available and safe. Avoid butter and other dairy products. All meat, poultry and seafood must be well cooked and served while hot. Pork is best avoided. Vegetables should be well cooked and served hot. Salads and mayonnaise are best avoided. Fruits with intact skins should be peeled by you just prior to consumption. Avoid cold buffets, custards, and any frozen dessert. First class hotels and restaurants in Bangkok (Krung Thep), Chiang Mai, and Sattahip serve purified drinking water and reliable food. However, the hazard is left to your judgement.

VACCINATIONS

Yellow fever—A vaccination certificate is required for travelers coming from infected areas and from or in transit through countries in the endemic yellow fever zone, see Chapter 6.63. A vaccination certificate is required for children over one year of age.

Routine immunizations should be current. For infants and children through 16 years of age, refer to Chapter 4.3. A rubeola (measles) booster should be considered. Persons age 16 to 65 should receive a booster of tetanus and diphtheria every ten years. Healthy adults under age 65 do not require pneumococcal vaccine, but it is appropriate for those with chronic medical conditions. Influenza vaccine may be considered for those providing essential community services, health care workers, and those wishing to reduce the likelihood of becoming ill with influenza. Adults over 65 years of age are urged to obtain yearly influenza immunization and to insure that their tetanus and diphtheria immunizations are current. Pneumococcal vaccination is also suggested for this age group.

The vaccinations listed are recommended for the traveler's protection.
Poliomyelitis—A poliomyelitis booster is indicated for this country.
Viral Hepatitis A—Vaccination is recommended for all travelers for their protection.

Typhoid fever—Vaccination is recommended for all travelers for their protection.

Selective vaccinations—These apply only to specific groups of travelers or persons on specific working assignments:
Viral Hepatitis B—Because of the high rate of healthy carriers of hepatitis B in this country, vaccination is recommended for persons on working assignments in the health care field (dentists, physicians, nurses, laboratory technicians), or working in close contact with the local population (teachers, missionaries, Peace Corps), or persons foreseeing sexual relations with local inhabitants.
Japanese encephalitis—Vaccination is indicated for persons traveling extensively in rual areas or living and working near rice growing rural and suburban areas and other irrigated land, when exposure to the disease carrying mosquitoes is high. Children are especially susceptible to the infection. Outbreaks occur mostly in the northern region (Chiang Mai valley), with sporadic cases reported from the areas of Sukhothai and Phitsanulok and the southern region. Period of transmission in the north: June to October; in the south: all year.
Rabies—In this country, where rabies is a constant threat, a pre-exposure rabies vaccination is advised for persons planning an extended stay or on working assignments (naturalists, agricultural advisors, archeologists, geologists, etc.). Although this provides adequate initial protection, a person bitten by a potentially rabid animal would still require post exposure immunization (see Chapter 6.40). Children should be cautioned not to pet dogs, cats, or other mammals.

U. S. Foreign Service:
95 Wireless Rd.
Bangkok, Telephone 252-5040/5171

Vidhayanond Rd.
Chiang Mai, Telephone 234566/7

9 Sadao Rd.
Songkhla, Telephone 311-589

35/6 Supakitjanya Rd.
Udorn, Telephone 221548

Canadian High Commission/Embassy Office:
Boonmitr Bldg.
11th Floor
138 Silom Road
Bangkok, Telephone 234-1561/8

TRAVEL ADVISORY

A U. S. Department of State Travel Advisory was in effect on 4 May 1990 when this book went to press. The entire text is included below. Travel advisories are subject to reissue, change, and cancellation at any time. Current travel advisory information is available by calling the U. S. Department of State Travel Advisory Hotline at (202) 647-5225. The current travel advisory status is also available from the Herchmer Database update system (see Chapter 2.8).

05/03/86 15:42
SECSTATE WSH
SUBJECT:
TRAVEL ADVISORY— THAILAND
1. THE DEPARTMENT OF STATE ADVISES U.S. CITIZENS TRAVELING TO NORTH THAILAND THAT TREKKING IN CERTAIN REMOTE AREAS ALONG THE THAI-BURMESE BORDER IN THE NORTHERN PARTS OF CHIANG MAI, CHIANG RAI AND MAE HONG SON PROVINCES CAN BE HAZARDOUS AND SHOULD BE AVOIDED. BANDITS AND ARMED DRUG TRAFFICKERS ARE KNOWN TO POSE A THREAT TO TRAVELERS IN THE AREA. IF TREKKING IN NORTH THAILAND IS CONTEMPLATED, THE DEPARTMENT RECOMMENDS U.S. CITIZENS FIRST CONTACT THE U.S. CONSULATE IN CHIANG MAI FOR AN ASSESSMENT OF THE CURRENT SITUATION AND FOR SPECIFIC AREAS WHICH ARE KNOWN TO BE DANGEROUS. TRAVEL TO THE MORE POPULATED AREAS OF CHIANG RAI, CHIANG MAI AND MAE KHONG SON, PARTICULARLY TO AND FROM THE PROVINCIAL CAPITALS, IS SAFE AND DOES NOT REQUIRE SPECIAL PRECAUTIONS.
2. EXPIRATION DATE: INDEFINITE.
3. TRAVEL ADVISORY CONTAINED IN STATE 15713 OF JANUARY 19, 1983 IS CANCELED.
DEPARTMENT OF STATE WASHDC 138992/0171L

_____ **Country number 8.193** _____
Togo

INFECTIOUS DISEASE RISK

Malaria Risk

Malaria is present in all parts of this country, including urban areas. The risk exists all year. The malaria in this country is resistant to chloroquine. The CDC recommends the use of mefloquine (Lariam) as described in Chapter 6.31 for chemical prophylaxis.

Falciparum malaria represents 85% of malaria, therefore there is a risk of p. vivax malaria exposure. Consider the use of primaquine upon return home.

Diseases of Special Risk

In addition to the worldwide hazard of tetanus and the routine and any special immunizations recommended below, the traveler should be aware that risk of exposure to the following diseases exists in this country. This list is not all inclusive, but it is a caution concerning the more likely endemic disease risks.

This country must be considered receptive to dengue fever. Intermittent epidemics in the past make renewed activity or reintroduction of the virus possible.

Schistosomiasis may be found in this country. Avoid contact with contaminated fresh water lakes, ponds, or streams.

DISEASE RISK PROFILE

Disease	endemic	risk	hazard
Dracunculiasis/Guinea Worm			x
Diarrheal Disease Risk			x
Dysentery, Amoebic/Bacillary			x
Echinococcosis		x	
Filariasis			x
Giardiasis			x
Helminthic Diseases (see Chapter 6.21)			x
Hepatitis, Viral			x
Lassa Fever	x		
Leishmaniasis			
Cutaneous	x		
Visceral	x		
Onchocerciasis			x
Polio			x
Rabies	x		
Relapsing Fever	x		
Trachoma			x
Trypanosomiasis, African Sleeping Sickness			x
Tungiasis			x

Disease	endemic	risk	hazard
Typhoid Fever			x
Typhus, Endemic Flea-Borne	x		
Typhus, Epidemic Louse-Borne	x		
Typhus, Scrub	x		

Food/Water Safety

All tap water used for drinking, brushing teeth, and making ice cubes should be boiled prior to use. Insure that bottled water is uncapped in your presence. Milk should be boiled to insure safety. Powdered and evaporated milk are available and safe. Avoid butter and other dairy products. All meat, poultry and seafood must be well cooked and served while hot. Pork is best avoided. Vegetables should be well cooked and served hot. Salads and mayonnaise are best avoided. Fruits with intact skins should be peeled by you just prior to consumption. Avoid cold buffets, custards, and any frozen dessert. First class hotels and restaurants in Lome serve purified drinking water and reliable food. However, the hazard is left to your judgement.

VACCINATIONS

Yellow fever—A vaccination certificate is required on arrival from all countries. A vaccination certificate is required for children over one year of age. CDC recommends vaccination for all travelers over 9 months of age who plan to go outside of urban areas.

Routine immunizations should be current. For infants and children through 16 years of age, refer to Chapter 4.3. A rubeola (measles) booster should be considered. Persons age 16 to 65 should receive a booster of tetanus and diphtheria every ten years. Healthy adults under age 65 do not require pneumococcal vaccine, but it is appropriate for those with chronic medical conditions. Influenza vaccine may be considered for those providing essential community services, health care workers, and those wishing to reduce the likelihood of becoming ill with influenza. Adults over 65 years of age are urged to obtain yearly influenza immunization and to insure that their tetanus and diphtheria immunizations are current. Pneumococcal vaccination is also suggested for this age group.

The vaccinations listed are recommended for the traveler's protection.

Poliomyelitis—A poliomyelitis booster is indicated for this country.

Viral Hepatitis A—Vaccination is recommended for all travelers for their protection.

Meningococcal meningitis—Vaccination is advised for persons traveling extensively or on working assignements in the meningitis belt of Africa's northern savannah, which stretches from the Red Sea to the Atlantic Ocean. Peak season is March and April. Local area of greatest danger is in the northern third of the country.

Typhoid fever—Vaccination is recommended for all travelers for their protection.

Selective vaccinations—These apply only to specific groups of travelers or persons on specific working assignments:

Viral Hepatitis B—Because of the high rate of healthy carriers of hepatitis B in this country, vaccination is recommended for persons on working assignments in the health care field (dentists, physicians, nurses, laboratory technicians), or working in close contact with the local population (teachers, missionaries, Peace Corps), or persons foreseeing sexual relations with local inhabitants.

U. S. Foreign Service:
Rue Pelletier Caventou and Rue Vouban
Lome, Telephone 29-91

Country number 8.194
Tokelau Islands

INFECTIOUS DISEASE RISK

Malaria Risk
There is no malaria risk in this country.

Diseases of Special Risk
In addition to the worldwide hazard of tetanus and the routine and any special immunizations recommended below, the traveler should be aware that risk of exposure to the following diseases exists in this country. This list is not all inclusive, but it is a caution concerning the more likely endemic disease risks.

This country must be considered receptive to dengue fever. Intermittent epidemics in the past make renewed activity or reintroduction of the virus possible.

DISEASE RISK PROFILE

Disease	endemic	risk	hazard
Diarrheal Disease Risk		x	
Encephalitis, Japanese	x		
Filariasis			x
Helminthic Diseases (see Chapter 6.21)		x	
Typhoid Fever		x	

Food/Water Safety
All tap water used for drinking, brushing teeth, and making ice cubes should be boiled prior to use. Insure that bottled water is uncapped in your presence. Milk should be boiled to insure safety. Powdered and evaporated milk are available and safe. Avoid butter and other dairy products. All meat, poultry

and seafood must be well cooked and served while hot. Pork is best avoided. Vegetables should be well cooked and served hot. Salads and mayonnaise are best avoided. Fruits with intact skins should be peeled by you just prior to consumption. Avoid cold buffets, custards, and any frozen dessert.

VACCINATIONS

Routine immunizations should be current. For infants and children through 16 years of age, refer to Chapter 4.3. A rubeola (measles) booster should be considered. Persons age 16 to 65 should receive a booster of tetanus and diphtheria every ten years. Healthy adults under age 65 do not require pneumococcal vaccine, but it is appropriate for those with chronic medical conditions. Influenza vaccine may be considered for those providing essential community services, health care workers, and those wishing to reduce the likelihood of becoming ill with influenza. Adults over 65 years of age are urged to obtain yearly influenza immunization and to insure that their tetanus and diphtheria immunizations are current. Pneumococcal vaccination is also suggested for this age group.

No vaccinations are required to enter this country.

—————————— Country number 8.195 ——————————
Tonga

INFECTIOUS DISEASE RISK

Malaria Risk
There is no malaria risk in this country.

Diseases of Special Risk
In addition to the worldwide hazard of tetanus and the routine and any special immunizations recommended below, the traveler should be aware that risk of exposure to the following diseases exists in this country. This list is not all inclusive, but it is a caution concerning the more likely endemic disease risks.

This country must be considered receptive to dengue fever. Intermittent epidemics in the past make renewed activity or reintroduction of the virus possible.

DISEASE RISK PROFILE

Disease	endemic	risk	hazard
Diarrheal Disease Risk		x	
Encephalitis, Japanese	x		
Filariasis			x
Helminthic Diseases (see Chapter 6.21)		x	
Typhoid Fever		x	

Food/Water Safety

All tap water used for drinking, brushing teeth, and making ice cubes should be boiled prior to use. Insure that bottled water is uncapped in your presence. Milk should be boiled to insure safety. Powdered and evaporated milk are available and safe. Avoid butter and other dairy products. All meat, poultry and seafood must be well cooked and served while hot. Pork is best avoided. Vegetables should be well cooked and served hot. Salads and mayonnaise are best avoided. Fruits with intact skins should be peeled by you just prior to consumption. Avoid cold buffets, custards, and any frozen dessert. Food, water, and milk products in Nuku'alofa on Togatapu Island are considered safe, however, the hazard is left to your judgement.

VACCINATIONS

Yellow fever—A vaccination certificate is required for travelers coming from infected areas. A vaccination certificate is required for children over one year of age.

Routine immunizations should be current. For infants and children through 16 years of age, refer to Chapter 4.3. A rubeola (measles) booster should be considered. Persons age 16 to 65 should receive a booster of tetanus and diphtheria every ten years. Healthy adults under age 65 do not require pneumococcal vaccine, but it is appropriate for those with chronic medical conditions. Influenza vaccine may be considered for those providing essential community services, health care workers, and those wishing to reduce the likelihood of becoming ill with influenza. Adults over 65 years of age are urged to obtain yearly influenza immunization and to insure that their tetanus and diphtheria immunizations are current. Pneumococcal vaccination is also suggested for this age group.

The vaccinations listed are recommended for the traveler's protection.

Viral Hepatitis A—Vaccination is recommended for all travelers for their protection.

Typhoid fever—Vaccination is recommended for all travelers for their protection.

Selective vaccinations—These apply only to specific groups of travelers or persons on specific working assignments:

Viral Hepatitis B—Because of the high rate of healthy carriers of hepatitis B in this country, vaccination is recommended for persons on working assignments in the health care field (dentists, physicians, nurses, laboratory technicians), or working in close contact with the local population (teachers, missionaries, Peace Corps), or persons foreseeing sexual relations with local inhabitants.

Country number 8.196
Trinidad and Tobago

INFECTIOUS DISEASE RISK

Malaria Risk

There is no malaria risk in this country.

Diseases of Special Risk

In addition to the worldwide hazard of tetanus and the routine and any special immunizations recommended below, the traveler should be aware that risk of exposure to the following diseases exists in this country. This list is not all inclusive, but it is a caution concerning the more likely endemic disease risks.

Dengue fever is active in this country. The World Health Organization reported 1,200 cases through mid-February 1990. No deaths were reported. Mosquito protection is important. See Chapters 5.4 and 6.9.

DISEASE RISK PROFILE

Disease	endemic	risk	hazard
Diarrheal Disease Risk		x	
Dysentery, Amoebic/Bacillary		x	
Hepatitis, Viral	x		
Rabies (esp mopngoose)	x		

Food/Water Safety

Water is probably safe, but due to local variations in bacterial counts, using bottled water for the first few weeks will help the traveler adjust and decrease the chance of traveler's diarrhea. Local meat, poultry, seafood, vegetables, and fruits are safe to eat. Milk is pasteurized and safe to drink. Butter, cheese, yogurt and ice-cream are safe.

VACCINATIONS

Yellow fever—A vaccination certificate is required for travelers coming from infected areas and from or in transit through countries with active disease. A vaccination certificate is required for children over one year of age. Vaccination is recommended when traveling outside the areas usually visited by tourists, traveling extensively in the interior of the country (trekkers, hikers) and for persons on working assignments in remote areas. CDC recommends vaccination for all travelers over 9 months of age who may travel outside of urban areas. Some countries will require a yellow fever vaccination to enter their country after visiting this country.

Routine immunizations should be current. For infants and children through 16 years of age, refer to Chapter 4.3. A rubeola (measles) booster

should be considered. Persons age 16 to 65 should receive a booster of tetanus and diphtheria every ten years. Healthy adults under age 65 do not require pneumococcal vaccine, but it is appropriate for those with chronic medical conditions. Influenza vaccine may be considered for those providing essential community services, health care workers, and those wishing to reduce the likelihood of becoming ill with influenza. Adults over 65 years of age are urged to obtain yearly influenza immunization and to insure that their tetanus and diphtheria immunizations are current. Pneumococcal vaccination is also suggested for this age group.

U. S. Foreign Service:
15 Queen's Park West
Port-of-Spain, Telephone 62-26371

Canadian High Commission/Embassy Office:
Huggins Building
72 South Quay
Port-of-Spain, Telephone 62-37254/8

Country number 8.197
Truk Islands
formerly Pacific Island Trust Territory

INFECTIOUS DISEASE RISK

Malaria Risk
There is no malaria risk in this country.

Diseases of Special Risk
In addition to the worldwide hazard of tetanus and the routine and any special immunizations recommended below, the traveler should be aware that risk of exposure to the following diseases exists in this country. This list is not all inclusive, but it is a caution concerning the more likely endemic disease risks.

DISEASE RISK PROFILE

Disease	endemic	risk	hazard
Dengue Fever	x		
Diarrheal Diseases		x	
Encephalitis, Japanese	x		
Filariasis			x
Helminthic Diseases (see Chapter 6.21)		x	
Typhoid Fever		x	

Food/Water Safety

On main islands: Local water is considered safe without further treatment. Milk is pasteurized and safe to drink. Butter, cheese, yogurt and ice-cream are safe. Local meat, poultry, seafood, vegetables, and fruits are safe to eat.

VACCINATIONS

Routine immunizations should be current. For infants and children through 16 years of age, refer to Chapter 4.3. A rubeola (measles) booster should be considered. Persons age 16 to 65 should receive a booster of tetanus and diphtheria every ten years. Healthy adults under age 65 do not require pneumococcal vaccine, but it is appropriate for those with chronic medical conditions. Influenza vaccine may be considered for those providing essential community services, health care workers, and those wishing to reduce the likelihood of becoming ill with influenza. Adults over 65 years of age are urged to obtain yearly influenza immunization and to insure that their tetanus and diphtheria immunizations are current. Pneumococcal vaccination is also suggested for this age group.

No vaccinations are required to enter this country.

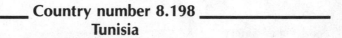

Country number 8.198
Tunisia

INFECTIOUS DISEASE RISK

Malaria Risk

There is no malaria risk in this country.

Diseases of Special Risk

In addition to the worldwide hazard of tetanus and the routine and any special immunizations recommended below, the traveler should be aware that risk of exposure to the following diseases exists in this country. This list is not all inclusive, but it is a caution concerning the more likely endemic disease risks.

Schistosomiasis may be found in this country. Avoid contact with contaminated fresh water lakes, ponds, or streams. Areas of infection are present in central and southern Tunisia. Risk exists in areas of (including towns) Gafsa, Sidi Mansour, Tozeur, the villages surrounding the Shott el Jerid, Gabes, Matmata and Foum Tataouine. The oases of southern Tunisia should be considered infected.

DISEASE RISK PROFILE

Disease	endemic	risk	hazard
Brucellosis		x	
Dengue Fever	x		
Diarrheal Disease Risk		x	
Dysentery, Amoebic/Bacillary		x	
Echinococcosis	x		
Giardiasis		x	
Helminthic Diseases (see Chapter 6.21)		x	
Hepatitis, Viral		x	
Lassa Fever	x		
Leishmaniasis			
Cutaneous	x		
Visceral	x		
Polio	x		
Rabies	x		
Relapsing Fever	x		
Sandfly Fever	x		
Trachoma	x		
Tungiasis			x
Typhoid Fever		x	
Typhus	x		

Food/Water Safety

All tap water used for drinking, brushing teeth, and making ice cubes should be boiled prior to use. Insure that bottled water is uncapped in your presence. Milk should be boiled to insure safety. Powdered and evaporated milk are available and safe. Avoid butter and other dairy products. All meat, poultry and seafood must be well cooked and served while hot. Pork is best avoided. Vegetables should be well cooked and served hot. Salads and mayonnaise are best avoided. Fruits with intact skins should be peeled by you just prior to consumption. Avoid cold buffets, custards, and any frozen dessert. First class hotels and restaurants in Bizerte, Hamamet, Jerba (Djerba), Sfax, Sousse, and Tunis serve purified drinking water and reliable food. However, the hazard is left to your judgement. The water, food, and dairy products in the city of Quairouan are considered safe.

VACCINATIONS

Yellow fever—A vaccination certificate is required for travelers coming from infected areas. A vaccination certificate is required for children over one year of age.

Routine immunizations should be current. For infants and children through 16 years of age, refer to Chapter 4.3. A rubeola (measles) booster should be considered. Persons age 16 to 65 should receive a booster of tetanus and diphtheria every ten years. Healthy adults under age 65 do not require pneumococcal vaccine, but it is appropriate for those with chronic medical conditions. Influenza vaccine may be considered for those providing essential

community services, health care workers, and those wishing to reduce the likelihood of becoming ill with influenza. Adults over 65 years of age are urged to obtain yearly influenza immunization and to insure that their tetanus and diphtheria immunizations are current. Pneumococcal vaccination is also suggested for this age group.

The vaccinations listed are recommended for the traveler's protection.
Poliomyelitis—Vaccination is recommended when traveling outside the areas usually visited by tourists, traveling extensively in the interior of the country (trekkers, hikers) and for persons on working assignments in remote areas.
Viral Hepatitis A—Vaccination is recommended when traveling outside the areas usually visited by tourists, traveling extensively in the interior of the country (trekkers, hikers) and for persons on working assignments in remote areas.
Typhoid fever—Vaccination is recommended when traveling outside the areas usually visited by tourists, traveling extensively in the interior of the country (trekkers, hikers) and for persons on working assignments in remote areas.

Selective vaccinations—These apply only to specific groups of travelers or persons on specific working assignments:
Rabies—In this country, where rabies is a constant threat, a pre-exposure rabies vaccination is advised for persons planning an extended stay or on working assignments (naturalists, agricultural advisors, archeologists, geologists, etc.). Although this provides adequate initial protection, a person bitten by a potentially rabid animal would still require post exposure immunization (see Chapter 6.40). Children should be cautioned not to pet dogs, cats, or other mammals.

U. S. Foreign Service:
144 Ave. de la Liberte
Tunis, Telephone 282-566

Canadian High Commission/Embassy Office:
3 Rue du Senegal
Place Palestine
Tunis, Telephone 286-577/337/619/004

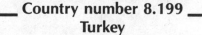

Country number 8.199
Turkey

INFECTIOUS DISEASE RISK

Malaria Risk
Malaria is found from March through October only in Cukorova/Amikova

areas and south east Anatolia. There is no risk of malaria is Istanbul, Ankara and other major cities. CDC recommends a weekly dose of chloroquine to areas of risk (see Chapter 6.31).

Falciparum malaria represents 1% of malaria, therefore there is a risk of p. vivax malaria exposure. Consider use of primaquine upon return home.

Diseases of Special Risk

In addition to the worldwide hazard of tetanus and the routine and any special immunizations recommended below, the traveler should be aware that risk of exposure to the following diseases exists in this country. This list is not all inclusive, but it is a caution concerning the more likely endemic disease risks.

DISEASE RISK PROFILE

Disease	endemic	risk	hazard
Brucellosis			x
Cholera	x		
Diarrheal Diseases		x	
Dracunculiasis/Guinea Worm	x		
Dysentery, Amoebic	x		
Echinococcosis	x		
Hepatitis, Viral		x	
Leishmaniasis			
Cutaneous	x		
Visceral	x		
Rabies		x	
Relapsing Fever	x		
Tapeworms	x		
Trachoma		x	
Typhoid Fever		x	
Typhus, Endemic Flea-Borne	x		
Typhus, Scrub	x		

Food/Water Safety

Water unsafe in Middle East, but may be safe in European Turkey (Istanbul, Edirne), but cautions are advised. Milk products and cold food is unsafe in Middle East, but considered safe in European Turkey.

VACCINATIONS

Routine immunizations should be current. For infants and children through 16 years of age, refer to Chapter 4.3. A rubeola (measles) booster should be considered. Persons age 16 to 65 should receive a booster of tetanus and diphtheria every ten years. Healthy adults under age 65 do not require pneumococcal vaccine, but it is appropriate for those with chronic medical conditions. Influenza vaccine may be considered for those providing essential community services, health care workers, and those wishing to reduce the likelihood of becoming ill with influenza. Adults over 65 years of age are urged to

obtain yearly influenza immunization and to insure that their tetanus and diphtheria immunizations are current. Pneumococcal vaccination is also suggested for this age group.

No vaccinations are required to enter this country.

The vaccinations listed are recommended for the traveler's protection.

Poliomyelitis—Vaccination is recommended when traveling outside the areas usually visited by tourists, traveling extensively in the interior of the country (trekkers, hikers) and for persons on working assignments in remote areas.

Viral Hepatitis A—Vaccination is recommended when traveling outside the areas usually visited by tourists, traveling extensively in the interior of the country (trekkers, hikers) and for persons on working assignments in remote areas.

Typhoid fever—Vaccination is recommended when traveling outside the areas usually visited by tourists, traveling extensively in the interior of the country (trekkers, hikers) and for persons on working assignments in remote areas.

Selective vaccinations—These apply only to specific groups of travelers or persons on specific working assignments:

Viral Hepatitis B—Because of the high rate of healthy carriers of hepatitis B in this country, vaccination is recommended for persons on working assignments in the health care field (dentists, physicians, nurses, laboratory technicians), or working in close contact with the local population (teachers, missionaries, Peace Corps), or persons foresceing sexual relations with local inhabitants.

Rabies—In this country, where rabies is a constant threat, a pre-exposure rabies vaccination is advised for persons planning an extended stay or on working assignments (naturalists, agricultural advisors, archeologists, geologists, etc.). Although this provides adequate initial protection, a person bitten by a potentially rabid animal would still require post exposure immunization (see Chapter 6.40). Children should be cautioned not to pet dogs, cats, or other mammals.

U. S. Foreign Service:
110 Ataturk Blvd.
Ankara, Telephone 26-54-70

104-108 Mesrutlyet Caddesi, Tepebasl
Istanbul, Telephone 143-6200/09

92 Ataturk Caddesi
Izmir, Telephone 14-94-26, 13-13-69

Ataturk Caddesi
Adana, Telephone 39-106, 42-145, 43-774

Canadian High Commission/Embassy Office:
Nenehatun Caddesi
75 Gaziosmanpasa Ankara,
Telephone 27-58-03/4/5

TRAVEL ADVISORY

A U. S. Department of State Travel Advisory was in effect on 4 May 1990 when this book went to press. The entire text is included below. Travel advisories are subject to reissue, change, and cancellation at any time. Current travel advisory information is available by calling the U. S. Department of State Travel Advisory Hotline at (202) 647-5225. The current travel advisory status is also available from the Herchmer Database update system (see Chapter 2.8).

9FB DN37 2-1 1LA71 2 07/15/89 03:21
SECSTATE WSH SUBJECT:
TRAVEL ADVISORY—TURKEY—CAUTION
1. THE DEPARTMENT OF STATE ADVISES U.S. CITIZENS THAT SPORADIC ATTACKS BY SEPARATISTS CONTINUE TO OCCUR AGAINST TURKISH JANDARMA, POLICE AND CIVILIANS IN SEVERAL SOUTH-EASTERN PROVINCES OF TURKEY. TRAVELERS TO THE SOUTH-EASTERN REGION ARE ADVISED TO COOPERATE WITH TRAVEL RESTRICTIONS OR OTHER SECURITY MEASURES IMPOSED BY TURKISH AUTHORITIES. TRAVELERS ARE FURTHER CAUTIONED NOT TO TRAVEL OFF MAIN HIGHWAYS IN REMOTE RURAL AREAS OR GENERALLY TO DRIVE AT NIGHT. U.S. CITIZENS COMTEMPLAT-ING TRAVEL SHOULD CHECK UPON ARRIVAL WITH THE U.S. EM-BASSY IN ANKARA OR THE U.S. CONSULATES IN ISTANBUL, IZMIR, AND ADANA TO LEARN WHETHER THERE ARE ANY SPECIAL TRA-VEL RESTRICTIONS IN PARTICULAR PROVINCES.
2. UNAUTHORIZED PURCHASE OR REMOVAL FROM TURKEY OF ANTIQUITIES OR OTHER IMPORTANT CULTURAL ARTIFACTS IS STRICTLY FORBIDDEN. VIOLATION OF THIS LAW MAY RESULT IN IMPRISONMENT. TRAVELERS WHO WISH TO PURCHASE SUCH ITEMS SHOULD ALWAYS OBTAIN FROM THE SELLER A RECEIPT AND THE OFFICIAL MUSEUM EXPORT CERTIFICATE REQUIRED BY LAW.
3. EXPIRATION: JULY 11, 1990.
4. THIS REPLACES THE PREVIOUS TRAVEL ADVISORY DATED AU-GUST 18, 1988 CONTAINED IN 88 STATE 272259.
DEPARTMENT OF STATE OC/T ROOM 5440 WASHINGTON DC 20520
4615/L0914

————————— Country Number 8.200 —————————
Tuvalu
formerly Ellice Islands

INFECTIOUS DISEASE RISK

Malaria Risk
There is no malaria risk in this country.

Diseases of Special Risk
In addition to the worldwide hazard of tetanus and the routine and any special immunizations recommended below, the traveler should be aware that risk of exposure to the following diseases exists in this country. This list is not all inclusive, but it is a caution concerning the more likely endemic disease risks.

This country must be considered receptive to dengue fever. Intermittent epidemics in the past make renewed activity or reintroduction of the virus possible.

DISEASE RISK PROFILE

Disease	endemic	risk	hazard
Diarrheal Disease Risk		x	
Encephalitis, Japanese	x		
Filariasis			x
Helminthic Diseases (see Chapter 6.21)		x	
Typhoid Fever		x	

Food/Water Safety
All tap water used for drinking, brushing teeth, and making ice cubes should be boiled prior to use. Insure that bottled water is uncapped in your presence. Milk should be boiled to insure safety. Powdered and evaporated milk are available and safe. Avoid butter and other dairy products. All meat, poultry and seafood must be well cooked and served while hot. Pork is best avoided. Vegetables should be well cooked and served hot. Salads and mayonnaise are best avoided. Fruits with intact skins should be peeled by you just prior to consumption. Avoid cold buffets, custards, and any frozen dessert.

VACCINATIONS

Yellow fever—A vaccination certificate is required for travelers coming from infected areas and from or in transit through countries in the endemic yellow fever zone, see Chapter 6.63. A vaccination certificate is required for children over one year of age.

Routine immunizations should be current. For infants and children through 16 years of age, refer to Chapter 4.3. A rubeola (measles) booster should be considered. Persons age 16 to 65 should receive a booster of tetanus

and diphtheria every ten years. Healthy adults under age 65 do not require pneumococcal vaccine, but it is appropriate for those with chronic medical conditions. Influenza vaccine may be considered for those providing essential community services, health care workers, and those wishing to reduce the likelihood of becoming ill with influenza. Adults over 65 years of age are urged to obtain yearly influenza immunization, and to insure that their tetanus and diphtheria immunizations are current. Pneumococcal vaccination is also suggested for this age group.

The vaccinations listed are recommended for the traveler's protection.
Viral Hepatitis A—Vaccination is recommended for all travelers for their protection.
Typhoid fever—Vaccination is recommended for all travelers for their protection.

Selective vaccinations—These apply only to specific groups of travelers or persons on specific working assignments:
Viral Hepatitis B—Because of the high rate of healthy carriers of hepatitis B in this country, vaccination is recommended for persons on working assignments in the health care field (dentists, physicians, nurses, laboratory technicians), or working in close contact with the local population (teachers, missionaries, Peace Corps), or persons foreseeing sexual relations with local inhabitants.

Country Number 8.201
Uganda

INFECTIOUS DISEASE RISK

Malaria Risk
Malaria is present in all parts of this country, including urban areas, below 1800 meters. The malaria in this country is resistant to chloroquine. The CDC recommends the use of mefloquine (Lariam) as described in Chapter 6.31 for chemical prophylaxis.
Falciparum malaria represents 82% of malaria, therefore there is a risk of p. vivax malaria exposure. Consider use of primaquine upon return home.

Diseases of Special Risk
In addition to the worldwide hazard of tetanus and the routine and any special immunizations recommended below, the traveler should be aware that risk of exposure to the following diseases exists in this country. This list is not all inclusive, but it is a caution concerning the more likely endemic disease risks.

Schistosomiasis may be found in this country. Avoid contact with contaminated fresh water lakes, ponds, or streams.

Louse-borne typhus is cosmopolitan in distribution and is present wherever groups of persons are crowded together under conditions of poor sanitation and malnutrition. Risk exists for persons living or working in remote areas of the country (anthropologists, archeologists, geologists, medical personnel, missionaries, etc.). Freedom from louse infestation is the most effective protection against typhus.

DISEASE RISK PROFILE

Disease	endemic	risk	hazard
Dracunculiasis/Guinea Worm	x		
Diarrheal Disease Risk			x
Dysentery, Amoebic/Bacillary			x
Echinococcosis		x	
Filariasis			x
Helminthic Diseases (see Chapter 6.21)			x
Hepatitis, Viral			x
Leishmaniasis			
Cutaneous	x		
Visceral	x		
Onchocerciasis			x
Polio			x
Rabies		x	
Relapsing Fever	x		
Trachoma			x
Trypanosomiasis, African Sleeping Sickness		x	
Typhoid Fever			x
Typhus, Endemic Flea-Borne	x		
Typhus, Epidemic Louse-Borne	x		
Typhus, Scrub	x		

Food/Water Safety

All tap water used for drinking, brushing teeth, and making ice cubes should be boiled prior to use. Insure that bottled water is uncapped in your presence. Milk should be boiled to insure safety. Powdered and evaporated milk are available and safe. Avoid butter and other dairy products. All meat, poultry and seafood must be well cooked and served while hot. Pork is best avoided. Vegetables should be well cooked and served hot. Salads and mayonnaise are best avoided. Fruits with intact skins should be peeled by you just prior to consumption. Avoid cold buffets, custards, and any frozen dessert. First class hotels and restaurants in Fort Portal, Gulu, and Kampala serve purified drinking water and reliable food. However, the hazard is left to your judgement.

VACCINATIONS

Yellow fever—A vaccination certificate is required on arrival from any country in the yellow fever endemic zone (see Chapter 6.63) children over one year of age. CDC recommends vaccination for all travelers over 9 months of age who will be traveling outside of urban areas.

Routine immunizations should be current. For infants and children through 16 years of age, refer to Chapter 4.3. A rubeola (measles) booster should be considered. Persons age 16 to 65 should receive a booster of tetanus and diphtheria every ten years. Healthy adults under age 65 do not require pneumococcal vaccine, but it is appropriate for those with chronic medical conditions. Influenza vaccine may be considered for those providing essential community services, health care workers, and those wishing to reduce the likelihood of becoming ill with influenza. Adults over 65 years of age are urged to obtain yearly influenza immunization, and to insure that their tetanus and diphtheria immunizations are current. Pneumococcal vaccination is also suggested for this age group.

The vaccinations listed are recommended for the traveler's protection.
Poliomyelitis—A poliomyelitis booster is indicated for this country.
Viral Hepatitis A—Vaccination is recommended for all travelers for their protection.
Typhoid fever—Vaccination is recommended for all travelers for their protection.

Selective vaccinations—These apply only to specific groups of travelers or persons on specific working assignments:
Viral Hepatitis B—Because of the high rate of healthy carriers of hepatitis B in this country, vaccination is recommended for persons on working assignments in the health care field (dentists, physicians, nurses, laboratory technicians), or working in close contact with the local population (teachers, missionaries, Peace Corps), or persons foreseeing sexual relations with local inhabitants.
Meningitis—Due to the increased number of cases of meningococcal meningitis in Kampala, the CDC has indicated that vaccination against meningitis is a reasonsable precaution, but has not issued a formal recommendation for routine vaccination for travelers.
Plague—Vaccination is recommended only for persons who may be occupationally exposed to wild rodents (anthropologists, geologists, medical personnel, missionaries, etc). The standard vaccination course must be completed before entering the plague infested area. Geographical distributions of the areas of risk for this country are present along the border with Zaire and Sudan.
Rabies—In this country, where rabies is a constant threat, a pre-exposure rabies vaccination is advised for persons planning an extended stay or on working assignments (naturalists, agricultural advisors, archeologists, geologists, etc.). Although this provides adequate initial protection, a person bitten by a potentially rabid animal would still require post exposure immunization (see

Chapter 6.40). Children should be cautioned not to pet dogs, cats, or other mammals.

U. S. Foreign Service:
British High Commission Building
Obote Avenue
Kampala, Telephone 59791

TRAVEL ADVISORY
A U. S. Department of State Travel Advisory was in effect on 4 May 1990 when this book went to press. The entire text is included below. Travel advisories are subject to reissue, change, and cancellation at any time. Current travel advisory information is available by calling the U. S. Department of State Travel Advisory Hotline at (202) 647-5225. The current travel advisory status is also available from the Herchmer Database update system (see Chapter 2.8).

10 DECEMBER 1989 SECSTATE WSH
SUBJECT:
TRAVEL ADVISORY—UGANDA—CAUTION
1. THE DEPARTMENT OF STATE ADVISES THAT WHILE TRAVEL TO KAMPALA AND OTHER PARTS OF UGANDA IS AT PRESENT GENERALLY SAFE, MOST OF NORTHERN UGANDA IS UNSAFE FOR AMERICAN TRAVELERS.
2. BECAUSE OF INTERMITTENT ACTIVITY BY BANDIT AND REBEL GROUPS, TRAVEL TO AREAS NORTH OF, AND INCLUDING, THE TOWNS OF KUMI, SOROTI, LIRA AND GULA TO THE KENYAN AND SUDANESE BORDERS, SHOULD BE AVOIDED COMPLETELY. MURCHISON FALLS NATIONAL PARK SHOULD BE AVOIDED. TRAVEL TO THE WEST NILE REGION (CITY OF ARUA) BY ROAD IS NOT ADVISED. TRAVEL IN THE FOLLOWING AREAS IS GENERALLY SAFE: MBALE, THE ROUTE FROM THE KENYAN BORDER THROUGH JINJA TO KAMPALA, AND WESTERN UGANDA, INCLUDING QUEEN ELIZABETH NATIONAL PARK AND THE RUWENZORI MOUNTAINS.
3. THE POLICE AND MILITARY ROADBLOCKS THROUGHOUT THE COUNTRY SHOULD PRESENT NO MAJOR PROBLEMS FOR TRAVELERS IF THEY PRESENT THEIR PASSPORTS WITH A VALID VISA. DO NOT PHOTOGRAPH SECURITY FORCES OR INSTALLATIONS. TRAVELERS SHOULD BE AWARE THAT THERE ARE REGULAR INCIDENTS OF DAYLIGHT HIGHWAY ROBBERY. NIGHT TRAVEL SHOULD BE AVOIDED ENTIRELY. ROADS THROUGHOUT UGANDA ARE POOR; OVERLAND TRAVELERS SHOULD PLAN ACCORDINGLY. FUEL MAY NOT BE READILY AVAILABLE OUTSIDE KAMPALA.
4. VISITORS ARE ENCOURAGED TO REGISTER WITH THE EMBASSY IN KAMPALA UPON ARRIVAL. JOURNALISTS MUST HAVE PROPER

CREDENTIALS FROM THE MINISTRY OF INFORMATION.
5. THE PREVIOUS TRAVEL ADVISORY CONTAINED IN STATE 097834,
DATED MARCH 14 1989, IS CANCELLED.
6. EXPIRATION DATE: DECEMBER 1, 1990.

Country Number 8.202
Union of Soviet Socialist Republics
(Russia)

INFECTIOUS DISEASE RISK

Malaria Risk
Malaria risk is present in a few scattered border areas with Iran and Afghanistan. See Chapter 6.31 for use of chloroquine.

Diseases of Special Risk
In addition to the worldwide hazard of tetanus and the routine and any special immunizations recommended below, the traveler should be aware that risk of exposure to the following diseases exists in this country. This list is not all inclusive, but it is a caution concerning the more likely endemic disease risks.
Giardia is a problem in the western portions of the country, especially in Leningrad.
Cutaneous leishmaniasis is encountered in southern sections of the country.
Scrub (tick borne) typhus is found in eastern and central Siberia.
Rabies is prevalent in many rural areas, especially in foxes.
The fish tape worm, diphyllobothrium, is common in the Baltic Sea area.
Hemorrhagic fever is encountered in southern Siberia.

Food/Water Safety
All tap water used for drinking, brushing teeth, and making ice cubes should be boiled prior to use. Insure that bottled water is uncapped in your presence. Milk is pasteurized and safe to drink. Butter, cheese, yogurt and ice-cream are safe. Cold foods may be safe, but are not recommended.

VACCINATIONS
Routine immunizations should be current. For infants and children through 16 years of age, refer to Chapter 4.3. A rubeola (measles) booster should be considered. Persons age 16 to 65 should receive a booster of tetanus and diphtheria every ten years. Healthy adults under age 65 do not require pneumococcal vaccine, but it is appropriate for those with chronic medical conditions. Influenza vaccine may be considered for those providing essential community services, health care workers, and those wishing to reduce the likeli-

hood of becoming ill with influenza. Adults over 65 years of age are urged to obtain yearly influenza immunization, and to insure that their tetanus and diphtheria immunizations are current. Pneumococcal vaccination is also suggested for this age group.

No vaccinations are required to enter this country.

The vaccinations listed are recommended for the traveler's protection.

Viral Hepatitis A—Vaccination is recommended when traveling outside the areas usually visited by tourists, traveling extensively in the interior of the country (trekkers, hikers) and for persons on working assignments in remote areas.

Typhoid fever—Vaccination is recommended when traveling outside the areas usually visited by tourists, traveling extensively in the interior of the country (trekkers, hikers) and for persons on working assignments in remote areas.

Selective vaccinations—These apply only to specific groups of travelers or persons on specific working assignments:

Japanese encephalitis—Vaccination is indicated for persons traveling extensively in rual areas or living and working near rice growing rural and suburban areas and other irrigated land, when exposure to the disease carrying mosquitoes is high. Children are especially susceptible to the infection. Outbreaks occur occassionally in the southeast between the border with China and the Sea of Japan, with prevalence in the area of Vladivostok. Period of transmission is June to October.

Plague—Vaccination is recommended only for persons who may be occupationally exposed to wild rodents (anthropologists, geologists, medical personnel, missionaries, etc). The standard vaccination course must be completed before entering the plague infested area. Geographical distribution of the areas of risk for this country are in Azerbaijan, Armenia and Georgia; in the Kazakh SSR; on the northern shores of the Caspian Sea, the northeastern shores of the Aral Sea and the southern shores of Lake Balkash. In Turkmen SSR a large focus of activity is present east of the Caspian Sea.

Tick-borne encephalitis—(Central European encephalitis) Vaccination is recommended for persons involved in recreational activities in forested areas (camping, hiking) or working in forestry occupations. Risk season: March to November. Risk is present in the western part of the country and in eastern Siberia (Russian Far Eastern encephalitis).

U. S. Foreign Service:

Ulitsa Chaykovskogo 19/21/23
Moscow, Telephone (096) 255-0019

Petra Lavrova St. 15
Leningrad, Telephone (812) 274-8235

Canadian High Commission/Embassy Office:
   23 Starokonyushenny Pereulok
   Moscow, Telephone (096) 241-9155/3067/5070

TRAVEL ADVISORY

A U. S. Department of State Travel Advisory was in effect on 4 May 1990
when this book went to press. The entire text is included below. Travel advisories are subject to reissue, change, and cancellation at any time. Current travel
advisory information is available by calling the U. S. Department of State Travel
Advisory Hotline at (202) 647-5225. The current travel advisory status is also
available from the Herchmer Database update system (see Chapter 2.8).

MARCH 14, 1990
USSR—CAUTION
ETHNIC AND POLITICAL UNREST:
ETHNIC CLASHES IN A NUMBER OF REGIONS OF THE SOVIET
UNION HAVE OCCURRED WITH GROWING INTENSITY OVER THE
PAST YEAR. WHILE SOVIET CITIZENS HAVE BEEN INJURED OR
KILLED IN SOME INSTANCES, THE VIOLENCE HAS NOT BEEN DI-
RECTED AT AMERICAN CITIZENS OR OTHER FOREIGNERS. THE
SOVIET GOVERNMENT HAS ON OCCASION TEMPORARILY CLOSED
AFFECTED AREAS TO FOREIGN TOURISTS, REQUIRING CHANGES
IN INTOURIST PACKAGE TOURS.
AMERICAN CITIZENS MAY WISH TO CHECK WITH INTOURIST OR
THE SOVIET EMBASSY OR CONSULATE GENERAL IN THE UNITED
STATES FOR INFORMATION CONCERNING CLOSED AREAS PRIOR
TO THEIR TRAVEL. AMERICANS TRAVELING TO AREAS OF POTEN-
TIAL POLITICAL UNREST OR VIOLENCE ARE ENCOURAGED TO REG-
ISTER WITH THE U.S. EMBASSY IN MOSCOW OR CONSULATE
GENERAL IN LENINGRAD BEFORE PROCEEDING TO THOSE AREAS.
CRIME AND PERSONAL SECURITY:
CRIME IS A VERY REAL THREAT IN THE SOVIET UNION. THERE
HAS BEEN A SUBSTANTIAL INCREASE IN VIOLENT STREET CRIME
IN THE USSR IN THE PAST YEAR, AS REFLECTED IN OFFICIAL SO-
VIET GOVERNMENT CRIMINAL STATISTICS. THE EMBASSY IN MOS-
COW AND CONSULATE GENERAL IN LENINGRAD HAVE RECEIVED
INCREASING NUMBERS OF REPORTS OF MUGGINGS ROBBERIES
AND PICK-POCKETINGS, BURGLARIES, SEXUAL ASSAULTS, AND
BEATING OF AMERICAN CITIZENS VISITING OR RESIDENT IN THE
SOVIET UNION.
HEALTH CARE AND UNEXPECTED EXPENSES:
TOURISTS IN FRAIL HEALTH ARE URGED NOT TO VISIT THE SOVIET
UNION. ORGANIZED TOURS IN THE USSR ARE STRENUOUS:DAILY
SCHEDULES ARE HEAVY, DISTANCES LONG, AND FLIGHT DELAYS

AND CHANGED DEPARTURE TIMES COMMON. MEDICAL CARE IN THE SOVIET UNION DOES NOT MEET WESTERN STANDARDS. THERE IS A SEVERE SHORTAGE OF BASIC MEDICAL SUPPLIES, INCLUDING DISPOSABLE HYPODERMIC NEEDLES, ANESTHETICS, AND ANTIBIOTICS IN THE SOVIET UNION. X-RAYS ARE OF POOR QUALITY, AND ADVANCED DIAGNOSTIC EQUIPMENT, SUCH AS CAT SCANNING MACHINES, IS NOT WIDELY AVAILABLE. PATIENT SUPPORT SERVICES, INCLUDING BASIC HYGIENE MEASURES, ARE INADEQUATE. FULL, FRANK, AND EMPATHETIC DISCUSSIONS BETWEEN DOCTOR AND PATIENT ARE HAMPERED BY LANGUAGE BARRIERS AS WELL AS LACK OF A TRADITION OF PATIENT RIGHTS.

IN MOSCOW, MEDICAL CARE WHICH APPROACHES WESTERN STANDARDS IS AVAILABLE AT A FRENCH-SOVIET JOINT VENTURE CLINIC, RECENTLY OPENED WITH FACILITIES AT A SOVIET HOSPITAL. IN LENINGRAD, SUCH MEDICAL CARE IS AVAILABLE AT A FINNISH-SOVIET JOINT VENTURE OUT-PATIENT CLINIC. PAYMENT IN BOTH MUST BE MADE IN HARD CURRENCY OR BY CREDIT CARD.

TRAVELERS ARE URGED TO ENSURE THEY ARE COVERED BY INSURANCE FOR UNEXPECTED MEDICAL EXPENSES, INCLUDING MEDICAL EVACUATION. THE COST OF MEDICAL EVACUATIN FROM THE SOVIET UNION TO THE U.S. OR A WEST EUROPEAN COUNTRY MAY BE TEN THOUSAND DOLLARS OR MORE. FURTHERMORE, LARGE UNANTICIPATED EXPENSES FOR CHANGED TRAVEL ARRANGEMENTS, INCLUDING FULL-PRICE PLANE TICKETS AND HOTEL ROOMS, ADD UP.

INTOURIST, THE SOVIET UNION TRAVEL ORGANIZATION, OFTEN WILL ABSOLVE ITSELF OF ALL RESPONSIBILITY FOR TOURISTS WHO BECAME SO ILL THEY CANNOT MAINTAIN THE TOUR SCHEDULE. THE TOURIST IS ABANDONED TO FEND FOR HIMSELF IN THE CONFUSING, FOR WESTERNERS, SOVIET MEDICAL SYSTEM.

CUSTOMS; IMPORTING AND EXPORTING

STRICT SOVIET CUSTOMS REGULATIONS SHOULD BE CAREFULLY OBSERVED. DETAILED CUSTOMS DECLARATIONS MUST BE MADE UPON ENTRY AND EXIT. SOVIET CUSTOMS OFFICIALS COMPARE THE LIST OF WHAT WAS BROUGHT IN WITH THE ITEMS BEING TAKEN OUT. IMPORT DUTIES MAY BE ASSESSED IF VALUABLES DECLARED ON ENTRY ARE NOT RE-EXPORTED, WHILE VALUABLES NOT LISTED AT THE TIME OF ENTRY ARE SUBJECT TO CONFISCATION ON DEPARTURE. SUCH ARTICLES GENERALLY CANNOT BE RECOVERED FROM CUSTOMS.

TRAVELERS SHOULD BE AWARE THAT SOVIET CUSTOMS OFFICIALS FREQUENTLY CONFISCATE THE FOLLOWING:

—SEXUALLY ORIENTED PHOTOS OR WRITINGS
ITEMS IN QUANTITIES BELIEVED TO BE GREATER THAN THAT RE-
QUIRED FOR PERSONAL USE, AND WHICH SOVIET AUTHORITIES
BELIEVE MIGHT BE DESTINED FOR THE BLACK MARKET. (THIS
APPLIES, FOR EXAMPLE, TO LARGE QUANTITIES OF RELIGIOUS
MATERIALS)
—LUXURY ITEMS SUCH AS RECORDS
—UNDECLARED CURRENCY OR VALUABLES, INCLUDING TRAV-
ELERS CHECKS AND JEWELRY
—AND,IN THE PAST, ANY MATERIAL CONSIDERED ANTI-SOVIET
ANTIQUES, DEFINED AS VIRTUALLY ANYTHING WHICH MAY BE
DEEMED OF HISTORICAL OR CULTURAL VALUE, EVEN WHEN
PROPERLY DOCUMENTED, ARE ALSO ON OCCASION SEIZED
FROM DEPARTING TRAVELERS. SOVIET AUTHORITIES ARE EX-
TREMELY SENSITIVE TO ATTEMPTS BY FOREIGNERS TO TAKE OUT
OF THE SOVIET UNION CORRESPONDENCE OR OTHER ITEMS FOR
SOVIET CITIZENS.
AMERICAN TOURISTS ACCUSED OR SUSPECTED OF CARRYING
ANY OF THE ABOVE "CONTRABAND" ITEMS HAVE SOMETIMES
BEEN DETAINED FOR SEVERAL HOURS AND SUBJECTED TO IN-
TERROGATION, INTIMIDATION AND HARASSMENT.
HARD CURRENCY PURCHASES IN THE USSR:
TRAVELERS TO THE SOVIET UNION ARE CAUTIONED THAT PAY-
MENT FOR GOODS AND SERVICES IN HARD CURRENCY(DOL-
LARS) IS PERMITTED UNDER SOVIET LAW ONLY IN SPECIALLY
DESIGNATED HOTELS AND RESTAURANTS AND HARD CURRENCY
STORES (BERIOZKA). TAXI DRIVERS, STREET ARTISTS, AND OTHER
MARKET VENDORS EXERT PRESSURE ON UNSUSPECTING FOR-
EIGNERS TO PAY FOR PURCHASES IN DOLLARS OR TO PURCHASE
RUBLES AT THE BLACK MARKET RATE. THE WIDESPREAD NATURE
OF THIS PRACTICE GIVES THE ILLUSION OF LEGITIMACY TO SUCH
TRANSACTIONS. IN FACT, PERSONS WHO USE HARD CURRENCY
ON THE STREET AND IN TAXIS VIOLATE SOVIET LAW AND RUN A
RISK OF BEING DETAINED.
VISAS AND TRAVEL DOCUMENTS:
STRICT SOVIET VISA REGULATIONS REQUIRE THAT A LOST OR EX-
PIRED VISA MUST BE REPORTED TO THE SOVIET SPONSORING
AGENCY IMMEDIATELY SO THAT A REPLACEMENT MAY BE ISSUED
IN TIME FOR SCHEDULED DEPARTURE. ANY AMERICAN CITIZEN
ENCOUNTERING PROBLEMS IN LEAVING THE SOVIET UNION
SHOULD IMMEDIATELY CONTACT THE AMERICAN EMBASSY AT 252-
2341 THROUGH 252-2459, OR THE AMERICAN CONSULATE GEN-
ERAL IN LENINGRAD AT 274-8235.
DUAL NATIONALITY

UNDER CURRENT SOVIET LAW ALL PERSONS (INCLUDING NATU-
RALIZED U.S. CITIZENS) WHO WERE BORN IN THE PRESENT TER-
RITORY OF THE USSR, AND THEIR CHILDREN (EVEN THOSE BORN
OUTSIDE THE USSR), ARE REGARDED SOLELY AS CITIZENS OF
THE USSR BY THE SOVIET GOVERNMENT.
SOVIET CONSULAR OFFICIALS SOMETIMES REFUSE TO ISSUE
SOVIET ENTRY VISAS IN THE U.S. PASSPORTS OF THESE
U.S. CITIZENS-PARTICULARLY IF THEY HAVE HELD SOVIET
PASSPORTS-UNLESS THEY RENOUNCE THEIR SOVIET CITIZEN-
SHIP IN ACCORDANCE WITH SOVIET LEGAL REQUIREMENTS. RE-
NUNCIATION OF SOVIET CITIZENSHIP GENERALLY TAKES AT
LEAST SIX MONTHS. IN MAY CASES THE REQUEST FOR RENUNCI-
ATION IS DENIED. IN SOME CASES, DUAL NATIONALS WHO HAD
PREVIOUSLY BEEN STRIPPED OF SOVIET CITIZENSHIP HAVE
BEEN TOLD BY CONSULAR OFFICIALS IN THE SOVIET EMBASSY IN
WASHINGTON, D.C. OR CONSULATE GENERAL IN SAN FRANCISCO
THAT IN ORDER TO TRAVEL TO THE SOVIET UNION THEY MUST RE-
OBTAIN SOVIET CITIZENSHIP AND A SOVIET EXTERNAL TRAVEL
PASSPORT AND RETURN TO THE USSR WITH A VISA FOR PERMA-
NENT RESIDENCE. UPON ARRIVAL IN THE SOVIET UNION USING
THE SOVIET PASSPORT, THESE U.S. CITIZENS HAVE DISCOVERED
THAT SOVIET OFFICIALS WOULD NOT ALLOW THEM TO LEAVE THE
COUNTRY USING THEIR U.S. PASSPORT (WHICH CONTAINED NO
SOVIET ENTRY VISA). FURTHER, SOVIET AUTHORITIES WOULD
NOT ISSUE THEM EXIT PERMISSION IN THEIR SOVIET PASSPORT.
DUAL NATIONALS WHO HOLD A VALID U.S. PASSPORT AND WHO
PLAN TO VISIT THE SOVIET UNION ARE CAUTIONED NOT TO TRA-
VEL ON SOVIET PASSPORT WITH A VISA FOR PERMANENT RESI-
DENCE IN THE SOVIET UNION, UNLESS THEY ARE PREPARED TO
RISK REMAINING PERMANENTLY IN THE USSR.
SOVIET AUTHORITIES HAVE CONSISTENTLY DENIED ANY OBLIGA-
TION TO PERMIT U.S. CONSULAR PROTECTION OF INDIVIDUALS
WHO, THEY BELIEVE, RETAIN SOVIET CITIZENSHIP. THIS SE-
VERELY LIMITS THE U.S. GOVERNMENT'S ABILITY TO ASSIST U.S.
CITIZENS WHO ARE DEEMED ALSO TO BE SOVIET CITIZENS, OR
EVEN TO OBTAIN CONSULAR ACCESS TO THEM. CONSEQUENTLY,
IT IS ADVISED THAT DUAL US/USSR CITIZENS REGISTER WITH THE
U.S. EMBASSY IN MOSCOW OR THE CONSULATE GENERAL IN LEN-
INGRAD UPON ARRIVAL AND CONTACT ONE OF THOSE OFFICES
IMMEDIATELY IF ANY QUESTIONS ARISE ABOUT CITIZENSHIP.
EXPIRATION: 6 MARCH 1991

Country Number 8.203
United Arab Emirates

INFECTIOUS DISEASE RISK

Malaria Risk

Malaria is present in all nearly parts of this country, including urban areas. The risk exists all year. See Chapter 6.31 concerning the use of weekly chloroquine for malaria prevention. There is no risk of malaria in the cities of Dubai, Sharjah, Ajman, Umm al Qaiwan and Emirate of Abu Dhabi.

Falciparum malaria represents 55% of malaria, therefore there is a risk of p. vivax malaria exposure. Consider use of primaquine upon return home.

Diseases of Special Risk

In addition to the worldwide hazard of tetanus and the routine and any special immunizations recommended below, the traveler should be aware that risk of exposure to the following diseases exists in this country. This list is not all inclusive, but it is a caution concerning the more likely endemic disease risks.

DISEASE RISK PROFILE

Disease	endemic	risk	hazard
Brucellosis			x
Cholera	x		
Diarrheal Diseases	x		
Dracunculiasis/Guinea Worm	x		
Echinococcosis	x		
Hepatitis, Viral		x	
Leishmaniasis			
Cutaneous	x		
Visceral	x		
Rabies	x		
Relapsing Fever	x		
Tapeworms	x		
Trachoma	x		
Typhoid Fever		x	
Typhus, Endemic Flea-Borne	x		
Typhus, Scrub	x		

Food/Water Safety

All tap water used for drinking, brushing teeth, and making ice cubes should be boiled prior to use. Insure that bottled water is uncapped in your presence. Milk should be boiled to insure safety. Powdered and evaporated milk are available and safe. Avoid butter and other dairy products. All meat, poultry and seafood must be well cooked and served while hot. Pork is best avoided. Vegetables should be well cooked and served hot. Salads and mayonnaise are

best avoided. Fruits with intact skins should be peeled by you just prior to consumption. Avoid cold buffets, custards, and any frozen dessert. First class hotels and restaurants in Dubai (Dubayy) serve purified drinking water and reliable food. However, the hazard is left to your judgement.

VACCINATIONS

Routine immunizations should be current. For infants and children through 16 years of age, refer to Chapter 4.3. A rubeola (measles) booster should be considered. Persons age 16 to 65 should receive a booster of tetanus and diphtheria every ten years. Healthy adults under age 65 do not require pneumococcal vaccine, but it is appropriate for those with chronic medical conditions. Influenza vaccine may be considered for those providing essential community services, health care workers, and those wishing to reduce the likelihood of becoming ill with influenza. Adults over 65 years of age are urged to obtain yearly influenza immunization, and to insure that their tetanus and diphtheria immunizations are current. Pneumococcal vaccination is also suggested for this age group.

No vaccinations are required to enter this country.

The vaccinations listed are recommended for the traveler's protection.
Poliomyelitis—A poliomyelitis booster is indicated for this country.
Viral Hepatitis A—Vaccination is recommended for all travelers for their protection.
Typhoid fever—Vaccination is recommended for all travelers for their protection.

Selective vaccinations—These apply only to specific groups of travelers or persons on specific working assignments:
Viral Hepatitis B—Because of the high rate of healthy carriers of hepatitis B in this country, vaccination is recommended for persons on working assignments in the health care field (dentists, physicians, nurses, laboratory technicians), or working in close contact with the local population (teachers, missionaries, Peace Corps), or persons foreseeing sexual relations with local inhabitants.
Rabies—In this country, where rabies is a constant threat, a pre-exposure rabies vaccination is advised for persons planning an extended stay or on working assignments (naturalists, agricultural advisors, archeologists, geologists, etc.). Although this provides adequate initial protection, a person bitten by a potentially rabid animal would still require post exposure immunization (see Chapter 6.40). Children should be cautioned not to pet dogs, cats, or other mammals.

U. S. Foreign Service:
Al-Sudan Street
Abu Dhabi, Telephone 336691
(Saturday—Wednesday)

Canadian High Commission:
Federal Commercial Bank Building
Tourist Club Area
Abu Dhabi, Telephone 723800

Country Number 8.204
United Kingdom

INFECTIOUS DISEASE RISK

Malaria Risk
There is no malaria risk in this country.

Food/Water Safety
Local water is considered safe without further treatment. Milk is pasteurized and safe to drink. Butter, cheese, yogurt and ice-cream are safe. Local meat, poultry, seafood, vegetables, and fruits are safe to eat.

VACCINATIONS
Routine immunizations should be current. For infants and children through 16 years of age, refer to Chapter 4.3. A rubeola (measles) booster should be considered. Persons age 16 to 65 should receive a booster of tetanus and diphtheria every ten years. Healthy adults under age 65 do not require pneumococcal vaccine, but it is appropriate for those with chronic medical conditions. Influenza vaccine may be considered for those providing essential community services, health care workers, and those wishing to reduce the likelihood of becoming ill with influenza. Adults over 65 years of age are urged to obtain yearly influenza immunization, and to insure that their tetanus and diphtheria immunizations are current. Pneumococcal vaccination is also suggested for this age group.

No vaccinations are required to enter this country.

U. S. Foreign Service:
24/31 Grosvenor Square
London, Telephone (01) 499-9000

Queen's House
14 Queen Street
Belfast, Telephone (0232) 28239

3 Regent Terrace
Edinburgh, Scotland, Telephone (031) 556-8315

Canadian High Commission/Embassy Office:
MacDonald House
1 Grosvenor Square, W1X OAB
London, Telephone (01) 629-9492

Ashley House
195 W. George Street, G2 ZHS
Glasgow, Telephone (041) 248-3026

TRAVEL ADVISORY

A U. S. Department of State Travel Advisory was in effect on 4 May 1990 when this book went to press. The entire text is included below. Travel advisories are subject to reissue, change, and cancellation at any time. Current travel advisory information is available by calling the U. S. Department of State Travel Advisory Hotline at (202) 647-5225. The current travel advisory status is also available from the Herchmer Database update system (see Chapter 2.8).

THE DEPARTMENT OF STATE ADVISES THAT TRAVELERS TO NORTHERN IRELAND SHOULD BE AWARE THAT FREQUENT BOMB THREATS AND SMALL EXPLOSIONS BY THE PROVINCIAL IRISH REPUBLICAN ARMY HAVE INTERRUPTED RAIL SERVICE, ESPECIALLY ON THE BELFAST-DUBLIN LINE. SINCE THE EXPLOSIVES HAVE BEEN PLACED ON THE TRACKS AND NOT ON THE TRAINS AND AUTHORITIES HAVE RECEIVED WARNINGS, THERE HAVE BEEN NO INJURIES OR DEATHS TO DATE. AUTHORITIES HAVE RESPONDED BY CLOSING THE TRACKS AND PROVIDING ALTERNATIVE TRANSPORTATION BY BUS; TRAVELERS SHOULD BE PREPARED FOR DELAYS AND SHOULD FOLLOW THE ADVICE OF AUTHORITIES.
ADVISORY POSTED 8/31/89
LIMIT: INDEFINITE

——————— **Country Number 8.205** ———————
United States of America

INFECTIOUS DISEASE RISK

Malaria Risk
There is no malaria risk in this country.

Diseases of Special Risk

In addition to the worldwide hazard of tetanus and the routine and any special immunizations recommended below, the traveler should be aware that risk of exposure to the following diseases exists in this country. This list is not all inclusive, but it is a caution concerning the more likely endemic disease risks.

DISEASE RISK PROFILE

Disease	endemic	risk	hazard
Encephalitis	x		
Giardiasis	x		
Helminthic Diseases (see Chapter 6.21)	x		
Hepatitis, Viral	x		
Lyme Disease	x		
Plague	x		
Rabies	x		
Rocky Mountain Spotted Fever	x		
Tularemia	x		

Food/Water Safety

Local water is considered safe without further treatment. Milk is pasteurized and safe to drink. Butter, cheese, yogurt and ice-cream are safe. Local meat, poultry, seafood, vegetables, and fruits are safe to eat.

VACCINATIONS

Routine immunizations should be current. For infants and children through 16 years of age, refer to Chapter 4.3. A rubeola (measles) booster should be considered. Persons age 16 to 65 should receive a booster of tetanus and diphtheria every ten years. Healthy adults under age 65 do not require pneumococcal vaccine, but it is appropriate for those with chronic medical conditions. Influenza vaccine may be considered for those providing essential community services, health care workers, and those wishing to reduce the likelihood of becoming ill with influenza. Adults over 65 years of age are urged to obtain yearly influenza immunization, and to insure that their tetanus and diphtheria immunizations are current. Pneumococcal vaccination is also suggested for this age group.

No vaccinations are required to enter this country.

The vaccinations listed are recommended for the traveler's protection.

Selective vaccinations—These apply only to specific groups of travelers or persons on specific working assignments:

Viral Hepatitis B—Because of the high rate of healthy carriers of hepatitis B among the local indigenous populations of Alaska, vaccination is recommended for persons working in health care, education, or in close contact with them.

Plague—Vaccination is recommended only for persons who may be occupationally exposed to wild rodents (anthropologists, geologists, medical personnel, missionaries, etc). The standard vaccination course must be completed before entering the plague infested area. Geographical distribution of the areas of risk for this country are in remote areas of many of the western states.

Rabies—Vaccination is recommended only for persons who may be occupational exposed to wild or rabid animals (vetenarians, select game wardens) or persons cave exploring in areas with rapid bat populations.

Canadian High Commission/Embassy Office:

1746 Massachusetts Avenue, N.W.
Washington, Telephone (202) 785-1400

900 Coastal States Building
260 Peachtree Stree, N.W.
Atlanta, Telephone (404) 577-6810

5th Floor
500 Boylston Street
Boston, Telephone (617) 262-3760/7767

Suite 3550
1 Marine Midland Center
Buffalo, Telephone (716) 852-1247

Suite 1200
310 South Michigan Avenue
Chicago, Telephone (312) 427-1031

Illuminating Building
55 Public Square
Cleveland, Telephone (216) 771-0150

Suite 1700
St. Paul Tower
750 N. St. Paul Street
Dallas, Telephone (214) 922-9806

_____ **Country number 206** _____
Uruguay

INFECTIOUS DISEASE RISK

Malaria Risk
There is no malaria risk in this country.

Diseases of Special Risk
In addition to the worldwide hazard of tetanus and the routine and any special immunizations recommended below, the traveler should be aware that risk of exposure to the following diseases exists in this country. This list is not all inclusive, but it is a caution concerning the more likely endemic disease risks.

Chaga's Disease is present in all rural and suburban areas except the Atlantic coastal areas.

Uruguay has generally good health conditions. Hepatitis and anthrax can be a risk and endemic diseases include tapeworms, typhoid fever, and echinococcosis.

Food/Water Safety
Local water is considered safe without further treatment. Milk is pasteurized and safe to drink. Butter, cheese, yogurt and ice-cream are safe. Local meat, poultry, seafood, vegetables, and fruits are safe to eat.

VACCINATIONS

Routine immunizations should be current. For infants and children through 16 years of age, refer to Chapter 4.3. A rubeola (measles) booster should be considered. Persons age 16 to 65 should receive a booster of tetanus and diphtheria every ten years. Healthy adults under age 65 do not require pneumococcal vaccine, but it is appropriate for those with chronic medical conditions. Influenza vaccine may be considered for those providing essential community services, health care workers, and those wishing to reduce the likelihood of becoming ill with influenza. Adults over 65 years of age are urged to obtain yearly influenza immunization, and to insure that their tetanus and diphtheria immunizations are current. Pneumococcal vaccination is also suggested for this age group.

No vaccinations are required to enter this country.

The vaccinations listed are recommended for the traveler's protection.
Viral Hepatitis A—Vaccination is recommended when traveling outside the areas usually visited by tourists, traveling extensively in the interior of the country (trekkers, hikers) and for persons on working assignments in remote areas.
Typhoid fever—Vaccination is recommended when traveling outside the

areas usually visited by tourists, traveling extensively in the interior of the country (trekkers, hikers) and for persons on working assignments in remote areas.

U. S. Foreign Service:
Calle Lauro Muller 1776
Montevido, Telephone 49-90-51

——————— Country Number 8.207 ———————
Vanatu
formerly New Hebrides

INFECTIOUS DISEASE RISK

Malaria Risk
Malaria is present in all parts of this country, including urban areas. The risk exists all year. The malaria in this country is resistant to chloroquinc. The CDC recommends the use of mefloquine (Lariam) as described in Chapter 6.31 for chemical prophylaxis.

Falciparum malaria represents 75% of malaria, therefore there is a risk of p. vivax malaria exposure. Consider use of primaquine upon return home.

Diseases of Special Risk
In addition to the worldwide hazard of tetanus and the routine and any special immunizations recommended below, the traveler should be aware that risk of exposure to the following diseases exists in this country. This list is not all inclusive, but it is a caution concerning the more likely endemic disease risks.

Potential risk of dengue fever exists. The virus is present in this country at all times and may give rise to major outbreaks.

DISEASE RISK PROFILE

Disease	endemic	risk	hazard
Diarrheal Disease Risk		x	
Dysentery, Amoebic Echinococcosis			
Encephalitis, Japanese	x		
Filariasis			x
Helminthic Diseases (see Chapter 6.21)		x	
Typhoid Fever		x	

Food/Water Safety
Water is probably safe, but due to local variations in bacterial counts, using bottled water for the first few weeks will help the traveler adjust and decrease the chance of traveler's diarrhea. Local meat, poultry, seafood, vegeta-

bles, and fruits are safe to eat. Milk is pasteurized and safe to drink. Butter, cheese, yogurt and ice-cream are safe.

VACCINATIONS

Routine immunizations should be current. For infants and children through 16 years of age, refer to Chapter 4.3. A rubeola (measles) booster should be considered. Persons age 16 to 65 should receive a booster of tetanus and diphtheria every ten years. Healthy adults under age 65 do not require pneumococcal vaccine, but it is appropriate for those with chronic medical conditions. Influenza vaccine may be considered for those providing essential community services, health care workers, and those wishing to reduce the likelihood of becoming ill with influenza. Adults over 65 years of age are urged to obtain yearly influenza immunization, and to insure that their tetanus and diphtheria immunizations are current. Pneumococcal vaccination is also suggested for this age group.

No vaccinations are required to enter this country.

The vaccinations listed are recommended for the traveler's protection.
Viral Hepatitis A—Vaccination is recommended for all travelers for their protection.
Typhoid fever—Vaccination is recommended for all travelers for their protection.

Selective vaccinations—These apply only to specific groups of travelers or persons on specific working assignments:
Viral Hepatitis B—Because of the high rate of healthy carriers of hepatitis B in this country, vaccination is recommended for persons on working assignments in the health care field (dentists, physicians, nurses, laboratory technicians), or working in close contact with the local population (teachers, missionaries, Peace Corps), or persons foreseeing sexual relations with local inhabitants.

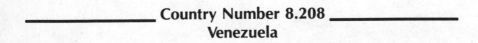

Country Number 8.208
Venezuela

INFECTIOUS DISEASE RISK

Malaria Risk

Malaria is present below 600 meters in the rual areas of Apure, Bolivar, Barinas, Merida, Tachira, and Zulia States. The risk exists all year. The malaria in this country is resistant to chloroquine. The CDC recommends the use of mefloquine (Lariam) as described in Chapter 6.31 for chemical prophylaxis.

Falciparum malaria represents 14% of malaria, therefore there is a risk of

p. vivax malaria exposure. Consider the use of primaquine upon return home.

Diseases of Special Risk

In addition to the worldwide hazard of tetanus and the routine and any special immunizations recommended below, the traveler should be aware that risk of exposure to the following diseases exists in this country. This list is not all inclusive, but it is a caution concerning the more likely endemic disease risks.

Current risk of dengue fever exists. The virus is present in this country at all times and is currently responsible for a major outbreak. The World Health Organization reported 5,416 cases with 51 deaths through 1/22/90. Cases have been reported from 16 of the 22 states and the Federal District.

Schistosomiasis may be found in this country. Avoid contact with contaminated fresh water lakes, ponds, or streams. Risk is confined to the central part of Northern Venezuela, from the coast to the northern border of the State of Guarico (San Juan de los Morros). In the west, the infection is present in the State of Carabobo (Valencia City, the areas of Lake Valencia including its tributaries) and extends to the east to the State of Miranda (along the rivers Tuy and Guaire) and to the Federal District including the outskirts of Caracus.

Chaga's Disease is present in rural areas of the following states: Anzoa'tegui, Barinas, Carabobo, Cojedes, Falcon, Gua'rico, Lara, Me'rida, Monegas, Nueva Esparta, Portugesa, Sucre, Yaracuy, and Zulia. The main vectors are known as vinchuca locally, but consist of two species of Rodnius and Triatoma beetles.

DISEASE RISK PROFILE

Disease	endemic	risk	hazard
Diarrheal Disease Risk		x	
Dysentery, Amoebic		x	
Echinococcosis	x		
Encephalitis, Venezuelan Equine	x		
Filariasis (Bancroftian)			x
Helminthic Diseases (see Chapter 6.21)	x		
Hepatitis, Viral	x		
Leishmaniasis			
Cutaneous	x		
Mucocutaneous	x		
Onchocerciasis	x		
Polio	x		
Rabies	x		

Food/Water Safety

Water is probably safe, but due to local variations in bacterial counts, using bottled water for the first few weeks will help the traveler adjust and decrease the chance of traveler's diarrhea. Milk is pasteurized and safe to drink.

Butter, cheese, yogurt and ice-cream are safe. Local meat, poultry, seafood, vegetables, and fruits are safe to eat.

VACCINATIONS

Routine immunizations should be current. For infants and children through 16 years of age, refer to Chapter 4.3. A rubeola (measles) booster should be considered. Persons age 16 to 65 should receive a booster of tetanus and diphtheria every ten years. Healthy adults under age 65 do not require pneumococcal vaccine, but it is appropriate for those with chronic medical conditions. Influenza vaccine may be considered for those providing essential community services, health care workers, and those wishing to reduce the likelihood of becoming ill with influenza. Adults over 65 years of age are urged to obtain yearly influenza immunization, and to insure that their tetanus and diphtheria immunizations are current. Pneumococcal vaccination is also suggested for this age group.

No vaccinations are required to enter this country.

The vaccinations listed are recommended for the traveler's protection.

Poliomyelitis—Vaccination is recommended when traveling outside the areas usually visited by tourists, traveling extensively in the interior of the country (trekkers, hikers) and for persons on working assignments in remote areas.

Viral Hepatitis A—Vaccination is recommended when traveling outside the areas usually visited by tourists, traveling extensively in the interior of the country (trekkers, hikers) and for persons on working assignments in remote areas.

Typhoid fever—Vaccination is recommended when traveling outside the areas usually visited by tourists, traveling extensively in the interior of the country (trekkers, hikers) and for persons on working assignments in remote areas.

Yellow fever—Vaccination is recommended when traveling outside the areas usually visited by tourists, traveling extensively in the interior of the country (trekkers, hikers) and for persons on working assignments in remote areas. CDC recommends vaccination for all travelers over 9 months of age who may travel outside of urban areas. Other countries may require a yellow fever certificate after visiting this country.

Selective vaccinations—These apply only to specific groups of travelers or persons on specific working assignments:

Viral Hepatitis B—Because of the high rate of healthy carriers of hepatitis B among the local Yucpa Indian population of western Zulia State on the Venezuela-Columbia border, vaccination is recommended for persons working in health care, education, or in close contact with them.

Rabies—In this country, where rabies is a constant threat, a pre-exposure rabies vaccination is advised for persons planning an extended stay or on working assignments (naturalists, agricultural advisors, archeologists, geologists, etc.). Although this provides adequate initial protection, a person bitten by a potentially rabid animal would still require post exposure immunization (see Chapter 6.40). Children should be cautioned not to pet dogs, cats, or other mammals.

U. S. Foreign Service:
Avenida Francisco de Miranda and Avenida
Pricipal de la Floresta
Caracas, Telephone 284-7111/6111

Edificio Sofimara
Piso 3
Calle 77 co Avenida 13
Maracaibo, Telephone 84-254/5

Canadian High Commission/Embassy Office:
Edificio Torre Europa
7th Floor
Avenida Francisco de Miranda

Country Number 8.209
Vietnam

INFECTIOUS DISEASE RISK

Malaria Risk
Malaria is present in all parts of this country. The risk exists all year. The malaria in this country is resistant to chloroquine. The CDC recommends the use of mefloquine (Lariam) as described in Chapter 6.31 for chemical prophylaxis. There is no risk, however, in urban areas. Prophylaxis is not necessary if your trip is confined to these areas. There is no risk of malaria in the delta region in the north.

Falciparum malaria represents 54% of the malaria encountered. There is therefore a risk of vivax exposure and consideration must be given to the use of primaquine upon returning home.

Diseases of Special Risk
In addition to the worldwide hazard of tetanus and the routine and any special immunizations recommended below, the traveler should be aware that risk of exposure to the following diseases exists in this country. This list is not all inclusive, but it is a caution concerning the more likely endemic disease risks.

Potential risk of dengue fever exists. The virus is present in this country at all times and may give rise to major outbreaks.

DISEASE RISK PROFILE

Disease	endemic	risk	hazard
Chikungunya Fever	x		
Cholera	x		
Clonorchiasis/Opisthorchiasis	x		
Dengue Fever	x		
Diarrheal Disease Risk		x	
Dysentery, Amoebic/Bacillary		x	
Encephalitis, Japanese	x		
Fasciolopsiasis	x		
Filariasis			x
Hepatitis, Viral	x		
Plague		x	
Polio	x		
Rabies	x		
Trachoma	x		
Typhoid Fever	x		
Typhus, Scrub	x		

Food/Water Safety

All tap water used for drinking, brushing teeth, and making ice cubes should be boiled prior to use. Insure that bottled water is uncapped in your presence. Milk should be boiled to insure safety. Powdered and evaporated milk are available and safe. Avoid butter and other dairy products. All meat, poultry and seafood must be well cooked and served while hot. Pork is best avoided. Vegetables should be well cooked and served hot. Salads and mayonnaise are best avoided. Fruits with intact skins should be peeled by you just prior to consumption. Avoid cold buffets, custards, and any frozen dessert. First class hotels and restaurants in Hanoi and Ho Chi Minh City (Saigon) serve purified drinking water and reliable food. However, the hazard is left to your judgement.

VACCINATIONS

Yellow fever—A vaccination certificate is required for travelers coming from infected areas. A vaccination certificate is required for children over one year of age.

Routine immunizations should be current. For infants and children through 16 years of age, refer to Chapter 4.3. A rubeola (measles) booster should be considered. Persons age 16 to 65 should receive a booster of tetanus and diphtheria every ten years. Healthy adults under age 65 do not require pneumococcal vaccine, but it is appropriate for those with chronic medical conditions. Influenza vaccine may be considered for those providing essential community services, health care workers, and those wishing to reduce the likelihood of becoming ill with influenza. Adults over 65 years of age are urged to obtain yearly influenza immunization, and to insure that their tetanus and diphtheria immunizations are current. Pneumococcal vaccination is also suggested for this age group.

The vaccinations listed are recommended for the traveler's protection.

Poliomyelitis—A poliomyelitis booster is indicated for this country.

Cholera—Cholera is present in this country. Risk to western travelers is low. Immunization is not required or recommended for travel to this country due to its low effectiveness. Avoid uncooked foods and untreated water. Vaccination is advised only for persons living or working under inadequate sanitary conditions and for those with impaired defense mechanisms.

Viral Hepatitis A—Vaccination is recommended for all travelers for their protection.

Typhoid fever—Vaccination is recommended for all travelers for their protection.

Selective vaccinations—These apply only to specific groups of travelers or persons on specific working assignments:

Viral Hepatitis B—Because of the high rate of healthy carriers of hepatitis B in this country, vaccination is recommended for persons on working assignments in the health care field (dentists, physicians, nurses, laboratory technicians), or working in close contact with the local population (teachers, missionaries, Peace Corps), or persons foreseeing sexual relations with local inhabitants.

Japanese encephalitis—Vaccination is indicated for persons traveling extensively in rual areas or living and working near rice growing rural and suburban areas and other irrigated land, when exposure to the disease carrying mosquitoes is high. Children are especially susceptible to the infection. The disease is endemic throughout the country during the entire year.

Plague—Vaccination is recommended only for persons who may be occupationally exposed to wild rodents (anthropologists, geologists, medical personnel, missionaries, etc). The standard vaccination course must be completed before entering the plague infested area. Geographical distribution of the areas of risk for this country are around Da Nang extending south to the areas around Cam Ranh.

Rabies—In this country, where rabies is a constant threat, a pre-exposure rabies vaccination is advised for persons planning an extended stay or on working assignments (naturalists, agricultural advisors, archeologists, geologists, etc.). Although this provides adequate initial protection, a person bitten by a potentially rabid animal would still require post exposure immunization (see Chapter 6.40). Children should be cautioned not to pet dogs, cats, or other mammals.

TRAVEL ADVISORY

A U. S. Department of State Travel Advisory was in effect on 4 May 1990 when this book went to press. The entire text is included below. Travel advisories are subject to reissue, change, and cancellation at any time. Current travel advisory information is available by calling the U. S. Department of State Travel

Advisory Hotline at (202) 647-5225. The current travel advisory status is also available from the Herchmer Database update system (see Chapter 2.8).

No.86-21   May 16, 1988
CANCEL
NO. 87-33A
NO. 87-33
NO. 87-31

VIETNAM—WARNING: THE DEPARTMENT OF STATE ADVISES THAT THE UNITED STATES DOES NOT MAINTAIN DIPLOMATIC OR CONSULAR RELATIONS WITH VIETNAM. NO THIRD COUNTRY REPRESENTS THE INTERESTS OF THE UNITED STATES IN VIETNAM. CONSEQUENTLY, THE UNITED STATES GOVERNMENT IS NOT IN A POSITION TO ACCORD NORMAL CONSULAR PROTECTIVE SERVICES TO U.S. CITIZENS IN VIETNAM AND DISCOURAGES TRAVEL TO VIETNAM.

U.S. PASSPORTS ARE VALID FOR TRAVEL TO VIETNAM. HOWEVER, IT IS THE TRAVELER'S RESPONSIBILITY TO APPLY FOR THE REQUIRED VISA. VIETNAMESE OFFICIALS IN THE PAST HAVE DETAINED AMERICAN CITIZENS WHO HAD ENTERED VIETNAM ILLEGALLY WITHOUT VISAS. THOSE DETAINED WERE HELD INCOMMUNICADO FOR MONTHS AT A TIME WITHOUT ANY CONTACT WITH U.S. AUTHORITIES AND RELEASED ONLY AFTER PAYMENT OF A LARGE FINE.

DUAL CITIZENSHIP: U.S. CITIZENS WHO WERE BORN IN VIETNAM OR WHO WERE AT ONE TIME CITIZENS OF VIETNAM, AND THE CHILDREN OF SUCH PERSONS, MAY BE DUAL NATIONALS AND MAY, THEREFORE, BE SUBJECT TO ALL VIETNAMESE LAWS THAT IMPOSE SPECIAL OBLIGATIONS UPON VIETNAMESE NATIONALS, SUCH AS MILITARY SERVICE, TAXES, ETC.

U.S. CITIZENS CONTEMPLATING TRAVEL TO VIETNAM SHOULD ONLY CARRY A U.S. PASSPORT WITH THE PROPER VISA AFFIXED. UNDER NO CIRCUMSTANCES SHOULD U.S. CITIZENS ACCEPT TRAVEL DOCUMENTS THAT IDENTIFY THEM AS CITIZENS OF VIETNAM.

SPECIFIC QUESTIONS ON DUAL NATIONALITY MAY BE DIRECTED TO THE OFFICE OF CITIZENS CONSULAR SERVICES, DEPARTMENT OF STATE, WASHINGTON, D.C. 20520.

U.S. TREASURY REGULATIONS: TRAVEL OF INDIVIDUAL U.S. CITIZENS: FOREIGN ASSETS CONTROL REGULATIONS ADMINISTERED BY THE TREASURY DEPARTMENT PERMIT U.S. CITIZENS TRAVELING TO VIETNAM TO ENGAGE ONLY IN CERTAIN TYPES OF FINANCIAL ACTIVITIES. NO WRITTEN AUTHORIZATION IS REQUIRED TO PERFORM THE FOLLOWING TRANSACTIONS:

—PAYMENT OF ORDINARY TRAVEL EXPENSES, INCLUDING LIVING EXPENSES AND PURCHASE OF GOODS FOR PERSONAL CONSUMPTION WHILE IN VIETNAM.

—PURCHASE AND IMPORTATION IN THE U.S. OF MERCHANDISE WITH A FOREIGN MARKET VALUE NOT TO EXCEED 100 DOLLARS PER PERSON. THIS MERCHANDISE MUST BE FOR PERSONAL USE, CAN BE BROUGHT INTO THE U.S. ONLY AS ACCOMPANIED BAGGAGE AND MAY NOT BE RESOLD. AN INDIVIDUAL MAY IMPORT THIS AMOUNT OF MERCHANDISE ONLY ONCE IN A SIX-MONTH PERIOD. SINGLE COPIES OF PUBLICATIONS DO NOT COUNT AGAINST THE 100 DOLLARS LIMIT.

U.S. CITIZENS MAY NOT USE CHARGE CARDS, INCLUDING, BUT NOT LIMITED TO DEBIT CARDS, CREDIT CARDS, OR OTHER CREDIT FACILITIES FOR EXPENSES WHILE IN VIETNAM.

TRAVEL OF MEDIA REPRESENTATIVES AND RESEARCHERS: PERSONS TRAVELING TO VIETNAM FOR THE PURPOSE OF GATHERING NEWS, MAKING NEWS FILMS, ENGAGING IN PROFESSIONAL RESEARCH, OR FOR SIMILAR ACTIVITIES ARE AUTHORIZED TO ACQUIRE AND IMPORT IN THE U.S. PUBLICATIONS, INCLUDING FILMS, PHONOGRAPH RECORDS, TAPES, PHOTOGRAPHS, ETC., DIRECTLY RELATED TO THEIR PROFESSIONAL ACTIVITIES WITHOUT MONETARY LIMITS. THE ITEMS MUST BE FOR PROFESSIONAL USE AND NOT FOR RESALE.

FURTHER INFORMATION: THIS ADVISORY PROVIDES ONLY GENERAL GUIDANCE REGARDING DEPARTMENT OF TREASURY REGULATIONS. INDIVIDUALS CONTEMPLATING TRAVEL TO VIETNAM ARE ENCOURAGED TO CONTACT THE DEPARTMENT OF TREASURY FOR FURTHER INFORMATION.

UNDER DEPARTMENT OF TREASURY REGULATIONS, NO PERSON SUBJECT TO U.S. JURISDICTION MAY ARRANGE, PROMOTE, OR FACILITATE GROUP OR INDIVIDUAL TOURS OR TRAVEL TO VIETNAM. TRAVEL SERVICE PROVIDERS SHOULD ALSO CONTACT THE DEPARTMENT OF TREASURY AT THE FOLLOWING ADDRESS FOR FURTHER INFORMATION:

LICENSING SECTION OFFICE OF FOREIGN ASSETS CONTROL DEPARTMENT OF THE TREASURY WASHINGTON, D.C. 20220 TELEPHONE: (202) 376-0236

EXPIRATION DATE: INDEFINITE

Country Number 8.210
Virgin Islands (UK)

INFECTIOUS DISEASE RISK

Malaria Risk
There is no malaria risk in this country.

Diseases of Special Risk
Potential risk of dengue fever exists. The virus is present in this country at all times and may give rise to major outbreaks.

Food/Water Safety
Water is probably safe, but due to local variations in bacterial counts, using bottled water for the first few weeks will help the traveler adjust and decrease the chance of traveler's diarrhea. Local meat, poultry, seafood, vegetables, and fruits are safe to eat. Milk is pasteurized and safe to drink. Butter, cheese, yogurt and ice-cream are safe.

VACCINATIONS
Routine immunizations should be current. For infants and children through 16 years of age, refer to Chapter 4.3. A rubeola (measles) booster should be considered. Persons age 16 to 65 should receive a booster of tetanus and diphtheria every ten years. Healthy adults under age 65 do not require pneumococcal vaccine, but it is appropriate for those with chronic medical conditions. Influenza vaccine may be considered for those providing essential community services, health care workers, and those wishing to reduce the likelihood of becoming ill with influenza. Adults over 65 years of age are urged to obtain yearly influenza immunization, and to insure that their tetanus and diphtheria immunizations are current. Pneumococcal vaccination is also suggested for this age group.
No vaccinations are required to enter this country.

Country Number 8.211
Virgin Islands (USA)

INFECTIOUS DISEASE RISK

Malaria Risk
There is no malaria risk in this country.

Diseases of Special Risk
In addition to the worldwide hazard of tetanus and the routine and any

special immunizations recommended below, the traveler should be aware that risk of exposure to the following diseases exists in this country. This list is not all inclusive, but it is a caution concerning the more likely endemic disease risks.

Potential risk of dengue fever exists. The virus is present in this country at all times and may give rise to major outbreaks.

Viral hepatitis, bacillary dysentery, amoebic dysentery, and other diarrheal diseases can occur.

Rabies, especially in the mongoose population, has been reported.

Food/Water Safety

Water is probably safe, but due to local variations in bacterial counts, using bottled water for the first few weeks will help the traveler adjust and decrease the chance of traveler's diarrhea. Local meat, poultry, seafood, vegetables, and fruits are safe to eat. Milk is pasteurized and safe to drink. Butter, cheese, yogurt and ice-cream are safe.

VACCINATIONS

Routine immunizations should be current. For infants and children through 16 years of age, refer to Chapter 4.3. A rubeola (measles) booster should be considered. Persons age 16 to 65 should receive a booster of tetanus and diphtheria every ten years. Healthy adults under age 65 do not require pneumococcal vaccine, but it is appropriate for those with chronic medical conditions. Influenza vaccine may be considered for those providing essential community services, health care workers, and those wishing to reduce the likelihood of becoming ill with influenza. Adults over 65 years of age are urged to obtain yearly influenza immunization, and to insure that their tetanus and diphtheria immunizations are current. Pneumococcal vaccination is also suggested for this age group.

No vaccinations are required to enter this country.

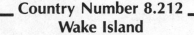

Country Number 8.212
Wake Island

INFECTIOUS DISEASE RISK

Malaria Risk

There is no malaria risk in this country.

Diseases of Special Risk

In addition to the worldwide hazard of tetanus and the routine and any special immunizations recommended below, the traveler should be aware that risk of exposure to the following diseases exists in this country. This list is not

all inclusive, but it is a caution concerning the more likely endemic disease risks.

DISEASE RISK PROFILE

Disease	endemic	risk	hazard
Dengue Fever	x		
Diarrheal Diseases		x	
Encephalitis, Japanese	x		
Filariasis			x
Helminthic Diseases (see Chapter 6.21)		x	
Typhoid Fever		x	

Food/Water Safety

Water is probably safe, but due to local variations in bacterial counts, using bottled water for the first few weeks will help the traveler adjust and decrease the chance of traveler's diarrhea. Local meat, poultry, seafood, vegetables, and fruits are safe to eat. Milk is pasteurized and safe to drink. Butter, cheese, yogurt and ice-cream are safe.

VACCINATIONS

Routine immunizations should be current. For infants and children through 16 years of age, refer to Chapter 4.3. A rubeola (measles) booster should be considered. Persons age 16 to 65 should receive a booster of tetanus and diphtheria every ten years. Healthy adults under age 65 do not require pneumococcal vaccine, but it is appropriate for those with chronic medical conditions. Influenza vaccine may be considered for those providing essential community services, health care workers, and those wishing to reduce the likelihood of becoming ill with influenza. Adults over 65 years of age are urged to obtain yearly influenza immunization, and to insure that their tetanus and diphtheria immunizations are current. Pneumococcal vaccination is also suggested for this age group.

No vaccinations are required to enter this country.

_____ **Country Number 8.213** _____
Wallis and Futuna Islands

INFECTIOUS DISEASE RISK

Malaria Risk

There is no malaria risk in this country.

Diseases of Special Risk

In addition to the worldwide hazard of tetanus and the routine and any

special immunizations recommended below, the traveler should be aware that risk of exposure to the following diseases exists in this country. This list is not all inclusive, but it is a caution concerning the more likely endemic disease risks.

DISEASE RISK PROFILE

Disease	endemic	risk	hazard
Dengue Fever	x		
Diarrheal Diseases		x	
Encephalitis, Japanese	x		
Filariasis			x
Helminthic Diseases (see Chapter 6.21)		x	
Typhoid Fever		x	

Food/Water Safety

All tap water used for drinking, brushing teeth, and making ice cubes should be boiled prior to use. Insure that bottled water is uncapped in your presence. Milk should be boiled to insure safety. Powdered and evaporated milk are available and safe. Avoid butter and other dairy products. All meat, poultry and seafood must be well cooked and served while hot. Pork is best avoided. Vegetables should be well cooked and served hot. Salads and mayonnaise are best avoided. Fruits with intact skins should be peeled by you just prior to consumption. Avoid cold buffets, custards, and any frozen dessert.

VACCINATIONS

Routine immunizations should be current. For infants and children through 16 years of age, refer to Chapter 4.3. A rubeola (measles) booster should be considered. Persons age 16 to 65 should receive a booster of tetanus and diphtheria every ten years. Healthy adults under age 65 do not require pneumococcal vaccine, but it is appropriate for those with chronic medical conditions. Influenza vaccine may be considered for those providing essential community services, health care workers, and those wishing to reduce the likelihood of becoming ill with influenza. Adults over 65 years of age are urged to obtain yearly influenza immunization, and to insure that their tetanus and diphtheria immunizations are current. Pneumococcal vaccination is also suggested for this age group.

No vaccinations are required to enter this country.

_____ **Country Number 8.214** _____
Yemen Arab Republic
(Sana'a')

SPECIAL NOTE: The Yemen Arab Republic and Yemen announced on 22 May 1990 that they were forming one nation, The Republic of Yemen. It was further announced that the republic would honor all treaties either of the former countries concluded. The database is listing the information currently available concerning the original two countries.

INFECTIOUS DISEASE RISK

Malaria Risk

Malaria is present from September through February below 1400 meters throughout the country, except Hajja and Sada provinces. See Chapter 6.31 concerning the weekly use of chloroquine for malaria prevention.

Falciparum malaria represents 99% of malaria, therefore there is only a slight risk of p. vivax malaria exposure. Consider use of primaquine upon return home only if heavy exposure to mosquitos was encounered.

Diseases of Special Risk

In addition to the worldwide hazard of tetanus and the routine and any special immunizations recommended below, the traveler should be aware that risk of exposure to the following diseases exists in this country. This list is not all inclusive, but it is a caution concerning the more likely endemic disease risks.

Schistosomiasis may be found in this country. Avoid contact with contaminated fresh water lakes, ponds, or streams.

DISEASE RISK PROFILE

Disease	endemic	risk	hazard
Brucellosis			x
Cholera	x		
Dracunculiasis/Guinea Worm	x		
Diarrheal Disease Risk		x	
Echinococcosis	x		
Hepatitis, Viral		x	
Leishmaniasis			
Cutaneous	x		
Visceral	x		
Polio			x
Rabies	x		
Relapsing Fever	x		
Tapeworms	x		

Disease	endemic	risk	hazard
Trachoma	x		
Typhoid Fever		x	
Typhus, Endemic Flea-Borne	x		
Typhus, Scrub	x		

Food/Water Safety

All tap water used for drinking, brushing teeth, and making ice cubes should be boiled prior to use. Insure that bottled water is uncapped in your presence. Milk should be boiled to insure safety. Powdered and evaporated milk are available and safe. Avoid butter and other dairy products. All meat, poultry and seafood must be well cooked and served while hot. Pork is best avoided. Vegetables should be well cooked and served hot. Salads and mayonnaise are best avoided. Fruits with intact skins should be peeled by you just prior to consumption. Avoid cold buffets, custards, and any frozen dessert.

VACCINATIONS

Yellow fever—A vaccination certificate is required for travelers coming from infected. A vaccination certificate is required for children over one year of age.

Routine immunizations should be current. For infants and children through 16 years of age, refer to Chapter 4.3. A rubeola (measles) booster should be considered. Persons age 16 to 65 should receive a booster of tetanus and diphtheria every ten years. Healthy adults under age 65 do not require pneumococcal vaccine, but it is appropriate for those with chronic medical conditions. Influenza vaccine may be considered for those providing essential community services, health care workers, and those wishing to reduce the likelihood of becoming ill with influenza. Adults over 65 years of age are urged to obtain yearly influenza immunization, and to insure that their tetanus and diphtheria immunizations are current. Pneumococcal vaccination is also suggested for this age group.

The vaccinations listed are recommended for the traveler's protection.
Poliomyelitis—A poliomyelitis booster is indicated for this country.
Viral Hepatitis A—Vaccination is recommended for all travelers for their protection.
Typhoid fever—Vaccination is recommended for all travelers for their protection.

Selective vaccinations—These apply only to specific groups of travelers or persons on specific working assignments:
Viral Hepatitis B—Because of the high rate of healthy carriers of hepatitis B in this country, vaccination is recommended for persons on working assignments in the health care field (dentists, physicians, nurses, laboratory technicians), or working in close contact with the local population (teachers,

missionaries, Peace Corps), or persons foreseeing sexual relations with local inhabitants.

Plague—Vaccination is recommended only for persons who may be occupationally exposed to wild rodents (anthropologists, geologists, medical personnel, missionaries, etc). The standard vaccination course must be completed before entering the plague infested area. Geographical distribution of the area of risk for this country is the northern half of the country.

Rabies—In this country, where rabies is a constant threat, a pre-exposure rabies vaccination is advised for persons planning an extended stay or on working assignments (naturalists, agricultural advisors, archeologists, geologists, etc.). Although this provides adequate initial protection, a person bitten by a potentially rabid animal would still require post exposure immunization (see Chapter 6.40). Children should be cautioned not to pet dogs, cats, or other mammals.

U. S. Foreign Service:
P O Box 1088
Sanaa, Telephone 271950/8

TRAVEL ADVISORY

A U. S. Department of State Travel Advisory was in effect on 4 May 1990 when this book went to press. The entire text is included below. Travel advisories are subject to reissue, change, and cancellation at any time. Current travel advisory information is available by calling the U. S. Department of State Travel Advisory Hotline at (202) 647-5225. The current travel advisory status is also available from the Herchmer Database update system (see Chapter 2.8).

1 NOVEMBER 1989
SECSTATE WSH SUBJECT: TRAVEL ADVISORY—YEMEN ARAB REPUBLIC—CAUTION

THE DEPARTMENT OF STATE ADVISES THAT TRAVELERS TO THE YEMEN ARAB REPUBLIC SHOULD BEWARE OF POSSIBLE PROBLEMS IN MORE REMOTE AREAS OF THE COUNTRY. MOST AMERICAN CITIZENS TRAVELING TO THE YAR EXPERIENCE NO DIFFICULTIES. HOWEVER, IN MORE REMOTE AREAS, THERE HAVE BEEN OCCASIONAL DISPUTES BETWEEN LOCAL TRIBES OR BETWEEN GOVERNMENT AUTHORITIES AND TRIBES. THESE DISPUTES HAVE OCCASIONALLY RESULTED IN ROAD CLOSURES AND DENIAL OF PERMISSION FOR TOURISTS TO VISIT CERTAIN AREAS. ON TWO OCCASIONS IN THE PAST YEAR, TOURISTS, TRAVELING OFF MAIN ROADS IN THE NORTHERN AND EASTERN SECTORS OF THE COUNTRY, WERE DETAINED BY TRIBESMEN. THERE ALSO HAVE BEEN PERIDIC SEIZURES IN THE SAME AREAS, OF VEHI-

CLES BELONGING TO EXPATRIATE COMPANIES.
BEFORE LEAVING SANAA, TOURISTS MUST OBTAIN TRAVEL PER-
MISSION DOCUMENTS, FROM THE YEMEN GENERAL TOURISM
CORPORATION, FOR SPECIFIC DESTINATIONS OUTSIDE THE CAPI-
TAL. TRAVELERS SHOULD MAKE SURE THEY OBTAIN PERMISSION
FOR ALL OF THE AREAS THEY WISH TO VISIT BEFORE LEAVING
SANAA. SPECIFIC PERMISSION ALSO IS REQUIRED FROM THE
GENERAL TOURISM CORPORATION FOR THE USE OF VIDEO CAM-
ERAS. PHOTOGRAPHY OF MILITARY INSTALLATIONS, EQUIPMENT,
OR TROOPS IS FORBIDDEN.
VISITORS SHOULD CONSULT THEIR PHYSICIAN BEFORE TRAVEL-
ING TO THE YAR DUE TO THE HIGH ALTITUDE OF MANY YEMENI
CITIES (SANAA IS AT 7,200 FEET) AND THE LACK OF ADEQUATE
MEDICAL FACILITIES FOR EMERGENCY TREATMENT.
ALL AMERICAN CITIZENS ARE STRONGLY ADVISED TO CONTACT
THE AMERICAN EMBASSY CONSULAR SECTION WHEN THEY AR-
RIVE TO OBTAIN CURRENT INFORMATION FOR TRAVEL OUTSIDE
THE CAPITAL. THE TELEPHONE NUMBER OF THE EMBASSY IS 271-
950/8. OFFICE HOURS ARE FROM 8:00 A.M. TO 4:00 P.M., SATURDAY
THROUGH WEDNESDAY.
EXPIRATION: OCTOBER 24, 1990

Country Number 8.215
Democratic Yemen
(Aden)

SPECIAL NOTE: The Yemen Arab Republic and Yemen announced on 22 May 1990 that they were forming one nation, The Republic of Yemen. It was further announced that the republic would honor all treaties either of the former countries concluded. The database is lisitng the information currently available concerning the original two countries.

INFECTIOUS DISEASE RISK

Malaria Risk

Malaria is present in all parts of this country, including urban areas. The risk exists all year. See Chapter 6.31 for the weekly use of chloroquine for malaria prevention. There is no malaria risk in Aden and the airport perimeter.

Falciparum malaria represents 99% of malaria, therefore there is very little risk of p. vivax malaria exposure. The use of primaquine upon return home is probably not indicated.

Diseases of Special Risk

In addition to the worldwide hazard of tetanus and the routine and any special immunizations recommended below, the traveler should be aware that risk of exposure to the following diseases exists in this country. This list is not all inclusive, but it is a caution concerning the more likely endemic disease risks.

Schistosomiasis may be found in this country. Avoid contact with contaminated fresh water lakes, ponds, or streams.

DISEASE RISK PROFILE

Disease	endemic	risk	hazard
Brucellosis			x
Cholera	x		
Dracunculiasis/Guinea Worm	x		
Diarrheal Disease Risk		x	
Echinococcosis	x		
Hepatitis, Viral		x	
Leishmaniasis			
Cutaneous	x		
Visceral	x		
Polio			x
Rabies	x		
Relapsing Fever	x		
Tapeworms	x		
Trachoma	x		
Typhoid Fever		x	
Typhus, Endemic Flea-Borne	x		
Typhus, Scrub	x		

Food/Water Safety

All tap water used for drinking, brushing teeth, and making ice cubes should be boiled prior to use. Insure that bottled water is uncapped in your presence. Milk should be boiled to insure safety. Powdered and evaporated milk are available and safe. Avoid butter and other dairy products. All meat, poultry and seafood must be well cooked and served while hot. Pork is best avoided. Vegetables should be well cooked and served hot. Salads and mayonnaise are best avoided. Fruits with intact skins should be peeled by you just prior to consumption. Avoid cold buffets, custards, and any frozen dessert. First class hotels and restaurants serve purified drinking water and reliable food. However, the hazard is left to your judgement.

VACCINATIONS

Yellow fever—A vaccination certificate is required for travelers coming from infected. A vaccination certificate is required for children over one year of age.

Routine immunizations should be current. For infants and children through 16 years of age, refer to Chapter 4.3. A rubeola (measles) booster

should be considered. Persons age 16 to 65 should receive a booster of tetanus and diphtheria every ten years. Healthy adults under age 65 do not require pneumococcal vaccine, but it is appropriate for those with chronic medical conditions. Influenza vaccine may be considered for those providing essential community services, health care workers, and those wishing to reduce the likelihood of becoming ill with influenza. Adults over 65 years of age are urged to obtain yearly influenza immunization, and to insure that their tetanus and diphtheria immunizations are current. Pneumococcal vaccination is also suggested for this age group.

The vaccinations listed are recommended for the traveler's protection.
Poliomyelitis—A poliomyelitis booster is indicated for this country.
Viral Hepatitis A—Vaccination is recommended for all travelers for their protection.
Typhoid fever—Vaccination is recommended for all travelers for their protection.

Selective vaccinations—*These apply only to specific groups of travelers or persons on specific working assignments:*
Viral Hepatitis B—Because of the high rate of healthy carriers of hepatitis B in this country, vaccination is recommended for persons on working assignments in the health care field (dentists, physicians, nurses, laboratory technicians), or working in close contact with the local population (teachers, missionaries, Peace Corps), or persons foreseeing sexual relations with local inhabitants.
Rabies—In this country, where rabies is a constant threat, a pre-exposure rabies vaccination is advised for persons planning an extended stay or on working assignments (naturalists, agricultural advisors, archeologists, geologists, etc.). Although this provides adequate initial protection, a person bitten by a potentially rabid animal would still require post exposure immunization (see Chapter 6.40). Children should be cautioned not to pet dogs, cats, or other mammals.

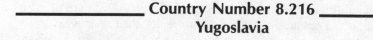

Country Number 8.216
Yugoslavia

INFECTIOUS DISEASE RISK

Malaria Risk
There is no malaria risk in this country.

Diseases of Special Risk
In addition to the worldwide hazard of tetanus and the routine and any

special immunizations recommended below, the traveler should be aware that risk of exposure to the following diseases exists in this country. This list is not all inclusive, but it is a caution concerning the more likely endemic disease risks.

DISEASE RISK PROFILE

Disease	endemic	risk	hazard
Diarrheal Diseases	x		
Dysentery, Bacillary	x		
Encephalitis	x		
Leishmaniasis			
Cutaneous	x		
Visceral	x		
Rabies	x		
Sandfly Fever	x		
Typhoid Fever	x		
Typhus, Endemic Flea-Borne	x		
Typhus, Scrub	x		
West Nile Fever	x		

Food/Water Safety

Water is probably safe, but due to local variations in bacterial counts, using bottled water for the first few weeks will help the traveler adjust and decrease the chance of traveler's diarrhea. Local meat, poultry, seafood, vegetables, and fruits are safe to eat. Milk is pasteurized and safe to drink. Butter, cheese, yogurt and ice-cream are safe.

VACCINATIONS

Routine immunizations should be current. For infants and children through 16 years of age, refer to Chapter 4.3. A rubeola (measles) booster should be considered. Persons age 16 to 65 should receive a booster of tetanus and diphtheria every ten years. Healthy adults under age 65 do not require pneumococcal vaccine, but it is appropriate for those with chronic medical conditions. Influenza vaccine may be considered for those providing essential community services, health care workers, and those wishing to reduce the likelihood of becoming ill with influenza. Adults over 65 years of age are urged to obtain yearly influenza immunization, and to insure that their tetanus and diphtheria immunizations are current. Pneumococcal vaccination is also suggested for this age group.

No vaccinations are required to enter this country.

The vaccinations listed are recommended for the traveler's protection.
Tick-borne encephalitis—(Central European encephalitis) Vaccination is recommended for persons involved in recreational activities in forested areas (camping, hiking) or working in forestry occupations. Risk season: March to

November. Risk is present in forested areas bordering Austria extending south to the areas around Ljubljana and Zagreb.

U. S. Foreign Service:
Kneza Milosa 50
Belgrade, Telephone (110) 645-655

Brace Kavurica 2
Zagreb, Telephone (041) 444-800

Canadian High Commission/Embassy Office:
Kneza Milosa 75
Belgrade, Telephone (110) 644-666

TRAVEL ADVISORY
A U. S. Department of State Travel Advisory was in effect on 4 May 1990 when this book went to press. The entire text is included below. Travel advisories are subject to reissue, change, and cancellation at any time. Current travel advisory information is available by calling the U. S. Department of State Travel Advisory Hotline at (202) 647-5225. The current travel advisory status is also available from the Herchmer Database update system (see Chapter 2.8).

JANUARY 31, 1990
YUGOSLAVIA—WARNING
THE DEPARTMENT OF STATE ADVISES U.S. CITIZENS THAT TRAVEL TO THE YUGOSLAV PROVINCE OF KOSOVO SHOULD BE DEFERRED UNTIL FURTHER NOTICE. THERE HAVE BEEN LARGE DEMONSTRATIONS THROUGHOUT THE PROVINCE AND A NUMBER OF FATALITIES IN CLASHES BETWEEN POLICE AND DEMONSTRATORS. ALSO THERE HAVE BEEN UNPROVOKED ATTACKS AND REPORTED INCIDENTS OF RANDOM SHOOTING AT, AND STONING OF, VEHICLES ON ROADS IN THE PROVINCE.
EXPIRATION: INDEFINITE

─────────── **Country Number 8.217** ───────────
Zaire

INFECTIOUS DISEASE RISK

Malaria Risk
Malaria is present in all parts of this country, including urban areas. The risk exists all year. The malaria in this country is resistant to chloroquine. The CDC recommends the use of mefloquine (Lariam) as described in Chapter 6.31

for chemical prophylaxis.

Falciparum malaria represents 93% of malaria, therefore there is a slight risk of p. vivax malaria exposure. Consider the use of primaquine upon return home.

Diseases of Special Risk

In addition to the worldwide hazard of tetanus and the routine and any special immunizations recommended below, the traveler should be aware that risk of exposure to the following diseases exists in this country. This list is not all inclusive, but it is a caution concerning the more likely endemic disease risks.

This country must be considered receptive to dengue fever. Intermittent epidemics in the past make renewed activity or reintroduction of the virus possible.

Schistosomiasis may be found in this country. Avoid contact with contaminated fresh water lakes, ponds, or streams. Risk of infection by S. mansoni is present in: —the northern and northeastern regions along the Kibali-Uele rivers and their tributaries, Lake Mobutu, Ituri River and tributaries;—the eastern part of the country, the areas of Lake Edward, Lake Kivu, and Lake Tanganyika;—the south of the country, the southeastern parts of Shaba (Katanga) and East Kasai;—a small area in lower Zaire, in the area of Kimpesi. Risk of infection by S. haematobium is present in the southeastern parts of the country, in the river basins of Lualaba (Congo) and Luapula, Province of Shaba. Risk of infection by S. intercalatum is present along the river Lualaba (Congo) from the area of Kongolo downstream to the confluence of the Lomani River north of Kisangani (Stanleyville).

Louse-borne typhus is cosmopolitan in distribution and is present wherever groups of persons are crowded together under conditions of poor sanitation and malnutrition. Risk exists for persons living or working in remote areas of the country (anthropologists, archeologists, geologists, medical personnel, missionaries, etc.). Freedom from louse infestation is the most effective protection against typhus.

DISEASE RISK PROFILE

Disease	endemic	risk	hazard
Dracunculiasis/Guinea Worm		x	
Diarrheal Disease Risk			x
Dysentery, Amoebic/Bacillary			x
Echinococcosis		x	
Filariasis			x
Giardiasis			x
Helminthic Diseases (see Chapter 6.21)			x
Hepatitis, Viral			x
Leishmaniasis			
Cutaneous	x		
Visceral	x		

Disease	endemic	risk	hazard
Loiasis			x
Onchocerciasis			x
Plague	x		
Polio			x
Rabies	x		
Relapsing Fever	x		
Trachoma			x
Trypanosomiasis, African	x		
Sleeping Sickness Typhoid Fever			x
Typhus, Endemic Flea-Borne	x		
Typhus, Epidemic Louse-Borne	x		
Typhus, Scrub	x		

Food/Water Safety

All tap water used for drinking, brushing teeth, and making ice cubes should be boiled prior to use. Insure that bottled water is uncapped in your presence. Milk should be boiled to insure safety. Powdered and evaporated milk are available and safe. Avoid butter and other dairy products. All meat, poultry and seafood must be well cooked and served while hot. Pork is best avoided. Vegetables should be well cooked and served hot. Salads and mayonnaise are best avoided. Fruits with intact skins should be peeled by you just prior to consumption. Avoid cold buffets, custards, and any frozen dessert. First class hotels and restaurants in Kinshasa (Leopoldville) and Lubumbashi (Elisabethville) serve purified drinking water and reliable food. However, the hazard is left to your judgement.

VACCINATIONS

Yellow fever—A vaccination certificate is required for travelers coming from infected areas. A vaccination certificate is required for children over one year of age. The reqirement applies to travelers arriving in or destined for that part of the country south of 10 degrees south latitude. CDC recommends vaccination for all travelers over 9 months of age who will be traveling outside of urban areas. The Embassy of Zaire reports that a yellow fever vaccination is rquired for all travelers over one year of age.

Routine immunizations should be current. For infants and children through 16 years of age, refer to Chapter 4.3. A rubeola (measles) booster should be considered. Persons age 16 to 65 should receive a booster of tetanus and diphtheria every ten years. Healthy adults under age 65 do not require pneumococcal vaccine, but it is appropriate for those with chronic medical conditions. Influenza vaccine may be considered for those providing essential community services, health care workers, and those wishing to reduce the likelihood of becoming ill with influenza. Adults over 65 years of age are urged to obtain yearly influenza immunization, and to insure that their tetanus and diphtheria immunizations are current. Pneumococcal vaccination is also suggested for this age group.

The vaccinations listed are recommended for the traveler's protection.

Poliomyelitis—A poliomyelitis booster is indicated for this country.

Cholera—Cholera is present in this country. Risk to western travelers is low. Immunization is not required or recommended for travel to this country due to its low effectiveness. Avoid uncooked foods and untreated water. Vaccination is advised only for persons living or working under inadequate sanitary conditions and for those with impaired defense mechanisms.

Viral Hepatitis A—Vaccination is recommended for all travelers for their protection.

Typhoid fever—Vaccination is recommended for all travelers for their protection.

Selective vaccinations—*These apply only to specific groups of travelers or persons on specific working assignments:*

Viral Hepatitis B—Because of the high rate of healthy carriers of hepatitis B in this country, vaccination is recommended for persons on working assignments in the health care field (dentists, physicians, nurses, laboratory technicians), or working in close contact with the local population (teachers, missionaries, Peace Corps), or persons foreseeing sexual relations with local inhabitants.

Plague—Vaccination is recommended only for persons who may be occupationally exposed to wild rodents (anthropologists, geologists, medical personnel, missionaries, etc). The standard vaccination course must be completed before entering the plague infested area. Geographical distribution of the areas of risk for this country are present in the notheastern corner of the country bordering Uganda and Sudan.

U. S. Foreign Service:
310 Avenue des Aviateurs
Kinshasa, Telephone 25-881/2/3/4/5/6

Bukavu, Telephone 2594

Lumbumbashi, Telephone 222324/5

Canadian High Commission/Embassy Office:
Edifice Shell
Coin Avenue Wangata et Boul. du 30-juin
Kinshasa, Telephone 22-706, 24-346, 27-839/551

Country Number 8.218
Zambia

INFECTIOUS DISEASE RISK

Malaria Risk

Malaria is present in all parts of this country, including urban areas. The risk exists from November through May. The malaria in this country is resistant to chloroquine. The CDC recommends the use of mefloquine (Lariam) as described in Chapter 6.31 for chemical prophylaxis.

Falciparum malaria represents 90% of malaria, therefore there is a slight risk of p. vivax malaria exposure. Consider use of primaquine upon return home.

Diseases of Special Risk

In addition to the worldwide hazard of tetanus and the routine and any special immunizations recommended below, the traveler should be aware that risk of exposure to the following diseases exists in this country. This list is not all inclusive, but it is a caution concerning the more likely endemic disease risks.

Schistosomiasis may be found in this country. Avoid contact with contaminated fresh water lakes, ponds, or streams.

DISEASE RISK PROFILE

Disease	endemic	risk	hazard
Cholera		x	
Dracunculiasis/Guinea Worm		x	
Diarrheal Disease Risk			x
Dysentery, Amoebic/Bacillary			x
Echinococcosis		x	
Filariasis			x
Giardiasis			x
Helminthic Diseases (see Chapter 6.21)			x
Hepatitis, Viral			x
Leishmaniasis			
Cutaneous	x		
Visceral	x		
Loiasis			x
Onchocerciasis			x
Plague	x		
Polio			x
Rabies	x		
Relapsing Fever	x		
Trachoma			x
Trypanosomiasis, African Sleeping Sickness	x		
Typhoid Fever			x

Disease	endemic	risk	hazard
Typhus, Endemic Flea-Borne	x		
Typhus, Epidemic Louse-Borne	x		
Typhus, Scrub	x		

Food/Water Safety

All tap water used for drinking, brushing teeth, and making ice cubes should be boiled prior to use. Insure that bottled water is uncapped in your presence. Milk should be boiled to insure safety. Powdered and evaporated milk are available and safe. Avoid butter and other dairy products. All meat, poultry and seafood must be well cooked and served while hot. Pork is best avoided. Vegetables should be well cooked and served hot. Salads and mayonnaise are best avoided. Fruits with intact skins should be peeled by you just prior to consumption. Avoid cold buffets, custards, and any frozen dessert. First class hotels and restaurants in Ndola serve purified drinking water and reliable food. However, the hazard is left to your judgement. Food, dairy products, and water is considered safe in Livingtone (Maramba) and Lusaka.

VACCINATIONS

Yellow fever—A vaccination certificate is required for travelers coming from infected areas and from or in transit through countries with active disease. A vaccination certificate is required for children over one year of age. CDC recommends vaccination for all travelers over 9 months of age who may travel outside of urban areas.

Routine immunizations should be current. For infants and children through 16 years of age, refer to Chapter 4.3. A rubeola (measles) booster should be considered. Persons age 16 to 65 should receive a booster of tetanus and diphtheria every ten years. Healthy adults under age 65 do not require pneumococcal vaccine, but it is appropriate for those with chronic medical conditions. Influenza vaccine may be considered for those providing essential community services, health care workers, and those wishing to reduce the likelihood of becoming ill with influenza. Adults over 65 years of age are urged to obtain yearly influenza immunization, and to insure that their tetanus and diphtheria immunizations are current. Pneumococcal vaccination is also suggested for this age group.

The vaccinations listed are recommended for the traveler's protection.

Poliomyelitis—A poliomyelitis booster is indicated for this country.

Viral Hepatitis A—Vaccination is recommended for all travelers for their protection.

Typhoid fever—Vaccination is recommended for all travelers for their protection.

Selective vaccinations—These apply only to specific groups of travelers or persons on specific working assignments:

Viral Hepatitis B—Because of the high rate of healthy carriers of hepatitis B in this country, vaccination is recommended for persons on working assignments in the health care field (dentists, physicians, nurses, laboratory technicians), or working in close contact with the local population (teachers, missionaries, Peace Corps), or persons foreseeing sexual relations with local inhabitants.

Plague—Vaccination is recommended only for persons who may be occupationally exposed to wild rodents (anthropologists, geologists, medical personnel, missionaries, etc). The standard vaccination course must be completed before entering the plague infested area. Geographical distribution of the areas of risk for this country are present in the western part of the country (near Bulawayo).

Rabies—In this country, where rabies is a constant threat, a pre-exposure rabies vaccination is advised for persons planning an extended stay or on working assignments (naturalists, agricultural advisors, archeologists, geologists, etc.). Although this provides adequate initial protection, a person bitten by a potentially rabid animal would still require post exposure immunization (see Chapter 6.40). Children should be cautioned not to pet dogs, cats, or other mammals.

U. S. Foreign Service:
Corner of Independence and United Nations Avenue
Lusaka, Telephone 214911

Canadian High Commission/Embassy Office:
Barclays Bank North End Branch
Cairo Road
Lusaka, Telephone 216161

TRAVEL ADVISORY

A U. S. Department of State Travel Advisory was in effect on 4 May 1990 when this book went to press. The entire text is included below. Travel advisories are subject to reissue, change, and cancellation at any time. Current travel advisory information is available by calling the U. S. Department of State Travel Advisory Hotline at (202) 647-5225. The current travel advisory status is also available from the Herchmer Database update system (see Chapter 2.8).

UNITED STATES DEPARTMENT OF STATE TRAVEL ADVISORY 26 JUN 1989
ZAMBIA—CAUTION
THE DEPARTMENT OF STATE ADVISES AMERICANS TO EXERCISE CAUTION AND PRUDENCE WHEN TRAVELING IN ZAMBIA. AS A RESULT OF A SERIES OF FOREIGN MILITARY INCURSIONS IN THE SOUTHERN AFRICAN REGION, ZAMBIAN POLICE AND SECURITY

FORCES ARE SUSPICIOUS OF FOREIGNERS. THERE HAVE BEEN INCIDENTS WHERE FOREIGNERS HAVE BEEN DETAINED AND THE ZAMBIAN AUTHORITIES HAVE BEEN VERY SLOW IN INFORMING EMBASSIES AND IN GRANTING CONSULAR ACCESS. WHILE ALL MAJOR ROADS ARE OPEN, POLICE ROAD BLOCKS ARE COMMON, AND VEHICLES AND PASSENGERS ARE COMMONLY SEARCHED. EXTREME CAUTION SHOULD BE USED WHEN GOING OFF MAJOR ROADS OUTSIDE OF TOURIST AREAS, AS MILITARY RESTRICTED ZONES ARE OFTEN UNMARKED. CAMERAS SHOULD NOT BE USED EXCEPT IN TOURIST AREAS OR LOCATIONS SPECIFICALLY AP-PROVED BY ZAMBIAN AUTHORITIES. VISITORS SHOULD AVOID WEARING CLOTHING THAT COULD BE CONSTRUED AS MILITARY IN NATURE.

VISITORS ARE ADVISED AGAINST TRAVEL TO THE AREAS WEST OF THE ZAMBEZI RIVER AND EAST OF THE GREAT EAST ROAD. SPE-CIAL CAUTION SHOULD BE EXERCISED ALONG THE ZAMBIA-ZAIRE FRONTIER BECAUSE OF POLICE AND MILITARY ACTIONS AIMED AT CURBING SMUGGLING. TRAVEL BY AIR DIRECTLY FROM LUSAKA TO ZAMBIA'S MAJOR GAME PARK, THE LUANGWA VALLEY, OR ITS MAJOR TOURIST ATTRACTION, VICTORIA FALLS, IS GENERALLY SAFE.

CRIME IS HIGH AND TRAVELERS SHOULD TAKE BASIC PRECAU-TIONS. TRAVEL AT NIGHT SHOULD BE AVOIDED EVEN ON MAJOR CITY STREETS AND MAIN HIGHWAYS. EXCEPT FOR AIRLINES, PUB-LIC TRANSPORT IS UNRELIABLE AND UNSAFE. MEDICAL TREAT-MENT AND PHARMACEUTICALS ARE IN SHORT SUPPLY. IN ADDITION, ZAMBIA HAS A HIGH INCIDENCE OF MALARIA, INCLUD-ING SOME STRAINS WHICH ARE RESISTANT TO THE MALARIA SU-PRESANT CHLOROQUINE.

THE BEST SOURCE FOR CURRENT INFORMATION WHILE IN ZAM-BIA IS THE U.S. EMBASSY, LOCATED AT THE CORNER OF INDEPEN-DENCE AND UNITED NATIONS AVENUES, LUSAKA; TELEPHONE 214911.

EXPIRATION: JUNE 30, 1990.

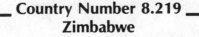

Country Number 8.219
Zimbabwe

INFECTIOUS DISEASE RISK

Malaria Risk

 Malaria risk is present from November through May, throughout the coun-try, including urban areas. Who reports that there is risk of malaria in the city of

Harare. The malaria in this country is resistant to chloroquine. The CDC recommends the use of mefloquine (Lariam) as described in Chapter 6.31 for chemical prophylaxis.

Falciparum malaria represents 91% of malaria, therefore there is a slight risk of p. vivax malaria exposure. Consider use of Primaquine upon return home.

Diseases of Special Risk

In addition to the worldwide hazard of tetanus and the routine and any special immunizations recommended below, the traveler should be aware that risk of exposure to the following diseases exists in this country. This list is not all inclusive, but it is a caution concerning the more likely endemic disease risks.

Schistosomiasis may be found in this country. Avoid contact with contaminated fresh water lakes, ponds, or streams.

DISEASE RISK PROFILE

Disease	endemic	risk	hazard
Dracunculiasis/Guinea Worm	x		
Diarrheal Disease Risk			x
Dysentery, Amoebic/Bacillary			x
Echinococcosis		x	
Filariasis			x
Giardiasis			x
Helminthic Diseases (see Chapter 6.21)			x
Hepatitis, Viral			x
Leishmaniasis			
Cutaneous	x		
Visceral	x		
Polio			x
Rabies	x		
Relapsing Fever	x		
Trachoma			x
Trypanosomiasis, African	x		
Sleeping Sickness			
Typhoid Fever			x
Typhus, Endemic Flea-Borne	x		
Typhus, Epidemic Louse-Borne	x		
Typhus, Scrub	x		

Food/Water Safety

Water is probably safe, but due to local variations in bacterial counts, using bottled water for the first few weeks will help the traveler adjust and decrease the chance of traveler's diarrhea. Local meat, poultry, seafood, vegetables, and fruits are safe to eat. Milk is pasteurized and safe to drink. Butter, cheese, yogurt and ice-cream are safe.

VACCINATIONS

Yellow fever—A vaccination certificate is required for travelers coming from infected areas and from or in transit through countries with active infection. A vaccination is required for children of all ages. Children under nine months of age should not be vaccinated due to health considerations. Please refer to the discussion in Chapter 6.63 on avoiding yellow fever vaccination in this age group.

Routine immunizations should be current. For infants and children through 16 years of age, refer to Chapter 4.3. A rubeola (measles) booster should be considered. Persons age 16 to 65 should receive a booster of tetanus and diphtheria every ten years. Healthy adults under age 65 do not require pneumococcal vaccine, but it is appropriate for those with chronic medical conditions. Influenza vaccine may be considered for those providing essential community services, health care workers, and those wishing to reduce the likelihood of becoming ill with influenza. Adults over 65 years of age are urged to obtain yearly influenza immunization, and to insure that their tetanus and diphtheria immunizations are current. Pneumococcal vaccination is also suggested for this age group.

The vaccinations listed are recommended for the traveler's protection.
Poliomyelitis—A poliomyelitis booster is indicated for this country.
Viral Hepatitis A—Vaccination is recommended for all travelers for their protection.
Typhoid fever—Vaccination is recommended for all travelers for their protection.

Selective vaccinations—*These apply only to specific groups of travelers or persons on specific working assignments:*
Viral Hepatitis B—Because of the high rate of healthy carriers of hepatitis B in this country, vaccination is recommended for persons on working assignments in the health care field (dentists, physicians, nurses, laboratory technicians), or working in close contact with the local population (teachers, missionaries, Peace Corps), or persons foreseeing sexual relations with local inhabitants.

Plague—Vaccination is recommended only for persons who may be occupationally exposed to wild rodents (anthropologists, geologists, medical personnel, missionaries, etc). The standard vaccination course must be completed before entering the plague infested area. Occasional cases are reported from the northeastern part of the country (Muchinga Mountains) and in the southwestern part bordering Botswana and Angola).

U. S. Foreign Service:
172 Rhodes Avenue
Salisbury, Telephone 70-58-35

Canadian High Commission/Embassy Office:
45 Baines Avenue
Harare, Telephone 79-38-01

TRAVEL ADVISORY

A U. S. Department of State Travel Advisory was in effect on 4 May 1990 when this book went to press. The entire text is included below. Travel advisories are subject to reissue, change, and cancellation at any time. Current travel advisory information is available by calling the U. S. Department of State Travel Advisory Hotline at (202) 647-5225. The current travel advisory status is also available from the Herchmer Database update system (see Chapter 2.8).

9FB DN37 1-1 1LA71 1 07/26/89 19:56
SECSTATE WSH SUBJECT: TRAVEL ADVISORY—ZIMBABWE—CAUTION
1. THE DEPARTMENT OF STATE ADVISES U.S. CITIZENS TRAVELING TO ZIMBABWE THAT, DUE TO UNCERTAIN SECURITY CONDITIONS, TRAVEL IN EXTREME EASTERN ZIMBABWE ALONG THE MOZAMBIQUE BORDER SHOULD BE UNDERTAKEN WITH SOME CARE. THIS REGION IS SUBJECT TO INCURSIONS FROM ARMED BANDS FROM MOZAMBIQUE. MAIN TOURIST AREAS FROM INYANGA TO VUMBA HAVE NOT BEEN AFFECTED, BUT TRAVELERS SHOULD CONSULT LOCAL OFFICIALS BEFORE TRAVELING BEYOND THESE MAIN TOURIST AREAS OR TAKING OFF-ROAD EXCURSIONS ANYWHERE NEAR THE EASTERN BORDER. THE GONAREZHOU NATIONAL PARK IN SOUTHEAST ZIMBABWE IS CLOSED TO ALL VISITORS DUE TO THESE SECURITY PROBLEMS. TRAVELERS SHOULD EXPECT TO ENCOUNTER POLICE AND MILITARY ROADBLOCKS THROUGHOUT THE COUNTRY.
2. TRAVELERS SHOULD BE AWARE THAT ZIMBABWE AUTHORITIES ARE EXTREMELY SENSITIVE ABOUT THE PHOTOGRAPHING OF CERTAIN INSTALLATIONS AND BUILDINGS, SUCH AS GOVERNMENT OFFICES, OFFICIAL RESIDENCES, AND EMBASSIES. VISITORS ARE STRONGLY ADVISED TO ASK POLICE FOR PERMISSION TO PHOTOGRAPH BEFORE ATTEMPTING TO TAKE PICTURES OF BUILDINGS OR INSTALLATIONS.
3. UNITED STATES CITIZENS SHOULD BE AWARE THAT THERE HAVE BEEN SEVERAL INCIDENTS IN WHICH THERE WERE LONG DELAYS BEFORE AUTHORITIES NOTIFIED THE U.S. EMBASSY OF THE ARREST OR DETENTION OF AMERICANS. U.S. OFFICIALS HAVE PROTESTED STRONGLY, BUT THERE IS STILL NO GUARANTEE THAT AMERICANS DETAINED FOR ANY REASON BY ZIMBABWE REPUBLIC POLICE WILL HAVE EARLY ACCESS TO U.S. CONSULAR OFFICIALS.

4. ALTHOUGH NO VISA IS REQUIRED TO ENTER ZIMBABWE, IMMIGRATION AUTHORITIES REQUIRE THE FOLLOWING: (A) A FIRM ITINERARY FOR THE PROPOSED VISIT, (B) SUFFICIENT FUNDS TO SUPPORT ONE'S NEEDS DURING THE VISIT, AND (C) A RETURN TICKET TO THE UNITED STATES. ONWARD TICKETS TO NON-U.S. DESTINATIONS WILL OFTEN NOT SUFFICE, AND IF THESE REQUIREMENTS ARE NOT MET, IMMIGRATION AUTHORITIES CAN ORDER DEPARTURE BY THE NEXT AVAILABLE FLIGHT.

5. CURRENCY TRANSACTIONS ARE STRICTLY REGULATED. TOURISTS MUST DECLARE TO ZIMBABWE CUSTOMS THE AMOUNTS OF CURRENCY AND TRAVELERS CHECKS THEY ARE CARRYING. FAILURE TO DECLARE CAN MEAN CONFISCATION AND A FINE.

6. THIS TRAVEL ADVISORY REPLACES THE PREVIOUS ADVISORY ISSUED ON AUGUST 16, 1988, CONTAINED IN 88 STATE 266875.

7. EXPIRATION DATE: AUGUST 1, 1990. DEPT OF STATE WASHDC 236950/L1712

Section 9

Glossary

The jargon and vernacular language of foreign travel experts will be explained in this dictionary of foreign medical travel. What is the difference between a toxin and a toxoid? This and many other mysteries are clarified in this important section. Listings in this section have been restricted to terms that have not been fully explained within the text and to terms that are referenced which might be unknown or confusing to the non- physician user of this book.

GLOSSARY

Absorption—The passage of a substance through some surface of the body into body fluids and tissues.

Acclimatize—To become accustomed to a different environment and climate.

Active immunization—The production of immunity in response to the administration of a vaccine or a toxoid.

Adsorption—Adhesion by a gas or liquid to the surface of a solid.

AIDS—Acquired Immunodeficiency Syndrome, a clinical diagnosis based upon several criteria which includes evidence of infection with the HIV virus and which has resulted in significant reduction of immune response and in the patient having thus acquired infections that a person with a normal immune response would not have acquired.

Ambient temperature—The surrounding, or environmental, temperature.

Anaphylactic shock—State of collapse resulting from exposure to a substance to which the person has become sensitized; pertaining to anaphylaxis.

Anaphylaxis—An exaggerated or extreme sensitivity resulting from the injection or exposure to a foreign protein that results in an asthmatic reaction, generalized skin rash (welts or urticaria), shock, and, sometimes, death.

Angina pectoris—Severe, constricting pain in the chest due to lack of oxygen in the heart muscle.

Antibiotic—A substance that inhibits the growth of microorganisms.

Antibody—A modified protein of an animal, usually formed in response to an infectious agent, such as a virus or bacterium, that causes a reaction in the host animal that destroys the infectious agent.

Antigen—Any of various types of substance (such as bacteria, virus, foreign protein) that causes an antibody to form, thus inducing an immune response.

Antitoxin—An antibody that is formed to defend the host animal against a foreign (usually protein) substance, such as snake venom or other poisonous substance, that neutralizes or otherwise prevents the toxic substance from causing harm, used to achieve passive immunity or to effect a treatment.

Antivenin—The active substance in an antiserum that protects an animal against another animal's, or insect's, venom.

ARC—Aids Related Complex; the definition given to a disease of a person infected with the HIV virus, who has demonstrated a decreased immunity from diseases, but who does not satisfy the full definition of having AIDS. A pre-AIDS state.

Arrhythmia—Irregularity, usually of the heart.

Bacillary—Relating to, or caused by, bacteria.

Bacteria—Plural form of bacterium.

Bacterium—Any one cell vegetable microorganism, some of which cause disease in man, animals, and larger plants.

Barotrauma—Injury, generally to the middle ear, resulting from imbalance between ambient pressure and that within the affected cavity; generally a term applied to injury to the ear drum from such a change in pressure.

Benign—A mild illness or nonmalignant tumor.

Catecholamine pathway—A biochemical process in the body that helps in the digestive use of proteins.

CDC—Centers for Disease Control.

Circadian rhythm or cycle—Relating to biologic variations or rhythms with a cycle of about 24 hours.

Cor pulmonale—Dilation and failure of the right side of the heart secondary to certain obstructing pulmonary diseases.

Cyanosis—A dark bluish or purplish coloration of the skin due to deficient oxygenation of the blood.

Deltoid muscle—The muscle at the upper part of the arm at the junction with the shoulder.

Direct transit area—A special area established in an airport, approved and supervised directly by the health administration concerned, for segregating passengers and crews breaking their air voyage without leaving the airport.

Diuretic—A substance that causes increased urination.

Emporiatrics—The science of the health of travelers visiting foreign countries.

Encephalitis—An infection of a layer of tissue covering the brain, frequently resulting in death or severe neurological damage, generally caused by a viral or bacterial infection.

Endemic—The usual frequency of occurrence of a disease, including possible seasonal variations, in a human population. Less precisely, a disease prevailing continually in a region.

Envenomate—To inject venom into, as a result of a poisonous bite or sting.

Enzootic—The usual frequency of occurrence of a disease, including possible seasonal variations, in an animal population.

Epidemic—The extensive prevalence in a community or region of a disease brought from without, or a temporary increase in a number of cases of an endemic disease.

Epidemiology—The science of epidemics and epidemic diseases.

Epizootic—The occurrence of a disease in a defined animal population at a higher than expected rate.

Eustachian tube—The tube connecting the space behind the ear drum to the throat, important in allowing the equalization of pressure of the middle ear and the ambient pressure.

FDA—Food and Drug Administration.

Glucagon—An injectable hormone of the pancreas that can elevate blood sugar, useful in treating low blood sugar as a result of insulin overdose, especially when in diabetic coma.

Gluteal—Relating to the muscle that forms the prominent portion of the buttocks.

Glycogen—A high energy fuel source that the body produces from blood sugar (glucose).

Hg—Mercury; when used to measure blood pressure, or atmospheric pressure, the figure is frequently reported in millimeters of mercury or mm Hg.

HIV—The abbreviation for the virus which causes AIDS, the Human Immunodeficiency Virus.

Hypertension—High blood pressure.

Hypoglycemia—Low blood sugar.

Hypoxia—Low oxygen level.

IM or i.m.—Intramuscular, as in giving a shot into the muscle. See also, subq and IV.

Immune globulin (IG)—A sterile solution containing antibody from human blood. It is primarily indicated for routine maintenance of certain immunodeficient persons, and for passive immunization against measles and hepatitis A.

Immunization—The process or procedure by which immunity is produced in a person or animal. Active immunity is the formation of antibodies by the human or animal in response to exposure to antigens. Passive immunity is acquired by injecting antibodies prepared in another organism (or otherwise manufactured), such as immune globulin.

Imported case—A person who acquired an infection outside of a specific area.

Indoleamine pathway—A biochemical process in the body which helps in the digestive use of carbohydrates.

Infected area—An area which harbors a particular agent of infection and which because of population characteristics, density, mobility, and/or vector and animal reservoir potential, could support transmission of disease(s) identified there. It is defined on epidemiologic principles by the health administration reporting the disease and need not correspond to administrative boundaries.

International Certificates of Vaccination—The official certificates used to document the vaccinations a traveler has received, when and where received, and who administered them.

IPV—Inactive poliovirus vaccine, injectable.

Isolation—The separation of a person or group of persons from others (except the health staff on duty) to prevent the spread of infection.

IV or i.v.—Intravenous, as in giving a medication directly into a vein.

Mal de mer—Motion sickness; a functional disorder thought to be brought on by repetitive motion and characterized by nausea or vomiting.

mm Hg—Millimeters of mercury; a measurement of pressure.

MMWR—Morbidity and Mortality Weekly Report, published by the CDC.

Morbidity—A diseased state; illness.

Mortality—Collectively, the death of large numbers, as by war or disease.

Murine—Relating to mice or rats.

Nanometer—A billionth of a meter.

Nape—The back of the neck.

OPV—Oral poliovirus vaccine; an active, or live virus, vaccine.

Pandemic—Denoting a disease affecting or attacking all, or a large proportion of the population of a region; extensively epidemic.

Parasitic disease—A disease caused by an organism that lives in or on another organism.

Passive immunization—The provision of temporary immunity by the administration of preformed antitoxin or antibodies.

Pathology—The medical science dealing with all aspects of disease; the results of a disease process.

Pharynx—The throat, the joint opening of the gullet and the windpipe.

Phobia—Irrational or exaggerated fear.

Pilot biscuits—A form of hardtack bread, used as a food ration.

Pneumothorax—Air in the chest, meaning a leak of air from the lungs, causing a partial or complete collapse of a lung.

Prophylactic—Preventing disease; relating to prophylaxis.

Prophylaxis—The prevention of disease.

Pulmonary cysts—A hollow area of the lung, devoid of normal lung tissue, caused by emphysema or infectious agent.

Quarantine—The state or condition during which measures are applied by a health administration to a ship, an aircraft, a train, road vehicle, other means of transport or container, or individuals to prevent the spread of disease from the object of quarantine to reservoirs, vectors of disease, or other individuals.

Quarantinable diseases—Cholera, plague, and yellow fever.

Recommended vaccination—Vaccination not required by International Health Regulations but suggested for travelers visiting or living in certain countries.

Required vaccination—Vaccination the traveler must have for entry into, or exit from, a country. The travelers must present a validated International Certificate of Vaccination which documents the vaccination(s) received.

Serology—A blood test for an antibody response, generally performed to check for syphylis exposure and presumptive infection; the branch of science dealing with serum, especially with specific immune serums.

Serotype—A subdivision of a species (generally a bacterium or virus) distinguishable from other strains therein on the basis of antigenic character.

Specific immune globulin—Special preparations obtained from donor pools preselected for a high antibody content against a specific disease.

Subq—Subcutaneous; a method of giving an injection, just under the skin into the subcutaneous fatty tissue.

Titer—The standard of strength per volume of a test solution; a measure of antibody response.

Topical—Applied to the skin surface, as with an ointment.

Toxin—A noxious or poisonous substance.

Toxoid—A toxin that has been treated so as to destroy its toxic property, but which is still antigenic, i.e., capable of stimulating the production of antibodies and thus of producing an active immunity.

Urticaria—A skin welt, a manifestation of an allergic reaction.

U.S.P.—United States Pharmacopeia, a book relating the purity and composition of certain medical substances; a compound with the purity as required by the United States Pharmacopeia.

U.S.P.H.S.—Initials of the United States Public Health Service.

Vaccine—The modified and attenuated virus (or bacterium) of any disease, incapable of producing a severe infection, but affording protection, when inoculated, against the action of the unmodified virus (bacterium).

Validation—Application of an official stamp or seal to the International Certificate of Vaccination by the health department or other appropriate agency. Approved validation stamps and seals in the United States are: 1) The Department of Defense Stamp, 2) the Department of State Seal, 3) the Public Health Service Seal, 4) the National Aeronautics and Space Administration Stamp, and 5) the Uniform Stamp.

Valid certificate—An International Certificate of Vaccination that has been fully completed, signed, and validated with an official stamp or seal.

Vasoconstriction—The constriction of the small arteries, generally in response to cold.

Vasodilation—The dilation of the small arteries, generally in response to warmth.

Vector—The term applied to an insect or any living carrier which transports a disease causing microorganism from the sick to the well.

Venom—A poisonous fluid secreted by snakes, spiders, scorpions, etc.

Vertigo—Dizziness.

WHO—The initials of the World Health Organization.

Yellow Fever Vaccination Center—A center designated under the authority of the health administration of a country to administer yellow fever vaccine.

Section 10

Index

In a resource book an index is the critical link between the consumer and the reason they obtained the book. This index is extensively cross referenced with both technical names and common names for diseases, organizational references, and medical and travel problems. Major listings are distinguished from minor references with the use of bold face type. Major listings will include descriptions of technical terms where they appear in the text. Minor listings cross reference the appearance of terms used throughout the book, with the exception of the Individual Country Database (Section 8). Section 8 has been indexed for country listings only as a full indexing of this section would unecessarily bulk up references to diseases, medications, and immunizations beyond reason. Minor listings include only cross-references of possible significance to the reader and exclude simple word appearances.

INDEX

A

Abbott Laboratories 5-8
abdominal pain 7-22
abrasion 7-5
    eye 7-11
Access America, Inc. 2-42
Actifed 7-73
    acute hypothermia 7-54
    acute mountain sickness 7-65
Aden 8-437
advice for travel, medical 2-23
Aedes aegypti mosquito 6-9
Afghanistan 8-1
African eyeworm 6-30
African sleeping sickness 6-62
after-drop 7-53
AIDS and travel 4-31
    entry testing 4-34
air squeeze 7-15
air travel 3-15
    squeeze on ear 7-15
    and children 4-18
airplane descent 7-15
Albania 8-3
Aleppo boil 6-27
Algeria 8-4
aloe vera 7-3
Amadiaquine 6-37
American leishmaniasis 6-27
American Samoa 8-6
Ames Uristix 4-5
AMS 7-65
Anakit 7-40
anaphylactic shock 7-39
Andorra 8-7
Angola 8-8
Anguilla 8-10
animal bites 7-37
ankle injury 7-32
anthrax 6-1
Antiqua 8-11
Antivert 7-30
appendicitis 7-24
Argentina 8-12
Argentinian hemorrhagic fever 6-19
Argonne jet lag diet 3-28
ARM Coverage Insurance 2-43

arrests, foreign 2-3
Aruba 8-14
assassin bug 6-63
assessment, post trip 4-41
assessment, emotional 4-45
assistance for travelers 2-39
AT&T 2-45
Atarax 7-31, 7-82
Australia 8-14
Austria 8-16
Avon 5-25
Azores 8-18

B

Bacillus anthracis 6-1
Bactrim DS 5-15, 7-26, 7-28, 7-80
    use while pregnant 4-9
Bahamas 8-19
Bahrain 8-20
Bang's disease 6-3
Bangladesh 8-22
Barbados 8-24
Barbuda 8-11
barnacle cuts 7-44
barotrauma 7-15
Bartonella bacilliformis 6-2
bartonellosis 6-2
Belgium 8-26
Beliza 8-27
Benadryl 7-39, 7-75
Benin 8-29
Bermuda 8-31
Bezruchka Steve 1-5
Bhutan 8-32
bilharziasis 6-53
bites
    animal 7-37
    insect 7-38
    snake 7-42
bladder infection 7-26
bleeding 7-4
    nose 7-19
blindness snow 7-12
    sun 7-12
blisters
    burns 7-2
    friction 7-1

Bolivian hemorrhagic fever 6-19
Bonaire 8-37
bones broken 7-34
Bonine 3-40, 7-30
books on travel 1-17
booster requirements 5-40
Borrelia 6-51
Borrelia burgdorferi 6-30
Botswana 8-37
Brazil 8-39
breakbone fever 6-9
British Honduras 8-27
broken tooth 7-21
brucellosis 6-3
Brugia malayi 6-17
Brunei Darussalam 8-43
bubonic plague 6-45
bug jacket 5-29
Bulgaria 8-45
Burkina Faso 8-46
Burma 8-48
burns 7-2
   sun 7-59
Burunda 8-52
butterfly closures 7-5

C

ings 6-30
Cambodia 8-97
Cameroon 8-54
Canada 8-57
Canal Zone 8-59
Canary Islands 8-59
Canicola fever 6-29
Cape Verde 8-60
Carafate 7-82
cardiac problems and travel 4-27
Carefree Travel Insurance 2-43
Carrion's disease 6-2
caterpillar rash 7-39
catfish stings 7-44
Cayman Islands 8-62
CDC Bulletins 2-13
Central African Republic 8-63
Ceylon 8-363
Chad 8-65
Chaga's disease 6-63
boards of health 2-17
boiling water 5-11
Bolivia 8-34

chagoma 6-63
chigoe 6-65
Chikungunya fever 6-3
Chikungunya hemorrhagic fever 6-20
children and travel 4-11
  air travel 4-18
  immunizations 4-17
  malaria 4-18
  protective clothing 4-19
Chile 8-68
China, People's Republic of 8-70
Chlamydia trachomatis 6-61
chloroquine 6-34
  use while pregnant 4-7
cholera 6-4
  immunization 5-34
  immunization adverse reactions 5-40
Christmas Island, Indian Ocean 8-76
chronic hypothermic 7-49
ciguatera poisoning 6-6
Cipro 5-18, 7-29
ciprofloxacin 5-18, 7-29
classic typhus 6-68
clinics, for immunizations 2-23
Clioquinol 5-15
clonorchiasis 6-7
Clostritium tetani 6-59
closure wound 7-4
Cocos Island 8-77
codiene 7-83
Colombia 8-78
Colorado tick fever 6-8
Comoros 8-82
complications, immunizations 5-45
Congo, People's Republic 8-84
Cook Islands 8-87
coral cuts 7-44
  stings 7-45
Corynebacterium diphtheriae 6-10
Costa Rica 8-88
Cote d' Ivoire 8-191
Cover Strips 7-5, 7-72
cramps heat 7-63
Crimea Congo hemorrhagic fever 6-20
cruise ship travel 3-35
Crysops deerflies 6-30
Cuba 8-90
Curacao 8-92
cutaneous leishmaniasis 6-27
cuts 7-4
  barnacle 7-44
  coral 7-44
Cyprus 8-92
cystitis 7-26

D

Dahomey 8-29
dairy safety 5-1
Dalmane 3-33
dandy fever 6-9
deaths 2-6
Dedoyan, Alan 4-6
deet insect repellent 5-23
Delhi boil 6-27
Democratic Kampuchea 8-97
Democratic People's Republic
    of Korea 8-205
Democratic Yemen 8-437
dengue fever 6-9, 6-20
dengue hemorrhagic fever 6-9
Denmark 8-101
dental pain 7-20
descent airplane 7-15
desoximetasone ointment 7-81
diabetes and travel 4-21
diarrhea 5-13, 7-26
    prevention 5-14
    treatment 5-15, 7-28
    while pregnant 4-9
Diasorb 5-16, 7-26, 7-77
dibucaine ointment 7-2, 7-20
dinoflagellates 6-44
diphenhydramine 7-75
diphtheria 6-10
    immunization
        adverse reactions 5-50
Diphyllobothrium latum 6-58
direct pressure 7-4
diseases
    helminthic 6-21
    sexually transmitted 6-55
    vector spread 5-22
dislocations 7-34
Djibouti 8-102
Dominica 8-104
Dominican Republic 8-104
doxycycline 5-15, 6-29, 6-37, 7-5, 7-7,
    7-26, 7-28, 7-79
    use while pregnant 4-9
dracunculiasis 6-10
Dramamine 3-40, 7-30
dumdum fever 6-27
dysentery
    amoebic 6-11
    bacillary 6-12

E

ear
    foreign body 7-18
    infection 7-16
    protection while flying 3-19
East Germany 8-135
East Timor 8-107
Ebola virue 6-19
echinococcus 6-12
Echinococcus granulosis 6-13
Echinococcus multilocularis 6-13
ECM rash 6-31
Ecuador 8-108
Egypt 8-111
Ehret Charles 3-28
Ellice Islands 8-403
embassy services 2-1, 2-4
emergency supplics 3-13
encephalitis
    California 6-16
    Eastern equine 6-16
    Japanese 6-13
    St. Louis 6-16
    tick borne 6-15
    Venezuelan equine 6-15
    Western equine 6-16
endemic typhus 6-67
endemic zone, yellow fever 6-75
Entamoeba histolytica 6-11
epidemic typhus 6-68
epinephrine 7-40
EpiPen 7-40
epistaxis 7-19
Equatorial Guinea 8-117
erythema chronicum migrans 6-31
erythromycin 7-29
espundia 6-27
Ethiopia 8-117
eugenol 7-85
Europe Assistance 2-42
European typhus 6-68
exhaustion heat 7-63
Extractor The 7-5
eye 7-9
    abrasion 7-11
    foreign body 7-9
    infection 7-12
    patch 7-11
    trauma 7-11

F

Falkland Islands 8-123
Fansidar 6-37
Fansimef 6-36
Faroe Islands 8-124
fasciolopsiasis 6-16
fear of flying 3-23
Federal Republic of Germany 8-136
fever 7-26
  reduction 7-2
fevers, viral hemorrhagic 6-19
Fiji 8-124
filariasis 6-17
filter, water 5-10
Finland 8-126
first degree burn 7-2
fluid replacement 7-28
fluke
  blood 6-53
  giant intestinal 6-16
  liver 6-43
flying, fear of 3-23
food for children 4-12
food safety 5-1
foreign body removal
  ear 7-18
  eye 7-9
forest yaws 6-27
fractures 7-34
France 8-127
Francisella tularensis 6-65
French Guiana 8-129
French Polynesia 8-131
friction blisters 7-1
frostbite 7-55
fugitive swellings 6-30
Futuna Island 8-432

G

Gabon 8-133
gall bladder pain 7-24
Gambia 8-134
gastitis 7-22
German Democratic Republic 8-137
German measles 6-41
Germany, Federal Republic 8-138
Ghana 8-140
Giardia lamblia 6-17
giardiasis 6-17
Gibraltar 8-143
Gibraltar fever 6-3
Gilbert Islands 8-204
glasses sun 7-13

glucagon 4-22
Greece 8-144
Greenland 8-146
Grenada 8-147
Grenadines 8-335
Guadeloupe 8-148
Guam 8-149
Guatemala 8-150
Guernsey, Alderney, and Sark 8-152
Guinea 8-153
Guinea-Bissau 8-155
Guyana 8-160

H

HACE 7-67
Haiti 8-162
Halazone 5-7
Halcion 3-33
handicapped travel 4-1
Hansen's disease 6-28
Hantaan virus hemorrhagic fever 6-20
HAPE 7-66
HDVC 6-50
HealthCare Abroad 2-44
hearing impaired 4-2
heart problems and travel 4-27
heat
  cramps 7-63
  exhaustion 7-63
  stroke 7-64
helminthic diseases 6-21
help
  embassy 2-1
  for travelers 2-39
hemorrhagic fevers 6-19
hepatitis A 6-23
  immunization 5-35
hepatitis B 6-24
  immunization 5-35
hepatitis C 6-25
hepatitis Non/A Non/B 6-25
Herchmer Country Database Program
  2-57, 8-1
Herchmer Medical Consultants 1-5
hiatal hernia 7-23
Hibiclens 7-71
high altitude
  acute sickness 7-65
  cerebral edema 7-67
  pulmonary edema 7-66
hijacking 3-10
home, return 4-41
Honduras 8-164

Hong Kong 8-168
hostage 3-10
hot line, State Department 2-1
Hungary 8-170
hydatid disease 6-12
hydrocortisone cream 7-76
hydroxyzine 7-82
hypothermia
  acute 7-54
  chronic 7-49
  signs, symptoms 7-51

I

IAMAT 2-40, 2-53, 5-24
ICAO 3-31
Iceland 8-171
illness, high altitude 7-65
immersion foot 7-56
immune globulin dose, hepatitis A 6-24
immunization 5-31
  booster requirements 5-40
  cholera 5-34
  complications from 5-45
  diphtheria 5-39
  for children 4-17
  hepatitis A 5-35
  hepatitis B 5-35
  influenza 5-37
  Japanese encephalitis 5-36
  meningococcal 5-37
  MMR 5-37
  plague 5-37
  polio 5-37
  tetanus 5-39
  typhoid 5-39
  yellow fever 5-40, 6-70
Imodium 5-18, 7-27, 7-78
  use while pregnant 4-10
impaired hearing 4-2
India 8-172
Indonesia 8-178
infantile paralysis 6-46
infection
  bladder 7-26
  ear 7-16
  eye 7-12
  wound 7-7
infectious hepatitis 6-23
influenza immunization 5-37
information, travel 2-9
injuries, environmental
  aquatic 7-44

  cold weather 7-48
  heat 7-57
  sun 7-57
  ultraviolet 7-57
injury 7-1
  and children 4-19
  ankle 7-32
  eye 7-11
  joints 7-32
  knee 7-32
  tooth 7-21
insect bites 7-38
  protection 5-21
  stings 7-38
insulin 4-23
insurance 1-9, 2-39
International Assoc. of
  Medical Assistance for
  Travelers 2-53
International SOS Assistance 2-43
iodochlorhydroxyquin 5-15
IPV 5-37, 6-47
Iran 8-181
Iraq 8-184
Ireland 8-187
Isle of Man 8-188
Israel 8-189
Italy 8-191
Ivory Coast 8-193
Ixodid tick 6-8, 6-52

J

jail fever 6-68
Jamaica 8-194
Japan 8-197
Japanese encephalitis
  immunization 5-36
jellyfish stings 7-45
Jersey 8-199
jet lag 3-27
  diet for prevention 3-28
jigger 6-65
joint injury 7-32
Jordan 8-199
Junin virus 6-20

K

kala azar 6-27
kaolin 7-26
Katadyn Filter 5-10
Keeling Island 8-77

Kenya 8-201
Kiribati 8-206
kissing bug 6-63
kit medical travelers 7-69
knee injury 7-32
knock out tooth 7-21
Korea, Democratic
   People's Republic 8-207
Korea, North 8-207

L

laceration 7-4
LaMosquitte neeting 5-24
Lao People's
   Democratic Republic 8-215
Laos 8-215
Lariam 6-36
   use while pregnant 4-7
Lassa fever 6-19, 6-26
Lebanon 8-217
Leeward Islands 8-10
legal concerns
   trip preparation 1-9
   trip problems 2-4
leishmaniasis 6-27
leprosy 6-28
leptospirosis 6-29
Lesotho 8-220
letter authorizing medications 1-3
Liberia 8-222
Libya 8-225
Liechtenstein 8-229
liver fluke 6-43
loa loa infection 6-30
Loiasis 6-30
lomotil 5-18, 7-27
   use while pregnant 4-10
loose stools 7-26
loperamide 5-18, 7-78
lost tooth 7-21
louse-borne typhus 6-68
lung problems and travel 4-27
Luxembourg 8-230
Luzindole 3-32
Lyme disease 6-30

M

Macao 8-231
Machupo virus disease 6-19

Madagascar 8-232
Madeira 8-235
mal morado 6-42
malaria 6-31
   prevention during pregnancy 4-7
Malawi 8-235
Malaya typhus 6-67
Malaysia 8-238
Maldives 8-242
Mali 8-243
Malta 8-246
Malta fever 6-3
Malvinas Islands 8-123
Mantoux test 6-64
Marburg virus 6-19
Marezine 3-40
marriages, during foreign
   travel 2-6
Martinique 8-247
Mauritania 8-249
Mauritius 8-252
McBurney's point 7-25
measles 6-41
   3 day 6-41
   German 6-41
   immunization
      adverse reactions 5-48
meclizine 3-40, 7-30, 7-75
Medic Alert 7-85
medical clinics, travel 2-23
medical kit
   commercial air 3-17
   travelers 7-69
Mediterranean fever 6-3
mefloquine 6-36
   use while pregnant 4-7
melatonin 3-32
melioidosis 6-40
   immunization 5-37
   immunization
      adverse reactions 5-48
meningococcus meningitis 6-40
Mexico 8-254
Miconazole cream 7-77
Miquelon 8-336
mite-borne typhus 6-69
MMR immunization 5-37
Mobigesic 7-76
Monaco 8-258
Mongolia 8-259
Montserrat 8-260
Morocco 8-261
motion sickness 3-39, 7-29

Mozambique 8-264
mucocutaneous leishmaniasis 6-27
mumps 6-41
   immunization
      adverse reactions 5-48
murine typhus 6-67
Myanmar 8-48
Mycobacterium bovis 6-64
Mycobacterium leprae 6-28
Mycobacterium tuberculosis 6-64

N

Namibia 8-268
Nauru 8-270
nausea 7-26
   motion induced 3-39
NEAR 2-42
Nepal 8-271
Netherlands 8-274
Netherlands Antilles 8-92, 8-275
Nevis 8-333
New Caledonia 8-277
New Hebrides 8-423
New World typhus 6-67
New Zealand 8-278
Nicaragua 8-279
Niger 8-285
Nigeria 8-287
Niue 8-290
Nix 5-27
norfloxacin 5-18
Norfolk Island 8-291
Noroxin 5-18
North Korea 8-207
Norway 8-292
nose bleed 7-19
nutrition for children 4-12

O

Okinawa 8-331
Oman 8-293
Omsk hemorrhagic fever 6-20
onchocerciasis 6-42
opisthorchiasis 6-7
OPV 5-37, 6-47
Oralyte 5-16, 7-26
Orbivirus 6-8
oriental sore 6-27
Oroya fever 6-2
otitis externa 7-17
   media 7-15
oxygen, supplemental 4-28

P

Pacific Trust Territory 8-398
pain
   abdomin 7-22
   bladder 7-26
   dental 7-20
   ear 7-15
   eye 7-9
   gall bladder 7-24
   urination 7-26
Pakistan 8-295
paludrine 6-38
   use while pregnant 4-7
Panama 8-301
pancreatitis 7-23
Papau New Guinea 8-303
paragonimiasis 6-43
Paraguay 8-306
paralytic shellfish poisoning 6-44
paregoric 7-27
passports 1-7
pectin 7-26
People's Republic of China 8-70
People's Republic of Congo 8-84
Pepto Bismol 5-16, 7-26
permethrin 5-27
Permone 5-27
personal security 3-5
Peru 8-308
Philippine Islands 8-313
phlebotomus fever 6-53
Pitcairn Island 8-318
plague 6-45
   immunization 5-37
Plasmodium falciparum 6-32
Plasmodium malariae 6-33
Plasmodium ovale 6-33
Plasmodium vivax 6-33
pneumonic plague 6-45
poisoning, scromboid 6-55
   shellfish 6-44
Poland 8-319
Polar Pure 5-10
polio 6-46
poliomyelitis 6-46
   immunization 5-37
      adverse reactions 5-49
Pontocaine ointment 7-81
Portugal 8-320
Portuguese Timor 8-107
post trip testing 4-44
Potable Aqua 5-8, 7-71
pregnancy

altitude 4-7
and travel 4-5
and malaria 4-7
risk factors 4-6
preparation, trip 1-2
pressure, direct 7-4
prevention
diarrhea 7-26
motion sickness 7-29
prickly heat 7-58
primaquine 6-38
use while pregnant 4-7
Principe 8-340
problems legal 2-4
proguanil 6-38
use while pregnant 4-7
Pseudomonas pseudomallie 6-40
Puerto Rico 8-322
pulmonary problems and travel 4-27
puncture wounds 7-5
purification water 5-7

Q
Qatar 8-323

R
rabies 6-48, 7-37
immunization
adverse reactions 5-49
rat-flea typus 6-67
Recombivax HB 5-35
red tide 6-44
Reduviidae 6-63
relapsing fever 6-51
removal foreign body
from ear 7-18
from eye 7-9
splinter 7-7
of tooth 7-21
replacement fluid 7-28
Republic of China-Taiwan 8-74
Republic of Korea 8-211
Republic of Yemen 8-436
return home 4-41
Reunion 8-325
Rickettsia prowazekii 6-68
Rickettsia rickettsii 6-52
Rickettsia tsutsugamushi 6-69
Rickettsia typhi 6-67
Rift Valley fever 6-20, 6-52
RIG 6-50
river blindness 6-42
Roble's disease 6-42

Rocky Mountain Spotted fever 6-8, 6-52
Romania 8-326
rubella 6-41
immunization
adverse reactions 5-49
rubeola 6-42
Russia 8-410
RVA 6-50
Rwanda 8-328
Ryukvu Islands 8-331

S
safari fever 6-53
safety
dairy 5-1
food 5-1
vehicle 3-1
water 5-1
Saint Christopher and Nevis 8-333
Saint Helena 8-332
Saint Kitts 8-333
Saint Lucia 8-334
Saint Martin 8-335
Saint Pierre and
Miquelon 8-336
Saint Vincent and
the Grenadines 8-337
Salmonella typhi 6-66
Samoa, American 8-6
Samoa 8-338
San Marino 8-340
Sana'a 8-436
Sandfly fever 6-53
Sao Tome and Principe 8-340
Saudi Arabia 8-342
scalpel blade 7-73
Schistosoma haematobium 6-54
Schistosoma japonicum 6-54
Schistosoma mansoni 6-54
schistosomiasis 6-53
scopolamine 7-84
scorpion fish injuries 7-45
scromboid poisoning 6-55
scrub, surgical 7-5
scrub, typhus 6-69
sea urchin injuries 7-45
second degree burn 7-2
security, personal 3-5
Senegal 8-345
Septra 5-18, 7-28, 7-80
use while pregnant 4-9
serum hepatitis 6-24
services, embassy 2-4

sexually transmitted diseases 6-55
Seychelles 8-348
shellfish poisoning 6-44
Shigella 6-12
shock 7-4
  anaphylactic 7-39
  treatment 7-6
sickness, motion 3-39, 7-29
Sierra Leone 8-350
Simulium black fly 6-42
Singapore 8-352
Skin So Soft 5-25
sleeping sickness, African 6-62
smallpox 6-57
snake bite treatment 7-42
Solomon Islands 8-354
Somalia 8-355
South-West Africa 8-268
South Africa 8-358
South Korea 8-211
Spain 8-363
Spenco 2nd Skin 7-1, 7-39, 7-70
splinter forceps 7-73
splinter removal 7-7
sponge rash 7-46
sprains 7-32
Sri Lanka 8-365
state boards of health 2-17
Steri Strips 7-5
sting ray injuries 7-46
stings
  catfish 7-44
  coral 7-45
  insect 7-38
stroke, heat 7-64
stye 7-12
sucralfate 7-82
Sudan 8-369
sulfamethoxazole trimethoprim 7-80
sun burn 7-2, 7-59
sun protective factor 7-60
sun screen 7-60
sun glasses 7-13
supplies emergency 3-13
Suriname 8-373
swamp fever 6-29
Swaziland 8-376
Sweden 8-378
swineherd's disease 6-29
Switzerland 8-379
syphilis 6-56
Syrian Arab Republic 8-380
syringe, bulb 7-74

T

Taenia saginata 6-58
Taenia solium 6-58
Tahiti 8-131
Taiwan-Republic of China 8-74
Tanzania 8-383
tapeworms 6-58
telephoning home 2-45
terrorism 3-8
testing AIDS 4-34
tetanus 6-59
  diphtheria immunization 5-39
  immunization
    adverse reactions 5-50
tetracaine ointment 7-81
testing after return home 4-44
Thailand 8-388
third degree burn 7-3
tick bites 7-39
Tobago 8-397
tobramycin 7-80
Tobrex ointment 7-80
Togaviridae 6-13
Togo 8-393
Tokelau Islands 8-394
Tonga 8-395
Tonga penetrans 6-65
tooth
  broken 7-21
  pain 7-20
Topicort ointment 7-81
trachoma 6-61
Transderm Scop 3-40, 7-30, 7-84
trauma 7-1
  aquatic 7-44
  eye 7-11
travel
  air 3-15
  and AIDS 4-31
  and heart problems 4-27
  and lung problems 4-27
  books 1-17
  cruise ship 3-35
  handicapped 4-1
  information 2-9
  medical advice 2-23
  medical clinics 2-23
  medical insurance 2-39
  while pregnant 4-5
  with children 4-11
  with diabetes 4-21
travelers diarrhea 5-13, 7-26
  prevention 5-14

treatment 5-15
Travelers Insurance Company 2-41
travelers medical kit 7-69
TravelMed 2-44
treatment
  cuts 7-4
  diarrhea 7-28
  motion sickness 7-29
  shock 7-6
  snake bite 7-42
  snow blindness 7-14
  splinter 7-7
  sun blindness 7-14
Trichinella spiralis 6-61
trichinosis 6-61
trimethoprim 7-28
Trinidad and Tobago 8-397
trip preparation 1-2
triple antibiotic ointment 7-5, 7-72
tropical sore 6-27
tropical typhus 6-69
Truk Islands 8-398
Trypanosoma cruzi 6-63
Trypanosoma gambiense 6-62
Trypanosoma rhodesiense 6-62
Trypanosomiasis, African 6-62
Trypanosomiasis, American 6-63
tsutsugamushi disease 6-69
tuberculosis 6-64
tularemia 6-65
tungiasis 6-65
Tunisia 8-399
Turkey 8-401
Tuvalu 8-405
tylenol #3 7-83
typhoid fever 6-66
  immunization 5-39
  immunization
    adverse reactions 5-50
typhus
  classic 6-68
  endemic 6-67
  epidemic 6-68
  European 6-68
  flea-borne 6-67
  louse-borne 6-68
  Malaya 6-67
  mite-borne 6-69
  New World 6-67
  rat-flea 6-67
  scrub 6-69
  tropical 6-69
  endemic flea-borne 6-67

murine 6-67

U

Uganda 8-406
ulcer 7-22
ultraviolet rays 7-12
  injuries 7-57
undulant fever 6-3
uniform stamp 5-33
Union of Soviet Socialist
  Republics 8-410
United Arab Emirates 8-416
United Kingdom 8-418
United Republic of Cameroon 8-54
United Republic of Tanzania 8-383
United States 8-419
urban typhus 6-67
urinary pain 7-26
Uristix 4-5
Uruguay 8-422
USADIRECT, telephone 2-46
USSR 8-410
uta 6-27

V

vaccination 5-31
  booster requirements 5-40
  complications 5-45
vaccine
  cholera 5-31
  diphtheria 5-39
  hepatitis A 5-35
  hepatitis B 5-35
  influenza 5-37
  Japanese encephalitis 5-36
  measles 5-37
  meningococcal 5-37
  MMR 5-37
  mumps 5-37
  plague 5-37
  pneumonia 5-37
  polio 5-37
  rabies 5-38
  rubella 5-37
  typhoid 5-39
  tetanus 5-39
  yellow fever 5-40
Vanatu 8-423
vehicle safety 3-1
Venezuela 8-424
veruga peruana 6-2
Vibrio cholerae 6-4
Vietnam 8-427

vinchuca bug 6-63
viral hemorrhagic fevers 6-19
Virgin Islands (UK) 8-432
Virgin Islands (USA) 8-432
visa 1-8
visceral leishmaniasis 6-27
volvulosis 6-42
vomiting 7-26

W

Wake Island 8-433
Wallis and Futuna Islands 8-434
water
    boiling 5-11
    emergency 3-12
    purification 5-7
    safety 5-1
Weil's disease 6-29
Weiss, Don and Phyllis 1-8
West Germany 8-138
West Nile fever 6-69
Western Samoa 8-338
WHO Bulletins 2-13
wind chill chart 7-50
wool sorter's disease 6-1
wound
    care 7-1
    closure 7-4
    infection 7-7
Wuchereria bancrofti 6-17

Y

yellow fever 6-20, 6-70
    active disease 6-73
    endemic zone 6-75
    immunization 5-40
        adverse reactions 5-50
        required for entry 6-73
Yemen Arab Republic 8-436
Yersinia pestis 6-45
Yugoslavia 8-441

Z

Zaire 8-443
Zambabwa 8-450
Zambia 8-447